PRINCIPLES OF LABOR LEGISLATION

FOURTH REVISED EDITION

BY

JOHN R. COMMONS, LL.D.

Professor of Economics, University of Wisconsin, Former Member Industrial Commission of Wisconsin and United States Commission of Industrial Relations

AND

JOHN B. ANDREWS, Ph.D.

Secretary of the American Association for Labor Legislation, Editor of "The American Labor Legislation Review," Author of "Administrative Labor Legislation"

REPRINTS OF ECONOMIC CLASSICS

AUGUSTUS M. KELLEY · PUBLISHERS
NEW YORK · 1967

FIRST EDITION 1916
(New York: Harper & Brother, 1916)
FOURTH REVISED EDITION 1936

Reprinted 1967 by

AUGUSTUS M. KELLEY · PUBLISHERS

By Arrangement With Harper & Row

LIBRARY OF CONGRESS CATALOGUE CARD NUMBER
66-22620

PRINTED IN THE UNITED STATES OF AMERICA
by SENTRY PRESS, NEW YORK, N. Y. 10019

CONTENTS

PREFACE TO FOURTH REVISED EDITION vii
CHAPTER I: EMPLOYMENT AND UNEMPLOYMENT 1
  I. REGULATION OF PRIVATE EMPLOYMENT AGENCIES 5
    1. Abuses of Private Agencies 6
    2. Restrictive Legislation 7
  II. PUBLIC EMPLOYMENT OFFICES 12
    1. State and Municipal Offices 12
    2. Foreign National Systems 17
    3. Federal-state System 21
  III. SYSTEMATIC DISTRIBUTION OF PUBLIC WORK... 27
    1. Emergency Work 27
    2. Adjustment of Regular Work 32
  IV. REGULARIZATION OF INDUSTRY............... 37

CHAPTER II: MINIMUM FAIR WAGE 43
  I. ECONOMIC BASIS 44
    1. Low Wage Scale 44
    2. Economic Weakness of Low-paid Workers .. 47
  II. HISTORICAL DEVELOPMENT 48
    1. Australasia 48
    2. Great Britain 51
    3. Other Countries 54
    4. The United States 54
  III. STANDARDS 58
    1. Australasia 58
    2. Great Britain 59
    3. The United States 60
      a. Definition of the Minimum Wage 60
      b. Wage Losses from Unemployment 62
      c. Profits of the Business 63
      d. Substandard Workers 63
  IV. METHODS OF OPERATION 64
    1. Flat-rate Laws 64
    2. Wage-board Laws 65

CONTENTS

V. RESULTS 68
   1. Changes in Wage Rates 69
   2. Changes in Wages Above the Minimum..... 70
   3. Effect on Employment 71
   4. Effect on Industry 72
   5. Effect on Trade Unionism 73
   6. Effect on Efficiency 73
VI. CONSTITUTIONALITY 74

CHAPTER III: HOURS OF LABOR 83
  I. MAXIMUM HOURS 95
    1. Children 95
    2. Women 99
    3. Men 116
      a. Public Work 117
      b. Private Employments: (1) Transportation; (2) Mines and Tunnels; (3) Factories and Workshops 121
      c. Constitutionality 132
  II. REST PERIODS 140
    1. Daily Rest and Mealtimes 141
    2. Night Work 142
    3. Saturdays and Legal Holidays 147
    4. One Day of Rest in Seven 149
    5. Annual Vacations 155

CHAPTER IV: SAFETY AND HEALTH 158
  I. REPORTING 160
    1. Accidents 161
    2. Occupational Diseases 164
  II. PROHIBITION 168
    1. Exclusion of Persons 169
      a. Children: (1) Age Requirements; (2) Physical Requirements; (3) Educational Requirements; (4) Special Problems in Enforcing Restrictions on Child Labor 169
      b. Women: (1) Prohibited Employments; (2) Childbirth Protection 186

PRINCIPLES
OF LABOR LEGISLATION

Also published in

> REPRINTS OF ECONOMIC CLASSICS

>> BY JOHN R. COMMONS
>> THE DISTRIBUTION OF WEALTH [1893]
>> LABOR AND ADMINISTRATION [1913]
>> PROPORTIONAL REPRESENTATION [1907]
>> RACES AND IMMIGRANTS IN AMERICA [1924]
>> SOCIAL REFORM AND THE CHURCH [1894]
>> THE SOCIOLOGICAL THEORY OF SOVEREIGNTY [1899-1900]
>> TRADE UNIONISM AND LABOR PROBLEMS
>> *First & Second Series* [1905 & 1921]

>> JOHN R. COMMONS *Et Al*
>> HISTORY OF LABOR IN THE UNITED STATES,
>> 4 VOLS. [1918, 1935]

CONTENTS

c. Men: (1) Physical Qualifications; (2) Technical Qualifications	189
2. Prohibition of Substances or Instruments	194
III. REGULATION	196
1. Factories and Workshops	197
a. Machine Guards	197
b. Protection against Fire	199
c. Lighting, Heating and Ventilation	200
d. Seats, Toilets, and Dressing-rooms	202
e. Protection from Infectious Disease	204
f. Tenement House Manufacture	205
2. Mines and Tunnels	208
a. Mining	208
b. Work in Compressed Air	211
3. Transportation	212
a. Navigation	213
b. Railroads and Street Cars	214
IV. DEVELOPMENT OF STANDARDS	219
1. Defects of Early Legislation	219
2. The Method of Administrative Orders	221
CHAPTER V: SOCIAL INSURANCE	224
I. INDUSTRIAL ACCIDENT INSURANCE	227
1. Rules of Employers' Liability	228
a. Duties of the Employer	228
b. Burden of Occupational Risks	229
c. Fellow Servant Rule	229
d. Contributory Negligence	230
e. Assumption of Risk	231
2. Beginnings of Industrial Accident Insurance	232
a. German System	233
b. Methods in Other Countries	234
c. Inclusion of Occupational Diseases	235
3. Compensation Legislation in the United States	236
a. Scope of Laws: (1) Employments Included; (2) Injuries Included; (3) Occupational Diseases	241
b. Scale of Compensation: (1) Medical Attendance; (2) Waiting Period; (3)	

viii CONTENTS

  Compensation for Total Disability;
  (4) Compensation for Partial Disability; (5) Compensation for Death 244
  c. Rehabilitation 250
  d. Method of Administration 251
  e. Security of Payment 253
 II. HEALTH INSURANCE 257
  1. Early Steps in Health Insurance 257
  2. Compulsory Health Insurance 258
  3. Maternity Insurance 264
  4. Need in the United States 267
 III. OLD-AGE AND INVALIDITY INSURANCE 273
  1. Unassisted Old-age Insurance 273
  2. Assisted State Plans 275
  3. Straight Pensions 276
  4. Compulsory Systems 280
 IV. WIDOWS' AND ORPHANS' INSURANCE 289
  1. Voluntary Life Insurance 289
  2. Compulsory Insurance 290
  3. Mothers' Pensions 291
 V. UNEMPLOYMENT COMPENSATION 293
  1. The Ghent System 293
  2. Compulsory Unemployment Insurance 294
  3. Unemployment Compensation in the United States 298
   a. Coverage 302
   b. Contributions 303
   c. Contribution Rates and Merit Rating... 305
   d. Set-up of Funds 307
   e. Benefits 309
   f. Administration 312
   g. Constitutionality 314

CHAPTER VI: INDIVIDUAL BARGAINING 315
 I. THE LABORER AS DEBTOR 315
  1. Servile Labor 316
   a. Slavery 316
   b. Serfdom 316
   c. Peonage 317

CONTENTS

2. From Master and Servant to Employer and
   Employee 320
   a. Indentured Service 320
   b. Apprenticeship 321
   c. Contract Labor 321
   d. Padrone System 325
   e. Imprisonment for Debt 326
   f. Wage Exemption 327
   g. Homestead Exemption 328
   h. Assignment of Wages 329
II. THE LABORER AS CREDITOR 329
   1. Time of Payment 330
   2. Place of Payment 331
   3. Basis of Payment 332
   4. Medium of Payment 332
      a. "Living In" 332
      b. Company Houses and Labor Camps... 333
      c. Company Stores 333
   5. Deductions 334
   6. Mechanics' Liens and Wage Preference 337
III. THE LABORER AS TENANT 339
   1. Classes of Agricultural Workers 339
      a. Hired Laborers 339
      b. Tenants 340
      c. "Croppers" 340
   2. Agricultural Labor Legislation 343
IV. THE LABORER AS COMPETITOR 345
   1. Protection against Immigration 346
      a. Induced Immigration 348
      b. The Quota System 350
      c. Exclusion of Orientals 353
      d. The Literacy Test 355
   2. Protection against Convict Labor 357
V. LEGAL AID AND INDUSTRIAL COURTS 361
   1. Private and Public Legal Aid............. 363
   2. Industrial Courts 367
VI. THE LABORER AS CITIZEN 370
   1. Voting 370
   2. National Guard Duty 371

CONTENTS

CHAPTER VII: COLLECTIVE BARGAINING 372
  I. GOVERNMENT AND COLLECTIVE BARGAINING 374
    1. Attitudes Toward Collective Bargaining..... 374
      a. Repression 374
      b. Toleration 374
      c. Encouragement 375
      d. Intervention 375
    2. Government Agencies Affecting Collective Bargaining 376
  II. EVOLUTION OF THE LAW OF COLLECTIVE BARGAINING IN THE UNITED STATES 379
    1. Origin of Collective Bargaining 379
    2. Development of Law in the United States.. 382
  III. THE LAW OF COLLECTIVE BARGAINING IN THE UNITED STATES BEFORE THE NEW DEAL..... 388
    1. The Rights of Labor 388
      a. The Right to Organize 388
      b. The Right to Bargain Collectively..... 389
      c. The Right to Strike 390
      d. Closed-shop Strikes 391
      e. Sympathetic Strikes 393
      f. Other Strikes 396
      g. Court Action Against Illegal Strikes... 396
      h. Methods of Conducting Strikes....... 397
      i. Picketing 397
      j. Boycotts 401
    2. The Rights of Employers 403
      a. The Right to Form Employers' Associations 403
      b. The Right to Lock Out 404
      c. The Right to Operate Their Plants.... 404
      d. The Right to Discriminate Against Union Workers 405
      e. The Right to Use Yellow-dog Contracts 406
      f. The Right to Blacklist............... 408
      g. The Right to Organize Company Unions 409
    3. Enforcement 411
      a. Prosecutions 411

CONTENTS xi

	b. Damage Suits	411
	c. Injunctions	413
4.	Toleration the Attitude of the Law	417
IV.	THE LAW OF COLLECTIVE BARGAINING UNDER THE NEW DEAL	419
1.	Precursors of New Deal Legislation	419
2.	Section 7a	423
3.	The National Labor Relations Act	424
V.	INTERVENTION BY GOVERNMENT	429
1.	State Mediation Laws	432
2.	Railway Labor Laws	433
3.	Compulsory Arbitration in Kansas	437
4.	Compulsory Arbitration in Australasia	439
	a. Operation of the New Zealand Act	441
	b. Operation of Australian Laws	444

CHAPTER VIII: ADMINISTRATION 448
   I. THE EXECUTIVE 449
   II. THE LEGISLATURE 452
   III. THE JUDICIARY 458
   IV. THE MODERN LABOR DEPARTMENT 465
      1. Administrative Investigations 466
      2. Representation of Interests 475
      3. Types of Labor Departments 482
      4. Civil Service 486
      5. Bill Drafting 488
      6. Penalties and Prosecutions 490
      7. Cooperation by Pressure 498

CHAPTER IX: THE BASIS OF LABOR LAW 502
   I. THE LABOR CONTRACT 502
      1. Industry 503
      2. Labor Law 504
      3. Politics 505
   II. INDIVIDUAL RIGHTS 506
   III. DUE PROCESS OF LAW 509
      1. Public Powers 510
         a. Power to Preserve Peace and Execute the Laws 510
         b. The Taxing Power 511

xii CONTENTS

  c. Guardianship 511
  d. Eminent Domain 512
  e. Proprietorship 513
  f. The Police Power 513
  g. Commerce Power and Federal Powers.. 515
  h. Police Power and the Constitution 515
 2. Public Authorities 517
  a. The Executive 520
  b. The Legislature 521
  c. The Judiciary 522
  d. The Administration 523
 3. Principles 523
  a. Public Benefit 523
  b. Equal Protection of the Laws 528

SELECT CRITICAL BIBLIOGRAPHY 535

TABLE OF CASES CITED 585

INDEX 597

PREFACE TO THE FOURTH REVISED EDITION

AMERICA'S FIRST LABOR LAW WAS ENACTED ONE HUNDRED years ago, yet the bulk of our effective and, indeed, revolutionary labor legislation is the fruit of the past twenty-five years. Since January, 1916, when this book was first offered to citizens and students, there have been remarkable developments. Despite a few temporary setbacks, a new sense of the worth, perhaps also of the power, of the ordinary man and woman of toil has influenced the thinking of lawmakers. Comparative indifference on the part of society to human welfare in industry has given way to a new and constructive course of social action. The result is written large upon the pages of the statute books.

The first important recent step in American labor legislation was that providing accident compensation for those injured in the course of employment. From this have developed other forms of social insurance which are now coming into operation. The second great advance has been in the provision for law enforcement. Both of these developments had their most significant beginnings as recently as 1911 with the first permanent adoption by the states of the principle of accident compensation, and the organization of the first modern state industrial commission. By 1936 workmen's accident compensation laws had been adopted in all of the states except two in the non-industrial South, and Congress had enacted compensation laws covering federal civilian employees, private employees in the District of Columbia, and longshoremen and harbor workers. The industrial commission form of administration of labor laws—resting upon the new basis of scientific investigation of facts, representation of employer, employee, and the public, a trained personnel, and the substitution of administrative rules for legislative statutes—has been extensively adopted.

This same period has witnessed the well-nigh universal spread of laws placing maximum limits upon the length of the working day of women. Prohibition of some form of night work has been written into the laws of more than a dozen states. Effective steps have been taken in several states to abolish the seven-day working week. Railroading has been put upon the basic eight-hour day. Seamen have been made free men in a federal act to promote the safety of crews and passengers on the high seas. Official commissions in a dozen states have made comprehensive investigations pointing to the need of workmen's health insurance legislation. A national employment service has been extended throughout the country. Billions of dollars have been expended on public works as one means of attacking unemployment. Mothers' pension laws have been enacted in forty-six states. The federal government in 1920 enacted a comprehensive old age insurance law for its civilian employees. The federal taxing power has been successfully invoked to abolish a dreaded occupational disease. Minimum wage laws for women and young persons have been adopted within a dozen years in nearly a score of states. Interstate compacts have been developed. Other progressive laws, as well as amendments strengthening and liberalizing existing statutes, have followed one another rapidly.

In addition to the continuous improvement and extension of outstanding measures just mentioned, there have been new and significant applications of the principles of protective legislation. Federal-state cooperation in the vocational rehabilitation of industrial cripples provided by Congress in 1920 has been adopted by forty-five states. Some states have provided in their workmen's accident compensation laws that in case a minor is injured while illegally employed his compensation award shall be doubled or trebled, a most effective measure not only for securing redress for the injured child but also for providing a strong incentive to comply with the child labor laws. An appalling increase in coal mine disasters has led to widespread interest in mine safety, particularly in the rock dusting of bituminous mines as an effective preventive of coal dust explosions, and by 1936 a number of states had provided by law for rock dusting, while the stimulus to voluntary adoption of this safeguard has greatly reduced the hazard. Provisions have been made for occupational disease compensation in a score of American compensation laws. Immigration has been radically restricted. Legislation against "yellow-dog" contracts, and restricting injunctions in labor disputes, has been enacted by many state legislatures and by Congress. A proposal for settling industrial disputes, inaugurated for the railroads in the Transportation Act of 1920, proved unsatisfactory to the bulk of the railroad workers and a considerable number of the managers, and it was replaced by the Railway Labor Act of 1926, which in turn was amended in 1934, a new and conspicuous experiment in giving legislative encouragement to collective bargaining and voluntary agreement in labor disputes.

The present revision of this book appears at a critical moment in the history of labor legislation in America. Largely under the leadership of the federal government, new labor laws of major importance have been enacted with almost unprecedented rapidity. Legislation providing for old age pensions, unemployment compensation, public employment offices, and child welfare has recently been enacted and is being put into effect in the states under the stimulus of federal cooperation. In addition, Congress has provided a unified national system of old age benefits for wage earners generally, as well as a pension system for railway workers. In the field of collective bargaining also, the federal government has extended to all businesses affecting interstate commerce, first in the National Industrial Recovery Act of 1933 and then in the National Labor Relations Act of 1935, a policy of encouragement with far-reaching implications. These advances in legislative enactments have created new administrative problems and, in many states, an urgent need for improved administrative organization and personnel in the labor departments.

The progress indicated in this brief outline of the more significant measures thus far adopted has not been without its checks and obstacles. The power exercised by the United States Supreme Court to declare laws unconstitutional has fallen with a heavy hand upon certain labor laws. Prior to the World War there appeared to be a growing disposition on the part of the Court to stretch the elastic police power of the states to protect the workers against new and increasingly serious hazards of industrial employment. Since the war several decisions of the Court have been markedly in keeping with the general post-war reaction. In 1923 the Supreme Court by a five to three decision held the minimum wage law of the District of Columbia to be unconstitutional, a precedent for its five to four decision in 1936 declaring the modern-type New York law unconstitutional. In

1922 the federal Child Labor Act of 1919 was declared unconstitutional by the Supreme Court. Congress in 1924 passed a constitutional amendment permitting federal action against child labor, but by 1936 only twenty-four states had ratified it. In 1922 the Supreme Court overturned for the second time in five years efforts by Congress to bring longshoremen and other harbor workers within the protection of state workmen's accident compensation laws when injured aboard a vessel at the dock. A federal accident compensation bill, designed to meet the Court's objections and to relieve a third of a million harbor workers of their desperate plight was adopted by Congress in 1927. Much of the recent social insurance and collective bargaining legislation adopted by Congress and the states still awaits the test before the highest court.

With its rapid development during the past fifteen years, the mere extent and multiplicity of labor legislation present to the citizen who would keep informed a task that is truly formidable. Obviously, only a few specialists can hope to keep pace with all the details of this growth. As in all the other sciences, it is necessary, finally, in the science of legislation to formulate fundamental principles which may be generally applied.

This book, therefore, is written from the standpoint of the citizen and the student rather than from that of the lawyer. With regard to each of the main phases of the modern labor problem—employment and unemployment, wages, hours, safety and health, social insurance, individual and collective bargaining, and administration—it endeavors not so much to expound technical questions of legality as to sketch the historical background of the various labor problems, indicate the nature and extent of each, and describe the legislative remedies which have been applied. Throughout, it is the principles of labor law, not the details which may change from legislature to legislature, which are emphasized. And this procedure has been followed because in a democracy it is the people themselves whose collective opinion finally determines what the laws shall be and how effectively they shall be enforced.

The work is intended to be both critical and constructive—critical in that it points out the good and bad features of the statutes, constructive in that it shows how, in the light of experience, the good is being strengthened and the bad remedied.

PREFACE xvii

Finally, it is in full recognition that a law is really a law only to the extent to which it is enforced that each chapter emphasizes efficient administration and that a chapter is entirely devoted to this complex and all-important problem.

In all the advances that have been made, it is only the details of the labor code that have changed. The fundamental principles on which the legislation is based remain as they were. No important stand taken in the first edition of this book twenty years ago has yet had to be modified. For additional statutes enacted year by year, the reader is referred to the publications of the United States Department of Labor and the *American Labor Legislation Review*, published by the American Association for Labor Legislation. This *Review* is so arranged as to serve as a convenient supplement to the present work.

In assembling facts and preparing chapters for the first edition, assistance was given by many valued co-workers, including E. E. Witte, Olin Ingraham, David J. Saposs, Anna Kalet, Margarett A. Hobbs, and the following students: W. H. Burhop, Mark Greene, Ora Harnish, A. P. Haake, Harry Jerome, Gladys Owen, and Stewart Scrimshaw. For painstaking reading of manuscript and proof, we were indebted also to Jean M. Douglas and Solon De Leon. Our further thanks were extended to the following persons, to whom various chapters were submitted, and who gave valuable criticisms and suggestions for improvement: Richard T. Ely and H. W. Ballantine of the University of Wisconsin, Ernst Freund of Chicago University, Edwin V. O'Hara of the Oregon Industrial Welfare Commission, Thomas I. Parkinson and Joseph P. Chamberlain of Columbia University, Louis D. Brandeis of Boston, and Arthur N. Holcombe and Frank W. Taussig of Harvard University. For aid in making the 1920 revision of this book acknowledgment was made to Margarett A. Hobbs, Olga S. Halsey, Irene Sylvester Chubb, and Solon De Leon, of the staff of the American Association for Labor Legislation; to Edwin E. Witte, secretary of the Industrial Commission of Wisconsin; to Mrs. Glenn Turner, of the Wisconsin Legislative Reference Library; and to Professor Don D. Lescohier, of the University of Wisconsin. In preparing the 1927 edition valuable assistance was given by Frederick W. MacKenzie, Helen Guttman Sternau, Margaret M. Shipman and Cornelius

Cochrane of the staff of the American Association for Labor Legislation, and by Edwin E. Witte of the Wisconsin Legislative Reference Library, A. J. Altmeyer of the Wisconsin Industrial Commission, Alfred W. Briggs, Anna Campbell Davis, and Frieda Auchter. In checking up the new experience and in bringing the text down to date for the present revised edition, much of which is completely rewritten as well as reorganized, we are primarily indebted to the invaluable cooperation of George H. Trafton, of the American Association for Labor Legislation. For two vitally important portions of the volume, on collective bargaining and on unemployment compensation, we are indebted to Elizabeth Brandeis, of the University of Wisconsin, assisted by three of her students, Marjorie Loomis, Paul Kuelthau and Paul Schuette. The preparation of a new edition of this book, owing to the multiplicity of legislative developments, court decisions and changes in provision for law administration, is a formidable task made possible only by the continuous thread of principles which connect and give consistency to this whole evolution of welfare measures.

JOHN R. COMMONS
JOHN B. ANDREWS

September, 1936

CHAPTER I

EMPLOYMENT AND UNEMPLOYMENT

UNEMPLOYMENT IS THE MOST SERIOUS LABOR PROBLEM. THIS has long been recognized by economists and social workers. Again and again it has been brought forcibly to general public attention by the tragic consequences of recurring industrial depressions which have deprived millions of wage earners of their only means of livelihood, creating a vast public and private relief burden. When "better times" have returned, however, the public and the legislatures have almost invariably been unwilling to think seriously of ways of dealing with unemployment. This fact has made permanent legislative provision especially important and, at the same time, very slow in coming.

Unemployment is chronic and the amount never insignificant even when industrial conditions are at their best. Douglas has estimated that for the thirty years, 1897 to 1926, unemployment in manufacturing, transportation, the building trades and mining combined averaged 10.2 per cent of the workers attached to these industries. In no year did it fall as low as 4 per cent and only in four years was it below 5 per cent.[1] It has been estimated that in no year from 1921 to 1927 did the average number of the unemployed in all industry fall below a million and a half, and in 1921 the average rose to more than four million.[2] In the depression beginning in 1929-1930, the conservatively estimated number of those out of work reached the unprecedented total of about 13,500,000 in March, 1933; and by March, 1936, the jobless still numbered at least 9,600,000.[3]

These unemployment figures, while carefully prepared upon

[1] Douglas, Paul H., *Real Wages in the United States, 1890-1926*, 1930, p. 459.
[2] Givens, M. B., and Wolman, Leo, in *Recent Economic Changes*, 1929, vol. ii, p. 478.
[3] These figures are approximately those released by the National Industrial Conference Board. The estimate of the American Federation of Labor showed 12,183,000 unemployed in March, 1936.

the basis of available statistics, are all estimates. In America there has been no regular collection of accurate information on the number unemployed. In 1890, 1900, and 1910, the federal census-takers inquired of all gainfully occupied persons whether they had been unemployed during the preceding year and, if so, for how many months. The returns were recognized to be not very reliable, and those for 1910 were never tabulated by the Census Bureau. In 1930, the Census Bureau sought to obtain a more accurate count of the unemployed, and, although also open to criticism, the resulting statistics are undoubtedly more nearly adequate than any that have ever been compiled on this subject in the United States. The only other attempts to determine the extent of unemployment by count have been those made by the sampling method in selected localities and for individual cities or states. For some years, a few states, notably Massachusetts and New York, published figures showing the per cent of trade union members unemployed. These were based on information secured regularly from trade union officials and, while perhaps useful as indications of unemployment trends, could not be regarded as accurate indication of total unemployment. The collection of this type of data has been continued by the American Federation of Labor.[4] Most statisticians, in estimating the extent of unemployment, have relied chiefly upon statistics of employment, using the census figures and those collected monthly from a large number of employers in selected industries by the United States Bureau of Labor Statistics.[5] With the results of the 1930 Census of Unemployment as a base, these figures showing the fluctuations of employment have provided one of the most satisfactory means available in this country for estimating current unemployment. More reliable statistics of unemployment will probably be obtained only through the adoption of systems of compulsory unemployment compensation.

Many factors combine to make unemployment a permanent problem, not confined only to periods of business depression. A large number of plants close their doors each year because of business failure; and sometimes whole industries are prac-

[4] These figures appear monthly in the *American Federationist*, published by the American Federation of Labor.

See the *Monthly Labor Review*, published by the Bureau.

EMPLOYMENT AND UNEMPLOYMENT 3

tically wiped out by the competition of new products and by changing customs and needs of consumers. The gradual shift of an industry from one part of the country to another throws wage earners out of work in the older section. Many industries, moreover, produce goods for which the demand is highly seasonal, often causing slack periods each year when employees are "laid off." Another cause of unemployment which operates in good times as well as in bad is the coming of new machines, new processes, new methods, and business mergers, all of which displace workers from their jobs by eliminating the need for special skill or by reducing the number of workers required to produce a given output. This so-called "technological" unemployment has occurred from the very beginning of the modern industrial era, but in recent years appears to have been unusually prevalent. These and other causes of unemployment[6] operate continuously; the "business cycle"[7] from time to time throws added millions into forced idleness.

The employee's loss from irregularity of work is twofold. Besides his immediate loss in wages and the resulting distress, there is the equally serious loss in the weakening of morale which comes with uncertainty, habits of irregular work, and occasional lapses into destitution. Unemployment is a culture bed for pauperism and all of its accompanying evils. As Lescohier has well stated, irregular employment "undermines the physique; deadens the mind; weakens the ambition; destroys the capacity for continuous, sustained endeavor; induces a liking for idlenesss and self-indulgence; saps self-respect and the sense of responsibility; impairs technical skill; weakens nerve and will power; creates a tendency to blame others for failures; saps courage; prevents thrift and hope of family advancement; destroys a workman's feeling that he is taking good care of his family; and sends him to work worried and underfed; plunges him in debt."[8]

Besides the losses to the worker and his family, there are other costs of unemployment affecting both employers and the

[6] See Douglas, P. H., and Director, A., *The Problem of Unemployment*, 1931.
[7] See Mitchell, W. C., *Business Cycles, the Problem and Its Setting*, 1927.
[8] Lescohier, Don D., *The Labor Market*, 1919, p. 107.

entire community. Overhead costs continue when plants are idle; and some equipment, notably that of mines, deteriorates more rapidly when not in use. Unemployment and fear of unemployment, moreover, impair the efficiency of workmen; and labor turnover, requiring the hiring and "breaking in" of new employees, has been shown to be expensive to the employer.[9] From the public point of view, unemployment represents a vast waste of productive capacity and, more directly, places a heavy burden upon public and private charity. It is one of the chief causes of destitution and often leads to crime.

Even this general statement of the wastes of unemployment indicates the imperative need of preventive measures. Hence we are asking with increasing insistence, is unemployment a necessary evil? If not, to what extent is legislation a solution?

In Chapter IX it is suggested that unemployment may be defined as the failure to make a labor contract. This failure may be traced to one of three causes: (1) cessation of work arising from trade disputes; (2) unemployability, or disability, owing to sickness, old age, or other personal conditions; and (3) inability of men who are willing and able to work to find employment.

The present discussion relates only to the third part of the whole problem of idleness. Legislation intended to minimize idleness caused by labor disputes is discussed in Chapter VII. The problems of unemployability and unemployment are by no means identical, but are related to the extent that much chronic unwillingness to work has resulted from the demoralizing influence of unemployment, and therefore a reduction of unemployment may decrease the additions to the ranks of the unemployable. Introduction of machinery and increasing speed of industry are constantly lowering the age limit and raising the standard of efficiency which divides the so-called unemployable from the unemployed, and thus adding to the number of people who are involuntarily idle. How to provide satisfactory means of caring for the shiftless and the criminal is primarily a problem of charity and correction, but the prevention of unemployment is a problem of industrial organization. In this chapter the purpose is to describe the

[9] Feldman, H., *The Regularization of Employment*, 1925.

EMPLOYMENT AND UNEMPLOYMENT

more direct legislative remedies for unemployment arising from the inability of normal workers to obtain positions. These remedies may deal with either: (1) the regulation of private employment agencies; (2) the establishment and operation of public employment offices; (3) systematic distribution of public work; or (4) the regularization of industry. A fifth important legislative remedy, unemployment insurance, will be discussed in the chapter on "Social Insurance."

1. Regulation of Private Employment Agencies

To the extent to which employers are seeking workers to fill available jobs while at the same time qualified unemployed workers are seeking jobs, the solution of unemployment is simply the proper distribution of the labor supply. Perhaps the commonest method of seeking to bring about this distribution is by unsystematic individual search. A man not recommended for a position by a relative or friend often follows the easiest course, that which involves the least immediate expenditure of money and thought. He starts from home and drops in at every sign of "Help wanted."

"Help wanted," scrawled on a piece of cardboard, is the symbol of inefficiency in the organization of the labor market. The haphazard practice of tramping the streets in search of work is no method at all. It assures success neither to the idle worker in his search for work, nor to the employer in his search for labor. On the contrary, by its very lack of system, it needlessly swells the tide of unemployment, and through the foot-weary, discouraging tramping which it necessitates often leads to vagrancy and to crime.

Another common method of connecting employer and employee is through the medium of advertising. Every large newspaper in the country carries yearly hundreds of columns of "Help wanted" and "Situations wanted," representing a total annual cost of hundreds of thousands of dollars. If the money spent brought commensurate results, there would be less ground for complaint. At present an employer advertises for help in several papers because not all the workers read the same paper. The employee lists the positions advertised and then starts on the day's tramp. At one gate fifty or a hundred men may be waiting for a single job, while in other places a hundred employers may be waiting each for a single employee. Unnecessary duplication of work and expense by both parties is evident. In addition to the expense, newspaper advertising also possesses inherent possibilities of fraud. It is difficult for the newspaper, even if it always tries, to detect misrepresentations, and the victimized employee very rarely seeks legal redress.

In recognition of the need of more systematic means of connecting the man with the job, private employment agencies of various sorts have long been established. Private bureaus which charge no fees are conducted by various philanthropic and semiphilanthropic agencies in all cities of importance, but their activities consist largely in finding casual employment for near unemployables. In addition, many trade unions and employers' associations maintain employment bureaus for workers in special occupations. Some of them are very efficiently organized and conducted. Notable examples are the printers' union "day rooms," and the chain of employment bureaus conducted by the National Metal Trades Association in the principal cities of the United States. The latter offices charge no fees, their registrations number into the hundreds of thousands, and it has been claimed by the employers that they are not strike-breaking or blacklisting institutions.[10] Nevertheless, the usefulness of employment bureaus under the partisan control of either trade unions or employers is limited by their potential or actual use as weapons in a trade dispute. They lack the neutrality essential to the satisfactory organization of the labor market.

Abuses of Private Agencies.—Private employment agencies charging fees and doing business for profit have sprung up in all large cities. In 1930 there were 1,036 of them licensed and in operation in New York City, 315 in Chicago, and 191 in Philadelphia. Recent reports show that in 1930 there were at least 1,149 such agencies in New York State, 352 in Illinois, and 235 in Pennsylvania; in 1931 there were 429 in California

[10] A. J. Allen, secretary of the Associated Employers of Indianapolis, in an address before the American Association of Public Employment Offices, 1914. A study of employment agencies published by the Russell Sage Foundation states: "The bureaus of this organization usually had as their aim the complete centralization of information about all the workers in their trade as a guard against the employment of men known to be 'union agitators.'" Harrison, Shelby M., and Associates, *Public Employment Offices*, 1924, p. 70.

EMPLOYMENT AND UNEMPLOYMENT

and 266 or more in Massachusetts. It is probable that in all states there were about 5,000 fee-charging agencies, the number varying considerably according to business conditions. Aside from a few specialized agencies, they handle chiefly unskilled, domestic, and theatrical labor. The best organized and most powerful are said to be those which supply the railroads with common labor.

Many abuses are charged against the commercial agencies, particularly misrepresentation of wages and conditions of work, exaction of extortionate fees, sending applicants to immoral resorts, and "splitting fees" with foremen and thus inducing frequent discharges in order to get fees from men employed to fill the vacancies. In the testimony in the hearing on the petition for an injunction against the Washington referendum practically abolishing commercial agencies, it was stated that some of the private offices were so conducted as to "have three men for one job; one upon the job, one going to the job, and one coming from the job, and receiving compensation from all." There are frequent instances, also, where the commercial agencies accept fees and send the workmen to distant points where there is no demand for laborers. By this and other methods some agents are able to obtain and keep fees without providing jobs. In the one year 1934, the license commissioner of New York City reported over two thousand complaints against licensed employment agencies in that city.

2. **Restrictive Legislation.**—In the majority of states the abuses of the profit-making agencies have brought about restrictive legislation designed to prevent fraud and extortion and to insure moral surroundings.[11] Under this legislation no one may carry on an employment agency for profit without depositing a bond with the state department of labor or the city authorities and securing a license. The amount of the bond varies from $500 to $5,000, and the annual license fee from $2 to $500, both often being graded according to the size of the city, the sort of labor handled, or the total amount of fees collected. In some of the southern states the license fee for agents hiring labor to transport from the state is much higher. In Virginia it is $5,000 for each county or city in which the

[11] See U. S. Bureau of Labor Statistics, "Laws Relating to Employment Agencies in the United States as of January 1, 1933," *Bulletin No. 581*.

8 PRINCIPLES OF LABOR LEGISLATION

agent operates.[12] Such fees are prohibitive, designed to obstruct migration of Negro labor.

Licenses are issued only if the premises are found proper, and they may, together with the bond, be forfeited for violation of the law. A number of states prohibit the location of agencies in saloons. Association with lodging houses or restaurants is also frequently prohibited, and Colorado extends the prohibition to gambling places. In more than a score of states the sending of minors or women to immoral resorts is forbidden. In many jurisdictions the law fixes a maximum charge, usually either a certain percentage of the first month's wages or a fixed amount. Other related provisions are requirements as to form of receipt, and provisions for return of all or part of the fee if work is not soon obtained or if a workman is discharged in a short time. In a dozen states traveling expenses as well as the fee must be returned. Frequently, it is specified that all advertisements or other information shall be truthful.[13] In a number of states a record of all applicants registered is required, but rarely are the requirements comprehensive enough to give information valuable for statistical purposes.

In Canada, fee-charging agencies are prohibited by law in all provinces except New Brunswick, Prince Edward Island and Ontario. Ontario requires annual licenses, and the lieutenant-governor is authorized by statute to fix the fees the agencies may charge and to make rules for the conduct of the business. The deputy minister of labor who issues the licenses is given broad discretionary power in granting and revoking them. The number of these agencies licensed in Ontario has gradually been reduced until there were in 1933 only eight. A ruling was then in force which prohibited the issuance of additional licenses. The efficient operation of the public employment office system, combined with strict regulation, has had the effect of greatly improving the character of the fee-charging agencies.

The validity of state regulation of private employment agencies has seldom been denied by the courts. The requirement of a license has been sustained, even when the license fee was placed so high as to be practically prohibitive. Thus a Georgia

[12] Virginia, Laws 1928, C. 45.
[13] Wisconsin (Laws 1915, C. 457) specifies in addition that advertisements of private bureaus must state the existence of a strike or lockout.

EMPLOYMENT AND UNEMPLOYMENT

law, fixing a fee of $500 for each county in which the agent operated, was upheld by the supreme courts both of the state[14] and of the United States,[15] the latter decision being followed in other southern jurisdictions.[16] The prevailing view is that license regulations have for their object the promotion of public health, safety, morals, and convenience, that they tend to prevent fraud and extortion, and hence that they are within the police power of the legislatures even though they may somewhat restrict the right to carry on a lawful business without legislative interference.[17]

The almost unanimous testimony of investigators and public officials, however, is that these provisions have not been successful in stamping out the abuses of private offices, and the result has been a widespread movement for the abolition of such offices altogether. The popular protest against the abuses of private commercial agencies was voiced by the adoption, in 1914 by the State of Washington, of an initiative measure prohibiting the collection of fees from workers by an employment agent. The reason assigned in the measure was that "The system of collecting fees from the workers for furnishing them with employment . . . results frequently in their becoming the victims of imposition and extortion and is therefore detrimental to the welfare of the state."[18] This measure was expressly based on the police power, and the United States District Court upheld the prohibition inasmuch as "The state, under its police power, can adopt any act which reasonably protects its citizens, or a class of citizens, from fraud and extortion."[19] But in 1917 the United States Supreme Court in a five-to-four decision held the law unconstitutional as "arbitrary and oppressive," and an undue restriction on the liberty of the appellants, and therefore a violation of the Fourteenth Amendment.[20] The minority opin-

[14] Williams v. Fears, 110 Ga. 584, 35 S. E. 699 (1900).
[15] Williams v. Fears, 179 U. S. 270, 21 Sup. Ct. 128 (1900).
[16] State v. Napier, 63 S. C. 60, 41 S. E. 13 (1902); State v. Roberson, 136 N. C. 587, 48 S. E. 595 (1904).
[17] People ex rel. Armstrong v. Warden of the City Prison of N. Y., 183 N. Y. 223, 76 N. E. 11 (1905); Price v. People, 193 Ill. 114, 61 N. E. 844 (1901).
[18] Initiative Measure No. 8, adopted November 3, 1914.
[19] Wiseman v. Tanner, 221 Fed. 694 (1914).
[20] Adams v. Tanner, 244 U. S. 590, 37 Sup. Ct. 662 (1917).

10   PRINCIPLES OF LABOR LEGISLATION

ion emphasized facts regarding the actual abuses of the private agencies rather than abstract principles of law.

The United States Supreme Court in 1928 went even further and held that the power of the states to regulate fee-charging employment agencies does not include the power to regulate the amount of the fees which these agencies may charge.[21] In this case, Ribnik v. McBride, the fee-fixing provision of the New Jersey statute was declared unconstitutional by a majority of the court on the ground that the employment agency business is not one having "that 'public interest' which the law contemplates as the basis for legislative price control." "That business," the court said, "does not differ in substantial character from the business of a real estate broker, ship broker, merchandise broker, or ticket broker." A strong dissenting opinion was delivered by Mr. Justice Stone, with the concurrence of Justices Holmes and Brandeis. The decisions in the Ribnik and earlier cases have been held by a lower federal court not to prevent states from prohibiting the charging of fees merely for the registration of applicants.[22]

In 1919 the Wisconsin legislature attempted to deal with the problem from a new angle, by giving the state industrial commission discretionary power to regulate fees and to refuse licenses to private employment agencies if the public bureau or private agencies in the community are sufficient to supply needs.[23] This amended the statute of 1913 which had given the commission such discretionary powers of refusal if in its judgment existing licensed agencies were sufficient for the needs of the community. Official reports show that the number of fee-charging agencies decreased from thirty-eight in 1913-1914 to twenty-six in 1918, to sixteen, of which nine served common labor, in 1919-1920, and to nine, of which three served common labor, in 1925-1926. In 1935, ten agencies were licensed, only one of which was for common labor, and they reported fewer than 5,000 placements in all.[24]

[21] Ribnik v. McBride, 277 U. S. 350, 48 Sup. Ct. 545 (1928).
[22] National Employment Exchange v. Geraghty, U. S. Circuit Court of Appeals, Second Circuit, July 29, 1932.
[23] Wisconsin, Laws 1919, C. 178.
[24] Industrial Commission of Wisconsin, *Biennial Report, 1918-1920*, p. 42, and *Wisconsin Labor Market*, January, 1926, p. 16, and January, 1936, p. 8.

EMPLOYMENT AND UNEMPLOYMENT 11

In many other countries, dissatisfaction with the private commercial agencies has led to their more or less complete abolition. By 1936 in Canada, such agencies had been prohibited in Saskatchewan (1919), Manitoba (1919), British Columbia (1919), Alberta (1920), Nova Scotia (1920), and Quebec (1932).[25] In Germany, a law of 1922 establishing a national system of public employment offices also provided that fee-charging agencies should be abolished in 1931. Such prohibition went into effect in that year, although at the end of 1930 there were 1,473 such agencies licensed.[26] In Italy a decree in 1929 prohibited the placement of workers for fee in occupations for which public employment offices have been set up. Other countries in which fee-charging agencies have been totally or partially abolished are Bulgaria, Chile, Finland, Rumania, and Yugoslavia. In the Netherlands and Poland gradual abolition is assured by laws providing that no new agencies shall be licensed.[27]

The official International Labor Organization has taken action looking toward the abolition of fee-charging agencies in all countries. At the first session of the International Labor Conference, held in Washington in 1919, a recommendation was adopted proposing that members take measures "to prohibit the establishment of employment agencies which charge fees or which carry on their business for profit." At the second session, in 1920, a convention was adopted whereby ratifying members agree "to take all practicable measures to abolish the practice of finding employment for seamen as a commercial enterprise for pecuniary gain as soon as possible."[28] Finally, the 1933 conference adopted a convention[29] under which fee-charging agencies conducted for profit are, with some exceptions, to be pro-

[25] Industrial Relations Counselors, Inc., *Administration of Public Employment Offices and Unemployment Insurance: Canada*, 1935, p. 58.

[26] Weigert, O., *Administration of Placement and Unemployment Insurance in Germany*, 1934, pp. 131-132.

[27] International Labor Office, *Abolition of Fee-Charging Employment Agencies*, 1932.

[28] International Labor Office, *Official Bulletin*, vol. i, pp. 419 and 556. By 1936, the Seamen's Convention had been ratified by twenty-four countries.

[29] *Ibid.*, vol. xviii, p. 299.

12 PRINCIPLES OF LABOR LEGISLATION

hibited within three years after ratification. Non-profit-making agencies may be permitted under public regulation.

II. PUBLIC EMPLOYMENT OFFICES

The agitation for public employment offices has been due partly to the search for a remedy for the abuses of private agencies and partly to a deepening conviction that it is a proper function of the state to help the unemployed find work. The first American state to make provision for employment offices was Ohio in 1890, followed by Montana in 1895, and New York in 1896.[30] The majority of the present laws have been enacted since 1900.

1. **State and Municipal Offices.**—Prior to the World War, the development of public employment offices in the United States was a function almost entirely carried on by states and cities. The depressions of 1907 and 1914 led to public demand for legislation creating such offices, and as a result numerous offices were established by laws in various states. Nevertheless, at the time the United States entered the war there were in this country fewer than one hundred public employment offices, located in twenty-six states.[31] A majority were operated by the states, more than a dozen by cities, and others by cities, counties and states cooperatively, with aggregate appropriations of approximately $400,000.[32]

Although many of these offices performed useful service within the limitations of their appropriations, and some of them developed methods of operation which have since been accepted as standard, their inadequacy became apparent when the war emergency created an unprecedented demand for workers to replace those who had left industry for war and to man the rapidly developing war industries. In this situation, the federal government was forced to step in and set up, almost over night, a nation-wide system of public employment offices; and when the armistice was declared in November, 1918, there were some eight hundred offices, operating in every state in the Union.

[30] The original Montana and New York laws were soon repealed.
[31] Herndon, John G., Jr., "Public Employment Offices in the United States," U. S. Bureau of Labor Statistics, *Bulletin No. 241*, 1918, p. 12.
[32] Harrison, Shelby M., and Associates, *Public Employment Offices*, 1924, p. 624.

EMPLOYMENT AND UNEMPLOYMENT 13

When federal appropriations were cut drastically, some of these offices were continued by the states. Early in 1920, there were 269 offices, located in 42 states, supported by appropriations totaling about $1,500,000. During the following decade, however, the number further declined so that by 1930 there were only 151 state offices in 24 states,[33] with expenditures slightly over $1,250,000.[34]

One of the most important lessons which these state employment offices taught from the very beginning was the fundamental necessity of a high type of managerial ability and technical knowledge on the part of the heads and staff members of these offices. The needed qualifications were not often found in states where appointments were not on a merit basis, and even in states with civil service laws the low salaries offered frequently failed to attract persons with adequate training and ability. Closely related and equally essential to effective operation is a strict policy of unswerving neutrality in matters relating to labor organization and industrial disputes. Employment offices are dependent for success upon the patronage of both workers and employers, and any suspicion of partisanship on the part of either group seriously impairs the usefulness of the service.

An administrative device which has helped to raise standards of employment office personnel and policy, where it has been used, has been the advisory committee made up of representatives of employers, employees and the general public. Although

---

[33] By 1930 the following thirty-four states had specific statutory provision for public employment offices: Arizona, 1917; Arkansas, 1917; California, 1915; Colorado, 1907; Connecticut, 1905; Delaware, 1929; Georgia, 1917; Illinois, 1899; Indiana, 1909; Iowa, 1915; Kansas, 1901; Kentucky, 1906; Louisiana, 1921; Maryland, 1902 and 1914; Massachusetts, 1906; Michigan, 1905; Minnesota, 1905; Missouri, 1899; Nebraska, 1897; Nevada, 1923; New Hampshire, 1917; New Jersey, 1915; New York, 1914; North Carolina, 1921; North Dakota, 1921; Ohio, 1890; Oklahoma, 1908; Pennsylvania, 1915; Rhode Island, 1908; South Dakota, 1913; Utah, 1917; Virginia, 1924; West Virginia, 1901; and Wisconsin, 1901. Of these, the following had no state employment offices in 1930: Arizona, Colorado, Delaware, Georgia, Kentucky, Louisiana, Maryland, Nebraska, North Dakota, South Dakota, and Utah. Maine, without specific legislative provision, had one office.

[34] U. S. Bureau of Labor Statistics, *Monthly Labor Review*, January, 1931, p. 22.

they usually are given no administrative authority, such committees, when truly representative of all three groups concerned with the effective operation of the employment offices, have exerted a healthy influence by keeping a critical eye upon personnel and placement policies. They have also been a source of helpful suggestions for improving the service, and a medium through which employers and workers may be educated to make use of the public offices. The first committee of this type was set up in Milwaukee, Wisconsin, in 1911, and has been credited in large measure for making the public employment office in that city one of the best in the country. Later, advisory committees were required by laws creating employment offices in other states, including Illinois[35] and Pennsylvania.[36] They were also introduced in the employment services of other countries, and were recommended by the first official International Labor Conference in 1919. They are now required in all states receiving federal grants under the Federal Employment Service Act of 1933.

Perhaps the most controversial point in the administration of an employment office is the policy to be pursued in time of strike or lockout. The first Illinois law establishing state employment offices in 1899[37] was four years later declared unconstitutional because of a provision that applications to fill places vacant because of a strike were not to be received.[38] The court held that this provision deprived citizens of the equal protection of the laws guaranteed by the Fourteenth Amendment, inasmuch as it discriminated between employers whose men were on strike and other employers, and also between workmen who wished to take places vacant because of a strike and workmen who did not. Wisconsin had a similar experience. The healthy instinct of which this prohibitory clause was an unskilled manifestation was later satisfied in most states by publicity. For example, in some states either party to a trade dispute has been permitted to file a statement, which, with any answer, must be exhibited at the employment office. The prospective employee is then informed of the statements at the same time that he is informed

---

[35] Illinois, Laws 1915, p. 414.
[36] Pennsylvania, Laws 1915, No. 373.
[37] Illinois, Laws 1899, p. 268.
[38] Matthews *v.* People, 202 Ill. 389, 67 N. E. 28 (1903).

of the position, and it is left to him to decide whether or not to take the work. It has even been a practice to stamp the introduction card which the employee is to present to the prospective employer with the words, "There is a strike on at this establishment." Under the publicity policy very few applicants take strike-breaking jobs. Employers and labor union representatives are thoroughly satisfied, and consequently the office escapes the rocks of disaster on either side. An important corollary to this method of handling a strike situation is, of course, that no applicant must suffer any disqualification or prejudice at an office if he refuses to accept an offered job on the ground that a strike or lockout exists or because the wages offered are lower than those current in the district for the same work.

A special feature of the public employment office system in New York has been the provision for special assistance to juveniles. In that state children of working age may register at the schools, and a special advisory committee is provided to assist in the management of the juvenile department of the employment offices and otherwise to aid parents and children with respect to the choice of employment. Special provisions for juveniles were also introduced in other states, sometimes operating in cooperation with school placement bureaus and school authorities generally.

Often, as has been recognized in the British and German systems, lack of railroad fare to reach an offered position is a serious obstacle to a willing but moneyless worker, yet no American state authorizes its employment bureau officials to advance the needed transportation. A few superintendents, however, have advanced fares in exceptional cases, and the Wisconsin offices frequently have turned over to applicants the transportation advanced by the prospective employer, checking the man's baggage to the employer as a safeguard. During the World War, the Minnesota Commission of Public Safety set aside $1,000 to be used as a revolving fund for advancing fares to men placed by the state employment office. Considerable care was exercised in selecting the men to receive these advances. In each of two years' experience the losses from the fund were less than 5 per cent, and arose ordinarily because the farmers to whom men were sent secured other help and then refused to reimburse the employment office.

One important shortcoming of state employment office systems was the lack of systematic clearing of labor between states. While some states provided for regular notification to each office of jobs not filled and workers not placed by other offices in the state, no agency existed to bring about such systematic interchange between states. The closest approach to it was the National Farm Labor Exchange, organized during the winter of 1914-1915 by several public employment offices and labor department officials in the grain-raising states, in cooperation with the United States Departments of Labor and of Agriculture, for the efficient placing of harvest hands. Since harvesting begins two months earlier in the southern than in the northern part of the country, and furnishes at most only a few weeks' work in any one place, it was felt necessary to develop some means for more carefully directing the large numbers of workers who "follow the crops," and for preventing hardship to them by loss of time and by congestion in districts already flooded with workers. The exchange had no administrative powers and represented simply a means of exchanging information and effecting personal contact between the offices in the several states. It did not constitute an organization of the Middle West market for harvest labor. But it was a short step in the right direction.[39] This organization met in annual convention for a number of years during the war and again in 1920, following the collapse of the federal employment service.

Notwithstanding the good work of a few, however, the state and municipal employment offices were still far from furnishing an adequate medium for the exchange of information on opportunities for employment. Only about half the states were represented. Because of lack of civil service requirements, many of the managers were political place-holders of worse than mediocre attainments. Some of the offices existed, as has been seen, only on paper, others were poorly located, in out-of-the-way places, and inadequately heated, lighted, and ventilated. Many had therefore driven away the better class of workers, and dealt only with casuals. Appropriations were usually too small for efficiency. A uniform method of record-keeping had yet to be adopted. Statistics were non-comparable, and frequently unreliable, if not wholly valueless. There was prac-

[39] Lescohier, Don D., *The Labor Market*, 1919, p. 173.

EMPLOYMENT AND UNEMPLOYMENT 17

tically no interchange of information between various offices in a state or between states.

It was evident that there was need for federal leadership and encouragement designed to provide additional financial support, higher standards in personnel and methods, and coordination of the various state systems.

2. **Foreign National Systems.**—The value of a coordinated national system of public employment offices had already been demonstrated in other countries. The neighboring Dominion of Canada provided a good example of such a system under a federal government.[40] Although the provinces of Ontario and Quebec had established a few public offices prior to the war, the Canadian employment service was developed to meet war needs. In 1918, the dominion legislature adopted the Employment Offices Coordination Act[41] requiring the Canadian Department of Labor to coordinate the provincial employment office systems, issue needed regulations, and distribute to those provincial governments which accepted the terms of the act, subsidies not to exceed 50 per cent of the amount expended by each upon its employment service. By 1923, all provinces except Prince Edward Island were cooperating under this plan. In 1934 there were seventy-six local employment offices, six clearing houses established by the provinces, and two interprovincial clearing houses established by the dominion government. In normal times this service has placed over 400,000 wage earners annually, a large number when it is considered that Canada is an agricultural country of less than 11,000,000 population. Regulations of the Department of Labor provided an advisory national council composed of representatives of provincial and dominion governments, employers', employees', farmers', and veterans' organizations. By special arrangement, the railways of Canada grant reduced transportation rates to workers who are referred by the service to distant jobs where the fares amount to $4 or more. Extension of federal participation in the operation of public employment offices was forecast by the adoption, in 1935, of the Employment and Social Insurance Act

---

[40] Industrial Relations Counselors, Inc., *Administration of Public Employment Offices and Unemployment Insurance: Canada*, 1935.
[41] Canada, Laws 1918, C. 21.

providing for a national system of unemployment insurance administered through a public employment service.

In Europe also, the war emergency, and subsequently the great increase in unemployment, led to a tremendous development in public employment offices. This was particularly true of countries in which compulsory systems of unemployment insurance, administered by the state, were adopted.[42]

The first European legislation to establish a well-unified and distinctly national system of employment offices was the British Labor Exchanges Act of 1909.[43] This act, which is still the legislative basis of the British system, gives the administrative authority—at first, the Board of Trade but beginning in 1917 the Ministry of Labor—broad discretionary powers as to the details of the system. It authorizes establishment of employment offices as needed, making of regulations for their management, assistance to offices maintained by other authorities, and creation of advisory committees to assist in the management of the offices. With the approval of the Treasury, loans may be made to cover traveling expenses of workers for whom employment has been found through an office.

The general regulations[44] made by the board under authority of the act set forth in great detail the rules of organization and management of the offices. Registrations of applicants must usually be made in person and renewed after seven days if employment is not obtained. During a labor dispute the parties are permitted to file statements in regard to the disagreement and applicants are to be informed of its existence. Applicants who refuse positions because of labor disputes, or because the wages offered are lower than those current in the trade, do not sacrifice any of their privileges to future services of the exchanges. The offices "shall undertake no responsibility with regard to wages or other conditions" beyond supplying what information may be in their possession.

The general regulations also prescribe the conditions on

[42] See pp. 294 ff.
[43] 9 Edw. 7, C. 8. For full text of the act and account of the British employment service, see Chegwidden, T. S., and Myrddin-Evans, G., *The Employment Exchange Service of Great Britain*, 1934.
[44] *General Regulations for Labour Exchanges Managed by the Board of Trade*, January 28, 1910.

which railroad fares may be advanced as loans to workmen who are sent to other towns to take employment. No advances are to be made unless the distance to be traveled is more than five miles, nor to points where a labor dispute is in progress or when the wages offered are below the current rates. Care is also to be taken to avoid "unduly encouraging rural laborers to migrate from the country to towns." The provisions for advances have been widely used. In 1929 their total for the year rose to £40,479, but then declined to £19,477 for 1932 owing to depression conditions. In the majority of instances part of the advances are repaid out of the unemployment insurance fund; sometimes the employer agrees to make repayment. Otherwise, the employee makes payments in installments.

Advisory committees have been organized consisting of equal numbers of representatives of employers and workmen; representatives of other groups such as the local authorities and ex-service men's associations, as well as persons with special knowledge or experience; and a chairman chosen by the Ministry of Labor. At first, only a few such advisory committees were created, each for a large area; but beginning in 1917, many local committees were set up with jurisdiction over one or more offices. By 1934 there were 333 such committees. They may consider and advise administrative officials on any matter connected with the operation of employment offices with a view to promoting their usefulness.

Special recognition has been given in Great Britain to the need for agencies to assist juvenile workers in choosing an occupation, finding employment in that occupation, and avoiding frequent changes in the early years of their working experience. This function, however, has been carried on by both the employment office system and the local school authorities. Establishment of employment bureaus for juveniles by local educational authorities was authorized by the Choice of Employment Act of 1910, while the employment exchanges were authorized by special rule in 1913 to establish juvenile departments in areas where the educational authorities did not provide such a service. Since 1923, the educational authorities have had the option of undertaking both placement work and administration of unemployment benefits for juveniles, or leaving both functions to the employment exchanges. In a majority of cases the work has been left to the employment offices; and where educational authorities do undertake placement activities, they are in this respect supervised by the Ministry of Labor.

There were sixty-one offices in 1910, but the number was increased until 391 were in operation during the war. Extension of unemployment insurance, under the act of 1920, necessitated a further increase, and by January, 1933, there were 420 exchanges and 747 branch offices in the system. The country is divided into seven districts—five for England and one each for Scotland and Wales. Each district has its divisional office or clearing house, which in turn is coordinated with the central office in London. Additional "intensive clearing areas" have been created in several large industrial centers. Notices of unfilled positions are first circulated among the offices of the clearing area, and then, if necessary, and if the position is one for which a worker may suitably be brought in from a distance, they are sent to the central office in London, from which a description goes next day to every exchange in the country. Since 1923, the British employment office system has filled over a million vacancies annually, almost reaching the two-million mark in 1931, when 1,952,057 vacancies were filled.

In France, although since 1904 municipalities of 10,000 or more population had been required to set up employment bureaus and in 1911 the subsidy plan was adopted, these offices were not coordinated nationally until the war. In 1933, the system consisted of a central office, seven regional offices, a departmental office in each of the ninety departments, a municipal office in each city of 10,000 or more population, and registries in all other municipalities. From 1925 to 1933, this system placed from about one-and-a-quarter to about one-and-a-half million workers annually.[45]

In Germany also, war necessities led to additions to and national control over the several hundred employment offices which previously had been maintained in loose federation by cities and voluntary associations which were granted subsidies from cities, states and the national government. A law of 1922 established a national system coordinated and supervised by

[45] Gilbert, A., *Administration of Public Employment Offices and Unemployment Insurance: France,* Industrial Relations Counselors, Inc., 1935.

EMPLOYMENT AND UNEMPLOYMENT 21

state and federal authorities, and in 1927 the employment offices were brought within the unemployment insurance system, with central control by the Federal Institution for Placement and Unemployment Insurance. In 1933 there were thirteen district offices and 363 local offices, and from 1928 to 1932 the system placed from three to six million workers annually.[46]

National subsidies have played an important rôle in foreign employment office legislation. Several countries have tried to raise the efficiency of local public employment offices by granting subsidies only to those which conformed to the standards fixed by the national government. Beginning with the World War period, many countries have increased the extent of national supervision or control. Some have made establishment of public employment offices compulsory upon local governments; in others this function has been taken over by the national government itself.[47] In 1919, the International Labor Conference adopted a convention[48] under which ratifying countries agree to establish a "system of free public employment agencies under the control of a central authority," with representative committees to advise on matters concerning their operation. It was also provided that the various national systems should be coordinated by the International Labor Office in agreement with the countries concerned. By January, 1936, this convention had been ratified by thirty countries.

3. **Federal-State System.**—Growing realization of the need for development of a nation-wide system of public employment offices in this country led to the creation of the United States Employment Service. During its first twenty-five years this service had a checkered career.[49] It had its beginnings in a program for placing immigrants on farms, inaugurated by

[46] Weigert, O., *Administration of Placement and Unemployment Insurance in Germany*, 1934.

[47] For a recent study of public employment office practice in other countries, see International Labor Office, *Employment Exchanges, an International Study of Placing Activities,* Studies and Reports, Series C, No. 18, 1933.

[48] International Labor Office, *Official Bulletin,* vol. i, pp. 417-419. See *Industrial and Labor Information* for latest chart on progress of ratifications.

[49] See Lescohier, Don D., *The Labor Market,* 1919; and U. S. Bureau of Labor Statistics, *Monthly Labor Review,* January, 1931, pp. 10-32.

the Federal Bureau of Immigration in 1907. In 1915 this service was extended by the bureau to cover all occupations and all classes of workers. By the middle of 1917, it operated over ninety offices in thirty-seven states. Although it made efforts to cooperate with state employment offices in various parts of the country, the service was handicapped by small appropriations, by its subordinate position in another bureau, and by the fact that many of its employees were immigration officials whose main line of work was not labor placement.

A few months after the United States entered the war, Congress appropriated $250,000, to which the President added $825,000 out of his security and defense fund, for the development of an employment service to meet the war emergency. In January, 1918, the Federal Employment Service was separated from the Immigration Bureau and made an independent division in the Department of Labor. There followed a feverish expansion of the service, and additional funds were provided by the President and Congress. By October, 1918, a total of 832 offices were in operation, covering every state, the District of Columbia and Puerto Rico. There were sixty-four offices in Illinois, sixty-nine in New York, and seventy-four in Pennsylvania.

In addition to offices doing general placement work, there were others which were specialized to deal with particular groups of workers. Some placed men or women exclusively; some were devoted to placing railroad, and others farm, labor; one Chicago office supplied demands for engineers and teachers. A plan for centralizing the hiring of longshoremen was put into operation in New York City, with a central clearing house and branch offices at every pier handling transatlantic trade. A special service for farm labor involved cooperation of postmasters in receiving and reporting applications, and of county agents of the Department of Agriculture in reporting shortages of help. During the harvest season, temporary offices were opened in the wheat belt to mobilize harvest hands. The central administrative machinery of the employment service was completely reorganized into five main divisions—Control, Field Organization, Clearance, Personnel, and Information—and in each state, responsibility was centered in a federal director of employment. State advisory boards were created, consisting at

EMPLOYMENT AND UNEMPLOYMENT

first of two representatives of employees and two of employers. Later the boards were asked to add two women members, also representing employers and employees, respectively.

Under its expanded organization the Federal Employment Service, between January, 1918, and March, 1919, received applications for no fewer than 10,164,000 workers, registered 5,323,509 persons, referred 4,906,556 to positions, and reported 3,776,750 positions filled. Far-reaching dependence of employers on the service began on August 1, 1918, when by presidential proclamation all employers engaged in war work who employed more than 100 persons were required to hire their unskilled laborers through the service.

Following the cessation of hostilities, the service attempted to direct the replacement of soldiers and war workers in civil pursuits. In cooperation with chambers of commerce, local councils of defense, and other agencies, it established 1,850 special bureaus for the placement of returning soldiers and sailors. Representatives of the service were stationed in the demobilization camps to help the soldiers go direct from the camp to employment.

But the service, in its expanded form, was entirely a creation of the war emergency, set up under the President's war powers and financed by war funds. It's machinery had to be built up and operated at the same time. In nine months it opened twice as many offices as England opened in four years. In the circumstances it was probably inevitable that certain weaknesses in organization and personnel should appear. Some employers also attacked the service on the alleged ground that it was dominated by organized labor, and it was charged that private fee-charging agencies carried on a subterranean campaign against it. In March, 1919, Congress refused to grant a deficiency appropriation of $1,800,000 to carry it to June 30, the end of the fiscal year. It was first stated that it would be necessary to cut down the offices 80 per cent, but through the cooperation of cities, states, and voluntary welfare organizations, the continuance of 364 offices was secured for a time. For the next fiscal year, however, the service asked Congress for $4,600,000 and received only $400,000. In October, 1919, it was announced that all the local offices were closed for lack of funds, and the only remaining activity would be the supplying of information to local public offices.

There followed a decade in which the Federal Employment Service was severely restricted in its activities by the small size of its appropriation, which was gradually cut from $225,000 in 1921 to $200,000 annually from 1928 to 1930. With these meager funds, the service functioned in a limited way as a coordinating and promotive agency for the various state and municipal offices. It published a monthly employment information bulletin and appointed the official head of each state service, or, where there was none, a representative of local offices, as federal director of the United States Employment Service, at a dollar a year. The appointment carried the franking privilege and, in some cases, small subsidies to help pay for clerical assistance. The most active branch of the service during these years related to farm labor, temporary field agents being employed during the harvesting season to help direct the placement of harvest hands. In 1930 a veterans' division was created in the service; this division opened placement offices in thirty cities.

Efforts to place the Federal Employment Service on a more permanent and effective basis began in 1919 as soon as it became evident that the war-time organization would have to be largely disbanded because of reduced appropriations. A conference called in Washington by Secretary of Labor Wilson early that year and composed of representatives of governors, federal and state employment services, employers and labor organizations, prepared the outline of a plan which was later drafted in the form of a bill by a subcommittee of the conference. This bill was introduced in Congress in 1919 and 1925, and with amendments in 1928. The coming of the depression in 1930 led to a vigorous campaign for this measure which was sponsored in Congress by Senator Robert F. Wagner of New York. Despite administration opposition, it was enacted by Congress in February, 1931, only to be vetoed by President Hoover after Congress had adjourned.

There immediately followed a reorganization and expansion of the Federal Employment Service with the use of a special $500,000 additional appropriation which had been made by Congress. At least one federal employment office was opened in each state, with a "state director," appointed from Washington, in charge. Seven industrial divisions were created, each with a superintendent. The new set-up was widely criticized by advocates of an effective public employment office system on the ground that it was a political maneuver; and private investigations showed that the type of appointments made appeared to corroborate the allegation. Claims of substantial accomplishment issued by Secretary of Labor Doak were challenged by state employment office officials, who pointed out that the federal offices were being opened in communities already served by state offices, thus causing needless duplication of effort. This reorganized service[50] continued to function until it was abolished by Secretary of Labor Frances Perkins soon after her appointment in 1933. On June 6, 1933, the Wagner measure, again adopted by Congress, was approved by President Roosevelt.

The 1933 act[51] established the United States Employment Service as a bureau in the Department of Labor. It authorized an appropriation of $1,500,000 for the year ending June 20, 1934, and $4,000,000 for each of the succeeding four years. One-fourth of the annual appropriation is made available for the expenses of the federal bureau. The remainder is allotted to the states on the basis of population, and is available on a dollar-for-dollar basis to states which maintain systems of employment offices in conformity with standards developed through the federal service. The function of the federal service as fixed by law is to provide the means for clearing labor between states and to promote the efficiency of public employment offices. The act provides for a Federal Advisory Council, consisting of representatives of employers, employees and the public, to assist the federal director, and requires similar councils to be set up in the states.

As provided in the law, the Federal Employment Service has prepared minimum standards which the states must maintain in order to receive the federal grants-in-aid. These stand-

[50] For a description of the "Doak reorganization," see articles in the *American Labor Legislation Review,* 1931, vol. xxi, pp. 85-93, 199-203, 297-299, and 393-394; also Kellogg, Ruth M., *The United States Employment Service,* 1933.

[51] Public No. 30, 73d Congress, 1933.

26 PRINCIPLES OF LABOR LEGISLATION

ards cover such matters as personnel, premises, statistical reports of operations, signs, telephone listings, terminology, use of the franking privilege, strikes or lockouts, and organization of state and local advisory councils. The standards include the requirement of merit tests in the selection of employment office personnel; in states having no civil service laws, these tests have been held under the supervision of the

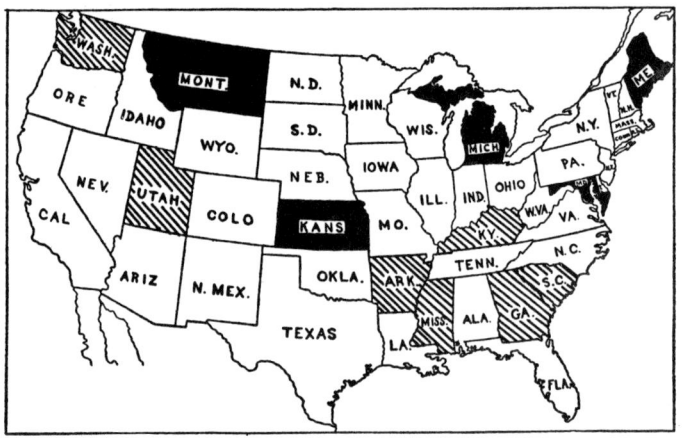

FEDERAL-STATE EMPLOYMENT OFFICE SYSTEM

All except the five black states by July 1, 1936, had enacted legislation to provide public employment offices cooperating through the United States Employment Service. Seven states (indicated by diagonal lines), although having such legislation, had not yet qualified for federal aid under the Federal Employment Service Act.

Federal Employment Service. Besides operation of the District of Columbia employment office, the service conducts a farm placement service and a veterans' placement service, both, however, operating in close cooperation with the state employment offices. All necessary forms for handling registrations and statistical reports are furnished to the state offices by the federal service.

Within a month after the law creating the Federal Employment Service was adopted, this service was called upon to provide the means of directing labor to jobs on public works projects and other types of employment provided in a nation-

EMPLOYMENT AND UNEMPLOYMENT

wide effort to overcome an unprecedented unemployment crisis. For this purpose a temporary "national reemployment service" was created which at the end of six months was operating 3,271 offices and had a personnel of 17,850. At least one office was opened in every county in the country not served by a state employment office. These temporary offices, which were financed by a special grant from federal relief funds, were closed or consolidated when the special need for them ended. On June 1, 1936, there were still 1,390 reemployment offices in operation.

Meanwhile, states were entering into agreements of affiliation with the Federal Employment Service in order to qualify for grants-in-aid as provided by Congress. By the end of the first year, eighteen states, with 166 offices in 132 cities, had thus affiliated, and by June 1, 1936, the number had increased to thirty-five states, with 296 district and local state employment offices. Thus, for the first time, the United States has made a substantial beginning in the development of a well-planned, permanent system of public employment offices. Enactment of state unemployment compensation laws greatly increased the importance of the continued improvement and expansion of this system.

III. SYSTEMATIC DISTRIBUTION OF PUBLIC WORK

A well-developed system of employment offices cannot, of course, create jobs; but in addition to bringing the jobless workers quickly and smoothly in contact with such opportunities as exist, it can register the rise and fall in the demand for labor. This knowledge would make possible intelligent action for the prevention and relief of unemployment through the systematic distribution of public work and the pushing of necessary projects when private industry's demand for labor is at a low level. Public work would then act as a sponge, absorbing the reserves of labor in bad years and slack seasons, and setting them free again when the demand for them increases in private business.

1. **Emergency Work.**—Probably ever since unemployment became a modern industrial problem there have been more or less insistent demands that the machinery of government be used for putting temporarily to work those who were displaced

28   PRINCIPLES OF LABOR LEGISLATION

from private industry during a period of depression. It was felt that supporting the unemployed in this way, or, rather, thus giving them the chance under community direction to support themselves, was preferable to supporting them either by public relief or by private charity. It was not likely to cost any more, the stigma of pauperism would not be fastened upon self-respecting persons out of work through no fault of their own, and, finally, some improvement of permanent value to the community would have been furthered.

As early as the panic year of 1857, when 70,000 were estimated to be unemployed in New York alone, Mayor Wood of that city sent to the common council a message in which he said:

"I recommend that the comptroller be authorized to advertise for estimates for furnishing the corporation with 50,000 barrels of flour and a corresponding quantity of corn-meal and potatoes, to be paid for by the issue of a public construction stock redeemable in fifty years, and paying 7 per cent interest; these provisions to be disposed of to laborers to be employed upon public works, at their cost price to the corporation, all these works to be commenced forthwith under the proper departments. Twenty-five per cent should be paid in cash. Every man who will labor should be employed at a fair compensation, and the supplies thus provided be distributed in return."[52]

Apparently the mayor's suggestion was not acted upon; but Central Park was then under construction and the city comptroller arranged to advance to the park commissioners $1,000 a day until such time as the city should take $25,000 of the bonds. The commissioners agreed in return to select not exceeding 1,000 of their workmen proportionally from the residents of each ward.[53] In this way a considerable portion of the work was made available when it could exert the largest influence in preventing destitution and demoralization.

During the severe unemployment crisis of 1914-1915, over 100 cities throughout the country made special provision for carrying on public work of various sorts, such as sewer-build-

[52] *Report of the Massachusetts Board to Investigate the Subject of the Unemployed,* 1895, Pt. IV, pp. 7-8.
[53] *Ibid.,* pp. 9-10.

EMPLOYMENT AND UNEMPLOYMENT 29

ing, street- and road-making, quarrying, forestry, drainage, waterworks, building, painting, and even clerical duties. The work was maintained for periods ranging from less than a month to more than six months, thousands of men were employed in from two-day to two-week shifts, and hours and rates of pay were as a rule the same as for regular employees on the same grade of labor. In the majority of cases the officials in charge declared that they had secured full efficiency from the workmen, and some even stated that necessary work had been done at a distinct saving.

In 1920-1922, when unemployment was again a matter of grave public concern, a survey by the American Association for Labor Legislation showed that, although many cities raised funds by bonds or loans with which to push forward public works as a means of relief, few had previously made efforts to reserve necessary improvements for periods of depression or maintained an emergency sinking fund.[54] The Conference on Unemployment called by President Harding at Washington in September, 1921, inaugurated the most thoroughgoing movement to meet the problem of unemployment that had yet been attempted in the United States. Its recommendations[55] included the expansion of public works to the fullest possible extent by concerted action of municipal, state, and federal authorities. Two months later it was reported to the standing committee of the conference that 209 out of 327 cities with 10,000 or more population, had organized "mayor's committees" or signified their ability to carry out the recommendations of the conference with machinery that already existed.[56] This effort resulted in an unprecedented expansion of public works by cities in the winter of 1921-1922.

This increased use of public works as a means of relieving unemployment brought city officials face to face with charter limitations on the expenditure of money. Many makeshift devices were adopted to overcome these restrictions, such as raising money by public subscription, borrowing without interest, or transferring funds between departments; and in some cases

[54] *American Labor Legislation Review*, September, 1921, pp. 207-210.
[55] President's Conference on Unemployment, *Report*, 1921, pp. 20 and 89.
[56] United States Bureau of Labor Statistics, *Monthly Labor Review*, December, 1921, p. 117.

business men had to furnish bonds to save the city officials from liability. It was evident that budgetary methods, and even city charters, needed modification in order to permit greater freedom in carrying out such emergency programs. A significant innovation in 1921 was a special appropriation, by Congress, of $75,000,000 to be distributed among the states for the purpose of expanding the federal-state road construction program.

Despite the experience of 1921-1922, the country again in 1930 found itself plunged into a new depression, unprepared to deal with the enormous unemployment relief burden. At the outset, there was general public inclination to ignore the growing need and to rely upon an effort, made under the leadership of the President, to revive industry by appeals for increased capital expenditures and maintenance of wage rates. Gradually, when private charity organizations found the relief burden growing beyond their ability to meet it, local communities were forced to provide public relief. By the winter of 1931-1932, failing municipal resources forced states to undertake a large share of the burden; and finally in July, 1932, when in some instances even state taxing and borrowing had reached its limit, the federal government began to lend its aid to meet the cost of relief.

From the outset, public works were an important part of the relief program. Cities and states were at first encouraged to undertake new public works projects, and the federal government accelerated its construction program. Local relief agencies sought to provide part-time work for many of the needy unemployed. In 1932, the federal government began to provide financial aid by offering loans to states and cities for relief and for public works projects. In 1933 federal participation was greatly extended. In addition to an initial $500,000,000 fund to assist states in meeting their relief needs, Congress appropriated $3,300,000,000 for federal public works and for loans and grants for state and municipal projects. In 1933 a temporary "Civil Works Administration," and in 1935 a "Works Progress Administration," each part of the federal relief program, attempted to provide practically all employable persons on relief with work. Workers on relief were at

EMPLOYMENT AND UNEMPLOYMENT

first paid full hourly wages but were employed only sufficient hours to provide necessary subsistence; but in 1935 a system of payment was introduced designed to assure a regular income somewhat above the subsistence level and with a full-time work week. Meanwhile, as the need continued, Congress made additional appropriations to support this nation-wide relief and public works program.

In extent and variety of undertakings, the emergency public works and relief work programs begun in 1933 were without precedent. The public works program included everything from road construction to hydro-electric power projects. It even embraced the resettlement of farmers and workers from declining rural and industrial areas by transferring them to more promising communities especially built for this purpose. It extended to the organization of a Civilian Conservation Corps, consisting of unemployed, unmarried men between sixteen and twenty-five years of age, who were quartered in camps constructed throughout the country and who worked on soil and forest conservation projects chiefly in the national and state parks. Work performed under the relief program was equally, or even more, varied. Besides small public works undertakings such as street resurfacing and park improvement, work relief included artistic, musical, theatrical, educational, and research projects designed to give suitable employment to the "white collar" group among the unemployed.

Experiences with emergency work relief have not always been gratifying. Poor work, increased expense to the community, and political favoritism in the selection of applicants are among the faults that have frequently interfered with its accomplishing what was expected of it. On the other hand, the tendency of direct relief to break down the moral fiber of the unemployed, in addition to the ill effects of long periods of idleness, has led most social workers and public officials to favor the work relief method despite its recognized difficulties. The opinion has been growing that the flaws are not inherent, but may be largely overcome by proper administration. Against the added cost, which admittedly is a serious problem, must be placed the value of the work accomplished and also the human resources which are conserved and even improved.

Public works not undertaken on a relief basis are, of course, free from many of the problems involved in relief work.

2. **Adjustment of Regular Work.**—It is fast becoming recognized, however, that to wait until the emergency has overtaken the community before the movement to provide public work is set on foot is wasteful and productive of unnecessary hardship. Public officials are therefore more and more turning their attention to preparing in ordinary times for the period of stress which experience has shown is likely to follow in a few months or a few years.

One of the earliest American experiments in this direction grew out of an attempt to meet a specific emergency. In the winter of 1910-1911 the city of Duluth, Minn., confronted by an unusual number of seasonal workers turned adrift by the closing of transportation on the Great Lakes, decided to anticipate its need and cut through a wall of rock which blocked the chief thoroughfare. Drilling and blasting were done by regular city employees, but preparation of the rock for the crusher was assigned to the unemployed, who were given an average of three days' work each. Applicants were hired and retained only if they were fit and willing to work, and wages were set at $1.20 a day, a little less than the current rate, in order not to attract those who could find employment elsewhere. Payment in meals, clothing, employment agency fees, or railroad fare was given by the associated charities, which referred the men to the work and was reimbursed by the city.[57] The plan worked so successfully that it was followed in subsequent years, and in addition the city shifted much of its sewer-building to the winter season to assist in equalizing the amount of employment.

Such foresighted arrangement of public work is capable of considerable extension, and may be efficaciously used to counteract cyclical as well as seasonal fluctuations. The English statistician Bowley in 1909 estimated that if in the United Kingdom a fund were set aside for public work to be pushed ahead in times of depression, an average of $20,000,000 yearly, or only 3 per cent of the annual appropriation for public works and services, would be sufficient to balance the wage loss from

[57] Leiserson, W. M., "The Duluth Rock Pile," *The Survey*, September 20, 1913, pp. 729-731.

EMPLOYMENT AND UNEMPLOYMENT 33

commercial depression.[58] If his suggestion were generally accepted, in each community or country a program of the amount of public work contemplated for several years in advance would be laid out and then carefully planned to be executed in the lean years. Thus public work, instead of declining and thereby accentuating the depression, as is now often the case, would exert a strong influence toward stability.

Americans seem particularly unwilling to prepare in advance for periods of industrial depression. They appear to think of the unemployment problem and to take action on it only in a crisis. Yet by 1930 a number of American cities had acted upon this principle of advance planning. Several progressive communities made definite plans to reserve work on unimproved parks, sewers, and streets for future dull periods. Several, also, without planning definite undertakings, issued bonds or established contingent funds to provide the resources when needed.

An interesting development in this direction was the Idaho law of 1915, which, probably for the first time in the history of the country, recognized the "right to work." Every United States citizen who had been a resident of the state for six months, and who did not possess more than $1,000 worth of property, was guaranteed sixty days' emergency employment on the highways or other public work yearly. But before being put into operation to any large extent, the law was declared unconstitutional on technical grounds involving the method of appropriating funds and not the general principle.[59] It has not been reenacted.

Pennsylvania, in 1917, was the first state to enact a law establishing a permanent fund to be used for public work in slack seasons.[60] The machinery for administering the fund was set up, and $40,000 appropriated. In 1919 an opinion by the state attorney-general, to the effect that the appropriation did not lapse at the end of the regular appropriation period, facilitated its operation. The fund was exhausted in 1922 and the

[58] Great Britain, Royal Commission on the Poor Laws, *Minority Report*, 1909, p. 1195.
[59] Epperson *v.* Howell, 28 Idaho 338, 154 Pac. 621 (1916).
[60] Pennsylvania, Laws 1917, No. 411.

law was repealed in 1923 when a general departmental reorganization was effected.

In May, 1921, California enacted a law[61] providing for "the extension of the public works of the state . . . during periods of extraordinary unemployment caused by temporary industrial depression and regulating employment therein." The state board of control is required to secure from the various departments, bureaus, boards, and commissions of the state tentative plans for such extension of public work; the bureau of labor statistics in cooperation with the immigration, housing and industrial welfare commissions is required to keep constantly advised of industrial conditions throughout the state and to report to the governor when it has reason to believe that a period of extraordinary unemployment exists. In such case, the board of control is authorized to make at its discretion distribution of the available emergency fund among the said several departments, bureaus, etc., for such extension of public work as will afford most relief to the unemployed and benefit to the public. California thus had the machinery started to relieve her unemployed, estimated to be over 100,000 in the winter of 1921, and was able to supply the President's Conference with data.[62] In 1923, Wisconsin enacted a law similar to that of California.[63]

The federal Congress of 1921-1922 responded to the recommendations of the President's Conference on Unemployment regarding expansion of public works to the extent of appropriating $75,000,000 to be distributed among the states for road construction as authorized by the amended act of 1916 providing aid in construction of rural post roads.[64] This was $50,000,000 more than any previous annual appropriation under the act. The Kenyon bill, however, providing for adoption of a permanent federal policy of long-range planning, met with little favor.

Although bills were introduced in succeeding sessions of Congress for the purpose of creating a "prosperity reserve"

---

[61] California, Laws 1921, C. 246.
[62] California Bureau of Labor Statistics, *Biennial Report, 1921-1922*, pp. 346-347.
[63] Wisconsin, Laws 1923, C. 76.
[64] United States, Laws 1921, C. 87.

EMPLOYMENT AND UNEMPLOYMENT 35

of public works to be undertaken when employment declined, no legislation for public works planning was adopted by Congress until early in 1931 when unemployment had already reached alarming proportions. The law then enacted[65] declares it to be the policy of Congress "to arrange the construction of public works so far as practicable in such manner as will assist in the stabilization of industry and employment through the proper timing of such construction." It provides that certain bureaus and departments of the government shall prepare and maintain a six-year "advance plan" of construction and also "a program for prompt commencement and carrying out of an expanded program at any time." A federal employment stabilization board was created, with a staff to cooperate in formulating methods of advance planning. The law further provides that when the President finds that a business depression exists or appears to be impending, he is to ask Congress for emergency appropriations for public works construction to aid in preventing unemployment. Although this legislation was enacted too late to serve its intended purpose in the already existing depression, it provides a basis for effective planning in the future.[66]

In Great Britain the use of public work on a national scale as an equalizing reservoir for the labor market was partially authorized by the Development and Road Improvement Funds Act of 1909.[67] This law set aside sums of money which might be advanced either as grants or as loans to associations not organized for profit, for the purpose of aiding and developing agriculture and rural industries, forestry, land reclamation and drainage, rural transportation, harbors, inland navigation and fisheries. The act was not passed primarily as an unemployment measure, but contained the provision that when the execution of any work involved the employment of labor on a considerable scale the commissioners must take into consideration "the general state and prospects of employment." Under this clause a certain amount of influence could be exerted toward

[65] Public No. 616, 71st Congress, 3d Session, 1931.
[66] For a program of state and local action to supplement the federal law, see Mallery, Otto T., "Public Works to Stabilize Employment and Industry," *American Labor Legislation Review*, March, 1931, pp. 97-101.
[67] 9 Edw. 7, C. 47.

the timely initiation of public improvements, but its scope was usually overestimated.[68]

Most European governments encouraged the pushing of public works for relief of the widespread unemployment following the war, both by granting subsidies and loans to municipalities for financing such works and by directly undertaking them. This was a particularly opportune method of relief, as public works had of necessity been neglected during the war. The severity and long continuance of the business depression revealed the difficulties of this method of relief. On the other hand, in many quarters the conviction is growing that when unemployment relief is necessary, it is better to render it in return for labor than as a straight pension. Some countries have initiated, on a large scale, enterprises to provide work for the unemployed that would not otherwise have been undertaken. For the same purpose, beginning with Germany in 1920, several countries enacted legislation providing for "productive insurance," that is, the use of part of unemployment insurance funds for financing public (or, in certain cases, private) enterprises.[69] In most countries, public works have furnished relief for manual labor only, but Swiss decrees of 1919 and 1922 included provisions for relief work for intellectual and artistic workers, such as research, drafting plans and decorating public buildings.[70]

The principle under discussion has taken firm hold among those interested in combating involuntary idleness; and in 1913, as the result of careful studies in many countries, the following recommendations were laid before the International Conference on Unemployment: (1) That public works be distributed, as far as possible, in such a way that they may be undertaken in dull seasons or during industrial depression; (2) that budget laws be revised to facilitate the accumulation of reserve funds for this purpose; (3) that permanent institutions be created to study the symptoms of depression in order

[68] Hall, A. D., "The Development Act and Unemployment," National Conference on the Prevention of Destitution (Great Britain), *Report of the Proceedings of the Unemployment Section*, 1911, p. 245.

[69] International Labor Office, *Studies and Reports*, Series C, No. 10, p. 61.

[70] *Ibid.*, No. 4, p. 5; and *International Labour Review*, February-March, 1923, "Employment and Unemployment," p. 319.

EMPLOYMENT AND UNEMPLOYMENT   37

to advise the authorities when to initiate the reserved work; (4) that such work as land reclamation and improvement of the means of communication, which would tend to increase the permanent demand for labor, be especially undertaken; and (5) that in order to secure the fullest benefits from the reserved work, contracts should be awarded not as units, but separately for each trade. The first International Labor Conference, meeting at Washington in October, 1919, recommended to member countries that they should "coordinate the execution of all work undertaken under public authority, with a view to reserving such work as far as practicable for periods of unemployment and for districts most affected by it." Several succeeding conferences adopted resolutions urging the application of the advance-planning principle, and the International Labor Organization has repeatedly pressed this proposal at international conferences held under the auspices of the League of Nations.[71]

IV. REGULARIZATION OF INDUSTRY

While methods of utilizing public work to counteract the fluctuations of employment in private industry have occupied the attention of lawmakers, legislative expression has also been given to the demand that private industry turn some attention to solving the problem at its source by reducing, if not eliminating, these fluctuations. Regularization of industry is demanded by the interests of employer and employee alike. The employer, with an expensive plant, requires steady production to keep down overhead expenses and to secure the best returns from the business; the employee needs steady work to prevent destitution and consequent demoralization. It is not surprising, therefore, to find governments exerting pressure to the end that, as far as possible, every job be made a steady job. Society has in the past attempted to adjust itself to the ups and downs of business; it is now beginning to insist that business avoid ups and downs.

The eventful period between 1914 and 1929 stimulated

[71] Two important studies of public works planning issued by the International Labor Office are *Unemployment and Public Works*, Studies and Reports, Series C, No. 15, 1931; and *Public Works Policy*, Studies and Reports, Series C, No. 19, 1935.

thought and action along this line. During the war, the temporary expansion of the administrative powers of governments brought to them a large amount of information and the necessity of putting it to immediate use. In their recommendations the President's Conference on Unemployment and the standing committee appointed to carry on its work stressed the responsibility of governments in collecting and distributing information and forecasting the probable fluctuations in business; the responsibility of the banking system in regulating the credit upon which business depends, and the responsibility of the various industries and corporations in making use of all available information and studying methods of management in order to avoid undue inflation in time of prosperity leading to collapse and depression.[72]

In carrying out the first of these recommendations, the collection and dissemination of information, much progress has been made by several departments of the government, particularly by the Department of Commerce and the Federal Reserve Board, both of which publish periodical bulletins for the guidance of the business world. Probably still more far-reaching has been the effect of the banking system in controlling loans, and particularly of the Federal Reserve System, established in 1913, in advancing rates on credit when in its judgment industry is approaching a "boom," and lowering rates when a depression is threatened or in progress. Central banks of other countries have taken similar action, especially during the general discontinuance in Europe of the gold standard. Governments and financiers have also increased their efforts to revive the industries of their various countries by high tariffs to shut off foreign competition, special guaranteed payment schemes for exports, and subsidies or loans on easy terms to private enterprises, in many cases with the avowed intention of relieving unemployment. For the same end, emigration has been encouraged and immigration checked.

Industry itself has been held particularly accountable for seasonal depressions. Perhaps the greatest advance toward mitigating these has been made by the construction industry, characterized as "the balance wheel of American industry."

[72] Committee of the President's Conference on Unemployment, *Business Cycles and Unemployment*, 1923, pp. xix to xxvii.

EMPLOYMENT AND UNEMPLOYMENT

In a special report of the committee of the President's Conference, it was urged that both public and private construction be transferred as much as possible from summer, the busiest season, to winter, the dull season. The main steps recommended to accomplish this were education of those who contemplate building in regard to advantages of prices and the labor market in winter, pecuniary inducement to place orders for the dull season, and perfection of devices to overcome weather difficulties. The principles embodied in these recommendations have been indorsed by builders' associations, and in the large centers some progress has already been made in putting them into execution. The fact that public works normally have formed one-fourth of the total value of yearly construction in the United States makes the proper timing of their execution a powerful factor in avoiding seasonal as well as cyclical depressions.[73] Among important contributions to technical information in regard to regularization of employment by efficient management is that by the American Engineering Societies in connection with their surveys of various industries.[74]

Methods of regularization are as various as the industries concerned, if not as various as the individual establishments. Many employers have found it economical to organize employment departments for the purpose of studying and remedying fluctuations in the size of the working force; and in Boston, New York, and Philadelphia, associations of employment managers were formed as early as 1912 to discuss their common problems. Through these departments considerable hardship has been avoided by reducing excessive "turnover" of labor, by transferring workers from slack departments to busy ones instead of discharging them, and by employing the whole force on part time rather than part of the force on full time. Careful planning of output for months or even for a year ahead, the development of supplementary lines such as tennis shoes and rubber tires in a rubber-shoe factory, and special measures to overcome weather conditions, such as the introduction of artificial drying in the brick industry, have also been found helpful. Through cooperation with other employers for the

[73] Committee of the President's Conference on Unemployment, *Seasonal Operation in the Construction Industry*, 1924, chap. xii.
[74] Federated American Engineering Societies, *Waste in Industry*, 1921.

40   PRINCIPLES OF LABOR LEGISLATION

maintenance of a common reserve of labor instead of a separate supply for each firm, the intermittent character of such occupations as the building trades and dock work has been effectually reduced. An increasing number of books have been written describing the methods that have been put into effect by various concerns to stabilize employment.[75]

Perhaps the most interesting experiment in "decasualizing" casual employment is the system now in force in England, where for more than half a century thousands of men eked out a precarious and irregular longshoreman's livelihood. Each ship company sought to attract enough men every day to meet the need on the busiest days, and it was alleged that some employers deliberately parceled out the work so that many more than the usual number employed were encouraged to be on hand and available when wanted.[76]

To counteract the demoralizing results of this chronic underemployment, what is known as the Liverpool dock scheme was inaugurated by the British Board of Trade in July, 1912, under authority of the unemployment insurance part of the National Insurance Act. In the first year of its operation sixty-eight employers became parties to the plan, and 31,000 dockers were registered.[77] A metal tally was issued to each man; only men holding tallies were employed, and new tallies could be issued only with the approval of the joint committees of workmen and employers which assisted in administering the scheme. Workmen who failed to be hired at the employers' regular stands were to go to one of fourteen "surplus stands," which were in communication by telephone with one another and with the six sectional clearing houses established in connection with the government labor exchange. The system sought to make it possible to do the same work with fewer men, but these employed much more regularly. The advantages of maintaining one reserve for the industry as a whole, instead of separately for each employer, are obvious. The adjustment caused tem-

[75] For example, Lewisohn, S. A., Draper, E. G., Commons, John R., and Lescohier, Don D., *Can Business Prevent Unemployment?* 1925; Feldman, H., *The Regularization of Employment,* 1925; and Smith, E. S., *Reducing Seasonal Unemployment,* 1931.

[76] Williams, R., *The Liverpool Docks Problem,* 1912, pp. 10-12.

[77] Beveridge and Rey, "Labour Exchanges," *Quarterly Bulletin on Unemployment,* July-September, 1913, p. 789.

EMPLOYMENT AND UNEMPLOYMENT

porary hardship for some workmen, but it was hoped that in time each employer would keep the nucleus of a force on regular wages and rely for extra men on a fluid reserve to be maintained jointly by all the employers of the port.[78] The Great War and subsequent conditions interfered with the normal working-out of the experiment. With minor modifications, however, it was still in force in 1934, and the principle of registration has been so widely approved by both employers and workers that plans embodying it have been introduced in nearly all British ports.[79] As a matter of fact, however, the scheme has not accomplished as much in decasualization as had been anticipated even on the Liverpool dock where it has been longest on trial. This is doubtless due partly to widespread unemployment but also partly to the fact that a large amount of surplus labor is necessary in an industry so irregular as the loading and unloading of ships. The idea first put forth by the transport workers' federation in 1918, and in the following year indorsed by the Shaw report on the inquiry into dockers' claims, that the industry should furnish each registered docker a minimum weekly maintenance wage, appears to be a promising solution of the difficulty.[80]

Under the war-time extension of the United States Employment Service, a similar scheme was started for New York longshoremen, but it had to be abandoned when the service was curtailed. A similar plan, inaugurated in 1921 by employers of dock labor in Seattle, Wash., is said to have improved conditions considerably.[81]

Employers, however, are frequently no more farsighted than are other persons in the community, and may neglect what is obviously to their own and other persons' economic advantage if it requires much additional exertion or forethought. Hence arises the need for governmental stimulus toward regularization

[78] See Williams, R., *First Year's Working of the Liverpool Dock Scheme*, 1914.

[79] See Chegwidden, T. S., and Myrddin-Evans, G., *The Employment Exchange Service of Great Britain*, 1934, pp. 165-168.

[80] Lascelles, E. C. P., and Bullock, S. S., *Dock Labour and Decasualization*, 1924, pp. 84-124.

[81] Foisie, F. P., *Proceedings of the National Conference on Social Work*, 1925, p. 306.

that is found in some of the newer legislation on unemployment.

Directly after the war, considerable legislation was enacted in European countries compelling employment of ex-soldiers or forbidding dismissal of employees in certain cases. These, however, were for the most part temporary measures designed to lessen hardship in the change from war to peace conditions. Of more permanent character is legislation enacted since 1919, not only in most European countries but also in Mexico and several South American countries, penalizing employers for dismissal of employees without due notice or just cause. This type of legislation varies widely in scope and character, being in some cases, as in the Belgian act,[82] designed primarily to prevent unemployment, and in others, as in several Mexican states,[83] also to prevent discrimination against union labor, and various injustices. In Europe there has also been considerable legislation since the war to compel employers in case of partial shut-down to furnish part-time work to a maximum number of employees.

Headway can be made to some extent against seasonal fluctuations also, under the proper encouragement of an efficient public employment office system. During the winter, for instance, it has been suggested that building laborers could be assisted to take up ice-cutting or logging, or to secure some of the less skilled work in shoe, textile, or other factories which are busier at that season. The Illinois and Pennsylvania laws of 1915 establishing state employment offices instructed the administrative authorities to take steps toward the regularization of employment, both public and private. Interesting possibilities are suggested by these measures, but in actual practice little, if anything, has been done under them. A more definite inducement to the regularization of industry on a comprehensive scale is offered through the establishment of unemployment reserves.[84]

[82] International Labor Office, *Legislative Series*, 1922, Belgium 2.
[83] *Ibid.*, 1923, Mexico 1.
[84] See p. 306.

CHAPTER II

MINIMUM FAIR WAGE

MINIMUM WAGE LEGISLATION MARKS A NEW STAGE IN THE long line of attempts to equalize the power of employer and employee in making the wage bargain. In contrast with conciliation and arbitration, either voluntary or compulsory, which take place only after a demand has been made by one party and refused by the other, minimum wage laws seek to regulate the wage rate before any dispute over the terms of the wage bargain has arisen. Moreover, interference by the state between the parties to the wage bargain through conciliation or arbitration usually implies the organization of the workers and the existence of collective bargaining.[1] But in any modern industrial community, large numbers of unorganized workers are found, still bargaining individually, employed at low wages and apparently unable to make any effective efforts themselves to improve their condition. If they are to be helped toward an equality in bargaining power with the employer, the state must take the initiative. This it does by setting standards below which wages may not be depressed—in other words, by passing minimum wage legislation.[2]

Minimum standards for safety and sanitation have been enacted in most states, and the maximum length of the working day has usually been fixed. Such safeguards have long been familiar and are generally accepted as necessary and beneficial to the health and welfare of the workers. There exists also a considerable group of laws which determine certain conditions of the wage *payment*. For instance, the weekly payment of wages may be required or payment in "store orders" may be

[1] The industrial courts of Europe employ conciliation in both collective bargaining and individual contracts.

[2] Modern minimum wage legislation is not comparable to the mediæval fixing of wages by justices of the peace which prescribed not a minimum, but the actual rates to be paid.

forbidden, as described in Chapter VI; but any legislative interference with the wage *rate* was long in making its appearance. Work may be done under safe and sanitary conditions for hours not too long, and payment of wages may be prompt and regular; but if the amount received is too small to secure the necessaries of life, the worker's health and welfare are menaced. Therefore, the same motives which have caused most of our states to establish minimum standards to guard the worker against unsafe and unsanitary conditions have caused many of them to attempt to set up standards for protection against the evils of low wages.

1. ECONOMIC BASIS

That a large proportion of unskilled workers are paid wages far too low for decent self-support is a fact confirmed by many wage investigations and well known even to those only slightly familiar with present-day industrial conditions.

1. **Low Wage Scale.**—Even before the era of unprecedentedly high prices ushered in by the war, it was the consensus of expert opinion that a weekly wage of $8 or more was necessary under urban conditions for the maintenance of a self-supporting woman in simple decency and working efficiency, and that a man with a wife and three children required at least $15 to $20 weekly for their proper support.[3] Yet a study made at that time of women's wages in the United States concluded that 75 per cent of female wage earners received less than $8 weekly, 50 per cent less than $6, and 15 per cent less than $4, and that these wages were further reduced approximately 20 per cent through lost time and unemployment.[4] The pay of unskilled male workers was at a correspondingly low level. Streightoff, in his discussion of American standards of living, estimated in 1912 that at least 6,000,000 adult men, married as well as single, received less than $600 a year, or $12 a week.[5] A little later the New York State Factory Investigating Commission examined the payrolls of over 2,000 stores and fac-

[3] See Woolston, Howard B., "Wages in New York," *The Survey*, February 6, 1915, p. 510.

[4] Persons, Charles E., "Woman's Work and Wages in the United States," *The Quarterly Journal of Economics*, February, 1915, p. 232.

[5] Streightoff, Frank H., *Distribution of Incomes in the United States*, 1912, p. 137.

tories during the fall, winter, and spring of 1913-1914. Out of 57,000 women and girls, approximately 34,000 or 60 per cent, earned less than $8 in a typical week. Seven thousand out of 14,000 married men, or 50 per cent, earned less than $15.[6]

During the war, the wage level was materially raised, but, owing to the unprecedented rise in prices that accompanied the change, it is doubtful whether real wages were materially altered for the better, except perhaps in a few war industries and in certain occupations covered by especially liberal government wage awards. The United States Bureau of Labor Statistics estimated that the cost of a family's living increased 80 per cent in the chief shipbuilding centers of the United States between June, 1914, and June, 1919, and 70 per cent in other localities. The National Industrial Conference Board, which is a federation of several large employers' associations, and likely, therefore, to be conservative in its estimates, put the increase at 71 per cent for the similar period of June, 1914, to July, 1919. According to the price statistics just quoted, the minimum "living wage" for a self-supporting woman, if assumed to be $8 a week in 1914, was $14 in 1919. It was, in fact, estimated to be $15 by the Consumers' League of New York City in January, 1919, and $16.50 by the District of Columbia Minimum Wage Commission in July of the same year.

On the average, wages had failed to reach these standards. The New York Industrial Commission, securing between November, 1918, and January, 1919, figures on the earnings of 32,000 women in the same industries which had been covered by the Factory Investigating Commission in 1913-1914, found that 60 per cent of those in factories and 61 per cent of those in stores still received less than $14 a week. In 1923, a similar investigation by the commission showed that 57 per cent of the factory women in four of the largest industries in New York were getting less than $16 per week. Similar investigations in ten states during the period of 1920-1924 by the Federal Women's Bureau showed such low averages as $14.95 in the important industrial state of New Jersey, $11.98 in Texas, $12.70 in Kansas, and for white workers $12.65 in Missouri and $11.60 in Arkansas.

[6] Woolston, Howard B., "Wages in New York," *The Survey*, February 6, 1915, p. 510.

46   PRINCIPLES OF LABOR LEGISLATION

The period of boom and depression in the following decade brought little change in the relative adequacy of women's wage rates. In 1928, the Texas Bureau of Labor Statistics reported that the cost of bare necessities for young women was $15 a week; in 1929, the New York Department of Labor found that in New York City room and meals alone cost girls at least $14.69 a week; and in 1930 the Colorado Industrial Commission estimated the minimum weekly living cost of women workers to be $17.20. In 1930, also, the Y.W.C.A. estimated the cost of a decent living standard to be $15 in Boston, $20 in Chicago, $16 in Kansas City, $9.96 in New Orleans, and $21 in Philadelphia. In 1932, the Minneapolis Y.W.C.A. estimated the minimum budget of a business girl as $22.50 a week. In 1935, the Welfare Council of New York City estimated $11 to be the cost of "subsistence" for a woman living alone in that city, and $16 to be the "minimum self-supporting level."

During this period, the Federal Women's Bureau found, in a study of the earnings of women laundry workers in 23 cities in 1927-1928, that half of the white women received less than $16.10 a week and half of the Negro women less than $8.85. In 1929, another Women's Bureau study showed half of the women employed in radio manufacturing to be earning less than $13.95. Other such "median week's earnings" of women reported by the Women's Bureau are $12.35 in the sewing trades of Connecticut in 1931-1932; $11.10 in Maine cotton mills and $7.70 in South Carolina cotton mills in 1932; and $8.45 in Arkansas factories, stores and laundries in 1932-1933. Investigations made by the Connecticut labor department prior to the establishment of minimum wage rates disclosed that in 1934 the earnings of women in the laundry industry of the state averaged $11.34 a week. A similar study of laundry wages by the Illinois labor department showed that in 1934 half of the women workers received less than $10.97, and more than a fifth less than $9 weekly. The New York Department of Labor, in a survey of women's wages in New York City in 1935, found that the percentage of women earning less than $10 weekly was 27.8 in the candy industry, 28.4 in the cotton garment industry, 30.8 in the handbag industry, 23.5 in the knit goods industry, 24.3 in the paper box industry, and

12.5 in retail stores. Those earning less than $16 weekly constituted more than 85 per cent in the candy industry, more than 70 per cent in the handbag, cotton garment and paper box industries, and more than 65 per cent in retail stores.

It seems no exaggeration to say that the majority of low-skilled industrial workers in the United States receive wages too small for decent self-support. This fact explains the demand for minimum wage legislation as necessary to social welfare.

2. **Economic Weakness of Low-paid Workers.**—The almost entire absence of strong labor organizations and collective bargaining among this group of wage earners is an important factor in producing the low wage scale. Many are women who are members of a family group and unable to move from place to place in search of better opportunities. They remain at home and overcrowd the few lines of work available in a given locality. Then, too, the majority of women workers are young and inexperienced, and their frequent withdrawal from industry on marriage makes them look upon their work as only temporary. On the whole, it has been extremely difficult to form stable unions among women workers. Experience both in England and in this country shows that organization among low-skilled men workers is almost equally difficult. In the absence of collective agreements it has sometimes been possible to compel the workers to keep their wages secret. An Oregon department store, for instance, required each applicant for employment to sign an agreement which included a promise to "keep my salary confidential."[7] Such secrecy obviously makes it easier to depress wage scales. Under the circumstances, it is also not surprising that among this group of workers the relation between wages and productivity is not traceable, but that "there are also great differences in wages for work that is apparently the same. Some firms pay constantly 25 per cent more than their rivals for similar operations."[8] In the United States the situation, until the outbreak of the European War, was further complicated by the stream of immigration, which

[7] *Report of the Social Welfare Committee, Consumers' League of Oregon,* 1913, p. 26.
[8] *Fourth Report of the New York Factory Investigating Commission,* 1915. "The Confectionery Industry," vol. ii, p. 312.

furnished an abundant supply of cheap labor and which put still another barrier, in the shape of divergent language and customs, in the way of union organization.

Another reason for the low wage scale, largely the result of the first, is the cutthroat competition of the workers for work. Among the unskilled, unorganized workers, the wage that the cheapest laborer—such as the partially supported woman, the immigrant with low standards of living, or the workman oppressed by extreme need—is willing to take, very largely fixes the wage level for the whole group.

Moreover, a socially undesirable type of competition among employers flourishes when the bargaining power of employees is weak. The encouragement of superior ability and invention has always been pointed out as one of the chief advantages gained by the community from the competitive system of production. When an employer can hire workers for practically his own price, he can be slack and inefficient in his methods, and yet, by reducing wages, reduce his cost of production to the level of his more able competitor.

Minimum wage legislation, therefore, is designed to answer the demands of social policy in two ways. By setting a barrier below which wages may not fall, it lightens the pitiful poverty and prevents the degeneration in body and spirit of those forced to live on a wage too small to supply the necessaries of life. Competition among them no longer takes the form of offering to work for lower wages, instead it tends to develop greater efficiency. At the same time, employers are forced to compete in efficiency of management, thus securing for society at large the many advantages of constantly improved methods of production. Minimum wage laws attempt neither to destroy competition nor to fix wages by law; they merely seek to set the lower limits to both in the interests of society as a whole.

II. HISTORICAL DEVELOPMENT

1. **Australasia.**—Australasia is the birthplace of minimum wage legislation. Though it is a new and prosperous country, as long ago as the 'eighties the sweating system, with its evils of low wages, long hours, and unsanitary conditions, was discovered to be alarmingly prevalent. The *Age*, the leading Mel-

bourne newspaper, carried on a crusade against these conditions, and a royal commission was appointed whose report in 1884 showed that hours were excessive and that wages were constantly reduced by the miserable rates paid to home workers. Public indignation was aroused until finally determined efforts were made to overcome these evils.

In 1894, New Zealand passed a law providing for the compulsory arbitration of labor disputes, which, while primarily intended to preserve industrial peace, may also be used for the prevention of sweating. The district conciliation boards established by this law have authority to fix minimum wages, and if sweated workers want their conditions improved, they need only file a statement of their claims in the office of the nearest conciliation board. By means of this machinery, underpaid workers, men more often than women, have secured wage increases.

The first Australasian law, however, whose main purpose was to end sweating, was passed by Victoria two years later; and since it is the Victorian method which Great Britain and the United States have adopted, the system deserves consideration at length. The public feeling against the sweating system in Victoria had resulted in the formation of an Anti-sweating League. Largely as a result of the league's efforts and in spite of bitter opposition from the employers under the leadership of the Victorian Chamber of Manufactures, Victoria passed the first minimum wage law in 1896. Sir Alexander Peacock, originator of the system and later minister of labor in Victoria, has written: "It was alleged, first, that all work would be driven out of the country; secondly, that only the best workers would be employed; and thirdly, that it would be impossible to enforce such provisions at all. . . . The government, however, managed to carry the bill, and the wage-board system was inaugurated."[9]

The law required that representative boards fix minimum wages in certain industries designated by the legislature. Moreover, being frankly an experiment, the act was to be enforced for only four years. Wage boards were first appointed in the

[9] Hammond, M. B., "The Minimum Wage in Great Britain and Australia," *Annals of the American Academy of Political and Social Science*, July, 1913, p. 28.

six especially sweated trades of boot-making and baking, which employed mostly men; clothing, shirt-making, and underclothing, which mostly employed women; and in furniture-making, in which the competition of Chinese labor was depressing wages. In 1900, when the first minimum wage law came to an end, the government brought in a bill providing for the extension of the wage-board system to other trades. The Victorian Chamber of Manufactures protested violently, urging, and with good reason, that the government's proposal meant the extension of the system to trades in which there was no evidence of sweating. The government, however, showed that it had received a number of applications from employers, asking for the appointment of special boards, and that sweating had disappeared in the trades in which boards had been established. Accordingly, the bill was passed and an extension of the system was begun. In 1932, nearly two hundred wage boards were in existence, fixing minimum wage rates for nearly 200,000 employees in a state whose total population is less than two million. Minimum wage rates have been established for all the important manufacturing occupations in the cities, and also for street railways, mercantile and clerical employments, mining, and even for certain agricultural workers. The wage-board system is regarded no longer as an emergency measure intended to secure a living wage where conditions are exceptionally bad, but as a satisfactory method of fixing the standard wage in any trade. The act was again renewed in 1903, and in 1904 was made permanent. While the scope of the law has been widely extended, the opposition of the employers decreased, until in April, 1912, as a result of first-hand investigations, M. B. Hammond, of the Ohio Industrial Commission, reported that both employers and employees "are now practically unanimous in saying that they have no desire to return to the old system of unrestricted competition in the purchase of labor."[10]

South Australia, Queensland, New South Wales, Tasmania, and Western Australia, between 1900 and 1912, also adopted minimum wage legislation, but in close relation to their systems of compulsory arbitration.[11] Frequent changes have since

[10] *Ibid.*, p. 35.
[11] See p. 439.

MINIMUM FAIR WAGE

been made in administrative organization, but from the first all of these states have made minimum wage legislation applicable to practically the whole range of employment and not merely to sweated trades.[12]

2. Great Britain.—One of the most important developments in the English social reform movement during the early years of the twentieth century was the acceptance of minimum wage legislation as a practicable policy. Today, after more than a quarter of a century of experience, the minimum wage principle is firmly established in that country.

Among the chief reasons for this development of public policy was the increased public knowledge of conditions among sweated workers. Investigations showed that large numbers of low-skilled unorganized workers were receiving less than the wage necessary for the maintenance of mere physical efficiency. Attempts were made to extend trade unionism among them, so that they might raise their wages as more skilled workers had done, by collective bargaining. But the formation of strong unions among these sweated workers was generally found to be impossible. The market for their labor was chronically overstocked and the struggle for bare existence was too severe to permit the development of stable organizations. The public was aroused to this menace of insufficient wages, which its victims themselves seemed powerless to remedy, mainly through the efforts of the National Anti-sweating League, which, with the Labor Party and certain other organizations, vigorously urged the adoption of minimum wage legislation. The agitation resulted first in a parliamentary inquiry and finally, in 1909, in the passage of a Trade Boards Act, modeled on the Victorian statute, which went into effect the following year.

This law provided that wage boards may be established by order of the board of trade, subject to ratification by Parliament, for all employees in any industry in which the prevailing rate of wages is "exceptionally low as compared with that in other employments."[13] The first four trades regulated were

---

[12] For later developments, see pp. 58-59. See also Anderson, George, *Fixation of Wages in Australia* (Melbourne, Macmillan & Co., Ltd., in association with Melbourne University Press, 1929).

[13] Trade Boards Act, 9 Edw. 7, C. 22, Sec. 1 (2).

tailoring, paper-box-making, the finishing of machine-made lace, and the manufacture of certain kinds of chain—industries which employed altogether about 250,000 operatives. By 1913 the successful operation of the law was so generally recognized that the formation of boards was ordered in five additional trades: sugar confectionery and food-preserving, shirt-making, certain kinds of tailoring, hollow-ware-making, and cotton and linen embroidery, employing nearly 150,000 more workers. The trades covered employ chiefly women, and before regulation the wage conditions were flagrantly bad.

The first extension of the wage-board system outside the sweated trades was also exceptional, but for an altogether different reason. There had been great unrest among the coal miners during the winter of 1911-1912, culminating in a strike in the spring of 1912 which paralyzed industry. One of the men's principal demands was a flat-rate weekly minimum wage. In the interests of industrial peace the government was forced to yield to the principle of this demand by passing a measure establishing representative district boards to fix minimum wages and other working conditions. While the operation of this act is said to have proved less satisfactory than the workings of the trade boards, it presents the issue of wage regulation in a wider form, not simply as a means of protecting the sweated workers at the very bottom of the industrial system, but as a supplement to voluntary collective bargaining for a comparatively well-placed economic group, the skilled men workers in a well-organized trade.

Up to the outbreak of the European War, then, English minimum wage legislation had reached some of the hardest pressed and some of the most fortunate groups of industrial workers. Throughout the war, numerous adjustments were made in the awards for the nine sweated trades which had been dealt with under the original act, but the increases hardly kept pace with the ever-soaring cost of living, the boards increasing rates only "by so much as they thought the industries concerned would be able to support after the war."[14] But in the latter years of the war, two important extensions of minimum wage legislation were made, in part with a view to

[14] Cole, G. D. H. and M. I., *The Regulation of Wages during and after the War,* p. 4.

MINIMUM FAIR WAGE

stabilizing wages during the transition from war to peace, which went far toward repeating in England the line of development which had been followed in Australia, and which transformed the trade boards from a special device for remedying unusually bad conditions to a common method for fixing wage standards for all wage earners. One was an amendment to the Trade Boards Act which, in brief, provided that boards to fix minimum wages might be formed wherever earnings were "unduly" low,[15] instead of "exceptionally" low, as under the original law. Before the war, the general wage level had been so low in certain groups of occupations that it was often difficult to prove that they were "exceptionally" so in cases where it was desired to take action. Provision was also made for having the awards come into force more quickly and for removing various administrative difficulties which had been experienced. The amending act likewise made the boards a possible instrument for industrial self-government by empowering them to make recommendations to government departments concerning improvements in industrial conditions in their trades and by requiring the government to consult them on industrial questions affecting the workers whom they represent. Following the signing of the armistice, the establishment of new trade boards proceeded rapidly, and by 1921 there were 63 boards in operation. The prolonged depression which began in that year had the effect of deterring the expansion of this method of wage-fixing into new industries. Practically all of the important industries employing women and children in Great Britain, however, had already been brought under the Trade Boards Act.

The other important extension of the minimum wage principle was the establishment of a minimum wage for agricultural laborers in connection with the Corn Production Act. The main purpose of this act was the stimulation of grain production through guaranteeing farmers a minimum price for their wheat for a considerable term of years. A demand was then made that wages in turn be guaranteed. Under this act the wage boards had, by the autumn of 1919, fixed minimum rates for men and women, boys and girls, through practically the whole of England and Wales.

[15] 8 and 9 George 5, C. 32 (1918).

The Corn Production Act was repealed in 1921, and wages were regulated by voluntary conciliation committees. But discontent over low wages and long hours finally resulted in the Agricultural Wages Act of August, 1924, which provides a central board with forty-seven local committees covering England and Wales.[16]

3. **Other Countries.**—Minimum wage legislation has been adopted in all the leading Canadian provinces, in most of the larger European countries, in Argentina and Uruguay and, in 1925, in South Africa. The administrative machinery is generally similar to that adopted by Great Britain, and usually applies to women and children. In Canada, most of the laws apply to females only. British Columbia in December, 1925, enacted a law providing for adult male employees generally minimum wages to be determined through investigations by the Board of Adjustment. Exceptions were made for farm laborers, fruit pickers and packers, fruit and vegetable canners, and domestic servants. Most of this foreign legislation applies to specified groups of workers, especially home workers and agricultural laborers, where collective bargaining cannot easily be enforced.

In addition to the development in Australia, already noted, in several European countries during and since the war the family wage system has been adopted for certain industries. Under this plan, a basic wage is allowed each adult male worker, with a supplementary allowance for dependent members of his family.[17] This plan is usually operated by individual employers or by groups through an "equalization fund," but in some instances the state governments cooperate either by direct participation or by supervision.

4. **The United States.**—In America, a widespread demand for minimum wage legislation dates back to about 1910. Two factors contributed to the rise of popular sentiment in favor of the legislation at this time. One was the increased knowledge of conditions among sweated workers, resulting from such investigations as that of the federal Bureau of Labor on *Condi-*

[16] Great Britain, Ministry of Labor, *Labour Gazette,* August, 1924, p. 278.

[17] Douglass, Paul, *Wages and the Family,* University of Chicago Press; and "The Family Allowance System: A Survey of Recent Developments," *International Labour Review,* March, 1930, pp. 395-416.

MINIMUM FAIR WAGE

tions of Woman and Child Wage-earners in the United States. The other was the enactment of the British Trade Boards Act. In public employment, to be sure, wages in America had for several years been regulated both by state laws and by city ordinances. Most commonly these regulations fix the wage rate or require that "prevailing rates" be paid, which are usually interpreted as union rates when a union exists in the locality. Several statutes and ordinances, however, establish a true minimum wage. In this country until 1912 wage rates in private employment were seldom considered a subject of possible legal regulation.

The first American state to pass a minimum wage law was Massachusetts. An investigating commission was appointed there in 1911, and its report resulted in legislation in 1912. In 1913, as a result of further investigations, eight states[18] followed the example of Massachusetts, and in 1915 two more were added.[19] Arizona enacted legislation in 1917 and Colorado revised its law; Congress legislated for the District of Columbia in 1918; North Dakota, Texas, and Puerto Rico passed laws in 1919, while South Dakota followed in 1923. The Nebraska law, under which no action had ever been taken on the ground that no complaints had been received, was repealed, apparently by accident, in codifying the laws in 1919, and the Texas Act, although declared constitutional by the state supreme court, was repealed in 1921.

Constitutional amendments specifically allowing minimum wage legislation were passed by California in 1914 for women and minors, and, contrary to American precedent, by Ohio in 1912 for all classes of workers, although no legislation was enacted in that state until 1933.

Despite the mass of evidence on the evil effects of low wages for women and children, the United States Supreme Court in 1923 held unconstitutional the minimum wage law of the District of Columbia,[20] thereby reversing its previous favorable action in the Oregon case as well as seven favorable decisions in state supreme courts. The District of Columbia

[18] California, Colorado, Minnesota, Nebraska, Oregon, Utah, Washington, Wisconsin.
[19] Arkansas, Kansas.
[20] Adkins *v.* Children's Hospital, 261 U. S. 525, 43 Sup. Ct. 394 (1923).

56 PRINCIPLES OF LABOR LEGISLATION

decision, however, applied only to women and left intact the laws as affecting children.

This decision was followed by two others invalidating the Arizona[21] and Arkansas[22] laws in similar manner, the Supreme Court in each case reaffirming its earlier opinion. Following this same precedent, adverse decisions were handed down by a Federal District Court on the Wisconsin law[23] and by the Kansas Supreme Court[24] on the law in that state. In 1925, Wisconsin amended her law with a view to meeting the objections raised by the courts; but in 1929 Utah repealed her law. As a result of the court decisions, no new minimum wage rates were fixed under any of the laws between 1923 and 1933, except in Massachusetts whose law was not mandatory. Moreover, rates already established were administered, if at all, chiefly by persuasion, although in California, where employer support made it possible, more active enforcement was attempted.

Thus by 1930, of the seventeen laws originally enacted, three had been repealed, five had been held unconstitutional by the courts as applied to women, and one of these had been amended. Following the decline in wage rates resulting from the depression which began in 1929, a new movement for minimum wage legislation led to the adoption of laws during 1933 in seven states.[25] Massachusetts, moreover, in 1934 replaced her non-mandatory law of 1912 with a mandatory act. These new laws, like the Wisconsin act of 1925, were designed to withstand court test. Nevertheless, in March, 1936, the New York law of 1933 was declared unconstitutional in a four-to-three decision by that state's highest court, which held that the Supreme Court's ruling in the District of Columbia case applied with equal force to this newer type of minimum wage law.[26]

[21] Murphy v. Sardell, 269 U. S. 530, 46 Sup. Ct. 22 (1925).
[22] Donham v. West Nelson Mfg. Co., 273 U. S. 657, 47 Sup. Ct. 343 (1927).
[23] Folding Furniture Works v. Industrial Commission of Wisconsin, 300 Fed. 991 (1924).
[24] Topeka Laundry Co. v. Court of Industrial Relations, 119 Kans. 12 (1925).
[25] Connecticut, Illinois, New Hampshire, New Jersey, New York, Ohio, and Utah.
[26] People ex rel. Tipaldo v. Morehead, 270 N. Y. 233 (1936).

MINIMUM FAIR WAGE

An appeal was taken from this decision to the United States Supreme Court which, on June 1, 1936, likewise declared the New York act unconstitutional as applied to women.[27]

Minimum wage laws resemble much other American labor legislation which also when first passed, in part for constitutional reasons, in part perhaps because of the more evident inability of this class of workers to protect themselves, applied only to women and minors. Then, too, many American representatives of labor oppose minimum wage laws for men, feeling that men workers can obtain better wages by organization without the aid of legislation.

A broader and more far-reaching experiment in minimum wage regulation resulted from the enactment by Congress of the National Industrial Recovery Act of 1933. In the 579 codes of fair competition set up under this act, minimum wage rates were established in each industry for men as well as women and minors. The entire law, however, was declared unconstitutional by the Supreme Court[28] in 1935, and the provisions of the codes immediately became inoperative. In 1936, the "prevailing wage" requirement, which had long been applied to public works contracts, was extended by Congress so that such provision must be included in every contract, entered into by a federal government department or other federal agency, "for the manufacture or furnishing of materials, supplies, articles, and equipment in any amount exceeding $10,000," except when these "may usually be bought in the open market" or are farm products "processed for first sale by the original producers." The prevailing wage must be determined by the Secretary of Labor, who enforces the act.[29]

In May, 1934, an interstate compact on minimum wage standards was indorsed by official representatives of seven eastern states.[30] This compact, which aims to secure uniformity in state laws by prescribing general standards substantially the same as those already enacted into law by several states in 1933,

[27] Morehead v. People ex rel. Tipaldo, 56 Sup. Ct. 918 (1936).
[28] Schechter Poultry Corp. v. United States, 295 U. S. 495, 55 Sup. Ct. 837 (1935).
[29] Public No. 846, 74th Congress, 1936.
[30] Connecticut, Maine, Massachusetts, New Hampshire, New York, Pennsylvania, and Rhode Island.

58 PRINCIPLES OF LABOR LEGISLATION

commits ratifying states to maintain such standards and to refrain from withdrawing ratification except after two years' notice. The terms of the compact make it operative when ratified by two states and consented to by Congress. Additional states may become party to the compact by ratification and with the consent of Congress. It was ratified first by Massachusetts in 1934, New Hampshire in 1935, and Rhode Island in 1936.

III. STANDARDS

The purpose of minimum wage legislation is the raising of excessively low wages. The question of the standards of wage awards is therefore an important one. How adequate is the minimum wage? Is it always a "living wage," and, if so, is account taken only of the bare physical necessities of life, or is allowance also made for the requirements of mental and moral welfare? Is provision made for the support of a family or for the needs of the individual worker alone? Is there any consideration of probable periods of unemployment? On what basis do wage boards fix the pay of young, inexperienced, and handicapped workers?

1. **Australasia.**—The statutes of the Australasian states except Victoria refer to the minimum wage as a "living wage." Since 1912, Western Australia has required every minimum prescribed to be "sufficient to enable the average worker to whom it applies to live in reasonable comfort, having regard to any domestic obligations to which such average worker would ordinarily be subject."[31] Tasmania and Victoria originally provided that the "wages paid by the reputable employer" should be taken as the basis, but this standard proved difficult to administer, and the clause was dropped. In New Zealand in 1921 and Tasmania in 1928, amendments provided for alteration of awards according to fluctuations in the cost of living. A significant step was taken in New South Wales in 1927, when a system of family allowances was introduced. As amended in 1929, this provides for a minimum wage rate fixed for a family with one child, and for special allowances to be paid for additional children out of a general fund raised by payroll tax. In New Zealand and Victoria special provision regulating wages

[31] Western Australia, Industrial Arbitration Act, 1912, No. 57, ¶ 84.

paid apprentices has been made in connection with acts governing apprenticeship generally.

The wage determinations of the Australian states have been much influenced by the decisions of the Commonwealth Arbitration Court which settles interstate trade disputes, and which early set as the minimum for unskilled laborers a sum sufficient to cover "the normal needs of the average employee regarded as a human being living in a civilized community." In other words, the minimum is a living wage in the broader sense of the term, not a mere subsistence wage. Above this "basic wage," which the court does not permit to be lowered for such considerations as international competition or the lack of profitableness of the enterprise, may be fixed an additional "secondary wage," "the extra payment to be made for trained skill or other exceptional qualities necessary for an employee exercising the functions required."

The question of differing wage standards for men and for women has been clearly worked out in Australia. Since a man must normally maintain a family, a living wage for male workers must cover the cost of such maintenance; a woman ordinarily supports herself alone, so that the minimum for female workers is fixed on that basis. "The minimum cannot be based on exceptional cases."[32] For the same reason, the partial support of some women workers by their families is not considered in fixing their wages. When both men and women are employed in the same occupation, the wage rate is fixed for the sex usually found therein. Allowance is also made in wage-fixing for time lost on account of irregular employment, and for any special expenses connected with the occupation, such as traveling expenses or the provision of uniforms.[33]

2. **Great Britain.**—In England, where no standard is set by the law itself, except the elimination of "sweating," the general practice at first was "to level the wage for the whole trade in each district up to the standard of the best employer in that district."[34] In the badly sweated trades this meant a considerable

[32] *Commonwealth Arbitration Reports,* vol. vi, p. 71.

[33] For an analysis of recent developments, see Anderson, George, *Fixation of Wages in Australia,* 1929.

[34] Hobson, John A., "The State and the Minimum Wage in England," *The Survey,* February 6, 1915, p. 503.

increase for most of the workers, but not necessarily a living wage. Since the World War, however, the trade boards have apparently given increased weight to the cost-of-living factor. Some have provided for an automatic adjustment of minimum wage rates in accordance with variations in the cost of living in certain trades.[35]

3. **The United States:** a. *Definition of the Minimum Wage.* —Nearly all the earlier American laws define in general terms the principle to be followed in fixing wages, usually that of a living wage. In a majority of these laws, phrases such as "the necessary cost of proper living" and "to maintain the health and welfare" are used.[36] In working out wage standards on this basis, the English practice of leveling up wages to those paid by the best employer in the trade in a given district is obviously not a sufficient guide. Then, too, since the laws apply only to women and minors, relative standards for the two sexes need not be considered, as in Australia. One finds, however, America on the whole using the Australian standard for women workers—namely, the cost of living of the entirely self-supporting woman. American employers have sometimes asked that the help received by many women workers from their families be taken into account in fixing the standard, but this request has been denied.

Earlier orders were in the neighborhood of $8 and $9 a week. Following the war-time price increases, the State of Washington was the first to break away from the traditionally low levels by establishing, in September, 1918, a flat rate of $13.20 for all experienced adult women for the period of the war, in practically all industries. Oregon followed in 1919 with the same wage, and both rates were still in effect at the end of 1935. In 1919 also, Wisconsin established the minimum hour rates of 18 to 22 cents for practically all industries. Later, in 1921, these rates were raised to 22 to 25 cents. The District of Columbia Commission, making provision for the high cost of living in the city of Washington, fixed minima of $15.50 in the printing and engraving industry, and $16.50—the highest award in the country at the time—in mercantile establishments. Massachusetts followed in 1920, with an order for a rate of $15.25 weekly in

[35] Great Britain, Ministry of Labor, *Labour Gazette*, July, 1925, p. 229.
[36] California, Laws 1913, C. 324.

MINIMUM FAIR WAGE

the women's clothing industry, and $15.50 in paper-box-making. But these awards, made when the cost of living was at its highest, were reduced in 1922 to $14 and $13.50 per week, respectively. California in 1923 set a weekly minimum of $16 for most of the important industries, and this minimum was reaffirmed in 1933 after further investigation. In the Middle West, rates ran slightly lower, except in North Dakota where the minimum was from $14 to $15 per week. In Minnesota, the minimum was $12 for adults in the larger towns, for 36 to 48 hours per week, and overtime payment was required as in several other states.

Even under the highest wage awards, strict construction has been placed by most wage boards upon the term "necessary cost of living." As a matter of fact, the budget, like the wage rate which it determines, is a compromise. The representatives of the employees present their budget and their proposal for a rate based on it; the representatives of the employers do likewise, and the two forces contend until they come to some agreement. The budgets provided for, even the most liberal, do little more than secure "not a wage so . . . women can live well, not enough to make life a rich and welcome experience, but just enough to secure existence amid drudgery in gray boarding houses and cheap restaurants."[37] That this is so is shown by an examination of two Massachusetts budgets, the earlier drawn up by a wage board in the boot and shoe industry in 1929, and the latter in 1932 for the pocketbook and leather goods worker.[38]

Following the Supreme Court decision in 1923 declaring unconstitutional the "living wage" standard for minimum wage determination as applied to women[39] Wisconsin in 1925 adopted a new law using terminology suggested by the language of Mr. Justice Sutherland's majority opinion. This Wisconsin law provides that: "No wage paid or agreed to be paid by any employer to any adult female shall be oppressive. Any wage lower than a reasonable and adequate compensation for the services rendered shall be deemed oppressive and is hereby prohibited."

[37] Lippmann, Walter, "The Campaign against Sweating," *New Republic,* March 27, 1915, Supp., p. 8.
[38] See table on page 62.
[39] See section below on "Constitutionality."

Weekly budget allowed certain women boot and shoe workers in Massachusetts, January, 1929.		Weekly budget allowed women pocketbook and leather goods workers in Massachusetts, June, 1932.	
Board and lodging	$ 8.42	Board and lodging	$ 7.75
Clothing	2.45	Clothing	2.00
Laundry	.45	Laundry	.20
Doctor, dentist, etc.	.50	Doctor, dentist, etc.	.30
Carfares	.54	Carfares	.60
Church	.15	Church	.15
Self-improvement	.25	Self-improvement	.20
Vacation	.35	Vacation	.25
Recreation	.44	Recreation	.40
Reserve	.40	Reserve	.40
Mutual association dues	.20	Mutual association dues	
Insurance	.25	Insurance	.25
Incidentals	.25	Incidentals	
Total	$14.65	Total	$12.50

This new standard was later further developed and embodied in the laws enacted by other states in 1933 and 1934. In most of these recent laws, it is declared contrary to public policy for an employer to employ women or minors at "an oppressive or unreasonable wage," and this is defined as a wage "both less than the fair and reasonable value of the service rendered and less than sufficient to meet the minimum cost of living necessary for health." Contracts or agreements in relation to employment at such a wage are declared null and void. The minimum wage to be established by administrative order is termed a "fair wage," that is, "a wage fairly and reasonably commensurate with the value of the service or class of service rendered."[40]

This new standard, although differing from the living wage principle, was expected in actual operation to produce similar results. In New York, for example, a minimum of 31 cents an hour, or $12.40 for a 40-hour week, was established for the laundry industry in 1933. In 1934, Ohio fixed an $11 weekly minimum for the laundry industry, and a $14 minimum for the cleaning and dyeing industry. These rates reflected in part the reduced wage levels of a depression period but also the unusually low standards prevailing in the industries covered.

b. *Wage Losses from Unemployment.*—In fixing standards

[40] New York, Laws 1933, C. 584. This and other laws adopted in 1933 were based upon a "model bill" prepared under the auspices of the National Consumers' League.

for minimum wages, the question of regularity of employment is of great importance. Whether or not a worker can secure steady employment in a given industry is the factor which determines whether the "living wage" prescribed in an award provides a "living income" throughout the year. Many low-paid industries whose wage rates are affected by minimum wage awards are notably irregular, as for example candy-making and paper-box-making.[41] A few states have attempted to meet the problem of irregular employment by requiring a higher rate per hour when full-time work is not provided.

c. *Profits of the Business.*—An important question likely to arise when wage standards are fixed is whether or not the financial condition of the industry should be taken into account. Most often the problem comes up in connection with the struggling business which claims it cannot survive if its workers are paid a living wage. The issue here is the lowering of the standard of wages in order to secure the continued existence of such an industry. Such a concession enables an industry to flourish without paying the whole cost of maintenance of those whose time and services it uses. Its workers must be partly supported by the earnings of others, who are thus practically subsidizing the underpaying industry. Such a trade has well been called "parasitic," since its existence depends on the bounty of others. It may be that other members of the woman's family (and the better-paying occupations in which they are employed) make up the deficit in her income; it may be that society as a whole pays the bill for the physical and moral deterioration of the workers by its expenditures for hospitals, charities, and reformatories. Only the repealed Nebraska law and the original Massachusetts law have provided that "the financial condition of the business" be considered along with the cost of living.

d. *Substandard Workers.*—Nearly all minimum wage laws permit the fixing of "suitable" wages for young workers and apprentices and for inexperienced workers. The usual practice is to name the rate for young workers and apprentices in the award with the regular minimum rate. In some cases where

[41] See Andrews, Irene Osgood, "The Relation of Irregular Employment to the Living Wage for Women," in *Fourth Report of the New York Factory Investigating Commission*, pp. 497-635; also in *American Labor Legislation Review*, June, 1915, pp. 287-418.

lower rates were set for minors and learners, especially in trades requiring little skill, there were attempts to substitute young girls and inexperienced workers for adults. To overcome this difficulty it was found necessary to specify the length of the apprenticeship and sometimes also the proportion of apprentices allowed. Learning periods specified in the orders vary from three weeks in the canning industry in one state to two years in the mercantile industry of another state.

The employment of slow or infirm workers at lower rates is generally permitted only by special license from the administrative authority. For further protection against the abuse of the privilege, certain of the laws specify the proportion of such workers in a single establishment for whom licenses may be issued.

The problem of piecework has caused considerable difficulty. Employers have been inclined to object to the hourly rates on the ground that their employees who are on piecework cannot make the hourly rate. The California commission worked out a method by which employers may test their piece-rates, by providing that if in an individual establishment the piece-rates do not yield the minimum wage to at least 66 2/3 per cent of the female employees engaged on each product, the piece-rates must be raised to the point where they will do so.

IV. METHODS OF OPERATION

There are two types of minimum wage law. One, the "flat-rate" law, prescribing the legal minimum in the statute itself, is very rare, while the other type, under which a board, commission or single official after proper investigation fixes rates for one industry or group of industries at a time, includes the vast majority of these laws now in existence.

1. **Flat-rate Laws.**—Laws which directly fix the flat minimum rate have been adopted only in certain of the Australian states, and in Arizona, Arkansas, South Dakota and Utah. In Australia, in addition to the system of wage boards, laws sometimes establish very low flat-rate minima, frequently of not more than 48 or 72 cents a week, intended principally to protect children, learners, and apprentices from being put to work without wages and dismissed when they ask for pay. In America, only the Arizona law, with a $16 weekly minimum, and the

MINIMUM FAIR WAGE 65

Utah act of 1913, which required a daily wage of 75 cents for females under eighteen, 90 cents for inexperienced women, and $1.25 for experienced women over that age, fixed universal flat rates, while South Dakota fixes a minimum of $12 per week for women and girls in a number of industries.[42] In Arkansas a flat rate of $1.25 a day for experienced workers and $1 a day for females having less than six months' experience was fixed by the law, but the commission was empowered, after investigation and public hearing, either to raise or to lower these rates.[43] This it did in a limited number of instances. The Arizona and Arkansas laws were declared unconstitutional as applied to women, and the Utah flat-rate law was repealed in 1929, leaving only the South Dakota law in full effect.

The method of fixing uniform flat rates prevents the more careful adjustment for various industries and localities which is elsewhere undertaken by wage boards, it fails to secure the active interest of the employers and employees concerned, and it makes revisions difficult during a period of rapidly changing prices such as occurred between 1916 and 1919. The flat-rate method is therefore held by most students of the problem to be disadvantageous.

2. **Wage-board Laws.**—Representative of the second type of minimum wage laws, those which fix rates for various industries through wage boards, are the laws of Great Britain and Canada and of most Australian and American states. In Great Britain, under the amending act of 1918,[44] the minister of labor is authorized to appoint representative "trade boards" to fix minimum rates in any industry "in which, on account of defective organization, wages are unduly low, or there is reason to apprehend an undue fall in wages when the special war conditions have passed."[45] New trades can be brought under the act without parliamentary confirmation, which was formerly necessary, though Parliament still reserves the right to veto such action. The boards may fix minimum time or piece-rates

[42] Arizona, Laws 1923, C. 3. Utah, Laws 1913, C. 63. South Dakota, Laws 1923, C. 309.
[43] Arkansas, Laws 1915, No. 291.
[44] 8 and 9 George 5, C. 32 (1918).
[45] Great Britain, Ministry of Labor, *Labour Gazette,* August, 1918, p. 308.

which may differ for different classes of workers, for different districts, for different processes, or for any combination of these factors. Rates may be arranged to come into operation successively at the end of specified periods, and variations in rates may be made, to remain in force only during specified periods. In short, under the new act, great flexibility in rate-fixing is secured.

In the United States, the administration of minimum wage laws has in most states been assigned to administrative departments which also enforce other—sometimes all other—labor laws of the state. The heads of these departments—either a commission or a single commissioner appointed by the governor —are authorized, usually with the aid of advisory wage boards, to make administrative regulations fixing the minimum wage rates. Their jurisdiction extends over females and usually over male minors up to eighteen or twenty-one, and over all industries, with the frequent exceptions of agricultural and domestic employments. The administrative authority is empowered to subpœna witnesses, administer oaths, and examine books and papers; and employers are required to keep records of the names, addresses, and wages of women and minor employees. If the administrative authority learns by investigation—which is sometimes compulsory on petition—that wages are insufficient to maintain the specified standard of living, it must proceed either to determine a minimum rate or to establish a subordinate wage board for the industry.

The subordinate board, which is provided for in all the laws, must be representative of employers, employees, and the "public." Unlike the foreign acts, which provide for the nomination of representatives by employers and employees, the older American laws generally leave the method of selection to be determined by the administrative authority. This authority may, of course, ask both parties to select, and this democratic method has often been used. It is required in the Minnesota and more recent laws "so far as practicable." While in theory it has been felt desirable that in the interests of democracy employers and employees should select their representatives to the wage boards, in practice it has proved exceedingly difficult to depend entirely upon election for securing proper representatives for unorganized workers. Their lack of acquaintance and the fear of

MINIMUM FAIR WAGE

losing their places on account of their service on the boards make them reluctant to serve, and timid in conference. Employers also have often been unwilling to choose their representatives.[46] For the present it has therefore been found more effective to leave the enforcing authority free to select representatives from lists submitted by the employers and employees or from those formerly in the trade.

The subordinate wage board may use the investigations of the administrative authority in determining wage rates or may make further investigations of its own. It must make a report of its work with recommendations to that authority, which may accept the recommendations in whole or in part or may refer them back to the board for further consideration, or may convene a new board. When the report of the wage board has been accepted by the department head, a public hearing must be held; if after public consideration no change in the recommendations is deemed necessary, they are promulgated as orders which become effective in thirty or sixty days. Nearly all the laws grant rehearings on petition of either side. Copies of orders issued must in most cases be forwarded to the employers concerned, who are required to post them in a conspicuous place. Minimum wage rates may apply either to time or to piecework, and in several states orders may be issued for a given locality or area. In Wisconsin the industrial commission has power to classify industries for the purpose of adjusting wage rates.

The interests of employers and employees are usually further safeguarded by provisions for a court appeal from the administrative authority's rulings, the procedure and the subjects for court review being carefully specified. In most of the states, rulings may be set aside if unreasonable or unlawful; in many states only questions of law may be reviewed. In most instances, the findings of fact by the administrative authority are held *prima facie* reasonable, and any new evidence must be referred back to them for consideration.

The administrative authorities are empowered to enforce their

---

[46] In Minnesota the commission was obliged to choose representatives of both employers and employees for the wage boards, and to select several of the latter from outsiders. See Ryan, John A., "The Task of Minimum Wage Boards in Minnesota," *The Survey*, November 14, 1914, p. 171.

own rulings. Under most of the laws enacted prior to 1923, employers who failed to pay the minimum wage, if convicted, could be punished by fines of $10 to $100. The Massachusetts law of 1912, however, provided only that the names of employers who were found to pay less than the minimum required should be published in a given number of newspapers throughout the state; but in 1924, the Supreme Judicial Court, while sustaining the law as a whole, held that the newspapers could not be compelled to publish lists of those not complying with the minimum wage decrees.[47] The most recent laws provide for two steps in enforcement. Minimum wage regulations must first be issued as "directory orders" whose violation is punishable only by publication of names as under the Massachusetts law of 1912. If, after the lapse of a given number of months, the administrative authority, following investigation and public hearing, finds that the "directory order" has not been generally complied with, the order may then be made "mandatory" and punishable by fine, and in some states by imprisonment as well.

It has also been found necessary to penalize by a fine of $25 to $5,000 employers who discriminate against employees because they have testified in wage investigations or served on wage boards. In most states employees who have not been paid the legal minimum rate may recover the unpaid balance through a civil suit, and this has proved an effective device for securing observance of the awards.

In America, then, under the most favorable conditions, the establishment of minimum wage rates has been a long and fairly complicated process. First there is the investigation by the administrative authority, then generally further investigations and deliberation by a representative wage board, next public hearings, and finally a possible court review before the minimum rate goes into effect.

v. Results

It is still alleged in some quarters that wages are fixed by economic laws, with which any legislative interference can

[47] Commonwealth v. Boston Transcript Company, 249 Mass. 477, 144 N. E. 400 (1924).

MINIMUM FAIR WAGE

result only in disaster. At present all that can be said is that experience covering forty years in Victoria and shorter periods elsewhere has failed to confirm these dire predictions.

1. **Changes in Wage Rates.**—Perhaps the first question to be considered is whether the laws have succeeded in raising wage rates. Nearly all the evidence so far collected goes to show that they have. Some instances of failure are known. In Victoria, for instance, it proved difficult to maintain the legal rate in the furniture trade among the Chinese, where neither employees nor employers welcomed the establishment of the wage board;[48] and in England the custom of distributing work through middlemen, and the depression of the industry, led to evasions in the lace-finishing trade.[49] Similar evasions have been suspected with regard to homeworkers in the British tailoring industry.[50] But on the whole, in the different countries and in the various industries, the awards of the wage boards have been found to be effective.

An exhaustive study of available evidence of the effect of minimum wage-fixing in the United States prior to 1927 led the Women's Bureau of the Federal Department of Labor to conclude:[51] "That every decree has raised a certain number of women's rates is not to be controverted. How large a proportion of women the decrees have advanced to the minimum and whether or not decrees have been instrumental in raising general rates are questions open to debate. . . . Notably underpaid women were brought up, but adjustments usually did not need to be made all along the line. After all, the purpose of minimum wage laws is not to raise rates in general but to help the most depressed group. The charge against the actual decrees is that often they have been set so low as to bring up only the most submerged women. Interestingly enough, the few rates that seem high enough to raise the entire depressed

---

[48] Hammond, M. B., "Where Life Is More Than Meat," *The Survey*, February 6, 1915, p. 498.

[49] *Sixth Annual Report of the Anti-sweating League*, p. 6.

[50] See Tawney, R. H., *Minimum Rates in the Tailoring Industry*, 1915, pp. 202-210.

[51] U. S. Department of Labor, Women's Bureau, "The Development of Minimum Wage Laws in the United States, 1912 to 1927," *Bulletin No. 61*, p. 370.

group to the cost-of-living level seem to have raised rates in general."

Experience under the most recently enacted minimum wage laws adds further confirmation to these conclusions. Comparative surveys made by the New York Labor Department in 1933 before and after a directory minimum wage decree had been issued for the laundry industry, showed that in six months, the percentage of women receiving less than $8 a week had been reduced from 22 to 12, and that those receiving $12 or more had increased from 31 to 52 per cent of those employed, in both cases despite a shorter work week. The median weekly earnings had increased from $10.77 to $12.54 in New York City laundries, and from $9.82 to $10.94 elsewhere in the state. In New Hampshire, where a directory minimum wage decree for the laundry industry became effective in August, 1934, studies of payrolls by the State Bureau of Labor showed an increase, in those receiving $16 or more, from 4 per cent in a week before, to 14 per cent in a week after the decree's effective date. In this same industry in Ohio, the median wage increased from $8.80 in September, 1933, to $10.61 in July, 1934, following a directory minimum wage decree effective in March, 1934, according to a study by the Ohio Department of Industrial Relations.

2. **Changes in Wages Above the Minimum.**—It is frequently declared that legal minimum wage rates tend to become maximum wage rates, thus injuring those whom they are expressly designed to benefit. This does not, however, appear to be generally the case. In California, for example, where a $16 minimum has been in effect for women since 1920, the percentage of women receiving $17 or more increased from 46.3 in October, 1920, to 65.9 in 1930, according to studies of wages paid in the mercantile, laundry and dry-cleaning, and manufacturing industries by the California Department of Industrial Relations.[52] Even in the depression year 1931, this proportion remained as high as 57.9 per cent. In Wisconsin, an official investigation in 1923 showed that 31.2 per cent of the women were receiving between 25 cents, the legal minimum, and 30 cents

[52] California Department of Industrial Relations, *Report for the Biennium 1930-32*, p. 108.

MINIMUM FAIR WAGE

an hour; 57.9 per cent were earning 30 cents and over.[53] In the laundry industry in New York, it was found that in 1934, soon after the minimum wage was made mandatory, 39 per cent of the women and minors employed were receiving more than the minimum rate, as compared with 31 per cent a year earlier.[54]

Although it is of course difficult to segregate the effect of a legal minimum upon wage rates when so many other influences are continually operating, the evidence available in this and other countries does not support the contention that wages above the minimum will be adversely affected.

3. **Effect on Employment.**—It is further argued against minimum wage laws that they force workers out of industry, either because the workers are considered by the employer unprofitable at the legal rate, or because they can be replaced by apprentices or by specially licensed workers at a lower rate, or perhaps because they have been active on the wage boards. While all three abuses have probably taken place at various times, they are not universal and are not inherent in the laws.

Actual experience with minimum wage regulation shows that while isolated instances of displacement of women workers may be found, they are exceptional, occurring usually in the "marginal" jobs where either men or women are suitable and "where the additional pay for women who are removed by the legislation from the class of exploited workers is the straw which tips the scale in favor of employment of men."[55] In reply to an inquiry as to whether any women or minors were displaced because of the minimum wage, 826 Wisconsin establishments replied "no," and 37 answered "yes," the latter sometimes adding comments indicating that in many instances the discharged employees were lacking in attention and discipline. In Massachusetts, in the four years ending in 1923 during which the wage rates of 123,543 women covered by wage orders were examined, only 90 women out of the 7.2 per cent found working for less than the minimum were discharged by employers

[53] Wisconsin Labor Statistics, May and June, 1923.
[54] Industrial Commissioner Elmer F. Andrews in a letter to the New York *Times*, January 8, 1936.
[55] Elinore M. Herrick in a letter to the New York *Times*, January 6, 1936.

who refused to adjust their rates as legally required.[56] That minimum wage regulation has little influence in restricting the employment of women is indicated by the 1930-1932 report of the California Department of Industrial Relations, which shows that in the mercantile, laundry, dry-cleaning, and manufacturing industries in that state the number of women employees more than doubled between 1919 and 1931, with minimum wage regulation in effect. The system of issuing special permits for less efficient workers to be employed at lower rates, which is provided for by most of the statutes, is undoubtedly helpful in making the adjustment. On the other hand, the displacement of adult skilled workers by apprentices or by defective workers at a lower rate can be checked by limiting the percentage of employees in any establishment who may work at such lower rates, as is already done in Minnesota with regard to defectives. The matter of discrimination against workers who serve on wage boards is more difficult to handle, although most American laws establish penalties for it. This discrimination is a severe handicap to securing a proper representation of the employees on wage boards. This is no serious argument against minimum wage legislation, however, as the same sort of discrimination often takes place against the leaders of the workers in any concerted movement for higher wages.

4. **Effect on Industry.**—From the side of employers it is frequently declared that minimum wage laws will put them under such a handicap that they will be forced to move to freer territory or be driven out of industry altogether. Neither seems to have taken place to any appreciable extent. The increase in wage rates resulting from minimum wage regulation usually affects so small a proportion of the employees and often only employers who are paying substandard wages, that the effect on total costs is in most instances very slight indeed. Only where an industry is generally "sweated" is the increase likely to be an important factor, but the value of such submarginal industries to the community is open to serious question. In Wisconsin, for example, the Industrial Commission found that in home-work manufacture, where workers are as a rule notori-

[56] See brief by Mary W. Dewson, Research Secretary, National Consumers' League, submitted to Ohio Legislative Committee to Investigate Minimum Wage Legislation, 1924.

MINIMUM FAIR WAGE

ously underpaid, the minimum wage apparently forced or kept such industry out of the state.[57] The record of industrial expansion in such states as California and Wisconsin tends to prove that such legislation has had little or no deterring influence. In this connection it is significant that despite doubt as to its ability to withstand attacks in court as to constitutionality, the California minimum wage law has continued to operate with employer support. The president of the California Canners' Association wrote:[58] "At the time the California minimum wage law was passed, more or less opposition was manifested by the canners, as well as other groups of employers of women and minors. As you know, this law has been in operation for several years, and I do not believe that you could find a reputable canner or owner, or large employer of women, who would ask to have this law repealed."

5. **Effect on Trade Unionism.**—Certain trade union officials, especially in the United States, at first feared that minimum wage legislation would hinder the trade union movement by enabling the workers to secure wage gains without the aid of organization. Their fears have not proved true. Instead, the formation of wage boards has often acted as a stimulus to the organization of unions, through which the workers have in some cases been enabled to make further gains above the legal minimum rate. In recent years, labor organizations have generally favored the enactment of this legislation; and they have usually been represented on the wage boards.

6. **Effect on Efficiency.**—A final point to consider is whether guaranteeing to every worker a legal minimum wage reduces incentive and output. The preponderance of evidence is that it does not, but that it even has the opposite effect, due in part to the employer's insistence on greater returns for increased wages, and in part to the workers' spontaneous response to the improved rate of remuneration.[59] In England and in the

[57] Frankfurter, Felix, Dewson, Mary W., and Commons, John R., *State Minimum Wage Laws in Practice,* New York, National Consumers' League, 1924.

[58] Brief of *Gainer vs. Industrial Welfare Commission of California,* prepared by Felix Frankfurter, New York, National Consumers' League, 1924, p. 58.

[59] " 'Output per head has increased,' said another [firm]; 'as a general rule the girls work better if they are paid more.' Indeed, the psychological

74 PRINCIPLES OF LABOR LEGISLATION

United States it is believed that efficiency has gone up rather than down. Thus the British Board of Trade declared that "there are indications that in many cases the efficiency of the workers has been increased,"[60] and the Industrial Welfare Commission of Washington concluded that "the whole standard of efficiency and discipline has been raised."[61] According to the president of the California Canners' Association, already quoted, "While it [minimum wage] has resulted in a very considerable increase in wages it has given us greater efficiency."[62] Besides affecting the attitude of the workers, the necessity of paying higher wages appears to have stimulated employers to reduce costs by better management. In fact, it may be said that the beneficial results of minimum wage legislation have been largely due to the transfer of emphasis from competition for low wages to efficiency on the part of both employer and employee.

Among the better-established results of minimum wage legislation, therefore, may be mentioned (1) that it has raised wages; (2) that minimum wage rates do not in general tend to become maximum rates; (3) that it does not necessarily force workers out of industry; (4) that it does not unduly handicap employers; (5) that it does not undermine trade union organization; and (6) that it does not decrease efficiency.

VI. CONSTITUTIONALITY

The constitutionality of minimum wage legislation involves a new application of the principle of the police power of the state. While it is an accepted constitutional principle that the employee's right freely to contract for the disposition of his own labor cannot be limited except by "due process of law,"

---

effect of relatively high and low rates on the workers would appear to be exactly the reverse of that often ascribed to them. So far from low rates 'making them work,' they often produce listlessness and despair. So far from high rates 'encouraging slackness,' they stimulate the workers to earn as much as possible while at work upon them." (R. H. Tawney, *Minimum Rates in the Tailoring Industry*, p. 133.)

[60] Quoted by Irene Osgood Andrews, *Minimum Wage Legislation*, p. 78.
[61] *First Biennial Report of the Industrial Welfare Commission,* State of Washington, p. 13.
[62] Brief of *Gainer vs. Industrial Welfare Commission of California*, prepared by Felix Frankfurter, New York, National Consumers' League, 1924, p. 59.

MINIMUM FAIR WAGE

yet the police power of the state can restrict the freedom of contract for the protection or betterment of the public health, morals, peace, and welfare. Enactments of the legislature which reasonably tend to that end have been commonly sustained by the courts. Are minimum wage laws a legitimate extension of this power?

The courts have already sanctioned under the police power principle state interference with the wage bargain by limiting working hours for all classes of employees, and by regulating certain conditions of the wage payment, such as the frequency of payment, store orders, or payment in cash.[63] Justification for state interference to fix minimum wage rates has been sought on the same grounds on which other protective legislation has been upheld.

In public employment, indeed, it has been frequently decided that the legislature may rightfully regulate wage rates as well as other conditions of labor both on direct work and on work done by contractors. On work done by contract the wage regulation has commonly taken the form of stipulating that the current rate of wages shall be paid, and the constitutionality of this form of regulation seemed to be well established.[64] In 1914, moreover, the Washington State Supreme Court sustained a more drastic wage regulation for public works. Spokane had fixed by ordinance a minimum wage rate of $2.75 a day for common labor on all public improvements. Though this rate was higher than the current rate for similar work, the court upheld the ordinance, even when applied to work done by contractors, as neither unreasonable nor in violation of the public policy of the state.[65] In January, 1926, the United States Supreme Court

[63] As early as 1859, in a wage exemption case, the court said: "The idea underlying the ultimately developed sentiment of the people upon that subject . . . is that the citizen is an essential elementary constituent of the state; that to preserve the state the citizen must be protected; that to live he must have the means of living; to act and to be a citizen he must be free to act and to have somewhat wherewith to act, and thus to be competent to the performance of his high functions as such. Hence it would seem, as no doubt it was, a matter of the gravest state policy to invest the citizen with, and to secure to him, those essential perquisites, without which the state could not demand of him at all times his instant service and devoted allegiance." Maxwell v. Reed, 7 Wis. 582 (1859).

[64] See Atkin v. Kansas, 191 U. S. 207, 24 Sup. Ct. 124 (1903).

[65] Malette v. City of Spokane, 77 Wash. 205, 137 Pac. 496 (1913).

in an Oklahoma case held the phrase "current rate of per diem wages in the locality" invalid as so vague and indefinite that "the constitutional guaranty of due process cannot be allowed to rest upon a support so equivocal."[66] Since this decision, however, other state laws that require public works contractors to pay the prevailing rate as determined in advance by an administrative authority have been sustained by state courts as sufficiently definite.[67]

These cases, however, were based on the proprietary power of government, and not on the police power. The legality of state regulation of wage rates in private employments was less certain. It was not until the Supreme Court of the United States, by an even division, left in force a previous decision of the Oregon Supreme Court in favor of the state's minimum wage law that the question seemed settled.[68] One justice did not vote because he had taken part in the preparation of the brief[69] in favor of the act. The Oregon court took judicial notice of the "common belief" that many women are employed at excessively low wages and that health, morals, and the public welfare are injured thereby. Accordingly, the law was held constitutional on the same grounds on which laws restricting the hours of labor for women have been sustained. The court held that "Every argument put forward to sustain the maximum hours law, or upon which it was established, applies equally in favor of the constitutionality of the minimum wage law as also within the police power of the state and as a regulation tending to guard the public morals and the public health."[70]

In answer to the argument that the minimum wage law was beyond the police power of the state, the court said: "Such

[66] Connally v. General Construction Co., 269 U. S. 385, 46 Sup. Ct. 126 (1926).

[67] See Metropolitan Water District v. Whitsett, 10 Pac. (2nd) 751 (California, 1932); and State v. Ankham, et al., 31 Pac. (2nd) 888 (Arizona, 1934).

[68] Stettler v. O'Hara, 243 U. S. 629, 37 Sup. Ct. 475 (1917).

[69] The brief is prepared in a similar way to those used in the defense of women's hour laws, and contains a mass of evidence on legislation providing a minimum wage for women, the experience on which such legislation is based, and citations to a large number of legal cases bearing on the subject.

[70] Stettler v. O'Hara, 69 Ore. 519, 139 Pac. 743 (1914).

MINIMUM FAIR WAGE

legislation must be taken as expressing the belief of the legislature and through it of the people. We think we should be bound by the judgment of the legislature, and if there is a necessity for this act, that it is within the police power of the state to provide for the health, morals, and welfare of women and children and that the law should be upheld as constitutional."

In another Oregon case[71] the objection was raised that the act was an infringement of the rights guaranteed by the Fourteenth Amendment, in that it abridged "the privileges or immunities of citizens." To this the court replied: "The right to labor for such hours and at such wages as would reasonably seem to be detrimental to the health or welfare of the community is not a privilege or immunity of any citizen."

In addition to the two favorable decisions of the Oregon Supreme Court in 1914, and that of the United States Supreme Court in 1917, favorable verdicts were handed down by the supreme courts of Arkansas and Massachusetts and twice by supreme courts in Minnesota and Washington. The Arkansas court, in upholding the state's flat-rate law, pointed out that while the legislature was under obligation not to fix an unreasonable or arbitrary minimum wage, there was no more appropriate standard than the normal needs of the employee, which was the basis upon which the legislature had proceeded.[72] In sustaining the Massachusetts law, the court especially noted the fact that it was not compulsory, and reserved opinion as to the legality of a compulsory law.[73] The Minnesota and Washington cases turned on the police power question, as had those in Oregon.[74]

Meanwhile the minimum wage law of the District of Columbia had come into the Court of Appeals of the District and its procedure through this court has been described as follows: "On the first hearing Mr. Justice Robb was unable to sit because of illness. Under statutory authority the other two Justices designated Mr. Justice Stafford of the Supreme Court

[71] Simpson v. O'Hara, 70 Ore. 261, 141 Pac. 158 (1914).
[72] State v. Crowe, 130 Ark. 272, 197 S. W. 4 (1917).
[73] Holcombe v. Creamer, 231 Mass. 99, 120 N. E. 354 (1918).
[74] Williams v. Evans, 139 Minn. 32, 165 N. W. 495 (1917); Miller Telephone Co. v. Minimum Wage Commission, 145 Minn. 262, 177 N. W. 341 (1920); Larsen v. Rice, 100 Wash. 642, 171 Pac. 1037 (1918); Spokane Hotel Co. v. Younger, 113 Wash. 359, 194 Pac. 595 (1920).

of the District to sit in his place. The decision, on June 6, 1921, was two to one in favor of the statute. Chief Justice Smyth and Mr. Justice Stafford were in favor; Mr. Justice Van Orsdel was opposed. Motions for a rehearing were denied on June 22, of the same year. Three days later, Mr. Justice Robb, who had now recovered, wrote the Chief Justice that he was considering an application for a rehearing. On July 1, he wrote that he had decided to vote for a rehearing and had so notified counsel and Mr. Justice Van Orsdel. Later Justices Robb and Van Orsdel instructed the clerk to enter an order granting a rehearing. The Chief Justice dissented. The case was reargued on February 14, 1922, and decided on November 6, 1922. The vote was two to one against the statute."[75]

Chief Justice Smyth in dissenting stated: "It would seem from the foregoing that the appellants, finding themselves defeated, sought a justice who had not sat in the case, but who, they believed, would be favorable to them, and induced him, by an appeal directed to him personally, to assume jurisdiction and join with the dissenting justice in an attempt to overrule the decisions of the court. I shall not characterize such practice; let such facts speak for themselves."[76]

The case was then appealed to the United States Supreme Court, which by a five-to-three decision rendered an adverse opinion written by Mr. Justice Sutherland, on April 9, 1923, in Adkins v. Children's Hospital.[77] In 1925 the Arizona minimum wage law came to the Supreme Court, which merely submitted a memorandum holding that it was bound by its decision in the Adkins case.[78] In 1927, the Supreme Court rendered a similar adverse decision on the Arkansas law.[79] These decisions applied only to working women, and left the laws intact as affecting minors.

The Constitution of the United States specifically provides that Congress shall legislate for the District of Columbia, and

[75] Powell, Thomas Reed, *Harvard Law Review,* March, 1924.
[76] Children's Hospital v. Adkins, 284 Fed. 613, 1922.
[77] 261 U. S. 525, 43 Sup. Ct. 394 (1923). Mr. Justice Brandeis, although technically eligible, did not vote, because he was of counsel in the Oregon cases.
[78] Murphy v. Sardell, 269 U. S. 530, 46 Sup. Ct. 22 (1925).
[79] Donham v. West Nelson Mfg. Co., 273 U. S. 657, 47 Sup. Ct. 343 (1927).

MINIMUM FAIR WAGE

by an unbroken line of decisions from Marshall to this case, an Act of Congress is presumed to be constitutional unless proved to the contrary beyond reasonable doubt. In the Adkins case, Chief Justice Taft pointed out: "But it is not the function of this court to hold congressional acts invalid simply because they are passed to carry out economic views which the court believes to be unwise or unsound." Mr. Justice Holmes added, "I am of the opinion that the statute is valid."

Mr. Justice Sutherland, however, considered the measure an infringement of freedom of contract and did not think that minimum wage legislation could be compared with restrictive legislation affecting public utilities, public work, or methods of wage payments. Neither could it be sustained, he argued, on the same ground as legislation regulating the hours of labor. He also pointed out that the passage of the Nineteenth Amendment had changed the political status of women and thereby tended to equalize the bargaining power of men and women. But Mr. Chief Justice Taft stated that "The Nineteenth Amendment did not change the physical strength or limitations of women upon which Muller *v.* Oregon rests," and Mr. Justice Holmes added: "It will need more than the Nineteenth Amendment to convince me that there are no differences between men and women or that legislation cannot take those differences into account." Probably the main objection of the majority was that this measure fixed wages without regard to the value of the services rendered. They did not indicate which one of the many wage theories they would be willing to accept.[80]

In the decade following the Adkins case in the District of Columbia, several state supreme and federal district courts were asked for opinions in reference to the status of state minimum wage laws, and in all cases these courts held that they were bound by the United States Supreme Court decision, although many of the judges specifically state that they do not agree with the economic philosophy advanced by Mr. Justice Sutherland in the Adkins case. Following these decisions, state authorities elsewhere continued to enforce the acts affecting adult women wherever the employers would voluntarily coöperate. Prosecution for violation, however, was no longer

[80] For a compilation of leading legal opinion on this case, see "The Supreme Court and Minimum Wage Legislation," *New Republic,* 1925.

80   PRINCIPLES OF LABOR LEGISLATION

possible, and the making of new regulations practically stopped, except in Massachusetts where the law of 1912 was not mandatory. As applied to minors, who comprise nearly half of the workers affected, the acts remained in full force.

With the beginning of more vigorous enforcement of minimum wage legislation after the enactment of 1933 of the "fair wage" standard in several states, the issue was again brought before the courts. In March, 1936, the highest court in New York in a four-to-three decision invalidated that state's minimum wage law of 1933, the majority holding that the new "fair wage" standard was "a difference in phraseology and not in principle" from the "living wage" legislation overthrown by the Supreme Court in the Adkins case. "Forcing the payment of wages at a reasonable value does not make inapplicable the principle and ruling of the Adkins case," the majority opinion declared.[81]

The United States Supreme Court, to which this case was appealed, in a five-to-four decision likewise ruled the New York act unconstitutional on the basis of the principles laid down in the Adkins case.[82] Justice Butler wrote the majority opinion, with Justices McReynolds, Roberts, Sutherland and Van Deventer concurring. He asserted that the ruling in the Adkins case, that the living wage standard set up by the District of Columbia act stamped that law as arbitrary and invalid, was "of subordinate consequence." He declared that this earlier decision clearly showed "that the State is without power to prohibit, change or nullify contracts between employers and adult women workers as to the amount of wages to be paid. . . . Any measure that deprives employers and adult women of freedom to agree on wages, leaving employers and men free to do so, is necessarily arbitrary." Two dissenting opinions were filed, one by Chief Justice Hughes, with Justices Brandeis, Cardozo and Stone concurring, and the other by Justice Stone, with Justices Brandeis and Cardozo concurring. Chief Justice Hughes held that the Adkins decision should not control since in it the court had not passed upon a statute like the New York act. He declared: "I can find nothing in the Federal Constitution which denies to the state power to protect women from being

[81] People ex rel. Tipaldo v. Morehead, 270 N. Y. 233 (1936).
[82] Morehead v. People ex rel. Tipaldo, 56 Sup. Ct. 918 (1936).

MINIMUM FAIR WAGE

exploited by overreaching employers through the refusal of a fair wage as defined in the New York statute and ascertained in a reasonable manner by a competent authority." Justice Stone went further and held that, regardless of the differences existing in the New York act, the Adkins case should not be followed. He said: "It is difficult to imagine any grounds, other than our own personal economic predilections, for saying that the contract of employment is any less an appropriate subject of legislation than are scores of others, in dealing with which this court has held that legislatures may curtail individual freedom in the public interest."

In the New York case, the majority opinion pointed out that the appellants had sought to differentiate the New York law from the District of Columbia act, but had not challenged the principles laid down in the Adkins case. While the court was preparing this decision, however, the Washington State Supreme Court handed down an opinion[83] upholding that state's minimum "living wage" law of 1913. The Washington court said: "Unless the Supreme Court of the United States can find beyond question that chapter 174, Laws of 1913, is a plain, palpable invasion of rights secured by the fundamental law and has no real or substantial relation to the public morals or public welfare, then the law must be sustained. The United States Supreme Court has not yet held that a state statute such as the one in the case at bar is unconstitutional, and until such time—*Adkins* v. *Children's Hospital,* 261 U. S. 525, is not controlling—we shall adhere to our holding in the case of *Larsen* v. *Rice,* 100 Wash. 642, 171 Pac., 1037; and *Spokane Hotel Co.* v. *Younger,* 113 Wash. 359, 194 Pac. 595. It does not appear upon the face of the minimum wage law or from any facts of which the Supreme Court of the United States must take judicial notice, that in the State of Washington evils did not exist for which our minimum wage law was an appropriate remedy. The action of the state legislature and of this court indicates that such evils do exist."

Whatever the future may bring, it seems fairly safe to say that the idea of a living wage for all workers has become a popular one. Our minimum wage laws have at least done this—they have called the attention of employers, employees, and the

[83] *Parrish* v. *West Coast Hotel Company,* 55 Pac. (2d) 1083 (1936).

public to some of the strange and unreasonable inconsistencies and discrepancies which exist in the wage system. They have been one of the most efficacious means of bringing to light facts of industry which are indispensable for the intelligent construction of economic and legislative programs. Whether we get away from chaotic methods of wage payment by means of greater equalization of power through organization of the workers, or by means of public intervention to fix a minimum wage, or by means of combinations of both methods, we can feel fairly well assured that the tendency is toward a guarantee of standards of living below which no worker should be allowed to fall.

CHAPTER III

HOURS OF LABOR

When American industry in 1933 and 1934 put into effect national "codes of fair competition" providing in most instances for a forty-hour work week, the United States temporarily assumed world leadership in the movement for the legal establishment of shorter hours of labor. For the first time in history a great industrial country adopted the forty-hour week as a national policy and attempted to enforce it by law. When in 1935 the system of codes was abandoned because of the Supreme Court's decision invalidating the National Industrial Recovery Act, a large number of employers had become convinced of the economic soundness of the forty-hour principle. Without legislative protection, however, a gradual breaking down of this standard began in many industries.

The forty-hour week was adopted in 1933 as an emergency measure to combat widespread unemployment by spreading available work and by checking overproduction in certain industries. This was recognition of a principle which the labor movement has for many years advocated as a permanent policy. In fact, the National Industrial Recovery Act was adopted by Congress partly as a substitute for a bill providing for a thirty-hour week which, at the insistence of the American Federation of Labor, had already passed the Senate. The reduction of hours has been organized labor's chief remedy for unemployment.

Some twenty years earlier, the United States had experienced a shorter-hours movement in the midst of a war-time boom. This was a movement for an eight-hour workday. Beginning in the spring of 1915 at Bridgeport, Connecticut, where a series of strikes put the war-supply industries on an eight-hour basis, the movement spread among machinists; and before the United States entered the war the anthracite coal miners had obtained a straight, and railroad workers a basic, eight-hour day. Eight-

84   PRINCIPLES OF LABOR LEGISLATION

hour agitation was strengthened during the war by the government's attitude and by the requirement of eight hours' work on government contracts, even though the latter was regularly waived and overtime at higher rates permitted. Between January, 1919, and the middle of 1919, according to figures compiled by the United States Bureau of Labor Statistics, the working hours of 3,462,000 persons were reduced to eight. This movement continued into the years immediately following the war, but was checked for the most part by the depression of 1921. During the following decade particular industries in a few instances reduced hours, but the average full-time work week increased slightly for industry as a whole.

The following table, compiled from data in the United States Census of Manufactures, shows the course of change in hours of labor in manufacturing industries from 1909 to 1929. "Prevailing hours" are the average usual working hours in the establishments, and take no account of varying hours for individuals or overtime operation which occurs at times in nearly

TABLE SHOWING COURSE OF CHANGE IN HOURS OF LABOR IN MANUFACTURING INDUSTRIES IN THE UNITED STATES FROM 1908 TO 1929

	Percentage Distribution of Wage Earners in Manufacturing According to Prevailing Hours of Labor per Week				Total Number of Wage Earners and Millions of Horse Power (Machinery)	
Year	48 Hours and Under	Between 48 and 54 Hours	54 and Under 60 Hours	60 Hours and Over	Total Wage Earners	Horse Power (Millions)
1909	7.9	7.3	45.6	39.2	6,615,046	18.8
1914	11.9	13.4	47.8	26.9	6,896,190	22.3
1919	48.7	16.5	22.8	12.0	9,000,056	29.3
1921	51.5	18.2	20.4	9.9	6,946,570	Not collected
1923	46.1	21.9	22.8	9.2	8,778,156	33.1
1929	45.9	25.1	21.4	7.6	8,838,743	42.9

all industries and is provided for in most agreements between organized labor and employers. The table also shows the total number of wage earners engaged in manufacturing, and the amount of machinery as measured by millions of horse power used.

HOURS OF LABOR

In 1909, of the 6,615,046 wage earners enumerated by the Census of Manufactures, only 7.9 per cent were employed in establishments where the eight-hour day prevailed. "Prevailing hours" for three-quarters of them were fifty-four to sixty weekly. No fewer than 344,011, or 5.2 per cent of the whole number, worked where prevailing hours were between sixty and seventy-two weekly; 116,083 worked where the prevailing hours were seventy-two per week; and 114,118 where the prevailing hours were more than seventy-two.

By 1921, over 50 per cent of the wage earners, more than 3,500,000 as compared with less than 1,000,000 in 1914, were working in establishments where the prevailing hours were forty-eight or less per week. The proportion of those working fifty-four hours or more had fallen to less than one-third, and of those working over sixty hours to 2.5.

From 1921 to 1929, the percentage of manufacturing wage earners working forty-eight or fewer hours a week decreased, and there was a slight decrease in the number working sixty or more. On the other hand, the group having a work week of between forty-eight and fifty-four, which includes those on a nine-hour day with a Saturday half-holiday, showed a substantial increase in this period. The picture was greatly changed, however, by the general adoption of the forty-hour week under the national codes of fair competition in 1933 and 1934. This resulted in widespread introduction of the eight-hour day and five-day week throughout all industry. Following the Supreme Court decision rendering the codes inoperative, however, many employers returned to the longer work week, although others continued, at least temporarily, to maintain the code standard. Although the NRA code experience gave the shorter-hours movement a strong push ahead, the coming of more normal business conditions may be expected to lead to strong pressure for a resumption of the hours of work prevailing before the depression.

The experience of the past twenty years has demonstrated that long hours do not pay. Shorter hours have not decreased total production. Labor shortage during the war and competitive conditions in the following decade stimulated employers to introduce more machinery, better equipment and improved methods, which, together with the heightened efficiency of the workers, led to a tremendous increase in the productivity of industry.

Under modern industrial conditions, excessive hours of work break down health. Even with short hours the strain of modern industry, with its speed, its piecework, its division of labor involving the monotonous repetition of the same process, sometimes even of the same movement, is a heavy tax on the worker. With the ten- or twelve-hour day or the seven-day week, a man must go back to his job before he has had sufficient rest to recover from the excessive fatigue of the long work period, and a progressive decline in health results. "In my judgment," said a former official of a large steel company, in 1914, "a large proportion of the steel workers, who from early manhood work twelve hours a day, are old men at forty."[1]

Though it is the health dangers of long hours which are most often emphasized, the lack of leisure for family life, for recreation, for all requirements of citizenship, is no less an evil. It should not be forgotten that the time spent in going to and from work and the dinner hour often add two hours to the length of the workday proper, so that an eleven-hour day is likely to mean thirteen hours away from home. Said a Pittsburgh steel worker of the results of such a workday, "Home is where I eat and sleep."[2] The beneficial effects on workers of the adoption of the eight-hour day in European countries was repeatedly emphasized in a report of the International Labor Office.[3] The good results included increased activity in education, decrease in alcoholism to which exhausted workers resorted for stimulation, and general improvement in health, morals, and devotion to family life.

For women workers, aside from their weaker physique, the "long day" is especially onerous because of the double burden of domestic duties and wage work which many of them carry. Ordinarily men rest when their day's toil is over, but there are few working girls who do not have at least mending

[1] Dickson, William B., former vice-president, United States Steel Corporation, *The Survey*, January 3, 1914, p. 376.

[2] Quoted by Fitch, John A., "The Steel Industry and the Labor Problem," *The Survey*, March 6, 1909, p. 1091.

[3] This report is summarized in the *International Labour Review* of February, 1926, p. 175: "Results of the Eight-hour Day: II. The Eight-hour Day and the Human Factor in Production," by Edgar Milhaud.

and laundering to do in the evenings, and many married women must take the entire care of their homes and children before and after work.

Long hours, moreover, do not make for the greatest efficiency of the worker in production. It is sometimes argued that if hours are reduced output will decline in proportion. This might be true if human beings were mere machines and not human beings who grow tired. As a matter of fact, as has been demonstrated by numerous investigations, the law of diminishing returns operates nowhere more strikingly than in regard to hours of labor. In Great Britain, in an effort to increase the supply of munitions early in the World War, the legal restrictions on the hours of women and children were relaxed, and night and Sunday work and days of twelve to fourteen hours became common for all classes of workers. Yet the supply of war materials failed to meet demands, and claims that the employees were "slacking" were met by counter charges that the workers were being driven beyond human endurance. To advise on the situation, the Health of Munition Workers Committee was formed, and as a result of its recommendations, as a means of improving output, Sunday work was practically abolished, hours were greatly reduced, and almost all the former peace-time restrictions on the hours of women and children were reintroduced. The whole history of this committee was of great educational value to officials, employers, and the public, in driving home the fact that excessive hours do not pay.[4]

The data supplied by these and many other studies were collected and analyzed by P. Sargent Florence in making a scientific estimate of business losses caused by fatigue and unrest of workers. Concerning hours of work he concludes: "A reduction of hours increases hourly output and decreases absence and accidents per hour. Reduction to eight hours per day also increases daily output in occupations where speed depends mainly on the human factor, but may fail to do so where the machine sets the pace or the completion of the operation

---

[4] A study undertaken by the Federal Public Health Service in America during the war also showed the eight-hour day to be more efficient than the ten-hour day.

depends on chemical process."[5] An authoritative report by a committee of the Federated American Engineering Societies on its investigation of continuous-process industries after the close of the war states that, in the overwhelming majority of plants that changed from the twelve- to the eight-hour shift, no technical difficulties were encountered; that, where good planning and care in execution were used, the effect upon quality and quantity of production was satisfactory, resulting in some plants in practically every major continuous-process industry in an increase in production of 25 per cent per man, and occasionally more, and that in practically every case the change reduced absenteeism and labor turnover in a marked degree.

Despite all this evidence of economic and social gain resulting from shortening of work periods, long hours have still prevailed in many American industries. Establishments which operate continuously have often combined the twelve-hour shift with the seven-day week, or required their employees to alternate weekly or fortnightly between day and night shifts, working twenty-four hours without rest when the change is made. The engineers' committee referred to above reported in 1922 that there were in the United States forty continuous-process industries in which 300,000 wage earners were working the twelve-hour shift. Approximately half of these were engaged in the manufacture of iron and steel. Among the principal industries in which the other half were distributed were manufacture of paper, ice, sugar, cottonseed and other vegetable oils, flour, salt, cement, lime, brick, pottery, rubber, and chemicals, and the metals industries, petroleum well drilling and operation, and mining.

After the publication of the engineers' report, a notable reduction in the twelve-hour shift but an increase in the seven-day week took place in the iron and steel industry. Before the war, the major branches of the industry were almost without exception operated on a two-shift basis. During the war, there was some tendency toward the three-shift system, but following the armistice, many of the plants which had adopted the eight-hour shift for emergency reasons returned to the old system. The great steel strike, which was to a large extent a protest against the excessive hours, was crushed in January,

[6] Florence, P. Sargent, *Economics of Fatigue and Unrest*, 1924, p. 348.

1920. The report of an investigation by a committee of the Interchurch World Movement, published in 1920, emphasized the long hours to which the workers were subjected.[6] In 1922 President Harding invited the principal steel manufacturers to meet in Washington to devise some means by which the twelve-hour shift could be abolished, as it had been in European countries at the close of the war. The report of the manufacturers' committee, of which Judge Gary of the United States Steel Corporation was chairman, stating that business and labor conditions rendered it inadvisable to reduce hours at that time, caused widespread popular indignation, voiced by the press and many organizations. The manufacturers soon reversed their decision and in the summer of 1923 began a systematic change from the twelve-hour to the eight-hour shift.

The report of a survey by the United States Department of Labor shows that in the blast furnaces the proportion of employees who labored seventy-two or more hours per week was reduced from 69 per cent in 1922 to 9 per cent in 1924, and of those who labored eighty-four hours per week from 17 to 5 per cent. In this and other continuous processes, weekly working hours of the majority were reduced from seventy-two or more to under sixty. Thousands in these processes, however, still worked eighty-four hours per week, and the proportion working seven days per week increased in blast furnaces from 29 to 45 per cent, and in open-hearth furnaces from 27 to 52 per cent. In this and other departments, there was also a large increase in the number working seven days once in two or three weeks. Between 1924 and 1929 the proportion of blast-furnace workers whose full-time work week was eighty-four hours increased from 5 to 8 per cent, but in the depression year 1933 had fallen to 1 per cent. The amount of seven-day labor, after a similar rise, had also declined by 1933 in this and other continuous operations. In that year, however, only 45 per cent of the blast-furnace workers and 50 per cent of the open-hearth workers had the straight six-day week. A large number worked on a schedule permitting a rest day not oftener than once in every nineteen days. This means that tens of thousands of wage earners in the steel industry were

[6] Commission of Inquiry, Interchurch World Movement, *Report on the Steel Strike of 1919,* chap. iii.

90 PRINCIPLES OF LABOR LEGISLATION

working regularly seven days each week and almost as many more had a rest day only once in every two or three weeks.[7]

In the petroleum industry, also, there has been much seven-day labor. After a thorough investigation of a large section of the industry in sixteen states, the United States Department of Labor reported that in 1920 three-fourths of all well drillers and operators, one-third of all pipe-line employees and 23 per cent of employees in refineries were working regularly seven days per week. For the whole industry, this would approximate 147,000 seven-day workers, of whom nearly 20,000, chiefly well drillers and operators, were also working the twelve-hour shift.[8] Between 1920 and 1926, the production of oil increased more than 50 per cent, which may have necessitated considerable increase in the number of employees. The engineers' committee in 1922 reported the twelve-hour shift continuing in the well-drilling section of the industry substantially as described above. The survey was not concerned with seven-day labor.[9] In the same year, Mr. Rockefeller publicly announced that he believed "that generally speaking the twelve-hour day and seven-day week should no longer be tolerated in industry, either from the viewpoint of public policy or of industrial efficiency."[10] Nevertheless, a study of hours worked in 1929 by oil-well and pipe-line employees in four important oil-producing states[11] showed that almost half of the oil-well employees and over a third of the pipe-line employees worked seven days a week when employed full time. For almost a fifth of the oil-well employees and a substantial number of the pipe-line employees, the seven-day week was combined with the twelve-hour day. Efforts to control overproduction in the oil industry through federal regulation authorized in the National Industrial Recovery Act of 1933 brought a general reduction of hours in this industry. Although federal regulation was declared unconstitutional by the Supreme

[7] United States Bureau of Labor Statistics, *Bulletin No. 567*, 1932.
[8] United States Bureau of Labor Statistics, *Bulletin No. 297*, 1922.
[9] Committee on Work Periods in Continuous Industry of the Federated American Engineering Societies, *The Twelve-hour Shift in Industry*, 1922, p. 143.
[10] *The Survey*, November 1, 1922, p. 147.
[11] U. S. Department of Labor, Bureau of Labor Statistics, *Monthly Labor Review*, March, 1930, p. 125.

HOURS OF LABOR

Court in 1935,[12] an effort has been made in the industry to continue the shorter work week. How successful this effort will be, cannot be predicted.

The manufacturing industries in each of which, according to the Census of Manufactures of 1929, more than 10,000 employees were working in establishments where the prevailing weekly hours were over fifty-four, are shown in the table below.

Logging and work in sawmills[13] employed in 1929 a total of 419,084 wage earners. This industry is scattered through the forests of a score of states, and involves arduous and dangerous labor. The seasons of its greatest activity are winter and spring, and many of its employees are migratory workers who harvest grain in summer and fall. The struggle of these men to organize and obtain decent working conditions has been one of the bitterest in the American labor movement. Thus far, excepting in the Northwest, they are largely unorganized. In 1914, four-fifths, and in 1923 over half, of them were working sixty hours or more per week; in 1929 only about one-fourth had gained the forty-eight-hour week, and more than half, 223,868, were still working sixty hours or more.

The cotton goods industry, located chiefly in the Northeast and South Atlantic States, employed in 1929 about 425,000 wage earners, a large proportion of whom were women and minors, which makes organization difficult. In 1914 nearly half its employees were working sixty hours or more, and less than 1 per cent had the forty-eight-hour week. By 1921 nearly 45 per cent had gained the forty-eight-hour or shorter week. After 1921 they lost ground, and in 1929 only 23 per cent retained the forty-eight-hour week, while the majority were working over nine hours a day. It is noteworthy that only one of the leading cotton-mill states, Massachusetts, has by law limited the working hours of women to forty-eight per week. Most of the northern states set the limit at fifty-four, while in the South several set it at sixty, and one state, Alabama, has no hour regulation for women. The cotton industry, how-

[12] Panama Refining Co. v. Ryan, 293 U. S. 388, 55 Sup. Ct. 241 (1935).
[13] Classified in the 1929 Census as "Lumber and Timber Products," not otherwise classified.

ever, was the first to adopt a code of fair competition under the National Industrial Recovery Act in 1933, with a forty-hour week maximum. Although this restriction became inoperative following the nullification of the Recovery Act by the Supreme Court in 1935, an effort was made by the better employers, in this as in some other industries, to retain voluntarily at least part of the gains made under the code.[14]

In many foreign countries, there has been a considerable decrease in working hours since the war. Forty-eight-hour week laws were enacted in New South Wales and Ecuador in 1916, the eight-hour day was established by constitutional provision in Mexico and by decree in Soviet Russia in 1917, and was introduced in most European countries in 1919-1920. The workers held out strongly for its continuance through the long period of business depression and unemployment that followed the war.

In some countries, as in Belgium and Switzerland, the eight-hour day is established for the great majority of workers by statute law; in others, as in Great Britain and Germany, less uniformly by trade agreements between employers' and employees' organizations, and by administrative orders; in still others, as in France, by a combination of trade agreements and legislation enunciating the principle and authorizing administrative orders to cover certain industries. In general, while the eight-hour day is recognized in principle all over Europe, employers have stood out for arrangements providing elasticity in length of hours according to occupation and business conditions.

An eight-hour law providing a number of exceptions has been in force in British Columbia since 1924. The official 1935 report on actual working hours in Canada showed great variation, the forty-four-hour week predominating in building, printing, and clothing trades, forty-eight-hours in laundries and coal mines, forty-eight to fifty-four in metal mines, fifty to fifty-five in textile mills, and sixty in lumbering. The tendency is to shorter hours in the western provinces. In some industries especially building and automobiles, the forty-hour week has been adopted to a considerable extent.

In Australia the forty-four and forty-eight-hour week pre-

[14] For hours of transportation workers and miners see pp. 122-129.

HOURS OF LABOR

TABLE SHOWING THE MANUFACTURING INDUSTRIES IN THE UNITED STATES IN EACH OF WHICH, IN 1929, MORE THAN 10,000 EMPLOYEES WERE IN ESTABLISHMENTS WHERE THE PREVAILING WEEKLY HOURS WERE OVER FIFTY-FOUR [15]

Industry	Total Employees	Number Working over 54 Hours
Boxes, wooden, except cigar	30,554	13,007
Bread and other bakery products	200,841	31,899
Butter	19,097	12,674
Canning and preserving, fruits and vegetables	98,866	38,015
Car and general construction, repairs, steam railroad repair shops	368,681	109,914
Cement	33,368	28,345
Chemicals	62,199	28,180
Cigars and cigarettes	105,308	10,192
Clay products (other than pottery)	93,336	27,925
Cotton goods	424,916	269,539
Dyeing and finishing textiles	79,327	17,112
Electrical machinery, apparatus, supplies	328,722	11,493
Engines, turbines, tractors, etc.	61,148	14,032
Fertilizers	20,926	15,898
Flour and other grain mill products	27,028	11,471
Foundry and machine shop products	454,441	77,810
Furniture	193,399	48,806
Gas	43,065	23,586
Glass	67,527	11,083
Ice cream	22,399	12,716
Ice, manufactured	32,184	25,850
Iron and steel:		
Blast furnaces	24,960	14,873
Steel works and rolling mills	394,574	158,748
Knit goods	208,488	55,968
Lumber and timber products	419,084	223,868
Meat packing, wholesale	122,505	11,302
Motor-vehicle bodies and parts	221,332	43,992
Non-ferrous metal alloys (except aluminum)	79,183	30,541
Oil, cake and meal, cottonseed	15,825	15,433
Paper	103,320	18,040
Petroleum refining	80,596	37,245
Planing mill products	90,134	21,304
Silk and rayon manufacture	130,467	19,944
Structural and ornamental iron work	54,947	17,594
Wire	22,467	14,269
Woolen goods	58,474	10,222

[15] U. S. Census of Manufactures, 1929, vol. i, pp. 52-56.

94   PRINCIPLES OF LABOR LEGISLATION

vail. Queensland in 1924, and New South Wales in 1925, enacted forty-four-hour laws covering nearly all classes of wage workers.

The eight-hour convention for industrial workers adopted by the official International Labor Conference at Washington in 1919, had been ratified by eighteen countries by January, 1936, but most of these were of secondary importance industrially.[16] Four countries—Austria, France, Italy and Latvia—had registered conditional ratifications which go into effect only when their chief competitor nations also ratify. The slowness of progress in ratifications of this convention has been the subject of lengthy discussion at the conferences at Geneva. By invitation of the British government the ministers of labor of France, Belgium, Germany, Italy, and Great Britain, and the Director of the International Labor Office, met in conference in London in March, 1926, and there drew up and signed an agreement accepting certain interpretations as to application of the convention and procedure in case of its ratification.[17] In 1935, the International Labor Conference adopted a convention favoring the principle of the forty-hour week, but leaving its specific application to be dealt with in separate conventions covering particular industries. The forty-hour week was made the rule in Italy in 1934 by agreement between the national organizations of employers and workers; and in 1936 France provided for the forty-hour work-week by statute.

Changing economic conditions, introduction of machinery, other modern equipment, and efficient management have made long hours unnecessary, and experience has proved them detrimental to industry and society. Many competent economists, moreover, believe that with present high industrial productivity, the short work week is a necessary means of reducing unemployment. In the United States, where industrial efficiency has been most highly developed, the movement for shorter hours was in some respects less advanced than in other industrial countries until 1933 when the national codes of fair

[16] Argentina, Belgium, Bulgaria, Canada, Chile, Colombia, Cuba, Czechoslovakia, Dominican Republic, Greece, India, Lithuania, Luxemburg, Nicaragua, Portugal, Rumania, Spain and Uruguay.

[17] International Labor Office, *Industrial and Labour Information*, March 29, 1926, p. 411.

HOURS OF LABOR

competition were inaugurated. When the codes became inoperative in 1935, the male workers in unorganized industries were again left without protection against excessive hours. The experience with legal hours limitation under the codes, however, has given added strength to the belief that the weaker groups—children, women and men who, owing to disadvantageous social conditions, personal handicaps, or the peculiar character of their work, are unable to secure reasonable hours —should receive the protection of legislation.

I. MAXIMUM HOURS

1. **Children.**—The first legislative regulation of the hours of labor in this country applied to children. In 1842 a petition was presented to the Massachusetts legislature by certain citizens of Fall River, who pointed out that the existing hours of labor must be permanently injurious to the health of children and detrimental to their education, and prayed that prohibitory legislation be enacted. The agitation resulted in the passage during the same year of a ten-hour law for children under twelve years of age in manufacturing establishments.[18] In the same year also, Connecticut enacted a ten-hour law for children under fourteen in cotton and woolen mills.[19]

By the beginning of the Civil War, laws limiting the hours of children in manufacturing establishments to ten a day had been enacted in the five additional states of New Hampshire,[20] Maine,[21] Pennsylvania,[22] New Jersey,[23] and Ohio.[24] The Connecticut statute of 1842 was, however, superseded thirteen years after passage by a new law which set back the limit to eleven hours,[25] followed within a year by an amendment which still further lowered the standard to twelve hours a day.[26] Like the first Connecticut law, the early Pennsylvania laws applied

---

[18] Massachusetts, Laws 1842, C. 60.
[19] Connecticut, Laws 1842, C. 28.
[20] New Hampshire, Laws 1846, C. 318.
[21] Maine, Laws 1848, C. 83.
[22] Pennsylvania, Laws 1848, No. 227; Laws 1849, No. 415; Laws 1855, No. 501.
[23] New Jersey, Laws 1851, p. 321.
[24] Ohio, Laws 1852, p. 187.
[25] Connecticut, Laws 1855, C. 45.
[26] Connecticut, Laws 1856, C. 39.

only to textile mills, but in the other states the acts covered manufacturing in general. The ages of the children affected varied from twelve in Massachusetts to twenty-one in New Jersey and Pennsylvania. In addition to the states already mentioned, Rhode Island enacted in 1853 an eleven-hour law for children from twelve to fifteen.[27]

These early laws were, however, to a great extent unenforced and even unenforceable. The frequent provision, for example, that only violations committed "knowingly" were punishable, which, to quote a government report, "put a premium on ignorance and . . . served to balk the intent of so much labor legislation,"[28] originated in the Massachusetts law of 1842 and was copied in New Jersey and Rhode Island. In New Hampshire, children under fifteen could work longer than the statutory ten hours if provided with the "written consent of the parent or guardian."[29] In New Jersey, and in Pennsylvania under the earliest laws, a child could not be "holden or required" to work more than ten hours a day, but if the child worked longer the employer, in order to escape all responsibility, needed only to declare that the extra labor was not required, but voluntary. Ohio even went so far as to legitimatize this subtle distinction by declaring that minors under eighteen might not be "compelled," but that minors under fourteen might not be "permitted," to work more than ten hours. Only in two states were any provisions made for enforcement: in Connecticut constables and grand jurors were to inquire after violations, and in Pennsylvania constables could take action—but only after complaint.

It is interesting to note that the early hour legislation for

[27] Rhode Island, Laws 1853, p. 245.

[28] *Report on the Condition of Woman and Child Wage-earners in the United States,* Senate Document No. 645, Sixty-first Congress, Second Session, 1910, vol. vi, "The Beginnings of Child Labor Legislation in Certain States," Elizabeth Lewis Otey, p. 78.

[29] Of this law Horace Greeley said: "Why should 'the consent of *the* (?) parent or guardian of such minor' 'be allowed to overrule the demands of Justice, Humanity, and the Public weal'? . . . We believe nothing less than a peremptory prohibition of the employment of Minors for more than 10 hours per day, without regard to the consent of parents or guardians, will effect much, if anything. Still, we are willing to see a trial made even of this milk and water enactment." (New York *Tribune,* August 11, 1847.)

children resulted almost altogether from interest in education and from the efforts of adult male workers to secure such regulations as a first step toward obtaining similar laws for themselves. Sometimes, also, the men workers undoubtedly believed that restrictions on the hours of women and children would result in decreased employment of these classes of wage earners, with consequent advantages to themselves. It was not until later that the main emphasis came to be put on the necessity of shortening children's hours to protect the health of the children.

The greatest progress in legislation regarding the hours of labor for children has been made in the last thirty years. Beginning with Illinois in 1903, the eight-hour standard for children under sixteen has been established in about four-fifths of the states.[30] The majority of these states have also a forty-eight hour or six-day weekly limit. Six—Mississippi, New Mexico, New York, Pennsylvania, Utah, and Virginia—have a forty-four-hour limit. In about twenty-five states the eight-hour standard applies to all occupations except domestic service and agricultural pursuits. All regulate hours in factories, though the laws of Georgia and South Carolina apply to cotton and woolen mills only. Fruit and vegetable canneries are exempted in half a dozen states. Several states, North and South, still permit the ten-hour day.

Legislation for shorter hours for children has sometimes been combined with that for women, but at present, except in states where there is an eight-hour law for females, the workday is nearly always shorter for children than for adult women. The child labor laws, however, not infrequently give more protection to young girls working under the ages of sixteen or even eighteen or twenty-one than to boys of the same ages. Hour limitations usually apply to all occupations except domestic service, agriculture, and frequently fruit and vegetable

[30] States in which the eight-hour standard for children under sixteen in factories has not been established are: Florida, Georgia, Idaho, Michigan, New Hampshire, South Carolina, South Dakota, and Texas where the age limit is fifteen. In Connecticut, Montana, Pennsylvania, Rhode Island, New York, and Utah, employment of children under sixteen in factories is prohibited. For specific regulations, which vary from state to state, see the latest report on Child Labor Facts and Figures, Children's Bureau, United States Department of Labor.

canneries. Occasionally the law covers factories, but not stores. The hours during which children may be employed are further regulated by the very common prohibition of night work.[31]

Opposition from employers against limitation of hours has been even stronger than against any other restriction on child employment, the common argument being that manufacturers will not be able to hold their own against competitors in neighboring states where longer hours are permitted. With regard to the eight-hour day, especially, an additional argument frequently advanced is that it would not be practicable to employ children for so short a period in a plant where adults work a longer day. After eight-hour legislation has been passed, however, it has usually been found that the industries soon adjusted themselves thereto.[32] Two laws, in 1916 and 1920, were passed by Congress for regulation of hours and other standards of child labor, but both were declared unconstitutional by the United States Supreme Court.[33] In 1924 an amendment to the federal Constitution authorizing Congress to legislate regarding child labor was passed by Congress and submitted to the states for ratification. By June, 1936, it had been approved by twenty-four states.[34]

[31] See "Night Work," pp. 142-147, for a fuller discussion of these prohibitions.

[32] In order to ascertain the grounds for the objection that children could not be worked shorter hours than adults in the same factory, a special investigation was made by an agent of the National Child Labor Committee in three states—Ohio, Illinois, and New York—where an eight-hour law for children had been in operation for several years. The report of the committee reads as follows: "Information was sought in factories representing the industries in which the largest numbers of children were employed. It was found that children were employed eight hours at the same kinds of work at which they had been employed before the law went into effect, while the adults continued to work for longer hours. With practical unanimity, employers reported that they had found no difficulty in readjusting schedules to obey the law, and the eight-hour day for children had not been a handicap upon business, and no cases of failure or removal from the state had resulted. On the contrary, the industries involved have steadily grown." (*Bulletin, National Child Labor Committee*, vol. ii, no. 4, February, 1914, p. 44.)

[33] See p. 172.

[34] Arizona, Arkansas, California, Colorado, Idaho, Illinois, Indiana, Iowa, Maine, Michigan, Minnesota, Montana, New Hampshire, New Jersey, North Dakota, Ohio, Oklahoma, Oregon, Pennsylvania, Utah, Washington, West Virginia, Wisconsin, Wyoming.

HOURS OF LABOR

Since all minors are for certain purposes wards of the state, which is empowered to act for their protection when necessary, the constitutionality of state laws limiting their working hours is not questioned. As a minor is legally incapable of entering into a free contract, such laws cannot be said to abridge without "due process of law" his freedom to dispose of his labor. The broad power possessed by the state to regulate the working

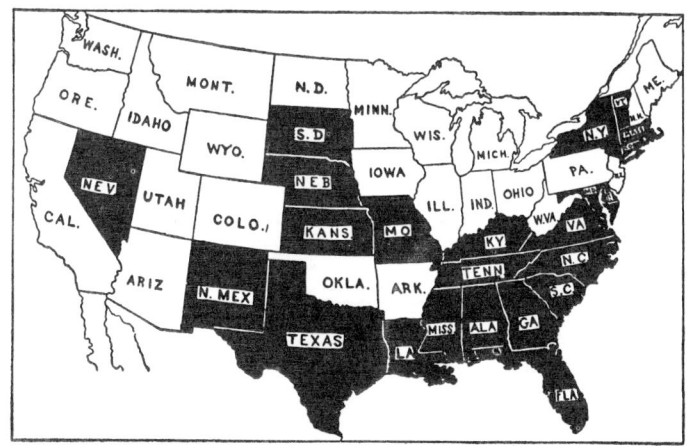

CHILD LABOR AMENDMENT RATIFICATIONS

By July 1, 1936, the twenty-four white states had ratified the proposed Child Labor Amendment to the federal Constitution.

conditions of minors was thus summed up by the judge in the case of People *v.* Ewer: "So far as such regulations control and limit the powers of minors to contract for labor, there never has been and never can be any question as to their constitutionality."[35]

2. **Women.**—In this country agitation for the limitation of women's hours followed close on the heels of the movement to regulate the hours of children. As early as the eighteen-thirties, the labor press had protested against the long hours of work, and strikes for reduction of hours had been called.[36] Naturally enough, the agitation centered around the textile

[35] People *v.* Ewer, 141 N. Y. 129, 36 N. E. 4 (1894).
[36] *Report on Condition of Woman and Child Wage-earners in the United States,* vol. ix, "History of Women in Industry," Helen L., Sumner, p. 67.

mills, as they were the earliest large factories and their working hours were twelve or more daily. In 1834 a delegate discussing the condition of women in factories before the Trades' Union National Convention in Boston, said of the mill-owners: "They must be forced to shut their mills at a regular hour; there must be a certain time over which they shall not work, that all the inmates may have an opportunity to rest their weary limbs and to enjoy free and wholesome air."[37]

By the 'forties, when many humanitarian movements were rife, the ten-hour cause had made progress, and legislative action was asked for. For example, in 1842, 1843, and 1844 petitions asking for a ten-hour law were presented to the Massachusetts legislature.[38] This early movement came almost entirely from the ranks of the workers themselves, who sought legislation limiting hours for both men and women. Organized working-women played a prominent part in the campaign. The New England Workingmen's Association, an organization of wage earners encouraged by a few public-spirited citizens, which soon became the New England Labor Reform League, was active in the agitation. Closely connected with it was the New England Female Labor Reform Association, formed in January, 1854, almost all of whose members were women workers in the textile mills and whose activities centered at Lowell. They organized meetings, wrote for the labor press, and petitioned the legislature for the ten-hour day. The association co-operated with other women workers and started branches in Fall River, Mass., Dover and Manchester, N. H., and perhaps other places. In 1845 the women textile workers of Pittsburgh were unsuccessful in a strike for a ten-hour day, but were told by their employers it would be given them when other localities also reduced their hours. Accordingly, the women wrote to New England for help. The girls of Lowell and Manchester responded and all resolved to work only ten hours after July 4, 1846. But on account of the opposition of the manufacturers their efforts failed, and they once more tried to secure legisla-

[37] National Trades' Union, September 13, 1834, p. 2. Quoted in *Documentary History of American Industrial Society*, John R. Commons and Helen L. Sumner, eds., vol. vi, p. 219.

[38] Persons, Charles E., "The Early History of Factory Legislation in Massachusetts," in *Labor Laws and Their Enforcement*, Susan M. Kingsbury, ed., pp. 24-27.

HOURS OF LABOR

tion. These organized women workers first succeeded in New Hampshire, where "by vigorous personal efforts they, more than any other group, secured the ten-hour law of 1847, the first of its kind in the country."[39] Similar acts were passed in Maine and in Pennsylvania in 1848, in New Jersey and in Rhode Island in 1851.[40] Massachusetts passed no ten-hour law until over twenty years later, perhaps partly because the leaders there insisted on effective legislation, which these earlier measures did not prove to be.

These first acts were all of a similar type. They set ten hours as the standard, generally for all workers, for "a day's work" in the absence of "an express contract requiring greater time."[41] In New Hampshire, three days before the law went into effect the manufacturers submitted such express contracts to their employees, and though meetings were held and active agitation carried on to prevent the operatives from signing, all who refused were discharged and their places were soon filled by new workers. In Pennsylvania and New Jersey, notably in Allegheny City, Gloucester, and Paterson, the operatives carried on severe and prolonged strikes to secure the enforcement of the laws. They were successful in some, though not in all, factories; but where the hours were shortened, they suffered a corresponding reduction in wages. On the whole, these early acts "were practically dead letters, owing to their contracting-out clauses."[42]

From the 'fifties until after the Civil War, social reform was largely forgotten in absorption in the anti-slavery question. After the Civil War, when the movement for protective legislation revived, the laws asked for applied only to women and children, and were of the modern type, forbidding employment in excess of a specified number of hours. The first of these had been passed in Ohio in 1852[43] and set a ten-hour

---

[39] *Report on Condition of Woman and Child Wage-earners in the United States,* vol. x, "History of Women in Trade Unions," John B. Andrews, p. 80.

[40] *Ibid.,* vol. ix, "History of Women in Industry," Helen L. Sumner, p. 69.

[41] See, for instance, New Hampshire, Laws 1847, C. 488.

[42] *Report on Condition of Woman and Child Wage-earners in the United States,* vol. ix, p. 73.

[43] Ohio, Laws 1852, p. 187.

day for women workers, but was rendered unenforceable by penalizing only when a woman was *compelled* to work in excess of legal requirements. As most employees will voluntarily work for twelve or more hours a day when they cannot find anyone to employ them for ten hours, the law became almost entirely inoperative. In Massachusetts, active agitation was recommenced by 1864. By that time the women in the mills were largely Irish and French Canadians, who took little or no part in the movement. After strong opposition a bill was passed in 1874[44] limiting the hours of women and minors in factories to ten daily and sixty weekly. Even this law was ineffective because only "willful" violations were penalized. It was not till 1879,[45] when an amendment removed the "willful," that an American state had an enforceable law limiting the hours of women's employment. By that time also, state bureaus of labor and factory inspection were being created in the principal industrial states and were aiding in the enforcement of labor laws.

Since that time, fairly enforceable hour limitation laws for women have been secured in one state after another. In 1908, when the Oregon ten-hour law for women was upheld by the United States Supreme Court, this legislation was placed upon a secure footing, and since that date the movement has gone steadily forward. By 1936 only four states had placed no restrictions on women's hours of work,[46] many had limited hours to eight or nine a day and about three-fourths had a weekly limit of less than sixty hours.

Present-day hour legislation for women runs in general along similar lines in the different states. Most statutes fix the same daily and weekly maximum hours for all occupations covered and generally include the principal industrial occupations for women. Thus in Pennsylvania, hours in "any establishment" are limited to ten daily and fifty-four weekly, and "any establishment" is defined as "any place within this commonwealth where work is done for compensation of any sort,

[44] Massachusetts, Laws 1874, C. 221.
[45] Massachusetts, Laws 1879, C. 207.
[46] These states were Alabama, Florida, Iowa, and West Virginia. Indiana merely prohibited night work by women in factories.

HOURS OF LABOR

to whomsoever payable,"[47] except homes and farms. In only about a dozen cases, however, do the laws define the time during which the work period must fall, either by naming the spread of hours allowed, by fixing opening and closing hours, or by forbidding night work.

American laws, therefore, seem extremely simple when compared with the mass of detail found in European legislation on this subject. General laws exist in most European countries, but either by special statutes or by administrative orders work periods longer or shorter than those of the general law are fixed for many industries and occupations, and frequently even for special processes. This principle is often so far extended as to prohibit entirely the employment of women in kinds of work especially dangerous to their health or safety. For example, the English Factory Act of 1901 gives the home secretary power to make any limitation of hours whatever or to forbid the employment of any class of workers in dangerous trades.[48] On the other hand, in certain cases, as where perishable materials must be handled at once to prevent spoiling, special orders lengthening the permitted period of employment may be issued.[49] In addition, night work is, in general, forbidden, and opening and closing hours, not necessarily the same for every trade, are almost always fixed.

The number of employments covered by hour legislation in America appears to depend largely on what occupations public opinion considers dangerous to the health of women. Thus the exclusion of farm work and domestic service from regulation is at least in part due to the belief that they in no way endanger health. The earlier laws, both those passed before the Civil War to fix a standard of hours and the first acts of the modern type, applied mainly to manufacturing establishments. Such a limitation in the scope of the early laws was natural enough. At that time women were employed in large numbers outside the home only in textile factories. The Census of 1870 shows that but 1 per cent of all the women "gainfully employed" were found in "trade and transportation." It was in the factories that complaint was made of the

[47] Pennsylvania, Laws 1913, No. 466, Secs. 1 and 3.
[48] 1 Edw. 7, C. 22, Secs. 79-83.
[49] *Ibid.*, Secs. 49-52.

overlong hours of work, and it was the factory operatives who carried on the bulk of the early agitation for legislation. Thus in New Hampshire the first hour limitation law, passed in 1847, applied only to manufacturing establishments,[50] and the Pennsylvania law of 1848 affected only "cotton, woolen, silks, paper, bagging, and flax factories."[51] Likewise the Massachusetts ten-hour law of 1874 covered only "manufacturing establishments."[52] It was not until the end of the 'seventies, when the number of saleswomen had largely increased, that the dangers of constant standing and long hours were noticed and agitation was begun for legislation covering this occupation.[53] In 1883 the Massachusetts law was amended to include "mechanical and mercantile establishments."[54] In the same way, as the field of women's employment broadened, the dangers of excessive hours and injury to health were discovered in one occupation after another, and the need for extending protective legislation became correspondingly apparent, until practically every form of industrial employment has been covered.

The Illinois ten-hour law of 1909 was one of the first to do this. It includes not only factories, mechanical and mercantile establishments, but also any "laundry, or hotel, or restaurant, or telegraph or telephone establishment or office thereof, or any place of amusement, or by any person, firm, or corporation engaged in any express or transportation or public utility business, or by any common carrier, or any public institution, incorporated or unincorporated."[55] Similarly inclusive acts are found in many other states, and almost every act now covers at least "manufacturing, mechanical, and mercantile establishments." When women entered such new occupations as street-car and elevator operation during the war, however, even the more inclusive of those acts which enumerated any list of specified occupations left the women without protection in their novel field of work. Laws such as that of Pennsylvania, which covers

[50] New Hampshire, Laws 1847, C. 488.
[51] Pennsylvania, Laws 1848, No. 227.
[52] Massachusetts, Laws 1874, C. 221.
[53] *Report on the Condition of Woman and Child Wage-earners in the United States*, vol. ix, p. 238.
[54] Massachusetts, Laws 1883, C. 157.
[55] Illinois, Laws 1909, p. 212.

HOURS OF LABOR

"any place . . . where work is done for compensation of any sort," except "private home and farming," and that of Wisconsin, which gives the administrative authorities power to modify the hour laws, are better suited to meet changing industrial conditions.

There are also occasional instances of classification by cities, exempting the smaller places from the operation of the law. The Missouri law of 1909[56] and the Texas law of 1913[57] both applied only to cities of more than 5,000 population. Establishments of various sorts employing fewer than three or five persons have also sometimes been excepted. Until 1914 the Louisiana law applied only to establishments employing more than five persons.[58]

Such exemptions may perhaps also be explained on health grounds. It might be expected that the need for legislation in smaller places would be lessened by a supposed easier pace of work and the greater personal contact between employer and employee. Investigation shows, however, that excessive hours are often worked in small establishments and out-of-the-way places where public opinion is not active, and such exceptions are becoming fewer.[59]

Certain exemptions have also been made because of special industrial requirements, the most important of which have to do with work in canneries. On account of the perishable nature of the materials, operators of canneries have vigorously opposed any legislation which would limit hours of work during the summer months, and because of this opposition a number of states, including many of those in which the industry is important, have allowed women and children to work unlimited hours in this industry.

In the degree of restriction placed upon hours of women's daytime labor, many American states have gone further than European countries. Several important industrial states still

[56] Missouri, Laws 1909, p. 616.
[57] Texas, General Laws 1913, C. 175.
[58] Louisiana, Laws 1908, No. 301, Sec. 1.
[59] For instances of bad conditions in the smaller establishments, see reports of the New York State Factory Investigation Commission, the Senate Wage Commission for Women and Children in the State of Missouri, the Oregon Social Survey, and similar investigations.

follow early English and American precedent and fix a daily limit of ten hours, though three-fourths of the states have reduced the working week to less than sixty hours. As the eight-hour day movement has spread and standards for protective legislation have risen, however, several progressive states have increasingly limited the workday to nine and even to eight hours. By the end of 1935, about thirty states had adopted the eight- or nine-hour day for women in at least some industries. The eight-hour limits are found in New York, in several western states and in the District of Columbia. In California, New York, Puerto Rico, Utah, Wyoming, and the District of Columbia, and in Kansas and New Mexico for certain industries, laws fix a forty-eight-hour week as well as an eight-hour day. Oregon in 1934 by administrative regulation established an eight-hour day, forty-four-hour week for the needlecraft and laundry industries. Among the states having eight-and-a-half- or nine-hour laws, Connecticut, Massachusetts, North Dakota and Oregon provide a forty-eight-hour week.

In Arizona and Utah the permitted hours must fall within a thirteen- and twelve-hour period respectively, but as a general rule regulations of this sort are not found in America.[60] Several states fix the incidence of the working day indirectly through the prohibition of night work.[61] In a majority of the states regulations contain some provision for overtime work. In most cases this is to meet pressure of special conditions like Saturdays or the week before Christmas in retail stores; emergencies, sometimes defined as flood, fire, storm or sickness, in telephone exchanges; and making up time lost because of stoppage of machinery in factories, or seasonal rushes, particularly in fruit and vegetable canneries. A number of laws

[60] In a few states the danger that a woman may be employed by two or more establishments a total length of time in excess of the legal maximum is recognized. In Massachusetts, for instance, some years ago, it was not uncommon in the textile mills for a woman to work ten hours during the day in one mill, and then for several hours in the evening in another. The practice was called "swamping." The Delaware statute (Laws 1913, C. 175, Sec. 2) contains a prohibitive provision in effective form, applying to all classes of work and placing the responsibility for discovering any previous employment in the same day entirely on the employer.

[61] See "Night Work," pp. 142-147.

allow overtime on one or more days to be deducted from the sixth day, providing the Saturday half-holiday. In most cases the amount of overtime is specifically limited, but in a few states no limit is set except by the stipulation of pay at extra rates. Extra wage rates are required in most cases, sometimes increasing, as in California, with the length of time worked. In general, the tendency seems to be to make overtime regulations more specific. This is particularly true of states which control hours by administrative orders.

As previously stated, American statutes usually set the same daily hour limit for a large and varied group of industries. That the requirements and the strain of various occupations may differ widely, and that the same limitation of hours may not equally well meet the needs of the workers in all of them, has been given but little consideration. For example, while it is apparent that in some occupations eight or even ten hours a day may not be physically injurious, in others, such as those involving exposure to poisons, extremes of temperature or humidity, or excessive nervous strain, a much shorter work period may be seriously harmful to health. In certain branches of the telephone service, for example, the nervous strain is particularly severe. An investigation of the telephone industry was made in the State of New York by the Bureau of Women in Industry in 1920. The basic working time was found to be eight hours, with one-fourth of the force working overtime to the extent of from three to six hours. A seven-hour shift was recommended, with compulsory rest periods at reasonable intervals and the elimination of all overtime work.[62] Yet, no American state has, on account of special dangers, placed the statutory restriction for any selected occupation in which women are employed below that stated in the general law.

But a few states have adopted a new method of regulating women's hours, together with minimum wages and working conditions. These states lay down in their statutes the general principle that a woman is not to be employed for any period of time dangerous to her health, safety, or welfare. A commission is then given the power to determine, after investiga-

[62] State of New York, Department of Labor, *Bulletin No. 100,* July, 1920.

108   PRINCIPLES OF LABOR LEGISLATION

tion, maximum periods for different industries and even for different localities, if desired. Such a law may become an instrument for the protection of the worker's health much superior to the ordinary fixed maximum law. A commission regulating hours, through its powers of investigating and setting standards, can take account of special factors in certain lines of work which might cause serious injury to the workers in the usual work period, and can adjust hours according to the strain of each specific occupation.

While all laws of this type conform to this same general principle, they differ in one important provision. California[63] and Oregon permit their commissions to fix only shorter hours than those established by the general statute. "No such order of said commission shall authorize or permit the employment of any woman for more hours per day or per week than the maximum now fixed by law."[64] In Ohio and Wisconsin the hours fixed may be either more or less than those of the general law. Kansas has no law limiting hours for women except the act empowering the commission to make regulations.

In California, Kansas, North Dakota, Oregon, Washington, and Wisconsin, the chief states in which really important action on hours of labor has been taken by these commissions, a considerable amount of flexibility has been secured in the determination of daily hours by commission rulings. In Kansas, for example, regulations vary from an eight-hour day and forty-eight-hour week in public housekeeping occupations, a basic eight-hour day and six-day week in telephone exchanges, to a nine-hour day and forty-nine-and-a-half-hour week with provision for limited overtime in laundries and factories, and a six-day week in the latter, and a nine-hour day and fifty-four-hour, six-day week in mercantile establishments. There are also varied provisions as to rest periods and time for meals.[65] A forty-four-hour-week limitation for women was fixed in

[63] California, Laws 1913, C. 324.

[64] Oregon, Laws 1913, C. 62, Sec. 9. In 1917 this law was amended to except women employed in harvesting, packing, curing, canning, or drying perishable fruit, vegetables, or fish; and the authority of the Industrial Commission to regulate the hours of women so employed was withdrawn. (Laws 1917, C. 163.)

[65] Commission of Labor and Industry, Orders No. 1 to 5, 1931.

HOURS OF LABOR

1934 by commission ruling in Oregon for the needlecraft and laundry occupations.[66]

The possibilities of still more detailed adjustment to the needs of specific industries are evident; and therefore the method of regulating hours through administrative rulings, provided the precaution is taken of preserving a statutory limit of hours, marks a decided advance toward accomplishing the real purpose of hour limitation, the prevention of fatigue by forbidding excessive hours of work.

The table below shows limitation of women's hours on January 1, 1936. For occupations to which laws apply, exemptions and other details, see the latest bulletin on Labor Laws for Women in the States and Territories, Women's Bureau of the United States Department of Labor.

Most of the special problems in the administration of women's work laws center about the enforcement of hour legislation. Violations of laws regulating a continuing condition like hours of work are obviously more difficult to detect than violations of safety or sanitary laws which can be discovered by a single inspection. Therefore, various aids to enforcement have long been found necessary. The most common of these is the posting of notices stating the permitted hours of work, a requirement which the United States Supreme Court sustained as constitutional in 1914.[67] Such a provision had long been in the laws of a number of states. Massachusetts, following English precedent, had found it necessary to require the posting of notices as early as 1880.[68] The law stipulated that printed notices containing the daily hours of work should be posted "in a conspicuous place" in every room where employees coming under the ten-hour law were at work. Immediately an attempt was made to evade the intent of the act. A report of the enforcing authority, the chief of the district police, says that notices were found illegibly written, "on cards four or five inches square, sometimes without a single break between the words, and placed over a doorway or some other inaccessi-

[66] State Welfare Commission, orders effective April 29, and May 5, 1934.
[67] Riley v. Commonwealth, 232 U. S. 671, 34 Sup. Ct. 469 (1914).
[68] Massachusetts, Laws 1880, C. 194.

PRINCIPLES OF LABOR LEGISLATION

State	Hours a Day	Hours a Week
I. Eight-hour states:		
Oregon	8, 9, 10	44[a], 48[a], 56, 70[b]
Arizona	8	48[a]
California	8	48[a]
District of Columbia	8	48[a]
Puerto Rico	8	48
Utah	8	48
Wyoming	8	48
Kansas	8, 9	48, 49½[a], 54[a]
New York	8, 9	48[a], 54[a]
New Mexico	8, 9	48[a], 54, 56
Washington	8	48[a], 56[b,a]
Nevada	8	56
Colorado	8	56[b]
Montana	8	56[b]
II. States allowing more than eight but less than ten hours:		
North Dakota	8½, 9	48[a], 54, 58
Massachusetts	9	48[a]
Connecticut	9,	48, 52, 58
Ohio	9	50[a]
Wisconsin	9, 10	50[a], 55[a]
Arkansas	9	54[a]
Maine	9	54
Michigan	9	54
Missouri	9	54
Nebraska	9	54
Oklahoma	9	54
Louisiana	9	54, 60
Texas	9, 11	54
Idaho	9	63[b]
III. States allowing ten or more hours:		
New Jersey	10	54[a]
Pennsylvania	10	54[a]
Rhode Island	10	54
South Dakota	10	54
New Hampshire	10¼	54
Minnesota	No limit	54
Delaware	10	55[a]
North Carolina	10, 11	55
South Carolina	10, 12	55, 60
Vermont	10½	56
Tennessee	10½	57
Kentucky	10	60
Georgia	10	60
Maryland	10	60
Mississippi	10	60
Illinois	10	70[b]
Virginia	10	70[b]

HOURS OF LABOR

State	Hours a Day	Hours a Week
IV. States placing no limit on daily and weekly hours: Alabama, Florida, Indiana, Iowa, West Virginia		

ᵃ Work limited to six days per week.
ᵇ No weekly limit set by law. This figure represents daily limit multiplied by seven.

ble place."[69] Extra time was also worked on the pretense that it was necessary to stop and start the machinery. Two amendments, in 1886,[70] and 1887,[71] were necessary in order to overcome these difficulties. The law then provided that the notices must be put on forms approved by the attorney-general and supplied by the enforcing authority, and must contain the hours of beginning and ending work and of mealtimes, as well as the number of hours worked each day. Similar provisions as to the posting of notices have been found essential in other states.

A more recent device which provides additional help in enforcing the law is that of a record book, open to inspection by the authorities and containing the actual hours worked each day by each female. Few states rely exclusively on this device for help in enforcing the law.[72] Several states, however, require the keeping of record books in addition to posting notices,[73] or as a substitute where daily hours are so irregular that they cannot be determined in advance.[74]

Even the wording of the penalty clause is of importance in relation to the enforceability of the law. Massachusetts' first ten-hour law could not be enforced so long as only "willful" violations were penalized. Several states still render their laws inoperative by similar clauses. For instance, in South Dakota only the employer who "compels" a woman to work overtime is responsible.[75] Experience shows that it is practically im-

[69] *Report of the Chief of the District Police*, 1884, pp. 14-18.
[70] Massachusetts, Laws 1886, C. 99.
[71] *Ibid.*, Laws 1887, C. 280.
[72] One of these is Illinois, Laws 1911, p. 328.
[73] See New York, Consol. Laws, C. 31, Sec. 174.
[74] See Kentucky, Laws 1912, C. 77, Sec. 5.
[75] South Dakota, Laws 1913, C. 240, Sec. 1.

possible to prove such compulsion and that convictions can be secured only when "permitting" excessive hours is also a violation of the law. The enforceability of the laws in a few southern states, which penalize only "contracting" to work overtime, also seems doubtful. Even among the enforceable laws there is a difference in effectiveness. It is clearly easier to obtain proof of violation in a state like New Hampshire,[76] where the employment of a woman "outside" the posted hours is a violation of the law, than where the inspector must prove that she worked longer than the posted number of hours, as in Tennessee.[77] It may also be of importance in successful prosecutions to note whether the employer alone, "his agent" or "any person" may be held responsible, and whether only the working of excess hours is penalized or, in addition, a failure to post notices, the making of false statements in notices and time books and the like.

Equitable and necessary as legal limitations on the daily hours of working-women are generally recognized to be, they have frequently been contested as out of harmony with our state and federal constitutions. Clearly, limiting the hours during which a woman may be employed does abridge her freedom to use her capacity for work to its utmost extent. The courts seem to hold in general that such a limitation may be made through the state's exercise of its police power only if excessive hours involve some appreciable danger to the class of workers involved or to the community.

The conflict of judicial decisions on the subject appears to arise from differing opinions as to the existence of such danger. Opinions opposed to legal restriction emphasized the interference with woman's freedom to contract to work each day as long as she pleases, implying that employer and employee stand on an equal footing in determining working conditions, and that an employee works long hours of her own free will. Such a restriction of freedom of contract, they hold, deprives a woman worker without due process of law of the valuable property right of disposing of her own labor as she sees fit, and furthermore is class legislation because it denies her privi-

[76] New Hampshire, Laws 1913, C. 156, Sec. 3.
[77] Tennessee, Laws First Extra Session, 1913, C. 12.

HOURS OF LABOR

leges accorded to men workers. The favorable decisions take cognizance of actual industrial conditions and point out that the labor contract is not freely made between equals, but that its terms are settled largely by the employer and that the state may therefore interfere in the interests of the public welfare.

The first important decision on the constitutionality of hour legislation for women was rendered in Massachusetts in 1876, upholding the ten-hour law. In this case, says Professor Ernst Freund,[78] "the court was obviously a good deal puzzled how to deal with the objections raised, disposing of them in a rather offhand and not altogether satisfactory fashion." In a brief opinion[79] the court pointed out that the legislature had evidently considered factory work "to some extent dangerous to health," and that the statute was therefore a health or police measure. This decision, however, held that the legislation did not prevent women from working as long as they saw fit, but only from working more than ten hours continuously in a factory.

The next important decision on the constitutionality of hour legislation for women was not rendered until 1895, almost twenty years later. During the interval the principle of entire freedom of contract between capital and labor had been developed.[80] This doctrine was reinforced by the idea that the right to dispose of one's labor freely is a property right, not to be abridged—according to the Fourteenth Amendment to the Constitution of the United States—"without due process of law." It was on this ground that in 1895 the Illinois Supreme Court declared invalid an eight-hour law for women in factories.[81] The court could see no "fair, just, and reasonable connection between such limitation and the public health, safety, or welfare proposed to be secured by it."

But three years later, in 1898, the United States Supreme Court showed the fallacy of the doctrine of freedom of con-

---

[78] Freund, Ernst, "Constitutional Limitations and Labor Legislation," in *Third Annual Meeting* of the American Association for Labor Legislation, p. 51.

[79] Commonwealth *v.* Hamilton Mfg. Co., 120 Mass. 383 (1876).

[80] First laid down in 1886 in Godcharles *v.* Wigeman, 113 Pa. St. 431, 6 Atl. 354; Millett *v.* People, 117 Ill. 294, 7 N. E. 631 (1886).

[81] Ritchie *v.* People, 155 Ill. 98, 40 N. E. 454 (1895).

tract between employer and employee,[82] and within the next few years, in 1900 and 1902, three decisions by state courts[83] brought out in addition reasons why women as a special class of workers particularly need protection. These decisions took into account the fact that women are physically weaker than men and that therefore their health is more likely to suffer from excessive hours of work. Any injury to the health of women workers is of particular social importance, since it is on their health that the vigor of the next generation directly depends.

The year 1908, however, finally settled the question as far as the restriction of daytime hours to a maximum of ten was concerned. The United States Supreme Court unequivocally upheld the constitutionality of the Oregon ten-hour law as a health measure.[84] "As healthy mothers are essential to vigorous offspring, the physical well-being of women becomes an object of public interest and care in order to preserve the strength and vigor of the race. The limitations which this statute imposes upon her contractual powers, upon her right to agree with her employer as to the time when she shall labor, are not imposed solely for her benefit, but also for the benefit of all." In this case and succeeding ones of a similar nature the influence of the method by which the legislation was defended should not be overlooked. Exhaustive briefs were prepared by Mr. Louis D. Brandeis and Miss Josephine Goldmark, not so much emphasizing the legal aspects of the case as presenting a mass of extracts to show the actual effects of excessive hours of work on the health of women. In 1909, Illinois, whose working-women had been left unprotected from excessive hours since its eight-hour law was overthrown in 1895, passed a ten-hour bill. The constitutionality of the statute was immediately attacked. This time, however, the Illinois Supreme Court did find a clear connection between the measure and the protection of the public health. It recognized not merely a theoretical freedom of contract, but, as well, the facts as to the effects of

[82] Holden v. Hardy, 169 U. S. 366, 18 Sup. Ct. 383 (1898). See "Hours of Labor, Men," p. 136.

[83] Commonwealth v. Beatty, 15 Super. Ct. (Pa.) 5 (1900); Wenham v. State, 65 Neb. 394, 91 N. W. 421 (1902); State v. Buchanan, 29 Wash. 602, 70 Pac. 52 (1902).

[84] Muller v. Oregon, 208 U. S. 412, 28 Sup. Ct. 324 (1908).

HOURS OF LABOR

excessive hours on the health of women. "What we know as men," said the court, "we cannot profess to be ignorant of as judges."[85]

The constitutionality of a ten-hour workday was now established, but the reasonableness of further restriction was still in doubt. In 1915, however, the United States Supreme Court upheld the constitutionality of the California law which fixed an eight-hour day as the maximum for women workers. The court said that the same principles were at stake as in the previous cases, and that while "a limitation of the hours of labor of women might be pushed to a wholly indefensible extreme . . . there is no ground for the conclusion here that the limit of the reasonable exertion of protective authority has been overstepped."[86]

Hour legislation for women has also been attacked on the ground that it is class legislation, discriminating unreasonably among various classes of workers, and denying that "equal protection of the laws" which was promised to all persons by the Fourteenth Amendment. The statutes have been attacked both because they included certain employments and because they failed to include certain others. The constitutionality of the Illinois law was questioned because it included employees in hotels and in public institutions. One of the chief points raised against the constitutionality of the California law was its inclusion of student nurses. On the other hand, different laws have at various times been called "class legislation" because they included only factories and laundries, and because they excluded mercantile establishments, canneries, stenography, and domestic service. The courts have given but little weight to this type of objection, asserting the freedom of the legislature either to use discretion in enlarging the scope of the laws[87] or to single out those groups of workers most in need of protection.[88]

In an Oregon case the constitutionality of regulation of women's hours by a commission has been attacked on the ground that substituting commission for court authority on

[85] Ritchie v. Wayman, 244 Ill. 509, 91 N. E. 695 (1910).
[86] Miller v. Wilson, 236 U. S. 373, 35 Sup. Ct. 342 (1915).
[87] People v. Elerding, 254 Ill. 579, 98 N. E. 982 (1912).
[88] See Withey v. Bloem, 163 Mich. 419, 128 N. W. 913 (1910).

questions of fact takes property without "due process of law." The state supreme court sustained the method, holding that it contained the essentials of due process, which it defined as "reasonable notice and a fair opportunity to be heard before some [proper] tribunal."[89] The case was appealed to the United States Supreme Court, where the judgment of the state supreme court was affirmed with costs by an equally divided court in 1917.[90]

Thus the working-woman's theoretical freedom of contract to dispose of her labor under whatever conditions she pleases has been restricted by the state through its police power. Such a limitation is rightfully applied to women workers as a class, because as workers they do not stand on equal footing with their employers in bargaining and because as women their health is more quickly injured by excessive hours of work. Furthermore, the community suffers if the health of any large number of women is endangered, for on the health of women depends the vigor of the race. The reasonableness of the range of employments included in the laws has been affirmed, and hours may now be limited to as few as eight in daytime work.

3. **Men.**—In contrast with the considerable development of hour regulations for women and children is the fragmentary condition of American legislation affecting the working hours of adult men. One of the main reasons for the halting growth of this type of law has been the doubtful attitude of the courts. In this matter, however, the courts have merely reflected prevailing public opinion, which has been slow to awake to the need of restricting men's hours in general employments. Even trade unionists have sometimes opposed shortening hours for men by the legislative method, through fear that it might weaken union organization.

In the midst of serious unemployment, however, the American labor movement strongly advocated hours limitation by law as a means of "spreading" work among a larger number of workers. In 1932 and 1933, labor supported a bill in Congress providing for a thirty-hour week, and in 1933 this measure was passed by the Senate. It was temporarily dropped, however,

---

[89] *Stettler v. O'Hara*, 69 Ore. 519, 139 Pac. 743 (1914).
[90] *Ibid.*, 243 U. S. 629, 37 Sup. Ct. 475 (1917). See "Minimum Fair Wage," p. 76.

upon enactment of the National Industrial Recovery Act in 1933.

Most men's hour laws cover employees on public works or in transportation. In the former case the state is merely fixing the working conditions of its own employees; in the latter, the element of public safety is involved. Where public safety is not directly concerned, legislation is common only for the peculiarly hazardous occupation of mining. As with other forms of protective legislation, however, and in view of our increasing knowledge of the dangers of overwork, especially in continuous industries, the principle of hour restriction, first established for women and children, may eventually be extended to cover all wage-earning men. This tendency has been strengthened by a widespread belief that shorter hours are necessary for the prevention of unemployment. The laws for one day of rest in seven; the favorable decision of the United States Supreme Court on the Oregon law for ten hours in manufacturing; and the hour restrictions in the codes that were adopted under the National Recovery Administration beginning in 1933, make extension of hours regulation for adult male workers a probable future development.

a. *Public Work.*—The first attempt legally to regulate the working hours of men in the United States was the executive order of President Van Buren in 1840, stipulating a ten-hour day in government navy yards.[91] Since the early 'thirties, special pressure had been brought to bear upon the federal government to shorten the working day, partly because it was felt that the short workday in public employments would have a strong influence in reducing hours in private industry, and partly because there was little doubt of the government's right to regulate the hours of its own employees. In 1840, therefore, while the eleven- and twelve-hour days were the rule in private industry, Van Buren was induced to issue the order referred to. Although this was done at a time of industrial depression, he requested that no corresponding reduction in wages be made.

It was not, however, until 1868 that Congress took action on the question and provided that "eight hours shall constitute a day's work for all laborers, workmen, and mechanics who may

[91] Commons, John R., ed., *Documentary History of American Industrial Society,* vol. viii, p. 85.

be employed by or on behalf of the government of the United States."[92] The law did not work as well as its advocates had hoped. Although it applied to contractors and subcontractors, it failed to prohibit agreements for overtime work. Its ineffectiveness in actually reducing the hours of any considerable number of government employees soon became apparent, but it was not until August 1, 1892, that a more effective law covering these classes of employees was passed. This act[93] was mandatory, applied to contractors and subcontractors, and provided a heavy penalty for violations. It did not, however, apply to work done on that very large class of goods or materials purchased by the government, such as army and navy equipment, vessels of war, clothing, boots, shoes and paper. The Attorney-general also ruled that the act did not apply to work done on materials purchased by contractors. Contractors themselves, moreover, were constantly making use of the undefined term "emergency" as an excuse for working employees overtime.[94] Agitation for a more inclusive measure was initiated and continued for twenty years before the law was rewritten. Finally, the Act of June 19, 1912, was passed; this required that an eight-hour provision be inserted in all contracts which may involve the employment of laborers or mechanics when made by, for, or on behalf of the federal government, its territories, or the District of Columbia. Exception was made in the case of contracts for transportation by land or water, for the transmission of intelligence, or for the purchase of supplies which could be bought in the open market, except armor and armor plate.[95] Provision was also made for "emergencies caused by fire, famine, or flood, by danger to life or property," or by any other extraordinary event or condition on account of which the President shall subsequently declare the violation to have been

[92] United States Revised Statutes, 1878, Title 43, Sec. 3738. See United States Commissioner of Labor, *Second Special Report*, 1896.
[93] United States Compiled Statutes, 1901, Sec. 3738.
[94] *Report of Industrial Commission*, 1902, vol. xix, p. 792.
[95] See opinions of the Attorney-general since 1912. One opinion held that under the Appropriation Act of June 6, 1912, where contracts for ammunition are made, the eight-hour provision relates to employees only when they are engaged on that particular government work and that they may work longer hours for their employers (when contractors) on non-government work.

HOURS OF LABOR

excusable. One year later dredging and rock-excavating in rivers and harbors of the United States, which had been excluded from the eight-hour law of 1892 by a Supreme Court decision,[96] were specifically brought under the operation of the new federal act. But Congress empowered the President during the war to suspend the eight-hour law "in case of national emergency," with pay at the rate of time and a half for all work in excess of eight hours; and this privilege was frequently exercised.

In 1936, Congress enacted a law requiring that contracts made by any agency or instrumentality of the federal government, including the District of Columbia and publicly owned corporations, for the manufacture or furnishing of materials, supplies, articles, and equipment in any amount exceeding $10,000, must include the stipulation that no person employed by the contractor in fulfilling such contract shall be permitted to work in excess of eight hours a day or forty hours a week. This law is enforced by the Secretary of Labor who is authorized to grant specific exceptions where necessary in the public interest; but in cases where longer hours are permitted, wages must be adjusted to provide time-and-a-half for overtime. The act does not apply to purchases that may usually be made in the open market or to agricultural products processed for first sale by the original producers.[97]

After the World War, the movement gained strength for a further reduction in hours for government employees to provide the forty-hour week by means of a Saturday half-holiday. This shorter work week had already been granted in a substantial part of private industry before Congress in 1931 enacted laws extending it to civil servants of the United States and the District of Columbia.[98]

Effective restriction of hours of labor was secured for certain groups of post office employees before it was for federal laborers and mechanics. As early as 1888 hours of city letter carriers were reduced from ten to eight, with the proviso that pay be not reduced and that extra remuneration at the new rate be given for overtime. In 1912 the eight-hour day was ex-

[96] Ellis v. United States, 206 U. S. 246, 27 Sup. Ct. 600 (1907).
[97] Public No. 846, 74th Congress, 1936.
[98] Public 672, 71st Congress, 3rd session.

tended to clerks in first- and second-class post offices, work to be performed within ten consecutive hours. Postal employees were given the forty-four-hour week along with other federal employees in 1931, and in 1935 Congress still further reduced their weekly hours to forty.[99]

In 1915 legislation to restrict the amount of work which might be exacted of federal employees took a new turn. In addition to the earlier laws limiting the number of hours a day that could be worked, clauses were enacted tending to limit the speed and intensity of the labor. In the appropriation bills for both the army and the navy, provisos were inserted that none of the money was to be used to pay any officer "while making or causing to be made, with a stop-watch or other time-measuring device, a time study of any job of any . . . employee . . . or of the movements of any such employee while engaged upon such work." It was also stipulated in both bills that money was not to be used to pay bonuses or cash rewards, except for suggestions resulting in improvements in the service.[100] Similar provisions against the methods of so-called "scientific management" were made annually thereafter.

The movement for a shorter workday on public employments was early taken up by the various states, until by the end of the 'nineties a dozen states and several cities had eight-hour enactments.[101] But the early state laws, like those of the federal government, were often faulty and unenforceable. The turning point was the Kansas law of 1891, which contained practically all of the essentials of an enforceable act. This measure not only fixed hours of labor on direct work for the state, but also extended its provisions to municipal corporations and to contractors for public works, and imposed a penalty for violations by any public official or contractor.

At present over half of the states have eight-hour laws for employees on public works.[102] In practically all cases the laws

[99] Public 275, 74th Congress, 1st session.
[100] United States, Laws 1914-1915, C. 83, section on "Increase of the Navy"; C. 143, section on "Ordnance Department."
[101] Baltimore (1866) was the first city, and California (1868) perhaps the first state, to adopt this legislation.
[102] When an eight-hour law of this kind went into effect in Ohio on July 1, 1915, during the last few weeks before that date contracts aggregating millions of dollars were let by state and city departments in order

apply to both direct and contract work, to "the state or any political subdivision thereof," and cover "all manual laborers" or all "laborers, workmen, and mechanics," and occasionally all classes of labor. Frequently certain classes of employees are excepted, such as firemen, policemen, and certain classes of workmen in state institutions. Provision is almost always made for overtime in case of "emergencies," frequently defined as "imminent danger to property, life, or limb"; but unless a clear definition of the term is given, advantage may easily be taken of the exception to permit unnecessary overtime.

In addition to the state laws regulating hours on public works, a large number of cities have embodied eight-hour provisions in their charters or have enacted eight-hour ordinances to cover municipal work. These measures follow the main lines of the state laws and in addition frequently specify, among other things, the kinds of work which may be done directly by the city and those which must be done by contract, rates of wages, the method of selecting employees—whether by civil service, citizenship, or trade-union membership—and occasionally provide for physical examination of applicants.

The two-platoon or twelve-hour shift system for city firemen has been adopted by a large majority of cities, occasionally as the result of state law, but generally through city ordinance. Agitation for an eight-hour, three-shift system was being carried on by 1919, but only a few cities had adopted it by 1936. The various organizations of firemen had been the leaders in carrying on the movement for limiting their hours.

b. *Private Employments.*—In private employments the movement for legislative restrictions upon the length of the working day for men, although associated with the ten-hour campaigns in the interests of both men and women in the reform agitations of the 'forties, did not attain national importance until the period of the Civil War, when Ira Steward, a Boston machinist, inaugurated a nation-wide movement for the universal eight-hour day by law.[103] Scores of eight-hour leagues sprang

---

to take advantage of the lower cost believed possible under the old ten-hour system.

[103] For a full description of the history and philosophy of this movement, see Commons, John R., and Andrews, John B., eds., *Documentary History of American Industrial Society,* vols. ix and x.

up; the National Labor Union, the predecessor of the Knights of Labor, indorsed Steward's plan, and during the next few years laws were actually passed by a number of states. First among these was Illinois in 1867. These laws were not enforceable, and the movement died down until it was revived by the growing Knights of Labor, which, however, soon turned the course of action away from the legislative to the trade union method.

During the past generation, progress has been made mainly through collective bargaining instead of by legal enactment.[104] There have been, however, important exceptions. Over half the states have enacted laws shortening the hours of employees on steam and electric railways, and more than a dozen states have eight-hour laws for the protection of workers in mines and smelters. Mississippi and Oregon have ten-hour laws for workers in manufacturing industries.[105] From 1933-1935, moreover, a most extensive program of hours regulation on a nation-wide basis was inaugurated through the codes of fair competition under the National Industrial Recovery Act, but these codes ceased to be operative when the law was declared unconstitutional in 1935.

(1) Transportation.—The regulation of hours of labor on railroads presents peculiar difficulties. Almost invariably employees in other industries live sufficiently near their work to enable them to return home at night. The engineer or fireman may find himself several hundred miles away from home or even away from food and shelter at the end of a stated number of hours' work. The problem, therefore, is to arrange "runs" so that employees may at the end of their work period find themselves in habitable quarters. The length of the "run"

[104] At the November elections of 1914 in the Pacific coast states of Washington, Oregon, and California, the Socialists secured a vote on initiated measures for the universal eight-hour day. All of these measures were defeated, largely through the opposition of the farmer vote. Resolutions favoring the legal eight-hour day for men were defeated at both the 1914 and 1915 conventions of the American Federation of Labor, although the vote on the second occasion was closer. This action was taken largely on the alleged ground that if the legislature may fix maximum hours of work it will also fix minimum hours. The real basis of opposition appeared to be the fear that legislative action would weaken the movement for trade organization.

[105] See p. 131.

must, of course, depend somewhat upon the length of the railway division and upon the character of the country through which the road extends.

One of the early court decisions dealing with hours on railroads involved the case of an engineer who, after he had been on duty for nearly seventeen hours, was summoned by the master mechanic of the road to take out another train, which it was assumed would require only five or six hours of work. In reality, the second run lasted for a much longer time, and on his return after thirty-one hours' service his train collided with another train on the company's road. On the ground of contributory negligence, the court denied the engineer's claim for damages for injuries he sustained.[106] Such situations were not infrequent, and runs of thirty-six, fifty, seventy, and at times even one hundred hours have been recorded.[107] These excessive hours often resulted in serious accidents and great loss of life; and accordingly the first decade of the twentieth century saw the enactment, under the influence of the powerful railroad brotherhoods, of many laws regulating the length of the working day for railroad employees.

By 1914 over half of the states of the Union had placed such acts upon their statute books. This legislation relates usually to two classes of employees, those directly connected with the handling of trains, such as engineers, firemen, conductors, and brakemen, and those connected with directing the movements of trains, such as dispatchers, telegraphers, and signalmen. Considerable uniformity exists in these legal restrictions. For men actually handling the trains, the majority of states make sixteen hours the maximum limit for a day's work, to be followed by eight or ten consecutive hours of rest. For those connected with the movement of trains, such as telegraphers, dispatchers, and signalmen, in the case of continuous employment, hours are usually limited to eight a day, and frequently the three-shift system is used, particularly in the larger railroad centers. If employment is not continuous, or if offices are open only in the daytime, hours are usually limited to twelve

---

[106] Smith v. Atchison, Topeka and Santa-Fe Railway Co., 39 Tex. Civ. App. 468, 87 S. W. 1052 (1905).
[107] For a vivid discussion of this subject, see paper by A. B. Garretson, *American Labor Legislation Review*, vol. iv, no. 1, pp. 120-128.

or thirteen a day, to be followed by a rest period of eight or ten hours, as with trainmen. Most states make a few exceptions or allow overtime for limited periods, while two or three restrict hours only where a certain number of trains, such as eight passenger or twenty freight trains, pass daily.

In 1907 Congress enacted an hour law applying to all "persons actually engaged in or connected with the movement of any train" in the District of Columbia, or in any territory of the United States or on interstate lines.[108] By this act, hours are limited to sixteen a day, with certain provisions for rest periods;[109] but no train dispatcher, telegrapher, or any employee who transmits messages or orders by telegraph or telephone "shall be required or permitted to be or to remain on duty for a longer period than nine hours" in places continuously operated day and night, or for more than thirteen hours in places operated only during the daytime. Overtime in cases of emergency, which is carefully defined in the act, may be permitted for four additional hours on not more than three days a week. The Interstate Commerce Commission is charged with the duty of enforcing the act, and it may require reports of violations and of the causes for overtime, and may, after full hearing, extend the period of permitted overtime in special cases. By the operation of the federal act the great majority of railroad employees, even in states without hour limitation laws, are protected, since but few employees are engaged in intrastate train service exclusively. In 1914 the United States Supreme Court declared unconstitutional the New York law which fixed an eight-hour maximum for telegraph operators and train dispatchers, where the federal law fixed a nine-hour day.[110] The court declared that "Where there is a conflict the state legislation must give way." Thus, state laws are now effective only on purely intrastate roads.

The law of 1907 was to some extent superseded by the so-called "Adamson law," providing a basic eight-hour day for railroad trainmen, which was adopted by Congress September 2, 1916.[111] Unusual public interest was attached to the passage

[108] United States, Laws 1906-1907, C. 2939.
[109] See "Rest Periods," p. 141.
[110] Erie Ry. Co. v. N. Y., 233 U. S. 671 (1914).
[111] United States, Laws 1916, C. 436.

HOURS OF LABOR

of the law, which was rushed through Congress at President Wilson's request in order to avert a nation-wide railroad strike which had been called for September 4, the issue being the basic eight-hour day which was demanded by the men and refused by the officials. The law fixed eight hours as the standard for a day's work, and forbade the reduction of wages because of the change until after an investigating commission created by the act had reported. It was immediately claimed by opponents of the law that it was not really a measure for reducing hours, but a subterfuge for increasing wages. The report of the commission created by the act, submitted to the President on December 29, 1917, showed that both wage increases and hour reductions had occurred among the more than 300,000 employees affected by the law.[112] The hour reductions were most frequent among employees working in railroad freight yards. Reports covering 175,744 miles of road showed that 11,390 yard crews had been placed on eight-hour shifts, and only 3,486 crews were still working more than eight hours. Overtime was paid pro rata until 1919, when time-and-one-half rates were introduced. This regulation and the policy of the United States Railroad Administration which managed the railroads during the war, led to much greater uniformity in working hours.

Somewhat akin to the problem of the trainmen is that of the motorman and conductor on street railways. Until the early 'eighties, hours for street-car employees were commonly from twelve to fourteen a day, and often ran as high as sixteen to eighteen. In 1864 a coroner's jury in the city of Philadelphia, passing upon a fatal accident, said: "Nor should we expect vigilance and attention from employees worn out by seventeen hours of incessant labor. . . . The constant occurrence of passenger railway accidents demands from this jury an unequivocal condemnation of the companies who compel men to do work to which the bodily and mental frame is not usually equal."[113] During the 'eighties the states began to enact legisla-

[112] United States Commission on Standard Work Day of Railroad Employees, Created by Act of Congress, approved September 3 and 5, 1916, Stat. L., p. 721, Sec. 2. *Report of the Eight-hour Commission,* Washington, 1918, 503 pp.

[113] United States Bureau of Labor, *Bulletin No. 57,* March, 1905, "Street Railway Employment in the United States," Walter E. Weyl, p. 610.

tion on the subject, until now about a dozen laws have been passed limiting hours usually to ten or twelve a day. Most of these acts provide for overtime in case of unexpected emergencies, and many require extra compensation for such emergency work, but very few give adequate attention to the equitable distribution of working time. Several states, however, definitely fix the maximum number of hours within which the legal day's work must be performed.

Another method of regulating hours of service on street railways is by the insertion of labor clauses in franchises granted to railway companies. This method is much less common in American than in European cities. In Paris, for instance, one of the labor conditions stipulated in the franchise for the subway was that daily hours should not exceed ten. Among the few American cities which have adopted this plan are Dallas, where a twelve-hour day, and Cleveland and Detroit, where a ten-hour day, were secured on local car lines. Hours have been shortened below the legal maximum by trade agreements.[114]

The increasing importance of motor vehicles in commercial transportation has led most states to limit the working hours of bus and truck drivers either by statute or by administrative regulation. Such laws have been adopted primarily as public safety measures, since a bus or truck driver who is exhausted from long hours and lack of sleep is a menace to other automobiles on the public highway as well as, in the case of the motor bus, to the bus passengers. The laws usually fix a maximum number of hours of continuous duty, in some states ten or twelve, but in others eight; and require a period of rest, usually eight hours, before resumption of duty. In 1935, Congress enacted a law giving the Interstate Commerce Commission power to regulate the hours of work for common and contract carriers by motor vehicle operating in interstate commerce.

Regulation of hours in water transportation was found in a federal act of 1913, limiting hours of deck officers to nine out of twenty-four while in port, and, except in emergencies, to twelve out of twenty-four while at sea.[115] Moreover, the federal law of 1915 regulating the working conditions of seamen pro-

[114] International Labor Office, *Studies and Reports,* Series D, No. 14, 1925, p. 46.
[115] United States, Laws 1912-1913, C. 118.

HOURS OF LABOR

vided that on merchant vessels of over 100 tons, sailors while at sea must be divided into at least two, and firemen, oilers and water tenders into at least three, watches. Also, when a vessel is in a "safe harbor, nine hours, inclusive of the anchor watch, shall constitute a day's work."[116] In 1936, this law was amended to extend the requirement of three watches to cover licensed officers, sailors and coal passers, and to limit the hours of officers and seamen, both at sea and in safe harbor, to eight a day.[117]

(2) Mines and Tunnels.—Beginning in the 1890's, several states have taken still another step and have enacted legislation regulating the hours of labor for men in private employments where the safety or welfare of the general public is not involved. This class of legislation has been applied particularly to mines, smelters, and related industries.

The mining industries occupy an important position in the industrial life of this country, since they employ about 800,000 workmen, practically all being adult males. Coal mining alone claims over three-quarters of the total number. Trade union organizations in both the coal and the metalliferous branches have been among the largest and most powerful in America.

The special dangers of mining from both accident and unhealthful conditions have been frequently pointed out, as well as the greater hazard in American than in foreign mines, and by 1936 had become so well-known that over a dozen states had passed eight-hour laws applying to some or all classes of work in mines.[118] These laws vary greatly in scope, from that of Pennsylvania, which applies only to hoisting engineers in anthracite mines, to that of Arizona,[119] which covers all classes of workers in underground, open-cut and open-pit mines, cement works, and all employment involved in mining, smelting, or refining ores. Most of the principal coal-mining states have failed to enact effective eight-hour laws.

The eight-hour day was nominally established in the anthracite coal mines in 1916 by agreement between operators and

[116] *Ibid.*, Laws 1914-1915, C. 153.
[117] Public No. 808, 74th Congress, 1936.
[118] Alaska, Arizona, California, Colorado, Idaho, Kansas, Maryland, Missouri, Montana, Nevada, North Dakota, Oklahoma, Oregon, Pennsylvania, Utah, Washington, Wyoming.
[119] Arizona, Laws 1912, C. 28.

128 PRINCIPLES OF LABOR LEGISLATION

miners, and is usually stipulated in bituminous coal-mine agreements where they exist; but in bituminous fields where miners have been unorganized hours have been very irregular. Reports of surveys made by the United States Bureau of Labor Statistics showed that in 1931 time actually spent underground by a considerable proportion of workers in both anthracite and bituminous mines exceeded nine hours per days.[120] Under the National Industrial Recovery Act of 1933, however, the bituminous industry adopted a code providing at first for an eight-hour and then by amendment for a seven-hour day. When this code became inoperative in 1935, Congress adopted the Bituminous Coal Conservation Act,[121] which provided for the adoption of a new code under which an agreement on hours reached by a majority of the workers and employers covering two-thirds of the industry's output was made binding on all. This act, however, was also declared unconstitutional by the Supreme Court in May, 1936.[122] In metalliferous mines also, there has been in practice considerable variation in hours. A Department of Labor survey in 1931[123] reported average full-time weekly hours from 48.2 in lead and zinc mines to 50.7 in western mixed ore and 58.4 in Alabama iron mines, the total average for all mines surveyed being 51.6 hours.

Hours in coal mines in Great Britain were fixed by law in 1919 at seven per shift underground and forty-six and a half per week on the surface; but on July 8, 1926, in the midst of a long struggle over disorganized conditions in the coal industry, the Parliament raised the daily maximum to eight hours. In 1931, the maximum was reduced to seven and one-half hours. In several provinces of Canada and in most European countries legal regulations limit miners' hours to eight per day, the time in Europe generally being reckoned from the moment of leaving the surface to that of return to it. The labor code of Soviet Russia limits work underground to six hours.[124] In 1931,

[120] United States Bureau of Labor Statistics, *Monthly Labor Review*, April, 1932, pp. 896-912; and September, 1933, pp. 634-650.
[121] Public No. 402, 74th Congress, 1st session, 1935.
[122] Carter *v.* Carter Coal Company, 56 Sup. Ct. 855 (1936).
[123] *Monthly Labor Review*, August, 1933, p. 366.
[124] International Labor Office, Legislative Series, 1922, Russia I, p. 14.

HOURS OF LABOR

the International Labor Conference adopted a convention limiting hours of work underground in mines to seven and three-quarters a day, with certain exceptions, and providing that its provisions should come into force six months after ratification by two of seven specified coal-producing countries in Europe. By 1935, none of these countries had ratified. The convention was therefore revised in 1935 to overcome objections which had prevented ratification.[125]

In hours regulations, surface excavations and work carried on at less than a specified depth, such as 150 feet in shaft work or 200 feet in tunnel work, are occasionally exempted. Although in some deeper mines the heat, moisture and the difficulties of proper ventilation make even eight hours of work a positive menace to health,[126] no mining law in this country has attempted to make any scientific adjustment of hours based on the degrees of danger in different classes of mines.

The beginnings of such adjustment are, however, to be seen in the laws of New York, New Jersey, Pennsylvania, and Louisiana, and in administrative regulations in California, Maryland, Massachusetts, and Wisconsin governing work in compressed air. Under these codes not only are daily working hours regulated by the degree of pressure under which the work is done, but they are divided into two equal periods, the rest interval between which also varies according to the pressure, for example:

If the Pressure Exceeds	But Does Not Exceed	Number of Hours' Work in 24	Interval Between Working Periods
Normal	21 pounds	8 hours	½ hour
21 pounds	30 pounds	6 hours	1 hours
30 pounds	35 pounds	4 hours	2 hours
35 pounds	40 pounds	3 hours	3 hours
40 pounds	45 pounds	2 hours	4 hours
45 pounds	50 pounds	1½ hours	5 hours

[125] The countries specified in the convention are Belgium, Czechoslovakia, France, Germany, Great Britain, The Netherlands, and Poland. See International Labor Office, *Industrial and Labour Information,* July 1, 1935, pp. 12-14.
[126] In the Comstock silver mines in Nevada, at a depth of 2,000 feet, work was carried on in short shifts at a temperature of 150° F., the men being freely supplied with ice water. The forty-four-hour law that went into effect in New South Wales, January, 1926, limited to six hours per day work underground where the temperature is over 81° F., while that of Queensland, 1925, set the temperature limit at 83° F.

(3) Factories and Workshops.—As indicated in the preceding section, when legal restrictions do not directly affect public health or safety, but apply mainly to the health of the individual adult male workers, we find fewer legal regulations in America. In foreign countries, especially since the end of the European War, many laws have been passed establishing an eight-hour day and generally a week of forty-eight hours or less in the majority of industrial occupations. The first annual session of the International Labor Conference arranged for by the peace treaty, which met at Washington in November, 1919, headed its program of subjects for discussion with the eight-hour day and adopted a draft convention for submission to its members through the League of Nations. This provides for the enactment of legislation for an eight-hour day and forty-eight-hour week in mines, factories, building, and transportation. Provision is made for overtime in certain emergencies, to be paid for at least at one-and-one-quarter times the regular rates of pay, for some flexibility in daily hours by agreement between labor and employers' organizations, and for a possible fifty-six-hour week in continuous industries. On account of alleged tardy development of industry, a fifty-seven-hour week was allowed in most Japanese factories and a sixty-hour week in India, while Greece and Rumania were allowed to delay in putting the eight-hour limitation into effect. In 1930, the conference also adopted an hours convention providing a forty-eight-hour week and an eight- or ten-hour day for commercial and office employees, not including hotels, restaurants, theaters and other places of amusement which were the subject of two recommendations. The enforcement of this convention, together with the recent spread of eight-hour laws, would put the industrial workers of western Europe practically on an eight-hour basis through legislation.

In 1935, a step was taken looking beyond the eight-hour day. In that year the International Labor Conference, influenced by developments under the American "codes of fair competition," adopted a convention approving the principle of the forty-hour work week. The conference, in accordance with a plan to put this principle into effect by means of separate conventions for each industry, also in 1935 adopted a convention providing for a forty-two-hour week in the glass bottle-making industry. It was proposed that similar conventions covering other industries should be adopted at succeeding conferences.

In contrast to the European situation, in the United States, Alaska alone has enacted any general eight-hour legislation. There the legislature in 1917, in response to an initiative vote of the people, passed a comprehensive eight-hour law,[127] which was, however, shortly thereafter declared unconstitutional.[128] The general declarations that eight or ten hours shall constitute a day's work in the absence of special contracts or agreements, found in the constitutions or statutes of about half the states, amount merely to a statement of principles. They have practically no effect upon the actual length of the working day, since they do not attempt to prevent either implied or written contracts for overtime, nor do they often provide a penalty for violation.

About a dozen states have succeeded in regulating by legislation the hours of adult males in one or more employments in factories and workshops. Eight-hour laws are found for electric plants and laundries in Arizona, for plate glass factories in Missouri, for stationary engineers in Montana, for plaster and cement mills in Arizona, Colorado, Montana, and Nevada, and for sugar refineries in Montana. A ten-hour limit is placed in saw- and planing-mills in Arkansas, in bakeries in New Jersey, in brickyards in New York, in certain textile mills in Georgia, Maryland, and South Carolina, and in a few states in drug and grocery stores. An eight-hour law for saw- and planing-mills, permitting limited overtime and not to go into effect until similar legislation is adopted in adjoining states, was enacted in Oregon in 1923. South Carolina in 1936 adopted a law limiting the hours of all employees in cotton, rayon, silk, and woolen mills to eight a day and forty a week, but this law does not become effective until similar laws are enacted in Georgia and North Carolina.

Mississippi in 1912[129] and Oregon in 1913[130] adopted ten-hour laws, and North Carolina in 1915[131] an eleven-hour law

[127] Alaska, Laws 1917, C. 55.
[128] See "Constitutionality," p. 140.
[129] Mississippi, Laws 1912, C. 157.
[130] Oregon, Laws 1913, C. 102.
[131] North Carolina, Laws 1915, C. 148.

132 PRINCIPLES OF LABOR LEGISLATION

for all workers in manufacturing establishments. The Oregon statute allows three hours overtime daily at time-and-one-half wage rate. The Mississippi act was amended in 1924[132] to provide a fifty-five-hour weekly limit. The North Carolina law was amended in 1931 to apply only to women.[133]

c. *Constitutionality*.—The two main legal principles involved in the constitutionality of maximum hour laws for women are equally important in connection with hour legislation for men. There is, on one side, the right of free contract for the disposal of one's own labor, and, on the other, the possible limitation of this right by the police power in the interests of social welfare. While it is now definitely settled that hour legislation for women is a rightful exercise of the police power of the state, the question is somewhat more uncertain in regard to hour laws for men. The constitutional status of the latter type of laws seems to depend on the purpose of the restriction and the class of workers covered. The courts usually uphold hour legislation which applies to public work, and to private business if the public safety is directly concerned, as with railroad trainmen; but opinions are conflicting on hour legislation for private employment where the safety, health, or welfare of the employees alone is involved.

Although several earlier decisions were unfavorable, in 1903 the United States Supreme Court upheld the Kansas Act of 1891, which established the eight-hour day in public employment both for direct and for contract work. "It belongs," said the court, "to the state, as guardian and trustee for its people, and having control of its affairs, to prescribe the conditions upon which it will permit work to be done on its behalf, or on behalf of its municipalities."[134]

But while this decision supported the right of the state to control the action of its political subdivisions, state courts have not always followed its precedent on this point. In New York, for instance, this right was denied on the ground that municipal corporations are local bodies supported by local taxes, and are therefore on the same footing as private corporations.[135] In

---

[132] Mississippi, Laws 1924, C. 314.
[133] North Carolina, Laws 1931, C. 289.
[134] Atkin *v.* Kansas, 191 U. S. 207, 24 Sup. Ct. 124 (1903).
[135] People *ex rel.* Cossey *v.* Grout, 179 N. Y. 417, 72 N. E. 464 (1904).

HOURS OF LABOR

order, therefore, that there might be no future question on these points, the people of the state in 1905 amended their constitution, expressly giving the legislature the power to fix all conditions of labor on public work whether done directly by the state or through contractors.[136] A similar amendment to the Pennsylvania constitution was voted down by the people in 1913. But on the whole, decisions have in recent years followed the main principles of the decision in Atkin v. Kansas.

In private employments, when the element of public safety is clearly and directly involved, as in most legislation regulating working hours in transportation, the courts have raised but few objections. Though during the early days of this class of legislation opinions varied considerably, the close connection between the safety and welfare of the traveling public and the physical condition of these employees has now been so well established that recent decisions almost invariably uphold the main principle of hour limitation as a valid exercise of the police power. In a decision given in 1911, the United States Supreme Court said: "The length of hours of service has direct relation to the efficiency of the human agencies upon which protection to life and property necessarily depends. . . . In its power suitably to provide for the safety of employees and travelers, Congress was not limited to the enactment of laws relating to mechanical appliances, but it was also competent to consider, and to endeavor to reduce the dangers incident to the strain of excessive hours of duty on the part of engineers, conductors, train dispatchers, telegraphers, and the persons embraced within the class defined by the act."[137]

Various related questions arise from time to time involving such points as the definition of emergency,[138] and the liability of the railroad company in case of accidents connected with overtime work. The courts have also had to consider the legality of the so-called "split trick." They have held that under the federal law the permitted hours of service may be divided into

[136] New York, Laws 1906, C. 506. Upheld in People ex rel. Williams Eng. & Cont. Co. v. Metz, 193 N. Y. 148, 85 N. E. 1070 (1908).

[137] Baltimore and Ohio Railroad Co. v. Interstate Commerce Commission, 221 U. S. 612, 31 Sup. Ct. 621 (1911).

[138] United States v. Chicago, Milwaukee and Puget Sound R. R. Co., 197 Fed. 624 (1912); United States v. Kansas City Southern R. R. Co., 202 Fed. 828, 121 C. C. A. 136 (1913).

two parts within the same twenty-four hours.[139] In some cases this rule has led to much practical difficulty in the enforcement of the law, and a number of cases have been brought into court in which train crews have had their time of service extended beyond the maximum sixteen hours by temporary "releases" at places where trains were delayed *en route*. In 1915 the United States Circuit Court of Appeals for the ninth circuit guarded against an abuse of this practice by ruling that such a "release," to constitute a break in the continuity of service, must be sufficiently long to insure "a substantial and opportune period of rest" in all circumstances. Whether or not a "release" was for such a period was a question for the jury to decide in each case.[140]

Another important point frequently raised is the division of jurisdiction between state and federal laws. In case of conflict between the provisions of a state law and the federal act, the higher courts have practically always given precedence to the federal act, largely because of the difficulty of separating interstate from intrastate operations. But where no conflict exists, both laws may operate at the same time. Among the later decisions on this subject is a New York case, carried to the United States Supreme Court, involving the validity of the New York eight-hour law for train dispatchers. In this case the New York court held that the act was a valid exercise of the police power, and that no conflict existed between state and federal authority since the federal law limiting hours to nine a day "prescribed a general minimum limit of safety applicable to average conditions throughout the country," whereas the New York statute limiting hours to eight a day "simply supplemented" the federal act by raising the limit of safety in response to conditions prevailing within the borders of the state.[141] On appeal the United States Supreme Court on May

[139] United States *v.* Atchison, Topeka and Santa Fe Railway Co., 220 U. S. 37, 31 Sup. Ct. 362 (1911). In this decision the United States Supreme Court upheld the practice of a railroad company in requiring telegraph operators to be on duty from 6.30 A.M. to 12 M. and again from 3 to 6.30 P.M.

[140] United States *v.* Southern Pacific Co., 136 C. C. A. 351, 220 Fed. 745 (1915).

[141] People *v.* Erie R. R. Co., 198 N. Y. 369, 91 N. E. 849 (1910). See also Smith *v.* Alabama, 124 U. S. 465, 8 Sup. Ct. 564 (1888).

HOURS OF LABOR

25, 1914, gave a unanimous opinion denying the constitutionality of the New York act, as in direct conflict with the federal act, holding that "Where there is conflict the state legislation must give way. Indeed, when Congress acts in such a way as to manifest its purpose to exercise its constitutional authority the regulating power of the state ceases to exist."[142] On the point made by the New York court, that the state law merely supplemented the federal act, the federal court said: "It is not that there may be a division of the field of regulation, but an exclusive occupation of it when Congress manifests a purpose to enter it. . . . It [the federal act] admits of no supplement; it is the prescribed measure of what is necessary and sufficient for the public safety and of the cost and burden which the railroad must endure to secure it." Another contention made by the New York court was that in any case the federal law had not become operative at the time of the alleged violation, November 1, 1907. But the federal court said that it "considered it elementary that the police power of the state could only exist from the silence of Congress upon the subject and ceased when Congress acted or manifested its purpose to call into play its exclusive power."[143] The important question as to whether the New York act was a valid exercise of the control reserved by the state over corporate charters was also raised in these cases, but no conclusive decision was reached in either court.

The Adamson law was treated by the majority of the Supreme Court as an extension of hour legislation for interstate railroad employees, the Chief Justice declaring that "the authority to permanently establish it [the basic eight-hour day] is so clearly sustained as to render the subject not disputable." The ground for the objection of the four dissenting judges was that the measure was not an hour but a wage-fixing statute. The majority upheld the regulation of wages contained in the law on the ground that the Constitution gave Congress power over interstate commerce to preserve it, and that any act necessary to its preservation is constitutional. They also characterized the

[142] Erie R. R. Co. v. New York, 233 U. S. 671, 34 Sup. Ct. 756 (1914). See also Minnesota Rate Cases, 230 U. S. 352, 33 Sup. Ct. 729 (1913).
[143] See also Northern Pacific Ry. v. Washington, 222 U. S. 370, 32 Sup. Ct. 160 (1912).

law "as the exertion by Congress of the power which is undoubtedly possessed to provide by appropriate legislation for compulsory arbitration."[144]

The right to limit the working hours of men in mines has been practically undisputed since the case of Holden *v.* Hardy in 1898, upholding the Utah eight-hour law for this group of workers.[145] This case has such an important bearing upon the right to limit the hours of adult men in general employments that it should be given special attention at this point. In connection with the custom of passing upon the validity of state legislation under the Fourteenth Amendment to the federal Constitution, the court said: "This court has not failed to recognize the fact that the law is, to a certain extent, a progressive science; that in some of the states methods of procedure which at the time the Constitution was adopted, were deemed essential to the protection and safety of the people, or to the liberty of the citizen, have been found to be no longer necessary; that restrictions which had formerly been laid upon the conduct of individuals, or of classes of individuals, had proved detrimental to their interests, while, on the other hand, certain other classes of persons (particularly those engaged in dangerous or unhealthful employments) have been found to be in need of additional protection."

Two far-reaching conclusions were set forth in the opinion

[144] Wilson *v.* New, 243 U. S. 332, 37 Sup. Ct. 289 (1917).

[145] Holden *v.* Hardy, 169 U. S. 366, 18 Sup. Ct. 383 (1898). Immediately after this favorable decision by the United States Supreme Court, Colorado enacted a law identical with the Utah statute. One year later the Colorado Supreme Court in an elaborate opinion refused to conform to the opinion of the United States Supreme Court and declared the act unconstitutional on the ground that public welfare was not involved, since only the employee himself is injured by long hours (*In re* Morgan, 26 Colo. 415, 58 Pac. 1071 [1899]). So determined were the miners of Colorado to have the shorter workday guaranteed them by legislation that they succeeded in 1902 in securing an amendment to the constitution providing for the eight-hour day (Art. 5, Sec. 25a). Despite this fact, it was not until 1905 that the legislature finally enacted an eight-hour law. Not until 1911 was an enforceable act passed, which was, however, immediately subjected by the efforts of the operators to a referendum vote. Not until 1913 was the question finally settled and an effective act in force. These unfortunate events played no small part in creating the bitter strikes of coal miners which occurred in Colorado in 1913-1914.

HOURS OF LABOR

given in this case. The first involved the question—Are the health dangers connected with the occupation of mining sufficiently serious to justify the legislature in separating out this class of employees and interfering with the right of free contract under the police power of the state? On this point the court said: "But if it be within the power of a legislature to adopt such means (provisions for proper ventilation, speaking-tubes, protection of cages, etc.) for the protection of the lives of its citizens, it is difficult to see why precautions may not also be adopted for the protection of their health and morals. It is as much for the interest of the state that the public health should be preserved as that life should be made secure. . . . While the general experience of mankind may justify us in believing that men may engage in ordinary employments more than eight hours per day without injury to their health, it does not follow that labor for the same length of time is innocuous when carried on beneath the surface of the earth, where the operative is deprived of fresh air and sunlight, and is frequently subjected to foul atmosphere and a very high temperature, or to the influence of noxious gases generated by the process of refining or smelting."

The second conclusion relates to inequality of bargaining power, which is treated in Chapter IX.

As to regulation of men's hours in general factory employments, the constitutionality of a ten-hour daily limit is now assured through favorable action by the United States Supreme Court on the Oregon ten-hour law.[146] Eight-hour legislation has not yet been passed on by the highest court in the land, and its status remains uncertain. In the argument against the ten-hour law, it was contended that the measure was not a health but a wage law, as it permitted three hours of overtime at increased rates of pay. But the court ruled that "apparently the provisions for permitting labor for the overtime on express conditions were made in order to facilitate the enforcement of the law, and in the nature of a mild penalty for employing one not more than three hours overtime." The decision of the state court upholding the act was quoted, to the effect that the hours in some other countries were less than those prescribed by the

[146] Bunting v. Oregon, 243 U. S. 246, 37 Sup. Ct. 435 (1917).

act, and that a ten-hour day was sanctioned by custom in local industries, so that the regulation could not be held to be unreasonable or arbitrary. The contention that the law discriminated against factories and other employments covered by requiring them to pay more for labor was disposed of by the fact that the law was an hours and not a wages act.

The decision in effect reversed the ruling of the court twelve years before in the celebrated Lochner case, in which a New York law providing a ten-hour day for bakers was overthrown.[147] A careful reading of the earlier opinion discloses, however, that the court did not feel sufficient evidence was presented to it indicating the injurious effect upon the health of bakers to justify the state in singling them out and interfering with their freedom of contract. Evidence on the health dangers of long hours and the beneficial effects of the short workday was amply supplied in the Oregon case in a brief prepared by Felix Frankfurter and Josephine Goldmark, similar in nature to the Brandeis-Goldmark briefs presented in the minimum wage and women's hour law cases.[148]

The Mississippi law of 1912,[149] limiting hours of all employees engaged in manufacturing or repairing to ten a day, but excepting cases of emergency or public necessity, was three times taken to the state supreme court and was each time upheld. The court held that it was not bound by Lochner v. New York, since in the law decided against in that case no provision was made for emergencies under which the "lightest violation of the provisions of the act would be innocent." The court also called attention to the physical and mental strain of present-day industry as compared with earlier methods. One of the few instances where a court has specifically recognized the right to leisure occurred in this case, when the court said:

We pause here to remark the notable fact that it is rare for the seller of labor to appeal to the courts for the preservation of his inalienable rights of labor; this inestimable privilege is generally the object of the buyer's disinterested solicitude. Some day, perhaps,

---

[147] Lochner v. New York, 198 U. S. 45, 25 Sup. Ct. 539 (1905).
[148] See pp. 76 and 114.
[149] Mississippi, Laws 1912, C. 157.

HOURS OF LABOR

the inalienable right to rest will be the subject of litigation, but as yet this phase of individual liberty has not sought shelter under the state or federal constitution.[150]

The constitutionality of eight-hour legislation for men in general employments had not, up to January, 1936, been passed upon by the United States Supreme Court. The early unenforceable eight- and ten-hour laws were generally upheld by the courts; but when Nebraska in 1891 attempted to make such a law enforceable by requiring double pay for all work in excess of eight hours, farm and domestic labor being excluded, the law was declared unconstitutional by the supreme court of the state in 1894, both on the ground of class legislation and as an interference with the right of free contract.[151]

In 1912 the Supreme Court of Lousiana declared an hour law unconstitutional on the ground of unwarranted classification of industries. This act limited the hours of stationary firemen to eight a day in manufacturing or business establishments, offices, or warehouses operating day and night, but exempted certain other industries, such as the petroleum, sawmill, and cotton-gin industries, and sugar plantations.[152] This classification of industries appeared to the court to be purely arbitrary, since it was difficult to see why long hours were not as injurious in sawmills as in warehouses or offices. On this point the judge said: "There is no suggestion in the record that the occupation of stationary firemen is dangerous or unhealthy to such a degree as to warrant the interference of the state. . . . The toil *per se* could not have warranted the interference of the legislature because it permitted unlimited toil in the plants excepted from the operation of the act. Whatever may have been the motive for the passage of the act, we are satisfied that it was not based on health considerations."[153] Here again the court did not feel that sufficient evidence was presented to justify the classification of industries as contained in the law, and after this decision the legislature amended the

[150] State *v.* J. J. Newman Lumber Co., 102 Miss. 802, 59 So. 923; 103 Miss. 263, 60 So. 215 (1912).
[151] Low *v.* Reese Printing Co., 41 Neb. 127, 59 N. W. 362 (1894).
[152] Louisiana, Laws 1912, No. 245.
[153] State *v.* Barba, 132 La. 768, 61 So. 784 (1913).

original law, making it apply to all stationary engineers in cities with a population of 50,000 or more.[154]

The Alaskan eight-hour law, which covered all workers, including partners and corporation officials, except in certain emergencies, was declared unconstitutional in 1918 in a federal circuit court.[155] The judge held that the statute, applying as it did to all occupations alike, was not shown to be a health measure, but was a "meddlesome interference" with individual rights. By interfering with the right to earn a living, which is a property right, it was held to have violated the Fourteenth Amendment to the federal Constitution. In addition, it was declared to be class legislation, which was forbidden by the organic act creating the territory. On similar grounds the Solicitor-general of the United States declined to allow the case to be appealed to a higher court, so that no final test was had on this, the only enforceable universal eight-hour law covering private employment enacted in America up to the beginning of 1936.

Even though the constitutionality of eight-hour laws for men in general is still undetermined, the Supreme Court decision in the Oregon ten-hour case opens the way for much larger regulation of the work of adult males than has heretofore been undertaken in this country. Equality of bargaining power may be secured in some cases by freeing labor organizations from existing restrictions upon acts, not in themselves unlawful, which are necessary to carry out effectively the purposes of organization.[156] But where organization fails to protect any considerable group of workers, or where this protection is not provided in a reasonable manner, the substitution of the power of the state becomes a justifiable and necessary interference with the right of free contract, for the protection of health, welfare, and citizenship. Such interference, an analysis of the various decisions shows, has been generally held legitimate by the courts.

11. REST PERIODS

In spite of the considerable development of maximum hour legislation in this country, only slight attention has been paid—

[154] Louisiana, Laws 1914, No. 201.
[155] U. S. v. Northern Commercial Co. and George A. Coleman (1918).
[156] See Chap. vii, "Collective Bargaining."

HOURS OF LABOR

except for the recent agitation for one day of rest in seven and some efforts to exclude women and children from night work—to the important question of legal rest periods.

1. **Daily Rest and Mealtimes.**—The most common form of legal requirement for daily rest periods in private employments is found in the laws regulating hours of labor for women. A number of states merely specify that from one-half to one hour shall be allowed for the noon meal. Under such laws as do not restrict the number of hours of continuous employment, women have been employed, with no time for rest and meals, for periods so long as to be definitely harmful to their health. Several states, therefore, make the provision more effective by prescribing that the noon rest period shall be given after five or six hours' work. If overtime is worked in the evening, a few states require a rest period of twenty or thirty minutes after 6 or 7 P.M. Most of the laws apply to all females and a few apply both to boys and to girls, but the inclusion of adult men workers is very rare.

In addition to the noon rest period, a few employers have voluntarily granted to employees, especially to women, a fifteen- or twenty-minute rest in the middle of the morning and again in the afternoon; but no legal regulations to this effect exist in America. In European countries, however, the beneficial effects of these shorter breaks in the workday have been recognized in legislative enactments. Such rest periods may, under the increasing strain and complexity of modern industry, add much to both the physical welfare and the efficiency of the worker.

For men workers in America a daily rest period is occasionally required by law in the interest of health or public safety. Thus a daily period as well as the maximum limit of daily hours is fixed by law for railroad employees. Trainmen must be allowed ten hours' rest after sixteen hours' consecutive employment, but if they have been at work for an aggregate of sixteen hours with brief intervals between, the rest period need be only eight hours. Several states make no distinction between consecutive and aggregate employment, but set a fixed period of eight or ten hours' rest after sixteen hours of work, while a few other states require this rest period after thirteen, fourteen, or fifteen hours on duty. In addition, a few states, including Massachusetts, Maryland, and New York, have enacted laws requiring that telegraphers, switchmen, and others directing the movement of trains be given a rest period of twenty-four consecutive hours twice each month, without reduction of pay.[157] In California, Maryland, Massachusetts, New Jersey, Pennsylvania, and Wisconsin, where tunnel and caisson operations have been scientifically regulated, the hours of workers in compressed air must be equally divided by a rest period varying in length according to the degree of air pressure.[158]

2. **Night Work.**—Night-work legislation applies only to women and minors, there being no regulation in the United States of the work of adult men in this respect.

The investigations of the International Association for Labor Legislation, begun in 1901, showed that serious physical and moral dangers surrounded the work of women at night. It was clearly demonstrated that recovery from fatigue is obtained mainly through rest and sleep, and that sound sleep can rarely be secured in the daytime, especially in the noisy and crowded homes of many working people in industrial cities. The lack of sunlight tends to produce anæmia and tuberculosis and to predispose to other ills. Night work brings increased liability to eyestrain and accident. Serious moral dangers also are likely to result from the necessity of traveling the streets alone at night, and from the interference with normal home life. From an economic point of view, moreover, the investigations showed that night work was unprofitable, being inferior to day work both in quality and in quantity. Wherever it had been abolished, in the long run the efficiency both of the management and of the workers was raised.[159] Furthermore, it was found that night-work laws are a valuable aid in enforcing acts fixing the maximum period of employment.

[157] The New York law was, however, held unconstitutional by the state appellate division, third department, in People v. N. Y. C. & H. R. R. R. Co., 163 App. Div. 79 (1914), on the ground laid down by the United States Supreme Court in Erie R. R. Co. v. New York, 233 U. S. 671, 34 Sup. Ct. 756 (1914), that "there can be no valid state legislation covering the same field where the federal authority has asserted its right to act." (See pp. 134-135.)
[158] See table, p. 129.
[159] See the brief in the case of People v. Charles Schweinler Press, 214 N. Y. 395, 108 N. E. 639 (1915), by Louis D. Brandeis and Josephine Goldmark, pp. 260-307.

As a result of these investigations, the association called, through the Swiss Federal Council, in Berne, in 1906, a conference on women's night work. This conference was attended by representatives of fourteen leading European powers,[160] and an international convention was drawn up by which the various countries agreed to provide as soon as possible that women industrial workers over eighteen be allowed at least eleven consecutive hours of rest at night, seven of which must fall between 10 P.M. and 5 A.M. In practically all of the signatory countries the necessary legislation was enacted and the prohibition was in force by January 1, 1912. By 1916 several of these countries had enacted legislation far beyond the provisions of the treaty, and a number of other states and dependencies, including India and Argentina, had passed similar laws. The International Labor Conference which met in Washington in November, 1919, reaffirmed in strengthened form the convention forbidding women's night work.[161] Where the war emergency had caused the temporary removal of the usual legal restrictions on such work, its evil effects had been once more demonstrated.[162] Nearly all industrial countries in the world have now enacted legislation beyond the provisions of this convention. Most European countries permit exceptions under certain conditions, especially when a delay in handling perishable materials would cause great financial loss, but such exceptions are, as a rule, very carefully safeguarded. The Mexican Constitution of 1917 prohibits night work by women and minors under sixteen between 10 P.M. and 6 A.M. In 1923, five countries of Central America signed at Washington a conven-

[160] Austria, Hungary, Belgium, Denmark, France, Germany, Great Britain, Italy, Luxemburg, Portugal, Spain, Sweden, Switzerland, and The Netherlands.

[161] International Labor Office, *Official Bulletin,* vol. i, p. 424. For list of countries which have ratified this convention, see *Industrial and Labour Information,* latest chart on progress of ratifications. In 1934, this convention, already ratified by thirty countries, was revised to exempt women in purely managerial positions and to permit administrative authorities to prohibit night work by women in certain industries and areas between 11 P.M. and 6 A.M., instead of between 10 P.M. and 5 A.M. as previously required.

[162] See Great Britain, Ministry of Munitions, Health of Munition Workers Committee, *Memorandum No. 4,* "Employment of Women," 1916.

tion for unification of protective labor laws[163] which agrees to prohibit within their territory employment of women and minors under fifteen between 7 P.M. and 5 A.M.

While the prohibition of night work by women is by no means universal in the United States, by 1936 more than a dozen states forbade some form of it,[164] and its dangers are coming to be better realized by the public. The standards for women's employment issued by the Women in Industry Service of the federal Department of Labor, which were based on wartime necessities, though issued in December, 1918, included prohibition of the work of women between 10 P.M. and 6 A.M. Massachusetts was the pioneer, forbidding in 1890 the employment of women in manufacturing and mechanical establishments between 10 P.M. and 6 A.M.[165] In 1907 the law was extended to forbid work in textile mills between 6 P.M. and 6 A.M.,[166] and Wisconsin, by administrative order of 1917, forbade work in manufactories and laundries for the same period—the strictest regulation found in the United States. Not one of the statutes, however, is an inclusive night-work prohibition. The Indiana law, for example, applies only to factories,[167] while the South Carolina law applies only to stores.[168] The New York statute covers factories, stores, laundries, restaurants, elevators, messenger service, and street railways,[169] while that of Nebraska omits the last three occupations but includes hotels and offices in cities of certain classes.[170] There is no statute law in Oregon forbidding night work, but the industrial commission by administrative order forbids it in mercantile, manufacturing and laundry occupations and on elevators.[171] The Kansas commis-

---

[163] Guatemala, El Salvador, Honduras, Nicaragua, and Costa Rica. International Labor Office, Legislative Series of 1923, International 2.

[164] California, Connecticut, Delaware, Indiana, Kansas, Massachusetts, Nebraska, New Jersey, New York, North Dakota, Ohio, Oregon, Pennsylvania, South Carolina, Washington, Wisconsin.

[165] Massachusetts, Laws 1890, C. 183.

[166] *Ibid.*, Laws 1907, C. 267.

[167] Indiana, Annotated Statutes 1926, Sec. 9411.

[168] South Carolina, Code, 1922, v. 2, Sec. 422.

[169] New York, Consolidated Laws 1930, C. 32, Secs. 2, 172, 182-185, and 391; and Laws 1931, C. 509.

[170] Nebraska, Laws 1931, C. 97.

[171] Industrial Welfare Commission of Oregon, Orders Nos. 37, 38, 39, 41, and 45, 1919.

HOURS OF LABOR

sion has taken similar action for stores, factories and laundries.[172]

In some cases, however, the laws have been so worded as to prove unenforceable. A Connecticut law of 1913 simply forbade the employment of women in certain lines of work "after ten o'clock in the evening."[173] Therefore, certain manufacturers observed the letter of the law by requiring women to stop work at 10 P.M., but calling them to their tasks again from midnight till early morning. It is reported that this practice became general in munition plants during the boom which began in 1915. It was not until 1919 that Connecticut passed an effective law specifying the entire period during which night work was forbidden.[174]

Another small group of states recognize the strain of employment at night for women and seek to discourage it by shortening the period which may be so worked. The Maryland statute is typical of this class of legislation. While by day women may work up to ten hours, if any part of their work falls between 10 P.M. and 6 A.M. the hours of employment are limited to eight.[175] With these exceptions, which are confined to a few states and a few industries, the night work of women is entirely unregulated in America.

Perhaps the slow progress of American laws forbidding night work of women may be in part accounted for by the doubtful attitude of certain of the courts. In 1907, eight months after the international agreement to forbid night work, the New York State Court of Appeals declared such a prohibition unconstitutional.[176] The doctrine of entire freedom of contract beween employer and employee applying alike to men and to women was emphasized, and the court was unable to trace any connection between the law and the promotion of health. No account was taken of inherent sex differences between men and women. After this decision, legislatures were naturally reluctant to pass night-work laws. As the dangers of night work for women have become more widely known, however, judicial

---

[172] Commission of Labor and Industry, Orders Nos. 1, 2, and 3, 1931.
[173] Connecticut, Laws 1913, C. 179.
[174] *Ibid.*, Laws 1919, C. 195.
[175] Maryland, Annotated Code, 1924, Art. 100, Sec. 54.
[176] People *v.* Williams, 189 N. Y. 131, 81 N. E. 778 (1907).

opinion has changed in respect to the constitutionality of prohibiting it. A brief by Mr. Brandeis and Miss Goldmark, bringing out the facts, was presented in defense of the new nightwork law passed by New York in 1913. The highest state court, the court of appeals, unanimously reversed its former decision, and, taking cognizance of the facts presented to it in regard to modern industrial conditions, upheld the law as a necessary protection to the health of women, both for their own sakes and for the sake of posterity.[177] In 1924 the United States Supreme Court upheld the New York statute of 1917 forbidding night work in restaurants.[178]

The injurious effects of night work are even more pronounced on children, whose strength and powers of resistance are not fully developed, than they are on women workers. The first of the annual International Labor Conferences, in 1919, recommended to its members the enactment of laws forbidding the employment of children under eighteen at night, with a limited number of exceptions for those between sixteen and eighteen.[179] In the United States children, fortunately, are better protected with regard to night work than women, there being no constitutional difficulty in their case. The standard proposed by the International Labor Conference has hardly been reached, however. By January, 1936, all except two states —Nevada and South Dakota—prohibited night work in factories, generally between 7 P.M. and 6 A.M., for children under sixteen.[180] Canneries are often excepted. About three-fourths of the states and the District of Columbia extend the prohibition to cover stores, and about twenty-five states to all occupations except agriculture and housework. A number of states extend the age limit to eighteen or to twenty-one, usually setting the age higher for girls than for boys. The greatest abuses in connection with the night work of children have been found in tex-

[177] People v. Charles Schweinler Press, 214 N. Y. 395, 108 N. E. 639 (1915). See also chap. viii, "Administration."

[178] Radice v. New York, 264 U. S. 292, 44 Sup. Ct. 325 (1924).

[179] International Labor Office, *Official Bulletin*, vol. i, p. 433. For list of states which have ratified this convention, see *Industrial and Labour Information*, latest chart on progress of ratifications. The conventions forbidding night work for women and young persons apply only to industrial undertakings.

[180] Texas sets the age limit at fifteen years.

HOURS OF LABOR

tile mills and glass works; and on account of the strong opposition of the manufacturers, the states where conditions were worst frequently were the last to pass the necessary legislation.

Special regulation of night work for adult men is a comparatively recent development. Some European countries have adopted laws placing special limitations on hours of night work for men, and others prohibit such work except in continuous processes.

The most general prohibition of night work for men is that in bakeries. This is due to the fact that such work is unhealthful and not really necessary, although customary owing to intense competition among bakers to meet the daily demand for freshly baked bread. Many European countries have laws providing for cessation of night work in bakeries for a period of from six to ten hours.[181] In other countries similar regulations have been made by municipalities. In 1925 the International Labor Conference adopted a convention which prohibits baking of commercial products, with certain exceptions, at night for a period of seven consecutive hours. The prohibition includes employers and one-man bakers, as well as employees, a point much discussed and one meeting with considerable opposition.[182] By January, 1936, this convention had been ratified by ten countries, most of them relatively small.[183]

3. **Saturday and Legal Holidays.**—While more than a dozen states have made Saturday afternoon a legal holiday, few, if any, have made effective provision for the enforcement of this or other laws fixing legal holidays. The extension of the Saturday half-holiday in private employment has often been due to voluntary action by employers. Occasionally, strong labor organizations, such as those in some of the building and garment trades, have secured the forty-four-hour week, which means the Saturday half-holiday. A 1933 official report on

[181] *International Labour Review,* "Night Work in Bakeries," April and May, 1924, pp. 558 and 680.

[182] *Ibid.,* August, 1925, pp. 153 and 185. For the favorable decision of the Permanent Court of International Justice on inclusion of working employers, see International Labor Office, *Industrial and Labour Information,* August 2, 1926, p. 175.

[183] Bulgaria, Chile, Colombia, Cuba, Estonia, Finland, Luxemburg, Nicaragua, Spain and Uruguay.

union scale of wages and hours[184] covering nearly half a million wage earners in organized trades showed that 78.3 per cent of these workers had gained the forty-four-hour week or a shorter one. The Census of Manufactures for 1929 reported 1,181,500 wage earners working in establishments where the prevailing hours per week were less than forty-five.

But probably women's hour laws were one of the strongest single influences in securing, though indirectly, a shorter workday on Saturday to certain workers. Many efforts to improve standards took the form of cutting down the sixty-hour week, though still retaining the ten-hour day; this in actual operation often meant a Saturday half-holiday. By 1936 about ten states allowed ten or ten and a half daily hours of work, but set a weekly limit of fifty-four to fifty-eight hours, while half a dozen by statute or administrative orders had adopted the same principle, with the higher standard of eight and a half or nine hours a day and a forty-eight- to fifty-hour week.[185] Several laws also permit an increase in daily hours to secure a shorter workday one day in the week. In public employment, as in private, the Saturday half-holiday has become the established practice.

In continental Europe the working week of five and a half days is generally known as "the English week" because it was widely enforced by law in England earlier than in any other country. So important is the Saturday half-holiday considered in Europe that it was proposed as a subject for international treaty at the meeting of the International Association for Labor Legislation in 1912, and discussed at the International Labor Conference of 1921.

Since 1926, a greatly increased number of workers have secured a full Saturday holiday through the extension of the five-day week. A survey by the federal Department of Labor[186] showed that in 1926, out of 764,600 union members covered, 40,400, or 5.3 per cent, had a work week not exceeding five days or forty hours for all or part of the year. The short week

[184] United States Bureau of Labor Statistics, *Bulletin No. 600,* 1934, p. 12.
[185] See p. 110.
[186] United States Bureau of Labor Statistics, *Monthly Labor Review,* December, 1926, pp. 1, 2.

HOURS OF LABOR

had gained greatest headway in the clothing industry, extending to 32 per cent of the workers; in the building industry, 6 per cent; and in newspaper printing, 5 per cent. The 1929 Census of Manufactures reported that 286,685 employees worked in establishments where prevailing weekly hours were forty or less. In 1933, in the midst of depression, the federal Department of Labor found that the proportion of union workers on the five-day week had increased to 85.3 per cent in the building trades and 63 per cent in newspaper printing.[187] Beginning in 1933, the adoption of codes of fair competition with the forty-hour standard extended this short week to a large proportion of workers in almost all industries. With the code restrictions removed and with increased industrial activity, some of these gains were lost. The extent of the permanent advance cannot be predicted.

4. **One Day of Rest in Seven.**—Under modern industrial conditions many thousands of wage earners are obliged to work seven days a week, a practice which deprives them of proper leisure and tends to break down their health. Remedial legislation in the United States has been of two kinds. The type of law found in nearly all the states is a descendant of the old Puritan "blue laws" and attempts to forbid all Sunday work, primarily from religious motives. Such laws, however, drafted before the rise of modern industry, generally fail to protect either the worker or the Sabbath. Many of them are meaningless because filled with exceptions; others remain dead letters on the statute books; all fail to provide proper means of enforcement. A few enforceable laws have been passed prohibiting Sunday employment in a single occupation, generally that of bakers or barbers, but have generally failed in their purpose because the courts have tended to declare them unconstitutional as making an arbitrary classification of industries, which violates the equal protection clause of the Fourteenth Amendment to the federal Constitution.[188] But it is hardly practicable or desirable, at the present day, to

[187] United States Bureau of Labor Statistics, *Bulletin No. 600*, pp. 14-16.
[188] See Clark, Lindley M., "Labor Laws Declared Unconstitutional," United States Bureau of Labor, *Bulletin No. 91*, November, 1910, pp. 951-952.

realize the aim of the old-time Sunday law and stop all Sunday work. Public necessity demands the continuous operation of such services as telephone and telegraph lines, heat, light, and power plants, steam and electric railways, and hotels and restaurants. Another large group of industries, important among which are iron and steel works, cement factories, paper and pulp, flour and grist mills, usually operate continuously on account of technical requirements or sometimes simply for economy. To remedy this situation an entirely new form of law has been devised which recognizes that much seven-day work is a necessity and that the objectionable feature is the seven-day worker. This type of law, therefore, simply requires that all employees be given a weekly day of rest, those employed on Sunday being given a free day at some other time in the week. Since such a law generally necessitates an addition of one-sixth to the working force, it tends to eliminate all unnecessary seven-day labor at the same time that it secures to every workman a weekly rest day.

This modern legislative movement began in Switzerland, where a law was passed in 1890 requiring each railway employee to be given, without loss of pay, fifty-two weekly rest days each year, seventeen of them to fall on Sunday. Between 1904 and 1911 enforceable rest-day measures were enacted in almost all the leading European countries. These laws generally name Sunday as the day of rest, but permit the operation of continuous industries on that day provided every employee gets some other day in the week free. As with many other classes of European labor legislation, only the general principle is laid down in the laws, and special extensions or exceptions are largely determined by administrative rulings. The International Labor Conference of 1921 adopted a convention providing for employees in industrial undertakings a weekly period of rest of at least twenty-four consecutive hours, with a provision that each ratifying country be allowed to make its own exceptions,[189] and a recommendation that such period of rest should also be established in commercial undertakings. The convention was made for one day of rest in seven, instead

[189] International Labor Office, *Official Bulletin,* Supplement vol. iv, no. 23. For list of states which have ratified this convention, see *Industrial and Labour Information,* latest chart on progress of ratifications.

HOURS OF LABOR

of specifically for Sunday, on account of both the exigencies of modern industry and varying religious customs. The importance of making the time of rest uniform for as many as possible of the workers of the same locality was, however, stressed. The office reported that legislation providing for a weekly rest day in commerce and industry had already been enacted in twenty-nine countries, three of which also extended the provision to agricultural workers.[190]

In the United States, eight states had by January, 1936, passed laws embodying this principle of one day of rest in seven. The California and Connecticut statutes are nullified by exempting "any case of emergency,"[191] and in addition the Connecticut law specifically excepts a long list of occupations. The Michigan act applies only to interurban motormen and conductors, but is interesting as the first attempt to apply legislation of this type to transportation.[192] There remain the Massachusetts and New York acts of 1913,[193] the Wisconsin act of 1919,[194] the New Hampshire act of 1933,[195] and the Illinois act of 1935,[196] which are similar in character and represent the most effective rest-day legislation yet passed in the United States. These laws apply to factories and mercantile establishments generally,[197] but exclude certain occupations, such as janitors, watchmen, superintendents, foremen in charge, employees caring for live animals, maintaining fires or making repairs to boilers or machinery, and employees working not more than three hours on a seventh day in setting sponges in bakeries. In addition, Massachusetts and New Hampshire exclude a long list of such occupations as those connected with newspaper work, restaurants, drug stores, livery stables or garages, the sale or distribution of gas, electricity, or milk, or any emergency which could not reasonably have been expected. Wisconsin excludes all workers in milk and cheese plants and in

[190] International Labor Office, *Questionnaire IV*, 1921, p. 6.
[191] California, Code 1906, p. 722; Connecticut, Laws 1911, C. 162.
[192] Michigan, Laws 1919, No. 361.
[193] Massachusetts, Laws 1913, C. 619; New York, Laws 1913, C. 740.
[194] Wisconsin, Laws 1919, C. 653.
[195] New Hampshire, Laws 1933, C. 30.
[196] Illinois, Laws 1935, p. 839.
[197] The Massachusetts act was extended to firemen and watchmen by amendments in 1933 and 1935.

flour mills. New York furthermore provides that if there are practical difficulties or unnecessary hardships in carrying out the law, the industrial commission may make variations "if the spirit of the act be observed and substantial justice done," and if the variations apply to all cases in which conditions are substantially the same.[198] An earlier amendment giving the commissioner of labor power to exempt necessarily continuous processes in which no one was employed for more than eight hours a day was declared unconstitutional by the court of appeals on the ground that it constituted a delegation of legislative power.[199] Under the clause just mentioned, however, which authorizes the industrial board to grant variations from the law in case of practical difficulty or unnecessary hardship, provided substantial justice be done, the board has from time to time, upon affirmative vote of the workers concerned, given exemption to necessarily continuous industries or processes where the eight-hour shift was in practice. As an aid to enforcement, employers are usually required to post a schedule containing a list of employees who are to work on Sunday, and designating the day of rest given them.

Investigations carried on by the American Association for Labor Legislation[200] in Massachusetts and New York after the law had been in force a year showed that its provisions were being generally observed and that many employees who had previously been obliged to work seven days a week were obtaining a weekly rest day without undue hardship to industry.

Women and children are also sometimes protected from seven-day labor through the provisions of those maximum hour laws which limit work to six days a week; other statutes seek to insure a weekly rest day by fixing weekly hours at six times daily hours or less. A few women's hour laws, however, leave the way open for seven-day labor by setting a daily but not a weekly limit, and one state, Nevada,[201] invites it by making the weekly working period seven times the permitted daily hours.

[198] New York, Laws 1921, C. 50, Sec. 161.
[199] People v. Klinck Packing Co., 214 N. Y. 121, 108 N. E. 278 (1915).
[200] *American Labor Legislation Review*, December, 1914, pp. 615-626.
[201] Nevada, Laws 1917, C. 14.

HOURS OF LABOR

It has been pointed out that Sunday laws applying to single occupations have sometimes been set aside as class legislation. General Sunday laws, however, have almost universally been upheld by the higher courts. Two distinct lines of reasoning have been followed. In the first half of the nineteenth century, beginning with a New York case in 1811,[202] the constitutionality of the laws was seldom directly involved, but was assumed on religious grounds in connection with the settlement of such questions as the scope of their application, the validity of contracts made on Sunday, the definition of "works of necessity or charity," or the classification of employments. In 1844 in North Carolina a case first came up which was sustained on the grounds of the police power of the state. For the next twenty years both lines of reasoning found their way into court decisions; but since 1866 the state courts in sustaining these laws have relied almost entirely upon the police power, and all acts passed upon by the federal Supreme Court have been upheld on this same ground.[203]

Representative of the reasoning by which Sunday laws have been held a legitimate exercise of the police power is the opinion of the state supreme court in Hennington v. Georgia,[204] later quoted by the United States Supreme Court:

"There can be no well-founded doubt of its being a police regulation, . . . for the frequent and total suspension of the toils, cares, and strain of mind or muscle incident to pursuing an occupation or common employment is beneficial to every individual, and incidentally to the community at large, the general public. Leisure is no less essential than labor to the well-being of man. Short intervals of leisure at stated periods reduce wear and tear, promote health, favor cleanliness, encourage social intercourse, afford opportunity for introspection and retrospection, and tend in a high degree to expand the thoughts and sympathies of people, enlarge their information, and elevate their morals.

[202] People v. Ruggles, 8 Johnson (N. Y.) 289, 5 Am. Dec. 335 (1811).

[203] As late as 1915 a general Sunday law was attacked in Oregon as class legislation and as a violation of the Fourteenth Amendment, but was upheld by the state supreme court (State v. Nicholls, 77 Ore. 415, 151 Pac. 473).

[204] Hennington v. State, 90 Ga. 396, 17 S. E. 1009 (1892); Hennington v. Georgia, 163 U. S. 299, 16 Sup. Ct. 1086 (1896).

"If a law which, in essential respects, betters for all the people the conditions—sanitary, social, and individual—under which their daily life is carried on and which contributes to insure for each, even against his own will, his minimum allowance of leisure, cannot be rightfully classed as a police regulation, it would be difficult to imagine any law that could."

In only two states had a test case on one-day-rest-in-seven laws reached a higher court by 1936. *A priori* it would seem that these laws could be sustained as police power regulations as the Sunday laws have been, and in the main such a position was taken by the New York State Court of Appeals on February 5, 1915. The court said:[205] "Can we say that the provision for a full day of rest in seven for such employees is so extravagant and unreasonable, so disconnected with the probable promotion of health and welfare, that its enactment is beyond the jurisdiction of the legislature? . . . We have no power of decision of the question whether it is the wisest and best way to offset these conditions and to give to employees the protection which they need, even if we had any doubt on that subject. Our only inquiry must be whether the provision on its face seems reasonable, fair, and appropriate, and whether it can fairly be believed that its natural consequences will be in the direction of the betterment of public health and welfare, and therefore that it is one which the state for its protection and advantage may enact and enforce." The classifications made by the act have likewise been upheld, as meeting the actual conditions of modern industrial life. Its limitation to employees of factories and mercantile establishments was reasonable because "We know as a matter of common observation that such labor is generally indoors and imposes that greater burden on health which comes from confinement, many times accompanied by crowded conditions and impure air." The exemption of dairies, creameries, and similar plants employing not more than seven workers was also reasonable, because of the perishable nature of the product, the heavier burden of the necessary increase in the force of a small establishment, and because of the closer personal relation between employer and employee and lessened strain in such small establishments. The power given to the commissioner of labor to exempt continuous industries

[205] People *v.* Klinck Packing Co., 214 N. Y. 121, 108 N. E. 278 (1915).

HOURS OF LABOR

in which daily hours were not more than eight, was held to be an unconstitutional delegation of legislative power, but similar action by the industrial board under a later amendment authorizing variations in certain cases has not been questioned. A law enacted in Minnesota in 1923 resembled in form the New York statute, but was rendered ineffective by the large number of exceptions provided. This law in 1925 was declared unconstitutional by the state Supreme Court on the ground that the classification of industries specified in the act was so arbitrary that it denied equal protection of the law.[206] This decision does not invalidate one-day-rest-in-seven legislation, but shows the necessity of greater care in drafting statutes. Thus the attitude of the courts is apparently favorable to the extension of laws securing industrial workers a weekly day of rest.

5. **Annual Vacations.**—The average salaried worker would consider himself ill-used if he failed to receive an annual paid vacation of two weeks or more. But ordinarily no such provision is made for the wage earner.[207] In this respect employees of state and federal governments fare better than workers in private employment. A survey by the New York Bureau of Women in Industry,[208] covering representative factories with fifty or more employees in all parts of the state, showed that 97 per cent of the plants gave annual vacations with pay to office workers, and 25 per cent to production workers. Length of vacation for office workers was usually two weeks; for production workers, one week. Eligibility was based on length of service, the minimum period in a majority of the plants being one year. The vacation policy was more common in larger than in smaller factories and was followed by a much larger proportion of plants in chemical and food industries than in the textile, wood, leather, stone, clay, and glass industries. Some states have laws providing annual vacations for several classes of public employees. The federal government likewise

[206] State v. Pocock, 161 Minn. 376, 201 N. W. 610 (1925).

[207] In May, 1915, the Milk Wagon Drivers' Union of Chicago signed an agreement with their employers which included a provision for two weeks' annual vacation with pay. This is said to be the first such provision in a signed trade agreement.

[208] New York Department of Labor, *The Industrial Bulletin*, vol. x, no. 3, December, 1930, pp. 76-78, 100.

provides annual paid leaves of absence for its civilian employees, amounting to twenty-six days, exclusive of Sundays and holidays, in addition to an annual sick leave of fifteen days.[209] In some states there is also legislative provision for vacations for employees of cities and towns. Another method sometimes used to secure vacations to city employees is that of inserting such provisions in city charters. For example, the New York City charter gives executive heads at their discretion power to grant employees annual vacations of not less than one week, but *per diem* employees may not be given more than two weeks.

Laws requiring annual vacations have in this country covered only public employments. In Europe, particularly since the war, compulsory annual vacations with pay for both public and private employees have become quite general, and in more than a dozen countries are established by law for larger or smaller groups of workers. In Russia, these include all employees; in other countries such as Austria, Czechoslovakia, Italy, Spain and Sweden, a large proportion; and in Greece, Denmark and other countries, certain groups. The length of vacation varies from one to five weeks, according to the country, occupation, and length of previous service. A number of laws make vacations longer for persons under eighteen.[210] In 1934 there were in Great Britain about one and a half million workers, provided with vacations of varying length.[211] In 1936, the International Labor Conference adopted a convention applying to most workers, providing for an annual vacation of at least six working days with full pay after one year of continuous service.

The foregoing discussion indicates that legal regulation of the working hours and of the rest periods for the different classes of employees in America has tended toward uniform provisions, the same limitations usually being applied to all industries covered by the law. In European countries, on the other hand, in addition to broad maximum and minimum regulations, frequent use is made of the method of determin-

[209] Public Nos. 471 and 472, 74th Congress, 2nd session, 1936.

[210] International Labor Office, "Holidays With Pay," Report V, First Discussion, International Labor Conference, 19th session, 1935.

[211] Great Britain, Ministry of Labor, *Labour Gazette,* July, 1934, pp. 232-233.

HOURS OF LABOR

ing the length of the work and rest periods in accordance with the special hazards of each industry of occupation. Scientific adjustment of hours of labor requires thorough and often continued investigations of actual conditions, and should combine the practical knowledge of workers and employers with the technical knowledge of experts. In many occupations, dusts and gases, poisons, or extreme temperatures make it safe to work consecutively for only short periods.[212] The presence in America of hazardous industries fraught with danger to the life and health of thousands of workers employed for long hours and frequently seven days a week, but as yet unregulated either by trade organizations or by state control, indicates the need for a system whereby permanent bodies will be authorized to investigate scientifically such conditions of employment, and fix varying hours of labor on a basis which will adequately protect the health and welfare of the employees and the state. As already noted, some of the leading states of the country have created industrial boards or commissions with authority to make special investigations and to regulate hours in the various industries. This method of meeting the problem, moreover, has been held constitutional by the Supreme Court of Wisconsin on the ground that "The authority thus conferred invests the commission with no arbitrary and uncontrolled discretion, but directs them to ascertain the facts and to apply the rules of law thereto under the prescribed terms and conditions. Such action is not legislative in character, but is the performance of an executive and ministerial duty within the regulations provided for in the act."[213] In these two facts lies some indication of the direction which future progress may be expected to take.[214]

[212] A strike in the oil plants of Bayonne, N. J., for instance, during the summer of 1915, brought to public knowledge the work of the still cleaners who must toil in a temperature of 200° F. cleaning the huge vats in which oil is refined.
[213] State v. Lange Canning Co., 164 Wis. 228, 160 N. W. 57 (1916), quoting State ex rel. Buell v. Frear, 146 Wis. 305, 131 N. W. 832 (1911).
[214] See chap. viii, "Administration."

CHAPTER IV

SAFETY AND HEALTH

PROMINENT AMONG THE PROBLEMS WHICH THE INDUSTRIAL Revolution brought in its wake is that of maintaining safety and health in work places. As long as industry was chiefly agricultural, or carried on about the family hearth, with tools relatively few and simple, the individual laborer might control the physical conditions under which he worked. But the drift during the late eighteenth and early nineteenth centuries from farming to manufacturing, and from homestead to factory methods, placed a growing proportion of wage earners in a new environment. They toiled now upon premises controlled not by themselves, but by another—the employer. Instead of working in isolation or in small groups, hundreds were collected under one roof where the error or illness of one might affect all his neighbors. New machinery, new chemical processes, new forces such as electricity and compressed air have been ceaselessly developed, each involving its own special dangers. Upon all production, speed, the ruling spirit of a machine age, has imposed its exactions. Nor have subjective factors been without their influence. Ignorance, recklessness, and inertia, manifested now by the leaders of technical research, now by the masters of industry, and not infrequently by the workers themselves, have contributed to create a situation in which the statistics of industrial accident and disease are often justly compared with those of the world's great battles.

Conservation of the life, health, and energy of our millions of wage earners is not an individual question. It is a social question, demanding social action. This does not mean that private or voluntary efforts of the workmen, or of industrial managers, or of physicians should be in any way discouraged. On the contrary, such voluntary efforts should be vastly increased. But the prevention of industrial accidents and diseases

SAFETY AND HEALTH

is too great an undertaking to be left entirely to individual action.

Although about half of the waking hours of the ordinary wage earner are spent at his place of employment, it is one of the fundamental disharmonies of present-day industry that he has little or no control over the conditions which there surround him, and which profoundly affect his well-being and even his life. Individual complaint frequently leads to loss of employment rather than to improvement of conditions. As a member of a labor union the worker's power is potentially increased, but often, for various reasons, is not effectively exerted. Regulation of the physical conditions of employment, on the other hand, cannot be safely intrusted to the individual employer, whose principal business, under competitive conditions, is to secure profits. While many employers are exercising the utmost consideration for their work people out of motives of humanity, and many more are doing so on grounds of efficiency, such motives cannot be said to have developed into a controlling principle of industrial life. Nor can the industrial accident and disease problem be left to medical treatment alone, for prevention and not after-care is the solution. Not only on account of the magnitude of the problem, but also because of its nature, the protection of the wage earner from dangerous conditions of employment is a proper function of government.

Frequently, it happens that without the aid of uniform legal regulations to force the recalcitrant minority into line, even a vast majority of the manufacturers in an industry are powerless to bring about reforms which they freely admit are desirable. A striking example of this was revealed by the three-year campaign which culminated successfully in the poisonous phosphorous prohibition act. Match manufacturers representing 95 per cent of the total product testified before Congress that they could not substitute a harmless compound for the slightly cheaper poison without a uniform law compelling all employers in that industry to abandon the poison. All of the other match manufacturers, representing the remaining 5 per cent of the product, stood out stoutly to the last, even declaring that they would close their factories before they would submit to this sanitary measure, already in compulsory operation in practically all civilized countries of the world.

It required labor legislation to end the use of this unnecessary deadly poison before "phossy jaw," the most loathsome of all industrial diseases, could be abolished.

Legislative activities for the control of industrial accidents and occupational diseases have developed in all important countries along four main lines, namely, (1) reporting, (2) prohibition, (3) regulation, and (4) compensation or insurance. All four lines of activity are closely interrelated, and depend for success largely upon one another. Reporting of accidents and diseases is purposeless unless it leads to prohibition or regulation of the sources of danger, and is likely to be incomplete if not made part of a proper system of compensation administration. Effort for prohibition and regulation gropes in the dark without the light of experience made available through thorough reporting, and is apt to be feeble unless stimulated by the cooperative financial pressure exerted by compensation. Compensation, in turn, is deprived, by lack of careful reports, of the necessary actuarial basis for successful operation, and accomplishes but the minor part of its purpose if the payment of benefits fails to lead to systematic efforts at prohibition or regulation. Upon the combined development of all four devices depends the efficacy of the modern legislative movement for the protection of the industrial worker's life, limb, and health. Leaving the fourth step, compensation, for treatment under "Social Insurance," we shall discuss in this chapter the first three methods of attack.

1. Reporting

While in many matters of social interest the gathering of statistics is well developed, in others only the beginnings have been made. In industry, for example, we know much about the value of the raw materials and of the product, but too little about the accidents and diseases which are entailed upon the workers in the creation of that product. Yet there can be no more important link in the whole chain of social effort for the prevention of industrial death and disability than securing accurate data as to the nature of the hazards, their extent, and the particular industries and establishments in which they are most rife. The acquisition of this knowledge is an integral part of the modern movement for the protection of life and

SAFETY AND HEALTH

health. It reveals the "sore spots" of industry. Not only does it point out conditions introduced by changing methods in manufacture and elsewhere which call for correction, but after corrective legislation has been secured it acts as a valuable guide to and index of the efficacy of the administrative authorities.

Such information, however, until comparatively recent years, had been intelligently sought, if at all, only incidentally by special commissions which investigated some more pressing phase of industrial abuse, submitted their reports, and disbanded. The idea of a permanent census on the matter has been of tardy development.

1. **Accidents.**—It was not until 1886 that any American state placed an accident-reporting law upon its statute books, and again, as in several other phases of early labor legislation, it was Massachusetts which took the lead. By the act of June 1, 1886, manufacturing and mercantile corporations were required to report to the chief of the district police, the organization which then had charge of factory inspection, accidents occurring in their establishments and causing death or four or more days' disability. A penalty was provided for failure to comply. Four years later the law was extended to apply to all proprietors of the designated classes of establishments, instead of only to corporations. Similar statutes were enacted in Ohio in 1888, Missouri in 1891, Rhode Island in 1896, and elsewhere during the same decade.

These early laws did not bring satisfactory results. Employers appeared reluctant to give their establishments an unenviable reputation for danger. Official enforcement, too, was lax. Prosecutions for failure to report were rare, and the imposition of the stated penalties still rarer. "In none of them," said a federal investigator, in 1897, of eight states which then had reporting laws, "is there any pretense that anything like complete returns of accidents are obtained."[1]

Since that time, in spite of its shortcomings and inadequacies, so useful has reporting proved itself as a guide for inspection, safeguarding, and advanced legislation, that it has steadily spread not only to new states, but to new branches of

[1] United States Bureau of Labor, *Bulletin No. 12*, September, 1897, p. 565.

industry.[2] The kind of accidents to be reported varies greatly, ranging from all injuries in the more advanced states to only those which result in death or in the incapacity of the injured workman for a stated length of time, as for two days, one week, and in rare cases for two weeks. The time of reporting is variously fixed at "immediately," twenty-four or forty-eight hours, two weeks, once a month, and, in Louisiana, "semiannually." Notification by mail, on a blank provided by the proper state authority, is in most cases sufficient; but in connection with fatal railway and street-car accidents a telephone or telegraph report, followed by a detailed written statement, is often obligatory. Reports are usually made to the state factory inspection or accident compensation authorities, and a wide range of questions must be answered. A standard schedule adopted for use in important industrial states containing about half the manufacturing wage earners of the country is divided into sections on (1) employer, place, and time; (2) injured person; (3) cause; and (4) nature and extent of injury; and each section asks a number of questions found by long experience and careful study to be most successful in eliciting the desired information.[3]

While much progress has been made since the beginning of the reporting movement in 1886, much remains to be done in the direction of extending and of introducing uniformity into the system. In a few states, and for a limited number of industries, good work is being done;[4] but the failure to cover

[2] A standard bill for industrial accident reports, drafted by the American Association for Labor Legislation in 1912, has been passed in several states.

[3] This schedule was prepared by the American Association for Labor Legislation, and was indorsed by the American Statistical Association, the United States Bureau of Labor Statistics, the Workmen's Compensation Service Bureau, and the National Safety Council. By October 1, 1915, it had been adopted by the labor departments of California, Iowa, Massachusetts, Minnesota, Nevada, New Hampshire, New York, Pennsylvania, and Washington. In 1920, it was adopted, with a few revisions, as a standard by the committee on statistics and compensation insurance cost of the International Association of Industrial Accident Boards and Commissions.

[4] Especially excellent is the reporting work done by several industrial accident or workmen's compensation boards, notably those of California, Massachusetts, New York, Ohio, and Wisconsin.

SAFETY AND HEALTH

all dangerous occupations and the wide differences in the meaning of reportable accident still render the data confusing and incomparable as between states. For a comprehensive view of the situation in all industries and throughout the country, dependence for the present must be placed on the more or less scholarly estimates which appear from time to time.

The United States Commission on Industrial Relations estimated that in 1915 there were 35,000 industrial deaths and 700,000 non-fatal injuries causing over four weeks' disability.[5] Mr. F. S. Crum, of the Prudential Insurance Company, set the number of industrial deaths in 1919 at 23,000.[6] Mr. Sidney J. Williams, secretary of the National Safety Council, estimated the number of industrial fatalities for 1919 at 23,000, and of non-fatal injuries as 2,977,000.[7] The late Mr. Carl Hookstadt, of the United States Bureau of Labor Statistics, estimated in 1923 that under normal industrial conditions there are annually some 2,453,418 industrial accidents in the United States, of which 21,232 are fatal.[8] In 1930, H. W. Heinrich, of the Travelers Insurance Company, estimated that the number of industrial fatalities in the United States was 25,000 annually, and the number of all lost-time injuries, including fatalities, 3,000,000.[9] Recently, the National Safety Council has issued an annual estimate of the number of occupational accidents. The estimate for 1935 was 16,500 killed and 1,403,000 injured.[10] This, however, was a depression year with decreased employment.

Some indication of the relative hazard of various industries is found in the data on accident severity and frequency rates compiled by the National Safety Council each year on the basis of reports received from a large number of establishments. The National Safety Council's figures for 1935, with industries arranged in order of accident frequency, are given in the table on page 165. The "frequency rate" represents the number of

[5] United States Commission on Industrial Relations, *Final Report*, p. 95.
[6] Quoted in United States Bureau of Labor Statistics, *Bulletin No. 304*, p. 59.
[7] United States Bureau of Labor Statistics, *Bulletin No. 304*, pp. 59-60.
[8] United States Department of Labor, *Monthly Labor Review*, November, 1923, pp. 1-9.
[9] United States Bureau of Labor Statistics, *Bulletin No. 541*, p. 314.
[10] National Safety Council, *Accident Facts*, 1936, p. 54.

disabling injuries per million man-hours of exposure. The "severity rate" is the number of days lost, as the result of disabling injuries, per thousand man-hours of exposure, including charges for permanent disabilities and deaths.

Lumbering and mining appear to be the most dangerous.[11] Meat packing, construction, and foundry work are high on the list, while rubber, textiles, and printing and publishing are found among the relatively less hazardous. Agriculture, which is not shown on the Safety Council's table, appears to be one of the more hazardous occupations, accounting for an estimated 4,400 deaths in 1935. What these thousands of accidents, occurring in every industrial state and country, mean in terms of suffering, interrupted wage earning, lowering of efficiency, and deterioration of standard of living, our compensation laws are at last beginning to reveal with something like scientific accuracy.

2. **Occupational Diseases.**—Hardly, if any, less serious than the misery and waste caused by industrial accident is that entailed through the more insidious danger of occupational disease.

Occupational disease has been defined as "morbid results of occupational activity traceable to specific causes or labor conditions, and followed by more or less extended incapacity for work."[12] American interest in the subject is mainly a product of recent years. In 1910 it was possible to record only the appointment of the Illinois Occupational Disease Commission, the completion of an investigation of phosphorous poisoning in the match industry, and the holding of the First National Conference on Industrial Diseases, an expert committee of which drew up a memorial on the subject for presentation to the President of the United States. Practically all of the many

[11] The inaccuracy of available accident statistics, as well as differences in classification and statistical method, makes tabulations of this type somewhat variable. Mr. Hookstadt's study (see United States Bureau of Labor Statistics, *Monthly Labor Review,* November, 1923, pp. 1-9) found the electric light and power industry most dangerous, for example, with lumbering, water transportation, and police duty all preceding mining in order of hazard.

[12] "Memorial on Occupational Diseases," *American Labor Legislation Review,* vol. i, no. 1, January, 1911, pp. 125-143.

SAFETY AND HEALTH

ACCIDENTAL INJURY RATES BY INDUSTRIES, 1935 [13]

Industry	Number of Units Reporting	Man-hours of Exposure (000's)	Accident Frequency Rate (per million hours' exposure)	Accident Severity Rate (per thousand hours' exposure)
Lumbering	33	23,272	62.69	3.83
Mining	134	54,978	49.46	10.14
Meat packing	70	147,276	29.22	1.51
Construction	73	135,872	28.24	4.52
Refrigeration	62	18,866	25.71	2.91
Foundry	120	68,475	25.37	1.40
Clay products	37	15,750	20.19	1.53
Automobile	56	266,606	19.68	1.11
Woodworking	96	29,002	18.17	.96
Electric railway	45	120,359	17.46	1.60
Paper and pulp	234	162,310	17.12	1.94
Food	411	263,079	15.52	1.08
Sheet metal	179	129,414	14.97	1.07
Miscellaneous metal products	158	125,799	14.06	1.03
Petroleum	133	643,524	14.04	1.61
Tanning and leather	70	52,108	13.38	.52
Non-ferrous metals	61	103,413	10.72	1.63
Marine	55	121,936	10.23	1.89
Quarry	119	12,332	10.22	1.72
Public utilities	558	541,415	10.20	1.91
Chemical	282	240,396	9.53	1.03
Glass	43	51,023	9.35	.79
Machinery	241	405,991	9.35	.79
Steel	106	422,327	8.86	2.04
Textile	125	147,863	8.38	.67
Printing and publishing	38	21,916	7.25	.46
Rubber	43	118,038	7.21	.53
Cement	119	31,042	6.73	2.78
Laundry	44	12,374	5.66	.08
Tobacco	25	23,804	1.89	.10
Total[a]	3,796	4,564,922	14.02	1.58

[a] Includes miscellaneous industries, and is corrected for certain duplications.

interesting American investigations and reports on this subject have been made since that time.

The principal industrial health risks, as far as we now know them, may be conveniently classified according to their nature as follows: (1) dangerous gases, acids, and dusts (poisonous

[13] Source: National Safety Council, 1936 Edition of *Accident Facts*.

and non-poisonous); (2) harmful bacteria and microorganisms; (3) compressed or rarefied atmospheres; (4) improper lighting; (5) extremes of temperature and humidity; (6) excessive strain. Almost every calling involves danger from one or more of these.

Considering merely the industrial poisons, "those raw materials and products, by-products, and waste products which, in their extraction, manufacture, and use in industrial processes, notwithstanding the exercise of ordinary precaution, may find entrance into the body in such quantities as to endanger by their chemical action the health of the workman employed," we find already prepared a careful list of ninety-four,[14] one of which alone, lead, is in daily use in about 150 trades, causing "painters' colic," "wrist drop," or even death. Connected with dusty trades of all sorts, from silk-weaving to quarrying, are found non-poisonous dusts which by infiltration and mechanical irritation produce various occupational lung diseases. One of the most common of these is silicosis, a disease of the lungs common among rock drillers, granite cutters and others who work over a period of years in an atmosphere loaded with fine silica dust. The bacillus of anthrax, moreover, may infect tanners and workers on hair goods, while ankylostomiasis, or "miners' hookworm," menaces those who toil in warmth and moisture underground. The tunnel and caisson worker dreads compressed-air illness. Less easy to trace, but perhaps even more widespread, are the obscure ailments which may arise in any industry, from insufficient or excessive lighting, from extremes of heat, cold, and humidity, or from work too heavy, too persistent, and too intense without adequate periods of rest.

Incomplete as is our information on the prevalence and seriousness of industrial accidents, even more incomplete is it with regard to specific trade maladies, some of which are now being recorded in our hospitals and dispensaries. The first American law for the compulsory reporting of these diseases was drafted by the Association for Labor Legislation after investigation of similar legislation in England, and was enacted in California in March, 1911. Within five years, as the result of vigorous and sustained effort, sixteen states enacted similar

[14] United States Bureau of Labor Statistics, *Bulletin No. 582,* "Occupation Hazards and Diagnostic Signs," 1933.

SAFETY AND HEALTH

legislation. In 1934 such disease reporting was required by law in twenty states.[15] The earliest of these laws called for reports on all cases of anthrax, compressed-air illness, and poisoning from lead, phosphorous, arsenic, mercury, or their compounds,[16] to which were later added brass and wood alcohol poisoning.[17] The more recent tendency, however, is to make the laws include "any ailment or disease contracted as a result of the nature of the patient's employment."[18]

The duty of reporting falls upon the physician, who may be either a general practitioner treating the case, or, in states requiring a monthly medical examination of workers in specially hazardous trades, the physician making such examination. A standard certificate adopted in a number of the reporting states[19] requires the name and address of both employee and employer, the nature of the business, the diagnosis and symptoms of the disease, and other pertinent information. In most cases reports must be made to the state labor department, but occasionally they go to the board of health, which transmits them to the labor department. Reporting of occupational diseases has been further stimulated by their inclusion as compensable injuries in a score of the American compensation laws.[20] In a number of these laws only specified diseases are covered; but under a dozen of them all occupational diseases clearly identifiable as such are compensable, and disease reporting covers a wide field.

Reliable statistical data for the country as a whole are, however, still lacking. Again we must fall back on estimates. Careful American authorities declared in 1910, on the basis of German experience, that if our gainfully occupied popula-

[15] Alabama, Arizona, Connecticut, Georgia, Illinois, Kansas, Maine, Maryland, Massachusetts, Michigan, Minnesota, Missouri, New Hampshire, New Mexico, New York, Ohio, Oregon, Pennsylvania, Rhode Island, and Wisconsin.
[16] California, Laws 1911, C. 485.
[17] Connecticut, Laws 1913, C. 14; New York, Laws 1913, C. 145.
[18] See Mettert, Margaret T., "State Reporting of Occupational Disease," U. S. Department of Labor, Women's Bureau, *Bulletin No. 114*, 1934.
[19] Like the standard accident schedule, this certificate was drafted after careful study by the Association for Labor Legislation.
[20] See chap. v, "Social Insurance."

tion was numbered at 33,500,000, no fewer than 284,000,000 days' illness occur annually, causing a social and economic waste of nearly $750,000,000.[21] Of this enormous waste, fully one-quarter, it was computed, could be prevented by deliberate effort, largely in the direction of greater care and cleanliness in the nation's workshops. The engineers' Committee on Elimination of Waste in Industry estimated in 1921 that "the 42,000,000 men and women gainfully employed probably lose on an average more than eight days each annually from illness disabilities, including non-industrial accidents—a total of 350,000,000 days," and that "the economic loss from preventable disease and death is $1,800,000,000 among those classed as gainfully employed— or over $700,000,000 among industrial workers in the more limited meaning of the term."[22] The report stated further that "there is experiential basis for the statement that this loss could be materially reduced and leave an economic balance in the working population alone, over and above the cost of prevention, of at least $1,000,000,000 a year." In 1936, an authoritative estimate placed the annual loss in earnings because of sickness at about $1,500,000,000, of which $900,000,000 represented losses to persons earning less than $2,500 a year. Medical costs to this lower-income group, it was estimated, amount to about a billion and a half dollars.[23] Many unhealthful conditions in industry, also, while they may not lead to actual absence from work, are nevertheless productive of unnecessary physical discomfort which reacts badly on the worker's health and strength. The effects of these daily minor drains upon industrial efficiency are necessarily difficult to trace or to measure, but they must in the aggregate be enormous.

II. Prohibition

The method of prohibition for the safeguarding of industrial workers is usually resorted to only under severe provocation. At times it appears to be the only effective way of removing

[21] *Memorial on Occupational Diseases.*

[22] Committee on Elimination of Waste in Industry of the Federated American Engineering Societies, *Waste in Industry*, 1921, p. 21.

[23] See Falk, I. S., *Security Against Sickness*, 1936, chap. ii, "The Cost of Sickness."

SAFETY AND HEALTH

an intolerable industrial hazard, and instances of its use are multiplying.

There are two ways in which the prohibitive method may be applied. First, it may be used to exclude from employment those most susceptible to danger, whether children, women, or certain classes of men. Second, it may be used to outlaw the substances or instruments which render employment dangerous.

1. **Exclusion of Persons**: a. *Children.*—Provisions for the exclusion of persons from industrial pursuits have been carried further with regard to children than with regard to any other group of wage earners, on the general theory that the child is the special ward of the state and most in need of special measures of protection. The dangers thus sought to be guarded against may be to the child's life, limb, health, or morals,[24] and the restrictions which have grown up are based on considerations of age, physique, and education.

(1) Age Requirements.—The past century has witnessed an almost complete reversal of public opinion as to the proper age at which children should become breadwinners. Without scruple, and even in the belief that they were acting charitably, the American colonists received from England as bound apprentices large numbers of orphans and children of the poor, ten to sixteen years of age, some even as young as seven years. Laws were passed to keep these boys and girls profitably employed, partly for the benefit of the community and partly to save them from the dangers of idleness. When manufactures arose, Alexander Hamilton approved of them as rendering children "more useful and . . . more early useful than they would otherwise be."[25]

These colonial traditions have now gone down before a standard of working age based on the observed harmful effects of premature labor. In 1848[26] Pennsylvania forbade the employment in textile establishments of children under twelve, a standard which it the following year[27] raised to thirteen.

Within the next decade a twelve-year limit was established

---

[24] See, for instance, Massachusetts General Laws 1921, C. 149, Secs. 61-66.
[25] Alexander Hamilton, *Works,* vol. iii, p. 207.
[26] Pennsylvania, Laws 1848, No. 227.
[27] *Ibid.,* Laws 1849, No. 415.

170   PRINCIPLES OF LABOR LEGISLATION

in Rhode Island,[28] and a ten-year limit in New Jersey[29] and Connecticut;[30] in all three states the law covered manufactures, and in Connecticut it covered mechanical establishments also. In none of these states was any proof of age required, and enforcement was everywhere very lax.

The first state to provide a special officer to see that its age restrictions on the employment of children were obeyed was Massachusetts, in its law of 1867.[31] The previous year, following a report by a commission on hours of labor, a law had been passed forbidding the employment of children under ten years of age in manufacturing establishments. The governor at his discretion might instruct the state constable and his deputies to enforce the law. It seems, however, that the governor did not see fit to give such instructions; and in 1867, when the act was amended to cover mechanical establishments as well as manufacturing, it was made a duty of the state constable to detail a deputy to enforce all laws regulating the employment of children.

About this same period the national labor organizations became active in demanding the legal prohibition of child labor below a minimum age limit. In 1876 laws against the employment of children under fourteen years of age were advocated by the Working Men's Party at a congress in Philadelphia, and about the same time the Knights of Labor took a stand for the prohibition by law of their employment under fifteen years of age in workshops, mines, and factories. The American Federation of Labor, organized later, indorsed the same standard. Since then many influential societies and women's clubs, as well as labor organizations, have supported and worked for the legal prohibition of child labor. In 1904 the National Child Labor Committee was formed to act as a clearing house for information on child labor, to investigate conditions, to educate public opinion, and to promote legislation.

The result of the work of this national committee and the

[28] Rhode Island, Laws 1853, p. 245.
[29] New Jersey, Laws 1851, p. 321.
[30] Connecticut, Laws 1856, C. 45.
[31] Massachusetts, Laws 1867, C. 285.
[32] The minimum age was sixteen in Connecticut, Montana, New York, Ohio, Pennsylvania, Rhode Island, Utah, and Wisconsin; and it was fifteen in California, Maine, Michigan, and Texas.

SAFETY AND HEALTH

various agencies that have cooperated with it is a large body of legislation restricting the employment of children. All states now forbid the employment of children in one or more kinds of work until they have passed a fixed age limit. A minimum age limit of at least fourteen years[32] was by 1936 established for general factory work in all the states except Wyoming,[33] but in two[34] the restriction applied only to work during school hours, and in four[35] children under fourteen could be exempted because of poverty. In most states documentary proof of a child's age is demanded, and working permits or employment certificates must be obtained by the children and placed on file in the establishment before they can be employed therein.

The age limit in some of the earliest child labor laws applied only to cotton and woolen factories and to a few other special industries where the evils of child labor were supposed to be most flagrant. In other laws the prohibition was general for all work in "manufacturing or mechanical establishments." It is only in comparatively recent years that the minimum age limit for employment has been applied in the majority of states to mercantile establishments and other places of employment as well as to factories. In most states children under fourteen years of age are excluded from employment in a list of establishments including—in addition to factories, mills, workshops, and stores—certain other places, such as hotels, restaurants, laundries, bowling alleys, and theaters, where conditions appeared to warrant such exclusion.

Nevertheless, most of the state laws are defective in that they fail to cover all the occupations from which children should be excluded. In fact, the rapidly changing industrial conditions render it practically impossible to draw up a list of occupations that will be complete for any length of time, even though it is complete at the time the law is enacted. The tendency of those who are experienced in drafting child labor laws

---

[33] Wyoming excludes children under sixteen from certain especially dangerous manufacturing processes and requires school attendance up to seventeen years.

[34] Nevada and New Mexico. In addition, many other states permitted work outside of school hours in specified cases. (See latest revision of "Child Labor Facts and Figures," U. S. Department of Labor, Children's Bureau.)

[35] Delaware, South Dakota, Texas, Washington.

now is to use the general term, "in any gainful occupation," instead of a specified list. Agriculture and domestic service are, however, frequently exempted from this general prohibition.

The fact that so much progress has been made in the enactment of child labor legislation, and that the fourteen-year limit has been so generally established, especially for factory work, does not mean that premature employment of children is eradicated. There is serious danger that since the most sensational stages in the fight against child labor have passed, public opinion will become apathetic and not perceive the inadequacies of laws that may have at one time been a great step in advance. Unfortunately, most of the laws bear the scars of conflicts with shortsighted legislators as well as with powerful interests who either looked upon the employment of children as necessary to their prosperity or considered prohibitive legislation an encroachment on their business rights. Exemptions—chief of which has been the exemption of the "poor widow's" child and children of "dependent parents," a relic of the days of the Elizabethan poor law—have been the curse of child labor laws.

Recognizing that securing and perfecting protective legislation state by state was likely to be a tedious process which would result at best in undesirable diversity of standards, opponents of child labor turned to federal action. Accordingly, in 1916 Congress enacted a measure which forbade the transportation in interstate commerce of the products of factories in which children under fourteen had been employed, or in which children between fourteen and sixteen had worked more than eight hours a day or six days a week or at night. The same prohibition was applied to products of mines employing children under sixteen.[36]

One day before the act was to have gone into effect a permanent injunction was secured restraining its enforcement in a North Carolina court district. The person who sued out the injunction was a poor cotton-mill operative who asked not to be deprived of the wages of his two boys. He was represented, however, by counsel from New York and from two North Carolina cities, and the strongest opposition to the measure while before Congress had come from southern mill-owners.

[36] United States, C. 432, Sixty-fourth Congress, First Session.

SAFETY AND HEALTH

The United States Supreme Court, to which the matter was appealed, held the law unconstitutional as an undue extension of the power to regulate interstate commerce.[37]

Undeterred by this reverse, the friends of child labor restriction continued their efforts. In 1919 Congress again enacted the protective standards which had been temporarily overthrown two years earlier. Instead of seeking authority through the power to regulate interstate commerce, the act was this time based on the taxing power. That is, a prohibitive tax of 10 per cent was levied on the annual net profits of any concern which employed children in violation of the standards named. As the "power to tax" had repeatedly been held to include the "power to destroy," it appeared probable that the court would uphold the new act. In so doing it would merely have sanctioned the same method for protecting children against premature or excessive labor that has already been upheld for protecting bankers against undue inflation of the currency, dairy farmers against attractively colored oleomargarine, and workers in the match industry against phosphorus poisoning.[38] However, the same North Carolina federal district judge who enjoined the enforcement of the earlier statute declared the second measure also unconstitutional, and in May, 1922, the United States Supreme Court upheld this decision.[39] The court argued that, though a tax law in form, the act was clearly regulatory in purpose and that Congress could not thus extend its powers into the field of social legislation. By these two decisions the court effectively blocked the use—for the protection of the country's children—of either of the two traditional sources of the federal police power.

But the problem still remained. The 1920 census showed more than a million[40] children between the ages of ten and fifteen gainfully employed in the United States; yet this census was taken in the winter months when agricultural employment

[37] Hammer v. Dagenhart, 247 U. S. 251, 38 Sup. Ct. 529 (1918).

[38] See Parkinson, Thomas J., "Child Labor and the Constitution," *American Labor Legislation Review,* June, 1922, pp. 110-113.

[39] Bailey v. Drexel Furniture Company, 259 U. S. 20, 42 Sup. Ct. 449 (1922).

[40] United States Department of Labor, Children's Bureau, "Child Labor in the United States," *Publication No. 114,* 1924, p. 5.

174 PRINCIPLES OF LABOR LEGISLATION

of children was at the lowest figure. Moreover, it represents conditions during the period when the second federal child labor law was in force. Available data indicate that the employment of children increased markedly after this law was invalidated.[41] The United States Children's Bureau reported in 1924 that only eighteen states measured up to the relatively conservative standards of the recent federal laws in regard to work in factories, canneries, mills, and workshops, and that only thirteen states measured up to these standards in all respects.[42] The need for federal action was still apparent, and the only remaining approach appeared to be through amendment of the federal Constitution. A constitutional amendment permitting Congress to prohibit and regulate the labor of children under eighteen years of age was accordingly prepared and urged by the supporters of child labor legislation and was passed by Congress in 1924. To become effective this amendment must be ratified by three-fourths of the states. By June, 1936, twenty-four states[43] had given their assent.

Ratification of the federal child labor amendment was stimulated[44] between 1933 and 1935 by the almost uniform adoption of a sixteen-year age minimum requirement in the codes of fair competition under the National Industrial Recovery Act. This temporary effort to "abolish child labor" gave the movement for a permanent sixteen-year minimum a strong foundation; and a gradual increase in the number of children employed following the nullification of the Recovery Act demonstrated the need for national legislation.

But even in the absence of federal legislation the country is fast approaching the basic standard of a draft convention adopted by the first International Labor Conference in October, 1919, prohibiting the employment of children under fourteen

[41] Testimony of Miss Grace Abbott, Chief of the Children's Bureau, United States Department of Labor, at the hearings on the proposed child labor constitutional amendment before the House Judiciary Committee, Sixty-eighth Congress, First Session, February and March, 1924. See especially pp. 37-39.
[42] *Ibid.*, p. 18.
[43] For list see footnote 34, p. 98.
[44] During 1933, twelve states ratified the amendment, followed by two in 1934, and four in 1935. Prior to 1933 only six states had ratified.

SAFETY AND HEALTH

years of age in industrial undertakings.[45] By January, 1936, this convention had been ratified by twenty-six countries.

In addition to the minimum age of fourteen for entrance to general factory work, many American states set a limit of sixteen years for certain more dangerous processes, and in some states an additional two years' maturity is required for entrance to a number of extra hazardous occupations. The first group of occupations may include such employments as the cleaning and oiling of machinery, the adjusting of belts, the operation of machine saws or of stamping, washing, grinding, and mixing machines, and the manufacture of lead products or of compositions containing poisonous acids; while in the second group is work in mines, at blast furnaces, or on railroads, in the outside erection of electric wires, and in the manufacture of explosives. Some states have established minimum limits as high as eighteen or even twenty-one for night messenger service or other morally dangerous work. A growing tendency is manifest to give to state boards of health or state labor departments power to add to the lists of dangerous and extra hazardous employments.[46]

Age restrictions for entrance to dangerous occupations have been repeatedly upheld as a valid exercise of the police power,[47] and the provision empowering health authorities and others to extend the lists of prohibited occupations for children of certain ages has been held not to be an unwarranted delegation of legislative authority.[48] In some states where illegally employed children are not covered by workmen's accident compensation or where they may sue for damages even though covered, illegal employment of a child deprives the employer of the defenses of assumption of risk and contributory negligence in case of a

---

[45] Conventions dealing with minimum age for employment at sea, in agriculture, and in trimming and stoking, and for non-industrial employment were adopted at the second, third and sixteenth International Labor Conferences, respectively.

[46] See "Report of Advisory Committee on Employment of Minors in Hazardous Occupations," U. S. Bureau of Labor Statistics, *Monthly Labor Review,* December, 1932, pp. 1315-1322.

[47] Lenahan *v.* Pittston Coal Mining Co., 218 Pa. 311, 67 Atl. 642 (1907).

[48] Louisville, Henderson & St. Louis R. Co. *v.* Lyons, 155 Ky. 39, 159 S. W. 971 (1913).

damage suit for accidental injury. Several states, in an effort to secure adequate redress for the injured child and at the same time to help enforce the child labor laws, have provided in their workmen's compensation laws that in case a minor is injured while illegally employed his compensation award shall be one-and-a-half, two, or even three times the normal amount.[49] In a majority, the employer must himself pay the extra amount.

All the important countries of Europe possess similar graduated restrictions upon engaging in remunerative employment at too extreme youth, and the principle of adding to the lists of prohibited occupations by administrative authorities is well established. Frequently, also, the authorities are permitted to allow exemptions from the application of the laws.[50]

A serious shortcoming of most of our child labor laws is their failure to deal adequately with child labor on city streets. We have more or less thoroughly prohibited the premature employment of children in factories, stores, and other places, but have inconsistently allowed boys and girls of tender years to be exposed to perhaps a worse moral and physical environment in vending newspapers, gum, and other articles on the streets, without sufficient regulation. In 1929 only one state, Kentucky, had the same age limit, fourteen years, for all street trades as for other employment. Several states have a fourteen-year limit for bootblacking and peddling, and a twelve-year limit for newsboys. So far only about half the states[51] have passed laws regulating the employment of children in street trades, and in these the prevailing age limit for newsboys is twelve years. Because

[49] Alabama (2), Illinois (1½), Indiana (2), Maryland (2), Massachusetts (2), Michigan (2), Missouri (1½), New Hampshire (2), New Jersey (2), New York (2), Pennsylvania (2), Utah (2), and Wisconsin (3).

[50] For discussion of such legislation, see Matthews, E. N., "The Illegally Employed Minor and the Workmen's Compensation Law," U. S. Department of Labor, Children's Bureau, *Publication No. 214*, 1932.

[51] By the beginning of 1936, legislation on this subject was found in Alabama, Arizona, California, Colorado (girls only), Delaware, District of Columbia, Florida, Iowa, Kentucky, Maryland, Massachusetts, Minnesota, New Hampshire, New Jersey, New York, North Carolina, Oklahoma (girls only), Pennsylvania, Puerto Rico, Rhode Island, Utah, Virginia, and Wisconsin.

SAFETY AND HEALTH

of the additional moral danger to girls, the age limit for them is usually four or six years higher than for boys.

Suggestions frequently have been made that a uniform age limit for all regular gainful occupations is not scientific, as some children are more mature and fit to work at thirteen years of age than others are at fifteen. No practical method has yet been found, however, of determining the physiological age of children, and the age limit will probably always prove the most satisfactory standard. The purpose of the minimum age is to prevent improper toil before the child has passed the most formative period of adolescence, and also to give the child a chance for a necessary minimum of education. Recent scientific studies of the physical effects of modern industry on children and of the educational needs of children in industry, indicate that the fourteen-year limit is not adequate in either of the above respects.[52] There is a strong tendency in the more advanced states to eliminate all children under sixteen from industry. By 1936, eight states had adopted the sixteen-year minimum age for employment—Connecticut, Montana, New York, Ohio, Pennsylvania, Rhode Island, Utah, and Wisconsin. Several of these, however, permitted employment at fourteen outside of school hours, and the Montana law applied only to factories. Four other states had a fifteen-year minimum—Texas for factories, and California, Maine and Michigan for most occupations during school hours. Almost all of the codes of fair competition in effect between 1933 and 1935 under the National Industrial Recovery Act prohibited employment of children under sixteen. Industries of the best type are finding that children under sixteen do not pay. Organized labor also has taken a determined stand for the sixteen-year minimum age for employment, and for a sixteen-year compulsory education limit. Educators are generally accepting this as the standard that must eventually be adopted, with the additional requirement

[52] See, for instance, Woolley, Helen T., *An Experimental Study of Children at Work and in School*, 1926; New York Department of Labor, Bureau of Women in Industry, "The Health of the Working Child," *Special Bulletin No. 147*, 1926; Fuller, Raymond G., *Fourteen Is too Early*, National Child Labor Committee, 1927; *Child Labor*, Report of the Subcommittee on Child Labor, White House Conference on Child Health and Protection, 1932.

of day continuation school classes for employed children under eighteen who have not completed high school.[53]

(2) Physical Requirements.—While it may be impracticable to substitute a physiological for the ordinary chronological age test, it is nevertheless true that physical development as well as age should determine the child's eligibility for employment. So far state laws have not designated any standard physical requirements, but have merely contained the general provision that children must be physically fit. At the beginning of 1936, a physical examination of all applicants for certificates was required by statute in twenty-five states.[54] In several other states the official granting employment certificates is authorized to ask for the physical examination of the applicant if he considers him of doubtful health and strength.

Because of the lack of definite standards, these examinations depend for their value almost entirely on the physician who happens to make them. In New York City, for instance, the physical examination of applicants for certificates is well standardized. Blanks are used in the examination of each child which include not only the height and weight, but a test of the eyesight and hearing, and an examination of the condition of the teeth, the heart, the lungs, throat, and nostrils, and the general physical condition. The same blanks are used throughout the state, but in smaller towns they are usually very poorly filled out. Similar uniform blanks are in use in several other states.

If the physical examination is to be a real test of the child's fitness, the medical examiner must know the prospective place of employment and have a knowledge of the conditions and processes in the various industries in which children are employed. Under the English law, accordingly, the certifying physician must examine the child in the factory where he is

[53] See, for example, recommendations of Subcommittee on Child Labor, White House Conference on Child Health and Protection (*Child Labor,* 1932, pp. 3-11).

[54] Alabama, Arizona, California, Connecticut, Delaware, Georgia, Illinois, Indiana, Iowa, Kentucky, Louisiana, Maryland, Massachusetts, Minnesota, Missouri, New Hampshire, New Jersey, New York, North Carolina, Ohio, Pennsylvania, Rhode Island, Tennessee, Virginia, West Virginia, and Wisconsin (Milwaukee only). The Massachusetts act (Laws 1906, C. 502) was the first of this type.

SAFETY AND HEALTH

entering employment, and if the child changes employment he must be reexamined in the same manner.[55] Wherever medical examination of children in the public schools is extensively developed, the records of the child's physical progress should be kept in such form that they may be compared with the examination at the time the child proposes to leave school. In smaller cities the simplest arrangement is for the school medical examiner to make the examinations of children applying for certificates. Whether school or health authorities are responsible for these examinations, it is desirable that the number of authorized examiners be small in order that uniform standards may be applied and that the examining physicians may acquire familiarity with the specialized industrial problems. It is also essential that some sort of state supervision be exercised.[56]

A single examination at the time of application for employment certificates, however, even when it has been put on a more scientific basis than at present, will not be sufficient protection for the health of working children. In order that children may not be injured by the work they do, examinations must be repeated periodically.

Theoretically, reexamination is automatically brought about in those states which require a new employment certificate or a personal renewal of the certificate with every change of employment. In practice, however, the procedure for reissuance of certificates to children who were once employed is frequently most perfunctory. A few states give children additional health protection by empowering child-labor-law-enforcing officials to require physical examination of employed children who appear physically unfit for their work, and to revoke employment certificates when necessary. In New York a medical inspector from the labor department selects the children who appear to need examination. But even a physician cannot detect all forms of serious disability by the mere appearance of the patient. All working children—if they are to be adequately protected and removed from occupations which are affecting

[55] Factory and Workshop Act, 1901 (1 Edw. 7, C. 22, Sec. 64 [3]).
[56] For discussion of this problem, see Woodbury, Helen Sumner, "Standards Applicable to the Administration of Employment Certificate Systems," United States Department of Labor, Children's Bureau, *Publication No. 133*, 1924, pp. 74-97.

them injuriously—should be regularly examined at least once a year.[57] Only one state, Virginia, requires annual physical examination of all children holding employment certificates. Similar provisions will probably be embodied in the laws of other states as public opinion gradually comes to realize the necessity of safeguarding the child's health after he has entered industry in the same way as is now being done to a large extent up to the time that he leaves school.

(3) Educational Requirements.—Merely to compel the child to go to school until he is fourteen or sixteen years of age does not guarantee the attainment of any definite minimum of education. Hence most states forbid the employment of children who do not come up to certain standards of knowledge. These standards, however, vary considerably. About half a dozen states require only that applicants for employment certificates be able to read and write English or show proficiency in certain other specified subjects. Many states require the attainment of certain grades in the public schools, or equivalent instruction. Completion of the eighth grade was by the beginning of 1936 the standard in more than a dozen states.[58] In January, 1936, the laws of eight states fixed no educational tests whatever for employment of children fourteen years of age or older.[59]

Several states require attendance at school for a minimum period either during the year previous to the birthday at which the child becomes old enough to go to work, or during the year previous to the time the certificate is issued. This required period of attendance may vary from the entire school year to twelve weeks or less. Instruction in certain specified subjects, usually reading, writing, spelling, geography, and arithmetic through common fractions, is required in some states.

[57] See "Physical Standards for Working Children," preliminary report of the committee appointed by the Children's Bureau of the United States Department of Labor to formulate standards of normal development and sound health for the use of physicians in examining children entering employment and children at work. United States Department of Labor, Children's Bureau, *Publication No. 79,* 1921, p. 11.

[58] For details of these requirements, see United States Department of Labor, Children's Bureau, *Child Labor Facts and Figures,* Chart I, October, 1933.

[59] Mississippi, Nevada, New Mexico, North Carolina, South Carolina, Tennessee, Virginia, and Wyoming.

SAFETY AND HEALTH

The provision that children who have been granted "working papers" but are under sixteen years of age shall attend school when not regularly employed is common, but little attention has been paid to its enforcement. Once an employment certificate has been secured, the child is usually forgotten by the school authorities. Even when the law requires that the certificate be sent direct to the employer and returned by him to the issuing office when the child's employment terminates, the certificate at no time becoming the property of the child, enforcement is often lax. Some of this difficulty is due to delay on the part of employers in reporting to certificating officials, or on the part of these officials in reporting to the school attendance departments. Frequently, it is due also to the belief of the school authorities that the child will profit little by the interrupted work and will act as a drag on those in regular attendance. Continuation schools, now operating in more than half the states for the part-time education of employed minors, are better adapted than the full-time schools to the handling of these irregular pupils. A few states, therefore, require that continuation school attendance, which is normally four to eight hours a week for employed minors under sixteen or eighteen years of age, shall be extended to twenty hours a week for those temporarily unemployed. These newer provisions should prove more nearly possible of strict enforcement. Continuation schools, however, exist for the most part only in the more populous communities.

Much of the time of the child under sixteen who drifts from one dull, monotonous job to another is wasted, as far as education and training are concerned. Consequently, the completion of the eighth grade seems little enough schooling to require of children who go to work under sixteen, and the continuation of part-time education during the first years of employment is most desirable.

(4) Special Problems in Enforcing Restrictions on Child Labor.—Difficult as it has been, and still is, to place comprehensive child labor laws on the statute books, it is even more difficult to build up their effective administration.

The principal agencies for the enforcement of child labor laws are the departments of labor, the school authorities, and in a few states child welfare commissions. Probation officers

182 PRINCIPLES OF LABOR LEGISLATION

and private child welfare agencies may sometimes aid. In some states special child labor inspectors are appointed; in fact, factory inspection was usually begun with the enforcement of the child labor law before other labor legislation was established. In most cases, however, enforcement rests primarily with the factory inspection bureaus.

Few, if any, states have an adequate corps of inspectors,[60] and in many of the southern states the provision for enforcement is most meager.[61] The experience of state after state has demonstrated that without official inspection child labor laws are dead letters.

The issuance of employment certificates is the first step in the administration of the minimum standards for entrance to industry. In most states where certificates are required they are issued by the local school authorities. In a very few states no employment certificates are required, the affidavit of the parent being accepted as proof of age.[62]

Under the prevailing method of issuance through the school authorities there is an attempt to secure uniformity by the use of standard blanks throughout the state, by regular monthly or more frequent reports either to the commissioner of labor or to the state superintendent of education, and by a certain amount of centralized supervision on the part of these officials. It is argued that this method is the most practical because the school office is the most convenient place for the children and their parents to go to obtain the certificates; because the local school authority knows the child through his record or through personal contact, and thus there is less likely to be falsification in regard to age; and because the local school authority is likely to be much more interested in keeping the child in school

---

[60] See chap. viii, "Administration," p. 450.

[61] In Georgia, for example, when the United States Children's Bureau investigated thirty-nine representative mills in November and December, 1922, it discovered 140 cases in which the *state* child labor law was violated, instances occurring in all but seventeen of the plants. Florida, Georgia, and Mississippi had, in 1925, only one inspector each to enforce their child labor laws.

[62] By January, 1936, Idaho was the only state with no employment certificate requirements. Wyoming, however, required certificates only for certain dangerous occupations, and Texas only for children between the ages of twelve and fifteen exempted from the regular restrictions because of poverty.

SAFETY AND HEALTH

and will make more of an effort to point out the inadvisability of allowing him to leave for some temporary and unnecessary employment. The enforcement of the compulsory education law, also, is so closely connected with the enforcement of the child labor law that the two should be coordinated under the school authorities in each community. The same sets of records are necessary for the issuance of certificates and for the enforcement of the compulsory education law. The school census, the record of the child's age on entering school, and his progress in school are equally important to the enforcement of both laws. Experience, however, reveals the danger that dependence on local school authorities may result in the creation of a large number of issuing officers whose respective jurisdiction may not be clearly distinguished, whose interpretation of the complex provisions of these laws may differ in many details, whose time may be so largely devoted to other school matters that the technical problems of certificating will not receive the proper study and attention, and whose very numbers make impossible effective cooperation with other child-labor-law-enforcing officials or effective supervision by the state authorities. A small number of full-time, well-trained certificating officers make for a better administered system.[63] In a few states such officers are appointed by the state department finally responsible for enforcement of child labor laws. The certificate-issuing officers, no matter how chosen, should be required to report promptly to the school attendance officials all applicants who have been refused certificates, in order that they may be returned to school. School principals, as well as inspection officials, should also be notified of the names of all children to whom certificates have been granted. In the regulation of children's work in street trades, badges to be worn conspicuously and renewed annually have been found essential to enforcement, and the responsibility for administration rests chiefly with the educational authorities.

Cooperation between the child labor inspectors and the schools is necessary that both may discharge their responsibility to

[63] For discussion of this problem, see Woodbury, Helen Sumner, "Standards Applicable to the Administration of Employment Certificate Systems," United States Department of Labor, Children's Bureau, *Publication No. 133*, pp. 18-44.

the best advantage of the child. A careful issuance of employment certificates and a thorough enforcement of the compulsory education law make the work of the labor inspector much easier. It is desirable, furthermore, that truant officers have the power to inspect establishments where children are employed, and they should be the local representatives of the state child labor inspectors, reporting to them all violations and aiding them in getting evidence to bring prosecutions. The actual presentation of evidence in the courts should always be done by the state inspector, who is more likely to be free from local pressure.

The important provisions of what is in most respects a model law in regard to employment certificates are as follows:[64] No child under eighteen should be engaged unless the child presents to the employer an employment certificate, which should be kept on file during the child's employment and returned to the issuing officer when the employment terminates. These certificates should be issued only by the local superintendent of schools, or by someone designated by him in writing, and should be given only after the following documents have been received and placed on file:

(1) The pledge of the employer that he expects to employ the child and will return the certificate to the issuing office as soon as the child leaves his employ.

(2) The child's school record, stating the age, ability to read and write, and school grade, signed by the principal of the school that the child last attended.

(3) Evidence of age, in the following order: (a) birth certificate; (b) baptismal record or passport; (c) school record or other documentary evidence; (d) in the absence of anything else, affidavit of the parent, with one or two disinterested citizens. The child should personally appear before the issuing officer for examination, and the officer should satisfy himself that the child is of legal working age, is able to read and write English, and has had a course of instruction equivalent to seven yearly grades in the public schools.

(4) A certificate from the school physician, board of health, or a licensed physician appointed by the board of education,

[64] Practically the provisions of the Ohio Law (General Code, 1910, Secs. 7765-7771).

SAFETY AND HEALTH

in the order named, showing that the child is physically able to do the work for which he is to be employed.

The certificate should be transmitted by the issuing officer to the employer, and should not at any time come into possession of the child, to be used as a license for idleness. The blanks should be furnished by the state commissioner of labor, to whom should be sent monthly a list of the names of children for whom certificates have been issued, returned, or refused. Such lists should give the names and addresses of the prospective employers and the nature of the occupations in which the children intend to engage. Factory inspectors and truant officers should be empowered to demand that certificates be obtained to prove the age of children apparently under eighteen who claim to be over that age.

Even more for the sake of uniformity in enforcement than for uniformity in restrictions on child labor, federal legislation is needed. Experience under the federal child labor laws before their invalidation by the courts indicates that state inspectors cooperated willingly with the federal authorities and that the state officials found their own work greatly facilitated by the existence of the federal standards.[65] Advocates of federal legislation believe, also, that the federal courts are more likely to find against a man who violates a federal law regarding the employment of children than the local courts are to convict for violation of state laws. This would be an important gain, because it is not at all an uncommon thing for the state factory inspector to have a case dismissed by the judge after the most careful evidence has been presented, merely because the judge does not see that any great injustice has been done the individual child.

For the better enforcement of child labor laws cooperation between all the different agencies that are interested is essential. The standards which have been and will be established in regard to the entrance of children into industry will never be thoroughly enforced until the problem of administration is

[65] Testimony of Miss Grace Abbott, Chief of the United States Children's Bureau, United States Department of Labor, at the hearings on the proposed child labor constitutional amendment before the House Judiciary Committee, Sixty-eighth Congress, First Session, February and March, 1924. See especially pp. 41 and 46-51.

186 PRINCIPLES OF LABOR LEGISLATION

taken up with the same enthusiasm and persistence which have marked the campaigns for legislation.

b. *Women.*—The exclusion of women from various branches of industry is based primarily on their inherently weaker resistance to certain health dangers, and sometimes upon moral grounds or upon their special need for protection at certain periods, as just before and after childbirth. Legislation to this end is much less extensively developed in America than in Europe.

(1) Prohibited Employments.—In America the most usual laws forbidding the employment of women in designated occupations or under designated conditions relate to work in mines, which is forbidden to women in most of the mining states.[66] In addition, a few scattered provisions of various sorts are found. Two or three states have forbidden the employment of women in cleaning moving machinery.[67] Arizona forbids the work of women "in any capacity" in which they must remain standing constantly[68]; and New York, in a law containing important exceptions, Michigan and Ohio forbid women to operate certain kinds of emery and other polishing wheels.[69] New York also forbids the employment of women coremakers in foundries if the cores are baked in the room where they are made,[70] and Minnesota prohibits women from lifting cores in and out of ovens.[71] Several states[72] exclude women from work involving repeated lifting of heavy weights. Ohio and Wisconsin were, in 1936, the only states with extensive provisions for the exclusion of adult women from dangerous occupations. Ohio prohibited their employment not only in the occupations specified above but also in quarries, blast furnaces, smelters,

[66] Alabama, Arizona, Arkansas, Colorado, Illinois, Indiana, Maryland, Missouri, New York, Ohio, Oklahoma, Pennsylvania, Utah, Virginia, Washington, Wisconsin, Wyoming.

[67] Louisiana, Minnesota, Missouri.

[68] Arizona, Revised Statutes 1913, Sec. 3115.

[69] New York Consolidated Laws 1930, C. 32, Sec. 146 (8); Michigan, Compiled Laws 1929, Sec. 8342-8346; Ohio, Annotated Code 1930, Sec. 1027.

[70] New York, Consol. Laws 1930, C. 32, Sec. 147.

[71] Minnesota, Statutes 1927, C. 32, Sec. 4073-4074.

[72] California, Massachusetts, Ohio, Pennsylvania, Washington, by the beginning of 1936.

SAFETY AND HEALTH

shoe-shining establishments, bowling alleys, pool rooms, delivery services, freight elevators, baggage or freight handling, and trucking.[73] Wisconsin prohibited the employment of women in any occupation prejudicial to their life, health, safety or welfare, and directed its industrial commission to classify employments and to issue orders embodying the specific exclusions.[74] The Pennsylvania labor department had also issued rules prohibiting or regulating employment of women in about a dozen dangerous occupations.

In Europe the evil effects of certain kinds of work are much better known than in this country, and it is well recognized that even the most careful regulation of working conditions in these occupations would not suffice to prevent injury to the health of women employed therein. Accordingly, European legislation forbids the work of women in a fairly wide list of occupations, most of which involve the presence of dusts, fumes, vapors, gases, or substances of a poisonous or clearly harmful character. Among women workers in white lead, for instance, it was discovered that a serious derangement of the reproductive organs frequently occurred, and that the percentage of miscarriages and stillbirths among married women was exceedingly high. Therefore, in most of the important European countries, and also in Argentina, India, and Japan, women are forbidden to work in many of the dangerous processes in which this poison is used. The International Labor Conference of 1919 recommended the exclusion of women, as well as children under eighteen, from work in a number of dangerous lead trades. By 1935, twenty-two countries had reported action taken toward putting this convention into effect.[75] In France females are forbidden even to enter a place in which any one of forty-six especially dangerous processes is carried on, and nearly one hundred additional occupations are forbidden except under special protective conditions. Similar lists are found in the more important European countries, and even Spain, long backward in social legislation, has forbidden the employment of women and minor children in a long list of

[73] Ohio, Laws 1919, p. 540.
[74] Wisconsin Statutes 1923, Sec. 103.05 (2).
[75] See International Labor Office, *Appendix to Report of Director,* 1935.

occupations. In 1935, the International Labor Conference adopted a convention to prohibit the employment of women in underground mines. While it is true that women in foreign countries often engage in work done only by men in this country, yet many women are undoubtedly at work here in industries so dangerous to their health that an extension of prohibitory legislation is urgently needed.

(2) Childbirth Protection.—It was not until 1911 that the prohibition of the industrial employment of women for a stated period before and after childbirth became the subject of legislation in America. Such statutes were passed by Massachusetts in 1911, New York in 1912, Connecticut and Vermont in 1913, Missouri in 1919, and the Philippine Islands in 1923. The Massachusetts act is a representative one. It forbids "knowingly" employing any woman in "a manufacturing, mechanical, or mercantile establishment" within two weeks before or four weeks after childbirth.[76]

The desirability of such additional protection for workingwomen at the time of childbirth has been recognized by most European countries and by several outside of Europe. The prohibited period is generally similar to that found in America, from two to four weeks before and from four to six or eight weeks after confinement. The International Labor Conference in 1919 drew up a draft convention prohibiting industrial employment of women for six weeks after childbirth, and permitting them to leave work, if they wished to, six weeks before confinement. By April, 1936, sixteen countries had ratified this convention.[77] The Third International Labor Conference at Geneva in 1921 recommended a similar standard for women in agricultural employments. European laws are rendered more effective than the American by their frequent connection with provisions for maternity insurance.[78] For instance, under the German system of health insurance, a woman worker is paid benefits of half-wages for four weeks before and six weeks following confinement. Such insurance is needed partly to make

[76] Massachusetts, Laws 1911, C. 229.
[77] Argentina, Brazil, Bulgaria, Chile, Colombia, Cuba, Germany, Greece, Hungary, Latvia, Luxemburg, Nicaragua, Rumania, Spain, Uruguay, Yugoslavia.
[78] See "Maternity Insurance," p. 267.

SAFETY AND HEALTH

up for the income loss during the enforced period of idleness, and may also be an important aid in the enforcement of the law.

c. *Men.*—Legal regulations for the exclusion of men from dangerous employments are never of universal application, as they are in the case of children and women, but are limited to certain classes or groups of individuals who must be excluded on definite grounds, usually ascertained by examination. The grounds of exclusion may be either physical or technical. Although the distinction does not always hold, physical requirements are in the main intended to protect the worker who is debarred, while in the case of technical qualifications the protection of fellow workmen or of the general public is an added if not the main consideration. Physical qualifications, also, are usually concerned with health; technical qualifications with safety.

(1) Physical Qualifications.—Physical qualifications established by law are of four kinds: (1) reasonable immunity from the trade malady characteristic of the employment; (2) freedom from a trade malady contracted in the course of employment; (3) freedom from a contagious disease which might be passed on to other workmen or to consumers of the product; and (4) freedom from physical defect of such nature as to interfere with the proper performance of duty. It will be noted that the first two qualifications look toward the health of the workman himself, and that the last two look mainly toward the health and safety of other persons.

The qualification of immunity from a particular occupational disease is found in only a few American states, but is more common abroad. The state laws and administrative rules regulating work in compressed air usually require that applicants must be found physically qualified by a physician paid by the employer, and these laws also exclude persons addicted to the excessive use of intoxicants. In Europe examinations for entrance to compressed-air work are required in Belgium, France, Germany, Holland, and Yugoslavia; several countries specify a long list of ailments, such as obesity, heart or lung diseases, and affections of the nose and ears, any one of which debars from the work. Austria, Czechoslovakia, and Yugoslavia bar from certain classes of work in paper-mills all workers with open wounds, persons with delicate respiratory organs, and consumptives. Still more common is the requirement of a medical certificate of fitness as a condition of entering the more dangerous lead trades, which is found in Austria, France, Germany, Great Britain, Russia, and Yugoslavia. Germany specifically prohibits the employment in these trades of applicants with lung, kidney, or stomach trouble, a generally weak constitution, or an addiction to alcohol; France, of those who exhibit symptoms of lead poisoning or of any complaint likely to be dangerously aggravated by plumbism. Belgium also forbids the employment of alcoholics in the white lead, lead oxide, or lead paint trades. Russia in 1922 empowered her Labor Commissariat to require physical examination of applicants for work in any trade dangerous to health, thus carrying to its logical conclusion the principle embodied in all of these laws.

It is obvious, however, that merely debarring from entrance to an unhealthy trade those demonstrably susceptible to its dangers is insufficient protection. The worker's real power of resistance to a specific hazard often cannot be determined until he has been exposed to it, and if he begins to show symptoms of succumbing he cannot be too quickly removed. Hence arises the necessity for the second qualification, freedom from a trade malady contracted in the course of employment.

Most common occupational diseases are of such slow inception that a capable physician can detect them in the early stages before their cumulative effects have become serious. To make sure, therefore, that the originally healthy employee is in fact successfully resisting the risk with which he is surrounded, the initial examination, when it is given, must be supplemented by periodic reexaminations at intervals graduated according to the degree of risk. Sometimes periodic examinations are required even when there are no restrictions upon entrance to the trade.

Such is the case with the monthly examinations required under the "lead laws" of the important lead-using states. The Ohio[79] and Pennsylvania[80] laws apply to the manufacture of certain of the more poisonous lead salts, such as white lead, red lead, and arsenate of lead (Paris green), while the later

[79] Ohio, Laws 1913, p. 819, as amended by Laws 1921, p. 181.
[80] Pennsylvania, Laws 1913, No. 851.

SAFETY AND HEALTH

New Jersey[81] statute covers also the manufacture of pottery, tiles, or porcelain-enameled sanitary ware in so far as lead is used.

In all three of these states the physician who discovers a case of lead poisoning must report it not only to the state departments of labor and of health, but also to the employer, who after five days must not continue the "leaded" employee in a dangerous process or return him thereto without a physician's written permit.[82]

Provision for regular reexamination is also found in the three American compressed-air laws already mentioned. Under these the examination must be repeated after the first half-day's work, on returning to work after ten days' absence from any cause, and after three months' continuous employment, and workmen who have ceased to be qualified must be excluded.

In the more dangerous lead trades workers are subject to regular examination in nearly all European countries, as well as in India and Western Australia. England and Germany, moreover, require examinations both in alkali chrome works, where corrosions of the mucous membrane are common, and in rubber vulcanizing works, where there is danger from the noxious gas, bisulphide of carbon. Belgium, France, Germany, and Yugoslavia require similar examinations in compressed-air work. The frequency of examination varies from once a week in the British white lead industry, to every six months among German painters, although once a month, as in the American lead trades, is the most usual period. In The Netherlands stone masons are entitled to medical examination at the employer's expense once a year. In Russia the Labor Commissariat may require periodic physical examinations in any trade dangerous to health. In order that the advantages of cumulative experience may not be lost, a factory record of the results of medical examinations, especially if they result in findings of disease,

---

[81] New Jersey, Laws 1914, C. 162.
[82] Similar laws in Illinois (Laws 1911, p. 330, as amended by Laws 1923, p. 351) and Missouri (Laws 1913, p. 402) cover wider ranges of related industries, including zinc smelting and work with arsenic, brass, mercury, and phosphorus, but do not require the removal from danger of workmen who show symptoms of the resultant diseases.

is nearly always required, and must usually be kept by the examining physician.[83]

Because they fear loss of employment if found to be suffering from some disqualifying ailment, workmen have at times protested against medical examinations conducted by the employer. Aside from possible abuse of such information, however, the advantages to be gained by the workman through exclusion or timely removal from a disease-breeding occupation would outweigh the hardship resulting from temporary loss of wages while awaiting recovery or securing other work. Even the wage loss, when exclusion is due to illness, can be in large part taken care of by the extension of workmen's compensation to embrace occupational diseases and by the institution of systems of universal health insurance.[84] For the physician, also, the practice of examining large bodies of men at the place of employment will lead to added insight into the trade causes of disease, an insight which unfortunately is as yet only rudimentary. In any compulsory system of medical examination the physician should be employed by the state.

The third physical qualification, absence of contagious disease, is applied occasionally in bakeshops and in other food establishments, while the fourth, freedom from physical defect which might interfere with proper performance of duty, is mentioned in a few states which require an examination of railroad employees for color-blindness or other defective sight.

(2) Technical Qualifications.—Far more numerous than the examinations to test an adult workman's fitness for a given occupation upon physical, or health, grounds, are those required in nearly all states for the licensing of men to carry on certain trades after a test of experience, skill, or general education. Laws for the examination and registration of barbers, horseshoers, plumbers, electricians, moving-picture machine

[83] In Germany this record is called a "control book," and must contain the name of the person keeping it, first and last name, address and age of each workman, date of his entering and leaving the employment, date and nature of his illness, date of his recovery, name of the factory physician, and dates and results of the medical examinations. The employer is responsible for the correctness of the record, and must show it to the factory or medical inspector on demand. The Austrian health register goes into even more detail.

[84] See "Health Insurance," p. 257.

SAFETY AND HEALTH

operators, chauffeurs, railroad, street-car, and steamboat employees, elevator operators, and even aviators, are designed primarily for the protection of the public, and need only be mentioned.[85] More closely related to the subject are technical examinations for miners and for firemen and engineers in charge of stationary boilers.

Statutes requiring the examination and registration or licensing of certain classes of coal mine employees exist in practically all of the important coal-mining states.[86] Managers, foremen or bosses, fire bosses, mine examiners, and hoisting engineers are the employees for whom licenses are usually required, but some laws cover all miners, each of whom, however, is allowed one unlicensed apprentice.[87] Candidates for the more responsible jobs must present affidavits attesting their good character and sobriety, must have a specified number of years' experience, must be residents of the state, and must pass the examination prescribed by an examining board. The problems created by foreign-born workmen among the miners is reflected by the number of states which require ability to read and speak English.[88] A fee ranging from $1 to $5 is charged for the examination and license. The examining boards are composed of from three to five men, one of whom is usually a state mine inspector, the others being miners and mine owners or superintendents in equal number.

Finally, in a number of states[89] and in the District of Columbia licenses are required for certain classes of firemen and engineers employed in connection with stationary boilers. Moral character and temperate habits, one to three years' experience,

---

[85] Similar in intent is the Wisconsin Industrial Commission order of 1917, fixing standards of technical skill for bricklayers as a prerequisite for giving a certificate to apprentices in the trade.

[86] Such statutes existed in 1932 in the twenty states of Alabama, Arkansas, Colorado, Illinois, Indiana, Iowa, Kansas, Kentucky, Missouri, Montana, North Dakota, Ohio, Oklahoma, Pennsylvania, Tennessee, Utah, Virginia, Washington, West Virginia, and Wyoming.

[87] Illinois, Laws 1913, p. 438, Sec. 1.

[88] See, for example, Kentucky, Laws 1914, C. 79, Art. XVI, Sec. 1.

[89] In 1932 licenses for stationary firemen and engineers (exclusive of those in mines) were required in the eleven states of Florida, Georgia, Maryland, Massachusetts, Minnesota, Missouri, Montana, Nevada, New Jersey, Ohio, and Pennsylvania. Many cities also require licenses under city ordinances.

and a minimum age limit are specified in a few instances, and the license is generally revokable for negligence, intoxication, or violation of law or regulations.

2. **Prohibition of Substances or Instruments.**—The most notable example of the application of the method of prohibition to a dangerous substance is the world-wide banishing of poisonous phosphorus from the match industry. Within eleven years after the commercial introduction of the phosphorus match in 1827, the disease known as "phossy jaw," or phosphorus necrosis, was attracting the attention of government investigators. Various efforts to eliminate the disease by regulation having signally failed, Finland in 1872 forbade the use of white phosphorus in match factories, and similar action was taken by Denmark in 1874. In France, where matchmaking is a government monopoly, the profits from the industry were wiped out by sickness and death claims until a harmless substitute was discovered and the dangerous ingredient prohibited in 1897. Other countries followed; and in 1906, on account of the difficulty of eliminating poisonous phosphorus in countries with an important export trade, the International Association for Labor Legislation secured an international conference at Berne which resulted in 1906 in the then unique expedient of an international convention[90] providing for the absolute prohibition of the manufacture, importation, or sale of matches made from white phosphorus. This treaty was signed at once by Denmark, France, Germany, Italy, Luxemburg, The Netherlands, and Switzerland, and a few years later by Great Britain, Spain, and numerous colonies.[91] Canada and Mexico also, without becoming signatories to the treaty, prohibited the poisonous substance in the match industry. A recommendation that nations which had not yet done so should adhere to this Berne convention was adopted by the International Labor Conference at Washington in 1919. By April, 1936,[92] seventeen additional countries had ratified, and three more, without formal ratification, had passed legislation to the same end.

---

[90] For text of this convention, see *Bulletin of the International Labor Office,* 1906, vol. i, pp. 275-276.

[91] For complete list see table, *ibid.,* 1912, vol. vii, following p. 503.

[92] See chart on *Progress of Ratifications,* published by the International Labor Office, April, 1936.

SAFETY AND HEALTH

In the United States the question was first given national prominence in 1910 by the report of a federal investigation.[93] Two years later, in April, 1912, Congress placed a prohibitory tax of 2 cents a hundred on matches containing white phosphorus, and prohibited their import or export.[94] The power of internal revenue taxation which Congress had previously exercised for the benefit of bankers and farmers was thus for the first time used for protecting the health of wage earners.

Against only one other industrial substance—lead—has the drastic method of prohibition been invoked, and in this case the prohibitory legislation is found only abroad. Austria was first to act, forbidding in 1908 the use of lead in all paints, colors, or cement used for interior work, and the same year the Swiss administrative departments were ordered to forbid the use of white lead in painting carried on in their behalf. France in 1909 declared that after July 20, 1914, the use of "white lead, of linseed oil mixed with lead, and of all specialized products containing white lead, will be forbidden in all painting, no matter of what nature, carried on by working painters either on the outside or on the inside of buildings."[95] By 1924 Greece, Tunis, and Czechoslovakia had been added to the list of countries prohibiting the use of white lead in interior painting and, in the case of Tunis and Greece, in some kinds of exterior work. Belgium, France, Germany, Greece, Yugoslavia, Tunis, Austria, and Czechoslovakia had also forbidden the removal of lead paint by any dry nibbing or scraping process. In 1925 Russia adopted a law prohibiting the sale, preparation and use of white lead in any form after 1929.

A convention adopted by the Third International Labor Conference in 1921 prohibited the use of white lead or lead sulphate in all interior painting—with certain specified exceptions —and eliminated the use of these substances in any other painting work unless employed in the form of a ready-mixed paint or paste. This convention also excluded women and young persons from work where the above-mentioned poisons were employed, and stipulated various precautions, including the

[93] Andrews, John B., "Phosphorus Poisoning in the Match Industry," United States Bureau of Labor, *Bulletin No. 86*, January, 1910, pp. 31-146.
[94] United States, Laws 1911-1912, C. 75.
[95] United States Bureau of Labor, *Bulletin No. 95*, July, 1911, p. 180.

elimination wherever possible of dry scraping down, for those operations in which white lead or lead sulphate paints were used. By April, 1936, this convention had been ratified by twenty-three countries.[96]

A few prohibitions apply not to substances, but to instruments of work. One of these is contained in the Massachusetts, Connecticut, and Rhode Island statutes, intended to protect textile mill operatives from "the kiss of death." These laws, in order to prevent the transfer from worker to worker of tuberculosis and other infections, prohibit the use of any form of shuttle in the use of which any part of the shuttle or any thread is put in the mouth or touched by the lips of the operator.[97] Contagious diseases among glass blowers are guarded against in France, Portugal, Yugoslavia, and the Mexican state of Jalisco by prohibitions against the use by more than one person of the same blowpipe.

III. REGULATION

The method of regulation, in the prevention of occupational accident and disease, as in other social problems, is based on the principle of toleration within limits. The majority of the people may believe that certain dangerous machines or processes are so necessary a part of our industrial life that their prohibition is at present undesirable or at least impracticable. In dealing with industrial accidents and diseases the adoption of this principle leads in the work *places* to the installation of machine guards, fire escapes, dust and fume removal systems, separate wash rooms and eating rooms; and for the work *people* to the limitation of working hours. As the latter point has been considered in the chapter on "Hours of Labor," only the regulation of work places need be treated here.

Furnishing a reasonably safe place in which to work is plainly the duty of the employer, and was so recognized under the common law and by the employers' liability statutes. Not all

[96] Austria, Belgium, Bulgaria, Chile, Colombia, Cuba, Czechoslovakia, Estonia, Finland, France, Greece, Hungary (conditionally), Latvia, Luxemburg, Nicaragua, Norway, Poland, Rumania, Spain, Sweden, Uruguay, Venezuela, Yugoslavia.

[97] Massachusetts, Laws 1911, C. 281; Rhode Island, Laws 1918, C. 1632; and Connecticut, Laws 1919, C. 27.

SAFETY AND HEALTH

industrial managers, however, are equally watchful and energetic, even if all were equally alive to their social responsibility in the matter, and hence has arisen the need of standards, drafted and enforced by public authority, which will throw about the workpeople the necessary protection. So diversified are the various branches of industry and the accident and disease hazards in each that separate codes have grown up about them. These codes deal in the main with (1) factories and workshops, (2) mines and tunnels, and (3) transportation.

1. **Factories and Workshops.**—Modifying to meet its own conditions a mass of legislation already existing in Great Britain, Massachusetts passed on May 11, 1877, the first American law requiring factory safeguards. This pioneer law touched on nearly all of the points now covered by our most advanced statutes for the prevention of factory accidents. It provided for the guarding of belting, shafting, and gearing, prohibited the cleaning of moving machinery, required elevators and hoistways to be protected, and called for sufficient means of egress in case of fire. Practically every state in the Union now has legislation prescribing minimum conditions of safety in industry or authorizing administrative officials to prepare and promulgate legally binding industrial safety regulations.

a. *Machine Guards.*—The point perhaps most frequently dealt with is safeguarding of machinery. Mechanism for the transmission of power, like belting, shafting, and gearing, as well as active parts of machines, such as saws, planers, mangles, and emery wheels, must usually be securely guarded, but if this is not considered possible it is sometimes required that notice of the danger be conspicuously posted. Set-screws or other projections must be countersunk beneath the level of the shaft or otherwise guarded, while shafts and belts, and floor openings through which they pass, must be cased or railed off. A statute found only in the great textile state of Massachusetts requires looms to be provided with guards which will prevent injury from flying shuttles.[98] In employers' liability suits it has often but not uniformly been held by the courts that failure to provide the required safeguards is negligence *per se*,[99] and that the worker does not assume the risk of the employer's

[98] Massachusetts, Laws 1909, C. 514, Sec. 101.
[99] Davis *v.* Mercer Lumber Co., 164 Ind. 413, 73 N. E. 899 (1905).

198 PRINCIPLES OF LABOR LEGISLATION

negligent disregard of duty, even though he is aware of it.[100] Under workmen's compensation laws the factor of negligence is not considered; but several states have provided for increased compensation awards to penalize employers in case of accidents caused by their failure to provide legally required safety devices.[101] Many safeguards can be applied best and most economically during the original building of the machine, and Minnesota has prohibited the manufacture or sale of mechanism with danger points unguarded.[102] The same idea is found in the laws of some European countries, and a growing number of American dealers are acting upon it without legislative compulsion.

It is not sufficient, however, for a safeguard to be attached to a machine. If the guard is to do its work it must be actually used. A number of states have therefore passed provisions forbidding any person to move, displace, or destroy any safety device except under rules established by the employer, and some specify immediate repairs as the only cause for which a machine guard may be removed during the active operation of the machine. A related clause forbids employees to operate or tamper with machines with which they are not familiar or which are not connected with their regular duties.

In case of accident it is important that the operative be able to stop the machine at once. It is commonly required, therefore, that shafting be fitted with tight and loose pulleys, and that belt-shifters or poles be supplied for shifting the belt quickly and safely from one to the other. Some states require friction clutches for stopping machinery, and also require speaking tubes, electric bells, colored electric lights or other means of communication between the workroom and the engine room. Other regulations governing moving machinery forbid cleaning or repairing it while in motion, and overcrowding. Closely related to the foregoing provisions are those dealing with covers or other safeguards on such stationary equipment as vats and pans.

Among other provisions against accident are frequent re-

[100] Evansville Hoop & Stave Co. *v.* Bailey, 43 Ind. App. 153, 84 N. E. 549 (1908).
[101] See "Accident Compensation," p. 243.
[102] Minnesota, Laws 1913, C. 316, Sec. 5.

SAFETY AND HEALTH

quirements that stairs must be properly screened at sides and bottom, must have rubber treads if thought necessary by the commissioner of labor, and must be furnished with substantial handrails. Stair openings on each floor must be closed, as well as entrances to elevator shafts. Trapdoors, fences, gates, or other safeguards may be required for hoistways, hatchways, and wellholes. It is often required that elevators be provided with automatic catches to prevent falling. In Wisconsin the industrial commission, in 1920, had issued more than seventy-five orders looking to the safe construction and operation of passenger and freight elevators.[103]

Protection against explosions of stationary boilers is best exemplified by the methods of the Massachusetts Board of Boiler Rules. This board, one of the earliest forerunners of the industrial commission plan of drafting and enforcing safety measures, was established in 1907.[104] It is composed of five members: the chief of inspections of the Department of Public Safety, who serves as chairman; one representative of the boiler-manufacturing interests; one representative of the boiler-using interests; one representative of the boiler-insurance interests; and one operating engineer. The duties of the board include the formulation of rules for the construction, installation, operation, and inspection of steam boilers. For this purpose public hearings and private conferences are held, and the rules as formulated are submitted to the governor for approval. When approved they are published and have the full force of law. The success of this system in reducing the number of boiler explosions has led to its adoption in many states and cities, even as far away as Manila.

b. *Protection against Fire.*—Though the prevention of fire is of far more importance than providing means of escape, legal provisions covering this point are of comparatively late development. It was not until 1911, for instance, that New Jersey ordered cans to be provided for combustible waste, and it was not until 1912 that New York required gas jets to be inclosed in globes, wire cages, or other protection, and forbade smoking

[103] Industrial Commission of Wisconsin, *Elevator Code*, 1918.
[104] Massachusetts, Laws 1907, C. 465, Secs. 24-28, as amended by Laws 1909, C. 393; Laws 1913, C. 610; Laws 1918, C. 257; and Laws 1919, C. 5 and C. 350.

200 PRINCIPLES OF LABOR LEGISLATION

in factories. Meanwhile, disastrous factory fires in both states, caused in part by lack of these safeguards, had attracted the attention of the country, and resulted in much legislation. In some states floors must now be swept daily and the sweepings removed; and the quantity of explosives that may be kept in a building is carefully regulated. Sometimes factories must be equipped with an automatic gas cock or appliance by which in case of fire the supply of gas may be shut off without entering the building.

Required means of extinguishing fires include pails of water or sand, a standpipe and hose of specified dimensions, fire extinguishers or automatic sprinkler systems. The major part of fire laws, however, is devoted to provisions for prompt escape. In the early days of this legislation, since no one had taken the time to study out what would constitute effective egress, lawmakers contented themselves in most cases with ordering "suitable and sufficient" exits and escapes. Now the most elaborate details as to material and construction are found. Balcony escapes, fire towers, or chutes or toboggans may be used in different states. Doors must be constructed to open out or slide, and must not be fastened in any way during working hours. Sometimes the number of employees to the floor is regulated, periodical fire drills are called for, and gongs, and red lights or other "Exit" signs, must be installed. An increasing number of states require plans for fire egress in new buildings to be passed upon by labor or building department officials.

c. *Lighting, Heating and Ventilation.*—Although proper lighting affects both the health and the comfort of the workman and his liability to accident, less attention has been paid to this phase of industrial safety and hygiene than to almost any other point of similar importance. About thirty states have enacted some legislation on the subject, but all except a dozen limit themselves to general provisions such as that factories must be "well and sufficiently lighted,"[105] meaningless and unenforceable

[105] Connecticut (General Statutes 1902, Sec. 4518) adds that painted, stained, or corrugated glass in factory windows must be removed, "where the same is injurious to the eyes . . . upon the order of the factory inspector." In other words, Connecticut permits any factory-owner to block out light by any one of the three methods named until ordered to desist by the inspector, who must, however, first prove that the darkness is injurious.

SAFETY AND HEALTH

except where industrial commissions have power further to define the standards in administrative orders. A long step in advance was made by the Oregon statute of 1919, requiring factories to be lighted according to a minimum scale of values to be recommended by the Illuminating Engineering Society, subject to modifications after public hearing.[106]

Artificial lighting in many factories is notoriously bad because of poor quality, insufficient quantity, haphazard distribution resulting in spots of excessive intensity separated by dangerous shadows, and glare caused by lack of shades or diffusing mediums. Many eye specialists assert that from 80 to 90 per cent of headaches are due to eyestrain, and in the production of eyestrain improper lighting is an important factor. The effects of poor illumination are particularly severe upon women workers because of their more delicate nervous organization. Yet at the present stage of the art all harmful light conditions in factories could be done away with easily and cheaply. "It can easily be shown," declares one expert, "that a workman earning only $2 per day of ten hours would have to lose but three minutes of his time to make a loss to the manufacturer equal to the cost of all the artificial light he could possibly require during the entire day."[107]

With the growth of industrial commissions in the United States there is now developing a body of regulations prescribing standards of factory lighting by administrative order. By 1934 codes of industrial lighting regulations had been issued by administrative officials in a dozen states. The Illuminating Engineering Society in 1930 adopted a standard code of lighting for mills, factories and other work places. These codes provide detailed standards for both natural and artificial illumination in terms of "foot-candles," with special provision for the avoidance of glare.[108]

Some states authorize the inspector to require changes in heating apparatus found dangerous to health, but no standards of proper or permissible temperature are set up. Massachusetts

[106] Oregon, Laws 1919, C. 181.
[107] Elliott, F. Leavenworth, "Factory Lighting," *American Labor Legislation Review*, June, 1911, p. 116.
[108] See Correll, Marie, "State Requirements for Industrial Lighting," U. S. Department of Labor, Women's Bureau, *Bulletin No. 94, 1932*.

has established for certain textile processes a graduated standard of humidity permissible at certain temperatures,[109] but only in a very few laws is the subject of humidity mentioned. Yet apart from the presence of dusts and fumes, the only atmospheric condition which has been thoroughly proved harmful is the combination of excessive heat with excessive humidity.

Recognition of the importance of ventilation is more widespread. Industrial dusts and fumes, whether metallic, mineral, chemical, vegetable, or animal in origin, and whether poisonous or not, are among the most insidious and serious of modern health hazards, and the illness and death of wage earners vary almost in direct proportion to the contamination of the air supply. Hence, more than half the states have enacted provisions that factories shall be ventilated. The wording, however, is in many cases so vague that it means but little. Among the first laws which attempted to establish even an elementary standard of ventilation was the Illinois statute of 1909. Under this act the amount of fresh air to be supplied depends upon the kind of illumination used, the cubic air space furnished for each employee, and the window area of workrooms.[110] Provisions for from 250 to 600 cubic feet of air space for every employee are now found in a few state laws, but more important are the newer regulations providing for the retention and removal of dangerous dusts and fumes at the point of production by specially constructed hoods, hoppers, exhausts, and fans. Regulations of this type, originally established either as statute laws or by administrative order principally in the large lead-using states, such as Illinois, Missouri, New Jersey, New York, Ohio, and Pennsylvania, have been adopted by more than twenty legislatures.[111] As additional precautions, the best of these laws require wet-cleaning methods, the use of respirators, and separate lunch-rooms, and forbid bringing any food or drink into the workrooms.

d. *Seats, Toilets, and Dressing-rooms.*—In safety and health legislation, as well as in legislation on hours and wages, a dis-

---

[109] Massachusetts, Laws 1910, C. 543.
[110] Illinois, Laws 1909, p. 202.
[111] For comprehensive regulations of this type, see *General Orders on Dust, Fumes, Vapors and Gases*, issued by the Wisconsin Industrial Commission, 1932, and reprinted in Andrews, John B., *Administrative Labor Legislation*, 1936.

SAFETY AND HEALTH

tinct tendency is noticeable to single out women for special protection, on the grounds of their greater physical weakness and their comparative helplessness as wage bargainers. The possibilities of injury from unsafe or insanitary conditions are more apparent and it is easier to make a conclusive case in their behalf. Not infrequently health and safety laws applied only to women when first passed, but were later extended to protect all workers. For instance, in Colorado a law which originally required handrails on stairways only in buildings where women were employed was extended in 1911 to cover all work places.[112] Or in some cases a law affording some protection to all workers may be of wider scope in its application to women. Thus, in Missouri mechanical means for dust removal must be installed in all factories carrying on dusty processes where three or more "persons" are employed, and also in dusty workshops if the three or more employees are "children, young persons, or women."[113]

Particularly striking is the special protection of women manifested in the factory and mercantile laws on seats, toilets, and dressing-rooms. In fact, except for provisions in about half a dozen states requiring seating arrangements for motormen and conductors on street cars, legislation with regard to seats exists almost entirely for women.[114] As far back as the end of the 'seventies the dangers of constant standing for salesgirls were recognized, and it was urged that they be furnished seats and allowed to use them. A law containing such provisions was passed by New York as early as 1881. Almost every state now requires suitable seats for females in at least mercantile establishments.[115] The majority of laws extend this requirement to manufacturing or to manufacturing and mechanical establishments, and several states cover practically all employments. The proportion of seats to workers is sometimes fixed, and in many cases the law specifies that employers must permit the use of the seats when work will not thereby be interfered

[112] Colorado, Laws 1911, C. 132.
[113] Missouri, Revised Statutes 1919, Sec. 6839.
[114] California, however, requires seats for passenger elevator operators regardless of sex (Acts 1921, C. 115); and Florida makes no sex distinction in its law requiring seats for employees in mercantile or other business pursuits. (Revised General Statutes, 1920, Sec. 5068.)
[115] By 1936 only Mississippi was without such legislation.

with. These laws are of little real importance in protecting health, however, since it is practically impossible to see that employers and foremen allow the seats to be used even when provided.

Some three-fourths of the states likewise require sanitary and separate toilets for women workers in addition to those for men, and about one-half make provision for women's dressing-rooms. These provisions form a very important factor in maintaining the health and morals of women workers in any establishment; the character of the employment frequently makes necessary a change from street clothes to work clothes, and it is also highly desirable that a suitable place be provided where women and girls may eat lunch, secure a little rest at the noon period, and retire in case of illness.

For the lead industries, especially, careful wash-room standards have been worked out, specifying hot and cold water, a definite ratio of basins or of trough length to the number of employees, and soap, nail brushes, and towels. In the best lead laws also, such as those of New Jersey, Ohio, and Pennsylvania, hot and cold shower baths are required, to be used at least twice a week on the employer's time; and to insure the use of the baths a bath register must be kept. A few states require a sufficient supply of pure drinking water to be kept in a readily accessible place. Sometimes, especially in connection with foundries and casting rooms, the lead trades and compressed-air work, the dressing-rooms must be properly heated and ventilated, and often supplied with lockers and with facilities for drying clothes.

e. *Protection from Infectious Disease.*—Modern industrial processes subject large numbers of employees not only to dangerous dusts and vapors, but also to a variety of disease-breeding organisms, carried either by fellow workmen or by the materials worked upon. As a protection against such infection a number of legal regulations have been adopted.

Several states, for example, forbid sleeping in workrooms, some require cuspidors to be furnished and to be cleaned and disinfected daily. Massachusetts in 1913 required that cloths or other material provided for cleaning printing presses must be sanitary,[116] and a California law of the same year laid down

[116] Massachusetts, Laws 1913, C. 472.

SAFETY AND HEALTH

the rule that all wiping rags must be sterilized.[117] Similar legislation was passed in Ohio in 1923.[118] In every industrial state hundreds of cases of infection or "blood poisoning" occur yearly, and about six out of every seven of these are the result of small scratches. The requirement now found in some states for a first-aid kit in factories, workshops, and mercantile establishments should assist in reducing this needless danger.

Prominent among the infectious diseases of industry is anthrax, which arises in the handling of infected hides or hair. By 1924[119] Austria, Belgium, France, Germany, Great Britain, India, Italy, Jalisco, and Russia all had turned their attention to eradicating this malady. Despite searching investigation, however, the United States remains nearly inactive.[120] The commonest legal safeguards are provisions for thorough washing, for overalls, neck coverings, and gloves, and for treating instantly scratches and slight wounds which offer an entrance to the bacillus. Disinfection of bristles and bales of hair from suspected localities before any work is done on them is insisted on in some countries. Another recommendation of the Washington International Labor Conference of 1919 was for the disinfection, either in the exporting country or at the port of importation, of wool contaminated with anthrax spores. By 1935, twenty-two countries[121] had reported action toward carrying out this recommendation.

f. *Tenement House Manufacture.*—Difficult as are the problems connected with the regulation of labor conditions in factories, they are not more troublesome than those encountered in the regulation of tenement workshops, where the work is done by the family group in its customary living quarters.

Tenement house manufacture is often looked upon as a pleasant and easy method whereby the mothers of the poor may

---

[117] California, Laws 1913, C. 81.
[118] Ohio General Code, Sec. 1011-1.
[119] See indices of the *Legislative Series* published by the International Labor Office.
[120] See Andrews, John B., "Anthrax as an Occupational Disease," United States Bureau of Labor Statistics, *Bulletin No. 267*, 1920.
[121] Albania, Australia, Belgium, Bulgaria, Czechoslovakia, Denmark, Estonia, Finland, France, Great Britain, Hungary, India, Italy, Japan, The Netherlands, Norway, Poland, Rumania, Siam, Spain, Sweden, and Switzerland.

add to the family income in their leisure moments. The fact is that such work has usually proved a menace to health, to wage standards, and to the existing labor laws. Congestion, insanitary quarters, lack of restriction on child labor, absolutely unregulated hours, and miserable pay combine to create a condition which endangers the lives not only of the workers, but of the purchasers of their product. Often tenement dwellers have been found at work on garments and articles of food while suffering from contagious diseases.[122]

As early as 1885 New York sought to end the "sweating" or tenement workshop system by prohibiting the manufacture of cigars and other tobacco products in tenement houses in cities of the first class. The law was declared unconstitutional, the court holding it an abuse of the police power and an infringement of the cigar-maker's liberties in that it sought to force him "from his home and its hallowed associations and beneficent influences, to ply his trade elsewhere."[123] Had this pioneer statute been sustained, the entire problem of tenement house labor might have been disposed of almost at its beginning.

The set back in the Jacobs case radically changed the method of attack on the sweating system. Prohibition having been declared invalid, for three decades nearly all effort was directed toward regulation and the imposing of minor restrictions through a licensing system. In 1891 Massachusetts passed "An act to prevent the manufacture and sale of clothing made in unhealthy places," and the following year New York inserted in its newly codified labor law a provision for the licensing and regulation of tenement workshops. Similar provisions exist in about a dozen states.

These statutes ordinarily require that home work on garments, foodstuffs, and tobacco must be done only in rooms licensed by the factory inspection department. Only members of the immediate family, which is carefully defined, may be employed, and licenses may be issued only if fire escape, toilet, and all other health and safety laws have been complied with.

---

[122] See *Second Report of the New York State Factory Investigating Commission,* "Manufacturing in Tenements," vol. i, pp. 90-123; *Report on Condition of Woman and Child Wage-earners in the United States,* vol. ii, "Men's Ready-made Clothing."

[123] *In re* Jacobs, 98 N. Y. 98 (1885).

SAFETY AND HEALTH

In case of disease, work must cease until the board of health has declared the illness at an end and has fumigated the apartment. A register must be kept of names and addresses of persons taking out work, and goods given out must be labeled with the name and address of the manufacturer. Licenses are revokable for failure to comply with the law, or, in some instances, "if the health of the community or of the persons employed thereunder requires it."[124]

The results of attempted regulation under even the best of these laws, however, have never been satisfactory. The difficulties involved in adequate enforcement through inspection have proved practically insuperable. Long hours, child labor and extremely low wages have continued, making industrial home work one of the worst forms of labor exploitation and in some industries a menace to the standards of factory workers.[125] In 1913, following studies by the state factory investigating commission, New York once more turned toward the prohibitory method in dealing with this question, and forbade work in tenement homes on food products, dolls or dolls' clothing, and children's or infants' wearing apparel.[126] This law, which was based upon considerations of public health and especially that of children, was upheld by the courts in 1915.[127] A similar provision was adopted by New Jersey in 1930.[128] Between 1933 and 1935 many of the codes of fair competition adopted under the National Industrial Recovery Act provided for the complete abolition of home work. Further investigations of conditions in New York and Connecticut led these states in 1934 and 1935, respectively, to adopt the most restrictive legislation yet enacted in this country. The New York law,[129] besides requiring each employer to pay a fee for a permit to send out home work, and each home worker to be certified, empowers the state industrial commissioner to restrict such work to those in-

[124] See, for instance, Maryland, Laws 1914, C. 779, Sec. 248.
[125] See Brown, Emily C., "Industrial Home Work," U. S. Department of Labor, Women's Bureau, *Bulletin No. 79*, 1930; and "The Commercialization of the Home through Industrial Home Work," *Bulletin No. 135*, 1935.
[126] New York, Laws 1913, C. 260.
[127] People v. Balofsky, 167 N. Y. App. Div. 913 (1915).
[128] New Jersey, Acts 1930, C. 26, Sec. 11.
[129] New York, Acts 1934, C. 825, as amended by Acts 1935, C. 182.

dustries where it will not unduly jeopardize wages and working conditions of factory workers and injure the health and welfare of the home worker. The Connecticut law[130] goes further and prohibits issuance of home work certificates to children under sixteen. It also requires that certificates be issued only to persons who must remain at home because of their physical condition or to care for some member of the household, unless the work requires no machinery and its discontinuance would work undue hardship on workers or industry.

2. **Mines and Tunnels.**—Underground work of any sort obviously subjects the workman to greater dangers, both as to health and to safety, than do most of the manufacturing industries. Distance beneath the surface, artificial light, poisonous gases, explosive dusts, dampness, intestinal parasites, extreme heat, and in some kinds of work abnormal air pressure amounting often to several atmospheres, all contribute to render underground occupations extraordinarily hazardous. It is for this reason that the validity of hour legislation for adult men has become thoroughly established in the mining industry, although in many other lines of work such restrictions are still subject to attack on the score of unconstitutionality.[131]

a. *Mining.*—In these circumstances it is not surprising that mining furnishes one of the highest fatal accident rates in industry. Metal mining has a higher death rate than coal mining, and employment in anthracite coal mines is more dangerous than in bituminous mines, since the former are deeper and more subject to accumulations of noxious and explosive gases.

Coal mining appears to be more dangerous in the United States than in any other country. In reality our mines are shallower and less hazardous to work; but our methods of mining, while enabling us to lead the world in productivity, have resulted in our leading it also in human sacrifice. Standing second with regard to the number of men employed, the United States exceeds all other important producing countries both in total number and in rate of occurrence of fatal accidents. During the five years ending with 1934 the average fatal accident rate per 1,000 men employed (full-time, or 300-day employees) in coal

[130] Connecticut, Acts 1935, C. 154.
[131] See, however, discussion of this point under "Maximum Hours, Men," pp. 127-129.

SAFETY AND HEALTH

mining was 4.26 for the United States with a production of 4.32 tons per man per day; 2.23 for Germany with productivity at 1.49 tons per man per day; 1.34 for Great Britain with production at 1.22 tons per man per day; 1.03 for France with a daily output of 0.77 tons per man; and 1.16 for Belgium with an output of 0.69 tons per man-day. The fatal-accident rate for the United States improved during 1934 and 1935, but the comparison with the leading countries of Europe is still unfavorable to the United States.[132]

Health dangers and occupational diseases among miners have been given much less legislative attention than has the subject of accidents. Accidents are usually more spectacular, their causes are more certain and more easily located, and, moreover, employers are required to provide compensation for accidental injuries to mine workmen, while most American states have not provided compensation for occupational diseases.[133] Among the more important legal provisions for safeguarding the life and health of miners are the requirements for detailed maps of mines showing all workings and open at all times to mine inspectors, for a sufficient number of escapement shafts, for proper ventilation, a supply of pure air, and frequently for a special employee to inspect the mine daily for explosive or poisonous dusts or gases. Precautions against falling rock or coal must also be taken by carefully timbering dangerous places as far as known. Rules are laid down in regard to proper methods of drilling and blasting, and hoisting gears and cages for carrying men in and out of the mine must conform to specific requirements. Safety lamps, shelter holes, fencing of machinery, telephone connections, safe electrical equipment, restrictions upon the storing of explosives and upon the quality of illuminating oils—these and many more safeguards are frequently required and carefully defined by law. Provision is usually made for a rather limited first-aid equipment.

One of the most serious hazards of coal mining, the explosiveness of bituminous coal dust, is still to be adequately dealt with in American legislation. Coal dust is inflammable,

---

[132] Data received from U. S. Bureau of Mines. See current bulletins on Coal Mine Fatalities issued by that bureau.

[133] For a further discussion of this subject see chap. v, "Social Insurance."

and its presence in the air serves to carry a slight spark or minor explosion throughout a mine in a series of devastating blasts. Some of our laws require periodic sprinkling with water in dusty mines, but this device, once considered a satisfactory precaution, has been shown by experience to be most undependable.[134] Research abroad and by our own Bureau of Mines, however, has disclosed a really adequate safeguard—sprinkling the mine with non-inflammable rock dust. Experience in European countries legally requiring the use of rock dust in bituminous mines,[135] as well as in many American mines[136] which have within recent years voluntarily installed this safety measure, proves conclusively that this constitutes a real protection. Fortunately, the experience shows also that the device is both simple and relatively inexpensive to put into operation.[137] It should unquestionably be required by law for bituminous mines. In 1924, following a catastrophic explosion at Castle Gate, which cost 172 lives, the Utah Industrial Commission issued a series of orders[138] making rock dusting mandatory in Utah coal mines. Several states have recently amended their codes to permit rock dusting instead of the previously required water sprinkling, and the continuously growing demand for mandatory legislation on this subject makes probable its general adoption in the near future.

The enforcement of mine safety provisions in the various states is usually intrusted to a special body of mine inspectors, who either form a separate bureau of mine inspection or are attached to the state bureau of industrial inspection. Mine inspection protects the property of the employer as well as the lives of the employees, and many states require of inspectors

[134] United States Department of the Interior, Bureau of Mines, Rice, George S., "Stone Dusting or Rock Dusting to Prevent Coal Dust Explosions as Practiced in Great Britain and France," *Bulletin No. 225*, 1924.

[135] *Ibid.*

[136] "Rock Dust Saves 1,050 Lives in a Single Accident," *American Labor Legislation Review*, March, 1926, pp. 67-68. See also other references cited in this article.

[137] "Cost of Rock Dusting to Prevent Coal Dust Explosions Is Remarkably Low," *American Labor Legislation Review*, September, 1924.

[138] *Supplement to General Coal Mines Safety Orders*, approved by the Industrial Commission of Utah, April 8, 1924.

SAFETY AND HEALTH 211

a certain number of years' experience and also civil service examinations conducted by an examining board frequently composed of representatives of employers and employees. The authority of the inspectors is sometimes far-reaching, extending even to the power of stopping work if the mine regulations have not been obeyed.

A significant step was the establishment by Congress in 1910 of the federal Bureau of Mines with the function, among others, of conducting "scientific and technologic investigations concerning mining," with a view to improving health conditions and increasing safety and efficiency. The bureau has no authority to do anything except conduct investigations, publish reports, and furnish advice, all enforcement of mine laws being left in the control of the states, but within its limited field it has already performed valuable services. Series of bulletins and technical papers distributed free present the results of the latest scientific inquiries into the causes and prevention of mine explosions and other accidents. Ten safety stations and three field offices have been established for advantageous service to the mining districts of the country. Each office is usually in charge of a district safety engineer with a staff of one or more safety engineers and one or more safety instructors. Their work includes giving training in first aid, mine rescue, and accident prevention; making mine safety inspections and reports; and assisting recovery work after mine fires and explosions. All stations are equipped with motor trucks for the rapid transportation of equipment and men. The bureau also has operated as many as eleven railroad mine rescue cars, but in 1936 only two were in active service because of lack of funds. These cars are equipped to give safety instruction and rescue work, and are dispatched at once to the scene of any disaster in their districts.

b. *Work in Compressed Air.*—An industrial hazard brought into prominence by the increasing construction of tunnels, subways, bridges, and skyscrapers is compressed-air illness, or the "bends." An investigator for the Illinois Commission on Occupational Diseases secured interviews with 161 men who had sustained attacks of the malady, and the medical director at the construction of the Pennsylvania-East River tunnels in New York in 1909 reported 3,692 cases, of which twenty were fatal.

By 1936, Louisiana, New York, New Jersey, and Pennsylvania, the states most concerned, had attempted to control the disease by legislation, and in other states similar steps have been taken through the method of administrative orders.[139] The customary provisions include physical examinations of all applicants for work and of all employees at stated intervals, a sliding scale of working hours, decreasing as the pressure increases,[140] and a period of gradual "decompression," ranging from one minute for emergence from a pressure of ten pounds above normal to twenty-five minutes for emergence from a pressure of fifty pounds above normal. Work under more than fifty pounds' pressure is forbidden. The employer must maintain dressing-rooms with lockers, hot and cold shower baths, and provision for drying clothes. Medical attendants are also required, as well as a hospital lock for the recompression and treatment of sufferers from the disease.

3. **Transportation.**—Protective legislation regulating working conditions in transportation relates mainly to safety. Commercial transportation by land and water is the subject of a large body of such legislation. The newest form of transportation, by air, presents new hazards, and already Congress and the states have enacted laws to promote aviation safety. Transportation safety laws either may be designed for the protection of employees, as in the case of automatic couplers on railroads and the provision for emergency exits for seamen, or they may be intended primarily for the protection of the traveling public, as in the case of boiler inspection in both kinds of transportation. A few measures, such as the full-crew laws on railroads and in navigation, have been urged as a direct protection for both laborers and travelers. As in the case of railroads, a number of states had already enacted laws requiring the licensing of aviators when Congress in 1925 undertook the regulation of interstate air transportation. The federal air safety program now includes not only the licensing of pilots and the regulation and inspection of equipment, but also the maintenance of radio and light beacons which in the airways serve a function similar to that of lighthouses and lightships in water transportation.

The majority of transportation employees are engaged in traffic which is interstate or international in character. The

[139] See p. 221.
[140] See "Hours of Labor, Men," p. 129.

SAFETY AND HEALTH

more important legislation affecting this class of workmen has therefore been federal rather than state. Railway employees have been more often brought under state laws than have seamen, but when any question has arisen over the respective jurisdiction of state or federal authority the latter has practically always been given precedence by the courts.

a. *Navigation.*—While slavery and serfdom have been abolished for the majority of the workmen in most civilized countries, until 1915 the seaman in America was kept in a position of semislavery through employment under a contract enforceable by imprisonment. This position of involuntary servitude gave him but little effective voice in regulating the conditions under which he worked. In the early days of sea travel a shipowner's interest impelled him to secure an intelligent and competent crew which could protect his cargo. With the substitution of steam for sails, the spread of lighthouses and channel markings, and the growth of marine insurance and limited liability legislation, the quality of seamanship greatly declined. The "seaman" was displaced by the "deck hand," the American by the northern European, and the latter by the immigrant of the southern races. In the majority of serious sea disasters in recent years the lack of both skill and numbers in the working force has been officially reported. There apparently was a steady increase in the size of the load carried, without a corresponding increase in the number and skill of those employed to handle it.

In a few states legislation looking toward general marine safety has been enacted, such as provisions for boiler inspection and signal lights, but most of the legislation affecting seamen has been federal. As early as 1798 Congress recognized the need of special protection for this class of workmen, many of whom are single and homeless. In that year the federal government established a marine-hospital fund to maintain hospitals for the care of disabled seamen of ships belonging to the United States. During the latter half of the nineteenth century Congress continued its protective policy toward seamen by legislation, regulating, among other matters, the conditions of living and working on shipboard, the size and experience of crews, and the construction and inspection of vessels. Despite these regulations the position of seamen was held to be most unsatisfactory, and it was not until the passage of the federal Seamen's Act of 1915 that the grosser injustices were removed.[141]

While the outstanding features of this act related rather to the personal freedom of seamen,[142] additional provisions were made for the health and comfort of employees through the requirement of proper washing places and sleeping rooms, hospital space, fumigation, heating, lighting, ventilation, and drainage.

It has been repeatedly pointed out that in case of accidents at sea, such as fires or boiler explosions, a ship cannot summon immediate assistance as a manufacturing establishment, for instance, is able to do on land, but must rely upon its own crew and the chance aid of near-by vessels. Despite the use of the radio as a means of notifying other ships in case of distress, experience has shown that the only way really to safeguard human life at sea is to provide an equipment and crew adequate to meet any reasonable emergency. The Seamen's Act of 1915, therefore, provided for a substantial increase in the size of the crews employed, for a certain percentage of able seamen, for "certified lifeboat men," and for properly constructed lifeboats, the number to be fixed according to the size and character of the ship and its cargo.

b. *Railroads and Street Cars.*—In the early days of railroading, reports of deaths and mutilations, particularly in connection with the coupling of cars, were repeatedly made public, and the need of protective legislation became apparent, especially as the length and complexity of lines developed and as speed increased. At the middle of the nineteenth century only about 9,000 miles of railroad existed. In 1869 a through route to California was opened, and by 1880 the total mileage had increased to 86,000. Between 1880 and 1890 more miles of new road were built than during the entire period previous to 1875, and in the early 'eighties a few states enacted protective legislation. It soon became apparent, however, that state legislation alone would result in long delays and in a great lack of uni-

[141] United States, Laws 1914-1915, C. 153, as amended by Public 141, Sixty-fourth Congress, First Session; Public 261, Sixty-sixth Congress, Second Session; and Public 808, Seventy-fourth Congress, Second Session.
[142] See "Contract Labor," pp. 324-325.

SAFETY AND HEALTH

formity. As the occurrence of serious accidents continued and as interstate commerce developed, the need of federal regulation became more apparent.

Many experiments were carried on in search of proper safety devices, and as early as 1868 a successful application of air brakes was made. The most serious danger to employees resulted from their being required to go between cars in order to couple or uncouple them. It was not until 1887 that a satisfactory automatic coupler was devised for general use. In order to compel the general adoption of the standard coupler the necessity of federal legislation was recognized.

Although the Interstate Commerce Commission, created by the federal Act of February 4, 1887, had power to investigate and regulate rates, the act made no mention of safety appliances or the protection of employees. The absence of authority over these matters was remedied by the federal act of March 2, 1893, and several subsequent acts[143] made it obligatory upon all roads engaged in interstate traffic to equip all cars and locomotives with approved automatic couplers, and to provide other safeguards such as power brakes and grab irons.[144] In this particular, American labor legislation was far in advance of European. The results of the coupler legislation are particularly striking. In 1890, when only about 10 per cent of railway cars were equipped with automatic couplers, accidents in the coupling of cars amounted to nearly half of all casualties to trainmen. By 1912, when over 99 per cent of all cars were so equipped, the proportion of accidents from this cause was reduced to about 8 per cent. The majority of early regulations imposed by the federal government, however, left open to the various roads the determination of the kind and character of devices to be installed. The absence of a central standardizing authority resulted in lack of uniformity, and at times in the

---

[143] United States, Laws 1892-1893, C. 196; Laws 1902-1903, C. 976; Laws 1906-1907, C. 225.

[144] For the further protection of employees and as a stimulus to the roads to use every possible safety precaution, Congress also provided that no employee injured on a train not equipped according to law could be held to have assumed the risk of his employment even though he knew of the violations. This provision has been upheld in the North Carolina case of Greenlee v. Southern R. Co., 122 N. C. 977, 30 S. E. 115 (1898).

adoption of inadequate or ineffective devices. In 1910, therefore, an act of Congress, in addition to making new safety provisions, gave to the Interstate Commerce Commission power, after proper hearings, to "designate the number, dimensions, location, and manner of application of the appliances," and thereafter such determinations were to remain as "the standards of equipment," and any failure to comply with any requirement of the commission was subject to a "like penalty as failure to comply with any requirement of this act."[145] At the same session of Congress the commission was given authority to investigate all collisions, derailments, or other accidents, to subpœna witnesses, administer oaths, take testimony, and to require the production of all papers, books, and other evidence. It might also make a public report "together with such recommendations as it deems proper." One year later $25,000 was appropriated for the use of the commission in making tests and establishing standards,[146] and a maximum of $300,000 a year was appropriated to provide for proper boiler inspection by a staff of fifty-three inspectors working in close cooperation with the commission.[147] Additional inspectors were provided and the maximum limit upon appropriations struck out by an amendment of 1924.[148]

Beginning with the great increase in railroad mileage in the early 'eighties, state legislation grew in volume and developed along two lines, one mainly for the protection of employees, and the other mainly for the protection of the traveling public. Measures for the protection of travelers are of two kinds. The first relates to mechanical devices for the prevention of accidents, such as automatic bell ringers, brakes, headlights, and signal lights, while the second relates to the qualifications and training of employees.

Among the measures which have been passed primarily for the protection of employees are found such requirements as those for the installation of grab irons, ladders, running boards, storm windows in engines, the maintenance of a proper temperature in mail or baggage cars, the regulation of the height

[145] United States, Laws 1909-1910, C. 160.
[146] United States, Laws 1910-1911, C. 285.
[147] *Ibid.*, C. 103.
[148] Public 277, Sixty-eighth Congress, First Session.

SAFETY AND HEALTH

of bridges or other overhead structures, the maintenance of a proper clearance around tracks, particularly in railroad yards, the blocking of frogs and switches, and, for employees engaged in repairing tracks, the erection of sheds to protect them from inclement weather. For the safety and convenience of employees who are frequently required to travel long distances on freight or stock trains caboose cars must be provided, which must be constructed according to certain specifications of size, strength, safety, and comfort.

Employees on street or interurban railways are also frequently protected through state legislation or municipal ordinance. Such measures relate usually to inclosed vestibules during the winter months, seats for motormen, and proper automatic brakes, and occasionally to equipment for the sanding of rails, to the examination of employees, and to minimum age limits.

During recent years the sharpest debate in matters of railway safety legislation has centered about the full-crew laws, which are held to protect both the public and the employee. More than twenty states have enacted such legislation, but in several cases the opposition of the railroads has resulted in its subsequent repeal. A few states fix no statutory limit but empower their railroad or public service commissions to determine the size of the crews. These acts usually apply to both passenger and freight service on roads of given lengths, and fix the number of employees—principally of brakemen—in proportion to the number and kind of cars in the train. Full-crew laws have been initiated by the railway men's organizations and have been vigorously opposed by the railroad owners, who have contended that as a rule larger crews are unnecessary because of the reduction in the amount of work required of employees since the introduction of safety devices, the formation of special switching crews, and the generally improved methods of handling trains. They point also to the increase in operating cost, resulting in reduced dividends and in curtailment of improvements.

On the other hand, the trainmen point to the large number of both fatal and non-fatal accidents, and to the increasing strain upon railway employees because of the increase in the weight of trains, in the number of tons per train, and in the number of cars per man. They hold that by these increases the railroads have made their greatest economies. The trainmen maintain, therefore, that full-crew legislation serves practically the same purpose as legislation restricting hours of labor, in that both reduce the physical strain and thereby the frequency of accidents.

This is the view which was adopted by the Supreme Court of Pennsylvania when in 1913[149] it upheld the full-crew law of that state, enacted in 1911,[150] as having a real and substantial relation to the safety of passengers and employees on railroad trains. The company presented evidence as to the cost of the legislation, but the court held that: "Uncompensated obedience to a regulation enacted for the public welfare or safety under the police power of the state is not taking property without due compensation, and any injury sustained in obeying such a regulation is but *damnum absque injuria*."

State provisions for railroad safety have frequently been contested on the ground that regulations which apply to interstate commerce are a subject for federal legislation; but the courts have uniformly held that where Congress has not legislated upon these questions the states were entirely within their rights. An interstate road, therefore, either might make such changes as were necessary, as it passed from one commonwealth to another, to meet the minimum requirements of each commonwealth, or it might comply everywhere with the maximum provision found in any of the states through which it passed.

Although much of the protective railroad legislation is mainly for the benefit of employees, it is recognized that the safety of the public depends in large part upon the safety of those who are intrusted with the care and management of trains. It is this aspect of the matter which has largely influenced the courts in rendering favorable decisions on safety and health laws for railway employees.

The enforcement of protective regulations in relation to railway labor has in the majority of states been intrusted to railway

[149] Pennsylvania R. Co. *v.* Ewing, *et al.*, 241 Pa. 581, 88 Atl. 775 (1913). A similar decision was rendered in Chicago, Rock Island and Pacific R. Co. *v.* Arkansas, 219 U. S. 453, 31 Sup. Ct. 275 (1911), upholding the 1907 law in that state.

[150] Pennsylvania, Laws 1911, No. 811. This law was repealed in 1921 and the public service commission was vested with authority in this matter. (Laws 1921. No. 184.)

SAFETY AND HEALTH 219

or public utility commissions created primarily to supervise or regulate rates. In this class of legislation, as in the regulation of conditions in factories, workshops, and mines, it has been found impracticable to embody in the statute law specifications which will be effective under diverse and constantly changing conditions. For this reason many legislatures have delegated to the railroad commissions power to work out details of provisions and to prescribe safety rules and regulations. This method of protection has repeatedly been sustained by the courts. In 1913 the law creating the Railroad Commission of Indiana and an early ruling of the commission fixing a 1,500-candle power standard for locomotive headlights were both attacked as unconstitutional. The case was carried to the supreme court of the state, which upheld the delegation of legislative powers, declaring that: "The decisions of this court and the courts of other states in this regard are clearly against the appellant's contention."[151] Subsequent appeal to the United States Supreme Court also resulted in the statute's being upheld.[152]

IV. DEVELOPMENT OF STANDARDS

A careful study of the early laws to preserve industrial safety and health, as passed by Congress and by the legislatures of the fifty American states and territories, discloses at once four fundamental defects.

1. **Defects of Early Legislation.**—First among these defects is *the incompleteness of these laws*. It was long the custom of legislatures to specify in the law the industries and danger points which were to be safeguarded, and to confine the inspectors' authority to the places and conditions mentioned. Under this method many industrial danger points were overlooked. Perhaps "buzz saw" or "dangerous dusts" or "foundry" was omitted from the law inadvertently or otherwise. Although often fraught with harm to the worker, these unmentioned points were outside the authority of the inspection officials, and the workers received no protection until the law could be

[151] Vandalia R. Co. *v.* Railroad Commission of Indiana, 182 Ind. 382, 101 N. E. 85 (1913). For a clear opinion on the delegation of legislative authority, see Minneapolis, St. Paul and Sault Ste. Marie R. Co. *v.* Railroad Commission of Wisconsin, 136 Wis. 146, 116 N. W. 905 (1908).

[152] Vandalia R. Co. *v.* Public Service Commission of Indiana, 242 U. S. 255, 37 Sup. Ct. 93 (1916).

changed. Frequently, too, a qualifying phrase greatly limited the operation of a good law. For example, the law in one state required poisonous fumes generated "in the course of the manufacturing process" to be removed. While varnishing the interior of vats in a brewery two men died and one was totally blinded for life, because they inhaled the poisonous fumes of wood alcohol used in the varnish; but because varnishing vats is in the nature of repair work and does not come "in the course of the manufacturing process," the inspectors could not legally remedy the dangerous situation. It was necessary to wait an entire year (in most states it would have been two years) before the legislature convened and the law could be amended. These illustrations indicate a common weakness of early safety and health laws in many states.

The second fundamental defect is *the absence of direct responsibility*. Many laws placed no obligation whatever upon an employer to safeguard danger points or upon the employee to aid in maintaining safety except "in the discretion of the commissioner of labor," or unless "the commissioner so directs," or "if in the opinion of the commissioner of labor it is necessary." This type of legislation placed no duty upon the employer to provide or upon the employee to maintain proper protection until required to do so by the inspector. No protective devices had to be provided until the inspector called and ordered them installed. Scarcely a state but has had laws of this character.

The third fundamental defect is *the absence of well-defined standards*. The old theory of factory inspection legislation assumed that the legislatures, often made up largely of lawyers and farmers, would define in the law the exact nature of protection to be provided in factory, workshop, or mine. But because of inadequate information, and possibly also because of fear of adverse court decisions, our lawmakers vaguely required merely that dangerous machinery be "sufficiently guarded," usually "where practicable," and left it to the poorly trained and poorly paid inspector to enforce these indefinite laws, usually "in his discretion." This discretionary power, when placed in the hands of uninformed officials, brought this method of lawmaking into disrepute among employers, employees, and the public.

SAFETY AND HEALTH

The fourth fundamental defect is *the lack of responsiveness to changing industrial conditions*. When it had become apparent that many of the early laws were failing of their purpose because of the foregoing blemishes, there followed a comparatively brief period during which efforts were made to frame comprehensive, scientific provisions, free from "jokers" and loopholes, and to secure their passage by the legislatures. Perhaps the most noteworthy example of such legislation was the standard law enacted in several states providing for the protection of workers in the lead trades. In this instance, after careful investigation by the federal government supplemented by private studies and many conferences, a very specific bill was drafted to apply to the various processes in the manufacture of lead salts, and the resulting legislation served a very useful educational purpose. In a few states also the laws undoubtedly hastened the efforts of employers to make their work places sanitary. But it was found that some specific safeguards minutely prescribed in the statutes were quickly out of date. In order that they might be superseded by improved devices or methods there was once more required the slow and expensive action of legislatures, which in most states might not be in session again for more than an entire year. The impracticability of embodying in statute law specific danger points and specific remedies became clear.

2. **The Method of Administrative Orders.**—Legislators themselves began to recognize the futility of attempting to formulate in the short and busy sessions, convening in most states only once in two years, proper protective measures. They saw that the proper persons to accomplish this work efficiently were those who had an opportunity to familiarize themselves with changing industrial conditions. Therefore, in several states, legislators decided that they would no longer attempt to enact laws specifying in detail what shall be done, but instead would ask that work places be made safe. To carry out the will of the legislature they provided a commission to work out with employers and employees the best possible methods of protection. After public hearings, the methods agreed upon were issued by the commission in the form of administrative orders or regulations to apply state wide and to have the force of law. Here we find the very foundation of effective safety inspection work. The keynote is *cooperation*. The experience of the worker,

the knowledge of the employer, and the critical constructive ability of the expert are all needed in the formation of effective standards of health and safety and in the enforcement of these standards.

By 1934, the legislatures of thirty states had authorized this type of administrative rule-making in at least some aspects of their labor legislation.[153] In a score, this authorization extended to practically the entire field of industrial safety and health. Although some labor departments had not made much use of this power, others—especially those of California, Massachusetts, New Jersey, New York, Pennsylvania, and Wisconsin—had promulgated detailed codes of regulations covering a wide variety of specific industries and processes. In such states, the administrative regulations, rather than the statutes, must be consulted to discover most of the safety laws. A movement to secure greater uniformity in the safety codes adopted in the various states has been led by the American Standards Association, organized in 1918. That association has drafted numerous standard codes for use by state officials in preparing state regulations.

This new method of regulating industrial conditions, through administrative orders cooperatively formulated and issued by a permanent commission, has resulted in several states in a progressive and accurate adjustment of factory inspection to the changing methods and new risks that accompany modern industry. Concerning this method, a former chief factory inspector has said: "As a state inspector, my experience has demonstrated that the arbitrary imposition of rules of law will not, in itself, produce satisfactory standards for the safety and health of employees in factories, mills, and workshops. . . . The observations which I have made emphasize the importance of cooperation and of education of both parties to the labor contract as to what are ideal factory conditions. This cooperation must be brought about if substantial results with reference to safety standards are to be obtained through state inspection." Fortunately, scientific accident prevention has been brought into the foreground by the adoption of workmen's compensation

[153] For a detailed discussion of this subject, see Andrews, John B., *Administrative Labor Legislation*, 1936.

acts, and it has quickened the movement for reorganization of administrative boards in many states.

No longer is it necessary in states like New York, Ohio, and Wisconsin, for example, to wait one or two years for a session of the legislature in order to submit proposals for the proper protection of the workers. No longer need specific rigid provisions be drafted into bills and thrust upon the bewildered attention of the legislators while temporarily in session at the state capital. The legislation has laid down the law in a broad way; the industrial commission, as rapidly as circumstances permit, may fill in the administrative detail. Under this new system the industry itself makes the laws for its own shop government. Employers and employees, with the aid of impartial experts, are learning through self-expression the importance and the practicability of safe working conditions. The prevention of industrial accidents and diseases, particularly when accompanied by social insurance, is becoming a matter of enlightened selfishness; the general and the specific statutory requirements of former years are being supplanted by scientific standards developed through administrative orders based on continuing investigations.[154]

[154] See chap. viii, "Administration."

CHAPTER V

SOCIAL INSURANCE

For most of the economic hazards of life there has been developed an appropriate method for the distribution of losses and the subsequent elimination of risks. Marine insurance, for the financial protection of those who send their goods down to the sea in ships, was the first to be developed on an extensive basis. Insurance against loss by fire is now a regularly accepted precaution in every community. By this common method of insuring against loss, each individual in the organized group is assured that in case of the destruction or damage of his property he will be reimbursed from a fund contributed little by little by the whole group. Insurance, accordingly, has been defined as an arrangement for distributing among many the losses sustained by a few.

By this thin spreading of individual losses over a large group, the man receiving an income from property destroyed by shipwreck or by fire is in a position to reinvest. Even more necessary than for the property owner is insurance for the workingman, whose ability to labor is his only asset and who is peculiarly liable to be deprived of his income. When the laborer, no matter how efficient he may be, has as a result of either individual or collective bargaining secured a job for himself even if at a wage and under hour limitations which are temporarily acceptable, his economic position is still precarious. He and his family are still face to face with exceptional economic risks, including the suffering and want following accident, illness, invalidity, premature or normal old age, premature death, and unemployment.

Peculiarly necessary, therefore, is this common arrangement for group or social action known as insurance, when those who suffer the losses are workingmen solely dependent for support upon their ability to labor. Such insurance may be developed by the initiative of individuals wishing to insure, or it may be developed through legislation. When such insurance provision is made through legislation, it marks the adoption by society of a settled policy of cooperative action to distribute among a group the losses suffered by individuals arising from their inability to work and thereby earn a livelihood. It is therefore natural to term this insurance *social insurance.*

While savings are sometimes urged as an alternative to workmen's social insurance, it is as true for the wage earner as for the merchant, that the provision by each person of a reserve sufficient to meet the possible maximum loss is extravagant, requiring as it does that each person shall be able to meet from his individual savings the hazard which will fall upon only a small number. Far more economical is the institution of insurance whereby the individual sets aside only enough to meet the average loss when distributed throughout the group.

The most substantial reason why wage earners do not voluntarily insure themselves against the risks of accident and illness, invalidity and old age, early death and unemployment, is insufficient income. Reliable information from conservative private and public reports amply confirms the statement that the average wage earner with a family is not receiving pay for his labor sufficient "to secure the elements of a normal standard of living."[1] It is unreasonable to expect such wage earners to provide against a possible future contingency at the sacrifice of present necessaries.

A further reason for the failure of the underpaid masses to insure themselves is indifference or lack of foresight concerning the problems of the future. Although thrift in the presence of subnormal living occasioned by low wages may at times become a positive social vice, provision for the future is on the whole necessary and beneficial. Furthermore, it is recognized that for millions of laborers saving will take place only under a distinct incentive. This "enforced saving" against the inevitable rainy day in the life of the workingman is most effectively brought about through the periodical collection of dues or premiums for the support of the various forms of social insurance. It has been discovered, moreover, that community of interest in directly bearing the financial cost of insurance

[1] See chap. ii, "Minimum Fair Wage."

furnishes a kind of cooperative pressure on employers[2] which can be utilized effectively in the elimination of risks in so far as they are preventable. The rapid development of the "safety first" movement which followed closely the enactment of workmen's compensation laws is sufficient evidence of the preventive power of social insurance.

There is a growing recognition, also, that industry is a contributing factor to the hazards of life among wage earners. For example, industry is responsible for work accidents, and is a contributing factor in illness. To the extent that men are idle because of industrial irregularities, industry and not the worker is responsible for unemployment. Social insurance plans generally recognize industry's share in creating hazards, the burden of which traditionally has rested upon the wage earners, and aim to distribute the cost in accordance with the responsibility. By this means social insurance not only spreads out the cost among wage earners as a group, but also distributes it between employers and workers. Experience with voluntary insurance has demonstrated that the only method of making insurance universal among wage earners, and of having employers assume their share of the cost, is to make it compulsory.

Thus, although beginning in each case with some form of private organization, there has been developed, to meet the peculiar risks which modern industrial workers must endure, a special kind of insurance, depending for its inclusiveness, its financial security, its economical administration, and its effectiveness in reducing the cause of each particular evil, upon an element of social compulsion.

Various countries have social insurance against accident and occupational disease, against sickness, against old age and invalidity, against death and the consequent dependency of widows and orphans, and finally against unemployment. In all of this social action an important element of self-defense is not lacking. It is clearly recognized that insurance is the most effective device for protecting society itself against the pressure of incapacitated individuals who otherwise would be thrown upon the community for maintenance. While attempting to avoid the demoralizing round of charity, by means of an insurance pro-

[2] See chap. viii, "Administration."

gram, there is consciously promoted a system of individual care aimed at the scientific promotion of the worker's efficiency.

1. Industrial Accident Insurance

The first kind of social insurance to be developed extensively through legislation in the United States, probably because of the comparative ease of recognizing both the industrial cause and the far-reaching extent of the evil, is insurance against occupational accidents and diseases, or, as it is more popularly termed in this country, workmen's compensation.

Compensation to the injured workman is based upon the theory that the consumer of economic goods should bear all the expenses incurred in the production of such goods. Among those expenses must be included the pecuniary losses from deaths and injuries occurring in the regular course of production. Wages lost, medical attendance, and burial expenses, in case of accidental injury or death, are all losses which should be considered as a part of the expense of production. If these losses are to be borne by the workman, he indirectly carries part of the expense of production. In order to avoid this, the expense of work accidents, it is now generally agreed, should be treated like all other expenses of production; it should be borne by the employer in the first instance, and be shifted by him, in the form of increased prices, upon the consumer of those goods in the production of which the injuries were sustained.

Our present compensation laws have passed through a long period of development, and have many precedents. As mining and navigation developed in Europe, the workmen of these two industries formed, in the eighteenth century and sometimes even earlier, mutual accident insurance associations for their own protection. The above industries were the pioneers in forming such mutual associations largely because each man was greatly dependent for his safety upon the care of his fellow workmen.[3]

In the handicraft production of the Middle Ages, not only were the workmen very closely related, but there was also a close connection between the master and his servants. Manufacturing in the gilds was conducted on a small scale, and each

[3] United States Commissioner of Labor, *Twenty-fourth Annual Report*, 1909, "Workmen's Insurance and Compensation Systems in Europe," vol. i, p. 977.

228 PRINCIPLES OF LABOR LEGISLATION

master had but few helpers. Accidents were not numerous because machinery was not developed, and production was carried on at low speed. When injuries did occur, the master, at least theoretically, took care of the disabled.

This personal relation of employer and employee disappears to a great extent with the development of large-scale industry. As the number of employees in each establishment increased, the owner could no longer give them his personal attention and care. The workman gained more personal freedom, but lost the aid of his employer in case of sickness and accident. To recover damages he now had to seek relief by legal proceedings, either under the common law or under statutes establishing employers' liability; he had to bring suit against his master.

1. **Rules of Employers' Liability.**—The conditions under which the injured could recover in court were based upon a series of rules which included (a) the duties of the employer; (b) the burden of occupational risks; (c) the fellow servant rule; (d) contributory negligence; and (e) assumption of risks.[4]

a. *Duties of the Employer.*—It was considered the duty of the employer to use reasonable care in protecting his employees against injury while engaged in his service.[5] Numerous court decisions defined this obligation of the employer in considerable detail. He was required to provide a safe place to work, to furnish safe tools and appliances, to conduct his business in a safe manner, and to select competent fellow servants. Reasonable care required the guarding of only those dangerous conditions of which the employer had knowledge or of which by the exercise of reasonable care he should have had knowledge.[6] It is held by many experts that no matter how great caution is taken against accidents, many mishaps will occur which result in death or injury to the workman. Establishments in which every machine is guarded and where safety work is carried on ably and conscientiously, nevertheless, it is declared, will have numerous accidents. These injuries are said to be due to the inherent hazards of the industry; nothing will prevent them.

[4] See Downey, E. H., *History of Work Accident Indemnity*, 1912, p. 17.
[5] Priestly v. Fowler, 3 Meeson and Welsby, 1, 6 (England, 1837).
[6] Magee v. Chicago & Northwestern R. Co., 82 Iowa 249, 48 N. W. 92 (1891).

SOCIAL INSURANCE

b. *Burden of Occupational Risks.*—It is to these accidents that the principle of the burden of occupational risks applies. The employee assumes the ordinary risks of the employment in which he engages. In an early American case the court stated that: "The general rule, resulting from considerations as well of justice as of policy, is that he who engages in the employment of another for the performance of specified duties and services, for compensation takes upon himself the natural and ordinary risks and perils incident to the performance of such services, and in legal presumption the wage is adjusted accordingly."[7] Freeing the employer from liability thus left a vast number of injuries and deaths as a direct burden upon the workmen and their dependents, with no chance of obtaining damages.

c. *Fellow Servant Rule.*—The rules holding the employer responsible for exercising reasonable care in protecting his employees, and exempting him from liability for inherent occupational hazards, were recognized uniformly by the courts. The third, or fellow servant rule, involved more serious difficulty. The usual rule of law is that a master is responsible for the negligence or carelessness of his servants in the course of their duties. Since many accidents to workmen can be traced to the carelessness or negligence of a co-employee, the application of the rule as between fellow servants was felt to be harsh.[8] Exception to the general rule was first taken by the English Exchequer Court in 1837 in the case of Priestly v. Fowler.[9] A butcher driver's helper was injured by the breaking down of the wagon. He brought suit against the butcher for damages on the grounds that the wagon was insufficient for its purpose, and that it had been overloaded. Damages were denied on the ground that if they were allowed the master's liability would extend very far. He might be held liable to the footman who was injured by a defective wagon because of the negligence of the coachmaker, or to the servant for the negligence of the cook in not properly cleaning copper vessels in the kitchen. Besides,

[7] Farwell *v.* Boston & W. R. Co., 4 Metcalf (Mass.) 49, 57 (1842).
[8] Consequently the courts, declare Shearman and Redfield in *The Law of Negligence,* "boldly invented an exception to the general rule of masters' liability, by which servants were deprived of its protection" (p. vi).
[9] Priestly *v.* Fowler, 3 Meeson and Welsby, 1, 6 (England, 1837).

the opinion states, the driver's helper "must have known as well as his master, and probably better," that the wagon was insufficient, or overloaded, and might have refused to use it.

A similar decision was rendered four years later in America, without mentioning the Priestly case. In this case[10] damages were denied a locomotive fireman who had been injured owing to the negligence of the engineer under whom he worked. It was held that the railroad company was not a guarantor to one employee against the negligence of other employees; that the fireman should have been aware of the perils of his employment, and that the plaintiff was paid for his labor and for the danger to which he was exposed.

In 1842 Chief Justice Shaw of Massachusetts gave the fellow servant rule a definite formulation and a wide application in deciding the case of Farwell v. Boston and Worcester Railroad Corporation[11] in favor of the defendant. An engineer brought action for damages because he had lost a leg owing to the switchman's neglecting to change a switch. Justice Shaw argued that any servant might reasonably anticipate that his associates at times will be careless and negligent; that this is one of the risks of employment to which, in legal presumption, the compensation is adjusted. Want of care can be anticipated as much as a coupling out of repair. The brakeman can guard against one as much as against the other—being powerless against both.

This chain of reasoning was accepted as sound and conclusive, and numerous later decisions were based on it. It relieved the master from all liability for an injury sustained on account of the negligence or carelessness of a fellow servant, provided the master had exercised reasonable care in his selection.[12]

d. *Contributory Negligence.*—According to the doctrine of contributory negligence, a plaintiff for damages for an injury occasioned by the fault of the employer, in order to win his case, must establish his own freedom from negligence. Any negligence on the part of the injured, no matter how slight in comparison with that of the employer, will cause him to lose the suit, if without that negligence the accident would not have

[10] Murray v. South Carolina R. Co., 1 McMullan 385 (1841).
[11] Farwell v. Boston and W. R. Co., 4 Metcalf (Mass.) 49 (1842).
[12] Thompson, Seymour D., *Commentaries on the Law of Negligence*, 1901-1905, vol. iv, p. 270, Sec. 4048.

occurred. Such negligence exists if the employee continues to work under conditions which are apparently dangerous and which a reasonably prudent man would avoid, or if his own want of due care contributed as a proximate cause to the accident.[13]

e. *Assumption of Risk.*—As a last resort to free himself from liability, the employer could set up the defense that the injured workman had "assumed" the risk. The risk referred to in this connection is not the ordinary inherent hazard of the occupation, but an abnormal danger of which the employee was fully aware, but in spite of which he continued to work. The principle of assumption of risk, however, has been modified in several states by statutes in favor of the workman. This is particularly true in case of children and of railroad workers.

It can easily be seen that with these last four rules, all aiming to relieve the employer of liability, it is extremely difficult for the injured workman to win a suit for damages. In order to gain a favorable verdict he must be able to show that the injury was the immediate result of the employer's failure to exercise ordinary care, and that it was not contributed to in any degree by his own want of ordinary care. Moreover, he cannot recover if the accident was due to an ordinary hazard of the employment, or to the negligence of a fellow workman, or to a defect arising from the negligence of the employer that was known to the injured and that created a condition under which a prudent man would not have continued to work.

Satisfactory statistics are not available to show definitely the proportion of injured men who received indemnity under these liability doctrines. From the meager investigations which have been made, however, it may be concluded that but few recovered damages, and that the amounts were in many cases shamefully small. Under the liability system insurance companies have engaged in carrying the employer's risk. They have expert legal advice, and are able to contest wage-earners' claims even more effectively than the average employer. It is true that numerous laws have been enacted in most countries attempting to place more liability upon the employer. Germany passed a law, wide in scope, to that effect in 1871, and Great Britain followed in 1880.

---

[13] Butterfield *v.* Forester, 11 East 60 (England, 1809); Haley *v.* Chicago & Northwestern R. Co., 21 Iowa 15 (1866).

The first American employers' liability law was passed in Alabama in 1885, followed by Massachusetts in 1887. Among the best of these laws was the federal statute establishing the liability of railroad companies for injuries to their employees.[14] Notwithstanding all attempted legal regulation, the position of the injured workman was not much improved. To recover, he had to go to the courts and had to meet the strong legal opposition of insurance companies or of his employer.

Not only are the injured man's chances to win his case very small and the machinery too slow to bring relief when it is most needed, but the system is extremely wasteful. The following figures taken from the records of ten insurance companies for a three-year period will substantiate this statement:[15]

Collected from employers	$23,523,585
Absorbed by companies in profits and expenses	14,963,790
Received by plaintiffs' attorneys (approximately)	1,900,000
Received by injured workmen or their dependents (approximately)	6,660,000

Of every $100 paid by the employer in premiums, only $28 reached the workman, and that amount only after a long legal action in many instances. In certain leading industrial states it was found that it required on the average from two to six years to reach final judgment in a fatal accident case under employers' liability.[16]

Without question, under the liability system only a small proportion of cases are taken to court, because the injured knows an attempted recovery is but a gamble, with all odds against him. As a rule, the insurance companies act as if their duty under employers' liability is not to compensate the injured, but to defeat their claims.

2. **Beginnings of Industrial Accident Insurance.**—The credit for first realizing that in order to furnish certain and adequate relief to the injured workman it was necessary to provide insurance for all laborers, and for all accidents, must be given to Germany. The original bill to this effect was introduced in the Reichstag in 1881, but failed to be adopted. The follow-

[14] United States, Acts 1907-1908, C. 149.
[15] New York Commission on Employers' Liability and Other Matters, *First Report*, 1910, pp. 29-31.
[16] Downey, E. H., *History of Work Accident Indemnity in Iowa*, p. 79.

SOCIAL INSURANCE

ing year a second bill was introduced providing for sickness and accident insurance. The sickness clauses, including provisions for accident compensation during the first thirteen weeks of disability, were passed in 1883, but the accident insurance was again defeated. Finally, in 1884 a bill providing compulsory insurance against accidents was passed which became effective in October, 1885.

a. *German System.*—The German law has been frequently amended and extended in scope, and today practically every industry of that country is included.

Under the German system the compensation of the injured workman for the first twenty-six weeks of disability comes from the sick funds which are maintained by contributions, two-thirds of which are paid by the workmen and one-third by the employers. Thereafter benefits are paid from the accident funds, and amount to two-thirds of wages until temporary disability ceases. This cost is met by employer contributions only.

In addition to the monetary benefit, free medical attendance, medicines, and appliances are provided. During the first twenty-six weeks these costs are paid by the sick fund, and after that by the insurance associations. To bring about a speedy recovery, and to avoid large pensions which would result if the injured were permanently disabled, the insurance associations have established numerous hospitals, convalescent homes, and similar institutions.

In case of permanent total disability the injured workman receives 66 2/3 per cent of wages for life. For permanent partial disablement he receives a pension in proportion to the degree of disablement. In computing the amount, the nature of his occupation and training are taken into consideration; for example, the loss of a finger would affect a linotype operator much more seriously than a foundry laborer, and accordingly he would receive a larger pension.

If the accident results in death, a funeral benefit is paid in all cases, whether the deceased has left dependents entitled to survivors' benefits or not. A liberal pension is provided for surviving dependents.

The most important branch of the administrative machinery of the German compulsory insurance law is the mutual trade associations. Employers in related trades organize their own associations, fix their own rates, and enforce their own safety requirements, and to the special facilities which this method affords is mainly due the conspicuous success of the German system in promoting accident prevention. Each *Berufsgenossenschaft*, or trade association, has its own constitution, but is closely regulated by the state and the federal insurance office. Subordinate to the federal insurance office is a system of local and superior insurance offices, each composed of public officials, with associates elected by and from employers and employees, respectively. Judicial and administrative matters passed upon by the local office may be appealed, subject to certain restrictions, to the superior office, and from that to the imperial office, whose decision is usually final.

b. *Methods in Other Countries.*—The German insurance system has been described in some detail because it was the first to be introduced, is one of the most efficient, and affords data based on experience from which, in various degrees, other countries gleaned hints to be utilized in drafting their own acts.

In 1897 Great Britain passed a compensation law which was frequently amended and amplified in scope until in its present form it covers all employments and all injuries arising out of and in the course of employment.

The principle of industrial accident insurance, or workmen's compensation as it is generally called, spread rapidly and is now so generally accepted throughout the world that by 1925 over seventy foreign countries and states, including practically all of any industrial importance, had laws of this character.[17]

The tendency in these laws is distinctly toward constantly broadening coverage, though there are still many limitations based on the supposed degree of hazard of the work or the number of persons employed. The waiting periods, during which no

[17] A study on *Compensation for Industrial Accidents* published by the International Labor Office in 1925 (Studies and Reports, Series M, No. 2) analyzes the following foreign laws: Argentina, Austria, six Australian states, Belgium, Bolivia, Brazil, Bulgaria, nine Canadian provinces, Chile, China, Colombia, Cuba, Czechoslovakia, Denmark, Ecuador, Estonia, Finland, France, Germany, Great Britain, Greece, Guatemala, Hungary, India, Irish Free State, Italy, Japan, Latvia, Lithuania, Luxemburg, The Netherlands, Newfoundland, New Zealand, Norway, Panama, Peru, Poland, Portugal, Rumania, Russia, Salvador, South Africa, Spain, Sweden, Switzerland, Uruguay, Yugoslavia.

SOCIAL INSURANCE 235

compensation is payable, are fixed at from three to seven days in the great majority of laws. Payments for total disability range from 33 per cent of wages in Peru to 100 per cent in Russia and Yugoslavia.[18] A few laws allow 70, 75, or 80 per cent of wages. Except in some half-dozen cases, medical care is provided in addition to cash compensation, occasionally through a cooperative arrangement with the health insurance scheme. To secure payment of benefits, employers are usually required to deposit in a special guarantee fund or to insure their risk, often in institutions prescribed and supervised or managed by the state.

c. *Inclusion of Occupational Diseases.*—Though workmen's compensation laws originally concerned themselves only with mechanical injuries, such as cuts, broken bones, or loss of members, it soon became obvious that elementary justice required the extension of similar relief to the victims of specific industrial diseases contracted in the course of employment. The first country to take this forward step was Great Britain, which in the act of 1906 included for compensation a schedule of six of the commonest occupational maladies, and provided for the extension of this schedule by the Secretary of State. It has been extended from time to time and after twenty years had grown to more than five times its original length. By 1933 occupational diseases were compensated to a greater or lesser extent in more than forty foreign countries.[19] Most of these countries still follow the British scheme and include under their compensation acts only certain specifically listed diseases, frequently, however, permitting the administrative authorities to extend the original list and, in some cases, leaving the formulation of the list entirely to such authorities. Great Britain and several of her dominions also grant compensation for certain respiratory diseases under entirely separate acts.[20] The International Labor Conference in 1925 adopted a draft convention providing for

[18] Permanent disability only.
[19] See International Labor Office, *Workmen's Compensation for Occupational Diseases,* Report V, International Labor Conference, Eighteenth Session (1933).
[20] Great Britain, Silicosis Act 1918; New South Wales, Silicosis Act 1920, and Broken Hill (tuberculosis and pneumoconiosis) Act, 1920; West Australia, Miners' Phthisis Act 1923; New Zealand, Miners' Phthisis Act 1915; South Africa, Miners' Phthisis Act 1919.

the compensation of workers with lead poisoning, mercury poisoning and anthrax infection. By April, 1936, this convention had been ratified by twenty-eight countries.[21] In 1934, the conference extended the list to include several other diseases, including silicosis. By April, 1936, the revised convention had been ratified by three countries.[22]

A few countries provide general coverage for all occupational diseases. The greater prevalence of "list laws" may be due in part to the existence of health insurance legislation in most of the industrially important countries. In the United States, in the absence of health insurance, experience in a dozen states appears to indicate the desirability of all-inclusive coverage of occupational disease disabilities in preference to the limited schedule plan.

3. **Compensation Legislation in the United States.**—As in other forms of social insurance, to be considered later, the United States acted much later than European countries to provide for the injured workman. The first legislation providing for stated benefits without suit or proof of negligence was enacted in Maryland in 1902, in the form of a cooperative insurance law.[23] The law was narrow in scope, covering only a small specific list of industries, and was declared unconstitutional in 1904.[24] In 1908 Congress enacted a law granting to certain employees of the United States the right to compensation for injuries sustained in the course of employment. In 1910 an act was passed in Montana providing for the maintenance of a state cooperative insurance fund for miners and laborers in and about mines. This also was declared unconstitutional.[25]

The first law of general application was passed by New York

[21] Austria, Belgium, Bulgaria, Chile, Colombia, Cuba, Czechoslovakia, Denmark, Finland, France, Germany, Great Britain, Hungary, India, Irish Free State, Italy, Japan, Latvia, Luxemburg, The Netherlands, Nicaragua, Norway, Portugal, Spain, Sweden, Switzerland, Uruguay, Yugoslavia.

[22] Austria, Hungary, Norway.

[23] United States Bureau of Labor Statistics, *Bulletin No. 126*, p. 30.

[24] Franklin *v.* United Railways and Electric Co. of Baltimore, Baltimore Common Pleas Ct., April 27, 1904. Summarized in United States Bureau of Labor, *Bulletin No. 57*, 1905, pp. 689, 690.

[25] Cunningham *v.* Northwestern Improvement Co., 44 Mont. 180, 119 Pac. 554 (1911).

SOCIAL INSURANCE

in 1910. It was made elective for most occupations, but compulsory for an enumerated list of hazardous employments. This statute was declared unconstitutional in 1911 in the case of Ives v. South Buffalo Railway Company,[26] but an amendment to the constitution made possible the enactment of a compulsory law in 1914. Other states followed. By 1920 compensation laws

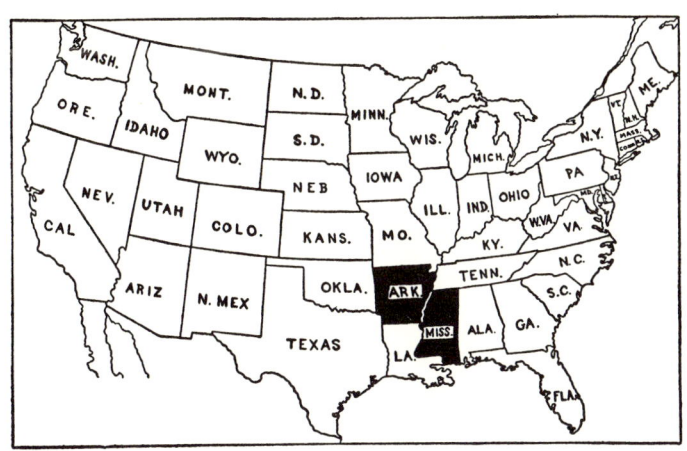

WORKMEN'S COMPENSATION LAWS

By July 1, 1936, only two states had failed to enact workmen's accident compensation laws. Such legislation was in effect in forty-six states, the District of Columbia, Alaska, Hawaii, the Philippines, and Puerto Rico. Congress had also enacted laws for the civil employees of the federal government, and for longshoremen and harbor workers.

were enacted in forty-three[27] states, Alaska, Hawaii, and Puerto Rico; and Congress, in 1916, replaced the limited act of 1908 by a compensation law covering all federal civilian employees. The Missouri act was twice repealed and reenacted, not going into effect until 1926. From 1920 to 1936, laws were enacted by three more states—North Carolina (1929), Florida (1935) and South Carolina (1935)—by the Philippines (1927), and by Congress for longshoremen and harbor workers (1927) and for private employees in the District of Columbia (1928). Only

[26] Ives v. South Buffalo R. Co., 201 N. Y. 271, 94 N. E. 431 (1911).
[27] All except Arkansas, Florida, Mississippi, North Carolina, and South Carolina.

two states—Arkansas and Mississippi—were without such laws in 1936.

In the early days one of the main obstacles to the enactment of effective compensation laws was the question of constitutionality. It was maintained that to require an employer to pay damages for an accident for which he was not to blame was taking property without due process of law, that both employer and employee were deprived of the right of trial by jury, and that the employer was charged with liability without fault.

In 1917, however, the constitutionality of the chief types of compensation laws was affirmed by the United States Supreme Court in three far-reaching decisions involving the New York, Iowa, and Washington laws.[28] The principal constitutional question under the New York compulsory law was whether the statute, by requiring the employer to make fixed payments for his employees' industrial injuries, deprived him of any rights of liberty and property guaranteed him by the Fourteenth Amendment to the federal Constitution. The Supreme Court ruled unanimously that the enactment of laws compensating for industrial accidents tended to promote the public welfare and was therefore within the police power of the state, saying: "We recognize that the legislation under review does measurably limit the freedom of employer and employee to agree respecting the terms of employment, and that it cannot be supported except on the ground that it is a reasonable exercise of the police power of the state. In our opinion it is fairly supportable upon that ground. And for this reason: The subject-matter in respect of which freedom of contract is restricted is the matter of compensation for human life or limb lost or disability incurred in the course of hazardous employment, and the public has a direct interest in this as affecting the common welfare. 'The whole is no greater than the sum of all the parts, and when the individual health, safety, and welfare are sacrificed or neglected, the state must suffer.'"[29] The Iowa elective law was sustained by a reference to the New York case.

[28] New York Central R. Co. v. White, 243 U. S. 188, 37 Sup. Ct. 247 (1917); Hawkins v. Bleakley, 243 U. S. 210, 37 Sup. Ct. 255 (1917); Mountain Timber Co. v. Washington, 243 U. S. 219, 37 Sup. Ct. 260 (1917).
[29] Holden v. Hardy, 169 U. S. 366, 397, 18 Sup. Ct. 383 (1898).

The Washington law presented a different issue. In that state employers in specified hazardous occupations are required to pay workmen's compensation premiums to a state insurance fund out of which injured workmen are compensated. In determining whether such enforced contributions were a "fair and reasonable exertion of governmental power" the court thought it "proper to consider: (1) Whether the main object of the legislation is, or reasonably may be deemed to be, of general and public moment, rather than of private and particular interest, so as to furnish a just occasion for such interference with personal liberty and the right of acquiring property as necessarily must result from carrying it into effect. (2) Whether the charges imposed upon employers are reasonable in amount, or, on the other hand, so burdensome as to be manifestly oppressive. And (3) whether the burden is fairly distributed, having regard to the causes that give rise to the need for the legislation."

In regard to the first point the court deemed the considerations advanced in the New York decision "sufficient to support the State of Washington in concluding that the matter of compensation for accidental injuries with resulting loss of life or earning capacity of men employed in hazardous occupations is of sufficient public moment to justify making the entire matter of compensation a public concern, to be administered through state agencies."

Upon the second point the court said: "No particular contention is made that the compensation allowed is unduly large; and it is evident that unless it be so the corresponding burden upon the industry cannot be regarded as excessive if the state is at liberty to impose the entire burden upon the industry."

On the third question, of fair distribution, the court found that: "The application of a proper percentage to the pay roll of the industry cannot be deemed an arbitrary adjustment, in view of the legislative declaration that it is 'deemed the most accurate method of equitable distribution of burden in proportion to relative hazard.' . . . As further rebutting the suggestion that the imposition is exorbitant or arbitrary, we should accept the declaration of intent that the fund shall ultimately become neither more nor less than self-supporting, and that the rates are subject to future adjustment by the legislature and the classifications to rearrangement according to experience, as plain evidence of an intelligent effort to limit the burden to the requirements of each industry."

Although the industry involved in the case, logging, is clearly hazardous, the court took occasion to demolish the objection that the act includes non-hazardous occupations, saying: "The question whether any of the industries enumerated in section four is non-hazardous will be proved by experience, and the provisions of the act themselves give sufficient assurance that if in any industry there be no accident there will be no assessment, unless for expenses of administration."

But most indicative of the attitude of the United States Supreme Court toward workmen's compensation legislation is the following statement: "The act cannot be deemed oppressive to any class of occupation, provided the scale of compensation is reasonable, unless the loss of human life and limb is found in experience to be so great that if charged to the industry it leaves no sufficient margin for reasonable profits. But certainly, if any industry involves so great a human wastage as to leave no fair profit beyond it, the state is at liberty, in the interest of the safety and welfare of its people, to prohibit such an industry altogether."

Owing, however, to the adverse decision on the early New York compulsory law in the Ives case, most American compensation acts have been made elective. That is, the employer is given his choice of accepting the act or of operating under the liability law; but as an encouragement to the employer to elect compensation, the old liability defenses of fellow servant's fault, contributory negligence, and assumption of risk, discussed earlier in this chapter, are abrogated or greatly modified. This is frequently called by its opponents "club" legislation, but the courts have sustained it as a valid exercise of legislative power for a public end.

The relief which a compensation act gives to the injured workman depends upon (a) the scope of the law, (b) the scale of compensation, (c) the provisions for rehabilitation, (d) the method of administration, and (e) the security for payment of awards. A liberal law, that is, one which provides a high rate of indemnity, will be of little service unless it applies to many cases of accidents, and, conversely, a law covering many or all

SOCIAL INSURANCE 241

cases will not accomplish what is intended unless the benefits provided are reasonably high. Again, the practical results obtained, no matter how liberal the law, will be seriously impaired unless means are provided for effective administration and for securing the actual payment to the injured worker or to his dependents of the amount awarded.

a. *Scope of Laws.*—A compensation system should apply to all employments and cover all injuries. In the early days of the movement, however, partly because of administrative difficulties and partly because of the incompleteness of public education on the subject, the exclusion of certain classes of workers and of certain sorts of injuries was found temporarily advisable.

(1) Employments Included.—Nine main groups of workers are commonly excluded from American state compensation laws. In the probable order of their importance these are: (1) employees in supposedly non-hazardous occupations; (2) agricultural laborers; (3) domestic servants; (4) employees in interstate commerce; (5) workmen in establishments employing fewer than a given number of persons; (6) public employees; (7) casual laborers; (8) those not engaged in the regular course of the employer's business; and (9) those in employments not conducted for gain. As a result of these exclusions, the proportion of employees protected in the various states in 1920 ranged from 99.8 per cent in New Jersey to only 20.5 per cent in Puerto Rico.[30] Altogether, it was officially estimated at the end of 1917, when compensation laws existed in forty states and territories, that there were in these states and territories alone over 8,500,000 American wage earners, or nearly 40 per cent of the total number within the area, who could "not possibly be covered under any existing compensation act."[31]

Of the various exclusions mentioned, that of workers in "non-hazardous" occupations is particularly indefensible. A laborer may be killed no matter how non-hazardous the occupation seems. As has often been stated, it is that industry in which a

[30] United States Bureau of Labor Statistics, *Monthly Labor Review*, January, 1920, p. 237.
[31] United States Bureau of Labor Statistics, Hookstadt, Carl, "Comparison of Workmen's Compensation Laws of the United States up to December 31, 1917," *Bulletin No. 240*, p. 29.

person is injured which is hazardous. The exclusion of casual workers has resulted in much confusion. The meaning of the term is not clear, and the various courts and commissions differ in construing it. Longshoremen, for example, who work only when a boat is to be loaded or unloaded, have been held not to be casual employees, as the irregularity of their employment is inherent in shipping by sea. On the other hand, waiters and teamsters, hired for particular jobs lasting only a day or thereabouts, have been held to be casuals. One state[32] has interpreted casual employment to mean all lasting less than ten days. Exemption of establishments with a small number of employees is based on the theory that in such work places the accident risk is less. When, however, the exemption is extended to all establishments with fewer than sixteen employees,[33] very few are left to benefit by the change from employers' liability to workmen's compensation. Employees in interstate commerce, numbering fully one million, do not come under state compensation laws because Congress took jurisdiction when it enacted its employers' liability law covering this field. By a five-to-four decision the United States Supreme Court held that the work of longshoremen was "maritime in nature," and that therefore they came under federal admiralty jurisdiction and were not covered by state workmen's compensation laws.[34] Twice Congress attempted to meet these objections and remedy the desperate condition of the longshoremen by specifically reserving to them the protection of state compensation laws.[35] These efforts, despite their characterization as "statesmanlike" by the minority justices, were held to be beyond the authority of Congress in that such power delegated to the states would interfere with the proper harmony and uniformity of the maritime law.[36] In 1927, therefore, Congress enacted a compensation law covering longshoremen and harbor workers when injured on board vessels.[37]

[32] California.
[33] Alabama, Laws 1919, No. 245.
[34] Southern Pacific Co. v. Jensen, 244 U. S. 205, 37 Sup. Ct. 525 (1917).
[35] Public 82, Sixty-fifth Congress, First Session, and Public 239, Sixty-seventh Congress, Second Session.
[36] Knickerbocker Ice Co. v. Stewart, 253 U. S. 149, 40 Sup. Ct. 438 (1920), and State of Washington v. Dawson & Co., 264 U. S. 219, 44 Sup. Ct. 302 (1924).
[37] Public 803, 69th Congress, Second Session, 1927.

When injured on the dock, these workers are covered by the state laws.

(2) Injuries Included.—All injuries sustained in the course of employment should be compensated, except those occasioned by the willful intention of the employee to bring about the injury or death of himself or his fellow workmen. These are clearly not a hazard of the industry, and should not be compensated. Some states also exclude accidents caused in part by the intoxication of the injured employee. Such exclusion is likely, however, to cause litigation over the question of whether or not the employee was "intoxicated"; and since compensation legislation aims at preventing litigation and securing prompt aid, limitations of this sort are to be deprecated. Moreover, the safety of fellow workmen requires that the employer be discouraged from hiring men who are prone to intoxication, and an excellent method of accomplishing this result is to make subject to compensation all accidents occurring to such employees.

In order to induce the workman to make use of the safety appliances supplied by his employer, the compensation may be reduced if he willfully fails to use such guards and appliances. On the other hand, the compensation should be increased in the same proportion if the employer fails to obey any safety law or to provide the proper devices, and the laws of some states include penalties of this nature. In Wisconsin, for example, the injured receives an increase of 15 per cent in compensation if the employer did not observe the safety laws, but, on the other hand, his compensation is reduced 15 per cent if he fails to use safeguards when they are provided.[38]

(3) Occupational Diseases.—Inclusion of occupational diseases in workmen's compensation laws is much discussed in America. Industry is recognized as the contributing cause in numerous disease cases and as practically the sole cause in others. In the absence of health insurance legislation in this country, workmen's compensation laws furnish the only relief for these injuries. While it is neither practical nor desirable for compensation laws to cover all sickness, industry should be charged with those disease disabilities for which it is clearly

[38] For reference to double and treble accident compensation as an incentive to compliance with child labor laws, see p. 176.

responsible. More than twenty[39] American laws provide occupational disease compensation. Nine cover only specified diseases, such as lead poisoning, anthrax, and caisson disease, while others compensate all disabilities clearly caused by the employment. The administrative commission determines in each case whether the industry is responsible. These are preferable to the "list laws" since, with ever-changing industrial processes, lists soon become incomplete, and constant legislative revision is impractical. The broadest occupational disease coverage, American experience shows, adds only a few per cent to the total cost of the law.[40]

b. *Scale of Compensation.*—The object of indemnity is twofold—first and more important, to restore the workman's earning power as completely and quickly as possible, so that society will not be burdened with disabled human beings; and, second, to provide for the support of the family while the surgical and medical treatment is being given. To effect the former it is imperative that he receive efficient medical and surgical care.

(1) M e d i c a l A t t e n d a n c e .—The importance of medical attendance is often underestimated. Proper, immediate care tends not only to reduce the period of disability, but also to diminish the number of serious, perhaps permanent, complications. Lifelong impairment of earning capacity frequently results from improper care of fractures; infections or "blood poisoning" could be almost eliminated by efficient immediate attention. Of 721 infections reported to the Wisconsin Industrial Commission during a two-year period, about 600 were the result of small scratches and breaks of the skin.[41] These cases represented a total of 12,500 working days lost, and, under the

---

[39] By 1936, there was all-inclusive coverage in California, Connecticut, District of Columbia, Hawaii, Illinois, Massachusetts, Missouri (by election), New York, North Dakota, Philippine Islands, Wisconsin, and the Federal Civil Service Employees' and the Longshoremen's and Harbor Workers' Acts. Limited coverage existed in Kentucky, Minnesota, Nebraska, New Jersey, North Carolina, Ohio, Puerto Rico, Rhode Island, and West Virginia.

[40] Andrews, John B., "Occupational Disease Compensation," United States Bureau of Labor Statistics, *Bulletin No. 389*, pp. 42-46; and Wilcox, Fred M., "The 'Schedule' Fraud in Occupational Disease Compensation," *American Labor Legislation Review*, vol. xxiv, no. 3, September, 1934, pp. 119-123.

[41] Industrial Commission of Wisconsin, *Shop Bulletin, No. 5.*

Wisconsin law, a compensation of about $40,000. Had proper care been provided, this large loss of time and money could have been avoided.

Full medical aid at the employer's cost is of benefit to the workman in that it relieves his suffering, reduces the period of disability, and permits his return to full earning capacity in a shorter time; at the same time, in virtue of this fact, it is beneficial to the employer inasmuch as the amount of compensation is reduced. If the wage earner is required to pay for his own medical treatment, he will not receive as good care. The average laborer has little means to pay for good service, even when earning full wages. When disabled and receiving only a part of his wages, he is even less able to provide himself with proper care.

The amount of medical aid, in proportion to the total indemnity, is large. In experience gathered by the National Council on Compensation Insurance[42] from thirty states for the three years 1918-1920 inclusive, medical care represented 20.7 per cent of the compensation payments, or $48,133,542 out of a total of $232,374,728. Thus it is evident that medical care is a very important factor in a compensation law and should not be underestimated. It is of such importance to the welfare of the injured and their dependents that the law should require the giving of full free medical attendance, medicines and appliances, and should impose a limit neither in time nor in amount. Where such a policy has been followed, besides vastly benefiting the injured it has achieved marvelous results in preventing permanent impairment.

America is gradually waking up to the economy of liberality in this respect, but while all states provide for medical care, the majority of them still impose either a time limit, an amount limit, or both. The time limits range from two weeks to one year, while the amount varies from $100 to $800. An increasing number of states, however, are giving their administrative boards discretion to increase the period or amount.

It is evident that in those states having low limits a large part of the medical care must be borne by the injured. The amounts may be sufficient to take care of the less serious in-

[42] Michelbacher and Nial, *Workmen's Compensation Insurance*, 1925, Appendix III, p. 380.

juries, but in case of accidents resulting in fractures, dislocations, and serious sprains a large part of the burden falls on the workman himself.

(2) Waiting Period.—It is customary, in compensation laws, to provide no monetary benefits for the first few days of disability. The intervening time is known as the "waiting period" and its object is to prevent malingering, that is, to prevent a slightly injured man from pretending inability to work, with the expectation of drawing part of his wages. On the other hand, if the period is too long it will prove a hardship to the injured. The danger of malingering, moreover, is greatly exaggerated by many inexperienced persons. Official commissions skilled in administration of workmen's compensation laws agree that a short waiting period is ample to check this tendency and that the reduction of originally long waiting periods in the laws of many important industrial states has resulted, in practice, in no increase in malingering. The proper length of the period is hard to determine and varies with individual cases, but it seems that three days is sufficient.[43] This view is upheld by actual accident experience. Studies of accidents made by Dr. I. M. Rubinow and by the Wisconsin Industrial Commission show that about three-quarters of all accidents requiring medical attendance terminate within two weeks, and that two-thirds terminate within one week. Of these two-thirds, one-half cause no disability other than on the day when the accident occurs, and one-quarter cause disability lasting from one to three days, while only one-quarter result in disability extending over more than three days. For example, a total of 36,000 accidents requiring medical attendance would be distributed about as follows:

Length of Disability	Number of Accidents	Per Cent
Two weeks and more	9,000	25
One week or more, but less than two weeks	3,000	8⅓
Three days or more, but less than one week	6,000	16⅔
More than one, but less than three days	6,000	16⅔
One day (day of accident)	12,000	33⅓
Total	36,000	100

[43] The American Association for Labor Legislation recommends a waiting period of not less than three nor more than seven days. See its *Standards for Workmen's Compensation Laws*.

Hence, if the waiting period is two weeks, only about a quarter, and if it is seven days, only one-third, of the injured receive compensation. By reducing the period to three days, one-half of those injured would be entitled to benefits.

In a small number of states there is no waiting period and compensation begins on the day of accident. More than three-fourths of the states set a period of seven days or less, and the others provide for from eight to fourteen days. In some, however, compensation is paid from the day of injury in case disability continues for more than a specified period, such as two, four, or eight weeks. Since the large majority of accidents cause disability which terminates in a short time, it is important that the period during which no compensation is paid be made short.

(3) Compensation for Total Disability.—Injuries for which compensation is paid may be divided on the basis of their severity into three large groups: namely, (a) death; (b) partial disability or impairment of earning capacity such as the amputation or loss of function of a member; and (c) total disability of either a permanent or a temporary nature. The vast majority of accidents result in total temporary disability.

The best American laws, of which the acts of North Dakota and Ohio, and the federal statute covering federal employees, are examples, award to the disabled workman 66 2/3 per cent of wages (within certain limits) during the entire period of disability. In permanent cases, of course, this means benefits for life. The limits referred to are, in North Dakota, a maximum payment of $20 a week and a minimum of $6 a week, except that if full wages be less than $6, full wages are paid. The Arizona act, adopted by vote of the people in 1925, fixes no maximum weekly limit.

Many of the laws, however, still contain provisions far less liberal. In some states the percentage of wages paid is 65, 60, or 55 per cent, and in over one-fourth of the American commonwealths which have compensation laws it was in 1936 still as low as 50 per cent. The weekly maximum, also, is often lower than in North Dakota, being sometimes $15, or in a few cases $12. Besides granting a low percentage of wages, frequently held down by a weekly maximum limit, most states still further restrict the total amount to be recovered, either directly or—what amounts to the same thing—by stating a maximum period beyond which compensation is no longer payable. Time limitations for total permanent disability vary from 260 to 1,000 weeks, and money limitations from $3,000 to $15,000.

The reason for these unprogressive restrictions is not hard to find. It is that our compensation laws are based upon the idea of merely keeping the injured and his family from starvation, rather than upon the principle of replacing wage loss. The common 50 per cent scale is obviously insufficient to keep a family from hardship. Despite spectacular instances to the contrary in some strongly organized trades, the majority of workmen hardly receive, when employed, enough to pay their current living expenses, and when their income is cut in two these expenses cannot be met. The low weekly maxima fixed in many states intensify the deprivation. A family whose head ordinarily receives $40 or $50 a week has a fairly high standard of living; and if in case of accident the maximum recoverable is limited to $12 or $15 weekly, that standard cannot be maintained. This is especially true if disability is of long continuance; yet some states which fix these low maximum limits for the first few years of disability reduce them further after stated periods, in some instances to "as little as $5 a week."

These excessive limitations upon the amount of compensation work considerable hardship to the cases which they affect, and should not be included in the law. If the accident results in permanent total disability, the injured should receive at least two-thirds of his wages for life. Nothing short of this will bring the proper relief. With a two-thirds normal income the family will be deprived of some things, but still the amount is sufficient to maintain about the same standard of living, and even in the lower-paid classes to keep the family from dependence on charity. Under our system of laws children are required to go to school until a certain age, which means considerable expense. If in case of accident causing a total loss of earning capacity no proper compensation is provided, or if the compensation period is limited, it frequently means disintegration of the family.

(4) Compensation for Partial Disability.—Compensation for permanent partial disability is based in most states upon a fixed schedule of a certain number of weeks' benefit

SOCIAL INSURANCE

for each specific dismemberment, such as fifteen weeks for the loss of a little finger, 125 weeks for an eye, or 215 weeks for a leg. While this system of a fixed charge for each dismemberment, regardless of its effect upon earning power, is easily administered, it is open to serious criticism on the grounds of arbitrariness and injustice. A system like that in use in California, in which partial disability is defined as a proportion of the loss of earning power, is more difficult to administer, but results in more equitable settlements. In response to the criticism that the number of weeks' benefit allowed by the fixed injury schedule is too small, there has been a tendency to increase the specific periods, but the best thought is now against this method and in favor of indemnifying on the basis of the loss of earning power. For this purpose and to facilitate administration, California has worked out a schedule showing the percentage of impairment in earning capacity which each specific injury may be expected to cause to a worker of any given age in any given occupation in the state. If the injured suffering a permanent impairment of earning capacity is a minor, his compensation should be increased until he reaches the age of twenty-one, as his wages would probably have increased had he not been injured. Many of our states already take cognizance of this fact, and the number is growing.

(5) Compensation for Death.—If the injury results in death a funeral benefit should be paid in all cases, whether or not the deceased had dependents entitled to compensation. About $150 has usually been regarded as sufficient to cover all essential funeral charges. Some states have laws providing funeral benefits only if there are no dependents entitled to compensation, but most grant funeral benefits in all cases.

Most states thus far have not been very liberal in prescribing the amount of compensation to be paid to dependents. A few, however, grant pensions to widows for life or until remarriage. North Dakota, one of the most liberal states, in 1936 prescribed 35 per cent of wages for the widow until death or remarriage, and 10 per cent additional for each child, the total not to exceed 66⅔ per cent. A few states limit the death benefit to a specified monthly amount, such as $35 or $50, while others set a maximum for the total, varying from $3,000 to $15,000.

A life benefit to the widow and additional amounts for each

child up to the age of eighteen is the only rational system to adopt. Statistics show that the average age of injured workmen is about thirty-two years. A young family which loses its supporter at such an age cannot exist very long on $3,000 or less. So small an amount will mean that the family must lower its standard of living, and that the children will not receive the proper care and education. Here again compensation is regarded more in the light of a means of preventing starvation than as a reimbursement for the loss of earning power. It may be expected that in the future more and more states will grant to the widow a pension for life or during the period of widowhood. If there are no dependents a substantial part of the death benefit should be paid into two special funds to be used (a) for maintenance of industrial cripples undergoing rehabilitation, and (b) for second-injury cases resulting in permanent total disability. These last provisions are found in a few laws; but if there are no dependents most states provide for funeral benefits only. The suggested system aids in the solution of two perplexing industrial problems—protecting both the employer and his permanently disabled worker from unfair treatment. It assists partly disabled workers in getting jobs and makes employers less hesitant to employ such workers.

The question as to whether alien non-resident dependents should be entitled to death benefit has been considerably discussed, and a few states still expressly exclude them. In most states they are expressly included, though often on a discriminatory basis, and elsewhere, though not mentioned, they are apparently included by implication. There seems to be little justification for excluding non-resident dependents or discriminating against them in any way; if our industry has been responsible for the loss of a family supporter, due remuneration should be made regardless of nationality or residence.

c. *Rehabilitation.*—Of recent years compensation for injuries has come to mean more than partial reimbursement for monetary loss. Considerations—perhaps economic in their origin, but humane in their outcome—have led to the view that no law truly compensates for injury which fails to rehabilitate. Rehabilitation includes all that can be done by surgery, general reeducation, technical retraining, and assistance in finding reemployment, to place the injured worker on his feet again as a self-supporting citizen. Prior to 1920 little progress had been made in this country in providing rehabilitation opportunities for disabled civilians. Massachusetts was the first state to act, establishing a rehabilitation program by a law of 1918. The next year nine other states followed her lead. When in 1920, however, Congress granted federal aid on a dollar-for-dollar basis to states carrying on rehabilitation work, great impetus

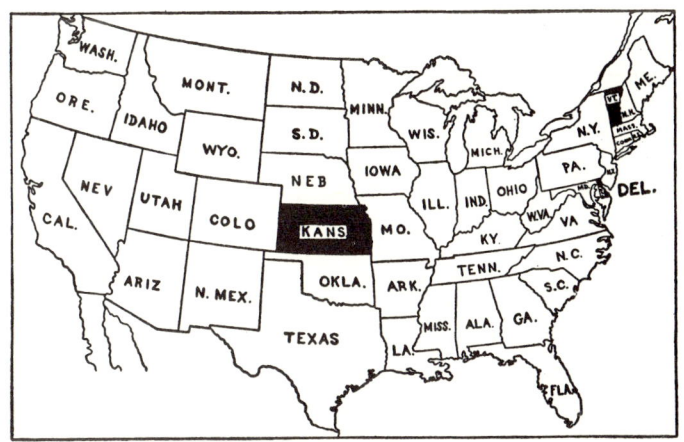

VOCATIONAL REHABILITATION LAWS

Only three states—Delaware, Kansas and Vermont—had failed by July 1, 1936, to make special provision for the vocational retraining of crippled workers. All other states had such laws and had qualified for federal aid under the Federal Rehabilitation Act of 1920.

was given to this movement. By July, 1936 all but three states—Delaware, Kansas and Vermont—had undertaken the work. Plans usually call for cooperation between the state compensation and education authorities and the federal government.

d. *Method of Administration.*—There are two general ways of administering compensation laws. One is to appoint a central board or commission with general powers of enforcing the law, and the other is to create no machinery for the administration of the act, but to provide that all questions arising shall be settled by the courts. Of the states having laws in 1936, only six—Alabama, Louisiana, New Hampshire, New Mexico, Tennessee and Wyoming—had no central administrative body and left the administration to the courts. All other states have adopted the central administrative plan. Five states—Kansas, Minnesota, Nebraska, New Jersey, and (in large measure) Rhode Island—abandoned court administration after finding it unsatisfactory in practice.

Investigations made by the National Civic Federation and the American Federation of Labor,[44] and by the American Association for Labor Legislation,[45] as well as by the United States Bureau of Labor Statistics, indicate that the administrative board plan is much superior to the court procedure scheme. The first two studies agreed in estimating that in New Jersey not over 60 per cent of the amounts payable under the statute were being paid, and the report of the Association for Labor Legislation made it clear that the court procedure plan was mainly responsible for this defeat of the legislative intent. The chief flaws in the court system were pointed out to be (1) the delay of court procedure, (2) the cost of court procedure, and (3) the unfitness of the courts for the settlement of compensation claims. The New Jersey statute was subsequently amended to provide for the board system of administration.

Prompt, honest, and full compensation, and medical aid as required, are the vital factors in bringing relief as desired by the law, and to achieve these purposes a central board with broad powers is essential. The essentials of prompt and inexpensive procedure, expert appraisal of the extent of injury and the resulting wage loss, and the continuous supervision of compensation payments are all best attained through commission administration. States with central boards having full power to make rules and regulations require receipts to be filed showing actual payment of compensation, and since they provide for arbitration hearings in cases of dispute there is little danger of fraud and deception of workmen, and payments are promptly made. The board should consist of three or five members ap-

[44] *Report upon Operation of State Laws,* Senate Document No. 419, Sixty-third Congress, Second Session.

[45] "Three Years under the New Jersey Workmen's Compensation Law," *American Labor Legislation Review,* March, 1915, pp. 31-102. For summary of this and other more recent studies of court administration, see Dodd, Walter F., *Administration of Workmen's Compensation,* 1936, Chapter iv.

SOCIAL INSURANCE

pointed by the governor and should have power to employ necessary assistants. To insure their adequate attention to the responsible duties of their position, its members should be required to devote their entire time to its work.

e. *Security of Payment.*—In order to protect the employer, as well as the workmen, liability under the compensation laws is commonly covered by some form of insurance. Should several of his men meet with a serious accident at one time, the small shop-owner or contractor would not be financially able to pay the compensation. For this reason nearly all states compel employers to insure their risk unless they can give satisfactory evidence that they are able to bear losses caused by accident, even if very serious. This, of course, means that practically all small employers will carry insurance, while many large companies will carry their risks themselves.

The carrying by a concern of its own risk is sometimes called "self-insurance," and in addition thereto three other methods have been developed: (1) insurance in a state fund; (2) insurance in a stock company; and (3) insurance in a mutual or interinsurance company.

State insurance funds are based on the principle that since the state, by the passage of a workmen's compensation act, has created a new obligation on the employer, it should provide him with the means of fulfilling it economically. Such funds have been established in seventeen states, including California, New York, North Dakota, Ohio, Oregon, and Washington. Sometimes insurance in such a fund is compulsory,[46] while some other states permit insurance in authorized private companies. Short as their experience has been, the success of efficiently managed state funds is undoubted. The federal government, through its workmen's compensation expert in the United States Bureau of Labor Statistics, has investigated the practical operation of workmen's compensation laws in twenty states and two Canadian provinces, and reported in 1920 that state funds are superior to private insurance companies in respect to cost, service, and security. The report[47] states: "The cost of compensation insurance to employers under different insurance systems may be

[46] By 1936, in Nevada, North Dakota, Ohio, Oregon, Washington, West Virginia, Wyoming.
[47] United States Bureau of Labor Statistics, *Bulletin No. 301*, p. 21.

254 PRINCIPLES OF LABOR LEGISLATION

indicated by their expense ratios. The average expense ratio of stock companies is approximately 38 per cent; of mutual companies, about 20 per cent; of competitive state funds, about 10.6 per cent; and of exclusive state funds, about 4 per cent. Under an exclusive state fund, therefore, the cost to employers would be 30 per cent less than under stock insurance and 15 per cent less than under mutual insurance. The total saving to insured employers of the United States, if all were insured in exclusive state funds, would be over $30,000,000 annually. . . . Thus far no injured workman has lost his compensation because of the insolvency of state insurance funds, nor has any large mutual company become insolvent. On the other hand, there have been several disastrous failures of private stock companies during the last three or four years. These failures have resulted in hundreds of thousands of dollars in unpaid claims." Recent growth of workmen's compensation insurance would make the saving to employers considerably greater than that estimated by Mr. Hookstadt in 1920. The Ohio Industrial Commission[48] reported July 1, 1925, that during the preceding year it had saved to employers in that state alone, more than $7,000,000. In 1933, the average country-wide compensation expense ratio for stock insurance companies was 47.2 per cent, and for mutual companies, 26.2 per cent. In that year, the comparable figure for New York's competitive state fund was 17.2 per cent. By 1934, according to an estimate by the state industrial commissioner, the New York fund had saved employers of that state a total of more than $28,000,000.[49]

The funds of Ohio, New York, and Pennsylvania were subjected in 1919 to critical examination by official commissions. The consulting actuary who was called in an advisory capacity by all three commissions stated, as a result of his examination into the accounts and administrative procedure of the funds: "State funds for workmen's compensation insurance are shown by my investigations to be extraordinarily successful. They are financially sound. They are operated on the strictest actuarial

---

[48] *Industrial Relations*—the official bulletin of the Ohio Industrial Commission—vol. ii, no. 7, p. 3.
[49] Andrews, Elmer F., "Exclusive State Fund Needed for Compensation Insurance," *American Labor Legislation Review*, vol. xxiv, no. 4, December, 1934, pp. 165-169.

principles. They reduce management expenses to a minimum. They have made steady progress even under competitive conditions. They permit increasingly liberal benefits for injured workers and their families. They result in enormous savings to industry."[50]

Stock companies carry on business for the profit of their stockholders. As a consequence of their large business soliciting organization, comprising thousands of agents, their managing expenses are excessively high.

Mutual insurance companies seek the protection of their own members, who are the policyholders. They do not need the large, expensive organization which a stock company must have, and therefore their managing expenses are lower. Mutual insurance is insurance at actual cost, any excess of premium remaining the property of the policyholder and being refunded in the form of dividends. A strong feature of the mutual insurance method, provided it be made general and brought under close supervision, is the added inducement to employers to do their own factory inspection. Such voluntary inspection, if stimulated by the financial inducement of reduced insurance rates for safer conditions, has sometimes been found even more effective than state inspection.

The premiums charged for workmen's compensation insurance obviously depend greatly upon the benefits provided by the compensation act, and thus we have different rates in the various states. Another factor which largely determines the insurance rate is the hazard of the industry. Thus, there is one rate for logging, one for machine shops, one for clerical pursuits, and so on. Even in establishments of the same industrial group widely different hazards will be found. One company may perhaps take great interest in safety work, while another does not. The former would be a better risk than the latter and is entitled to a lower rate. This allowance is accomplished under a merit rating system. Instead of one flat rate for an entire industry, this system seeks to adjust the rate of each employer to the hazard of his particular establishment. A schedule of credits and charges is provided, so that the employer receives

[50] Dawson, Miles M., "State Accident Insurance in America a Demonstrated Success," *American Labor Legislation Review*, March, 1920, pp. 8-14.

credit for conditions tending to reduce or prevent accidents, and, conversely, he is charged for conditions conducive to accidents.

The feature of accident prevention just alluded to is too often underestimated when discussing compensation laws. After all, to prevent the injury is of greater significance than to provide compensation for it; accident prevention is the greatest feature of a comprehensive accident indemnity plan.

The accident prevention or safety movement has spread rapidly and with persistency, and the chief factor in this development is the growing correlation between accident prevention and compensation. State agencies are usually effective in accident prevention work to the degree that they secure the cooperation of employers and of workmen. Their main function consists in educating these two in methods of safety. State agencies can order the application of mechanical safeguards. Their rules afford standards. But their inspectors can do but little in comparison with what the employer and employee can do, under the stimulus of an adequate compensation system.

Neither insurance companies nor state funds have power to compel the safeguarding of machinery, but they can frequently attain the same end by increasing or reducing the insurance rates under the merit rating system previously discussed. Many companies now have a force of inspectors who investigate the risk before the final rate is computed. During 1924 the amount expended on inspection and rating by insurance companies in the United States equaled 2.9 per cent of the total earned premiums[51] on compensation business. It is impossible to measure statistically the preventive force of compensation laws. Our accident statistics are far from perfect and, moreover, many non-measurable social forces contribute to the final accident rate. Authorities agree, however, that compensation laws have been among those forces making for safety.[52] In 1920, C. W. Price, then general manager of the National Safety Council,

[51] New York State Superintendent of Insurance, *Report, 1925*, pt. iii, p. 77.
[52] Andrews, John B., "The Relation of Workmen's Compensation to Accident Prevention," *Annals of American Academy of Political Science*, January, 1926, pp. 205-209.

SOCIAL INSURANCE

stated that during the five years when he was connected with the Wisconsin Industrial Commission accidental deaths were reduced 61 per cent. "One-half of the credit for this accomplishment," he says, "must be given to the stimulus which the compensation laws gave to the whole safety movement."[53]

In order to secure more satisfactory industrial accident and occupational disease statistics for purposes of prevention as well as for rate-making, a number of government bureaus and interested organizations have jointly engaged in working out uniform industry classifications and uniform methods of reporting.[54] If the classifications agreed upon are finally adopted in all states, the occupational accident and disease statistics will be comparable, and a vast amount of valuable information will then be available.

II. HEALTH INSURANCE

The development of machinery, the expansion of industry, and the growth of the wage-earning class have not only brought into existence the problem of industrial accidents, but have also added importance to the question of the wage-earner's ill health. Since a large amount of the worker's time and energy are expended in the workshop, it is natural that industry and the conditions connected with it are among the important factors seriously affecting his health. Foresight, consequently, has led to the introduction of health insurance, which is gradually being extended to cover all occupations, even those in which the risk to health is less obvious.

1. Early Steps in Health Insurance.—The importance of adequate provision in case of illness or invalidity was recognized by the workers long before the era of social insurance. As early as the Middle Ages the insufficiency of individual action was realized, and a more satisfactory arrangement, that of insurance, was initiated by the mediæval gilds. Under these early plans insurance was purely voluntary and the workers had to bear the full cost. This optional unassisted form of health insurance still exists in many civilized countries. In this country it is provided to a limited extent by trade unions, fraternal

[53] *American Labor Legislation Review,* March, 1920, p. 26.
[54] See "Reporting," pp. 160-168.

societies, establishment funds,[55] and insurance companies. Except for the device of "group insurance," by which a few large concerns have insured their employees in a commercial company without charge to them, it is the only form of health insurance so far in operation here. But under optional insurance most workers are either unwilling or unable to make regular outlays for the premium, and thus are left without the much-needed insurance protection. Other weaknesses frequently charged against the system are inefficiency of management, inadequacy, lack of state supervision, financial instability, and, in the case of profit-making insurance companies, excessive cost.

A remedy for these defects was offered in the device of government subsidies and control. This measure marked the beginning of the second stage in the history of health insurance and directly prepared the way for the compulsory principle. The aim of government subsidies is to relieve the worker from a part of the burden and thus to stimulate insurance; the aim of control is to secure efficient management. Subsidies are usually given to the so-called recognized societies, that is, health insurance organizations which answer certain requirements and submit to government regulations.

The system of subsidized insurance was first introduced in Sweden in 1891, and existed in 1935 in six countries: Sweden, Denmark, Belgium, France, Iceland, and parts of Switzerland. Government regulation of voluntary schemes, without direct subsidy, existed in several other countries. The financial assistance granted in these countries and the government supervision, potent though they are, cannot be expected to be a very vigorous stimulus to insurance among the classes most in need of it. Obviously, compulsory insurance, transferring a considerable part of the burden to industry and including in the system those workers who most require this protection, is a more effective way of meeting the need.

2. **Compulsory Health Insurance.**—Long before 1883, the first date in the official history of social insurance, there existed in several states of Europe insurance associations in which the

[55] Funds organized among the workers in one plant or establishment, usually under the control of the employer.

elements of compulsory state supervised insurance were found. It was left, however, for Germany first to gather, in the year mentioned, these dispersed components into one coordinated unit. By 1935[56] widely applicable compulsory legislation had been enacted in Austria, Bulgaria, Chile, Czechoslovakia, Estonia, France, Germany, Great Britain, Greece, Hungary, Irish Free State, Japan, Latvia, Lithuania, Luxemburg, The Netherlands, Norway, Poland, Portugal, Rumania, Russia, and Yugoslavia; and a number of other countries maintained compulsory systems for individual industries. In 1935, the province of Alberta in Canada enacted a health insurance law providing elective coverage by localities, and in 1936, British Columbia adopted a compulsory law.

Health insurance legislation has generally recognized the existing mutual sick benefit funds of various kinds, such as fraternal societies, trade unions, and establishment funds, which were allowed to continue business, provided they complied with the regulations imposed upon them by the new law. In many countries the law also brought into existence new insurance associations, the local sick funds, for the insurance of persons not claiming membership in any other society. In a few countries, where mutual benefit funds had reached no appreciable development of the compulsory law, government agencies have been organized to insure all persons subject to the act.

The scope of health insurance legislation varies in the different countries. The early legislation was rather restricted, but later amendments have in many cases increased the numbers covered. Thus, for example, the German legislation which, in 1885, covered 4,671,000 persons, or 10 per cent of the total population, in 1911 was amended to include 14,000,000, or 22 per cent of the population, and its scope was further broadened after the revolution of 1918.

Many of the more recent acts, moreover, have permitted broad coverage from the time of their original enactment. By 1935 the compulsory health insurance laws of thirteen coun-

[56] International Labor Office, *Sickness Insurance* (Studies and Reports, Series M, No. 4, 1925), and *The International Labor Organization and Social Insurance* (Studies and Reports, Series M, No. 12, 1936).

260 PRINCIPLES OF LABOR LEGISLATION

tries[57] covered practically all persons doing paid work in the service of others even including in most cases apprentices, home workers, and independent workers, but usually excluding public employees as well as blood relatives of the employer, casual workers, and certain other numerically unimportant groups. The laws of France, Germany, Great Britain, Irish Free State, The Netherlands, Norway, Poland, and Portugal exempted, in addition, special classes of workers—usually non-manual—earning over specified amounts. One country, Portugal, had an even broader sickness insurance act which included all persons between the ages of fifteen and seventy-five engaged in any occupation "recognized as worthy and honest by custom and tradition and sanctioned by law." The criterion of paid work did not apply. Though practically the whole adult population contributed to this scheme, however, only persons whose annual incomes were below 900 escudos were eligible for benefit.

On the other hand, the compulsory health insurance laws of several countries exclude certain important groups of workers. The most usually excluded group are agricultural laborers[58] and domestic servants,[59] but in a few countries exclusions apply to commercial[60] and railway[61] workers. Public service workers are not covered in several countries.[62]

The cost of insurance is usually distributed between the worker and the employer, and in some countries the government also contributes a share. By this device the employer is compelled to bear some portion of the cost of sickness among his employees, and the worker receives larger benefits than he could purchase unaided. In Russia, however, the employer—which there is the state—bears the full cost and in Rumania it is met entirely by the employee. In other countries employees contribute from 40 to 66⅔ per cent. In Norway the worker contributes six-tenths, the employer one-tenth, the commune one-tenth, and the state the remaining two-tenths. In continental

[57] Austria, Bulgaria, Czechoslovakia, France, Germany, Great Britain, Irish Free State, The Netherlands, Norway, Poland, Portugal, Russia, Yugoslavia.
[58] Estonia, Greece, Hungary, Japan, Latvia, Lithuania, Rumania.
[59] Estonia, Greece, Japan, Luxemburg, Rumania.
[60] Estonia, Japan.
[61] Estonia, Rumania.
[62] Chile, Estonia, Greece, Japan, Luxemburg, Rumania.

SOCIAL INSURANCE

legislation the premium is frequently calculated as a percentage of wages. The employees are divided into wage groups, and the premiums and benefits vary with an increase in the worker's income. Great Britain, however, has not followed the continental practice, but has adopted a uniform rate of contributions, regardless of wage differences. The insured male worker pays weekly ten cents, the female worker eight cents; in either case the employer adds ten cents. The state pays part of the cost of the benefits and local administration—one-seventh for men and one-fifth for women—and all the cost of central administration. To mitigate any hardship on the low-paid worker, special provisions are made for those earning less than at the rate of $1 a day, whereby the worker's contribution is diminished, and that of the employer increased. If the worker earns less than 75 cents, the employer bears the whole cost.

In return for their contributions, workers usually receive both a money benefit and medical care. The cash benefits paid in time of sickness are not equal to the full wage, but in most laws are calculated as a certain percentage of the basic wage, the figures ranging from 50 to 100 per cent.[63] England has been consistent with her flat rate contributions and has adopted a system of uniform benefits of $3.75 a week for men, $3 a week for unmarried women, and $2.50 a week for married women.[64] In general, benefit is not allowed for the first three days of illness, and is paid for only twenty-six weeks in a year. Benefit is usually made conditional upon a doctor's certificate stating that the applicant is incapable of work. When the attending physician certifies that the patient has recovered, sick benefit ceases.

The German and British acts differ in the character of the disabilities which they include. Germany is typical of the countries which have included "invalidity"—chronic illness or impairment of earning capacity—in the old-age insurance act, so that only temporary illnesses are covered by health insurance.

[63] The latter figure is allowed in Russia, where, however, the central social insurance authorities may, in case of shortage of funds, reduce the benefit for temporary disability to not less than 66 2/3 per cent of wages.

[64] The original benefits and contributions of the British act were somewhat lower. The figures given here were fixed by the amending acts of 1920, 1924 and 1932.

Great Britain, on the other hand, has included "invalidity" in the provision for health insurance. The invalidity contemplated by the British legislators, however, is limited to incapacity for work because of disease or disablement, as distinguished from reduction in earning power. The British invalidity benefit consists of a weekly payment of $1.87 for men, $1.50 for unmarried women, and $1.25 for married women.[65] as long as incapacity for work continues, though it ceases when the beneficiary becomes entitled to an old-age pension.

Medical attendance was furnished by almost all compulsory health insurance systems in force in 1935. If an insurance system is to accomplish its ultimate object of improving the health of the workers, it is of great importance that they receive treatment whereby they may be restored to health. Furthermore, it is financially important to the insurance funds that sick members shall recover as quickly as possible and so reduce the amounts expended upon sick benefit.

The medical care provided usually includes not only physicians' services, but also hospital treatment when needed, and the necessary medicines and appliances, such as spectacles, trusses, and crutches. In some countries it includes medical care to all members of the immediate family. In Great Britain, where medical care was from the beginning less liberal and where specialist services and hospital care were not provided, the inadequacy at once became manifest and by 1920 a strong movement for more liberal benefits was under way. In 1926, however, a Royal Commission which investigated this question submitted a majority report opposing further extension of medical benefits at that time.

In providing medical care for insured persons, two fundamental safeguards to the economic interest of the medical profession have developed which are observed in the best practice, namely, free choice of doctor by the patient, and collective agreements between the doctors and the administrative authorities. Free choice of doctor prevents insurance practice from being monopolized by a few physicians and also permits the insured to apply for treatment to practitioners in whom they place confidence. Collective agreements between the doctors and the authorities have the same value for the medical pro-

[65] *Ibid.*

fession that collective bargaining has for organized workers. In Great Britain, for example, free choice of doctor is recognized by legislation, while the more detailed arrangements with the doctors are made between the medical men and the local insurance committees. In practice the details of the agreement are settled by negotiations between authorized representatives of the physicians and of the insurance authority for the entire country. Various methods of remunerating the physician have been adopted. While doctors generally urge payment by the visit, the system of "capitation," or a lump-sum payment for each person for the year, has been adopted in Great Britain and is preferred by the physicians. In some other countries a combination of the two principles is effected by setting aside for the payment of medical services a definite sum for each insured person for the year and distributing this amount among the doctors upon the basis of the actual services rendered by each.

In the organization of the carriers of insurance each country has adapted itself to existing conditions. Germany found already in existence mutual aid funds and an effective system of compulsory insurance among miners. The former it allowed to serve as a substitute for compulsory insurance, providing that employers might be exempted from contributing for workers so insured; it also permitted establishment funds, under certain conditions, to carry the insurance. The system, however, was based in the main on self-governing local mutuals, organized by the law, which it has been the policy to encourage, so that they are now overwhelmingly predominant. This system, with some modifications, has been adopted by most of the central European countries.

Great Britain built its insurance system around the voluntary friendly societies, utilizing their organization and permitting them to establish separate sections for national insurance. Accordingly, many societies have both a "private" and a "state" section. In contrast to the German method, the insured are not grouped according to trade or locality, but are given unrestricted choice of society. As a result of this freedom, the members of some of the large societies are distributed throughout the kingdom and through various industries. Segregation by locality, and in some large cities by trade, which is not possible under the British system, has many practical and technical advantages, such as more precise distribution of the risk and greater ease of administration. In a few countries, of which Russia and Yugoslavia are typical, there had been practically no development of voluntary mutual schemes prior to the passage of the compulsory act, and consequently completely new organizations founded and operated by the government became the sole insurers.

There are two typical methods of establishing security of payments. In Germany the dues are calculated so as to cover the current expenditure on benefits and to accumulate a small reserve fund. It is, however, a recognized fact that sickness increases with age and that any voluntary fund organized on this basis would be compelled to increase its dues as the members advanced in years in order to cover the increasing costs—unless the fund is able to attract a sufficient number of young people. These younger members, paying the same dues as the older members, do not claim the same amount of sick benefit; hence from their contributions a surplus would accrue which could be devoted to making up the deficit caused by the older members. This system is practicable in Germany, since each local or trade society is practically assured of a due proportion of young members which will pay for the older members.

In Great Britain the contributions are calculated so that the surplus accumulated during the early life of each worker may be applied for his own benefit in later years. That is, contributions are calculated not on the simple basis of covering expenditures, but upon the basis of covering the estimated liability for the average person throughout life. This involves the accumulation of an "actuarial reserve" for each insured person. This method of financing has not been satisfactory in Great Britain, where it has been combined with a flat rate of premium and free choice of society. The German system is followed by most of the other countries.

3. **Maternity Insurance.**—Insurance provision for the needs of mothers at the time of childbirth is found in many countries. Such provision has been made through compulsory health insurance in all countries having comprehensive health insurance systems. In a few countries separate compulsory maternity insurance laws have been adopted, and others have provided for

SOCIAL INSURANCE

voluntary systems through subsidized sickness insurance or state grants.

In Sweden, Denmark, Belgium, and Switzerland, government grants are made to sickness societies which voluntarily provide maternity benefits. In Sweden and Switzerland the government subsidizes approved sickness insurance carriers and gives an especially liberal grant toward meeting the expenditure for maternity care, thus trying to encourage provision for this need. In Switzerland the federal legislation for voluntary insurance may be made compulsory by the individual communes and cantons. In Belgium and Denmark government subsidies are given sick funds which provide maternity care among their benefits.

In the countries which provide maternity benefits as part of compulsory health insurance legislation, the benefits thus provided are available for insured women. In some countries, as in Great Britain, a money benefit only is provided, but more frequently both cash and medical care are furnished. The cash maternity benefit is usually equal to the regular cash sick benefit, varying from 50 per cent to the full amount of the basic wage. The period during which the cash benefit is paid varies from a few weeks up to the entire period of incapacity for work. Most frequently, however, benefit is paid during the period before and after confinement during which employment is prohibited by law. The legislation of many countries provides an additional allowance—a nursing benefit—during a limited period, provided the mother nurses her child.

Health insurance legislation in some countries also makes provision for the uninsured wife of an insured man, usually for medical care at confinement, and sometimes for a modest cash benefit in addition. Great Britain, contrary to the usual continental developments, provides no medical care but a cash benefit of $20 for an insured married woman (regardless of whether or not her husband is insured), $10 for the uninsured wife of an insured man, and $10 for an insured unmarried mother. An insured woman unable to work during pregnancy is entitled to her usual cash sickness benefit.

The World War with its emphasis upon the importance of adequate care for mothers and young children stimulated development in this field. In Germany, during the conflict, maternity provisions voluntarily undertaken by the funds in addition to the required six weeks' maternity benefit were curtailed, and an extensive system of maternity grants financed partly by the state but administered by the insurance funds was substituted. In September, 1919, Germany placed the extended provision for maternity care upon a permanent legal basis as part of the regular health insurance scheme. In addition, uninsured women of small means were granted maternity benefits from the treasury. In Great Britain the emphasis was laid upon more extended provision for consultation centers where mothers might go for advice and treatment. In a number of other countries maternity benefits were liberalized or came into being for the first time in the post-war period.

Compulsory maternity insurance, independent of any health insurance scheme, existed in 1935 in Argentina, Cuba, Italy and Spain. Italy, in 1910, established a system of compulsory maternity insurance applicable to women industrial workers of from fifteen to fifty years of age. Contributions are divided between employee and employer in the ratio of 3 to 4, and the state pays a fixed amount for each confinement. In Spain, beginning in 1931, a compulsory system has provided, in addition to medical care, cash benefits for six weeks prior to confinement. The costs are met by employer and employee contributions of equal amount, with additional state subsidies.

Direct state aid early in 1935 was in existence in several countries, including Australia, Denmark, France, and Germany. In Australia legislation first adopted in 1912 provided for a payment from government funds of $20 to every woman upon the birth of a living child. Danish legislation of 1913 provided that any public relief given lying-in women during the four weeks following confinement, when their industrial employment is prohibited, shall not be considered poor relief. A French act of 1913 provided a grant from public funds to women employed by others for wages. This grant is given upon condition that the mother give up her usual gainful employment, that she take all practicable rest, and that she follow health instructions given her. An additional allowance is made if the mother nurses her child. In 1918 this act was extended to include all women with insufficient means. Germany, beginning in 1919, granted maternity allowances from public funds to women of small

SOCIAL INSURANCE 267

means not included under its compulsory health insurance scheme.

Although in this country several states, beginning with Massachusetts in 1912, prohibit the industrial employment of women for a period of several weeks immediately before and after childbirth,[66] no American state has legislatively recognized the justice and necessity of furnishing maternity benefits during such periods of enforced idleness. The International Labor Conference of 1919, held in Washington, adopted a draft convention providing that during the six weeks' rest which a wage-earning woman may take preceding confinement and the similar rest which she is to be required to take following confinement, she shall be paid "benefits sufficient for the full and healthy maintenance of herself and her child provided either out of public funds or by means of insurance, the exact amount of which shall be determined by the competent authority in each country, and as an additional benefit shall be entitled to free attendance by a doctor or certified midwife." By April, 1936, this convention had been ratified by sixteen countries.[67] If insurance is to accomplish its object of conserving the health and life of a nation, it is desirable that maternity benefits be extended as widely as possible.

4. Need in the United States.—By 1920 universal workmen's health insurance was eagerly discussed in America, a bill having been passed by the New York Senate in April, 1919. Nine states,[68] through official investigating commissions, had reported, thus making available to the public a wealth of data concerning the need for this type of social insurance. Despite these revelations, however, the selfish and highly organized opposition of commercial insurance companies and medical societies succeeded in so misleading the public mind as to the true purposes and merits of health insurance, that legislative work in this field became totally impossible for more than a decade. No serious effort to enact health insurance was again

[66] See "Childbirth Protection," p. 188.
[67] Argentina, Brazil, Bulgaria, Chile, Colombia, Cuba, Germany, Greece, Hungary, Latvia, Luxemburg, Nicaragua, Rumania, Spain, Uruguay, and Yugoslavia.
[68] California, Massachusetts, New Jersey, Connecticut, Wisconsin, Ohio, Illinois, New York, and Pennsylvania.

made in the United States until 1935, when a bill was unsuccessfully pressed for adoption in the California legislature.

The facts, unperverted by propaganda, however, are available and convincing. Official investigations have disclosed that in the course of a year approximately 20 per cent of the workers are sick, the illnesses lasting on the average about thirty-five days. Other investigations show that at any one time 2.25 per cent of the workers are so sick as to be unable to work, and that sickness when distributed over a group means an average of about eight days of sickness a year for each person. Although the hazard has been measured with a fair degree of accuracy, existing forms of insurance have so far been unable to meet the situation. Official investigations have shown that only a small minority of the workers carry health insurance, and that what they do carry is usually for small amounts and often unaccompanied by any medical benefit. Low-paid workers, among whom there is most sickness, carry the least insurance. Savings from wages are too frequently inadequate to meet the strain of a period of sickness. It is not surprising, therefore, that in normal times sickness is a factor in more cases of dependency than any other one cause, being involved in at least one-third of the cases which seek relief from voluntary charity.

Although the burden is borne by the workers and those philanthropically inclined, there is accumulating evidence that industry is also a factor in causing sickness and that it should justly bear a portion of the expense. Investigation has also shown that the medical needs of sick wage earners are inadequately met, partly on account of inability to pay the customary fees. As a result, many go without proper care, or obtain medical charity where it is available. The recent advances in medicine resulting in increased specialization have increased the expensiveness of medical service and the need for its organization. Among those familiar with the social side of medicine there is a keen realization that a reorganization of medical practice and new methods of financing it are urgently needed. On the medical side, health insurance will distribute the cost of medical care between industry and the workers and enable the worker to pay his share of the cost in advance during periods of good health. It will also facilitate the organization of group practice which is required by the recent advances in medicine.

After a careful survey, the California Social Insurance Commission as early as 1917 concluded that: "Health insurance to be effective must be made compulsory upon the individual worker."[69] The Pennsylvania Health Insurance Commission stated two years later: "Your commission believes that the best way to close this sickness highroad to poverty and dependency is to make available immediate and adequate medical care for sickness cases and to prevent the financial burden of sickness from falling entirely on the person least able to bear it—the sick worker. In some way the burden should be distributed among all wage workers, or shared by industry and by the community as a whole."[70] The New York State Federation of Labor, in recommending compulsory health insurance, pointed out that only through this method could a portion of the cost be passed on to industry. The bills which were introduced in the various state legislatures follow in the main the standards for health insurance formulated by the American Association for Labor Legislation in 1914.[71] They usually provide for a cash sickness benefit during twenty-six weeks, medical care, maternity benefits, and a funeral benefit. The cost is divided equally between worker and employer, while the state bears the cost of central supervision. The insurance is to be carried by mutual democratically managed associations of workers and employers, called "funds," which the state will supervise.

In addition to their relief value, such measures contain important possibilities for the prevention of illness. After a century of rapid industrial growth and increasing urban population we are just beginning to value as a social factor the sanitation which drains cities, provides pure water and pure milk, and quarantines infectious diseases. We have too long failed to realize that the ill health of the individual, even though he may not be suffering from a contagious disease, is a matter of public concern. Medical care of adults is no less important for a state which values the lives of its citizens than is the medical examination of school children which we have already adopted in the larger cities.

[69] *Report of the Social Insurance Commission of California*, 1917, p. 121.
[70] *Report of the Health Insurance Commission of Pennsylvania*, 1919, p. 9.
[71] *American Labor Legislation Review*, December, 1914, pp. 595-596.

More general medical consultation will reveal unsuspected tendencies which, if allowed to develop, will have as pernicious effects as the adenoids we are careful to remove from school children. There are many wage earners who are unable to afford a doctor's fee. Nor· is the dispensary service given in the large cities sufficient to meet the need. A socialized medical service, whereby all who require the services of a physician may have access to the necessary treatment, has been found very effective in many countries. Great Britain's health insurance act has revealed a mass of human suffering, especially among women, which hitherto had received no medical attention. Because of the increased use of doctors, a far larger number of persons have been discovered who need operations and hospital care—persons whose ills previously would have gone without treatment until the suffering had become acute and the chances of recovery had been diminished. The need revealed has been so great that there is strong sentiment in favor of extending medical care under the insurance act to the dependents of the insured. Socialized medical service has resulted in prophylactic treatment for the individual and in the conservation of national vitality.

Great Britain's health insurance act has been an incentive for undertaking a national campaign against tuberculosis. By means of a sanatorium benefit for insured workers suffering from this disease, more adequate treatment is being provided.

Furthermore, the necessity of spending money on preventable disease is in itself a stimulus to prevention. Various English bodies have been aroused by this factor to a keen interest in the relation between tuberculosis and housing. The financial pressure on "approved societies" is a direct inducement to demand thorough inspection of dwellings and work places, especially since the delinquent authority can be made to pay the cost of the sickness produced by the poor sanitary conditions which it has allowed to exist. In its report on public health, after the war, the British Ministry of Reconstruction stated of the workings of the insurance act: "The attention thus drawn to these [sickness] conditions not only stimulated provision for the direct alleviation of existing suffering, but also encouraged the rediscovery, as it were, following the course

SOCIAL INSURANCE

of evolution of medical science, to a humaner principle of prevention, as the means by which the sufferings of the individual could best be relieved or averted. In another general respect the insurance act entirely altered the previous position. It created a new body of organized public opinion, with a financial interest in the improvement of the national health."[72]

Some of the American plans have proposed the levying of a higher premium upon the industry or particular establishment in which the sickness rate is higher than normal. This is a means tending to persuade the employer of the economy of factory sanitation which will improve the health of the worker and thereby reduce his insurance premium. It is the same inducement of low insurance premiums for workmen's compensation which is partially responsible for the "Safety first" movement and the installation of safety appliances. Without a compulsory health insurance system, the economy of health preservation cannot be made an effective lever for reform.

A revival of interest in health insurance followed the publication from 1928 to 1932 of a series of reports by the Committee on the Costs of Medical Care. This committee, organized in 1927 and financed by several large foundations, included forty-eight members representative of the medical professions and other special groups, as well as the social sciences and the general public. In its final report and recommendations, published in 1932, the committee urged "that the costs of medical care be placed on a group payment basis, through the use of insurance, through the use of taxation, or through the use of both these methods."[73] Although eleven members were recorded as favorable to compulsory health insurance, the majority hesitated to recommend more than voluntary measures. The committee's factual findings, however, like the official reports of a dozen years earlier, clearly indicated the need. One of its members, Walton H. Hamilton, in a separate statement accompanying the report, declared that "compul-

---

[72] Great Britain, Ministry of Reconstruction, *Reconstruction Problems*, 23, "Public Health, I—A Survey," 1919, pp. 6-7.

[73] *Medical Care for the American People—The Final Report of the Committee on the Costs of Medical Care*, University of Chicago Press, 1932, p. 120.

272 PRINCIPLES OF LABOR LEGISLATION

sory health insurance is the very minimum which this committee should have recommended."[74]

After the Committee on the Costs of Medical Care had issued its final report, the Milbank Memorial Fund, which had helped finance the committee's work, for a time undertook, with the aid of some of the committee's experts, to carry on further studies looking toward the practical application of its findings.[75] Moreover, a variety of voluntary schemes for group payment of medical costs were brought forward by various organizations and individuals throughout the country, and a few were put into operation. In California, however, where some of the most extensive of such voluntary experiments had been in operation for several years, a state senate investigating commission, created in 1933 to study health insurance, submitted a report in 1935 recommending the adoption of a compulsory law. The California Medical Association also in 1935 adopted a resolution in favor of such legislation. A bill was introduced, but the senate voted to continue the study and to postpone action until the 1937 session. At the same time, health insurance bills were before the legislatures of several other states. The medical profession, however, as represented by the American Medical Association, has continued its stubborn opposition to health insurance; but the American College of Surgeons, the American Hospital Association, and several local medical societies, including the state organizations in California, Colorado, Michigan, Oregon, and Washington, have openly advocated some form of insurance against medical costs.[76] In 1935 the American Federation of Labor, which in earlier years had opposed compulsory insurance, adopted a resolution urging the enactment of "socially constructive health insurance legislation through Congress and the individual states."[77]

Although not included in the Federal Social Security Act

[74] *Ibid.*, p. 196.

[75] This study was discontinued in 1935 following pressure from organized opponents of health insurance. See Rorty, James, "The Case of John A. Kingsbury," in *The Nation*, June 24, 1936.

[76] See Falk, I. S., "Formulating an American Plan of Health Insurance," *American Labor Legislation Review*, vol. xxiv, no. 2, June, 1934. Pp. 87-94.

[77] *Report of the Proceedings of the Fifty-fifth Annual Convention of the American Federation of Labor*, 1935, p. 593.

SOCIAL INSURANCE

of 1935, health insurance was one of the subjects studied by the President's Committee on Economic Security. Taking over the experts employed by the Milbank Memorial Fund, that committee in 1934 began the preparation of a national program dealing with the sickness problem. While recommending the immediate extension of public health services, as subsequently adopted in the Social Security Act, the committee's report in January, 1935, declared[78] that "The nature of this problem and the nature of the risks which it involves calls for an application of the insurance principle to replace the variable and uncertain costs for individuals by the fixed and predictable costs for large groups of individuals." It stated, moreover, that "Voluntary insurance holds no promise of being much more effective in the near future than it has been in the past." The committee announced that it had prepared a tentative plan for health insurance which it had submitted to its advisory committees for further study. By July 1, 1936, the details of this plan had not yet been made public. Meanwhile, in March, 1936, in the Canadian province of British Columbia, there was adopted the first compulsory health insurance law on the North American continent.

III. OLD-AGE AND INVALIDITY INSURANCE

The rapid development of industry, among its other results, has placed emphasis on the individual's physical vigor and wage-earning capacity. It has deprived old age of the esteem bestowed upon it under more primitive patriarchal conditions, and after a life of productive toil it relegates to the background the aged or incapacitated man as a useless, uneconomic factor. Failing health, inability to find employment, lack of means, often absence of friends willing or able to help him—such is the prospect which confronts, in the great majority of cases, the aged worker.

1. **Unassisted Old-age Insurance.**—In response to the gravity of this situation three main measures of relief have been developed: charity, saving, and insurance. Charity has been known since ancient times, and no doubt has relieved a deal of destitution; but the modern opinion is that charity, both

[78] *Report to the President of the Committee on Economic Security,* 1935, pp. 41-43.

private and public, is insufficient in amount and unsatisfactory in quality; that it exercises a degrading effect upon the recipient and is repugnant to the self-respecting person. The serious difficulties in the way of saving are also well known. The low standard of wages seldom, if ever, allows any surplus; most often the immediate demands outweigh the arguments in favor of saving. Besides, the very remoteness of old age and the uncertainty of attaining it discourage many people from making preparation for the future at the expense of the present. In this problem, as in that of provision for illness, the collective process of insurance is considered much more satisfactory than the individualistic method of savings. Professor Seager has said: "For every wage earner to attempt to save enough to provide for his old age is needlessly costly. The intelligent course for him is to combine with other wage earners to accumulate a common fund out of which old-age annuities may be paid to those who live long enough to need them."[79]

The development of old-age and invalidity insurance is similar to that of health insurance. The first stage in the movement was marked by optional unassisted insurance, which is still furnished by some fraternal societies, trade unions, establishment funds, and insurance companies. However, the number of fraternal societies and trade unions, either here or abroad, which undertake the complicated business of old-age and invalidity insurance is small. In many states of this country fraternal societies are prohibited from dealing in it. As to American trade unions, out of about 150 existing national organizations, in 1932 less than a dozen were known to pay old-age benefits.[80] In addition, some old-age benefits are paid by individual locals, and a number of national unions pay permanent disability benefits. Business concerns furnishing old-age insurance or straight pensions for their employees are also relatively few, especially in this country.

A careful study of industrial pension plans made under the auspices of the Industrial Relations Counselors, Inc.,[81] shows

[79] Seager, Henry R., *Social Insurance*, 1910, pp. 118, 119.
[80] Latimer, Murray W., *Trade Union Pension Systems*, Industrial Relations Counselors, Inc., 1932.
[81] Latimer, Murray W., *Industrial Pension Systems*, vols. i and ii, 1932.

that in 1932 there were in the United States and Canada a total of 434 companies with pension schemes in normal operation. It was estimated that the number of persons receiving pensions under these plans did not exceed 140,000, with total payments for 1931 of not more than $97,000,000. About two-thirds of the plans in operation were of the non-contributory type, and less than half offered any form of guarantee of pension payments. The social value of these schemes has been questioned, first, because of the relatively small group affected, and, secondly, because of defects of most of the schemes, such as uncertainty as to receipt of the pension, arbitrary action by the employer, and restriction of the independence and mobility of labor. Insurance companies do a considerable old-age annuity business in Europe, chiefly among the middle class; in the United States, on the contrary, commercial annuity insurance for wage earners is negligible.

2. **Assisted State Plans.**—Obviously, voluntary unassisted old-age insurance reaches only a small part of the wage earners. As a consequence, as in the other branches of social insurance, it came to be considered the duty of the state to assist its aged citizens; and the principle of state insurance, sometimes aided by subventions, was devised.

Many countries, among them Belgium, France, Italy, Portugal, and Spain, had at one time, voluntary schemes of this type which have since been superseded by compulsory insurance. Voluntary old-age insurance, not supplemented by other schemes, existed in 1935 in Japan and two Swiss cantons, while practically all foreign countries having modern old-age legislation maintain voluntary schemes for persons or groups not covered by their compulsory insurance or straight pension laws.

In the United States there has been little development of such voluntary systems. Massachusetts and Wisconsin alone have taken steps in this direction. The Massachusetts plan is a system of voluntary old-age insurance through the savings banks under state supervision, while the Wisconsin system provides for the issuance of annuities by the state life fund under the supervision of the insurance commissioner.

Even state assistance and supervision, however, failed to secure for old-age and invalidity insurance any large measure of popular acceptance. Experts commonly agree that even generous subsidies do not seem to attract more than a small part of the wage earners; that in a large number of cases the payments either are made irregularly or are after a while suspended, and that the benefits paid are very small.

In view of the insufficiency of state control and subsidy, two other very significant elements of social insurance were added, namely, compulsion and the requirement of the employer's contribution.

3. Straight Pensions.—One widely adopted method of meeting the problems of old-age poverty is that of "straight," or non-contributory, old-age pensions. Such pensions have been granted sometimes for the performance of a definite period of service and sometimes to all persons meeting certain personal requirements. The first country to adopt such a plan for all of its needy aged citizens was Denmark in 1891. Similar laws have also been enacted in other foreign countries—New Zealand (1898), France (1905),[82] Australia (1908), Great Britain (1908),[83] Iceland (1909), Newfoundland (1911), Uruguay (1919), Belgium (1920),[84] Norway (1923), Greenland (1926), Canada (1927),[85] and the Union of South Africa (1928).

Under most of these foreign laws a definite period of both residence and citizenship is required. Moreover, only worthy citizens are eligible—family or child desertion, drunkenness, vagrancy and previous prison sentence being among the moral grounds which disqualify applicants either permanently or temporarily. Requirements as to economic status of the pensioner vary widely. Australia and New Zealand aid persons whose incomes do not exceed $380 and $474, respectively, there being additional limitations with respect to value of property owned.

[82] Largely superseded in 1910 by a compulsory contributory insurance plan.

[83] This act was supplemented by a compulsory contributory scheme of old-age and widows' pensions adopted in 1925. The pension plan was continued in the Irish Free State after it became self-governing by treaty in 1921.

[84] Superseded in 1926 by the compulsory insurance law of 1924.

[85] A federal aid law. By 1932 it had been accepted by all of the Canadian provinces except Quebec. In New Brunswick, the act of 1930 providing pensions was not made effective until July 1, 1936. In Quebec, a bill to provide pensions was introduced early in 1936.

SOCIAL INSURANCE 277

In other countries, yearly income limits are much lower. Pensions vary with the income of the pensioner but usually may not exceed a fixed maximum limit, as much as $253 a year in Australia and as little as $50 a year in Newfoundland.

In the United States the movement for more systematic and humane provision for the aged found legislative expression as early as 1907 in the creation of an investigating Commission on Old Age Pensions in Massachusetts. This commission's report in 1910, however, was unfavorable. In 1914, Arizona's voters by initiative petition adopted a measure providing not only public old-age pensions but also mothers' pensions. That law, a crudely drafted measure, was soon declared unconstitutional because of its technical defects.[86] In 1915, however, Alaska enacted a law providing pensions up to $25 a month for men and $45 a month for women as an alternative to care in the "pioneers' home," an old folks' home created by an earlier statute. This was the first permanent American old-age pension law. Beginning in 1915, several states created investigating commissions, some of which, notably those of Ohio and Pennsylvania, made valuable reports which stressed the extent of old-age dependency and the inhuman conditions that existed in many almshouses where old folks were found herded together with the diseased and mentally defective. No further legislation, however, was enacted until after the World War.

Renewed interest was aroused in 1922 by the preparation of a standard bill by the Pennsylvania Commission on Old-age Pensions, the American Association for Labor Legislation and the Fraternal Order of Eagles. Further investigations, official and unofficial, of almshouse conditions gave added emphasis to the need. In 1923, three states—Montana, Nevada and Pennsylvania—enacted pension laws; but the Nevada act did not become operative, because of inadequate appropriations, until reenacted in amended form in 1925; and the Pennsylvania law was held invalid because of an unusual provision of the state constitution prohibiting state grants to individuals or communities for benevolent purposes. During the next six years, old-age pension laws were enacted in eight additional

[86] State Board of Control *v.* Buchstegge, 18 Ariz. 277, 158 Pac. 837 (1916).

states.[87] The number of such laws then increased rapidly and by July, 1936, all except eight states—Georgia, Kansas, New Mexico, North Carolina, South Carolina, South Dakota, Tennessee, and Virginia—had laws providing for old-age pensions.

The effectiveness with which these old-age pension laws were administered varied greatly from state to state. In some states, lack of appropriations rendered the laws inoperative, or nearly

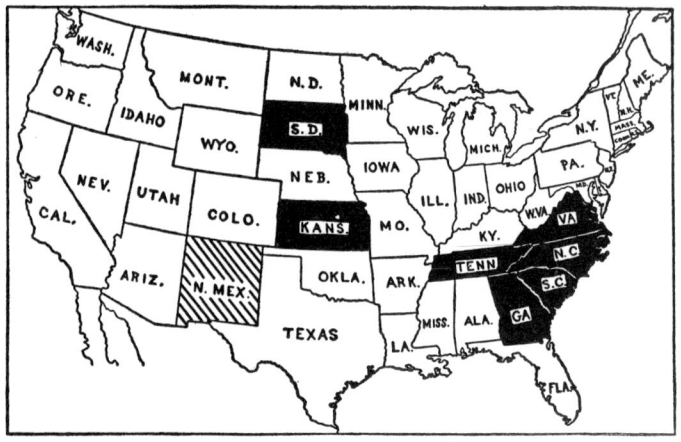

STATE OLD-AGE PENSION LAWS

By July 15, 1936, laws providing pensions for the needy aged had been adopted by all except eight states. New Mexico, with no pension law, had qualified for federal aid under the Social Security Act by adopting an old-age assistance plan under the state poor-relief law.

so. During 1934, of the twenty-eight states having pension laws, three paid no pensions. In the remaining states, a total of 235,397 persons were receiving pensions at the end of the year, payments during that year varying from an average of $26.08 a month in Massachusetts to an average of 69 cents a month in North Dakota. In only five states was the average monthly pension more than $20; in thirteen, it was less than $10. Administration of the pension laws differed widely in quality not only between states but also within the same state when no state

[87] California (1929), Colorado (1927), Kentucky (1926), Maryland (1927), Minnesota (1929), Utah (1929), Wisconsin (1925), Wyoming (1929).

SOCIAL INSURANCE

supervision of county administration was provided. In several states pensions were paid only in those counties which elected to do so.

The Federal Social Security Act of 1935, by providing financial aid and by fixing certain minimum standards for state pension laws, was a long step toward liberalizing and improving the administration of state old-age pension laws. Under the act the federal government pays one-half of each old-age pension granted under an approved state law, not counting amounts in excess of $30 a month per pensioner. To receive approval from the Social Security Board and thus be eligible for federal aid, a state law must provide for pensions to needy persons 65 years of age or older (70 years, until 1940) who have resided in the state five years or more out of the previous nine. No more than one year's residence in the state immediately prior to application may be required. The law must be state-wide and mandatory, with direct financial participation by the state, and with administration by the state or under state supervision. Persons whose claims for pensions have been denied must be given opportunity for fair hearing before the state administrative or supervisory agency. Reports concerning the operation of the law must be made to the Social Security Board. By June 1, 1936, the laws of thirty-one states and the District of Columbia had been approved by the Federal Social Security Board as conforming to the federal law.

Under most state old-age pension laws, needy persons 65 years of age or older may be granted pensions amounting to $30 a month or $1 a day. On June 1, 1936, a dozen state laws fixed the minimum age at 70. In California the maximum pension allowed was $35 a month, but the laws of Massachusetts, Mississippi, New York, and the District of Columbia specified no maximum. In five states the maximum pension was $25 a month, while in four states it was even smaller, the smallest being $150 a year (North Dakota). In most states, a pensioner may not have an income from all sources, including the pension, in excess of an amount usually equal to the maximum pension payable under the law. There is generally a limit to the value of property a pension recipient may hold, varying from none at all (West Virginia) to $5,000 as in Illinois. The applicant must not have transferred property to another in order to qualify for a pension. Upon the death of the pensioner, moreover, the laws as a rule give the state a lien on the estate of the deceased for the total amount of the pensions he has received. Most state laws also have citizenship, residence, and character requirements.

Straight pension systems have been attacked as destroying the habit of thrift, but thrift can hardly be destroyed by the remote and uncertain possibility of attaining old age with a pension which is hardly sufficient to keep body and soul together. A more substantial objection, advanced by some champions of social insurance, stresses the point that a straight grant conditioned upon proof of need resembles charity and is therefore less desirable than an insurance system under which the worker is asked to contribute. On the other hand, it is pointed out that contributory plans involve complicated administrative machinery for collection of contributions and preservation of individual records over long periods of time. The great advantage of straight pension plans is their marked simplicity. Although there has been a world-wide tendency toward contributory systems, the need will continue to exist for straight pensions to provide for those who cannot be covered by the insurance method.

Straight pensions for service are granted both by governments and by private employers. In America such pensions are provided by some state and municipal governments for certain classes of employees, such as policemen, firemen, and teachers, though contributory pension systems for such public servants are more usual. The federal government has also established pensions in the army and navy, with particular generosity toward Civil War veterans. In several European countries, furthermore, workers in the government-owned industries are granted pensions, as, for example, in the tobacco works of Italy and France. Finally, pensions are granted to their employees by some private concerns but their social importance is not great.

4. **Compulsory Systems.**—Compulsory old-age and invalidity insurance in other countries was slower in developing than health insurance, but after the World War it made rapid advances. In this branch of social insurance, as in the two previously discussed, Germany took the lead, enacting its first law

SOCIAL INSURANCE

in 1889. All German wage earners of the designated ages and occupational groups, regardless of size of income, are compelled to insure. Salaried workers of the lower income groups are also included. Other classes may take out voluntary insurance. Contributions are of eight grades, according to the worker's income, and are paid in equal parts by employer and employee. The pensions equal a fixed basic amount plus an increment varying with the number of contribution weeks and rate of contribution. The state's contribution consists in the payment of a fixed sum annually to each person in receipt of a pension. The age qualification for receiving an old-age pension, first set at seventy years, is now sixty-five.

Provisions for old age are subsidiary, in the German law, to those for invalidity insurance. An insured person of any age, who on account of diminished strength is unable to earn one-third of the wages usually paid to normal workers in his occupation, is entitled to an invalidity pension. The law also provides a benefit to an invalided wife or husband upon the death of the insured wage earner and a benefit to the fatherless orphan of an insured person.

Two unusual points in the German old-age invalidity insurance system are sickness pensions and sanatorium treatment. Sickness benefits, equivalent in amount to invalidity benefits, are paid to persons not permanently incapacitated, who have exhausted their claims to sick pay and are still unable to work. It is entirely apart from cash payments, however, and in the realm of prevention, that the most significant feature of the whole German social insurance plan is to be found. Under the local pension boards is maintained a country-wide network of sanatoria, rest homes, and health resorts. Persons who have drawn all their sick benefits but who are still unable to work are entitled to maintenance in these institutions, and the timely and efficient care there furnished to the patients has proved a powerful factor in the prevention of invalidity.

By 1935 wage earners in twenty-five foreign countries[88] were

[88] The following countries had compulsory old-age insurance laws with broad coverage: Argentina, Austria, Belgium, Bulgaria, Chile, Czechoslovakia, France, Germany, Great Britain, Greece, Hungary, Iceland, Irish Free State, Italy, Luxemburg, The Netherlands, Poland, Portugal, Rumania, Russia, Spain, Sweden, the Swiss cantons of Glarus, Appenzell and Basle, Uruguay and Yugoslavia. For description of foreign laws and

covered by compulsory old-age insurance laws, many of which, like Germany's, provided invalidity benefits also. Occasionally, these laws are restricted to special groups, "industrial and commercial wage earners," or "manual workers," and frequently wage earners of the higher income groups are exempt from the compulsory features of the law. A few countries provide compulsory old-age insurance for persons other than wage earners; for example, Sweden and the Swiss canton of Glarus for "all subjects" within certain age limits; Portugal for "all persons gainfully employed"; and Austria, Czechoslovakia, Germany, and Poland for certain groups of "non-manual workers." Under most of these laws the employer, employee, and state share the cost. In some cases the state does not contribute at all, employers and employees dividing the cost, while under a very few laws the employees do not contribute and the costs are borne by the employers and the state, as in The Netherlands and Spain. In Russia the employer, which is the state, alone bears the cost. Pensions for old age provided under most of these laws vary with the wage rate, the amount contributed, and the duration of insurance membership or employment. In a few countries, however, among them Rumania, Spain, and the Swiss canton of Glarus, the pension is uniform for all insured persons. Invalidity allowances are uniform under some laws, vary with wage rate and contribution value under others, or in still others are computed on the basis of a uniform minimum pension supplemented by varying amounts depending on contributions. Several countries—for example, Austria, Czechoslovakia, Germany, and Sweden—provide additional family allowances to supplement invalidity and old-age pensions.

The earliest compulsory old-age and invalidity insurance laws in the United States were enacted to cover all federal government employees in the classified civil service and public employees in a number of states and most large cities. In a few cases the state and municipal laws cover practically all civil service employees; but more often only special groups, particularly policemen, firemen, and teachers, are included.

The American law establishing compulsory contributory old-

experience, see International Labor Office, *Compulsory Pension Insurance* (Studies and Reports, Series M, No. 10, 1933).

SOCIAL INSURANCE 283

age and invalidity insurance for the federal government's employees in the classified civil service[89] was enacted in 1920 after years of agitation. The age of retirement was fixed at sixty-two for railway mail employees, sixty-five for mechanics, letter carriers, and post office clerks, and seventy for all others. Any employee able and willing to carry on his duties efficiently, in the discretion of the head of his department and on approval by the Civil Service Commission, may be continued in his position beyond the retirement age for two periods of two years each, but no longer. On retirement an employee becomes eligible to a yearly pension varying according to previous salary and length of service. No one who has not been employed by the government at least fifteen years is eligible to benefits under the law. In addition to the old-age pension provisions, the act establishes the same benefits for those who, after five years' service but before the retiring age, become totally disabled because of disease or injury "not due to vicious habits, intemperance, or willful misconduct." Recipients of disability benefits, unless their incapacity is known to be permanent, are to be examined annually by a United States medical officer or a designated physician to determine whether they are still eligible to the benefit. The employees' contribution toward the benefits is made through a deduction of 3½ per cent from all salaries. The balance of the cost is to be paid from general taxation.[90] Persons who leave the government service or die before reaching the age or length of service necessary for retirement are entitled to receive all moneys paid in by them, with interest compounded at 4 per cent annually. If, however, they are over forty-five years of age, have served at least fifteen years when involuntarily separated from the service, they may receive either an immediate annuity reduced in amount or a full pension de-

[89] Numbering, when the act was passed, about 300,000. Active membership of the fund on June 30, 1935, was estimated to be 407,200.

[90] The normal annual contribution required from the government to meet its currently accruing liability to the fund was estimated, as of June 30, 1935, to equal 2.71 per cent of payroll. Because Congress had failed in earlier years to appropriate a sufficient amount to cover its accruing liability, an additional annual contribution of 5.58 per cent was estimated to be needed to meet the existing deficiency. See *Fifteenth Annual Report of the Board of Actuaries of the Civil Service Retirement and Disability Fund*, 74th Congress, 2d Session, Doc. No. 196, 1936, p. 8.

ferred until the normal retirement date. Administration of the act is mainly lodged with the commissioner of pensions under the Secretary of the Interior.

The first compulsory old-age insurance law applying to workers in private industry in the United States was the Federal Railroad Retirement Act adopted in 1934.[91] Because the seniority rule in force in that industry resulted in the retention of an unusually large proportion of older workers, railroads employing about 90 per cent of all railway workers had earlier adopted voluntary pension schemes. The railway labor organizations, however, were critical of these voluntary arrangements because of the long service requirements, the high retirement age and the small amount of the pension usually afforded. Moreover, the payment of pensions was left wholly at the discretion of the companies, which could arbitrarily modify or discontinue them; and employees who went on strike or violated a company rule sometimes lost their pension rights. The railway labor organizations urged the enactment of a compulsory pension plan also as a means of relieving the existing serious unemployment among railway workers by expediting the retirement of the older employees.

The Railroad Retirement Act of 1934 provided for employer and employee contributions and for pensions beginning at age sixty-five, or after thirty years of service. It was, however, declared unconstitutional in 1935 by the United States Supreme Court in a five-to-four decision.[92] The court found that certain details of the law failed to meet the "due process" test. More broadly, however, the court held that the law was "in no proper sense a regulation of the activity of interstate transportation." Soon after this decision, Congress reenacted the pension plan, this time in two separate laws, one[93] levying taxes on employers and employees, and the other[94] providing for the payment of pensions. The new pension plan was essentially the same as that provided in the law of 1934, except for a few

[91] Public No. 485, 73rd Congress, approved June 27, 1934.
[92] Railroad Retirement Board v. Alton Railroad Co., 295 U. S. 330, 55 Sup. Ct. 758 (1935).
[93] Railroad Retirement Act of 1935, Public No. 399, 74th Congress, approved August 29, 1935.
[94] Public No. 400, 74th Congress, approved August 29, 1935.

detailed amendments designed to meet the objections raised by the court. These companion measures of 1935, however, were based upon the power of Congress to levy taxes and to appropriate money, and not upon the power to regulate interstate commerce. In this it was like the old-age benefit plan which Congress had just adopted in the Social Security Act.[95]

Under the tax measure, railway workers are taxed 3.5 per cent of their wages and their employers are taxed an equal amount. The receipts go into the general treasury fund, no special pension fund being created because of constitutional obstacles. The Retirement Act provides for the payment by the federal government of annuities to railroad employees beginning at age sixty-five. A worker with thirty years of railroad service may retire at an earlier age, but with reduced annuities; or a worker may elect to continue in service after sixty-five but his annuity is then also reduced for each such year of employment up to age seventy. The amount of the monthly pension is determined by multiplying the employee's years of service up to thirty by the following percentages of his basic monthly wage: 2 per cent of the first $50, 1½ per cent of the next $100, and 1 per cent of the next $150. Provision is made for a continuation, at half-rate, of pension payments to the widow of a pensioned employee for one year after his death. Taxes, payable beginning March 1, 1936, are collected by the Treasury Department; but benefits, beginning ninety days later, are administered by a specially created Railroad Retirement Board. This legislation was promptly challenged in court by the railroad companies, but by July 1, 1936, final decision on its validity had not been rendered.

Proposals for compulsory contributory old-age insurance with broad coverage had received scanty attention in the United States prior to 1934. The efforts of old-age pension proponents had been directed chiefly to securing straight pension laws. Separate state systems of contributory insurance, it was pointed out, would be costly, and there would be special difficulties arising out of the interstate movement of labor. On the other hand, a single national plan was believed to have little chance of enactment, and no measure had been brought forward which was thought capable of meeting the test of constitutionality.

[95] See below, p. 287.

Nevertheless, President Roosevelt's Committee on Economic Security appointed in 1934 recommended, and in 1935 Congress adopted as part of the Social Security Act, a national system of old-age benefits comparable in its coverage to the old-age insurance schemes already in effect in many foreign countries. This plan in its original form was prepared by members of the staff of the President's Committee and was developed with the assistance of the committee's technical and representative advisory boards. In urging early enactment of a contributory system, the Committee on Economic Security[96] stressed the point that the future cost of adequate provision for the aged on a non-contributory basis would place heavy burdens upon the taxpayer. Moreover, it was held that a contributory plan providing old-age annuities as a right would be preferable to the usual straight pension system which resembles poor relief in that it imposes a needs test. Foreign experience with old-age insurance and American experiments with voluntary industrial pensions were cited as demonstrating the worth of, and providing the factual basis for, a comprehensive system in this country. In enacting the old-age benefit plan into law, Congress is believed to have been influenced also by the substantial proportions of the nation-wide movement for the so-called "Townsend Plan" which proposed the payment of pensions as high as $200 a month to all persons beginning at age sixty.

The old-age benefit provisions of the federal Social Security Act[97] do not, strictly speaking, create a system of contributory old-age insurance, although the President's Committee on Economic Security recommended such a system and so provided in the bill as originally introduced. In the course of passage through Congress, however, the plan was amended in a manner which eliminated any direct connection between "contributions" and old-age benefits. Instead of a contributory insurance system, the act provides for old-age annuities paid on a non-contractual basis out of funds appropriated by Congress for that purpose. The amount of the annuity or benefit paid to any qualified individual is determined, not by the number or amount of tax payments made, but by the amount of wages

[96] See *Report to the President of the Committee on Economic Security*, 1935, pp. 23-35.
[97] Public No. 271, 74th Congress, 1935, Titles II and VIII.

received by him after the law's effective date. The act levies upon employers and employees taxes in amounts intended to cover the estimated cost of the old-age benefits provided, but nowhere does it provide that these taxes shall be used to pay such benefits. It is, on the contrary, provided that the tax receipts under the act shall be paid into the general treasury.

Congress carefully avoided creating any direct legal relationship between the taxes imposed and the benefits provided. These two features of the act are placed in two entirely separate "titles" or subdivisions. The reason for this separation was basically a constitutional one. Congress decided that its power to levy taxes "for the general welfare" did not include power to tax for the special purpose of old-age insurance. Therefore, instead of requiring "contributions" to an insurance fund, the law was made to levy taxes to be paid into the general treasury. Under its broad powers to make appropriations, on the other hand, Congress authorized an annual appropriation of an amount "sufficient as an annual premium to provide for the payments required" under the old-age benefit provisions. Such authorization merely sets a maximum to the annual appropriation Congress may make under the act, but it does not fix the amount of the appropriation. Much less does it determine whether the annual appropriation will be the same as, or larger or smaller than, the amount of the taxes collected under the act. These are all matters which Congress is left to determine each year.

In many respects, nevertheless, the old-age benefit plan provided has the appearance of a contributory insurance system. The employments subject to the tax provisions are identical with those covered by the benefit provisions. All employments are included except agricultural, domestic and casual labor, employment on a vessel or by an interstate carrier, public employments, and employment by certain non-profit institutions. Every employee in an employment not thus excluded is required to pay an income tax beginning at the rate of 1 per cent of wages received in 1937 and increasing by ½ of 1 per cent of wages at three-year intervals until a maximum of 3 per cent is reached in 1949. Each employer, moreover, is required to pay an excise tax on his payroll equivalent to the taxes levied on his employees. Thus, the combined taxes amount to

2 per cent of wages in 1937, increasing to 6 per cent in 1949. In both cases, however, that portion of an employee's wage in excess of $3,000 a year is not to be counted for tax purposes.

Benefits are payable to workers at age sixty-five who have worked in an employment covered by the act within each of five years after December 31, 1936, and before reaching sixty-five; and who have received at least $2,000 in wages for such employment. The amount of the monthly benefit is fixed as a percentage of the total amount of wages received after December 31, 1936, and before age sixty-five—½ of 1 per cent of the first $3,000; 1/12 of 1 per cent of the next $42,000; and 1/24 of 1 per cent of all amounts over $45,000. A minimum benefit of $10 a month and a maximum of $85 are fixed. Workers who are over sixty in 1937, and so will not have worked five years before reaching sixty-five, and others who for any reason are not qualified for benefits upon reaching that age, will thereupon be paid a lump sum equal to 3½ per cent of all wages received after December 31, 1936. If a worker dies before reaching sixty-five, his estate will be paid an amount equal to 3½ per cent of the total wages he received after tax payments begin; or if he dies after sixty-five his estate will receive this same amount less the sum of the benefits already paid him. Payment of benefits will be withheld from a qualified worker aged sixty-five or over, for each month during which he has regular employment.

A feature which aroused much controversy while the measure was pending in Congress was the question of the amount and rapidity of increase in the rate of the taxes. As drafted by the President's Committee on Economic Security,[98] the taxes on employees and employers each began at ½ of 1 per cent (total 1 per cent) and increased at five-year intervals, reaching a maximum of 2½ per cent (total 5 per cent) at the end of twenty years. Before the bill was enacted, these rates were increased at the request of the Treasury so as to begin at 1 per cent (total 2 per cent) and increase at three-year intervals to a maximum of 3 per cent (total 6 per cent) at the end of twelve years.

This increase in tax rates was designed to make it possible for Congress to avoid the necessity of large future appropria-

[98] S. 1130 and H. R. 4142, 74th Congress, introduced January 17, 1935.

tions for old-age benefits out of other general tax revenues. Under the bill as first introduced it was estimated by the President's Committee that such appropriations would have been necessary beginning about 1965, and the amount required would have risen to a maximum of nearly one and a half billion dollars in 1980 and each year thereafter. Under the law as enacted, it is estimated that if Congress should appropriate each year for the reserve account an amount equal to the tax collections under the act, this annual amount plus interest on the resulting reserve would be sufficient to cover the entire cost of the benefits. This, however, would involve the building up of a reserve amounting by 1980 to almost forty-seven billion dollars, which many believe might create serious investment and financial problems.

It cannot be predicted what policy Congress will adopt in the future with respect to financing old-age benefits. In determining this policy Congress will undoubtedly be guided to some extent by the accumulating experience derived from the administration of the act. As in all other forms of labor legislation, amendments will doubtless be made as the need arises. The old-age benefit features of the Social Security Act, it is evident, in no way commit Congress to a fixed, irrevocable policy with respect to either taxes, reserves or benefits.

IV. WIDOWS' AND ORPHANS' INSURANCE

Insurance for the protection of widows and orphans, or, as it is ordinarily called, life insurance, is furnished by practically all fraternal societies, many trade unions, some establishment funds, and by private life insurance companies. In some countries, such as Great Britain, France, Italy, Russia, and Canada, the government has undertaken the business of life insurance; in the United States we have state life insurance in Wisconsin, and in Massachusetts there is a system of life insurance administered by savings banks under state supervision.

1. **Voluntary Life Insurance.**—Life insurance, sometimes for enormous amounts and paid for by annual or quarterly contributions or premiums, is now a well-established method of providing for the future among the moderately well-to-do and the wealthy. In order to bring the poorly paid wage earner under the system, a special form of life insurance had to be

devised, known as "industrial" or "prudential" insurance, as opposed to the "ordinary" type. Under industrial insurance the policy amounts are much smaller, usually providing only for the burial of the insured, and, to facilitate payment, premiums are collected weekly or monthly by a vast army of agents. This method of collection, however, results in the increase of administrative expenses and, consequently, in higher rates. Another cause of higher rates in industrial insurance is the higher death rate among wage earners. Thus, even in purchasing decent burial the wage earner is obliged to pay a higher rate of insurance than does his more prosperous neighbor.[99] The more recently developed system of "group" insurance, by which the employees of a plant are covered under a group of policies sold through the employer and paid for collectively by him, usually with partial reimbursement from the workers, eliminates this excessive overhead cost, but depends on the good will of the employer for its inception and continuance and so is available to only a relatively small number of wage earners.

State insurance, as well as insurance furnished by fraternal societies, trade unions, establishment funds, and mutual assessment societies, is less expensive but still outside of the reach of many working people. Moreover, because the insurance is voluntary, the very families most in need of protection are often left without it. These defects, as in the other branches of social insurance, have led to the introduction of the compulsory principle.

2. **Compulsory Insurance.**—Compulsory widows' and orphans' insurance, also called survivors' insurance, is the newest branch of social insurance. This provision had been adopted by 1935 in nineteen countries,[100] most of which had passed such legislation since the World War. Several other countries had

[99] See Taylor, Maurice, *The Social Cost of Industrial Insurance*, 1933.
[100] Austria, Belgium, Bulgaria, Czechoslovakia, France, Germany, Great Britain, Greece, Hungary, Irish Free State, Italy, Luxemburg, The Netherlands, Poland, Rumania, Russia, the Swiss canton of Basle, Uruguay, Yugoslavia. A survey of widows' and orphans' insurance made by the International Labor Office was published as the "First Discussion" report on *Invalidity, Old Age and Widows' and Orphans' Insurance*, International Labor Conference, Sixteenth Session, 1932. See also, *Compulsory Pension Insurance*, Studies and Reports, Series M, No. 10, 1933.

compulsory systems covering limited groups of workers in specific occupations.

In Germany, survivors' insurance is combined with the old-age and invalidity insurance system and is supported by contributions from employees, workers and the state. Upon the death of the insured worker, his children receive a pension until fifteen years old or, if they continue in school, up to twenty-one. The widow of a manual worker receives a pension only if she is an invalid or is sixty-five years old. The amount of the survivors' pension is fixed for children at one-half the pension due the deceased, and for widows at six-tenths of such pension, the combined total not to exceed 80 per cent of the earnings of the basic wage group. In Great Britain, contributions and benefits are fixed at flat rates, as under the old-age insurance system. A widow receives $2.50 weekly until death or remarriage, with $1.25 paid on behalf of one child, and 75 cents for each additional child, until sixteen years of age if in school.

The laws of other countries have also established these survivors' pensions as a branch of the old-age and invalidity insurance schemes. The pensions are usually equal to a specified fraction of the old-age or invalidity pension received by or due the deceased, but under a few laws the survivors' pensions are determined directly by the contributions of the insured or in proportion to his scale of wages.

3. **Mothers' Pensions.**—Another method of dealing with the problem of widowhood and orphanhood is by means of mothers' or widows' pensions, paid to certain classes of mothers with dependent children. These pensions, however, are straight grants by the government. Such systems exist in Denmark, New Zealand, New South Wales, several Canadian provinces, and most American states.

The movement in this country is particularly interesting. Here the pressing problem of widows' and orphans' poverty and helplessness, instead of giving rise to social insurance measures, resulted in a sudden wave of legislation providing straight pensions, usually upon condition that the mother is found capable of providing a proper home for her child. Indeed, a leading argument in behalf of this legislation is that it is better to pay the mother for taking care of her

292 PRINCIPLES OF LABOR LEGISLATION

child than to expend the same amount in financing institutions, in even the best of which the death rate is abnormally high. In the nine years 1911-1919 thirty-nine American states and the two territories enacted such laws. By 1936, all except two states —Georgia and South Carolina—had such legislation, as had the District of Columbia, Alaska, Puerto Rico and Hawaii.

In many of the states, however, this legislation was unfortunately restricted in its operation. Only twenty state laws were

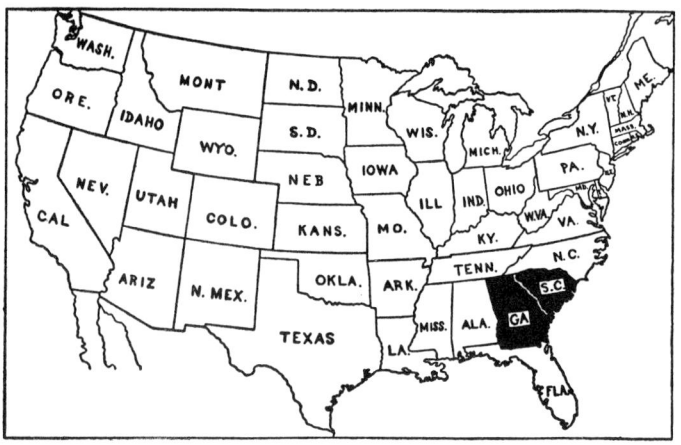

MOTHERS' PENSION LAWS

Only the two black states had failed by July 1, 1936, to adopt legislation for the payment of pensions to widowed mothers to enable them to maintain homes for their young children.

mandatory on the counties, with the result that many counties made no such provision, and the amount of aid granted was often inadequate. In 1935, therefore, provision was made in the federal Social Security Act for grants-in-aid to states which adopted state-wide mothers' aid systems. Under this law states with approved laws receive from the federal government one-third of all mothers' aid payments, not counting amounts in excess of $18 a month for one child and $12 a month for each additional child. Improvements in many state mothers' pension laws have resulted from this legislation.

SOCIAL INSURANCE

v. Unemployment Compensation[101]

Finally, the destitution arising from unemployment, in the past considered a matter of purely individual concern or, at best, an occasion for private charity, is now recognized as an evil which must be dealt with by the coordinated forethought of society as a whole. The demoralization of individuals and communities by prolonged or widespread deprivation of income because of involuntary idleness, it is now almost universally agreed, should not be allowed to continue unchecked. Seventeen countries in Europe provide some system for compensating the unemployed, and Queensland, Australia and the Dominion of Canada have similar legislation. In the United States, by May 1, 1936, twelve states and the District of Columbia had enacted unemployment compensation laws, and the federal Social Security Act contains provisions designed to stimulate the passage of similar legislation in the other states.

1. **The Ghent System.**—In warding off the financial hardships of unemployment, individual action and charity have been found just as inadequate as they were in protecting against the financial hardships caused by accident, ill health, or old age. Unemployment insurance originated among labor organizations. In this form it achieved considerable success in the important European countries. In the United States, on the contrary, only a few unions were known to pay out-of-work benefits. Unassisted trade union unemployment insurance with the cost borne by the workers alone proved a heavy burden on them; comparatively few were able or willing to insure; and adequate benefits could seldom be paid. In order to encourage insurance, a plan was devised by which governments, most often municipal, granted subsidies to trade unions furnishing unemployment insurance. This is the principle of the famous Ghent System, which was first introduced in the city of Ghent in Belgium in 1901. The Ghent idea was rapidly adopted, with some modifications, not only in many cities in Belgium, Germany,

[101] In Europe the term ordinarily used is unemployment *insurance*. Wisconsin, in enacting the pioneer American law in 1932, used the term *compensation* because its law is definitely not an insurance law. (See below, p. 308). The federal Social Security Act uses the term *compensation* so that this may now be regarded as the standard American term.

France, Switzerland, Italy, and The Netherlands, but also on a state-wide basis in Denmark, France, and Norway before the World War;[102] and since then in seven additional countries, The Netherlands, Finland, Spain, Belgium, Czechoslovakia, Switzerland, and Sweden. In many cases the trade union funds are subsidized by both the state and the municipality. Subsidies are based either on benefits payable or on contributions received, and sometimes represent as much as one-half to two-thirds of the total allowance received by the insured.

The system of government-subsidized unemployment insurance undoubtedly stimulated provision against unemployment.[103] On the other hand, it is generally recognized that the advantages of optional subsidized insurance are not far-reaching enough to offset its limitations, perhaps the most important of which is its failure to attract a sufficiently large number of workers. This limitation was partly offset by the practice among European unions of requiring all their members to join the unemployment insurance schemes. Unless, however, a country is practically 100 per cent unionized, even this form of compulsion leaves many workers unprotected. The exemption of employers from any direct share in the cost of the insurance, with the consequent loss of a valuable stimulus to unemployment prevention, is another serious disadvantage of voluntary subsidized schemes.

2. **Compulsory Unemployment Insurance.**—Compulsory unemployment insurance was first introduced in the city of St. Gall, Switzerland, in 1894. After a two years' trial the system, owing to defective administration, was adjudged a failure and was discontinued. The first country to adopt a system of compulsory unemployment insurance was Great Britain, whose act went into effect in 1912. Following her example, six more European countries have since established nation-wide compulsory unemployment insurance. These countries and the years of enactment are as follows: Italy, 1919; Austria, 1920; Irish Free State, 1920; Poland, 1924; Bulgaria, 1925; and Germany,

---

[102] It was also adopted in Great Britain for certain trades and continued for these trades until the scope of compulsory unemployment insurance was broadened by the act of 1920.

[103] See Gibbon, I. G., *Unemployment Insurance*, London, 1911, pp. 104, 105.

SOCIAL INSURANCE

1927. Russia also enacted such insurance, but later repealed it on the grounds that unemployment no longer existed in that country. In addition, Queensland, Australia, enacted a law in 1922, and thirteen cantons of Switzerland also have such laws, the first of which was passed in 1925. In Canada, on June 28, 1935, a compulsory system was enacted to cover the entire dominion.

In its original form the British act applied to seven groups of trades, and included about 2,500,000 workmen out of 15,000,000 in the country, or about 16⅔ per cent. The provisions of the act were frankly experimental in nature, and it has been frequently and extensively revised since its initiation. The various modifications were incorporated in a consolidated unemployment insurance act which was passed on February 26, 1935.[104] The provisions of the law cover England, northern Ireland, Scotland, and Wales. All manual workers and all non-manual workers earning less than £250 a year are now included, except agricultural and domestic workers, and certain public employees. The minimum age is the school-leaving age and the maximum age is sixty-four.

The employer, employee, and the government all contribute equal amounts to the insurance fund. The amounts of both contributions and benefits are based on sex and age differentials rather than on wages. The amount of the contribution ranges from 2d. for workers under sixteen, to 10d. for male workers from 21 to 65 years of age. The total contributions therefore are three times this amount. In 1931 when the rates now in effect were established, the total weekly contribution of worker, employer, and state for a man over twenty-one represented 4.6 per cent of average weekly earnings.

The weekly benefit rates to which these workers are entitled in case of unemployment range from 5s. for females under seventeen, to 17s. for males between 21 and 65 years of age, with slight additions for dependents of the contributor. Benefits are payable to workers unemployed and unable to find other work, for twenty-six weeks in the twelve months following the date of application. No benefit is paid for the first week of unemployment, and it is required that not less than thirty contributions must have been made during the two years previous

[104] 125 Geo. 5, C. 8, Chetty's *Eng. Stat.* vol. xxix, p. 760.

to the date of a claim for benefits. However, special provisions permit persons with good employment records in insured occupations to receive benefits for up to fifty-two weeks in a twelve-month period.[105] When a claimant has exhausted his right to benefits, ten contributions must be made before he may again be entitled to benefits.[106]

To safeguard the workers' interests, an unemployed man does not forfeit his right to benefits if he refuses work in a place where a trade dispute is on, or at wages below those he usually received, or less than those current in the community. On the other hand, he is not entitled to benefits if he is unemployed because of a labor dispute. If he quits voluntarily or is discharged for misconduct he is disqualified from benefits for a certain period.

The administrative machinery of the act is simple. The employee is required to secure an unemployment insurance book which, on his taking employment, is deposited with the employer. The latter pastes in the book on pay day stamps representing his own and the employee's contribution, deducting the worker's portion from his wages. The weekly payments are transmitted through the post office, which sells the stamps, to

[105] If the contributor has been insured for five years previous to the date of application for benefits, he is allowed three additional days of benefits for each five weekly contributions made in his behalf during the five-year period, except that one day is subtracted for every five days of benefits received during the five years.

[106] During the depression years the British system was liberalized to give "extended" or "uncovenanted" benefits beyond the specified maximum periods. This, of course, destroyed the actuarial basis of the fund and necessitated large loans from the Treasury. The act of 1934 put an end to these extensions of the unemployment insurance system by creating a new agency to handle this problem. It set up the Unemployment Assistance Fund, financed in small part (5 per cent) by local funds but in the main by the exchequer, to care for all employables who are in need but who have no right to covenanted insurance benefits. This provision has the dual function (1) of freeing the unemployment insurance system of a burden which is beyond its financial capacity and scope, and (2) of arranging for a form of government emergency relief which will keep able-bodied unemployed workers from local poor-law relief. For an account of the new British Act, see Davison, Ronald C., *The New Unemployment Act Popularly Explained,* Longmans, Green & Co., London, 1934, pp. 19-26.

SOCIAL INSURANCE

the unemployment insurance fund. If the insured worker loses his place, he gets his insurance book from his employer and deposits it in the nearest labor exchange or insurance office, one of which is within five miles of every considerable group of workers in the kingdom. He is thus automatically registered as looking for work, and so an abuse of the system by the "work-shy" man is avoided.

Most of the other compulsory unemployment insurance acts are not unlike Great Britain's in general plan. They usually cover the whole adult wage-earning population, with certain specified exceptions. Agricultural workers, domestic servants, public employees, independent workers, and home workers are frequently excluded, as also, occasionally, are workers earning over specified amounts. Expenses are usually divided among employees, employers, and the state, the proportions contributed by each varying somewhat. In every law except that of Poland, the employee and employer contribute equal amounts, but in Poland the employee contributes only one-third as much as the employer. In Italy the state makes no contributions, while in the Irish Free State, in Bulgaria, and in Queensland it contributes one-third of the total. In the other countries its contribution ranges somewhere between these two extremes. Benefits are calculated under some laws on the basis of the wages of the insured, and under others there is a flat rate for each of several specified wage groups. Most of the laws adjust the benefit to the family status of the insured. Some distinguish merely between married and unmarried men, while others make a more careful adjustment to the actual size of the family. The duration of benefits is limited to a specified period, the normal periods varying from twelve to twenty-six weeks. Many of the laws, however, provide for prolongation of the benefit in times of industrial crisis or severe individual hardship. Practically all these unemployment insurance schemes are coordinated with extensive systems of public employment offices.[107]

[107] For a brief account of foreign unemployment insurance systems, see United States Bureau of Labor Statistics, "Operation of Unemployment Insurance Systems in the United States and Foreign Countries, 1931-1934," *Monthly Labor Review,* August and September, 1934, vol. xxxix, no. 2, pp. 273-307, and no. 3, pp. 571-601. For more detailed accounts, see Gilson, Mary, *Unemployment Insurance in Great Britain,* Industrial

298   PRINCIPLES OF LABOR LEGISLATION

3. Unemployment Compensation in the United States.— The movement for unemployment compensation in the United States may be said to have begun as early as 1914 when a brief industrial depression with its resulting volume of unemployment led to an interest in the recently installed British system of dealing with this problem. A bill modeled on the British unemployment insurance act was prepared by the American Association for Labor Legislation and introduced in Massachusetts in 1916. In 1921 the post-war depression led to a renewed and increased concern with the unemployment problem. In that year the first unemployment compensation bill to receive serious consideration was introduced in Wisconsin. In the following decade interest in the subject survived only in that state, where the bill was reintroduced at each session of the legislature. Elsewhere the prosperity of the 'twenties, though it by no means solved the unemployment problem, blinded the general public to its importance.

After the crash in 1929 the mounting volume of unemployment inevitably attracted public attention and concern. While relief on an ever-increasing scale was seen to be the only way of meeting the emergency situation, in state after state serious consideration began to be given to permanent measures which should provide a more orderly and adequate way of compensating able-bodied workers unemployed through no fault of their own. In 1931 unemployment compensation bills of one kind or another were introduced in many states, and a half dozen official investigating commissions were created to study the problem and make recommendations.[108] In that year also, under the leadership of Franklin Roosevelt, then Governor of New York, an interstate commission representing the governors of six of the leading industrial states was set up to recommend action on

Relations Counselors, Inc., 1931; Lubin and Hill, *The British Attack on Unemployment,* Brookings Institution, 1934; Carroll, Mollie Ray, *Unemployment Insurance in Germany,* Brookings Institution, 1930, 2nd Edition Revised.

[108] See reports of some of these commissions: The Ohio Commission on Unemployment Insurance, *Report,* 1932; California State Unemployment Commission, *Report,* November, 1932; Massachusetts Special Commission on Stabilization of Employment, *Final Report,* December, 1932.

SOCIAL INSURANCE 299

the subject of unemployment compensation.[109] In February, 1932, that commission recommended state legislation along the same lines as the act which had passed the Wisconsin legislature in the preceding month—the first American unemployment compensation law.[110] In the next three years the movement for unemployment compensation gained momentum in many parts of the country; in 1933 bills were introduced in twenty-seven states. But the opposition was strong, and in each state it used the argument that to enact such a law would seriously burden the industry of the state in competition with industry in states lacking such legislation.

The Federal Social Security Act passed in 1935 contained provisions which put an end to that argument and provided a powerful stimulus to the enactment of state unemployment compensation laws.[111] The unemployment compensation sections of the federal act provided a nation-wide tax of 3 per cent on the payroll[112] of employers of eight or more individuals, against 90 per cent of which tax employers may offset contributions paid to unemployment compensation funds set up under state laws.[113] The act further provides for a federal subsidy for the administration of these state laws.[114] Obviously this tax,

[109] For the report of the Interstate Commission, see "Governors' Interstate Commission Urges Unemployment Reserves," *American Labor Legislation Review*, vol. xxii, March, 1932, pp. 19-23.

[110] Wisconsin Laws of Special Session, 1931-32, C. 20; Wisconsin Statutes, 1935, C. 108.

[111] 49 U. S. Stat. at Large 639, Secs. 901-910, 42 U. S. C. A., Secs. 1101-1110 (1935).

[112] One per cent for 1936, 2 per cent for 1937, and 3 per cent thereafter.

[113] To permit state laws to provide for reduction of contributions on the basis of various forms of "merit rating" (for explanation of that term, see below, p. 306), the Social Security Act contains an "Additional Credits" section which provides that the employer can offset against the federal tax (up to 90 per cent of that tax) not only contributions actually made under a state unemployment compensation act but also contributions which he is permitted *not* to make under such act because under its merit-rating provisions his contribution is reduced. Thus if the standard contribution rate under the state act is 2.7 per cent, but some employers contribute only 2 per cent or 1 per cent on the basis of their unemployment experience, they can receive credit for the full 2.7 per cent. See 49 U. S. Stat. at Large 643, IX, Sec. 909, 42 U. S. C. A., Sec. 1109.

[114] 49 U. S. Stat. at Large 626, Secs. 301-303, 42 U. S. C. A., Secs. 501-503.

with the provisions for its offset, offers a strong inducement for the enactment of state legislation. Since the employers of the state will be taxed in any case, many of them will prefer to pay the money to a state fund to be used to compensate the unemployed in their own state, rather than pay a tax to the federal government to be used for general purposes.

The federal act sets up only a few minimum standards which these state laws must meet in order to entitle the employers of

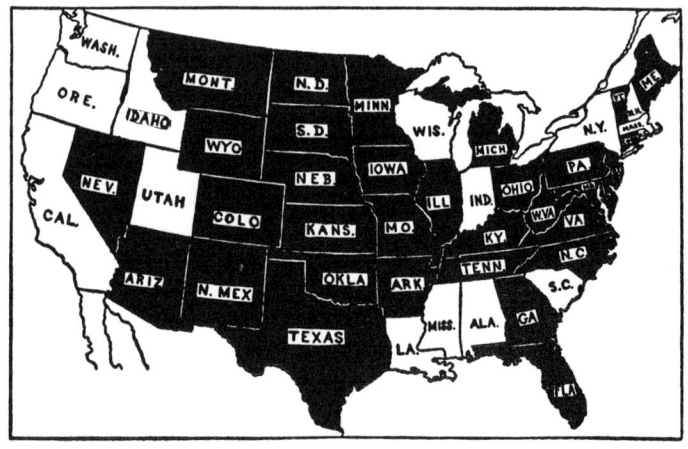

UNEMPLOYMENT COMPENSATION LAWS
By September 1, 1936, the fifteen white states and the District of Columbia had adopted compulsory unemployment compensation laws.

the state to the tax offset. All the money contributed must be used to pay compensation, and must be deposited in a national unemployment compensation fund. Each state act must protect labor standards by providing that workers shall not forfeit compensation benefits by refusing to take jobs under certain circumstances. For the most part, the states are left free to enact any type of unemployment compensation act they choose.

Under the stimulus of this federal act, laws were passed in a number of states during 1935 and early 1936. By May 1, 1936, thirteen unemployment compensation laws were on the statute books—in Alabama, California, District of Columbia, Indiana,

SOCIAL INSURANCE 301

Massachusetts, Mississippi, New Hampshire, New York, Oregon, Rhode Island, Utah, Washington, and Wisconsin.[115]

The American unemployment compensation laws so far enacted differ widely among themselves in a number of important respects, and none of them is modeled on European precedents. In some ways they more nearly resemble American accident compensation legislation. Laws in this field are inevitably complex in character and run to many pages in length, for they necessitate complicated administrative machinery and detailed provisions as to how the contributions are to be determined and collected and how the benefit payments are to be fixed and disbursed. Amid a welter of detail, six problems may be seen as basic to this type of legislation: (a) Who shall be covered by the act; what employers and what employees shall be excluded? (b) How shall the money be raised to finance the benefits; who shall contribute to the funds—employers only, or employers and employees, or, as in most European countries, employers, employees and the state? (c) How much money shall be raised; what shall be the rate or rates of contribution; shall the rate be uniform or vary on the basis of some form of "merit rating"? (d) How shall the money be

[115] Alabama, General Acts, 1935, No. 447, p. 950.
California, C. 352 Laws of 1935.
District of Columbia, Public No. 386, 74th Congress.
Indiana, C. 4 Laws of 1936.
Massachusetts, C. 479 Laws of 1935.
Mississippi, C. 176 Laws of 1936.
New Hampshire, C. 99 Laws of 1935, as amended by C. 142 Laws of 1935.
New York, C. 468 Laws of 1935; Article 18, Secs. 500-531 of C. 31 Consol. Laws of New York.
Oregon, C. 70 Laws of 1935, special session.
Rhode Island, C. 2333 Laws of 1936.
Utah, C. 38 Laws of 1935.
Washington, C. 145 Laws of 1935.
Wisconsin, C. 108 of Wis. Statutes of 1935.
By September 1, 1936, the following three states had been added: Idaho, C. 12, Acts of 1936; Louisiana, No. 97, Acts of 1936; South Carolina, No. 768, Acts of 1936.
Up to July 1, 1936, no benefits had been paid under any of these acts. Collection of contributions under the Wisconsin act was originally to start July 1, 1933. Because of business conditions the date was postponed to July 1, 1934. The Federal Social Security Act requires two years of contribution payments before benefits can start. The first benefit payment was made in Wisconsin on August 17, 1936.

kept—in state funds or by insurance companies; in insurance pools or in individual employer accounts? (e) How much shall be paid in benefits, for how long, and under what conditions? (f) How shall the act be administered; what agencies must be set up to carry it into effect?

a. *Coverage.*—As to coverage, unemployment compensation is like other types of labor legislation. Ideally, it should cover all wage earners. But political pressures and administrative difficulties cause various exclusions which deprive a large number of workers of this protection. Agricultural workers are usually excluded, for both political and administrative reasons. Domestic workers also, chiefly for administrative reasons; no government agency is equipped to supervise all the households employing servants. For the same reason employers with very few employees are often excluded. Government employees and those employed by non-profit educational, religious, and charitable institutions are frequently excluded. There is some justification perhaps for excluding government employees on the ground that most of them have regular employment; there is none whatever for excluding the employees of non-profit institutions. Certainly "charity should begin at home"; and no matter how worthy the work of a school or hospital it should not "do good" at the expense of its employees. Casual workers are sometimes excluded, largely for administrative reasons. Such an exclusion is dangerous and unless very carefully limited may be a means of avoiding liability under the law.

The coverage of the different American unemployment compensation laws is rather similar. They all excluded agricultural and domestic workers. Six exclude employers of fewer than eight workers (following the coverage of the tax under the Social Security Act); six exclude employers of fewer than four; and only the District of Columbia act covers all employers employing one or more employees.[116] Public employees and the employees of non-profit institutions are excluded under all the laws.[117]

[116] States excluding employers of less than eight: *Alabama, California, Indiana, Massachusetts, Mississippi, Wisconsin.* States excluding employers of less than four: *New Hampshire, New York, Oregon, Rhode Island, Utah, Washington.*

[117] There is no definite exclusion of non-profit institutions under the Utah act, but the general exclusion of "employment not in the usual

SOCIAL INSURANCE 303

b. *Contributions.*—Who should contribute to unemployment compensation funds has been in the United States a highly controversial question. Of course it is generally recognized that employers should contribute. In theory it is frequently urged that the state should contribute. But actually the pressure on general revenue has been so great that state contributions have not been seriously considered except in the District of Columbia. The real contest has arisen over whether or not employees should contribute. Employers generally favor employee contributions; labor is generally opposed. In Wisconsin the original bill introduced in 1921 was largely modeled on accident compensation and, disregarding European precedents, provided for contributions by employers only. This feature was retained in the act passed in that state in 1932. On the other hand, in Ohio the official investigating committee reported later that year in favor of contributions from employees as well as employers.

The usual arguments for employee contributions are four: (1) Such contributions are urged on the score of justice—the workers should share with their employers the burden of providing benefits for those who become unemployed. (2) It is said that only through contributing can workers maintain their self-respect; if they do not contribute, the compensation they receive when unemployed is a "dole" or a form of charity, with all its demoralizing consequences. If they contribute they are exercising (under compulsion, to be sure) the moral virtue of thrift. (3) It is argued that only through contributing to the funds can the workers gain the right to participate in the administration of the law and have an interest in so doing—an interest in detecting malingering and preventing the payment of benefits to persons not really entitled to them. (4) The argument of expediency is frequently heard, that only with the addition of employee contributions can enough money be raised to pay adequate benefits.

The opponents of employee contributions take the position that unemployment, at least that part of it made compensable under unemployment compensation laws, is an industrial hazard.

---

course of trade . . . carried on by the employer for pecuniary gain" will probably operate as such exclusion. See Utah Laws of 1935, C. 38, Sec. 3 (b).

Therefore the employer should be required to make provision for compensation in this field just as he does in the field of industrial accidents. They see no justice in requiring the worker to contribute, since he does nothing to cause unemployment and can do nothing to prevent it. Incidentally they point out that under all the American compensation laws the worker will certainly continue to carry more than half the burden of unemployment anyway, since he will get no benefits during a two- to four-week "waiting period," will frequently be unemployed after his right to benefits is exhausted, and will practically never receive more than 50 per cent of his wages while drawing compensation. The opponents of employee contributions insist that there is no resemblance to doles in specified benefits paid as a matter of right, and assert that accident compensation payments have never been regarded as demoralizing to the recipient. As for the argument that workers must contribute to win the right to participate in administration, the facts in Wisconsin and New York are the most effective refutation. The laws passed in these two states, though they do not require employee contributions, provide (as do all the other unemployment compensation laws) for the use of advisory committees with labor and employer representation. And in practice in these two states labor is taking an active part in administration. As for worker interest in preventing unjust claims, the opponents of employee contributions cannot see why such contributions would give workers such an interest; perhaps the feeling is rather to the contrary—that anyone who has contributed has a right to get something out of the fund whether legally entitled to benefits or not. Finally, the opponents of employee contributions question the necessity of such contributions to secure adequate funds. It depends of course on the rate of contribution by employers.[118]

Of the thirteen American compensation laws enacted before May 1, 1936, five provide for contributions by employers

[118] For arguments against employee contributions, see Green, William, "Why Labor Opposes Forced Worker Contributions in Job Insurance," *American Labor Legislation Review*, vol. xxiv, no. 3, September, 1934, pp. 101-105; and Trafton, George H., "Should Workers Be Compelled to Contribute?" *Law and Contemporary Problems*, vol. iii, no. 1, January, 1936, pp. 49-53.

SOCIAL INSURANCE

only,[119] seven for contributions by employers and employees,[120] one for contribution by employers and general tax payers.[121]

c. *Contribution Rates and Merit Rating.*—American compensation laws all measure contributions as a percentage of payroll. Somewhat complicated questions arise in defining payroll for this purpose. It may be the total paid in wages and salaries, or only the amount paid to these workers *covered* by the act—i.e., entitled to benefits under any circumstances. The federal payroll tax has a very broad definition of payroll for this purpose, and most of the state acts have used a similar basis in order to make the contributions of the individual employer under the state act approximate the offset or credit allowable to him under the federal act. As for the contribution rate, after the first two years the federal tax is to be 3 per cent, 90 per cent of which (or 2.7 per cent) can be offset. There is therefore some tendency for the states to set 2.7 per cent as the standard rate of contributions for employers. Eight of the thirteen acts do this; the other five set 3 per cent.[122] The acts which provide for employee contributions provide (unlike most European laws) that employees shall pay less than employers, usually setting a rate for them at 1 per cent or not to exceed 50 per cent of the employer's standard rate.[123]

The most important thing about contribution rates in Amer-

[119] Mississippi, New York, Oregon, Utah, and Wisconsin.

[120] Alabama, California, Indiana, Massachusetts, New Hampshire, Rhode Island, Washington.

[121] District of Columbia. For citations to these statutes, see above, p. 301.

[122] Two and seven-tenths per cent, Alabama, California, Indiana, Massachusetts, Mississippi, Oregon, Rhode Island, Wisconsin.

Three per cent, District of Columbia, New Hampshire, New York, Utah, Washington.

These acts following the federal example all provide for lower contribution rates for the first two years.

[123] Alabama, 1 per cent.

California, 1 per cent—not to exceed 50 per cent of general employer rate.

Indiana, 50 per cent of employer's rate, not to exceed 1 per cent.

Massachusetts, 50 per cent of amount contributed by employer.

New Hampshire, 1 per cent not to exceed 50 per cent of general employer rate.

Rhode Island, 1½ per cent.

Washington, 1 per cent.

ican legislation (in contrast to European) is that all of these acts make some provision for varying the rate paid by employers on the basis of the unemployment risk in the industry or the specific establishment.[124]

In Europe all employers in all industries pay a flat rate of contributions entirely regardless of the regularity or irregularity of the employment they provide. In the United States, on the other hand, all the acts passed make some provision for "merit rating" in respect to the contributions of employers,[125] i.e., for varying the rate of contribution as between employers on the basis of their performance in giving regular employment. Merit rating in American unemployment compensation legislation is not derived from European precedents.[126] Rather, it is based on American accident compensation laws, under which there has always been a wide differentiation in premium rates among industries, based on variation in occupational risks; and within the last decade a differentiation among individual plants on the basis of actual accident experience or an appraisal of their safety appliances and the like. In fact, the term "merit rating" is borrowed from accident compensation.[127] The purpose of differentiating contribution rates in both accident and unemployment compensation may be said to be twofold: First, to allocate the cost of compensation so that each industry or plant will pay somewhat in proportion to its share of the total cost; second, to provide a stimulus to prevention—to give a financial inducement to the employer to reduce accidents or unemployment to its smallest possible compass. It is generally agreed that accident compensation has been very important in stimulating the safety movement.[128] It is hoped that merit rating under unemployment compensation will be similarly effective.

[124] The Mississippi, New York and Rhode Island provisions on this point merely call for recommendations to the legislature which will have to act before any departures from flat rates can be made.

[125] In most of the states where employees contribute they pay a flat rate. In some their rate may fluctuate with those of their employers.

[126] In fact, both England and Germany made some provision for similar variation in rates when their laws were first enacted but speedily abandoned it without any real trial. See references to books on the English and German systems given above, p. 297.

[127] See p. 255.
[128] See p. 256.

The provisions for merit rating in the various American unemployment compensation laws differ markedly in effectiveness and definiteness. At the one extreme are the provisions in the laws of New York, Mississippi and Rhode Island which as passed merely provide that within a given period the administrative body shall make recommendations to the legislature as to the establishment of a merit-rating system. Next are five states in which the administrative body is instructed under the statute to classify employers in accordance with their benefit experience and to adjust their contribution rates accordingly. The statute merely sets the limits to such variation in rates—a minimum and maximum rate.[129] A more definite provision for merit rating is contained in the California and New Hampshire laws, under which the basis for differentiation in rates and the specific contribution rates are set forth in the statutes.[130]

The Indiana, Utah, and Wisconsin acts go the furthest and are the most definite in their merit rating. The employer reserve set-up of the fund in these states (to be described below) provides an automatic method of measuring the performance of the individual employer in providing steady work for his employees or repeatedly laying them off. In Utah his contribution rate may vary from zero to 3 per cent; in Indiana, from zero to 3.7 per cent; in Wisconsin, from zero to 4 per cent.

d. *Set-up of Funds.*—American unemployment compensation laws are all alike in providing for state handling of funds and in completely barring private insurance companies from the field. Further, under the provisions of the Social Security Act no state law can be approved unless the fund is deposited in the Federal Unemployment Compensation Trust Fund set up in the United States Treasury. This exclusion of private insurance is of course in marked contrast to the situation in accident compensation.[131] Fortunately, when unemployment com-

---

[129] The states with this type of provision are Alabama, District of Columbia, Massachusetts, Oregon, and Washington. The Alabama and District of Columbia acts set a minimum of 1½ per cent and a maximum of 4 per cent; Massachusetts sets a minimum of 1 per cent and no maximum; Oregon, a minimum of .7 per cent and a maximum of 4.7 per cent; Washington, a minimum of 2 per cent and no maximum.

[130] See below, p. 309.

[131] See p. 253.

308   PRINCIPLES OF LABOR LEGISLATION

pensation was first discussed, the insurance companies were themselves a little afraid of this new field. Moreover, proponents of the new form of social insurance realized clearly the abuses of private insurance in accident compensation and were unanimous in insisting on exclusive state funds for unemployment compensation.

As to the set-up of these funds, however, there is a wide diversity of opinion. The controversy is between a "pooled fund" and "employer reserves." In the former set-up the contributions of all employers are merged and benefits will be paid to eligible unemployed workers from the general fund, regardless of which employer laid them off. Under the latter system each employer has a separate "account" in the state fund (like an individual's account in a bank) to which he contributes and from which *his* employees and no others will be compensated.

The pooled fund is based on the insurance principle of distributing the risk of unemployment as widely as possible; under such a fund industries or employers with little unemployment will thus help to finance compensation for employees laid off by industries or employers with much unemployment.[132] The individual worker, if eligible, is entitled to benefits as long as there is any money left in the pool.

On the other hand, under employer reserves each employer is required to set up, under state supervision and control, a reserve from which his employees are to be compensated if he is unable to keep them continuously employed. He does not help finance compensation for workers laid off by other employers. The employer reserve set-up thus automatically allocates the cost of compensation to the employers who make it necessary.[133] Under this system a laid-off worker may fail to receive the benefits to which he was otherwise entitled, if his employer's reserve becomes exhausted.[134]

[132] Pooling and merit rating are really contradictory. To the extent that these laws provide for merit rating, the pooling of the risk is thereby diminished.

[133] Under all American laws unemployment compensation is paid only to workers previously employed and in proportion to that employment. See below, section on "Benefits."

[134] Some protection against this danger has been provided by amendment to the Wisconsin act under which an employer's contribution rate is raised above the standard rate as soon as the reserve falls below a

SOCIAL INSURANCE

The employer reserve system provides a basis for the simplest and most thoroughgoing system of merit rating, for the employer's contribution rate is made to depend on the size of his reserve account. If he avoids lay-offs and compensation payments, his reserve accumulates. When it reaches a certain point he is permitted to reduce his contributions; when it reaches a higher point he may suspend his payments entirely. If, on the other hand, he provides irregular employment, his reserve will tend toward depletion and his contribution rate will be raised.

The Wisconsin unemployment compensation act is of the employer reserve type. Utah has a similar statute. The Indiana act also provides for separate reserves,[135] combined with a small "partial pool,"[136] to be used to pay benefits to laid-off workers where the reserve of their employer has become exhausted. The remaining ten unemployment compensation laws are of the pooled fund type. New Hampshire and California, though setting up pooled funds, have tried at the same time to secure the advantage of a reserve law in providing a definite and clear-cut basis for merit rating. Under the New Hampshire and California acts, employer contributions are pooled for benefit purposes. That is, so long as the pool is solvent, any eligible worker draws the benefits to which he is entitled. But a "paper account" is kept for each employer—to which his contributions are to be credited and against which benefits paid to workers laid off by him are charged. His contribution rate is to vary on the basis of a theoretical "balance" in this paper account. However, presumably to protect the safety of the pool, this merit rating is not carried as far as under the Wisconsin, Utah and Indiana laws. Both the California and New Hampshire acts provide that the employer's rate of contributions shall in no case fall below 1 per cent.

e. *Benefits.*—In their benefit provisions the American unemployment compensation laws enacted to date draw both on

---

given point and seems in danger of depletion. The Indiana act, in addition to providing a "partial pool" (see below), also provides for stepping up the employer's rate.

[135] The Indiana act provides for employee as well as employer contributions to these reserve accounts.

[136] One-sixth of the contribution made by each employer and each employee is to be deposited in the partial pool.

310   PRINCIPLES OF LABOR LEGISLATION

American accident compensation and on European unemployment insurance. These benefit provisions are immensely complicated—covering elaborate computation of benefit rates and benefit periods, and detailed requirements as to the conditions under which workers are "eligible" for benefits. Only a few major points can be indicated here, without any attempt at a real comparison of the provisions in the different laws.

Under American laws, as under European, the length of the benefit period depends on the length of previous employment. In the United States, typically, one week of benefits is to be paid for each four weeks of employment within the preceding year. There is no right to benefits unless a worker has been employed a given number of weeks in the preceding year or two years. There is usually a maximum benefit period—in many acts set at sixteen weeks per year. The amount of benefit payable each week is not a flat amount as in England (where one benefit rate is fixed for men, another for women, and another for minors); nor is it one of a number of flat amounts, depending on which of several broad wage classifications the individual belongs in. Instead, the benefit rate, as in accident compensation, is fixed as a percentage of "average full-time wages" limited by a stated maximum and minimum amount. The percentage of wage in unemployment compensation is usually 50 per cent; the maximum benefit ranges from $10 to $18; the minimum is usually $5. (In accident compensation the percentage and the maximum and minimum are frequently higher.) The computation of the "average full-time wage" for a given worker will prove a complicated task. And since presumably many more individuals will receive compensation than under accident compensation laws, this method of fixing the weekly benefit to be paid may perhaps prove excessively cumbersome.[137]

An unemployed worker is "eligible" for benefits only after a "waiting period" (of two to four weeks), and only if physically able to work and available for work, and if no "suitable employment" can be found for him. Some acts bar benefits entirely to a worker who refuses suitable employment; others disqualify him for a further period. Suitable work is that for which the worker is reasonably well fitted and that

[137] This will be determined by experience when benefits are payable generally under various American laws.

SOCIAL INSURANCE

which is not too far from his residence. The purpose of these provisions is to deny compensation to a worker (at least for a time) if he refuses to take another job if available. Such a requirement seems essential to any unemployment compensation system. Workers should not be paid compensation if they refuse to work and choose to remain idle. But organized labor in the United States was very much afraid of such a requirement. It was, in fact, a chief reason for their long-continued opposition to unemployment compensation. Labor feared that this "suitable employment" provision would be used to break down labor standards—union men might be forced to take non-union jobs or forfeit benefit rights. To protect labor standards, there was included in the Social Security Act a provision as to suitable employment which must be made part of any state act if it is to secure approval by the Social Security Board and be the basis of tax credits. This section provides that no employment shall be deemed suitable:

(A) If the position offered is vacant due directly to a strike, lockout or other labor dispute; (B) if the wages, hours, or other conditions of work offered are substantially less favorable to the individual than those prevailing for similar work in the locality; (C) if as a condition of being employed the individual would be required to join a company union or to resign from or refrain from joining any *bona fide* labor organization.[138]

On the other hand, if unemployment is due to voluntary quitting or discharge for misconduct, a worker may be barred from benefits, or be disqualified for a further period beyond the regular waiting period. If he is unemployed because of a strike, under most acts he can draw no benefits while the strike is in active progress.

The preceding has related to benefits payable for total unemployment. In addition, most of the unemployment compensation laws provide for benefits for "partial unemployment"—the most common provision being that when a worker earns less than his weekly benefit rate (based on his average full-time earnings) he is entitled to enough in benefits to make up the difference. Benefits for partial unemployment are of course limited by the provisions as to the total amount he can draw in benefits on the basis of previous employment.

[138] 49 U. S. Stat. at Large 640, Sec. 903; 42 U. S. C. A., Sec. 1103 (5).

f. *Administration.*—The foregoing discussion of unemployment compensation laws indicates something of the magnitude of the administrative task. Until the advent of this newcomer in the field of American labor legislation, accident compensation was accepted as creating the biggest administrative problem, because the government agency had to deal not only with all the employers of the state, but with a very large number of individual employees, namely, all those injured in the course of their employment; and had to take up in detail the case of any injured worker whose right to compensation was questioned. But unemployment compensation bids fair to be an even bigger administrative task: first, because the government agency performs the work of the insurance company[139] and, second, because it will have to deal with many more individual workers. The number laid off in a given year will presumably be far greater than the number injured. Even more strikingly than in accident compensation, government will be not merely supervising employers to see that they comply with the law; it will also be engaged in an immense business undertaking.

Most of the state laws provide for new administrative agencies—unemployment compensation boards or commissions—to administer the new law. The others set up a new division within the present agency for enforcing the labor laws of the state. A complete system of public employment offices is an essential, since all the laws provide that the unemployed worker must register at the public employment office in order that suitable employment may be found for him if possible. Further, all the laws provide machinery for settling disputed claims to benefits—usually setting up tripartite "appeal boards" with employer and employee representation. The central administrative agency ordinarily will serve as an appellate tribunal, with a further right of appeal to the courts on questions of law. In the first few years of benefit payments many difficult questions will undoubtedly arise in deciding disputed claims. Eventually, no doubt, precedents will be built up to aid in determining such questions as when a dismissal is a discharge for misconduct and whether a new job is or is not "suitable." Even in undisputed cases the problem of computing the benefits due will be

[139] Of course this is also true under state funds for accident compensation.

considerable because of the elaborate benefit provisions sketched above, and the necessity (under all laws with merit-rating provisions) of charging each benefit payment to a given employer as part of the record on which his contribution rate is to be based.

Most of the acts provide for the use of advisory committees with labor and employer representation, to assist the administrative agency. In states where such committees have been used in connection with other labor legislation they can be expected to play an important part—as they have already done in New York and Wisconsin. Elsewhere it is to be hoped that a genuine effort will be made to constitute such committees an integral part of the administrative machinery, for the help of such committees will be sorely needed. Experience in the states with the best record in labor law administration indicates the value of securing the intelligent participation of labor and employers through the use of representative advisory committees.

What part the Federal Social Security Board will play in the administration of state unemployment compensation laws remains to be seen. Under Title III of the federal act the board is to make such grants to the states for the administration of these laws as it determines "to be necessary for the proper administration of such law." The board is not to make such grants unless (along with certain other standards) it finds that the state statute contains provisions for "such methods of administration (other than those relating to selection, tenure of office and compensation of personnel) as are found by the board to be reasonably calculated to insure full payment of unemployment compensation when due." And the board is further empowered to deny grants for administration when it finds, after notice and opportunity to be heard, that the state agency is not living up to the administrative standards set up in the act.[140] Obviously this puts a very powerful weapon into the hands of the board—a weapon which may be used wisely to hold the states to reasonable administrative performance, or may be abused by too great insistence on uniform methods, and too great interference with experimentation in this untried field, and with the development in each state of the methods best

[140] 49 U. S. Stat. at Large 626, Secs. 301-303; 42 U. S. C. A., Secs. 501-503.

suited to its particular problems and the rest of its administrative set-up.

g. *Constitutionality.*—At the present writing the United States Supreme Court has not passed on the unemployment compensation sections of the Social Security Act or on any one of the state unemployment compensation laws. The New York Court of Appeals in April, 1936, upheld the New York act, and an appeal was taken to the United States Supreme Court.[141] If this state law is upheld and if the federal act is upheld in the near future, unemployment compensation can be expected to spread rapidly over the whole country.

[141] Chamberlin *v.* Andrews, *et al.,* 241 N. Y. 1 (1936).

CHAPTER VI

INDIVIDUAL BARGAINING

IN THE BROADEST SENSE OF THE TERM, A DEBT IS THAT WHICH is due from one person to another, whether money, goods, or services.[1] The laborer as debtor may therefore be looked upon as owing either labor or money to another. Modern law does not force a laborer to work out his debt. It converts a labor debt into a money debt, or "damages," and enforces payment of the latter. Furthermore, under "exemption" laws, the law does not always enforce even the total payment of a money debt.

On the other side, the laborer is a creditor to the extent that the employer owes him money for his labor. Here, too, modern legislation gives him certain privileges or protection, not usually given to other creditors.

In this twofold relation of debtor and creditor we may trace the history of labor law from the servile stage, through the stage of master and servant, to the modern stage of employer and employee.

1. THE LABORER AS DEBTOR

If we classify the legal relations of the laborer as debtor we shall begin with the employment of labor in its elementary form of slavery, where all of the rights were on the side of the owner and all the obligations on that of the laborer. This, and a succeeding or contemporary stage of serfdom, are known as a period of *status*. The laborer is born to the position; he does not enter it by agreement or contract. But status often merges into contract, or the fiction of a contract, and we may therefore speak of a servility stage, or a stage of servile contracts, preceding that of free contracts. Here would be classified slavery, serfdom, and peonage. These conditions of labor, even if based on contract, may be so evidently the outcome of

[1] Kimpton v. Bronson, 45 Barb. 625 (1866).

coercion that they may rightly be considered as belonging to a pre-contract or servile stage.

A second stage, which we may designate as that of master and servant, emerges gradually from the more liberal forms of servile contracts, although retaining vestiges, of servile relations. Some of the contracts of this stage, especially the seaman's contract, have continued down to the present day, while others, such as apprenticeship, indentured service, and contract labor, can with difficulty be distinguished from those of the servile stage. The ameliorating character of both the servile and master stage is that of paternalism, and both of them are closely connected with the institution of the family, in which the wife and children occupy a position of status, afterward modified by contract, express or implied.

Modern labor legislation begins with a conscious effort on the part of the legislature to remove both the servile and paternal vestiges of the master and servant stage and to substitute a stage of real equality, as far as possible. This we designate as the employer and employee stage.

1. **Servile Labor:** a. *Slavery.*—The worker under primitive slavery is regarded as the property of his master. In Roman law a slave was regarded not as a person, but as a thing.[2] In 1776 Mr. Justice Chase of Maryland said: "Negroes are property, and no more members of the state than cattle."[3]

In England, in 1772, it was held by the court that slavery could not exist in the mother country. The slave trade was abolished by statute there in 1807, and in the colonies in 1833. The example of Great Britain in regard to her colonies was gradually followed by other European states, by France in 1848, Portugal in 1858, Holland in 1863. Spanish-American states abolished slavery after securing indenpendence. In the United States the slaves were freed in 1865 by the Thirteenth Amendment to the federal Constitution, as an outcome of the Civil War; and Brazil, the South American state which retained slavery longest, abolished it by decree of the Chambers in 1888.

b. *Serfdom.*—Slavery aims at the subjection of the whole

[2] Sohm, *Institutes of Roman Law,* tr. Ledlie, 1901, p. 171.
[3] Wilson, *History of the Rise and Fall of the Slave Power in America,* n. d., vol. i, p. 15.

man. Another degree of unfreedom, namely, serfdom or villeinage, does not attempt to cover the entire range of human life. It is concerned only with certain relations, generally economic in character. Compulsory labor—compulsion as to the kind of service and the time and place where it is to be rendered—is the essential note of serfdom or villeinage. A serf was bound to the land and bought and sold with it, like cattle, but he might secure freedom by "commutation," that is, by paying to the lord or master who had the title to the soil a sum of money or an annual payment presumably equivalent to the value of the service which he rendered his lord. He substituted a money debt for a labor debt—in other words, he bought his freedom. Serfdom appears as a corollary of feudalism. It grew up as a consequence of customary subjection in an agricultural system and melted away with the advent of the industrial age.

c. *Peonage.*—Peonage has been defined as a "status or condition of compulsory service based upon the indebtedness of the peon to the master."[4] The basic fact is indebtedness. In Mexico, after the Spanish conquest, slaves were used in mines and on roads, while serfs or peons were used for agriculture. The condition of the latter, though differing little from slavery, was theoretically more humane and right-respecting. Together with peonage, a system of large estates grew up. The peons got food and clothing from their masters.[5] These Mexican peons were descendants of natives enslaved by the Spaniards, and were often merely bondsmen.[6] Their wages were low and they were compelled to deal at the store of the estate. They were always kept in debt, and until the Mexican Constitution of 1917 abolished involuntary servitude except as a punishment for crime, an Indian workman owing his employer became the property of the latter.[7] Sometimes peons have been induced to contract for work to be done in tropical parts, and here they get into debt at once and are prevented by armed guards from escaping.[8]

[4] Clyatt *v.* U. S., 197 U. S. 207, 25 Sup. Ct. 429 (1904).
[5] United States Bureau of Labor, *Bulletin No. 38,* 1902, p. 23.
[6] Carson, W. E., *Mexico,* 1914, p. 185.
[7] *Ibid.,* pp. 188, 189.
[8] *Ibid.,* p. 191. See also Ely, *Property and Contract,* 1914, chap. x.

318   PRINCIPLES OF LABOR LEGISLATION

In the United States, after the abolition of slavery by the Thirteenth Amendment in 1865, the proprietors, being deprived of their property right in the services of the slave, sought in some cases to effect the same purpose by indirect means, such as enforcing indebtedness and compelling the working out of the debt. These subterfuges gave added impetus to the agitation which led to the adoption, two and a half years later, of the Fourteenth Amendment, which created a citizenship of the United States in addition to that of the state, and prohibited any state from depriving a citizen of the United States of "life, liberty, or property without due process of law," or denying "to any person within its jurisdiction the equal protection of the laws."[9]

In 1875 the United States Congress passed statutes which have been thought to enforce the meaning of the Thirteenth Amendment. That they do not entirely accomplish this was pointed out by the Immigration Commission of 1911.[10] One statute provides heavy fines for those who "conspire to injure, oppress, threaten, or intimidate any citizen in the free exercise or enjoyment of any right or privilege secured to him by the Constitution or laws of the United States";[11] and another for "whoever kidnaps or carries away any other person, with the intent that such other person be sold into involuntary servitude, or held as a slave."[12] But, as the Immigration Commission showed, "if a person simply places or holds another in slavery, it is impossible for the federal courts to impose penalties under statutes at present in vogue [1911], unless the placing or holding be for the purpose of forcing the settlement of a debt, no matter how great may be the abuses perpetrated upon the person held. In the Clyatt case, the Supreme Court decided unmistakably that the peonage statute (R. S. 5526) referred only to cases where the return or arrest or holding has been for the purpose of paying a debt."[13]

The chief origins of the enforced indebtedness upon which

[9] Constitution of the United States, Fourteenth Amendment, Sec. 1, in force July 28, 1868.
[10] Immigration Commission, *Abstracts of Reports*, 1911, vol. ii, p. 446.
[11] United States Statutes at Large, 35: 1092, Sec. 19.
[12] *Ibid.*, 35: 1141, Sec. 268.
[13] Immigration Commission, *Abstracts of Reports*, vol. ii, p. 446. See also Clyatt v. U. S. 197 U. S. 207, 25 Sup. Ct. 429 (1904).

peonage rests are advances made by the employer to the laborer, misrepresentations made to laborers by unscrupulous employment agents, the payment by an employer of fines and costs in cases of misdemeanor, especially violations of vagrancy laws, and the operation of contract labor laws. Advances to laborers might include payments for transportation, working equipment of various sorts, and any payment in kind, such as food, clothing, or housing, accomplished through company stores and land ownership. An example was found in the State of Maine, where advances were made to laborers sent out by the employment agents who "misrepresent conditions in the woods, and frequently tell the laborers that the camps will be but a few miles from some town where they can go from time to time for recreation and enjoyment. Arriving at the outskirts of civilization, the laborers are driven in wagons a short distance into the forests, and then have to walk sometimes sixty or seventy miles into the interior, the roads being impassable for vehicles. The men will be kept in the heart of the forest for months throughout the winter, living in the most rugged fashion and with no recreation whatever."[14] Similar practices of deceit were exercised by the agencies which send labor from New York to the South.

Abuses of the vagrancy laws were found to occur in the South, involving both Negro and white laborers.[15] In Florida, for instance, "common pipers and fiddlers, common railers and brawlers" may be arrested under the vagrancy law of 1905, and fined not more than $250 or imprisoned not more than six months. Other states of the South make it quite easy for arrests to be made under these statutes. The victim is usually a Negro who, for a trivial offense, or no offense at all except being unemployed, will be arrested and charged with vagrancy. He gets little consideration from the local justices, and his fines are so high that he is unable to pay them. An employer appears and advances the fine on the condition that the laborer will work out his debt. When the debt is worked out and the Negro is again unemployed, perhaps, he will be rearrested on similar charges, and in such manner becomes virtually a

[14] *Ibid.*, p. 447.
[15] United States Department of Justice, *Annual Report of the Attorney-general,* 1907, Exhibit 17, pp. 207-213.

peon. Occasionally, a victim is not allowed to pay the fine when he has the money; he will be imprisoned and word sent to a planter, who comes in and pays his fine and then takes possession of the unfortunate criminal, who is obliged to work off his debt. In most cases this is as hopeful a proceeding as borrowing from a mediæval usurer, for at the end of months of toil the laborer may find himself as deeply in debt as ever.[16]

Although the Immigration Commission reported that in every state except Connecticut and Oklahoma there had occurred sporadic cases which, if supported by legal evidence, would constitute peonage as the Supreme Court has defined it, nevertheless no general system of peonage and no sentiment supporting it were found. In the South, where such practices were most frequent, prosecution by United States district attorneys was vigorous and usually successful.[17] The evil, however, has continued to exist in some parts of the South.[18]

2. **From Master and Servant to Employer and Employee.**—In the master and servant stage we have the beginnings of the contract. In some cases the contract is very elementary in form, while in others it approximates closely the free labor contract. It is the first expression of the idea of equality between the laborer and his employer. The master was at liberty to hire whomsoever he wished, and, on the other hand, the servant could work for any master he chose. The master was not free to discharge his servant during the term of the contract, nor the servant free to quit his master and to work for another. The laborer was to serve the master faithfully, keep his secrets, obey his lawful commands, and guard his interests. On the other hand, the master was to give his servant a living, to protect him, and look after his welfare.

a. *Indentured Service.*—The slave, the serf, and the peon perform their labor under a fixed status, and the individual has little or nothing to say about it. The indentured servant had in some particulars the right of a servant in making a contract, and in other respects he was little more than a slave, except that his chances for ultimate freedom were more real.

[16] Terrell, M. C., "Peonage in the United States," *Nineteenth Century and After*, 1907, vol. lxii, pp. 312, 313.
[17] Immigration Commission, *Abstracts of Reports*, vol. ii, p. 445.
[18] Wilson, Walter, *Forced Labor in the United States*, 1933.

INDIVIDUAL BARGAINING

Indentured labor is peculiar to new countries where labor is scarce and where opportunity for individual enterprise is great. People were shipped from the Old World to the American colonies to supply the need for young, healthy, energetic laborers for the development of the new. Children were sometimes shipped under the Elizabethan statute of apprentices.[19] White indentured service is mentioned in laws of all the thirteen colonies.[20] The dates 1619 to 1819 may be taken as indicating roughly the beginning and end of the system. Competition with slavery destroyed it in the South before the end of the eighteenth century, but it continued to exist in the northern states into the nineteenth century. White servitude was hampered by too many considerations in favor of the laborer; above all, the white servant's labor belonged to his master only for a term of years, after which he was as free as anyone else, while the slave's services were property during the term of his life.

b. *Apprenticeship.*—Apprenticeship proper differs from indentured service in that the master obligates himself to teach the apprentice a trade. If this obligation does not appear in the contract, or is not enforced, the apprentice becomes in fact an indentured servant.[21] Thus many who came to America under what purported to be apprenticeship contracts were in reality indentured servants. The two merged into each other in another direction, in that an apprentice could be bound for seven years to learn a trade which could be learned as well in three. Four years' enforcement of such a contract would be really indentured service, and only three years' would be true apprenticeship.[22] Where regulated by the state, as in Wisconsin, these objectionable features are eliminated and the period of indenture is wholly educational.[23]

c. *Contract Labor.*—Midway between indentured service, on

---
[19] 5 Eliz., C. 3 and 4 (1563).
[20] Hurd, *Law of Freedom and Bondage in the United States*, 1858, chap. vi.
[21] Abbott, *Women in Industry*, 1910, p. 331.
[22] See Motley, J. M., *Apprenticeship in American Trade Unions*, "Governmental Regulation of Apprentices," Johns Hopkins University Studies, 1907, vol. xxv, p. 494.
[23] Wisconsin Statues—1925, Sec. 106.01, Sec. 9. See also Scrimshaw, Stewart, *Apprenticeship*, 1932.

the one hand, and the padrone system on the other, is contract labor. This form of labor, although apparently built on freedom of contract, results in compulsory service or in peonage practices. It is the kind of labor contract whose performance can be enforced at law, and it has been quite common where large numbers of natives of backward races have been employed, as in the Hawaiian Islands, the Philippines, the West Indies, and in South Africa, where Chinese coolies were employed in the mines.

In many respects, contract labor closely resembles peonage, as we have previously suggested, for it places the laborer in the position of a debtor owing services; yet there is a difference between the two. Peonage involves continuous or indefinite service as long as a balance of debt continues, which may be permanent. Contract labor pertains to a term of years only, after which the laborer cannot be compelled to work. Furthermore, should the laborer renew his contract because of economic pressure, still it is only for another term of years. Contract labor results in servitude for a definite period only while it leaves the way open to freedom. It is possible, however, that abuses of the system may lead very easily to a state almost as bad as peonage, and it is this possibility that has made contract labor unpopular in freedom-loving countries and has led to legislation aiming at its restriction and abolition.

In the Hawaiian Islands, a condition of contract labor existed for fifty years. In order to solve the problem raised by the scarcity of labor combined with the opportunity for industrial development, the employing class got a law enacted in 1850 by which laborers over twenty years of age could contract themselves to service for not more than five years. Refusal to work on the part of such a person was punished by imprisonment with hard labor. The man who tried to escape and was caught could be bound to double the original term of service. A later amendment added to the punishment for a second desertion three months' hard labor for the state.[24] This condition of contract labor was abolished in 1900 by a clause in the organic act settling the conditions of annexation to the United States.

[24] Coman, Katherine, "Contract Labor in the Hawaiian Islands," *American Economic Association,* 1903, 3d Series, vol. iv, pp. 492-493, 531.

INDIVIDUAL BARGAINING

While the performance of labor cannot be compelled by direct means except where life and property are endangered, or public necessity and convenience demand it, yet indirect devices are invented to effect the same thing. Statutes which deal with "employers' advances" make it a misdemeanor for the employee to fail in the performance of his contract to work off a debt. As imprisonment for debt has been prohibited by law, the only means by which these contract labor laws can be made effective is to couch them in such terms as to make the laborer breaking his contract appear to be guilty of getting money or provisions under false pretenses. Intent to defraud must be shown, since a mere breach of the labor contract is not a crime.[25]

The law of Mississippi provides that "the refusal or failure of any person who enters into such contract to perform such act or service, or refund such money, or pay for such property without just cause, shall be *prima facie* evidence of the intent to injure or defraud his employer."[26]

Prosecutions under such statutes, however, have been invalidated by a sweeping decision of the United States Supreme Court in a leading case.[27] Here the court stated: "The fact that the debtor contracted to perform the labor which is sought to be compelled does not withdraw the attempted enforcement from the condemnation of the statute [prohibiting peonage]. The full intent of the constitutional provision could be defeated with obvious facility if, through the guise of contracts under which advances had been made, debtors could be held to compulsory service. It is the compulsion of the service that the statute inhibits, for when that occurs the condition of servitude is created, which would be not less involuntary because of the original agreement to work out the indebtedness. The contract exposes the debtor to liability for the loss due to the breach, but not to enforced labor. . . . The act of Congress [Act of 1875] deprives of effect all legislative measures of any state through which, directly or indirectly, the prohibited thing, to wit, compulsory service to secure the payment of a debt,

---

[25] *Ex parte* Riley, 94 Ala. 82, 10 So. 528 (1891).
[26] Mississsippi Code of 1906, Sec. 1148.
[27] Bailey *v.* Alabama, 219 U. S. 219, at p. 242; 31 Sup. Ct. 145 (1910).

may be established or maintained." This decision delivered in 1910 invalidated laws of like nature in other states,[28] for the court observed: "No question of a sectional character is presented and we may view the legislation in the same manner as if it had been enacted in New York or Idaho. Opportunities for coercion and oppression in varying circumstances exist in all parts of the Union, and the citizens of all these states are interested in the maintenance of the constitutional guarantees the consideration of which is here involved."[29]

Until 1915, seamen generally stood on a different footing from other employees, for with them enforced contracts were permitted and the law as to involuntary servitude was not applicable. In the case of Robertson v. Baldwin,[30] the court in 1897 stated: "Seamen are treated by Congress as well as by the Parliament of Great Britain as deficient in that full and intelligent responsibility for their acts which is accredited to ordinary adults, and as needing the protection of the law in the same sense in which minors and wards are entitled to the protection of their parents and guardians." Since the date of that case, however, the law of the United States affecting seamen has been changed and more freedom has been granted. A federal law[31] in 1915 abolished arrest and imprisonment as a penalty for desertion. This act goes so far as to stipulate that it shall be unlawful in any case to pay any seaman wages in advance of the time when he has actually earned them, or to pay any person for the shipment of seamen when payment is deducted or to be deducted from seamen's wages. This is a clear effort to prevent the obligation of indebtedness on which involuntary servitude is based.

The law goes further and provides that for quitting the vessel without leave after her arrival at the port of her delivery

[28] Arkansas, Florida, Georgia, Louisiana, Michigan, Minnesota, New Hampshire, New Mexico, North Dakota, South Carolina, and Virginia.
[29] Bailey v. Alabama, 219 U. S. 219, at p. 231; 31 Sup. Ct. 145 (1910).
[30] Robertson v. Baldwin, 165 U. S. 287, 17 Sup. Ct. 326 (1897).
[31] United States Laws 1914-1915, C. 153; Revised Statutes, Sec. 4529, 4530, 4596, 4610, 4611. Title: An act to promote the welfare of American seamen in the merchant marine of the United States; to abolish arrest and imprisonment as a penalty for desertion, and to secure the abrogation of treaty provisions in relation thereto; and to promote safety at sea.

and before she is placed in security, a seaman forfeits from his wages not more than one month's pay. This approaches the free contract perhaps as far as the conditions of seafaring will permit. Congress regulates the nature of the contract, the term of service, the payment and assignment of wages, advance payments and credits, sailors' lodging houses, shipping masters, quarters on board ship, rations, and many other details.

Railroad employees also come within the power of Congress; and it was a federal court which, while reiterating the general right of employees to quit work, suggested by way of dicta that "his quitting would not be of right and he would be liable for any danger resulting from a breach of his agreement and perhaps in some cases subject to criminal prosecution for loss of life and limb, by passengers or others, directly resulting from his abandoning his post at a time when care and watchfulness were required upon his part in the discharge of a duty he had undertaken to perform."[32] Laws on this subject as a rule connect the cessation of work with combinations and strikes, and forbid engineers and railroad employees to abandon locomotives under circumstances of this nature, under penalty of fine and imprisonment.

d. *Padrone System.*—The padrone system is one step removed from contract labor. Those who work under this system permit a leader, the padrone, to make their contracts, yet the agreement is not enforceable at law. It is enforced only by their own necessities. The system started first with Italian laborers. The padrone brought over laborers from Italy, advancing the cost of their transportation, and hired them out to a contractor. He rented to them the shanties in which they lived while at work, and sold them supplies of food.

Italian laborers formerly made contracts with their padrone to serve him for one to three years, and occasionally for a longer period.[33] The report of the Immigration Investigating Commission of 1895 shows that Italians and other foreigners had been imported "by the cargo" into the Michigan iron mines and worked on the padrone system in the early 'nineties.[34] This

[32] Arthur *v.* Oakes, 11 C. C. A. 209, 63 Fed. 310 (1894).
[33] Industrial Commission, *Report,* vol. xv, 1901, pp. 430-432.
[34] Immigration Investigating Commission, *Report,* 1895, p. 26.

was probably the time when the padroni were most numerous and flourishing.

Formal agreements among the laborers and the padroni have since become less common, and for this there are perhaps three reasons. First, the alien contract labor laws made their agreements not only unenforceable at law, but actually punishable if discovered by the government. Secondly, spontaneous immigration from Italy became so great before 1920 that it was not worth the padrone's while to risk a conviction under the contract labor laws, so that he became merely a middleman. Thirdly, there was a condition of dependence on one side and assistance on the other. The padrone did not establish his control over a man, strictly speaking, by either force or fraud. Dr. Rossi has called the padrone system "the forced tribute which the newly arrived pays to those who are acquainted with the ways and language of the country."[35] The system was founded on an inequality more deeply rooted than the usual inequality between the employer and the laborer. The races which work under this method are ignorant and accustomed to be commanded, and it is on their dependence and lack of knowledge that the power of the padrone rests. From the standpoint of the immigrant, a remedy is to be found not so much in legal rights, as in better education, American habits of thought, efficient employment bureaus, and more adequate administration of existing laws.

e. *Imprisonment for Debt.*—Not only as a debtor-laborer, but also as a debtor-consumer, the laborer receives consideration. Imprisonment for debt originally had no particular bearing on the labor contract or its history. The fundamental idea in the ancient German imprisonment for debt is the indirect compulsion to pay. The debtor was to be encouraged to pay what he owed by being made uncomfortable until he did so. Compulsion to work had given place to compulsion to pay.[36]

The abolition of imprisonment for debt was one of the issues raised by the early workingmen's parties in 1827. Kentucky, the first state to abolish imprisonment for debt, had already done so in 1821. New York followed ten years later, and a

[35] Industrial Commission, *Report*, vol. xv, 1901, p. 432.
[36] Niemeyer, Th., "Schuldhaft," *Handwörterbuch der Staatswissenschaften*, 1911, vol. v, p. 593.

INDIVIDUAL BARGAINING 327

series of legislative and constitutional provisions followed at intervals throughout the country. Inability to pay one's debts, if not accompanied by embezzlement or other fraudulent conduct, is now no longer a reason for imprisonment in civilized countries.

f. *Wage Exemption.*—Following the abolition of imprisonment for debt is the wage exemption legislation which took on large proportions in the United States in the 'forties. At the present time every state in the Union has legislation exempting wages from attachment and execution for debt. In other words, the authority given to the sheriff or other administrative officer to seize from the property of the defendant (debtor) an amount sufficient to satisfy the judgment in favor of the creditor, is invalid when applied to wages under the exempt amount. The persons covered by these laws are differently specified in different states. Several provide for exemption applying to "all persons," as in Georgia; "resident of the state," as in Idaho; "resident debtor," as in Iowa; all "householders," as in Indiana; "judgment debtor," as in New York; and "any person or persons having a family dependent upon him or them for support," as in Wisconsin.

The amount of wages exempted varies somewhat from state to state. Some exempt ninety days' wages, as in Iowa; others, sixty or thirty; while still others stipulate the percentage which may be collected for a given period. In Missouri and Kansas, 90 per cent of a worker's earnings for the preceding three months is exempt. The exempted amount runs from $15 in Illinois to not more than $180, as in Wisconsin. The usual period of exemption, in so far as the time is specified at all, is the two to three months preceding attachment. The wages of a minor child are exempt in many of the states. In all cases, it is clear that the purport of the laws is to protect the minimum earnings of the workingman who has nothing to depend upon except his wages.

Wage exemption applies not only against execution or attachment, but also against garnishment.[37] This is a proceeding by which the plaintiff in an action seeks to reach the rights and effects (wages, in this case) of the defendant by calling into court some third party (employer) who has such effects

[37] Clark, *Law of the Employment of Labor*, 1911, p. 56.

(wages) in his possession or who is indebted to the defendant.[38] Should the employer unwarrantedly make payments from his employee's wages, he will still be left liable to the employee himself for a second payment of the wages.[39]

g. *Homestead Exemption.*—All American states have provided that the means of earning a livelihood, that is, the tools of one's trade or profession, shall be exempt from execution. Along with the exemption of personal property goes homestead exemption. This legislation is designed to keep intact the family unit in society, to prevent entire destruction, and to encourage a debtor who has been reduced to the last term to try again. These laws, however, are not for laborers alone, but for any person. In most states a man must be a householder or the head of a family in order to get the exemption, but in a few states any person may be entitled to the exemption. The limitations on the homestead exemption are in both acreage and value. Rural homesteads may vary in acres from 40 to 100, and city homesteads from one lot to one acre (five acres in one state). Maximum monetary limits are $500 to $5,000. In Nebraska, homesteads are not exempt from execution of judgments on debts secured by mechanic's, laborer's, or vendor's liens upon the premises.[40]

In 1848 English statutes provided only that tools and actual necessaries of judgment debtors were not to be seized in execution. In 1883 a statute carried the exemption a little further, so as to include "the tools (if any) of his trade and the necessary wearing apparel and bedding of himself, his wife and children, to a value, inclusive of tools and apparel and bedding, not exceeding twenty pounds [$100] in the whole."[41] These provisions have parallels in most of the British colonies, and the exempted property amounts to about the same. Nowhere, however, is the exemption as liberal as in the United States. Home-

---

[38] *Cyclopædia of Law and Procedure* 1901-1914, vol. xx, p. 978, "While a garnishment proceeding accomplishes the same purpose as an attachment or execution, it is in no sense a levy on property, but a judicial proceeding by which a new judgment is obtained."

[39] See Clark, *op. cit.,* p. 55, and cases cited. Also, Clark, L. D., and Tracy, S. J., "Laws Relating to Payment of Wages," U. S. Bureau of Labor Statistics, *Bulletin No. 408,* 1926.

[40] Nebraska, *Compiled Statutes,* 1922, Sec. 2818.

[41] 46 and 47 Vict., C. 31, Pt. IV, Sec. 44.

stead exemptions are peculiar to the United States, but the tools of a debtor's trade, at least, are exempted in most English-speaking countries.

h. *Assignment of Wages.*—Assignment of wages grows out of the legal act of transferring or making over to another the whole or part of any property, real or personal, in possession or in action, or of any estate or right therein. But if the wage earner is to have effective exemption of wages from attachment and garnishment, it is consistent that he be prevented from making an assignment of his future wages. Assignments of unearned wages are safeguarded in various ways, as by requirement that they must be recorded, that copies must be filed with the employer or even that the employer's consent must be obtained, or that the wife must join in the husband's assignment, or *vice versa*. Missouri affords a good example of the effort to modify this evil. An act of 1911 provides that "all assignments of wages, salaries, or earnings must be in writing with the correct date of the assignment and the amount assigned, and the name or names of the party or parties owing the wages, salaries, and earnings so assigned, and all assignments of wages, salaries, and earnings not earned at the time the assignment is made shall be null and void." Assignments to secure loans or future advances are void in Georgia and Massachusetts, and all assignments of future earnings are prohibited in Indiana.[42]

II. THE LABORER AS CREDITOR

Modern industry is conducted mainly "on credit." The employer is the middleman, whose creditors are those who advance the capital he uses, and whose debtors are those who buy his product. When the laborer starts to work for him, he also becomes, for a time, a creditor. He contributes his services in advance of compensation. He is a temporary investor in the business. While he works, he passes over to the employer the title to his product, and retains a claim for wages. When his wages are paid his investment is liquidated.

Other investors advance money or "credit." Their contracts are secured by notes, bonds, mortgages, giving to them a preferred claim on the property and earnings of the business. They invest "capital"—the laborer invests "labor." Laws regulat-

[42] See Clark and Tracy, "Laws Relating to Payment of Wages."

ing the time, place, and medium of payment, laws providing for mechanics' liens, wage preference, and so on, are intended to guarantee to the laborer as creditor, regardless of contract, that certainty of payment which the capitalist as creditor secures in the ordinary enforcement of contracts.

1. **Time of Payment.**—Legislation has not ventured far in interfering directly to set the amount of wages,[43] but it makes the amount of wages greater or less by indirect methods. Whatever the nominal amount may be, the frequency of the time of payment is a matter of concern to the laborer. The longer he must wait for his wages the greater is the extent of his need for credit, and, accordingly, the higher will be his cost of living and the lower his real wages. The advantages of fewer pay days are obvious to the employer. His cost of bookkeeping is less, and his required circulating capital will be less.

Over the entire world in industrial states there are statutes requiring a regular pay day, which may be once a month, semimonthly, or weekly. Many of the European laws are so phrased that modifications may be introduced according to local custom. Almost all of the states and territories of the United States have laws dealing with time and mode of payment of wages. Most of these laws provide for semimonthly payment, but several require weekly payment. Most of them stand without being contested in the courts to determine their constitutionality. Some cases have reached the courts, and different decisions have been rendered.

In favor of the validity of such laws, it has been argued that semimonthly payment of wages is required by the actual necessities of employees, and that regular payment of wages at short intervals is much more a matter of life and death to a workingman with a family dependent on him than to the employing corporation.[44] The purpose of the Rhode Island weekly payment law was laid down by the court as being protection of the worker from "the greed of corporate capital." Poverty and weakness, it was said, "can wage but an unequal contest with corporate wealth and power"; and the act was considered to be for the prosperity and comfort of the workingmen who

[43] See chap. ii, "Minimum Fair Wage."
[44] Arkansas Stave Co. v. State, 94 Ark. 27, 125 S. W. 1001 (1910).

INDIVIDUAL BARGAINING 331

depend entirely on their weekly wages, and are, like other people, obliged to pay for credit.[45]

The cases in which laws relating to time of wage payment have been held unconstitutional show, as might be expected, that less consideration was given to the practical economic facts of the situation. In these cases appears the usual argument, that the liberty of contract of the workingman is encroached upon by legislation. In the case of Johnson v. Goodyear Mining Co.[46] an indignant protest was raised by the court against any interference with the liberty of contract. "The workingman of intelligence," it was said, "is treated as an imbecile. Being over twenty-one years of age, and not a lunatic or insane, he is deprived of the right to make a contract as to the time when his wages shall fall due."

There are several states which legislate to the effect that wages shall be paid during working hours. This accomplishes two things: it saves the time of the employee and precludes payment in barrooms. Most of the states provide that an employee shall be paid immediately upon discharge, and for delay thereafter is entitled to interest charges—in the case of Iowa $1 a day penalty up to the amount of the wages due. In some cases this penalty is 5 per cent a year to be added for the cost of the delay, and the attorney's fee if his services are necessary to procure wages withheld from an employee. The Supreme Court of Indiana,[47] however, held that the provision that the employer must pay wages within seventy-two hours after discharge or leaving, with a penalty of $100 to $500, was an unreasonable deprivation of property. When an employee quits, the law generally stipulates that he shall be paid at the next regular pay day.

2. **Place of Payment.**—The evil attached to the payment of wages in saloons and other places where intoxicants are sold needs no elaboration. This evil is partly taken care of by providing that wages shall be paid upon the premises, as is the case with most of the legislation in the United States on the subject. Wage payment in barrooms, however, has been specifically pro-

---

[45] State v. Brown & Sharpe Mfg. Co., 18 R. I. 16, 25 Atl. 246 (1892), at p. 252.
[46] Johnson v. Goodyear Mining Co., 127 Cal. 4, 59 Pac. 304 (1899).
[47] State v. Martin, 193 Ind. 120, 139 N. E. 282 (1923).

hibited in California for any worker not employed therein, and in Nevada for miners. Other countries have legislated against payment of wages in public houses and taverns.

3. **Basis of Payment.**—In the United States there are some statutes that prohibit the screening of coal before it is weighed, the loss of coal through the screen being regarded as causing an unjust loss to the miner, whose contract calls for payment by the weight of coal mined. The validity of such laws has been both upheld and denied by different state courts, but in the case of McLean v. State of Arkansas[48] the Supreme Court held the law to be within the police power of the states.

4. **Medium of Payment.**—Carlyle declaimed against a modern civilization whose only bond of union is the cash nexus. Yet, from a different point of view, it may be said that liberty depends on cash. Indeed, the transition from slavery to freedom is a transition from payment in lodging, board, and goods, or "truck," to payment in legal tender or in a medium convertible into money on demand at its face value. Cash means freedom. It permits the wage earner to buy what and where he wants. It also means earnings, for it exposes and corrects unwarranted deductions, such as high prices, through bookkeeping accounts.

a. *"Living In."*—Under systems of slavery, serfdom, indentured service, and apprenticeship the laborer lived on the premises of his master. The most complete survival of these systems in modern industry is known in England as "living in," where the employee receives part payment in board and lodging at his place of employment. The system is encountered in all countries, and is characteristic of domestic service. Very often, "living in" is made a condition of employment, either express or implied, and the board and lodging accommodations provided are often inferior and inadequate. The system may rob the employees of their sense of personal responsibility and check individuality and independence of character. There is frequently no freedom of complaint, for, if the workers venture to remonstrate about food or lodging, they render themselves liable to dismissal and "spoiling" their references.

In some countries "living in" has been regulated as to quantity or quality of food and adequacy of accommodations; but

[48] McLean v. Arkansas, 211 U. S. 539, 29 Sup. Ct. 206 (1909).

INDIVIDUAL BARGAINING

in the United States this problem has not yet come into the realm of legislation, although it exists in hotels, restaurants, bakeries, and clubs.

b. *Company Houses and Labor Camps.*—The employer may build "company houses" for his workmen which they must occupy, and the rent is then deducted from wages. Frequently these houses are better than those which the employees would provide, but they have counteracting disadvantages in contractual ties of dependence. In New York where factory operatives are given living quarters, these may be regulated by the industrial board,[49] and the labor department has power to enter and inspect. Labor camps for certain kinds of work have been brought under regulation in certain states, as California,[50] New York,[51] and Pennsylvania.[52] In California the state labor department is ordered to secure the abatement of any camps which are dangerous to public health. After 1920, Idaho, Montana, Nevada, New Mexico, Oregon, Utah, and Alaska passed laws prohibiting coercion as to boarding houses.

c. *Company Stores.*—The "truck system," or "truck" in English usage, is the term which denotes payment in kind, or otherwise than in cash.[53] In the United States this is generally treated under such terms as "store orders," "payment in scrip," or "company stores." Legislation respecting the truck system falls into three classes: (1) Laws that would eliminate it altogether, at least in business establishments where it is a real evil, such as mining, manufacturing, and railroad corporations. (2) Laws which permit the system, but which regulate the prices charged and the quality offered. (3) Laws which allow the institution to exist, but which endeavor to eliminate coercion of employees to make use of the system.

Among the first class would come the laws of many of the leading industrial states, such as Colorado, Maryland, New Jersey, New York, and Pennsylvania. The second class includes Connecticut, Indiana, and Virginia. Here prices must not be unreasonable, or higher to the employees than to others who

[49] New York, Consol. Laws, C. 78, Sec. 298.
[50] California, Laws 1913, C. 182, as amended.
[51] New York, Consol. Laws, C. 78, Sec. 298.
[52] Pennsylvania, Laws 1915, No. 397, Sec. 18.
[53] Great Britain, Departmental Committee on the Truck Acts, *Report,* 1908, p. 4.

are not employees. Of course, if the town should be owned by the corporation, the law could not have much effect, and, for that matter, no anti-truck legislation can accomplish much for the laborer in a town where the land and buildings are all owned by the employing corporation. In the third class would fall the laws of a dozen other states, mainly in agricultural areas.

The last two groups have this in common, that both regulate prices. Although penalties provided seem to be ample, yet in the United States the administrative features are sometimes weak, as typified by the case of Colorado,[54] where, if the attorney-general should fail, neglect, or refuse to act after a demand by a responsible party, any citizen has a right to institute proceedings upon giving bonds for cost of suit. Obviously, the workman is in no position to give bonds or to bring suit, for he can afford neither the expense nor the loss of the job which such a procedure would entail.[55]

5. **Deductions.**—The problem of deductions from wages involves: (a) Deductions in respect to fines. (b) Deductions as payment for damages. (c) Deductions for use of material and tools. (d) Deductions for benefits.

Fines are imposed, presumably, for disciplinary reasons, and vary in application and amount in different establishments and with the caprice of the individual employer. They may not always be a real deterrent, but may on the other hand lead to carelessness, suggesting to the worker that he has paid for what he has done. They may be unfairly imposed, creating a sense of injustice and irritating the workers, and they may even prove to be a source of petty profits to the unscrupulous employer. At all events, they decrease the income of the wage earner.

Deductions as payment for damages may be for bad or negligent work, injury to materials and to other property of the employer. Abuses are very general, for the employer determines the amount of damage done and puts the price on materials spoiled. It is humanly impossible to do perfect work, and no

[54] Colorado, Compiled Laws 1923, Sec. 4240.

[55] Respecting the variety of decisions on the constitutionality of this class of legislation, see Freund, *Police Power,* 1904, pp. 305-308; Clark, *Law of the Employment of Labor,* pp. 65-72; Stimson, *Handbook to the Labor Laws of the United States,* 1896, pp. 104-110; and Clark and Tracy, "Laws Relating to Payment of Wages," pp. 24-27.

INDIVIDUAL BARGAINING

matter how good a worker may be at his trade, faults will occur at times. Such faults are part of the manufacturer's risk and should be dealt with as such. The employer is himself often to blame for setting an inexperienced hand to do work for which he is not competent.

The case of charges for materials and tools used by employees involves the same principle as in the previous case. This system is intended to secure economy in the use of material by making the worker responsible. From the point of view of the worker, however, the system is objectionable because of the possibility of overcharge, which no regulation, however strict, can altogether prevent.

Deductions for benefits received, such as medical attention, hospital care, and sickness insurance, are allowed by all states and countries, but some provide that the deduction must not exceed the value of the thing supplied, and, when not stated, this is generally implied by all countries. Usually, also, these deductions from wages are in pursuance of a previous contract. About half a dozen states, including New York, New Jersey, and Ohio, specifically legislate against forced contributions for certain enumerated benefits as a condition of employment. Utah prohibits forced contributions for political campaign expenses.[56] Oregon is an example of a state which has legalized deductions for hospital benefits, but which requires that such deductions must be approved by the industrial accident commission.[57] A further development in the regulation of deductions for benefit funds is found in a type of law enacted first in Minnesota in 1919, which requires employers who make deductions from wages for the purpose of furnishing medical or hospital care, or accident, sickness, or old-age insurance, to secure a license for the benefit plan from the state insurance commissioner.[58]

A corporation may furnish insurance, lessening many hardships of life for the workingman and his family; but this insurance is enjoyed only as a result of continuous employment, which in turn often involves oppressive dependence. Especially is this true when after a number of years the workingman has acquired rights which may be lost by change of em-

[56] Utah, Compiled Laws, 1917, Sec. 2379.
[57] Oregon, Laws 1917, C. 393.
[58] Minnesota, Laws 1919, C. 388.

ployment. Thus the burden may become great with increasing years, as new employment with insurance becomes more and more difficult to secure.

Provisions are found in some laws, enacted under the old system of employers' liability, and sometimes confined to railroads, which regulate or prevent the payment of benefits to injured employees as a means of escaping from such liability. Thus about half the states, the Philippine Islands, and the federal government have enacted that no contract of insurance or relief benefit shall constitute a bar to action by an employee for damages in case of injury or death.[59] These measures, however, have for the most part been superseded by workmen's compensation laws which have abolished the damage-suit system in such cases.[60]

In the act of 1896[61] the first attempt was made in England to protect the worker from harsh and unreasonable fines. This act provided that there must be formal agreement for the fines; that the fine must be for something which causes, or is likely to cause, damage or loss to the employer or interruption or hindrance to his business; that it must be fair and reasonable, having regard to all the circumstances of the case; that written particulars must be given to the worker each time a fine is exacted; and, finally, that there shall be a register of fines open to inspection.[62]

In the United States legislation dealing with deductions as fines is found in about fourteen states and two dependencies.[63] Massachusetts says fines shall not be levied except for imperfect work,[64] and Louisiana prohibits them except when employees

[59] See, for instance, Ohio, Laws 1910, p. 195.
[60] See section on Workmen's Compensation in chap. v.
[61] 59 and 60 Vict., C. 44.
[62] Great Britain, Departmental Committee on the Truck Acts, *Report*, 1908, vol. i, p. 6.
[63] Arkansas, California, Connecticut, Hawaii, Indiana, Louisiana, Maryland, Massachusetts, Michigan, Mississippi, New Jersey, Nevada, Ohio, Puerto Rico, Wisconsin, and Wyoming.
[64] Massachusetts, Laws 1909, C. 5140, Sec. 114. Under the terms of this act, fines for imperfect weaving may be levied only after the imperfections have been pointed out and the amount agreed upon by both parties. Apparently these provisions did not sufficiently protect the weavers, for in 1911 another act was passed stating that "No employer shall impose a fine upon an employee engaged at weaving for imperfec-

INDIVIDUAL BARGAINING 337

willfully or negligently damage goods or property of the employer. Arkansas limits the rate of discount to 10 per cent of wages because of early payment. Connecticut, Mississippi, Nevada, New Jersey, and Puerto Rico prohibit discounting at all for early payment of wages. The California law prohibits a deduction from the wages of an employee, on account of the employee's coming late to work, of a sum in excess of the proportionate wage which would have been earned during the time actually lost; provided, that for a loss of time less than thirty minutes, a half hour's wage may be deducted.[65] A clause dealing with deductions not levied for inferior work or for destruction of property, appears in Massachusetts,[66] where no deductions are to be made from the wages of women and minors when there is a stoppage of work owing to a breakdown of machinery, and the workers are not allowed to leave the mill.

6. Mechanics' Liens and Wage Preference.—The idea that wages are to receive special treatment, that they are to be paid before other claims, that security is to be given for their payment, and that they shall be exempt up to a certain amount from execution, underlies legislation on mechanics' liens, on wages as preferred claims, and on wage exemption. The last of these subjects is treated elsewhere;[67] here we consider the preferential treatment of the laborer as creditor.

Mechanics' lien laws represent a stage in the progress toward wage preference, but they should not be confused with it. They are founded on the still older practice of giving contractors and builders a claim for payment on houses they built and the land that these were built on.

In 1830 the first mechanics' lien law was passed by the New York legislature[68] and was based on the following considerations, set forth in a committee report:

"The committee are credibly informed that the severe and heavy losses sustained by the laboring interests have arisen far

---

tions that may arise during the process of weaving" (Laws 1911, C. 584). The court, however, rendered the new law nugatory by its limited interpretation of the word "fine." (Commonwealth *v.* Lancaster Mills, 212 Mass. 315, 98 N. E. 864 [1912].)

[65] Session Laws 1921, C. 901.
[66] Massachusetts, Laws 1909, C. 514, Sec. 119.
[67] See "Wage Exemption," p. 327.
[68] New York, Laws 1830, C. 330.

more frequently from insufficient, reckless contractors, having nothing to lose, than from contractees. . . . They would be distinctly understood, declaring it as their undivided opinion, that a mortgage given to secure the payment of money lawfully borrowed, the justice of which no one will presume to dispute, is not a more equitable claim than that of the mechanic and laborer on the dwelling house and other buildings, and ground on which the same are erected, so far as their claim and demand can be correctly ascertained."[69]

Mechanics' lien legislation seeks to give the laborer a claim for the payment of what is due him, backed by the security of the structure or land on which he has been employed. Contractors on public works are in most states required to give bond to secure the payment of wages. Mechanics' lien legislation exists in all the states, and extends to labor performed on public works, railroads, in mines, and on the land, as well as to lumbering, construction, and repair of vessels, sawmilling, and other occupations. Such liens are generally ranked as coming before other payments; and in many cases where contractors and subcontractors are entitled to benefit in a similar way, the wage-earner's claim is put first. A type of law which is hardly designated a lien but intends to give security to the payment of wages is that which makes stockholders in certain designated corporations liable for debts owed employees for labor. Indiana, Massachusetts, Michigan, New York, North Carolina, North Dakota, Oklahoma, Pennsylvania, Tennessee, and Wisconsin have such laws, the law in the last-mentioned state applying to every corporation other than railroads.[70]

The next step was the provision that wages should be considered as preferred claims. All the states and the federal government have laws providing that in cases of assignments, administrations, and receiverships caused by death or bankruptcy, the wages of servants and employees, up to a definite sum and for work done within a limited time, shall be paid next after fees, costs, and taxes.[71] France has a law giving preference to wage payments. Great Britain and her colonies include in their

[69] New York Assembly, *Documents,* 1830, No. 24.
[70] Wisconsin Statutes 1925, Sec. 182.23.
[71] Also, Alaska, District of Columbia, Hawaii, and the Philippine Islands.

INDIVIDUAL BARGAINING

bankruptcy laws preferential payment claims, providing usually that salaries of clerks and wages of laborers not exceeding fixed amounts shall have equal claim to payment with taxes and expenses. The British bankruptcy law includes in this category national insurance contributions and amounts due for workmen's compensation. New Zealand has a *bona fide* contractors' and workmen's lien act resembling the American legislation.

III. THE LABORER AS TENANT

1. Classes of Agricultural Workers.—Of the 48,829,920 persons over ten years of age engaged in gainful occupations in 1930, more than one-fifth, or 10,471,998, were employed in agriculture. Of this number, something less than 3,600,000 were owners operating their own farms. More than 2,500,000 were tenants,[72] and 4,392,764 were laborers working for owners and tenants. These figures do not represent the actual proportions of wage earners and employers in the sense of the wage bargain as understood in manufacturers and other industries. Of the 4,392,764 laborers, 1,659,792 were members of the family of the owner or tenant, and therefore their labor contracts do not exhibit the strictly business relation of employer and employee in the modern wage bargain. Such labor problems as they present, from the standpoint of legislation, are mainly those of child labor.

a. *Hired Laborers.*—The remaining 2,732,972 were hired laborers, and to them would be applicable labor laws similar to those enacted to protect laborers in other industries. As a matter of fact, however, labor legislation in the United States has had very little to do with farm labor. Laws like those regarding workmen's compensation, safety, health, or hours of labor sometimes either specifically exclude agricultural labor from their operation or are not applicable. Other laws, such as laborers' liens, wage exemption, prohibition of involuntary servitude, and the like are so general or fundamental that they apply to farm labor. Hired laborers are of two classes, considerably different in their condition. Casual laborers are usually hired by the day, whereas others are hired by the month.

---

[72] Fifteenth Census of the United States, 1930, vol. iv, p. 146. The census distinguishes the number of *farms* operated by owners and tenants, not the number of *owners and tenants*; hence these numbers are estimated.

The number of 2,732,972 farm hands is understated, because an uncertain number of tenants are really hired laborers under a special form of tenant contract and should be classed as employees rather than tenants.

b. *Tenants.*—The Fifteenth Census classified the 2,664,365 tenant-operated farms into two groups—489,210 farms whose tenants paid a cash rental, and 2,175,155 farms whose tenants compensated the landlord in whole (share tenants) or in part (share-cash tenants) by turning over to him a share of the crop, or paying a stated amount of farm products (standing renters). Tenant-operated farms represented 42.4 per cent of the total number of farms in 1930.[73] Evidently, the "cash" tenant (and also the "standing renter") is a small capitalist, a contractor, or an employer, since he invests his own money or labor and takes all of the risks of the business. His gains are profits rather than wages; his bargain with the landlord is a price bargain, not a wage bargain. Share-cash tenants are those who pay a share of the products for a part of the land and cash for a part.

The share tenants are more difficult to classify. They may be either small capitalists or simply farm laborers, and the census does not distinguish between the two. A share tenant pays the landlord as rental a certain share of the product, such as one-half, one-third, or one-quarter. In making such a contract, the tenant would appear to be a contractor or capitalist, who takes not indeed the whole risk of the business, but a part of the risk. Such is the case if he actually invests his own capital, such as horses, cattle, implements, and so on, and runs the risk of losing his capital on the chance of increasing it. He would figure the outcome as profit or loss.

c. *"Croppers."*—If, on the other hand, the tenant "invests" nothing but his own labor and the landlord furnishes all of the working capital, then the landlord is the capitalist-employer, the tenant is a laborer, and the bargain is a wage bargain. His wages, however, are not the stipulated daily or monthly wages received by a "hired man," but they are contingent wages, similar to those paid to a pieceworker, or, rather, to a sailor on a whaling ship who receives a share of the product at the end of

[73] Fifteenth Census of the United States, *Agriculture*, 1930, vol. iv, p. 146.

INDIVIDUAL BARGAINING 341

the voyage. This system of wage payment is spoken of as "product sharing" to distinguish it from "profit sharing."

The terms "cropper" and "cropping contract" will be used herein to designate this kind of labor tenant under the system of share tenancy. The terms originated in the southern states, where share contracts are most prevalent and where they account for the high percentage of tenancy. In popular usage, the term "cropper" includes both the share farmer, or small capitalist, and the share laborer. Both are croppers. The courts, however, have settled upon the term "cropper" to indicate the laborer,[74] and, adopting this usage, we can distinguish the cropper, as a laborer whose wages are measured by a share of the product under the guise of a lease, from the share tenant, as a small capitalist paying rent.

The 1930 census, which reported the number of croppers for the southern states only, adopted the definition of a cropper as a share tenant whose landlord furnished all the work animals. The term being thus defined for purposes of enumeration, it was found that of the 1,790,783 tenant-operated farms in the South, 776,278—nearly a fourth of all farms in those states— were operated by croppers. A little more than half of the croppers were colored, these representing about 45 per cent of all colored farm operators in the states covered.[75]

In most of the states it has been left to the courts to decide in specific cases who were croppers and who were farmers. Indeed, the amount of capital owned by the farmer may be so small that he would be looked upon in other industries as scarcely more than a mechanic furnishing his tools and taking out work on a contract. The law of Texas, enacted in 1915,[76] is the first American law designed to regulate the rents of share tenants. It attempts to prevent the landlord from charging more than one-half of the value of the product if he furnishes everything except labor, and more than one-third of the grain and one-fourth of the cotton if the tenant furnishes all of the

---

[74] Steel v. Frick, 56 Pa. St. 172 (1867); Harrison v. Ricks, 71 N. C. 7 (1874); Almand v. Scott, 80 Ga. 95, 4 S. E. 892 (1888); Hammock v. Creekmore, 48 Ark. 264, 3 S. W. 180 (1886).

[75] Fifteenth Census of the United States, *Agriculture*, 1930, vol. iv, p. 156.

[76] Texas, Laws 1915, Art. 5475 (3225).

operating capital. Thus it distinguishes and regulates both the rent of the farmer and the wages of the cropper.

In other states, where the legislature has not attempted to standardize or regulate the share contracts, the courts have been compelled to decide in each case as it arises whether the laborer is a cropper working for wages under a labor contract, or a tenant farmer paying rent under a lease. If he is a cropper, then, in case of dispute, he would be awarded what similar laborers in the locality receive as wages, regardless of the value of the crop. If he is a tenant farmer he is awarded his share of the crop, regardless of what he might earn as wages.

In order to decide the point, the courts look into the contract to discover which party has the control and direction of the farming operations and the legal possession of the crop at the end of the season. In brief, if the landlord gives orders as to cultivation, and has legal possession and the right to divide the crop and give the tenant his share, the contract is a labor contract.[77] If the tenant is "his own boss" and has legal possession of the crop, and gives the landlord his share, the contract is a lease.[78] In Oklahoma, it was held that a "cropper" is a hired hand paid for labor with a share of the crop he works to make and harvest, and has no exclusive right and no estate in the land until the landowner assigns him a share, but that a "tenant" has exclusive right to possession of lands he cultivates and an estate therein for the term of his contract and right of property in the crop.[79] Generally, it turns out that, in proportion as the tenant advances a larger and larger share of the working capital, the contract which he is able to make is a lease and gives him not only a larger share of the product, but also a chance to make a profit in addition to wages; while the smaller the proportion of capital which he advances, the lesser is his share and the more nearly the contract becomes a labor contract.

If the contract is a lease, the landlord has a preference lien

[77] Shoemaker v. Crawford, 82 Mo. App. 487 (1900); Kelly v. Rummerfield, 117 Wis. 620, 94 N. W. 649 (1903); Bowman v. Bradley, 151 Pa. St. 351, 24 Atl. 1062 (1892); Chase v. McDonnell, 24 Ill. 237 (1860); Cutting v. Cox, 19 Vt. 517 (1847).

[78] Taylor v. Bradley, 39 N. Y. 129 (1868); Neal v. Brandon, 70 Ark. 79, 66 S. W. 200 (1902); Almand v. Scott, 80 Ga. 95, 4 S. E. 892 (1888).

[79] Halsell v. First National Bank, 109 Okla. 220, 235 Pac. 532 (1925).

INDIVIDUAL BARGAINING 343

on the crop for his rent.[80] If it is a labor contract, the laborer has a laborer's lien on it for his wages.[81]

2. **Agricultural Labor Legislation.**—The foregoing distinctions indicate differences in the kind of legislation needed to protect agricultural labor, compared with that protecting industrial labor. The one modifies mainly the law of landlord and tenant, the other that of employer and employee. Farming is, for the most part, a small-scale industry, and there is opportunity for individuals to rise to the position of independent owners. Beginning, perhaps, as a casual laborer, the person's next step is that of the farm laborer hired by the month or by the year, and living with the family of the owner. Next, with a family of his own, the steps upward are cropper, share tenant, cash tenant, owner with mortgage, and, finally, ownership unencumbered. Legislation may aid or obstruct this upward movement.

If the share tenant, whether cropper or farmer, is not permitted to acquire any title to such permanent improvements as he adds to the land, his condition is practically the same as that of the wage earner who has no title to his own product. Like the laborer, he tends to be kept permanently in that class. This is the condition of croppers and share tenants in the United States, and the result is seen in their frequent movement from farm to farm. Such tenants, without title to their "savings" in the form of improvements, can do but little in the way of accumulating the capital necessary to rise to the higher steps, and their instability and lack of incentive are equally serious factors in their own deterioration and in that of the soil.

This condition received legislative attention first in England. There had been a strong agitation favoring the enactment of legislative measures to compensate tenants for improvements made on the landlord's estate, but not until 1850 was a bill introduced into Parliament favoring a reasonable allowance for such improvements. The bill did not pass, but similar measures were brought before that body several times, and in 1875 an

[80] Randall v. Ditch, 123 Ia. 582, 99 N. W. 190 (1904); Hopper v. Haines, 71 Md. 64, 18 Atl. 29, 20 Atl. 159 (1889); Keoleg v. Phelps, 80 Mich. 466, 45 N. W. 350 (1890); Wilson v. Stewart, 69 Ala. 302 (1881); Noe v. Layton, 69 Ark. 551, 64 S. W. 880 (1910).
[81] Grisson v. Pickett, 98 N. C. 54, 3 S. E. 921 (1887).

act was obtained stipulating the conditions under which an outgoing tenant was to be paid for improvements. No provision was made, however, compelling landlords to contract under the law, and as a consequence the statute was ineffective.

In 1883, a new bill, known as the Agricultural Holdings Act, was passed, compelling all landlords to make their leases with tenants subject to compensation for improvements.

Even with compensation for improvements, it requires time and trials for the tenant or purchaser to find a suitable farm. Finding the tenant a farm has a direct relationship with finding the laborer his job.[82] The importance of this problem is keenly felt, and some states have special information services to aid persons seeking to rent or purchase farms. In 1935, as part of its emergency relief program, the federal government through a Rural Resettlement Administration undertook to assist farmers located on land too poor for profitable cultivation to move to land in more fertile regions.

Legislation of various countries also provides credit agencies to enable the tenant or farmer to acquire advances of capital necessary to secure permanency in his position. The Schultze Delitsch and Raiffeisen banks in Germany and Austria, the Crédit Foncier in France, and the cooperative banks in other countries are private cooperative credit systems operating under government supervision.[83] Governments in many countries, including several states and the federal government in the United States, have provided special encouragement to cooperative agricultural credit enterprises, and have set up special farm credit agencies under government auspices.

Since the World War, the central European states have attempted to break up the large landholdings either by voluntary sale or by expropriation, and to pass the land on in smaller tracts to cooperative societies of farmers, to small landowners whose holdings were too small for family independence, and to the landless for homestead dwellings. In this last class were industrial workers, employees in the public service, ex-service men, workers on the expropriated estates, and the disabled who

---

[82] See "Public Employment Offices," pp. 12-27.
[83] See Whitney, E. L., "Cooperative Credit Societies (Credit Unions) in America and in Foreign Countries," U. S. Bureau of Labor Statistics, *Bulletin No. 314, 1922.*

INDIVIDUAL BARGAINING

were not capable of full-time work. Credit facilities have been extended and other steps taken to assist the new owners in holding their land.[84]

In regulating the contract of landlord and tenant, the problem of administration is similar to that of regulating the contract of employer and employee. At first, the matter is left to the courts; but the tenant, like the wage earner, is unable to avail himself of the aid of the courts. An administrative body or commission is needed to deal with each contract as it arises. In the case of the tenant contract, it is the highly inflated value of land that offers the chief obstacle to the laborer or cropper in advancing to the position of owner. This obstacle was attacked in Ireland in 1881, by the creation of a land commission to fix rents. The commission reduced rents 15 to 20 per cent. Later, when the government began to make loans at low rates of interest in order to encourage farm ownership, and then began to compel the landlords to sell to their tenants, the land commission fixed the fair value of the land. Otherwise, the government loans at 3 per cent interest would have served only to inflate land values further, and the landlord would have absorbed the benefit intended for the tenant. Thus the Irish Land Commission does for landlord and tenant what a public utility commission does for corporation and consumer, or a minimum wage commission for employer and employee.[85]

IV. THE LABORER AS COMPETITOR

From one point of view, all labor legislation has as its object the protection of the laborer as a competitor. The wage-bargaining power of men is weakened by the competition of women and children; hence a law restricting the hours of women and children may also be looked upon as a law to protect men in their bargaining power. The same is true in a different way of industrial education and free schools, for they tend to reduce the competition for the poorly paid jobs by increasing the efficiency and wage-earning power of laborers who otherwise would be serious competitors. But for these classes

[84] "New Agrarian Legislation in Central Europe," *International Labor Review*, September, 1922, vol. vi, no. 3, p. 344.

[85] See Irish Land Acts of 1881, 1885, 1903, and 1909 in the English statutes; Cant-Wall, *Ireland under the Land Acts*.

of legislation the protection of the laborer as a competitor is not the main object. There are two classes of legislation, however, of which it may be said that the main purpose has been to protect the American workman from competition of poorly paid laborers: (1) legislation on immigration, especially the laws against induced immigration and the Chinese exclusion laws; (2) legislation as to the sale of goods manufactured by convicts.

1. **Protection against Immigrants.**—Immigration legislation tends more and more to develop along protective lines. At first a country encourages people to come in order to develop its resources; later, means have to be found to safeguard the interests of the existing population.

There are four protective purposes which are served by immigration legislation. The first is the social protection of the community generally. It is obvious that every state will regard certain classes as objectionable; hence the prohibitions that the United States puts on the landing of prostitutes (since 1875), criminals (1875), professional beggars (1903). Polygamists (1891) and anarchists (1903) are excluded, partly on social and partly on political grounds. By the act of 1918, power was given to expel and exclude aliens who were anarchists; who taught opposition to all organized government, the overthrow of government by force, etc.; who wrote, published, or gave pecuniary assistance to any organization furthering these aims.[86] The exclusion of Orientals (1882), again, may be justified on the principle that they are unlikely to live successfully together with the other races in America. Since political offenders are on a different level from ordinary offenders against the law, they have always been exempt from such exclusion (1875).

A second kind of protection, that of the national health, is afforded by the laws which attempt to keep out those immigrants suffering from contagious disease (1891), especially from tuberculosis (1907).

A third type of excluded class is made up of those persons who are looked upon as constituting a danger to the taxpaying classes. Legislation designed to keep out persons likely to be-

[86] 41 United States Statutes at Large, C. 251, p. 1008.

INDIVIDUAL BARGAINING   347

come a public charge (1882) aims at protecting the taxpayer from having to support such individuals. The fear that lunatics, idiots, or epileptics may also become charges on the community is chiefly accountable for the prohibition (1891) against their coming into the country. Again, the repeated efforts which were made to introduce a literacy test, culminating in success, over the President's veto, in 1917, may have been inspired partly by a feeling that the illiterate are more likely to become destitute than others. A head tax, generally used for revenue alone, may at times become a sort of property qualification. In the United States it was at first 50 cents (1882) and has been gradually raised to $8 (1917), which is not exactly a prohibitive figure. Finally, persons traveling on assisted passages who cannot prove that they do not belong to any of the excluded classes are not allowed to land (1891); after being dependent on others, such persons might easily come to be dependent on the state.

The fourth kind of protection put forth by the law over the people of this country is, from the standpoint of labor legislation, the most important. The contrast between the protection afforded to American goods in the commodity market and the lack of any such effort to lessen the competition of labor in the labor market was early noticed, and efforts have been made since 1868 to control immigration after the example of the tariff. In that year the act of 1864 encouraging immigration was repealed,[87] and a start was given to a new negative policy with regard to immigration. This new policy had particular reference to what is commonly but inaccurately called "contract labor," or induced immigration. The percentum Act of May 19, 1921, went further than merely refusing to induce immigration and positively limited the number of aliens admissible in each year. This was necessary to ward off the post-war influx of aliens during a period of business depression and unemployment. The 1921 act expired by limit on June 30, 1922, but by the act of May 11, 1922,[88] it was extended to June 30, 1924. In

[87] United States, Laws 1868, C. 38, Sec. 4.
[88] "An act to Limit the Immigration of Aliens into the United States," approved May 19, 1921, and amended May 11, 1922. 42 United States Statutes at Large, May 19, 1921, C. 8, p. 5. C. 187, 42 United States Statutes at Large, 540 (Sixty-seventh Congress, Second Session).

this year a new law was enacted changing the percentage and the base. This will be discussed later.[89]

a. *Induced Immigration.*—The eighteenth-century type of immigration had been very largely due to inducement—sometimes, indeed, to compulsion. After the first quarter of the nineteenth century indentured labor[90] had practically ceased to exist; but in 1864 a stimulus was given (owing to the war-time scarcity of labor) to a similar system of bringing numbers of Europeans here to work under contract, by a law[91] which provided that such contracts should be valid and enforceable in the United States courts. This, it must be remembered, was before the passage of the Thirteenth Amendment. Employers took advantage of the law in order to bring over foreign laborers. Companies were formed for the same purpose, and the American labor market was threatened with a huge oversupply of cheap foreign labor. In spite of agitation in Congress and feeling in the country, it was not until 1868 that this act was repealed, nor until 1885 that the inducement of immigration was formally forbidden by law.

The Contract Labor Law of 1885[92] forbade the assistance or encouragement of immigrants coming here under contract to work. The act applied solely to laborers, for those professions which send representatives abroad were expressly exempted, as were also domestic servants and skilled workmen in new industries, provided labor of the same kind could not be obtained otherwise. Individuals were allowed to assist friends and relatives to come to America. This successful reversal of policy from the act of 1864 was due in a large measure to the efforts of the Knights of Labor and the trade unions. It answered the demand of the working class as a whole, and especially that part of it which was organized, for effective protection against the competition of the masses of immigrants who were now entering the country. The number of immigrants, which had decreased during the 'seventies, rose to 457,257 in 1880, 669,431 in 1881, and 788,992 in 1882.[93] Another immigration act

[89] 43 United States Statutes at Large, 1923-1925. C. 190, p. 153.
[90] See "Indentured Service," p. 320.
[91] United States, Laws 1864, C. 246.
[92] United States, Laws 1885, C. 164.
[93] Immigration Commission, *Reports,* 1911, vol. iii, p. 4.

INDIVIDUAL BARGAINING 349

was passed in 1891, which had as one of its objects the prevention of induced immigration.[94] The government was beginning to make it more difficult for a man who had previously obtained work to come into the United States. Transportation companies were now forbidden to solicit or encourage immigration, and the practice of issuing advertisements in foreign countries promising employment here was prohibited. At the same time the efforts of Congress to make the Contract Labor Law a real deterrent were met by a silent opposition from the courts, which continued to construe the law strictly and to treat it as of limited application until 1907, when the terms of the law itself were changed.

But during the 'eighties and 'nineties the change from the "old immigration" to the "new immigration" was taking place; that is, the great bulk of the people no longer came from Germany, the United Kingdom, and Scandinavia, but from southern Italy, Austria-Hungary, Russia, and latterly Greece. These people had, in general, a lower standard of life than the Americans and the earlier immigrants. While it is true that in many cases where they replaced native labor this adjustment was favorable to the Americans, in that these were raised thereby to more responsible and better-paid positions, or else went farther West or Southwest—as did the coal miners, attracted by better wages—still it cannot be denied that the newer immigrants were as a rule willing to work for less wages, to endure harder conditions, and to lower the general plane of living of unskilled laborers. It is on account of this displacement of American labor by immigrant labor, a phenomenon which has been at times emphasized to the point of exaggeration, that the working class has so eagerly desired the restriction of immigration;[95] and the contract labor laws were the first attempt to do this. It was not necessary to enforce the law against farm laborers, because from them no such competition was feared.

A later revision of the Contract Labor Law was made in the General Immigration Act of 1917.[96] This time the scope of the words "contract laborer" was enlarged to include anyone "in-

[94] United States, Laws 1891, C. 551.
[95] For a discussion of the economic effects of immigration from opposite points of view, see Jenks, J. W., and Lauck, W. J., *The Immigration Problem*; and Hourwich, I. A., *Immigration and Labor*.
[96] United States, Laws 1916-1917, C. 29.

duced, assisted, encouraged, or solicited" to immigrate by any kind of promise or agreement, express or implied, true or false, to find employment. The Immigration Commission of 1911 said of even the less sweeping law of 1907 that "it is difficult to conceive how the letter of the law respecting the importation of contract laborers could be more stringent than at present"; and in consequence of this trend in the law the courts have been obliged to give up their attitude of considering as prohibited by the law only those transactions in which a contract could be proved.

The cases on the subject bring out the increasing strictness of the law. In United States v. Edgar,[97] decided under the law of 1885, the prosecution of an employer who had imported labor from abroad failed because no contract could be proved. In United States v. Gay[98] it was held that the law of 1891 was intended to exclude only unskilled manual laborers. After the act of 1907, as already pointed out, these doctrines could no longer be held, and in 1914 there was a case in which a fine of $1,000 was exacted for each of forty-five contract laborers brought across the Mexican border for the purpose of helping to construct a railway.[99]

In November, 1919, the first official International Labor Conference called under the League of Nations, in session at Washington, adopted as part of its proposed program on unemployment the recommendation that "recruiting of bodies of workers in one country with a view to their employment in another country should be permitted only by mutual agreement between the countries concerned and after consultation with employers and workers in each country in the industries concerned."[100]

b. *The Quota System.*—That laws against induced immigration, although in force for thirty-five years, did very little to protect the American laboring man from the competition of immigrants is evident from two facts: the enormous numbers of unskilled laborers who entered the United States, and the efforts that were constantly being made to secure other means,

---

[97] United States v. Edgar, 1 C. C. A. 49, 48 Fed. 91 (1891).
[98] United States v. Gay, 37 C. C. A. 46, 95 Fed. 226 (1899).
[99] Grant Bros. Construction Co. v. U. S., 232 U. S. 647, 34 Sup. Ct. 452 (1914).
[100] *American Labor Legislation Review,* December, 1919, vol. ix, no. 4, pp. 533-534.

INDIVIDUAL BARGAINING

notably a literacy test, for creating a "labor protective tariff."[101] With regard to the first point, it may be mentioned that during the fiscal year ending June 30, 1914, the latest before the war, the number of "laborers" who entered the United States was 226,407, and the number of skilled workmen was 173,208.[102]

The demand for protection was answered more fully by the 1921 Quota Act than by any previous one. The total immigrants to be admitted in any fiscal year was limited to 3 per cent of the number of persons of such nationality who were resident in the United States according to the Census of 1910. This act was supplemental to, and not a substitution for, other immigration laws. It did not apply to countries regulated in accordance with treaties or agreement relating solely to immigration, i.e., China and Japan. Preferences within the quota were to be given to wives and certain near relatives of citizens of the United States. This act was extended at its expiration in 1924.

The act of 1924[103] had two purposes—one to limit the total influx, and the other to select the type of immigrant which most easily fitted into American institutions and whose standard of living was not below that of the American worker. The act provided for the first few years a limit of 2 per cent of the number of persons of such nationality resident in 1890. The "new" immigration commenced after 1890 so that by taking that year as a base a greater proportion of north European immigrants were admissible. The provisions were extended to the entire world except Canada, Newfoundland, Mexico, Cuba, Haiti, Dominican Republic, Canal Zone, or an independent country of South America.

Since July 1, 1929, as provided in the act of 1924, the quota has been determined by the number which bears the same ratio to 150,000 as the number of inhabitants in continental United

---

[101] In the effort to secure the desired protection by another method, the people of Arizona in 1914 enacted by initiative and referendum a law requiring employers of more than five persons to engage at least 80 per cent qualified electors or citizens. This statute was declared unconstitutional by the United States Supreme Court as denying the equal protection of the laws. Truax v. Raich, 239 U. S. 33, 36 Sup. Ct. 7 (1915).

[102] Commissioner General of Immigration, *Report,* 1914, pp. 40, 41.

[103] Public No. 139, 68th Congress, 1924.

352 PRINCIPLES OF LABOR LEGISLATION

States in 1920 having that national origin bears to the number of inhabitants in continental United States in 1920. The minimum quota is 100.

Immigrants are now divided into quota and non-quota. Those in the latter group are: (1) Wives and unmarried children under twenty-one years of age of a citizen of the United States. (2) Lawfully admitted aliens temporarily abroad. (3) Immigrants from excepted countries and wives and children under eighteen. (4) Certain of the professional classes. (5) Students. Quota immigrants are those not included under the non-quota groups.

Preferences within the quota are given to unmarried children under twenty-one, father, mother, husband, or wife of a citizen of the United States, to wives and minor children of legally resident aliens, and to immigrants skilled in agriculture. These preferred groups, however, may not exceed 50 per cent of the quota.

A very practical provision was embodied in the law of 1924. Every immigrant must now secure a visa from the American consul in the country of departure. The consul cannot issue a visa if from any of the statements it appears that the alien is inadmissible or if the quota for that country has already been filled. This provision prevents the rush of aliens at the beginning of each month and at the end of the year, and does away with the discomforts caused by excessive congestion at Ellis Island. Furthermore, the number of rejections of aliens inadmissible under our laws has decreased as the consuls have learned their duties and have been more careful about granting visas.

Section 13 of the law provides that "no alien ineligible to citizenship shall be admitted to the United States." This is important when it is recalled that the naturalization laws state that the provisions thereof "shall apply to aliens being free white persons and to aliens of African nationality and to persons of African descent." This means persons other than Caucasian, or white race, and African, or black race, are ineligible to citizenship through naturalization and therefore not eligible as immigrants. This excludes Chinese, Japanese, East Indians, and other people indigenous to Asiatic countries and the adjacent islands. These new provisions may in time become a substitution for the other exclusion acts as to these classes.

The effect of the present law is that it now allows at the most between 150,000 and 160,000 new alien immigrants from Europe to enter annually. The total number of aliens legally entering the country for permanent residence in 1925 was 294,314, less than half the number who came the previous year under the earlier law. In 1930, following the going into effect of the "national origins" provision, the number fell to 241,700. About two-fifths of this immigration was from the Western Hemisphere, chiefly Canada and Mexico. With respect to European immigration, distribution among the various nationalities was fairly in accordance with the racial composition of this country's population. Instead of about 80 per cent from southeastern Europe, nearly that same proportion came from northern and western Europe.

Beginning in 1930, because of the extent of unemployment, immigration was drastically reduced by the adoption of the policy of refusing visas to many applicants on the legal ground that they were "likely to become a public charge." Under this policy the amount of permanent immigration in 1931 fell below 100,000 for the first time since the Civil War, and reached the low point of 23,068 in 1933. In 1935, the number of immigrants was only 34,956. As a result, beginning in 1932, emigration of aliens from this country exceeded the alien immigration—by 67,719 in 1932, and 3,878 in 1935.

c. *Exclusion of Orientals.*—The danger to the laborer from the competition of European immigrants may be lessened and gradually done away with as these become Americanized. Trade unionism, especially, is a force which is giving the immigrant the same standards as the American. In the case of the Oriental races, however, this "happy ending" to the story is not to be expected. Individual Chinese, Japanese, and Hindus may settle down to lead western lives and adopt western ideas; but the great mass of their countrymen who emigrate do so without any desire to change their ways of living. It is a well-known fact that these ways are much more economical than those of an American or European, and that therefore an Oriental can accept wages which to a white man would mean starvation. No doubt, race feeling enters to some extent into the composition of laws excluding Chinese, Japanese, and Hindus; but more deep-lying is the fear of the competitive worker. This is shown by the fact that the employing classes welcome Orientals, whom they find efficient, polite, and contented. Miss Eaves says of the early Californian opposition to the Chinese:

> The legislation on Oriental labor sprang from the people. . . . The laws . . . were the product of the actual experiences—sometimes of the race prejudices—of those in the humblest ranks of society. For thirty years the working people persistently made known their needs, winning at last a practically unanimous support in the state, so that all classes united to urge the tardy federal legislation for exclusion.[104]

The report of the federal Joint Special Committee to Investigate Chinese Immigration, which was published in 1877, is filled with complaints against the Chinese on the part of American workingmen who asserted that they could not compete with Chinese. A point very often made was that the average American workman is a married man with a family, while Chinese would come to California alone and expect to earn only what would keep a single man. Others said that Chinese labor was less efficient than white labor.[105] One witness asserted that he used to earn from $20 to $21 a week at broom-making, but that in competition with the Chinese he could make only $14.89.[106]

It was this agitation by the people on the Pacific coast, who had learned to fear the industrial competition of the Chinese, that led to federal legislation and finally to the exclusion of the Chinese laborers. The Burlingame Treaty of 1868 had settled nothing, for it merely proclaimed the right of the Chinese to settle where they would, while denying them the right of naturalization.[107] Another treaty, concluded in 1880, gave the American government the right "to regulate, limit, or suspend" Chinese immigration, but not absolutely to prohibit it. Two years later the exclusion of Chinese laborers went

---

[104] Eaves, Lucile, *History of California Labor Legislation* 1910, p. 115.
[105] Joint Special Committee to Investigate Chinese Immigration, *Report*, pp. 346, 347, Forty-fourth Congress, Second Session, Senate Report No. 689, 1877.
[106] *Ibid.*, p. 360.
[107] Immigration Commission, *Reports*, 1911, vol xxxix, p. 69.

INDIVIDUAL BARGAINING 355

into effect when an act was passed forbidding them to enter the country for the next ten years.[108] This policy has been kept up ever since in laws and treaties which have gradually grown more strict. On the same principle Japanese laborers not coming to the United States in order "to resume a formerly acquired domicile, to join a parent, wife, or children residing there, or to assume active control of an already possessed interest in a farming enterprise in this country," were refused passports by the Japanese government, in accordance with a treaty agreement of 1907.[109] In 1924, however, the Japanese were excluded by a provision of the immigration act of that year which forbade immigration of persons ineligible to citizenship.[110]

The British self-governing colonies have had a similar experience to that of the United States, and have met it by practically the same means. Canada excludes Chinese laborers; the Japanese, by an agreement with the government of that country, that not more than 150 Japanese are to enter Canada annually; and the Hindus, by a head tax of $250 and the requirement that they shall come by a "continuous journey" from India, which cannot be done by the existing routes. Australia uses a literacy test to keep out Chinese, who must write fifty words in a European language.

d. *The Literacy Test.*—The British self-governing colonies early found in the literacy test a weapon against Asiatic immigration. In this country a long struggle was made to apply to all immigrants a test of this kind, succeeding in 1917 over the Presidential veto which had three times defeated earlier Congressional action in this direction.

First introduced unsuccessfully in Congress in 1892, the principle of the literacy test was embodied in a bill of 1895 and survived through numerous modifications until two years later it had passed the House and Senate.[111] The intention of the bill was to keep out not only the criminal and pauper classes, but also the southern and eastern Europeans, many of whom were illiterate. President Cleveland, however, vetoed

[108] United States, Laws 1882, C. 126.
[109] United States, Laws 1907, C. 1134.
[110] Public No. 139, 68th Congress, Sec. 13 (c).
[111] Immigration Commission, *Reports,* vol. xxxix, p. 47.

it as being un-American and illiberal, and also as unlikely to have any good effect on the prevailing depression or on violence in labor troubles and racial degeneration. The House passed the bill over the President's veto by a majority of 193 to 37, but no action was taken in the Senate and the bill was consequently not enacted into law.

The next attempt to secure a literacy test was made under the Taft administration. A bill was introduced into the Senate in 1911, containing a clause which was practically copied from the bill mentioned before.[112] It was passed by the House and Senate, but President Taft vetoed it in 1913. The Senate thereupon passed the bill again, but in the House the vote fell short of the required two-thirds majority and the bill therefore had to drop.[113]

Another bill including a literacy test of the usual type was introduced in the House in 1913.[114] The House and Senate voted favorably on this bill and it went to President Wilson on January 16, 1915. He returned the bill with his veto, giving as his reason the fact that this bill embodied a radical departure from the traditional policy of the country, in almost entirely removing the right of political asylum and in excluding those who have missed the opportunity of education, without regard to their character or capacity. He did not believe, moreover, that the bill represented the will of the people, and for these reasons he refused to sign it.[115] The House again could not raise a two-thirds majority in favor of the bill, and so, like its predecessors, it came to nothing.[116]

Finally in 1916 an immigration measure containing the literacy test was again introduced and passed by Congress. It was again vetoed by President Wilson,[117] but this time the necessary two-thirds majority was secured in both houses to adopt it over his veto, and it became a law on February 5, 1917.[118] Persons physically capable of reading, and over six-

[112] *Congressional Record*, 1911, vol. xlvii, p. 3669.
[113] *Ibid.*, 1913, vol. xlix, p. 3429.
[114] *Ibid.*, 1913, vol. l, p. 2013.
[115] Sixty-third Congress, Third Session, H. R. Document No. 1527.
[116] *Congressional Record*, 1915, vol. lii, p. 3078.
[117] Sixty-fourth Congress, Second Session, H. R. Document No. 2003.
[118] United States, Laws 1916-17, C. 29.

INDIVIDUAL BARGAINING

teen years of age, are excluded if they cannot read some language, except near relatives of admissible aliens and those seeking entrance to escape religious persecution. During the first fiscal year after its going into effect, the reading test served to exclude 1,598 immigrants.[119]

2. **Protection against Convict Labor.**—The latest survey of the number of convicts engaged in productive industry was made by the United States Department of Labor in its study in 1932.[120] There were 158,947 convicts in the 104 state and federal prisons studied; 82,276, or 52 per cent, were employed at productive labor as follows:[121]

[119] Commissioner General of Immigration, *Report*, 1918, p. 23.
[120] United States Department of Labor, Bureau of Labor Statistics, *Bulletin No. 595*, "Prison Labor in the United States, 1932."
[121] Six systems of employment are generally recognized, as follows:

The lease system.—Under this system the contractors assume practically the entire control of the convicts, including their maintenance and discipline, subject, however, to the regulations fixed by statute. In general, the prisoners are removed from the prisons and are employed in outdoor labor, such as mining, agriculture, railroad construction, etc., though manufacturing is sometimes carried on. The nature and duration of the employment are, within the restrictions of the law, fixed by the lease. (The lease system was not reported in effect in any of these institutions.)

The contract system.—The employment under this system is usually within the prison shops or yards, discipline and control remaining in the hands of the officers, only the labor of the convicts being let to, and directed by, the contractors for manufacturing purposes. The state usually furnishes shop room, and sometimes also provides power and machinery.

The piece-price system.—Not only the discipline of the convicts, but the direction of their labor as well, is retained by the state under this system, the contractors furnishing the material to be made up and receiving the finished product, an agreed price per piece being paid for the labor bestowed.

The public-account system.—There is no intervention of outside parties under this system, the employment of the convicts being in all respects directed by the state, and the products of their labor being sold for its benefit.

The state-use system.—This system is similar to the above, except that such articles are produced as will be of service to the state in supplying and maintaining its various institutions, and are appropriated to such use instead of being put on the general market.

The public-works-and-ways system.—Under this system convicts are employed in the construction and repair of public buildings, streets, highways, and other public works.

358 PRINCIPLES OF LABOR LEGISLATION

Convicts	Value
18,697, or 23 per cent, were working under the public-works-and-ways system and produced goods with a value of....................	$25,159,152
34,894, or 42 per cent, under state-use system.............	21,260,411
15,249, or 19 per cent, under public-account system........	12,367,646
9,081, or 11 per cent, under piece-price system............	10,522,200
4,355, or 5 per cent, under contract system..............	6,060,062
Total...	$75,369,471

About thirty-eight per cent ($28,889,908) of the goods were destined for direct competition on the open market. Of the goods sold, forty per cent (in value) was sold within the state of origin, and about sixty per cent without. The industries mainly affected by this competition are:

Shirts................	$7,847,313	Dresses..............	$ 859,276
Pants................	4,674,994	Pajamas and night gowns.............	796,984
Binder twine..........	4,050,123	Brooms..............	708,153
Farm, garden and dairy	1,474,651	Overalls.............	523,469
Chairs (wood).........	1,009,826	Shoes...............	498,564
Cotton yard goods, heavy..............	916,207	Roads, new and repaired (under public-works-and-ways system)..............	15,474,951
Underwear............	889,334	Buildings, new (under same system)......	7,378,924

Of the 116 state institutions studied, fifty paid no money compensation to the prisoners, and sixty-six paid some compensation to all or part of the inmates. Twelve federal prisons paid wages to prisoners and five did not. In most of the institutions, the amounts paid were nominal, generally ranging from two to fifteen cents a day.

The problem raised by permitting convicts' work to be sold in the open market in competition with the product of free labor has been expressed as follows:

The two investigations [of the Bureau of Labor, 1885 and 1895] showed that the convict product as a whole was very small when compared with the entire product of free labor in the United States. But the employers of free labor and their workmen unite in affirming that when any convict-made product is placed in competition with the product of free labor the market becomes demoralized, even a small sale affecting prices far out of proportion to the amount of the sale. . . . Every state objects to being made the market for convict-made goods produced in other states.[122]

The prisons do not stand in the normal relation of producers to the commodity market; they go on working, regardless of the fluctuations of business; they can undersell any competitor, for they do not have to meet the usual costs of production and in the last resort they can always fall back on the taxes. Manufacturers sometimes assert that they do not feel the competition of convict labor except in times of depression.[123] When concentrated on one article, prison-made goods may dominate that market. This would not affect goods sold to a world market, such as cotton and wheat. It is specialization as well as volume that counts.

The employer of "free labor" can meet this competition in several ways. He may adulterate or otherwise lower the quality of his goods so as to lower his cost of production, or he may give up the particular branch of his trade in which the competition of convict labor is felt. Instances can, however, be given of whole industries which were practically absorbed by convict labor in certain localities, such as the cooperage industry in Chicago during the 'eighties.

The problem of convict labor competition takes an even more serious aspect when it is considered in respect to interstate commerce. Pressure brought to bear on the government of any one particular state is often successful in getting a law passed forbidding the sale of convict-made goods within that state, but this has often meant that convict-made products from other states are brought in and sold there. In fact, the publicity given to the system of convict contract labor when a bill to abolish it is being discussed is apt to attract attention to the fact that a new market will be opened for the convict-made goods of other states.

Many states have laws designed to minimize competition between convict and free labor.[124] Some have prescribed in gen-

---

[122] United States Commissioner of Labor, *Twentieth Annual Report*, pp. 11, 23.
[123] *Ibid.*, p. 59 (statement of a Minnesota shoe manufacturer).
[124] See Sharkey, C. F., and Patterson, G. D., Jr., "Laws Relating to

eral terms that convicts are not to be employed where their work conflicts with free labor; others have prohibited convict labor in certain branches of industry. Still other states have required that prison industries be distributed among diversified lines, sometimes limiting the number of convicts to be employed in a given industry; a few specify the industries in which convicts must be employed. Another group of laws regulates the sale of convict-made goods, requiring that such goods be labeled, or providing that they be sold at not less than wholesale prices. The most effective kind of law is probably the provision that all goods manufactured in prison shall be for the use of the state (the "state-use" system). This system, together with the "public-works-and-ways" system, has been adopted almost exclusively in a number of states, including Illinois, New Jersey, New York, Ohio and Pennsylvania, and by the federal government. A federal law provides for the employment of convict labor in federal prisons on public works and ways, and in industries producing goods "for consumption in United States penal and correctional institutions or for sale to the departments and independent establishments of the federal government and not for sale to the public in competition with private enterprise." The federal departments and agencies are required to purchase such prison-made goods "as meet their requirements" at not more than current market prices.

For many years, the states were unable, because of federal constitutional restrictions, to prevent the sale of convict-made goods shipped in from other states. Attempts to deal with the problem by laws requiring all convict-made goods to be labeled as such, failed when such legislation was declared unconstitutional. After years of agitation by both labor and manufacturers' organizations, however, Congress in 1929 adopted the Hawes-Cooper Act[125] which beginning in 1934 divested prison-made goods, manufactured in one state and shipped into another, of their interstate character and rendered them subject to the laws of the state where they are offered for sale. This led immediately to the enactment in many states of laws designed to end this form of unfair competition—by prohibiting

Prison Labor in the United States," U. S. Bureau of Labor Statistics, *Bulletin No. 596,* 1933.

[125] United States, 45 Stat. 1084.

INDIVIDUAL BARGAINING

the sale of prison-made goods, by requiring that such goods be labeled, or by subjecting such goods from other states to the existing state laws. Although challenged on constitutional grounds, the Hawes-Cooper Act was upheld by the United States Supreme Court in 1936.[126] Enforcement of the Hawes-Cooper Act was strengthened by the Ashurst-Sumners Act of 1935,[127] which forbids the transportation of convict-made goods into a state which forbids the sale of such products in the open market, and furthermore requires that all prison-made goods shipped in interstate commerce be clearly marked to show the name and address of the shipper, the consignee, and the prison in which the goods were produced.

The Hawes-Cooper Act, and the state legislation that followed, created a crisis in many states with respect to prison labor. Besides the cost of maintaining prisoners in idleness, it is generally agreed that the welfare of the prisoners and the maintenance of prison discipline requires that prisoners be given employment. In an attempt to deal constructively with the problem of prison employment, the President in 1935 by executive order created the Prison Industries Reorganization Administration for the purpose of developing a national program in cooperation with the states. Progress appears to lie in the direction of further expansion and improvement of the "state-use" system.

v. Legal Aid and Industrial Courts

We have seen how modern legislation has attempted to give to the individual wage earner increasing privileges and to place him more nearly on an equality with his employer. Yet these privileges are available to him only so far as the state actually enforces them. We have seen that, in the case of factory legislation,[128] the early statutes assumed that the employee would initiate proceedings in court, with the aid of the ordinary officers of law, to enforce the safety and health laws. Not until many years had passed did the state provide special police, the factory inspectors, to relieve the laborer of this impossible obligation. So in these more fundamental

---
[126] Whitfield v. State of Ohio, 56 Sup. Ct. 532, 1936.
[127] Public No. 215, 74th Congress.
[128] See chap. viii, "Administration."

rights growing out of the labor contract the state leaves to the laborer the duty of realizing upon them through the ordinary means of prosecution in court.

Poverty, ignorance, and the technicalities of law often combine to set the remedies beyond his reach. "From birth to death," says a report of the New York Legal Aid Society,[129] "the poor man is the prey of a host of petty swindlers. He is educated to believe that justice is free, and he finds that, to get it, he must pay a lawyer a price he cannot afford." To realize justice he must appeal to charity. In countless individual cases, attorneys have given their aid without price, but it cannot be expected that they can meet the need without neglecting their regular clients. Yet without their aid the chance of the laborer's success in the legal battle is negligible.

The reports of legal aid societies are filled with cases of injustice that calls for an attorney. Wages are withheld. Pawnbrokers and "loan sharks" command usurious rates of interest on small loans, and compel their victims to sign papers, such as chattel mortgages and wage assignments, of whose contents they are ignorant. Wage exemption laws are nullified by garnishment proceedings brought against the employer to attach wages not yet paid. The laborer must then have an attorney to secure the release of his wages, and he may lose his position, for employers often make it a rule to discharge employees whose wages are garnisheed. Thus, even the threat of garnishment may serve not only to nullify his exemptions, but to force him to pay unjust claims out of wages not exempt. The foreign-born are a class especially exposed to fraud. The abuses of peonage, vagrancy laws, and the padrone system have already been mentioned.[130]

Against these invasions of their legal rights wage earners are for the most part helpless to defend themselves. The majority of their grievances involve small amounts which do not justify the employment of a lawyer. Besides, there are the initial court costs, such as fees for filing, fees for serving summonses and subpœnas and for attaching property, and fees to clerks of court in contested cases. To the man with a small claim the remedy may cost more than the result.

[129] *Thirty-eighth Annual Report*, 1913, p. 23.
[130] See "Peonage," p. 317; "Padrone System," p. 325.

INDIVIDUAL BARGAINING 363

1. **Private and Public Legal Aid.**—To remedy these abuses, private charity has found a large field. Legal aid societies have been organized in some sixty American cities in about thirty different states. Their object is "to render legal aid and assistance gratuitously to all who may appear worthy thereof, and who from poverty are unable to procure it."[131] The first was started by certain German merchants in New York in 1876 to help poor German immigrants, and was called the German Law Protection Society, but it soon extended its aid to others. In 1890 Arthur von Briesen, called the "father of the legal aid society movement," became president, and the name was changed to the Legal Aid Society of New York. The society has confined its work to wage earners, but without regard to nationality, race, or religion. The applicant must be one whose claim is too small or who is too poor to hire an attorney, a poor man being defined as one whose income may be just sufficient to maintain him, but not sufficient for extraordinary demands. It is the aim of the society to cooperate with and not to compete with other lawyers. Its attorneys are under agreement to have no other legal business and they are not permitted to recommend any particular attorney to applicants whom the society may reject. A case to be accepted must be unquestionably meritorious, and this is ascertained by investigation and an impartial hearing of both sides. Finally, the society makes every effort to settle cases out of court, and, up to the moment of trial, if a reasonable offer of settlement is made, advises its client to accept. The policy is to discourage litigation in such a way as to protect the rights of all. In 1935 there were only 1,256 cases taken to court out of a total of 28,601 cases handled.[132]

From New York, legal aid societies have spread throughout the United States and Europe. In 1933, fifty-six legal aid societies in the United States reported 331,970 new cases recorded during that year. Since its organization to 1936 the New York Society had collected $4,999,027 for its

[131] Legal Aid Society of Philadelphia, *Thirteenth Annual Report,* 1906, Constitution, Art. I, Sec. 2. For a general survey of legal aid, see Smith, R. H., and Bradway, J. S., "Growth of Legal Aid Work in the United States," U. S. Bureau of Labor Statistics, *Bulletin No. 607,* 1936.

[132] Sixtieth Annual *Report* of the Legal Aid Society of New York for the year 1935.

clients.[133] In the United States they are generally unincorporated voluntary associations, conducted by private individuals. In 1911 the first national conference of legal aid societies was held in Pittsburgh, thirteen of the forty organizations in the country being represented. The second was held in New York in 1912, with delegates from sixteen societies. At this time the National Association of Legal Aid Organizations was established, the objects being to give publicity to the work, to bring about cooperation and increased efficiency, and to encourage the formation of new societies.

The legal aid movement has flourished especially in Germany. There it has been developed extensively as a public function as well as by private organizations. In London, the "Poor Man's Lawyer's Association," with "centers" in settlements and missions, gives gratuitous legal advice to persons who cannot afford a solicitor, but does not furnish assistance in court.[134] It is sometimes objected that legal aid will encourage litigation, but the record of cases settled out of court by legal aid societies does not support this view.

So far, legal aid in the United States is almost entirely a private enterprise, and, excellent as has been the work, it is restricted to a few of the larger cities. Even there the work has been seriously hampered by lack of funds, a handicap repeatedly mentioned in the reports. There is, accordingly, an increasing demand that legal aid be made a function of government and thus put within the reach of all. Several attempts in this direction have been made in the United States. Kansas City, Mo., has the distinction of having created the first municipal free legal aid bureau in the United States. It was organized as a department under the board of public welfare, in 1910.[135] Los Angeles County, Cal., was the first to establish the office of public defender,[136] the duties in civil cases being the prosecution of actions for the collection of wages and other demands of persons who cannot afford counsel, in cases where the sum in-

[133] See *ibid.*
[134] See Gurney-Champion, F. C., *Justice and the Poor in England*, 1926.
[135] See Board of Public Welfare, Kansas City, Mo. *Reports.*
[136] Los Angeles County Charter, Sec. 23. This became effective July 1, 1913.

INDIVIDUAL BARGAINING

volved does not exceed $100. This officer also defends such persons in civil litigation when they are being unjustly harassed. Costs are paid from the county treasury. Similar officers were within the next few years appointed in half a dozen other cities, including Portland, Ore., and Minneapolis, Minn., while elsewhere, as in New York City, committees of "voluntary defenders" sprang up. Work of this nature is efficacious in obtaining justice and reducing its expense for the poor man. A plan has been worked out for the cooperation of students in the law school and the legal aid society in several of the larger cities, notably Chicago, whereby the students devote a definite portion of their training period to work in the legal clinic, which is generally under the direction of both the faculty of the law school and the Legal Aid Society. Under this plan, a larger volume of work may be handled by the society, and the students receive practical experience.

In several states labor departments have been given special powers to assist workers in collecting unpaid wage claims, and in other states labor departments have performed this function under the general wage payment laws.[137] California offers an outstanding example. Its Payment of Wages Act[138] provides for immediate payment of wages due to a discharged employee, and for payment within three days to an employee who quits unless he gives a three-days' notice, in which case wages are due immediately upon quitting. All other wages must be paid twice a month on regular pay days. If an employer willfully refuses to pay wages when due and payable, the law provides that as a penalty the wages of the employee shall continue at the same rate until paid, or until action is commenced, but in no case longer than thirty days. No employee who refuses or avoids payment is entitled to benefit under the act for such time as he avoids payment. Willful refusal to pay for labor, with intent to secure a discount, or to harass or defraud, constitutes a misdemeanor. The labor department, whose duty it is to enforce the act, is authorized to take assignments of wage claims and to prosecute actions on behalf of wage claimants.

[137] See "Work of State Labor Offices in Behalf of Wage Claimants," U. S. Bureau of Labor Statistics, *Monthly Labor Review,* October, 1933, pp. 776-790.
[138] California, Laws 1919, C. 202, as amended.

In 1932, no fewer than 35,400 claims for wages were filed with the department; 16,517 were settled, and a total of $775,254 collected. In 1934, New Jersey enacted a law[139] giving the state commissioner of labor power to investigate wage claims, with authority to summon defendants, subpœna witnesses and administer oaths. An award made by the commissioner after hearing, when filed with the appropriate court, becomes a judgment with the same effect as a judgment rendered by a court. A wage claim division was created in the labor department to administer the act.

In 1910, following the recommendation of a state immigration commission appointed to investigate the condition of aliens in the state, the legislature of New York created a bureau of industries and immigration subordinate to the department of labor, whose object was to give newly arrived immigrants a fair start. This was to be done by securing to aliens a hearing for complaints in their own language, the bureau to act as mediator in securing the enforcement of existing laws to prevent exploitation. This system of state legal aid for immigrants was extended to all wage earners in 1915. The industrial commissioner is required[140] to "cooperate with any employee in the enforcement of a just claim against his employer and for his protection against frauds and other improper practices on the part of any person public or private." This function is carried out through a special Bureau of Labor Welfare in the labor department.

Through the influence of Dean John H. Wigmore, the League of Nations has become interested in legal aid societies. A meeting was arranged in Geneva in 1924, to which was invited one expert from each of the following countries: America, England, Norway, Denmark, France, Italy, and Japan. Plans for taking care of international cases, i.e., where one party is a foreigner, and for coordinating the work of similar character being done in other countries, were discussed.[141] One result of this effort was the publication in 1927 by the League

[139] New Jersey, Laws 1934, C. 91.
[140] New York, Consolidated Laws, C. 78, Sec. 211.
[141] "International Arrangements for Legal Assistance for the Poor," *Legal Aid Review,* January, 1925.

INDIVIDUAL BARGAINING

of Nations of a compilation of all legal aid legislation and a list of practically all legal aid organizations in the world.[142]

2. **Industrial Courts.**—In Europe, a different type of legal aid has been evolved, taking the place not of the lawyer, but of the judge. This is the industrial court, or *conseil de prud'-hommes*. Industrial courts are special courts for the settlement of disputes arising out of labor contracts between employers and employees, and their purpose is "to settle by conciliation whenever possible and by legal judgment when conciliation fails, but in any event cheaply, quickly, and by means of a court composed in part or in whole of elected representatives of the two classes, all individual legal cases which arise from the relations of employer and employed."[143] The first industrial court was founded at Lyons, France, in 1806, for the silk industry. The law creating the Lyons court provided that similar courts might be established in all the factory cities of France, and accordingly their number has increased steadily. When the left bank of the Rhine in 1815, and Alsace-Lorraine in 1871, became German territory, the industrial courts were retained, and in 1890 a general law provided for their establishment throughout the empire. Industrial courts similar to the French were introduced in Belgium in 1859, while Austria followed in 1869, Italy in 1893, and Spain in 1908. In Switzerland, Geneva was the first canton to take up the idea, creating an industrial court on the French model in 1882. Systems of industrial courts have now been introduced in most European countries. In 1932, provision for such courts was made in Brazil.[144]

There are, in general, three types of industrial courts: (1) The French, in which only employers and workers are represented, and the number of members is even. (2) The German, in which the president is neither an employer nor a worker, and the number of members is odd. (3) The Swiss, which is an adaptation of the ordinary court, with the addition of special

[142] League of Nations, *Legal Aid for the Poor* (Publications, V, Legal, 1927, vol. vii).

[143] United States Bureau of Labor *Bulletin No. 98*, January, 1912; "Industrial Courts in France, Germany, and Switzerland," Helen L. Sumner, p. 273.

[144] International Labor Office, *Industrial and Labour Information*, March 20, 1933, pp. 339-340.

"assessors," or advisers, to the judge.[145] In all three types the employers and workmen are equally represented.

With respect to jurisdiction, a labor contract of some kind is essential, but the idea is interpreted to cover any relationship between wage givers and wage receivers. The great majority of cases are for wages due, but discharge without notice is also a frequent cause of complaint. By far the greater number of complaints are made by workers, mostly for small sums.

Conciliation being the chief object of industrial courts, the procedure is a radical departure from that of the ordinary court. Personal appearance of the parties is required, except for a good excuse, such as illness or absence from the city. In some countries lawyers are not permitted to take part in the proceedings, which are much less formal than in an ordinary court. Preliminary hearing for the purpose of conciliation before a section of the court is sometimes provided. A substantial proportion of the cases are settled by conciliation.

The salient advantages of the industrial courts are rapidity and cheapness. Cases are set for as early a hearing as possible after complaint, and only necessary delays are permitted. Expenses exceeding the fees collected are met by the municipalities over which the court has jurisdiction, or, in the case of courts with wider jurisdiction, by the state. In some cases there are no fees; in others the fees are low. Wherever established, industrial courts are held indispensable, the fact that no dispute is too insignificant for them being regarded as a special advantage.

No such institution exists in English-speaking countries.[146] In Great Britain the Arbitration Act of 1824 was designed to cover individual disputes, but the procedure was too intricate and costly ever to be applied. The "Councils of Conciliation" Act of 1867 permitted industrial courts like the French, but no true judicial tribunal was ever created under it. In the United States, a Pennsylvania law, enacted in 1883, attempted to establish a sort of industrial court, but none was ever created

[145] Some cantons have courts based on the French or the German model.

[146] See also "Intervention by Government," p. 429. The above description applies to industrial courts in their relation to the individual bargain. In some cases they also deal with the collective bargain.

INDIVIDUAL BARGAINING 369

and ten years later the law was repealed. The constitutions of New York and a few other states contain provisions for courts of voluntary arbitration, but no courts were ever established.

In the United States, the courts of small claims, as they are most often called, have developed along quite different lines. The first of these was the conciliation court of Cleveland, Ohio. It grew out of a provision in the Municipal Court Act, designating a clerk to assist persons unable to hire a lawyer in preparing and filing papers, and, if possible, to bring about a settlement. An experienced man was selected by the chief justice, and he often acted successfully as a mediator. All services were free. Since 1913, a conciliation branch of the court has been in operation. The costs to the litigant are small, averaging in 1933 approximately $1.50 per case. Lawyers are not prohibited from representing the parties, but their appearance is discouraged. No set procedure is required. Each party is allowed to state his case in his own way. When both sides have been heard, the judge must seek to effect an amicable adjustment of the differences between the parties. Ordinarily, he obtains their consent that he shall adjust the issue himself. The Cleveland court differs from the European industrial courts in that neither employers nor workmen are represented on the bench, the judge is not elected by the two classes, and the court does not confine itself to disputes arising out of the labor contract. It resembles them in that it is an authoritative tribunal, instead of being merely a private society, like the legal aid agencies of the United States. By 1934, small claims courts had been created by state law in sixteen states and by local action in four large cities in other states.[147]

To what extent it would be possible to apply the European industrial court system in the United States is as yet an open question. People have not awakened to the need, and they are not prepared for such a system by habits of organization and joint action of interests. It is improbable that industrial courts would be created generally by local initiative, as in France; and even if the system were made mandatory by the state govern-

---

[147] The states were California, Colorado, Connecticut, Idaho, Iowa, Kansas, Massachusetts, Minnesota, Nevada, New Jersey, New York, Oregon, Rhode Island, South Dakota, Utah, and Vermont. The cities were Chicago, Cleveland, Philadelphia, and Spokane.

ment, as in Germany, it would require a state agency to guide local governments in starting them.

VI. THE LABORER AS CITIZEN

1. **Voting.**—There is a growing tendency among the states to recognize the civil rights of the employee by providing holidays on election days, compelling time to be allowed employees to vote, and providing means for absent voting.

Forty states[148] and territories have declared that no employee shall be compelled to labor during the afternoon—and some include the whole day—upon which there is a general election in progress. Some states and territories have such a law applying to primary election days.

In line with election-day-holiday laws are those guaranteeing the exercise of the voting privilege. The majority of these laws provide that the employer must, upon prior notification, permit employees to leave the establishment some time between the opening and closing of the polls, for the purpose of voting, and that the employee shall not be subject to any penalty because of the exercise of the privilege. In Illinois the provision for absence was held valid, but the portion of the law providing that the employee should not be subject to penalty or deduction of wages was held unconstitutional on the ground that it was an unlawful attempt to regulate private contracts, that it was not a proper exercise of the police power, and that it was taking property without due process of law.[149] Twenty-three states and Alaska have laws upon this subject.[150]

Laws that probably originated in a desire to permit railroad employees to exercise their franchise right at some point most convenient for them, whether in their home precinct or not, have now become general. Although the labor aspect of these "absent voters" laws has been somewhat swallowed up,

---

[148] Every state and territory except Alaska, Connecticut, District of Columbia, Hawaii, Illinois, Maine, Massachusetts, Mississippi, Ohio, the Philippines, and Vermont.

[149] R. S. of 1917, C. 46, Sec. 312; People v. Chicago, Milwaukee and St. Paul Railway Company, 306 Ill. 486, 138 N. E. 155 (1923).

[150] Alaska, Arizona, Arkansas, California, Colorado, Illinois, Indiana, Iowa, Kansas, Kentucky, Maryland, Massachusetts, Minnesota, Missouri, Nebraska, Nevada, New Mexico, New York, Ohio, Oklahoma, South Dakota, Utah, West Virginia, Wyoming.

INDIVIDUAL BARGAINING

yet railroad and similar employees may still enjoy the benefits. A majority of the states permit all absent voters to vote by mail; some specifically indicate that their laws were enacted for employees of railroad companies and similar employees, while another group permit absent voting, but limit it to voting within the state itself. In these states the laws are more of the nature of labor legislation than in those which extend the law to other jurisdictions.[151]

Some effort has been made to protect the employee as a voter from coercion by the employer. More than three-fourths of the states have laws which in general provide that any employer who attempts by coercion, intimidation, or threats to discharge or to lessen the remuneration of an employee to influence his vote in any election, etc., is guilty of a misdemeanor and is liable to a fine. Some of the methods prohibited are solicitation of funds, printing political advertisements on the pay envelopes, or distributing printed matter carrying a threat of discharge unless a certain party or candidate is supported.[152]

2. **National Guard Duty.**—About one-third of the states have provided that members of the National Guard shall not be willfully obstructed in their business nor deprived of employment because of such membership.

---

[151] "Labor Laws of the United States with Decisions of Courts Relating Thereto," United States Bureau of Labor Statistics, *Bulletin No. 370.*
[152] Colorado, Acts 1923, Sec. 7830; Wisconsin, Statutes 1923, Sec. 1219.

CHAPTER VII

COLLECTIVE BARGAINING

COLLECTIVE BARGAINING IN THE LABOR FIELD MEANS THAT wage earners as a group, acting through their chosen representatives, bargain with one or more employers as to the wages, hours, and conditions under which they are to be employed.[1] Where a collective bargain is made, each individual worker is employed on the terms contained in that bargain. He virtually makes no individual bargain at all, unless through individual bargaining he is able to secure better terms than those contained in the collective bargain. Workers cannot bargain collectively unless they can choose representatives to bargain for them and unless the employer recognizes these representatives as such. Either the power to strike or the possibility of arbitration is an essential concomitant of collective bargaining. One or the other must be available as an alternative if no collective bargain can be reached. The significance of this potential alternative becomes apparent from an analysis of the bargaining process as it is carried on between individuals.

Bargaining rests on the power to withhold. When two individuals bargain, they know that if they cannot agree on the terms of an exchange, no exchange will occur. Or possibly a third party may step in and fix the terms on which the exchange is to be made. Under individual bargaining in the labor field, if the worker is not satisfied with the best terms the employer offers, he withholds his labor, i.e., he refuses the job or quits. Under collective bargaining, if the workers are not satisfied, either they must be in a position to withhold their labor collectively, that is, to strike; or a third party—presumably the government—must step in and impose terms of employment to be accepted by both workers and employers. The

[1] At the present time a single employer is rarely an "individual" except in a fictitious sense. Most employers are corporations. That is, they are really combinations of capitalists who bargain collectively through the corporation.

COLLECTIVE BARGAINING 373

possibility of a strike (or arbitration) is integral to the process of collective bargaining. A strike may in a sense be a step in that process. For a strike usually continues until one side or both are willing to accept terms which were unacceptable before the strike started. (A strike does not always produce a collective bargain, of course. It may fail completely and workers may go back to work as individuals, making individual bargains.)

Obviously, collective bargaining cannot take place unless the workers are organized in some kind of association—usually called a union. Only then can they select representatives to bargain in their behalf; only then can they be in a position to withhold or threaten to withhold their labor.

The need for collective bargaining arises from the serious discrepancy in "withholding power" between the individual employer and the individual wage earner, a discrepancy which tends to result in terms of employment highly oppressive to the worker and injurious to society in general. It is obvious that the individual laborer is at a great disadvantage in bargaining with an employer. The employer is usually a corporation, which is itself a combination of capital; but the disadvantage of the laborer is even more fundamental. Being propertyless, he has no opportunity to make a living except by working on the property of others. Having no resources to fall back upon, he cannot wait until he can drive the most favorable bargain. It is a case of the necessities of the laborer pitted against the resources of the employer.

The increasing size of the typical industrial concern and the spread of mass-production methods have enhanced the need for collective bargaining. For the larger the employer, the more the worker is at his mercy in bargaining as an individual as to his terms of employment. And the more automatic the machine, the less the need for skill in the man who tends it, and the weaker in consequence the economic position of the worker who applies for a job. Since anyone can learn to be a machine tender in a few days, if one man is not satisfied with the wage which is offered, another equally competent can probably be found who will be. Moreover, the constant displacement of men by machines tends to create a continuous oversupply of workers even at times when industry is expanding. And this oversupply weakens still further the bargaining position of the individual job seeker.

In short, today "individual bargaining" in any real sense cannot exist. In the absence of collective action, the inequality in withholding power between employer and employee is so great that the term bargaining is a misnomer as applied to the process by which wages and other terms of employment are arrived at. Only through organized group action by workers can equality in withholding power be even approximated.

1. Government and Collective Bargaining

1. **Attitudes Toward Collective Bargaining.**—Society's attitude toward collective bargaining expresses itself in law, both common and statute, and its enforcement through policemen, courts and administrative agencies. In its actual operation in the United States in recent years, the law of collective bargaining presents a complex and somewhat confused picture—a maze of varied statutes and conflicting court decisions, frequently clothed in legal verbiage which tends to conceal their real economic meaning. A comprehensive view of the situation may be facilitated by a preliminary analysis of the different attitudes which society acting through government can take toward collective bargaining. Roughly speaking, there are four such attitudes: (a) repression; (b) toleration; (c) encouragement; (d) intervention.[2] These terms require brief explanation.

a. *Repression.*—This attitude is only historically important in English-speaking countries. It means that organizations of workers designed to raise wages or improve conditions are treated as illegal conspiracies to be restricted or even prohibited. Strikes are severely restricted or forbidden.

b. *Toleration.*—This means that workers are allowed to organize and bargain collectively *if they can*. But employers are allowed to prevent such organization if they can, and to refuse to bargain collectively if they choose. It follows that while many of labor's activities in pursuit of these aims are legal,

[2] For a somewhat similar analysis of governmental attitudes toward collective bargaining, see Perlman, Selig, "The Principle of Collective Bargaining," in the *Annals of the American Academy of Political and Social Science*, March, 1936, pp. 156-158.

COLLECTIVE BARGAINING

not all of them are, for employers' rights must be protected too. Thus some strikes are legal, but not all strikes. This position is based on a *laissez-faire* philosophy. It is an attempt to maintain a "hands-off" attitude. Government is supposed to confine itself to policing, to protecting property rights and preventing violence.

In practical effect this attitude favors the employers who are trying to prevent the organization of labor unions and refusing to bargain collectively. For employers have physical property and intangible property rights which are capable of being protected both by the police and by the courts. The rights of the workers to organize and bargain collectively are rights which courts, even if they wished, have not known how to protect. Moreover, because the corporation is treated at law as a person, equal treatment by the law of individuals on both sides of the wage bargain leads to anomalous results. When the individual worker applies for a job, the corporation is a huge and powerful combination with which he is entirely powerless to "bargain." Yet the law has regarded it as individual like himself, who in the name of equality must be permitted to fire him for any or no reason, so long as he is free to quit for any or no reason.

c. *Encouragement.*—This means that collective bargaining is regarded as good public policy to be encouraged by government. Unions and efforts to organize them are legal. Strikes are legal, but not necessarily all strikes. More than that, government assumes the duty of protecting workers against interference with their right to organize and bargain collectively. Such protection involves restrictions on employers who seek to prevent organization or refuse to meet with the chosen representatives of their workers. This governmental attitude probably cannot be made effective without an administrative agency to protect the worker in the exercise of rights and liberties which are not susceptible of protection by courts or police. But the existence of such an agency does not involve any limitation on the right to strike. If no collective bargain can be arrived at, the strike may still be resorted to.

d. *Intervention.*—This means that collective bargaining is encouraged by government, but if no agreement can be reached, the government intervenes to adjust the dispute and prevent a strike. If even with government help no collective bargain can be arrived at, the government itself settles the terms and conditions of employment. This in the final stage is compulsory arbitration. It substitutes government action for the resort to a trial of economic strength through the strike. Compulsory arbitration rests on two assumptions: (1) that strikes are a kind of warfare and arbitration the peaceful and orderly way of adjudicating disputes; (2) that the public has a right to interfere because it has a paramount interest in the uninterrupted operation of the industrial machine.

Repression of collective bargaining is no longer practiced in any English-speaking country. *Toleration* may be said to characterize the attitude prevailing in this country before 1933; *encouragement* the attitude under New Deal legislation;[3] *intervention* is exemplified in Australasia. How these attitudes have expressed themselves in laws and court decisions is the content of the following pages.

2. **Government Agencies Affecting Collective Bargaining.**—In the United States, government impinges in various ways on labor's struggle to secure and maintain collective bargaining. All the branches of government play a part—the executive, the legislature, the courts, and sometimes special administrative agencies.

Theoretically, the executive merely carries out the law as written. Actually, persons in executive positions exercise considerable discretion, and their attitude toward collective bargaining and activities in connection therewith often makes more differences than statutes or court decisions. Mayors and governors are important elements in public opinion. They may exert pressure on employers to accept arbitration in case of strike. The attitude of the police, particularly in time of strike, may be even more important. "Intimidation" and even violence are terms susceptible of widely varying interpretation. If the police are friendly—if their attitude is one of "encouraging" collective bargaining rather than merely "tolerating" it—they let strikers and pickets do things which in another city would

[3] This is a rough statement. The Railway Labor Act of 1926 and the Norris-La Guardia Act of 1932 were in some respects precursors of the New Deal in this field. For further discussion on this point see below, pp. 419 ff.

COLLECTIVE BARGAINING 377

lead to speedy arrests for obstructing traffic, inciting to violence, or what not. It is possible that, by and large, what the executive arm of government does during a strike (which depends only in part on acts of the legislature and decisions of the courts) is the most important expression of the government's attitude toward labor's struggle.

Statutes enacted by legislatures are important in defining the rights and liberties of employers and workers. They modify the common law on this subject built up by court decisions. A statute may be passed in the interest of employers, to enhance their common law rights and liberties and restrict those of workers. Or it may be passed in the interest of the workers, to enhance their rights and liberties at the expense of employers. Finally, a statute may affect not directly the substantive rights of workers or employers but the procedures through which courts enforce these rights.

The courts are in many respects the dominant branch of government so far as the law of collective bargaining is concerned. In the first place, much of that body of law has never been formulated in statutes, but has been built up through a long line of court decisions. Moreover, even where a statute is involved, the courts still must exercise a wide discretion in applying it to a specific situation. Statutes in this field are necessarily general in their terms. It is their interpretation by the courts which may determine whether they actually encourage collective bargaining or the reverse. Where the rights of employers and workers are in conflict, courts must decide the issue. Finally, the courts exercise ultimate control through their power to invalidate statutes. A number of very important statutes affecting the law of collective bargaining have been declared unconstitutional.[4]

The procedures through which courts enforce the law of collective bargaining are three: (a) prosecutions; (b) damage suits; (c) injunctions. Workers (or, much less frequently, employers) may be prosecuted by the government for viola-

[4] Anti-discrimination statutes in Adair v. U. S., 208 U. S. 161, 28 Sup. Ct. 277 (1908); anti-yellow-dog statutes in Coppage v. Kansas, 236 U. S. 1, 35 Sup. Ct. 240 (1915); anti-injunction statutes in Truax v. Corrigan, 257 U. S. 312; 42 Sup. Ct. 124 (1921); compulsory arbitration in Wolff Packing Co. v. Court of Industrial Relations, 262 U. S. 522, 43 Sup. Ct. 630 (1923); 267 U. S. 552, 45 Sup. Ct. 441 (1925).

tions of criminal law, with possible penalties of fine or imprisonment. Or employers may sue individual workers or unions for damages for wrongs done to them.[5] Employers (or, less frequently, unions) may secure injunctions prohibiting specified unlawful conduct—usually in connection with a strike. Of these three forms of procedure, prosecutions are by far the most numerous and probably on the whole have had the most effect on the success or failure of strikes. But injunctions have received much more attention both from labor and from students of the subject. It is the use of injunctions in labor disputes against which organized labor has protested vehemently and sought legislative protection.[6]

Administrative or quasi-judicial agencies may also be used in translating government attitudes toward collective bargaining into action. These agencies play the dominant rôle where government *intervenes* in labor disputes. Australasia has a variety of such agencies known as conciliation boards, arbitration courts, etc. They are also important, possibly indispensable, where government seeks to *encourage* collective bargaining. As discussed in a subsequent section, Section 7a of the National Industrial Recovery Act[7] and the National Labor Relations Act[8] necessarily involved the functioning of administrative agencies. The rights embodied in these statutes could not be enforced without the use of administrative agencies.

To add to this complicated picture of the ways in which government impinges on collective bargaining, it must be remembered that in the United States we have a dual system of government—federal and state—with local governing units besides. The executive which affects a given situation may be federal, state or local. And federal and state statutes both play a part, and sometimes local ordinances as well. A number of federal statutes have had an important effect on collective bargaining—the Sherman and Clayton Anti-Trust Acts,[9] the Nor-

[5] Suits by workers against employers are rare.
[6] For a further discussion of the different forms of court procedure and their use in enforcing the law of collective bargaining, see below, pp. 411-417.
[7] 48 U. S. Stat. at Large 198 (1933), 15 U. S. C. A., Sec. 707 (a).
[8] 49 U. S. Stat. at Large 457 (1935), 29 U. S. C. A., Secs. 151-166.
[9] 26 U. S. Stat. at Large 209 (1890), 15 U. S. C. A., Secs. 1-7; and 38 U. S. Stat. at Large 730 (1914), 29 U. S. C. A., Sec. 52.

COLLECTIVE BARGAINING 379

ris-La Guardia Act,[10] the famous 7a of the National Industrial Recovery Act,[11] the new National Labor Relations Act,[12] and a long series of acts relating to railway labor.[13]

In the application of these statutes the federal courts, of course, decide many cases involving collective bargaining. In addition, many cases unrelated to these statutes are tried in the federal courts, for under the federal Constitution diversity of citizenship between the parties can bring a case into a federal court.[14] So where a concern has its factory in one state and is incorporated in another, the litigation growing out of a labor dispute is frequently carried on in the federal courts. The workers are citizens of one state, the corporation a citizen of another. Federal administrative agencies also have an important place in the collective bargaining picture.

Thus society's attitude toward collective bargaining is expressed through a complex of agencies. It follows, perhaps inevitably, that its attitude is not always a self-consistent whole. The different agencies may even express divergent attitudes. Moreover, the law of collective bargaining differs from state to state and even the court decisions in a single state are sometimes difficult to reconcile. Consequently it is very difficult to make general statements as to what the law is on any given point. In the following pages we shall attempt to sketch the law of collective bargaining in the United States: (1) its evolution; (2) as it prevailed before the New Deal; and (3) as it stands at the present writing. By way of contrast we shall describe briefly the attitude of government intervention in action, as practiced in a limited field in the United States and as fully developed in Australasia.

II. Evolution of the Law of Collective Bargaining in the United States

1. Origin of Collective Bargaining.—In a broad sense, collective bargaining may be said to date back as far as individual bargaining. Its first examples in England are town charters and

---

[10] 47 U. S. Stat. at Large 70 (1932), 29 U. S. C. A., Secs. 101-115.
[11] 48 U. S. Stat. at Large 198 (1933), 15 U. S. C. A., Sec. 707 (a).
[12] 49 U. S. Stat. at Large 457 (1935), 29 U. S. C. A., Secs. 151-166.
[13] For references to these statutes see pp. 385-387, 415, 423-429.
[14] U. S. Const., Art III, Sec. 2, Clause 1.

merchant gilds. The townspeople through a collective contract secured certain rights from the king in return for a money payment. Among these rights none was more valuable than the doctrine, "City air makes free." Under this doctrine if a serf had been in a free city for a year he became a free man. Thus freedom was established through collective bargaining; until freedom was attained there could be no individual contracts. Historically, then, individual and collective bargaining have been interdependent; the one was necessary to maintain the other.

Yet collective bargaining for a long time was viewed with suspicion. All associations were treated as conspiracies. They were much more powerful than individuals, and hence were considered dangerous. Collective bargaining meant interference with free bargaining by individuals—both the individual members of the organization and non-members. So collective action was permitted in early law only under grant of a special charter from the king. Thus the king granted charters to free citizens, and to merchant and craft gilds. Armed with a charter, the association could not be prosecuted as a conspiracy, and was conceded the great privilege of acting as a unit with continuous existence through the right of succession.

Of these early associations, the craft gilds were the nearest approach to the trade unions of today; yet their functions were very different. They were composed of three classes: the masters, the journeymen, and the apprentices. The masters and the journeymen worked side by side, with the same tools. It was easy for an apprentice to become first a journeyman, then a master. Hence the relations of the masters to the journeymen and apprentices received but little attention in the charters which created gilds. The *wage bargain* which the master made with the journeyman and the apprentice was as yet not a matter of public concern. The public was interested primarily in the other bargaining function of the masters—their merchant function, the making of the *price bargain* with consumers. The consumers dominated the government; and it was their concern to prevent extortionate prices and the substitution of "bad ware."[15]

[15] See Commons, John R., *Labor and Administration,* 1913, "American Shoemakers," pp. 219 ff.

COLLECTIVE BARGAINING

With the gradual expansion of markets, the merchants gained recognition in society. Charters were granted to the merchant adventurers who risked their capital in foreign enterprises, and patents of monopoly were granted to merchants in the domestic trade. Later came the special charters to banks, canal, turnpike and railway companies and other companies. Thus the right of association was granted to capital. With freedom from the taint of conspiracy, the company charter conferred upon the incorporators the privilege of "limited liability." Each of them was liable usually only to the extent of his subscription or stock. This was in contrast to the partnership where each member was responsible to the full extent of his resources for the contracts and torts of the partnership.

At first, incorporation could be secured only through special act of the legislative body. Finally, in the middle years of the nineteenth century, general incorporation laws were enacted in England and most of the states of the United States. It is now the privilege of all persons to combine their capital and form corporations with but few restrictions. So complete is the right of association of capitalists that the law has introduced the fiction that corporations are persons, entitled to many of the advantages of natural persons—with important consequences in relation to collective bargaining between employers and labor, as we shall see in the following pages. Collective action by capital has not stopped with the corporation. The corporations have themselves become members of associations which act collectively in many ways.

Labor did not win the right of collective bargaining as early as capital. When in the eighteenth century in England the laborers combined to enforce their demands for higher wages, they were prosecuted for "conspiracy." In the journeyman tailors' case,[16] for example, all combinations to raise wages were held to be conspiracies. This case was followed by the enactment of statutes to penalize combinations to raise wages. In 1824 and 1825 these statutes were repealed and a considerable degree of freedom to combine was conceded to labor.[17] In 1871 trade unions were declared not to be illegal combinations in

---

[16] 8 Mod. 10, 88 Eng. Reprint 9 (1721).
[17] Combination Act, 5 Geo. 4, C. 95, and Combination Act, 6 Geo. 4, C. 129.

382   PRINCIPLES OF LABOR LEGISLATION

restraint of trade.[18] In 1875 labor was entirely freed from the conspiracy law in its criminal aspects.[19] Finally, in 1906 the law of civil conspiracy was also swept away, and the trade unions were conceded complete exemption from the responsibility for damages growing out of tortious acts alleged to have been committed in their behalf.[20]

2. Development of Law in the United States.—In the United States, also, prosecutions for "conspiracy" often followed the early strikes for higher wages. In the indictment or in the charge to the jury in some of these cases, there was presented the doctrine of the common law that all combinations of workingmen, including even those to raise wages, are illegal.[21] This was never unchallenged law in the United States, and in only one case did a court of final jurisdiction hold this view.[22] Yet it was considered that there was something unlawful about combinations of laborers. They were denounced as being injurious to the public because they were injurious to employers and made it difficult for them to compete in distant markets. Naturally the journeymen looked upon all of these cases as prosecutions brought by the masters to resist increases of wages. This was undoubtedly the real motive of the prosecution; but in most of these cases the restrictive rules and practices of the unions were emphasized, not the effort to raise wages.

In the earliest cases the juries always convicted; but as unions became more frequent public sentiment ceased to regard them with alarm. In nearly all conspiracy cases of the eighteen-thirties the juries acquitted, although in most of them the defendants were guilty of conduct which would now be described as "intimidation." As a climax, the Massachusetts Supreme Court, in the famous case of Commonwealth v.

[18] Trade Union Act, 34 and 35 Vict., C. 31.
[19] Conspiracy and Protection Act, 38 and 39 Vict., C. 86.
[20] Trade Disputes Act, 6 Edw. 7, C. 47. For a good history of the law of collective bargaining in England, see Hedges, R. Y., and Winterbottom, A., *The Legal History of Trade Unionism*, 1930; and Slesser, H. H., and Baker, C., *Trade Union Law*, 1921.
[21] For these early cases, see *Documentary History of American Industrial Society*, vols. iii and iv.
[22] People v. Fisher, 14 Wendell 9, N. Y. (1835).

COLLECTIVE BARGAINING 383

Hunt in 1842,[23] held that even a strike for the closed shop is lawful.

For two decades thereafter there were few unions and few strikes. With the revival of unionism in the 'sixties, however, prosecution for conspiracy again became quite frequent. In these cases there were many convictions and not a few severe sentences. This led to a demand by the labor organizations of the day for "the repeal of the conspiracy laws," and to the enactment of laws in several of the industrial states which expressly legalized combinations of workingmen to raise wages or to reduce hours of labor.[24] Despite these statutes, however, criminal prosecutions for conspiracy continued to be quite frequent until about 1890, and thereafter ceased to be of much importance only because injunctions had become the most usual form of action in labor disputes.

The development of the law of labor combinations in this country thus differed radically from that of England. In England all combinations of workingmen were at the outset regarded as criminal conspiracies, but by parliamentary enactments labor has been freed entirely from the restrictions of the conspiracy doctrine. In the United States the early English doctrine that combinations to raise wages are unlawful was never generally accepted as good law. On the other hand, labor in this country never gained complete relief from the conspiracy doctrine.

For many years the tendency in this country, with but rare exceptions, was toward increasing restrictions upon the activities of labor unions in their combats with employers and employers' associations. This tendency was particularly pronounced during the 'eighties and early 'nineties. During this period, boycotts were first condemned as unlawful, strikes for many different purposes fell under the ban of the courts, and anti-trust laws were applied to the acts of labor unions. Most important, however, was the gradual identification of "business" with "property." "Good will," by which is meant the established relationships of a going business, had been recognized

---
[23] Commonwealth *v.* Hunt, 4 Metcalf 111, 45 Mass. 111 (1842).
[24] See Oakes, *Organized Labor and Industrial Conflicts* (1927). ʞ Mass. General Laws, 1932, C. 180, Sec. 15 (enacted 1888). New Jersey Compiled Statutes, 1910, Sec. 128, p. 3051 (enacted 1883). Wisconsin Statutes, 133.04 (enacted 1893).

as property at an earlier date. Not until this period, however, did the courts recognize as property, also, the right *to enter or do business,* by which is meant unhindered access to the commodity and labor markets.[25]

This right *to do business* is of great importance in labor disputes. Strikers may attack the physical property of employers; but the police, the military, and the criminal laws are usually adequate to deal with this menace. But without any destruction of physical property the employer's business may be ruined. Picketing may prevent his getting new employees, and boycotting may keep him from selling his products. While the modern manufacturer can often survive the destruction of his physical property, obstruction of access to the labor market or to the commodity market brings with it certain ruin.

The recognition of "business" as "property" ushered in the era of injunctions in labor disputes. Injunctions were sought primarily to protect the expectancies which are embraced in the right *to do business.* In fact, nobody thought of injunctions in connection with labor disputes until these expectancies were recognized as property.

The first injunction was issued in either 1883 or 1884; but not until the Debs case, ten years later,[26] did the public generally know anything about the use of injunctions in labor disputes. After that, the injunction was the legal remedy most usually sought by employers when menaced by strikes or boycotts. Much of the distrust of the courts and the bitterness manifested by workingmen in labor disputes arose from the use of injunctions. For many years organized labor made relief from "government by injunctions" its foremost legislative demand. Injunctions probably hurt labor less than was generally represented and certainly often proved disappointing to employers; but as a source of friction and as a cause of complaint they ranked among the most serious of problems in industrial relations.

In 1908 organized labor was suddenly aroused to a new

[25] See Duplex Printing Press Co. *v.* Deering, 254 U. S. 443, 465, 41 Sup. Ct. 172 (1921); Truax *v.* Corrigan, 257 U. S. 312, 42 Sup. Ct. 124 (1921); also Holmes' dissent in Truax *v.* Corrigan on page 342. See also Commons, John R., *Legal Foundations of Capitalism,* 1924 pp. 17-18.

[26] *In re* Debs, 158 U. S. 564, 15 Sup. Ct. 900 (1895).

COLLECTIVE BARGAINING

menace which, at that time, appeared even more serious than the injunction and the conspiracy doctrine. This was the damage suit and the Sherman Anti-Trust Act.[27] The occasion for this alarm was a decision rendered by the United States Supreme Court in the Danbury Hatters' case,[28] in which a hat manufacturer was allowed in excess of $200,000 damages for losses sustained through an interstate boycott of his goods. This decision was based upon the Sherman Anti-Trust Act, particularly the section allowing treble damages to anyone injured through an illegal restraint of trade.

The Sherman Anti-Trust Act was passed in 1890, and at the time of its passage was generally thought to have no application to labor unions or their activities.[29] Almost immediately thereafter, however, this act was held applicable to labor disputes, and as early as 1900 the American Federation of Labor sought legislation to exempt labor unions from its provisions. Not until the decision in the Danbury Hatters' case, however, was the situation regarded as really serious. Then a great fear arose that the Sherman Act might be construed as rendering unlawful labor unions and all their activities. No case actually went this far, but labor lost no time in fighting vigorously for "relief from the anti-trust laws."

Labor believed it had won such relief when Congress in 1914 passed the Clayton Act.[30] Section 6 of this act declared that "labor of a human being is not a commodity or article of commerce," and provided that the anti-trust laws should not be construed to forbid the existence of labor organizations, or to restrain their members from carrying out the "legitimate objects" thereof.

Through this same act, organized labor at the time believed it had won, also, relief from injunctions, as far as the federal courts were concerned. This hope was based principally upon Section 20 of the Clayton Act, which provides that no injunction shall prohibit the quitting of work, the refusal to patronize, peaceful picketing or peaceful persuasion, whether these acts

[27] 26 U. S. Stat. at Large 209 (1890), 15 U. S. C. A., Secs. 1-7.
[28] Loewe v. Lawlor, 208 U. S. 274, 28 Sup. Ct. 301 (1908).
[29] For a thorough analysis of whether or not Congress intended the Sherman Act to apply to labor, see Berman, Edward, *Labor and the Sherman Act*, Harpers, 1930.
[30] 38 U. S. Stat. at Large 730 (1914), 29 U. S. C. A., Sec. 52.

386 PRINCIPLES OF LABOR LEGISLATION

are done "singly or in concert," and, further, that these acts shall not be considered "violations of any law of the United States." Hardly less important did labor consider the provisions allowing jury trial to persons accused of violations of injunctions through acts indictable as criminal offenses.[31]

Even before the Clayton Act was passed by Congress, organized labor began a drive to secure similar legislation in all states. Nine state "anti-injunction" laws were secured, most of them modeled on the labor provisions of the Clayton Act.[32]

In actual operation, however, both the Clayton Act and the state anti-injunction laws proved very disappointing to labor. The Clayton Act did not exempt labor from the anti-trust laws, and there were at least as many successful prosecutions of workingmen under these laws after its passage as before.[33] Similarly, the Clayton Act failed to bring about either a reduction in the number of injunctions issued by the federal courts or the elimination of sweeping and drastic clauses.[34] Both Sections 6 and 20, in fact, which labor regarded as the most im-

[31] 38 U. S. Stat. at Large 730, Secs. 21 and 22.

[32] Arizona, Laws Second Special Session, 1913, C. 41; Illinois, Acts 1925, S. B. 442; Kansas, Laws 1913, C. 233; Massachusetts, Laws 1914, C. 778; Minnesota, Laws 1917, C. 493; New Jersey, Laws 1925, C. 169; North Dakota, Laws 1919, C. 171; Utah, Laws 1917, C. 68; Wisconsin, Laws 1919, C. 211, Laws 1923, C. 208. In addition, two states in 1913 passed laws intended to legalize peaceful persuasion: Massachusetts, Laws 1913, C. 690; New Hampshire, Acts 1913, C. 211. A similar act was passed in Wisconsin in 1923 (C. 55).

[33] U. S. v. Norris, 255 Fed. 423 (1918); Boyle v. U. S. 259 Fed. 803 (1919); Belfi v. U. S., 259 Fed. 822 (1919); U. S. v. Bricklayers' Union, 4 *Law and Labor* 95 (1922); Curran Printing Co. v. Printing Council, 5 *Law and Labor* 91 (1923); O'Brien v. U. S., 290 Fed. 185 (1923); Vandell v. U. S., 6 Fed. (2d) 188 (1925); Coronado Coal Co. v. United Mine Workers, 268 U. S. 295, 45 Sup. Ct. 551 (1925).

[34] Nearly 300 injunctions were issued by federal courts during the railroad shop crafts' strike in 1922 (address of U. S. Senator George W. Pepper to the American Bar Association on "Injunctions in Labor Disputes" (1924). This was undoubtedly the largest number of injunctions issued in connection with any single strike. One of the injunctions issued during this strike, procured at the instance of Attorney-general Daugherty from Judge Wilkerson at Chicago (U. S. v. Railway Employees' Dept., 283 Fed. 479 [1922], 290 Fed. 978 [1923]) was one of the most sweeping and one of the most criticized of injunctions ever allowed in this country.

portant in the Clayton Act, were construed as having made no change in the law as previously interpreted by the courts.[35] Only the sections relating to jury trial, in cases where the act constituting the contempt is also a criminal offense, made any change in the law. Doubt existed whether these sections were constitutional, but they were upheld in 1924.[36]

As for the state "anti-injunction" laws, they proved of no greater value than the Clayton Act. In most states they were narrowly construed; and when the Arizona Supreme Court gave a broad construction to the law of that state, the United States Supreme Court in Truax v. Corrigan held that, as thus interpreted, this act violated the Fourteenth Amendment.[37]

The American Federation of Labor had hailed the Clayton Act as "Labor's Magna Charta" and "Bill of Rights." In its convention of 1925, however, it frankly acknowledged that this act had fallen far short of its expectations. In that year it started a campaign to secure a new federal statute to restrict the issuance of injunctions in labor disputes by the federal courts. This campaign finally bore fruit in the Norris-La Guardia Act, passed in 1932.[38]

Another type of law passed in many states to protect the rights of labor was invalidated by the courts. Beginning in the 'nineties, a large number of states passed statutes forbidding employers to discriminate against union members either by discharging them for this reason or by using "yellow-dog" contracts—that is, by requiring as a condition of employment that workers sign individual agreements not to join a union while employed.[39] A federal provision forbidding railroads to discharge men for union affiliations[40] was declared unconstitutional by the United States Supreme Court in 1908,[41] and a state statute prohibiting under penalty the use of yellow-dog con-

---

[35] American Steel Foundries Co. v. Tri-city Central Trades Council, 257 U. S. 184, 42 Sup. Ct. 72 (1921); Duplex Printing Press Co. v. Deering, 254 U. S. 443, 41 Sup. Ct. 172 (1921).
[36] Michaelson v. U. S., 266 U. S. 42, 45 Sup. Ct. 18 (1924).
[37] Truax v. Corrigan, 257 U. S. 312, 42 Sup. Ct. 124 (1921).
[38] 47 U. S. Stat. at Large 70 (1932); 29 U. S. C. A., Secs. 101-115. This act is discussed below; see p. 415.
[39] For a list of states and citations to statutes, see below, pp. 405-407.
[40] Erdman Act of 1898, 30 U. S. Stat. at Large 424.
[41] Adair v. U. S., 208 U. S. 161, 28 Sup. Ct. 277 (1908).

tracts received the same treatment in 1915.[42] These decisions were based on the legal theory that workers and employers must be treated with formal "equality" by the law. The Supreme Court held that as long as the worker was free to quit for any or no reason the employer must be free to fire him for any or no reason. The court entirely ignored the effect of these decisions in denying to government the power to protect the workers' legal right to organize. Beginning in Wisconsin in 1929, a new type of anti-yellow-dog legislation was passed in a good number of states, and a similar provision was included in the Norris-La Guardia Act.[43]

III. THE LAW OF COLLECTIVE BARGAINING IN THE UNITED STATES BEFORE THE NEW DEAL

The law of collective bargaining consists of the rights and liberties of employers and workers (derived from common law or statutes) which government agencies will protect from infringement. As previously noted, the law varies considerably from state to state, and even within a given state the decisions of the courts are sometimes difficult to reconcile. In this section an attempt is made to describe briefly the law of collective bargaining as it stood just before the advent of the New Deal. In many respects the law today stands unchanged. In others, if the National Labor Relations Act is upheld by the courts, it has been substantially altered.

The law of collective bargaining will be analyzed under two main heads, the rights of labor and the rights of employers.

1. **The Rights of Labor**: a. *The Right to Organize.*—Everywhere in the United States labor is accorded the right to organize (if it can) into permanent combinations known as trade unions or labor unions.[44] Labor unions are not only

[42] Coppage v. Kansas, 236 U. S. 1, 35 Sup. Ct. 240 (1915).
[43] For a fuller discussion of yellow-dog contracts and the new legislation relating thereto, see below, p. 407.
[44] This statement applies to "regular" unions, i.e., those affiliated with the American Federation of Labor, the railroad unions and other independent non-communist unions. It does not apply to revolutionary or communist or I. W. W. unions. These have come under the ban of anti-syndicalism statutes. Such statutes have been frequently held to be constitutional. Representative cases are: Gitlow v. People of New York, 268 U. S. 652, 45 Sup. Ct. 625 (1925); Whitney v. California, 274

COLLECTIVE BARGAINING 389

lawful.[45] They have to some extent been favored and protected by statutes. Many states have laws to protect union labels, union cards, and union funds.[46] The legal status of unions is very similar to that of fraternal organizations. They cannot be compelled to admit anyone to membership.[47] They may settle disputes between the members on questions of policy, discipline or internal government, so long as the government of the society is fairly and honestly administered in conformity with its laws and the laws of the land, and no property rights or civil rights are involved. And even when property or civil rights are involved, members must first exhaust their remedies within the organizations before the courts will give them relief.[48]

As regards their internal affairs, labor organizations have thus been very free and unrestricted. When it comes to their outside activities, their rights have naturally tended to come into conflict with the rights of others, either employers or non-unionists. Hence government has necessarily taken a far more active part.

b. *The Right to Bargain Collectively.*—The right to bargain collectively (if employers are willing) and to make collective agreements, usually known as "trade agreements," is everywhere recognized. As for the attitude of the courts toward such agreements, some courts regard them not as contracts but as "usages" which are assumed to be incorporated in every individual contract between members of the parties to the collective bargain.[49] In recent years more courts have regarded trade

---

U. S. 357, 47 Sup. Ct. 641 (1927); State *v.* Hennessy, 114 Wash. 351, 195 Pac. 211 (1921); People *v.* Steelik, 187 Cal. 361, 203 Pac. 78 (1921); State *v.* Kassay, 126 Ohio St. 177, 184 N. E. 521 (1932).

[45] Hitchman Coal & Coke Co. *v.* Mitchell, 202 Fed. 512 (1912), *reversed* as to point that the United Mine Workers of America was an unlawful organization, in 245 U. S. 229, 38 Sup. Ct. 65 (1917).

[46] Representative of laws protecting union labels and the union name are: Mass. Gen. Laws 1932, Ch. 266, Secs. 69, 71, 72; New York, McKinney's Consolidated Laws, V. 5, Labor Law, Secs. 15, 16.

[47] For an excellent discussion of the rights of labor unions in selecting their own membership, see Mayer, *et al., v.* Journeymen Stone-Cutters' Ass'n, *et al.,* 47 N. J. Eq. 519, 20 Atl. 492 (1890).

[48] Stivers *v.* Blethen, 124 Wash. 473, 476, 215 Pac. 7, 8 (1923); Crisler *v.* Crum, *et al.,* 115 Neb. 375, 213 N. W. 366 (1927).

[49] Hudson *v.* Cincinnati, etc., Ry. Co., 152 Ky. 711, 154 S. W. 47

agreements as enforceable contracts. Damages have seldom or never been recovered by either party against the other for breach of such agreements, but individual workers have recovered under such contracts as "third-party beneficiaries."[50] Injunctions have frequently been granted to compel observance of trade agreements by employers or unions.[51]

c. *The Right to Strike.*—But what if no agreement can be reached without a trial of economic strength? Have laborers the unqualified right to quit work collectively in an effort to force the employer to accede to their terms? The courts in the United States have held that the legality of strikes is not unqualified.[52] It depends on the purpose for which the strike is called. The rule most generally applied is that when the purpose of the strikers is primarily to injure the employer or nonunion workmen the strike is illegal. The Massachusetts Supreme Court has best stated this rule:[53]

To justify interference with the rights of others the strikers must in good faith strike for a purpose which the court decides to be a legal justification for such interference. . . . A strike is not a strike for a legal purpose because the strikers struck in good faith for a purpose which they thought was a sufficient justification for a strike. As we have said, to make a strike legal, the purpose of the

(1913); Gregg v. Starks, 188 Ky. 834, 224 S. W. 459 (1920); Moody v. Model Window Glass Co., 145 Ark. 197, 224 S. W. 436 (1920), 150 Ark. 142, 233 S. W. 1092 (1921). See Rice, William G., Jr., "Collective Labor Agreements in American Law," 44 *Harv. L. Rev.* 572, 581-593 (1931).

[50] Wages were recovered by individuals in Blum & Co. v. Landau, 23 Ohio App. 426, 155 N. E. 154 (1926); Yazoo & M. V. R. Co. v. Sideboard, 161 Miss. 4, 133 So. 669 (1931).

[51] Gulla v. Barton, 164 App. Div. 293, 149 N. Y. Supp. 952 (1914); Tracey v. Osborne, 226 Mass. 25, 114 N. E. 959 (1917); Schlesinger v. Quinto, 201 App. Div. 487, 194 N. Y. Supp. 401 (1922); Goyette v. Watson Co., 245 Mass. 577, 140 N. E. 285 (1923); Metzler v. Kaminer, 131 Misc. 813, 227 N. Y. Supp. 459 (1927); Ribner v. Racso Co., 135 Misc. 616, 238 N. Y. Supp. 132 (1929); Weber v. Nasser, 286 Pac. 1074 (Cal. App. 1930); Suttin v. Unity Button Works, Inc., 144 Misc. 784, 258 N. Y. Supp. 863 (1932). Trade agreements have been accorded greater effectiveness in some foreign countries. See Rice, William G., *op. cit.,* note on pp. 575-581.

[52] The only state in which all strikes are accounted lawful is California. See Parkinson Co. v. Building Trade Council, 154 Cal. 581, 98 Pac. 1027 (1908).

[53] De Minico v. Craig, 207 Mass. 593, 598, 94 N. E. 317, 319 (1911).

COLLECTIVE BARGAINING 391

strike must be one which the court, as a matter of law, decides is a legal purpose of a strike, and the strikers must have acted in good faith in striking for such a purpose.

What purposes do the courts regard as legal justification for striking? Higher wages and shorter hours are accepted in all states as legal purposes, and strikes undertaken to secure them are everywhere regarded as lawful.[54] But many strikes are not carried on primarily or solely for these ends. Along with wage and hour demands there is frequently the demand for the closed shop; or groups of workers may carry on sympathetic strikes to help other groups gain their ends—perhaps by refusing to work on non-union material. Strikes for such purpose have frequently been the subject of court action and the courts of different states have taken different positions as to their legality.

d. *Closed-shop Strikes.*—A closed shop means that the employer agrees to employ only union members. Unions justify their demand for a closed shop on two grounds: (1) They allege that only workers who support the union financially and otherwise are entitled to the benefits which it secures. (2) They insist that if the shop remains open to non-unionists collective bargaining will be endangered. For the union will be seriously weakened, both because workers will not feel the need of retaining membership, and, perhaps more important, because the employer will be able imperceptibly to discriminate in favor of non-unionists, and thus eventually be able with impunity to break the collective agreement or refuse to renew it. In order, then, to maintain the wages and hours won through union effort, many unions seek to achieve the closed shop.

On the legality of strikes carried on for this purpose the courts have diverged widely. In Massachusetts strikes for the closed shop have frequently been condemned.[55] Agreements

---

[54] For an exhaustive citation of authorities relative to legality of strikes for higher wages, shorter working hours, better working conditions, etc., see Oakes, *Organized Labor and Industrial Conflicts* (1927), pp. 376-402.

[55] Plant *v.* Woods, 176 Mass. 492, 57 N. E. 1011 (1900); Berry *v.* Donovan, 188 Mass. 353, 74 N. E. 603 (1905); Aberthaw Construction Co. *v.* Cameron, 194 Mass. 208, 80 N. E. 478 (1907); Reynolds *v.* Davis, 198 Mass. 294, 84 N. E. 457 (1908); Folsom *v.* Lewis, 208 Mass. 336, 94 N. E. 316 (1911); Snow Iron Works *v.* Chadwick, 227 Mass. 382, 116 N. E. 801 (1917); Bausch Machine Co. *v.* Hill, 231 Mass. 30, 120 N. E.

for the closed shop are not necessarily illegal in Massachusetts. If voluntarily entered into and not monopolistic in character, they have been held to be lawful.[56] But a strike to secure the closed shop is a different matter, for it usually involves a demand that certain non-union workers be discharged, and the Massachusetts courts hold that it is for the courts to decide whether strikers are entitled to demand that other workmen be discharged. They have never regarded strengthening the union as justifying this demand. In fact, the Massachusetts Supreme Court has held unlawful a strike to gain the preferential shop (where union members are merely given preference over non-unionists).[57] Inferior Massachusetts courts have even taken the same position toward strikes for "recognition" of the union.[58] Strikes in which the demand for the closed shop was but one of several demands made by the strikers have also been condemned.

The New York courts have been much more liberal in regard to closed-shop strikes. The decisions of the New York Court of Appeals on the point are somewhat difficult to reconcile; but apparently a closed-shop strike is lawful so long as it is not designed to give the union a monopoly in a particular community.[59] In contrast to Massachusetts, the court has definitely

---

188 (1918); Smith v. Bowen, 232 Mass. 106, 121 N. E. 814 (1919); A. T. Stearns Lumber Co. v. Howlett, 260 Mass. 45, 157 N. E. 82 (1927). Slightly contra, Pickett v. Walsh, 192 Mass. 572, 78 N. E. 753 (1906); Minasian v. Osborne, 210 Mass. 250, 96 N. E. 1036 (1911); Shinsky v. O'Neil, 232 Mass. 99, 121 N. E. 790 (1919).

[56] Hoban v. Dempsey, 217 Mass. 166, 104 N. E. 717 (1914); Shinsky v. O'Neil, 232 Mass. 99, 121 N. E. 790 (1919); Ryan v. Hayes, 243 Mass. 168, 137 N. E. 344 (1922); Henry v. Century Shoe Co., 12 *Law and Labor* 7 (Mass. Super. Ct., 1929).

[57] Folsom Engraving Co. v. McNeil, 235 Mass. 269, 126 N. E. 479 (1920).

[58] Thomas G. Plant Co. v. Gould, 2 *Law and Labor* 276 (1920); Jackson v. Brown, 3 *Law and Labor* 53 (1921).

[59] Curran v. Galen, 152 N. Y. 33, 46 N. E. 297 (1897); National Protective Assoc. v. Cumming, 170 N. Y. 315, 63 N. E. 369 (1902); Jacobs v. Cohen, 183 N. Y. 207, 76 N. E. 5 (1905); Kissom v. Printing Co., 199 N. Y. 76, 92 N. E. 214 (1910); McCord v. Thompson-Starrett Co., 198 N. Y. 587, 92 N. E. 1090 (1910); Cusumano v. Schlessinger, 152 N. Y. Supp. 1081 (1915); Exchange Bakery & Restaurant, Inc., v. Rifkin, 245 N. Y. 260, 157 N. E. 130 (1927).

COLLECTIVE BARGAINING

stated that strengthening the union is a legitimate motive for a strike.

In other states there have been fewer cases involving closed-shop strikes. A majority of state supreme courts have never passed on the question. Where it has come up, the courts are about evenly divided as between the Massachusetts and the New York positions.[60] In the federal courts, there have been few cases involving this issue, and the United States Supreme Court has never passed on it.

e. *Sympathetic Strikes.*—A sympathetic strike is a strike by the workmen of one employer or craft in aid of the employees of another. Such strikes occur most frequently in the building trades where labor is organized along craft lines and each craft frequently has a different employer (i.e., a different subcontractor). Where one craft goes out on strike all the other crafts working on the same building may go out too, though they have no immediate grievance of their own. Perhaps the most frequent and most important type of sympathetic strike is the refusal to work on non-union material. Strikes against non-union material are often called boycotts, though they are carried out, not by a refusal to patronize, but by a refusal to work.[61]

The courts are somewhat divided on the legality of sympathetic strikes; but they have held them illegal more frequently than closed-shop strikes.[62] Strikes against non-union mate-

---

[60] *California:* Greenwood v. Building Trades Council, 71 Cal. App. 159, 233 Pac. 823 (1925). *Illinois:* O'Brien v. People, 216 Ill. 354, 75 N. E. 108 (1905); Kemp v. Division 241, 255 Ill. 213, 99 N. E. 389 (1912). *Pennsylvania:* Erdman v. Mitchell, 207 Pa. 79, 56 Atl. 327 (1903); Bausbach v. Reiff, 244 Pa. 559, 91 Atl. 224 (1914). *New Jersey:* Baldwin Lumber Co. v. Local 560, 91 N. J. Eq. 240, 109 Atl. 147 (1920); Gevas v. Greek Restaurant Workers' Club, et al., 99 N. J. Eq. 770, 134 Atl. 309 (1926).

[61] Such strikes may be called workers' boycotts.

[62] Thomas v. Cincinnati, etc., R. R. Co., 62 Fed. 803 (1894); Beattie v. Callanan, 67 App. Div. 14, 73 N. Y. Supp. 518, (1901), 82 App. Div. 7, 81 N. Y. Supp. 413 (1903); Gray v. Building Trades Council, 91 Minn. 171, 97 N. W. 663 (1903); Pickett v. Walsh, 192 Mass. 572, 78 N. E. 753 (1906); New England, etc., Co. v. McGivern, 218 Mass. 198, 105 N. E. 885 (1914); Grant Construction Co. v. St. Paul Building Trades Council, 136 Minn. 167, 161 N. W. 520 (1917); Lehigh Structural Steel Co. v. Atlantic, etc., Works, 92 N. J. Eq. 131, 111 Atl. 376 (1920); Burgess v. Stewart, 112 Misc. 347, 184 N. Y. Supp. 199 (1920), 114 Misc. 673, 187 N. Y. Supp. 873 (1921); Bricklayers', Masons', and

394 PRINCIPLES OF LABOR LEGISLATION

rials have been upheld by the supreme courts of California, North Carolina and New York,[63] but declared illegal in Florida, Massachusetts, New Jersey and Pennsylvania.[64] The United States Supreme Court held such strikes illegal under the anti-trust acts in two important decisions, Duplex Printing Company v. Deering,[65] and Bedford Cut Stone Co. v. Journeymen Stone Cutters' Association.[66] The legal basis for these Supreme Court decisions was complicated, of course, by the issue of interference with interstate commerce and the question whether such interference was "reasonable" or "unreasonable" within the meaning of the anti-trust act. But the practical effect was to make strikes against non-union material illegal.

The Bedford case went furthest in condemning this type of sympathetic action, for the strike was confined to members of the same national union—the stone cutters. The members of locals in different parts of the country, in accordance with a rule of their union, simply refused to work on stone from the Bedford Cut Stone Company because that company had refused to renew its union agreement. The United States Supreme Court held that this was a combination which

deliberately adopted a course of conduct which directly and substantially curtailed or threatened thus to curtail the natural flow in interstate commerce of a very large proportion of the building limestone production of the entire country . . . and it must be held

---

Plasterers' International Union v. Seymour Ruff & Sons, Inc., 160 Md. 483, 154 Atl. 52 (1931).

[63] *California:* Parkinson v. Building Trades Council, 154 Cal. 581, 98 Pac. 1027 (1908). *North Carolina:* State v. Van Pelt, 136 N. C. 633, 49 S. E. 177 (1904). *New York:* Bossert v. Dhuy, 221 N. Y. 342, 117 N. E. 582 (1917); Newton Co. v. Erickson, 126 N. Y. Supp. 949 (1911), 129 N. Y. Supp. 1111 (1911), 221 N. Y. 632, 117 N. E. 1059 (1917); Aeolian Co. v. Fischer, 27 F. (2d) 560 (1928).

[64] *Florida:* Jetton-Dekle v. Mather, 53 Fla. 969, 43 So. 590 (1907). *Massachusetts:* Burnham v. Dowd, 217 Mass. 351, 104 N. E. 841 (1914); Stearns Lumber Co. v. Howlett, 260 Mass. 45, 157 N. E. 82 (1927), 163 N. E. 193 (1928). *New Jersey:* Booth v. Burgess, 72 N. J. Eq. 181, 65 Atl. 226 (1906). *Pennsylvania:* Patterson v. Building Trades Council, 11 Pa. Dist. 500 (1902); Purvis v. Carpenters, 214 Pa. 348, 63 Atl. 585 (1906).

[65] 254 U. S. 443, 41 Sup. Ct. 172 (1921).

[66] 274 U. S. 37, 47 Sup. Ct. 522 (1927).

COLLECTIVE BARGAINING 395

to be a combination in undue and unreasonable restraint of such commerce within the meaning of the Anti-trust Act as interpreted by this court.[67]

In a dissenting opinion Mr. Justice Brandeis asserted that the interference with interstate commerce practiced by the members of the Stone Cutters' Union was not "unreasonable" since it was the only way in which the members of the union could protect themselves. And only unreasonable restraint of trade is forbidden by the anti-trust laws. He pointed out that the Sherman Law had been held by the court to permit capitalists to combine in a single corporation fifty per cent of the steel industry of the United States, and to permit a combination of practically the whole shoe machinery industry of the country, and he added:

It would, indeed, be strange if Congress had by the same Act willed to deny to members of a small craft of workingmen the right to cooperate in simply refraining from work, when that course was the only means of self-protection against a combination of militant and powerful employers. I cannot believe that Congress did so.[68]

State decisions condemning sympathetic strikes or strikes against non-union material are based on the legal theory that the sympathetic strikers have no legitimate interest in the dispute and hence no legal justification for striking. This line of reasoning, along with that holding such strikes an "unreasonable" interference with interstate commerce, involves a disregard of economic realities pertaining to collective bargaining. For "sympathetic" action is frequently essential. Workers cannot possess sufficient economic strength to induce employers to accept collective bargaining or reasonable terms in a collective agreement unless their concerted action is allowed to extend beyond the narrow range of a craft local. No doubt there must be a limit somewhere; but workers in another craft or in another local of the same national union frequently are "interested parties" in a labor dispute—in economic fact, if not in law. If that strike is lost, their own organization will be seriously weakened and the success of their own future collective

---

[67] Bedford Cut Stone Co. v. Journeymen Stone Cutters' Association, 274 U. S. 37, 54, 47 Sup. Ct. 522, 527 (1927).
[68] 274 U. S. 37, 65, 47 Sup. Ct. 522, 531 (1927).

bargaining will be imperiled. A decision holding such a strike illegal really constitutes an interference with the right to bargain collectively.

f. *Other Strikes.*—Many other kinds of strikes have been held unlawful. Wherever the question has arisen, the courts have condemned strikes to collect fines imposed upon employers, and strikes in violation of collective agreements, or in disregard of individual contracts.[69] A strike to enforce a doubtful private claim was declared illegal by the United States Supreme Court.[70]

g. *Court Action Against Illegal Strikes.*—What difference does it make if a strike is declared illegal? It does not mean that by court action the strike will be directly prevented or terminated, for no court in the United States will enjoin workmen from quitting work or order them back to work.[71] The furthest the courts have gone is to order union officials to call off an illegal strike.[72] But the legality of a strike is very important, none the less. For if a strike is held illegal, methods used to carry it on which would otherwise be lawful become

[69] Illegality of strikes to collect fines: Carew v. Rutherford, 106 Mass. 1 (1870); People v. Barondess, 133 N. Y. 649, 31 N. E. 240 (1892); Burke v. Fay, 128 Mo. App. 690, 107 S. W. 408 (1908); People v. Walczak, 315 Ill. 49, 145 N. E. 660 (1924). Illegality of strikes in violation of collective agreements or individual contracts: Reynolds v. Davis, 198 Mass. 294, 84 N. E. 457 (1908); Gilchrist Co. v. Metal Polishers, 113 Atl. 320 (N. J. Ch. 1919); Cook v. Wilson, 108 Misc. 438, 178 N. Y. Supp. 463 (1919); Best Service, etc., Co. v. Dickson, 121 Misc. 416, 201 N. Y. Supp. 173 (1923); Metzler v. Kaminer, 131 Misc. 813, 227 N. Y. Supp. 459 (1927).

[70] Dorchy v. Kansas, 272 U. S. 306, 47 Sup. Ct. 86 (1926).

[71] This has been regarded as settled law since Arthur v. Oakes, 11 C. C. A. 209, 63 Fed. 310 (1894).

[72] The best known of such injunctions is the case of U. S. v. Hayes, in which, at the instance of the Attorney-general of the United States, Judge Anderson, in November, 1919, directed the officers of the United Mine Workers to "call off" a nation-wide strike of the bituminous coal miners. This direction was complied with, but the strikers did not return to work until they knew that at least part of the wage increases for which they were striking would be secured to them through the Bituminous Coal Mining Commission instituted by President Wilson to adjust this dispute. See also, Burgess v. Ga., etc., Ry. Co., 148 Ga. 415, 96 S. E. 864 (1918); Western Union v. International Brotherhood, 2 F. (2d) 993 (1924). (Both of these strikes involved public utilities. It is doubtful whether courts would go so far in other fields.)

COLLECTIVE BARGAINING

illegal and are frequently forbidden by injunction. Thus all picketing may be prohibited. Or the payment of strike benefits,[73] or even meetings of strikers to sing hymns,[74] may be enjoined.

h. *Methods of Conducting Strikes.*—Even more important in practice than the legality of strikes is the legality of methods used in carrying them on. If the strike is to succeed, the strikers must be able to keep other workers from taking their places or (probably less important) to keep customers from dealing with their employer. In general, the courts agree that in the furtherance of these ends the strikers may use *persuasion* but not threats, coercion or intimidation. The differences arise in deciding where persuasion ends and intimidation or coercion begins. However, even persuasion is illegal in connection with an illegal strike. And, except in states which have passed statutes making yellow-dog contracts void and unenforceable (and in the federal courts, which are now governed by similar provisions in the Norris-La Guardia Act), the courts may hold that it is illegal to "persuade" a worker under a yellow-dog contract to join the union.[75]

i. *Picketing.*—The principal method used by strikers is the stationing of pickets near the employer's premises. Upon the legality of picketing the courts have been and, to a lesser degree, still are seriously divided.[76] The question is whether picketing is merely persuasion or whether it constitutes intimidation. All courts agree that the conduct of pickets may be such as to

---

[73] U. S. *v.* Railway Employes' Dept., A. F. L., 286 Fed. 228 (1923); International Organization, etc., *v.* Red Jacket C. C. & C. Co., 18 F. (2d) 839 (1927).

[74] Such an order was given by Judge Langham of the Pennsylvania State Court in September, 1927, during a strike in the bituminous coal fields. See Frankfurter and Greene, *The Labor Injunction,* 1930, p. 101, note 91.

[75] For a full discussion of the law as to yellow-dog contracts, see below, pp. 405-408.

[76] Early conflict as to legality of picketing illustrated by: (1) Decisions that *all* picketing is illegal: Vegelahn *v.* Guntner, 167 Mass. 92, 44 N. E. 1077 (1896); Barnes *v.* Typographical Union No. 16, 232 Ill. 424, 83 N. E. 940 (1908). (2) Picketing by lawful means for a lawful purpose upheld: White Mountain Freezer Co. *v.* Murphy, 78 N. H. 398, 101 Atl. 357 (1917).

render the picketing unlawful.[77] Abusive language, threats, even though veiled, and an unreasonable number of pickets, constitute intimidation and are clearly unlawful. Some courts even hold that speaking to employees against their will is intimidation;[78] and one court has held that silence is intimidation.[79] In other cases the offer made by the pickets to pay strike benefits or transportation back to the place from which the new employees came has been considered bribery and an illegal method of picketing.[80]

The most serious disagreement, however, has arisen upon whether all picketing is illegal. On the one hand, it has been held that there is no such thing as "peaceful" picketing and that the establishment of a picket line is of itself intimidating and, hence, unlawful.[81] It has been asserted, on the other hand, that peaceful picketing is not a mere fiction and that there is no warrant in law for enjoining all picketing. Prior to 1921, the view that all picketing is unlawful was held by the supreme courts of California, Illinois, Massachusetts, Michigan, New Jersey, Pennsylvania, and Washington, and by many federal courts;[82] while in Alabama, Colorado, and Washington all

[77] Thus, all picketing was forbidden when a previous injunction against violence had been violated in Nann v. Raimist, 255 N. Y. 307, 174 N. E. 690 (1931). And picketing in a narrow area in front of a theater was found to be an obstruction of the streets and unlawful in Bomes v. Providence Local No. 223, 51 R. I. 499, 155 Atl. 581 (1931).

[78] Frank v. Herold, 63 N. J. Eq. 443, 52 Atl. 152 (1901); Jersey Printing Co. v. Cassidy, 63 N. J. Eq. 759, 53 Atl. 230 (1902); Goldfield Consolidated Mines Co. v. Miners' Union, 159 Fed. 500 (1908); Segenfeld v. Friedman, 117 Misc. 731, 193 N. Y. Supp. 128 (1922).

[79] Gevas v. Greek Restaurant Workers' Club, 99 N. J. Eq. 770, 134 Atl. 309 (1926).

[80] Jersey Printing Co. v. Cassidy, 63 N. J. Eq. 759, 53 Atl. 230 (1902); Tunstall v. Stearns Coal Co., 192 Fed. 808 (1911); McMichael v. Atlanta Envelope Co., 151 Ga. 776, 108 S. E. 226 (1921). To contrary, Levy v. Rosentein, 66 N. Y. Supp. 101 (1900); Everett Waddey Co. v. Typographical Union, 105 Va. 188, 53 S. E. 273 (1906).

[81] Atchison, Topeka & Santa Fe Ry. Co. v. Gee, 139 Fed. 582 (1905).

[82] Pierce v. Stablemen, 156 Cal. 70, 103 Pac. 324 (1909); *ex parte* Williams, 158 Cal. 550, 11 Pac. 1035 (1910) (but as to California see also Southern California Iron & Steel Co. v. Iron & Steel Workers, 186 Cal. 604, 200 Pac. 1 [1921], which may be construed as modifying the earlier decisions cited); Franklin Union v. People, 220 Ill. 355, 77 N. E. 176 (1906); Boston Store v. Retail Clerks, 216 Ill. App. 428 (1920); Vegelahn v. Guntner, 167 Mass. 92, 44 N. E. 1077 (1896); *In re* Langell,

COLLECTIVE BARGAINING 399

picketing was forbidden by statute, and in some cities by municipal ordinances.[83] In a yet larger number of jurisdictions, however, it was recognized that picketing may be peaceful and, hence, lawful. This view was held in Arkansas, Arizona, Indiana, Minnesota, Missouri, Montana, New Hampshire, New York, Ohio, Oklahoma, Oregon, and Wisconsin, and, again, by many federal courts.[84]

In 1921 the United States Supreme Court delivered two opinions which, while they have not brought all courts into agreement, have yet had the effect of rendering more definite

---

178 Mich. 305, 144 N. W. 841 (1914); Glass Co. v. Glass Blowers, 77 N. J. Eq. 219, 79 Atl. 262 (1911); Keuffel & Esser v. Machinists, 93 N. J. Eq. 429, 116 Atl. 9 (1922); O'Neil v. Behanna, 182 Pa. 236, 37 Atl. 843 (1897); St. Germain v. Bakery Workers, 97 Wash. 282, 166 Pac. 665 (1917); Otis Steel Co. v. Molders, 110 Fed. 698 (1901); Kolley v. Robinson, 109 C. C. A. 247, 187 Fed. 415 (1911); Vonnegut Machinery Co. v. Toledo Machine & Tool Co., 263 Fed. 192 (1920).

This view is now modified to allow peaceful picketing at least in California, Illinois, and Pennsylvania. See Lisse v. Local Union No. 31, 2 Cal. (2d) 312, 41 Pac. (2d) 314 (1935); Fenske Bros., Inc., v. Upholsterers' Union, 358 Ill. 239, 193 N. E. 112 (1934); Kirmse, et al., v. Adler, et al., 311 Pa. 78, 166 Atl. 566 (1933).

[83] Haskins v. Royster, 70 N. C. 601 (1874); Bixby v. Dunlap, 56 N. H. 456 (1876); Beekman v. Marsters, 195 Mass. 205, 80 N. E. 817 (1907); Flaccus v. Smith, 199 Pa. 128, 48 Atl. 894 (1901); Employing Printers' Club v. Doctor Blosser Co., 122 Ga. 509, 50 S. E. 353 (1905); and the Indianapolis ordinance by the Indiana Supreme Court in Walters v. City of Indianapolis, 191 Ind. 671, 134 N. E. 482 (1922). For decisions holding anti-picketing ordinances to be unconstitutional, see *In re* Sweitzer, 13 Okla. Crim. 154, 162 Pac. 1134 (1917); and Hall v. Johnson, 87 Ore. 21, 169 Pac. 515 (1917).

[84] Local Union v. Stathakis, 135 Ark. 86, 205 S. W. 450 (1918); Truax v. Bisbee Local, 19 Ariz. 379, 171 Pac. 121 (1918); Shaughnessy v. Jordan, 184 Ind. 499, 111 N. E. 622 (1916); Steffes v. Motion Picture Operators, 136 Minn. 200, 161 N. W. 524 (1917); Hughes v. Motion Picture Operators, 282 Mo. 304, 221 S. W. 95 (1920); Empire Theatre Co. v. Cloke, 53 Mont. 183, 163 Pac. 107 (1917); White Mt. Freezer Co. v. Murphy, 78 N. H. 398, 101 Atl. 357 (1917); Butterick Publishing Co. v. Typographical Union, 50 Misc. 1, 100 N. Y. Supp. 292 (1906); La France Electrical & Supply Co. v. Electrical Workers, 108 Ohio St. 61, 140 N. E. 899 (1923); *In re* Sweitzer, 13 Okla. Crim. 154, 162 Pac. 1134 (1917); Greenfield v. Central Labor Council, 104 Ore. 236, 192 Pac. 783 (1920); A. J. Monday Co. v. Automobile Workers, 171 Wis. 532, 177 N. W. 867 (1920); Allis Chalmers Co. v. Iron Molders, 166 Fed. 45 (1908).

the law as to picketing. In the first of these cases, American Steel Foundries Co. v. Tri-City Central Trades' Council,[85] the court held all "picketing" to be unlawful, but also held that whether efforts strikers may make to persuade employees and prospective employees to join them are lawful, depends upon the circumstances and facts in each case. In this particular case the court allowed the union to place one representative (picket) at each factory entrance to present the strikers' case peaceably. In the second case, Truax v. Corrigan,[86] the court held that mass picketing violates the constitutional guarantees of liberty and property and that no state can legalize such conduct.

Because of the unfortunate use of the term "picketing" in a narrower sense than this term is popularly used, the American Steel Foundries Company decision has been cited in some cases since as absolutely prohibiting the employment of any pickets in strikes. It is authority, rather, for the proposition that peaceful picketing may be lawful, and that it is the duty of the court to examine all the facts in each case and determine and definitely prescribe what conduct is permissible under the particular circumstances presented. This is the interpretation which has been adopted in nearly all cases since 1921 involving the law as to picketing. The courts still differ in their statements as to whether there is any such thing as "peaceful" picketing, but even the courts which hold that all "picketing" is unlawful usually permit one or more pickets. Similarly, the courts which hold that peaceful picketing is lawful, now generally follow the United States Supreme Court in definitely prescribing how the picketing shall be conducted. The disagreement over whether all picketing is necessarily unlawful seems to have resolved itself into little more than the use of the term "picketing" in two different meanings. However widely the statements of the courts may differ, the conclusions are generally not far apart.

In fact, in probably a majority of all injunctions issued since 1921, the same number of pickets have been allowed as in the American Steel Foundries Company case, namely, one at each factory entrance. In other cases this precise number has not been treated as a fetish; but, more correctly interpreting the

[85] 257 U. S. 184, 42 Sup. Ct. 72 (1921).
[86] 257 U. S. 312, 42 Sup. Ct. 124 (1921).

COLLECTIVE BARGAINING 401

decision of the Supreme Court, the courts have examined the particular circumstances presented and have varied their orders accordingly, but always definitely prescribing both the number of the pickets permitted and the manner in which they must conduct themselves.[87]

j. *Boycotts*.—The boycott is another means used by strikers to bring employers to their terms. Boycotts sometimes arise without strikes, but usually they grow out of strikes and are frequently continued after the strike is lost. One difficulty in the law of boycotts is that the term has no standard meaning.[88] In its simplest form it means a collective refusal to purchase specified commodities.[89] But it usually involves pressure on third parties to induce them to refuse to buy the boycotted product. The boycott was condemned as unlawful as early as 1886.[90] Many decisions confirmed this view. As the United States Supreme Court has said, the courts are nearly unanimous in condemning boycotting as wrongful.[91] In a few states it is specifically prohibited by statute.[92]

In some cases an effort is made to distinguish the primary boycott from the secondary boycott, the latter being the boycott of a third party, usually a merchant who sells the product of the employer primarily boycotted. Many courts, in fact, use the term boycott as embracing only secondary boycotts. This dis-

---

[87] Great Northern Ry. Co. *v.* Brosseau, 286 Fed. 414 (1923); Reed Co. *v.* Whiteman, 238 N. Y. 545, 144 N. E. 885 (1924); United Chain Theaters *v.* Philadelphia M. P. M. O. Union, 50 F. (2d) 189 (1931).

[88] See Oakes, *Organized Labor and Industrial Conflicts*, note 4, pp. 603-605, for definitions of the term and extensive citation of cases. "The definitions of 'boycott,' as the word has been defined in the various cases, are nearly as varied as the cases defining the term." Truax *v.* Bisbee Local No. 380, 19 Ariz. 379, 171 Pac. 121 (1918).

[89] This is known as the "consumers' boycott." What might be called a "workers' boycott" is the refusal to work upon or with non-union materials. This kind of boycott is carried on through strikes or the threat of strikes. It was discussed above under sympathetic strikes.

[90] People *v.* Wilzig, 4 N. Y. Crim. 403 (1886); People *v.* Kostka, 4 N. Y. Crim. 429 (1886).

[91] Loewe *v.* Lawlor, 208 U. S. 274, 28 Sup. Ct. 301 (1908).

[92] Boycotting is generally brought under the ban of conspiracy and anti-trust statutes, which are found in most states. For typical statutes, specifically penalizing boycotting, see Wis. Stat. 1935, Secs. 343.681, 343.683; Illinois, Revised Stat. 1935, Ch. 38, Sec. 116. See also Witte, E. E., *The Government in Labor Disputes*, 1932, pp. 77-78.

tinction in practice amounts to little. Few employers of labor sell directly to consumers. Hence there can be but few primary boycotts. To boycott a manufacturer, pressure must usually be brought to bear upon the dealers who handle his products. This introduces the third party and the element of the secondary boycott.

In Arizona, California, and Montana the courts of final jurisdiction have held that boycotts if conducted peaceably are lawful.[93] In New York also some inferior courts have sustained the boycott.[94] In Missouri the legality of boycotting is doubtful, but it is established that the printing and distribution of boycott circulars may not be enjoined, the Supreme Court holding that such a prohibition violates the constitutional guarantees of free speech and free press.[95]

Though held illegal, boycotts continued to be conducted openly and fearlessly until 1908. Prior to that date injunctions were sometimes taken out against boycotts, but they only increased their effectiveness by giving them wider publicity. But in 1908 the Danbury Hatters' case[96] brought home to labor for the

[93] Truax v. Bisbee Local, 19 Ariz. 379, 171 Pac. 121 (1918); Truax v. Corrigan, 20 Ariz. 7, 176 Pac. 570 (1918); Parkinson Co. v. Bldg. Trades Council, 154 Cal. 581, 98 Pac. 1027 (1908); Pierce v. Stablemen's Union, 156 Cal. 70, 103 Pac. 324 (1909); Lisse v. Local Union No. 31, 2 Cal. (2d) 312, 41 Pac. (2d) 314 (1935); Lindsay & Co. v. Montana Federation of Labor, 37 Mont. 264, 96 Pac. 127 (1908); Empire Theatre Co. v. Cloke, 53 Mont. 183, 163 Pac. 107 (1917).

[94] Sinsheimer v. Garment Workers, 77 Hun. 215, 28 N. Y. Supp. 321 (1894); People v. Radt, 15 N. Y. Cr. 174, 71 N. Y. Supp. 846 (1900); Cohen v. Garment Workers, 35 Misc. 748, 72 N. Y. Supp. 341 (1901); Foster v. Retail Clerks, 39 Misc. 48, 78 N. Y. Supp. 860 (1902); Butterick Publishing Co. v. Typographical Union, 50 Misc. 1, 100 N. Y. Supp. 292 (1906); Englemeyer v. Simon, et al., 148 Misc. 621, 265 N. Y. Supp. 636 (1933). Contra: Matthews v. Shankland, 25 Misc. 604, 56 N. Y. Supp. 123 (1898); Sun Printing & Publishing Assoc. v. Delaney, 48 Ap. Div. 623, 62 N. Y. Supp. 750 (1900); Mills v. U. S. Printing Co., 99 App. Div. 605, 91 N. Y. Supp. 185 (1904). See also, Auburn Draying Co. v. Wardell, 227 N. Y. 1, 124 N. E. 97 (1919), in which the appellate court condemned a boycott carried on by a city-wide confederation of unions as being unreasonable and oppressive in scope.

[95] Jeans Clothing Co. v. Watson, 168 Mo. 133, 67 S. W. 391 (1902); Lohse Patent Door Co. v. Fuelle, 215 Mo. 421, 114 S. W. 997 (1908); Root v. Anderson, 207 S. W. 255 (Mo. App. 1918); Hughes v. Motion Picture Operators, 282 Mo. 304, 221 S. W. 95 (1920).

[96] Loewe v. Lawlor, 208 U. S. 274, 28 Sup. Ct. 301 (1908).

COLLECTIVE BARGAINING

first time that damages could be collected for losses sustained through boycotts. The American Federation of Labor at once discontinued its "We Don't Patronize" list. Fewer boycotts were undertaken thereafter and they were conducted much less openly. There can be no doubt that the attitude of the courts toward the boycott seriously restricts labor's use of this collective weapon.

2. **The Rights of Employers.**—What are the rights of employers in dealing with their employees? These rights have been substantially affected by the recent legislation discussed in the following section which deals with the law of collective bargaining under the New Deal.[97] Here the rights of employers will be summarized as they stood before the enactment of the Norris-La Guardia Act of 1932,[98] state laws patterned thereon,[99] 7a of the National Industrial Recovery Act,[100] and the National Labor Relations Act of 1935.[101] Because this legislation has effected substantial changes, this section is written in the past tense although much of it still remains true at the present writing.

a. *The Right to Form Employers' Associations.*—The right of employers to combine in employers' associations was unquestioned in the courts.[102] Employers might refuse to enter into trade agreements with unions and might agree among themselves to operate under the open-shop plan. They might bind themselves with penalties not to deal with labor unions, and such penalties were enforceable at law and through injunctions.[103] Further, it was held, in the only case raising this ques-

[97] To what extent this recent legislation will be upheld by the courts remains at this writing an open question.
[98] 47 U. S. Stat. at Large 70 (1932), 29 U. S. C. A., Secs. 101-115.
[99] For a list of these state laws, see below, p. 415.
[100] 48 U. S. Stat. at Large 198 (1933), 15 U. S. C. A., Sec. 707 (a).
[101] 49 U. S. Stat. at Large 457 (1935), 29 U. S. C. A., Secs. 151-166.
[102] See, for example, Cote v. Murphy, 159 Pa. 420, 28 Atl. 190 (1894).
[103] City Trust, etc., Co. v. Waldhauer, 47 Misc. 7, 95 N. Y. Supp. 222 (1905); United Hat Manufacturers v. Baird-Unteidt Co., 88 Conn. 332, 91 Atl. 373 (1914); State v. Employers of Labor, 102 Neb. 768, 169 N. W. 717, 170 N. W. 185 (1918); Middleton v. Stark, 2 *Law & Labor* 121 (Super. Ct. Wash. 1920); Dyer Bros., etc., v. Central Iron Works, 182 Cal. 588, 189 Pac. 445 (1920); Trade Press Publishing Co. v. Milwaukee Typographical Union, 180 Wis. 449, 193 N. W. 507 (1923);

tion, that unions might not combine to prevent employers from belonging to employers' associations.[104]

b. *The Right to Lock Out.*—The right of employers to lock out their employees (the counterpart of the strike) was not questioned.[105]

c. *The Right to Operate Their Plants.*—As for employers' rights during a strike, their right to continue to operate their plants—if they could—was also not questioned.[106] They were entitled to police protection in so doing.[107] They might employ strike breakers—either local men or men brought from a distance.[108] The only restriction was in a few states where statutes required that in advertising for labor when a strike was on, the strike must be mentioned.[109] To protect strike breakers, employers might hire strike guards. Statutes entirely *forbidding*

Androff v. Building Trades Employers Assoc., 7 *Law & Labor* 178 (Ind. App. 1925).

[104] Parker Paint & Wall Paper Co. v. Local Union, 87 W. Va. 631, 105 S. E. 911 (1921).

[105] Sinsheimer v. United Garment Workers, 77 Hun. 215, 28 N. Y. Supp. 321 (1894); Cote v. Murphy, 159 Pa. 420, 28 Atl. 190 (1894); Atkins v. Fletcher, 65 N. J. Eq. 658, 55 Atl. 1074 (1903); City Trust, etc., Co. v. Waldhauer, 47 Misc. 7, 95 N. Y. Supp. 222 (1905); McGrath v. Norman, 221 App. Div. 804, 223 N. Y. Supp. 288 (1927).

[106] A city ordinance was adopted in Milwaukee, Wisconsin, in September, 1935, authorizing city officials to close factories where labor disputes threatening to lead to violence are in progress. The ordinance is only to be invoked in those situations in which collective bargaining has been refused. See Comment (1936), 11 *Wis. Law Rev.* 254.

[107] Failure to provide protection gives the employer a cause of action against the municipality in many states. A typical statute imposing liability upon the local governmental unit for damages caused by riotous assemblies is Wis. Stat. 1935, Sec. 66.07. For discussion of such statutes, see City of Chicago v. Sturges, 222 U. S. 313, 32 Sup. Ct. 92 (1911); Yalenezian v. City of Boston, 238 Mass. 538, 131 N. E. 220 (1921). According to the Massachusetts case cited, "Persons whose property is destroyed or injured by members of a riotous or tumultuous assembly have no common-law right of action against the city for damages." Accord, McQuillin, *Municipal Corporations* (2d ed., 1928), vol. vi, Sec. 2821.

[108] American Steel & Wire Co. v. Davis, 261 Fed. 800 (1919); Swift v. Hague, 2 *Law & Labor* 9 (1919); Mullins Body Corp. v. International Assoc., 3 *Law & Labor* 149 (1921).

[109] For a typical statute, see Wis. Stat. 1935, Sec. 103-43. See also, Witte, *The Government in Labor Disputes,* p. 209, note 3.

COLLECTIVE BARGAINING 405

the use of strike guards had been held unconstitutional, but laws *regulating* the use of such guards had been upheld.[110]

Thus employers had certain rights useful in defeating strikes. In addition, they had many rights which might be used to prevent the growth of labor organization among their employees. It is primarily these rights which were restricted by New Deal legislation, to be discussed in the next section. Just what is left of these rights under the new legislation is not entirely clear.

d. *The Right to Discriminate Against Union Workers.*—In the first place, the employer had the unlimited right to discriminate against union members. He could refuse to hire union men, or could fire workers who joined the union. Legislation restricting this right had been passed in at least eight states,[111] and by Congress in an act covering railway workers.[112] These acts had made it a criminal offense to fire a man for belonging to a union. They were declared unconstitutional in the state courts in six states,[113] and in 1908 the federal act applying to the railroads was declared invalid by the U. S. Supreme Court in Adair *v.* United States. The court held that for Congress to restrict the right of discharge would be contrary to the Fifth Amendment, declaring:

The right of a person to sell his labor upon such terms as he deems proper is, in its essence, the same as the right of the purchaser of labor to prescribe the conditions upon which he will accept such labor from the person offering to sell it. So the right of the employee to quit the service of the employer, for whatever reason, is the same as the right of the employer, for whatever rea-

[110] See *ibid.*, pp. 210-211 and notes following, for lists of states with such legislation and cases interpreting the same.

[111] Anti-discrimination statutes were enacted in the following states: *Illinois*, Laws 1893, p. 98; *Kansas*, Laws 1897, C. 120; *Ohio*, Laws 1892, p. 269; *Pennsylvania*, Laws 1897, p. 116, no. 98; *South Carolina*, Laws 1909, p. 15, Sec. 6. In addition, three states passed anti-discrimination acts which also specifically prohibited "yellow-dog contracts"— *Indiana*, Laws 1893, C. 76; *Missouri*, Laws 1893, p. 187; *Wisconsin*, Laws 1899, C. 332.

[112] In the Erdman Act of 1898, 30 U. S. Stat. at Large 424.

[113] State *v.* Julow, 129 Mo. 163, 31 S. W. 781 (1895); Gillespie *v.* People, 188 Ill. 176, 58 N. E. 1007 (1900); State *v.* Kreutzberg, 114 Wis. 530, 90 N. W. 1098 (1903); Coffeyville, etc., Co. *v.* Perry, 69 Kan. 297, 76 Pac. 848 (1904); Jackson *v.* Berger, 92 Ohio St. 130, 110 N. E. 732 (1915); Commonwealth *v.* Clark, 14 Pa. Super. 435 (1900).

son, to dispense with the services of such employee. . . . In all such particulars the employer and the employee have equality of right and any legislation that disturbs that equality is an arbitrary interference with the liberty of contract which no government can legally justify in a free land.[114]

e. *The Right to Use Yellow-dog Contracts.*—In the second place, the employer could prevent the growth of unionism through the use of "yellow-dog contracts." This was a contract which the employer required the individual worker to sign as a condition of employment. In its simplest form it stated that the employee agreed not to join a union while employed. The deterrent effect of such a contract on the individual worker was largely psychological, for the employer could virtually never recover anything from an employee who broke the contract—he could merely fire him. And an employer was free to fire a worker who joined a union in any case.

But the yellow-dog contract proved an immensely effective weapon against union organization campaigns. For some courts, including the United States Supreme Court, held such contracts the grounds for sweeping injunctions against any kind of "persuasion" of workers to join unions. The legal basis for such injunctions was that persuasion under such circumstances was inducing the worker to break a contract. And "inducing breach of contract" is a legal wrong against which the employer is entitled to protection. Because the Hitchman Coal and Coke Company employed its miners under yellow-dog contracts, the United States Supreme Court upheld a sweeping injunction which practically barred United Mine Worker organizers from entering the towns in which Hitchman employees lived.[115]

[114] Adair *v.* U. S., 208 U. S. 161, 174, 28 Sup. Ct. 277, 280 (1908).

[115] Hitchman Coal and Coke Co. *v.* Mitchell, 245 U. S. 229, 38 Sup. Ct. 65 (1917). Cases following the Hitchman case: Eagle Glass & Mfg. Co. *v.* Rowe, 245 U. S. 275, 38 Sup. Ct. 80 (1917); International Organization, U. M. W. A. *v.* Leevale Coal Co., 285 Fed. 32 (1922); Montgomery, *et al., v.* Pac. Ry. Co., 293 Fed. 680 (1923); Bittner *v.* West Virginia-Pittsburgh Coal Co., 15 F. (2d) 652 (1926); International Organization, U. M. W. A. *v.* Red Jacket Consol. C. & C. Co., 18 F. (2d) 839 (1927); Floersheimer *v.* Schlesinger, 115 Misc. 9, 187 N. Y. S. 891 (1921); Rice, Barton & Fales Machine, etc., Co. *v.* Willard, 242 Mass. 566, 136 N. E. 629 (1922). See Oliphant, "Present Status of the Hitchman Case" (1929), 29 *Col. L. Rev.* 441.

In some states the courts refused to grant injunctions based on

COLLECTIVE BARGAINING

Thirteen states had passed laws making the use of yellow-dog contracts a criminal offense.[116] But in 1915 the United States Supreme Court had held these acts unconstitutional in Coppage v. Kansas,[117] refusing to distinguish anti-yellow-dog provisions from the general anti-discrimination provisions invalidated in Adair v. United States. After the Hitchman decision the use of yellow-dog contracts spread rapidly as a most effective defense against unions.

Alarmed at the effectiveness of this weapon, labor sought some way of preventing the use of these contracts which could stand court test. A new type of statute was first passed in Wisconsin in 1929,[118] which did not attempt to *prohibit* yellow-dog contracts but merely made them unenforceable in the courts. That meant that they could not be made the basis of sweeping injunctions against all forms of union activity. In the following years similar laws were passed in eighteen other states,[119]

---

yellow-dog contracts. This was especially true in New York, where the courts held that no contract existed. See Interborough Rapid Transit Co. v. Lanvin, 247 N. Y. 65, 159 N. E. 863 (1928), and Interborough Rapid Transit Co. v. Green, 131 Misc. 682, 227 N. Y. Supp. 258 (1928).

[116] *California*, Stats. 1893, p. 176; *Colorado*, Laws 1911, C. 5; *Connecticut*, Laws 1899, C. 170; *Idaho*, Laws 1893, p. 152; *Kansas*, Laws 1903, C. 222; *Louisiana*, Acts 1914, No. 294, p. 602; *Massachusetts*, Laws 1892, C. 330 and C. 410, Sec. 2; *Minnesota*, Laws 1895, C. 172 and C. 174; *Nevada*, Laws 1903, p. 207, C. 111, Sec. 1; *New Jersey*, Laws 1894, p. 327; *New York*, Laws 1887, C. 688; *Oklahoma*, Laws 1907-08, p. 513, Sec. 1; *Oregon*, Laws 1903, p. 137. In addition, three states had yellow-dog provisions in their anti-discrimination statutes. See above, note 111, p. 405.

[117] 236 U. S. 1, 35 Sup. Ct. 240 (1915). Many state courts took the same position. See People v. Marcus, 185 N. Y. 257, 77 N. E. 1073 (1906); State v. Daniels, 118 Minn. 155, 136 N. W. 584 (1912); Bemis v. State, 12 Okla. Crim. 114, 152 Pac. 456 (1915); People v. Western Union Tel. Co., 70 Colo. 90, 198 Pac. 146 (1921); Goldfield Consolidated Mines Co. v. Goldfield Miners' Union No. 220, 159 Fed. 500 (Nev. 1908); Montgomery, et al., v. Pac. Elec. Ry. Co., 293 Fed. 680 (Cal. 1923).

[118] Wis. Statutes 1935, Sec. 103.46, Laws of 1929, C. 123.

[119] The following states have passed anti-yellow-dog legislation modeled on the Wisconsin act: *Arizona*, Revised Code 1928, Sec. 1360a, Laws 1931, C. 19; *California*, Deering 1933 Supp. 1819, Stats. 1933, p. 1478, Act 4104, C. 566; *Colorado*, Laws 1931, C. 112; *Illinois*, Ill. Rev. Stat. 1935, C. 48, Sec. 237, Laws 1933, p. 588, S. B. No. 394; *Massachusetts*, Laws 1933, C. 351; *New Jersey*, Laws 1932, C. 244; *Ohio*, Laws 1931,

and the Norris-La Guardia Act of 1932 contained a provision along the same line.[120] The constitutionality of this kind of legislation has not been passed on by any court of last resort, but these new anti-yellow-dog laws are generally assumed to be valid. What they mean as to a changing attitude toward collective bargaining will be discussed in the next section.

f. *The Right to Blacklist.*—The theory of the absolute right of the employer to discharge also resulted in the virtual legalization of the black list. Most of the states of the Union had laws prohibiting blacklisting, but before the New Deal they were dead letters.[121] The explanation lies in the fact that these laws could not be effective so long as employers were free to discharge or to refuse to employ any workman who belonged to a union. Anti-black-list laws which merely prohibited the circulation of information as to who were union members were probably constitutional, although one federal decision did not even grant that much.[122] He who circulated this information might be punished, but the employer who acted upon it was entirely within his rights. His reason for refusing to employ or for discharging could not be questioned in any court. In the day of the telephone, the telegraph, watermarked paper, and the card system, it was well-nigh impossible to prove who fur-

---

p. 562, Sec. 6241-1; *Pennsylvania,* Laws 1933, C. 219. In Wisconsin, Illinois and Arizona this protection extends to agricultural organizations as well as to labor unions.

Of these states, Colorado and Wisconsin have also adopted a general anti-injunction measure containing a similar yellow-dog feature while still retaining the earlier section. The anti-yellow-dog measure exists only as a part of the more comprehensive statute in Idaho, Indiana, Louisiana, Maryland, Minnesota, New York, North Dakota, Oregon, Utah, and Washington. (See note 149, p. 415.)

See Fraenkel, "Recent Statutes Affecting Labor Injunctions and Yellow-dog Contracts" (March, 1936), 30 *Ill. L. Rev.* 854, 855-864.

Federal legislation making non-union contracts unenforceable is a part not only of the Norris-La Guardia Act but of the Railroad Reorganization and of the Corporate Reorganization sections of the Federal Bankruptcy Act. 47 U. S. Stat. at Large 1474, 1481, Sec. 77 (p), (q) (1933), 11 U. S. C. A., Sec. 205 (n); 48 U. S. Stat. at Large 912, 922, Sec. 77B (1), (m) (1934), 11 U. S. C. A., Sec. 201 (1), (m).

[120] 47 U. S. Stat. at Large 70, Sec. 3 (1932), 29 U. S. C. A., Sec. 103.

[121] These statutes are listed and decisions analyzed in Witte, *op. cit.,* pp. 213-216 and notes following.

[122] Boyer *v.* Western Union, 124 Fed. 246 (1903).

nished the information upon which a blacklisted workman was discharged. Moreover, the supplying of such information by a former employer upon the request of the present employer was regarded as "privileged" at law. It was expressly declared legal in the anti-black-list laws of many states. This is the simplest and most common manner in which an employer secures information about the records of his employees.[123] A workman discharged for union activity as a result of information secured in this manner had no redress against either his employer or his former employer. If the information was supplied by an employers' association or furnished gratuitously by the former employer, the blacklisted workman could not recover unless he proved who furnished the information and that he was discharged as a result thereof. He could not establish either proposition unless the employer who discharged him was in sympathy with him.[124] This was obviously not the case where the reason for the discharge was membership in a labor union. As a result, blacklisting was legal throughout the United States to all intents and purposes.

g. *The Right to Organize Company Unions.*—Until 1933 in every industry except railroading, the employers' right to set up a "company union" was entirely unquestioned. Many employers found this an effective device for preventing the growth of genuine labor unions. Employees were often satisfied with the illusion of collective bargaining which these organizations provide.

A company union or employee representation plan cannot by its very nature operate as an effective collective bargaining agency. Under the constitutions of many such plans, dealings with the employer are limited to the adjustment of grievances, the arrangement of benefit plans, and discussion of minor matters of "plant housekeeping." Wages, hours and working conditions are entirely outside the scope of the organization's

---

[123] Lists of employees to be blacklisted are seldom used today.

[124] This explains why workmen who were discharged upon the demand of employers' liability insurance companies have sometimes been able to recover from these companies. See Hilton *v.* Sheridan Coal Co., 132 Kan. 525, 297 Pac. 413 (1931). But see Johnson *v.* Aetna Life Ins. Co., 158 Wis. 56, 147 N. W. 32 (1914), in which the employer refused to testify on behalf of the employee and the court held for the defendant insurance company.

functions. Under other company union plans, the chosen representatives of the workers do go through the form of making an agreement with the employer covering these basic matters. However, no real collective bargaining is possible. In the first place, under company union plans, the representatives of the workers must themselves be employees of the employer.[125] Hence they lack the knowledge and skill in collective bargaining of regular union agents. Even more important, they are afraid to fight too aggressively for their constituents, for fear the employer will discharge or otherwise discriminate against them. In the second place, the company union ordinarily has no independent treasury for use in financing a strike. It has no affiliations with the labor movement to help it in carrying on a strike. Hence there exists no possibility of effectively withholding labor if no satisfactory collective terms can be arrived at.[126]

The number of company unions grew very rapidly in the decade following the war.[127] Some impetus was given by the War Labor Board, which actually set up shop committees or employee representation plans as a method for adjusting grievances and preventing disputes in concerns which had not previously dealt with labor organizations.[128] The Transportation Act of 1920[129] and the decisions of the Railroad Labor Board created by that act also encouraged the growth of company unions. The board held that the carriers should deal collectively with their employees. So the carriers proceeded to set up organizations of their employees which they could dominate.[130]

Restriction of the right of employers to organize company unions was foreshadowed by the Railway Labor Act of 1926 which specified that the workers should be free to select their

[125] The only exception to this statement known to the writer is in the Nunn Bush shoe factory in Milwaukee.

[126] For a more extensive analysis of the weakness of company unions, see Twentieth Century Fund, Inc., *Labor and the Government*, 1935, part i, chaps. iv and v.

[127] See *ibid.*, p. 77.

[128] See *ibid.*, pp. 76-77; and Lescohier, D. D., *History of Labor in the United States*, 1935, vol. iii, Working Conditions, pp. 341-345.

[129] 41 U. S. Stat. at Large, 456, 49 U. S. C. A., Secs. 71-74.

[130] See *Labor and the Government*, pp. 179-181.

COLLECTIVE BARGAINING 411

representatives for collective bargaining purposes.[131] In 1930 the United States Supreme Court interpreted this provision to warrant enjoining a railroad from setting up a company union among its employees, on the ground that such action by an employer interfered with the free choice by employees of their representatives for collective bargaining purposes.[132] Though this decision affected only employers and workers covered by the Railway Labor Act, it indicated a possible line of development in the law of collective bargaining.[133]

3. **Enforcement.**—The law of collective bargaining as outlined above is enforced through the three types of court action: prosecutions, damage suits and injunctions.

a. *Prosecutions.*—Prosecutions are the most numerous.[134] In most strikes there are many arrests: some on criminal charges of assault, rioting, or even murder; and many for petty misdemeanors, such as disorderly conduct, obstructing traffic, or intimidation. As indicated earlier in this chapter, the numbers of arrests vary considerably with the attitude of the police in the particular city where the strike occurs. If they are friendly to the strikers they let them "demonstrate" rather freely and employers complain that they get no police protection. If the police are unfriendly, even one or two pickets silently marching to and fro may be arrested for intimidation.[135]

b. *Damage Suits.*—While damage suits against unions or their members have been very infrequent as compared with criminal prosecutions, there are many instances in which this remedy has been sought. A leading authority on labor law states knowledge of 314 cases in which damages were sought against unions or their members for acts committed by or in behalf of the

[131] 44 U. S. Stat. at Large, Sec. 2 (3), 45, U. S. C. A., Sec. 152 (3).
[132] Texas & N. O. R. Co. *v.* Brotherhood of Railway and Steamship Clerks, 281 U. S. 548, 50 Sup. Ct. 427 (1930).
[133] For a more detailed discussion of this case and its significance, see below, p. 421.
[134] The following are representative figures: New York furriers' strike in 1926, 884 arrests and 477 convictions; ladies' garment workers' strike in Chicago in February, 1917, 1,400 arrests out of 2,500 strikers; and in 1929, in the textile workers' strike at Elizabethton, Tenn., there were 300 arrests in a single day. See Witte, *op. cit.*, p. 152.
[135] Gevas *v.* Greek Restaurant Workers' Club, 99 N. J. Eq. 770, 134 Atl. 309 (1926).

union, and at least 66 cases in which damages were recovered.[136] The most important damage suits were the Danbury Hatters' Case,[137] decided by the United States Supreme Court in 1908, and the Coronado Case, first decided in that court in 1922.[138]

In the Danbury Hatters' Case, 197 members of the hatters' union were sued under the Sherman Act for damages caused by the boycott called by their union against the product of the Danbury hat factory. The triple damages asked for were $240,-000. Many of the individual hatters testified that they knew nothing of the boycott. But as members of the union they were all held liable, and their savings accounts and homes were placed under attachment to pay the damages awarded. Eventually, after further litigation, the case was settled for $234,000, most of it furnished by the American Federation of Labor. But the individual hatters lost their savings, and the danger of damage suits as a means of enforcing the law of collective bargaining was amply demonstrated.

In 1922 in the Coronado Case, the United States Supreme Court held that an unincorporated union could be sued as an entity and damages collected from it if its responsibility for illegal acts could be established.

These decisions have established that labor unions and their individual members are responsible without limit for all unlawful actions of the union officers and agents which they have in any manner authorized or sanctioned. Such antecedent authorization or subsequent approval of unlawful acts does not have to be expressed, but may be inferred from all the facts in the situation. Continued membership in the union after publicity has been given to unlawful acts done in its behalf is of itself sufficient to constitute approval thereof.[139]

Once liability is established against a union, none of its funds is exempt from seizure. With liability of the union goes also

---

[136] See Witte, *op. cit.*, pp. 138, 139.

[137] Loewe v. Lawlor, 208 U. S. 274, 28 Sup. Ct. 301 (1908).

[138] United Mine Workers v. Coronado Coal Co., 259 U. S. 344, 42 Sup. Ct. 570 (1922).

[139] Illinois Central R. R. Co. v. International Association of Machinists, 190 Fed. 910 (1911); Church Shoe Co. v. Turner, 218 Mo. App. 516, 279 S. W. 232 (1926). Contra, Lawlor v. Loewe, 187 Fed. 522 (1911); Michaels v. Hillman, 112 Misc. 395, 183 N. Y. Supp. 195 (1920).

COLLECTIVE BARGAINING 413

liability of all members of the union. Unions, being unincorporated associations, are, as far as responsibility for torts is concerned, much like partnerships. In the case of a tort committed on behalf of a corporation, the stockholders can be held only to the extent of their stock subscriptions (or double the amount in case of banks and similar corporations). In contrast, the responsibility of each member of a labor union is unlimited for tortious acts committed in his behalf, except for the personal exemptions allowed him by statute.

c. *Injunctions.*—The injunction has been the most publicized method of enforcing the law of collective bargaining. An injunction is an order issued by an equity court ordering named parties to do, or more generally to refrain from doing, certain specified acts. Anyone violating an injunction is charged with contempt of the injunction and may be punished by fine or imprisonment.

Since the beginning of the century there has been frequent use of injunctions in connection with strikes. Employers have sought and secured sweeping injunctions forbidding many kinds of activities important and even essential in the conduct of a strike. Labor has bitterly resented the use of injunctions in labor disputes and has repeatedly sought by statute to restrict their use. In the past such legislation proved notoriously ineffective. It was either so interpreted by the courts as to amount to nothing, or else held unconstitutional.[140] Within the past few years a new kind of anti-injunction law has been passed—by Congress applying to the federal courts, and by more than a dozen states.[141] To what extent this new legislation will allay labor's criticism it is as yet too early to say. The following pages will sketch what have been labor's chief objections to the use of injunctions, and give a brief summary of the main provisions of the new statutes.[142]

Labor's attitude was due in part to certain characteristics of injunction procedure which seemed grossly unfair to the average worker; and in part to the fact that injunctions appeared in

[140] See above, p. 385.
[141] The Norris-La Guardia Act and state laws modelled thereon. For summary and citations to statutes, see below, p. 415.
[142] For a full account of injunction procedure see Witte, Edwin E., *The Government in Labor Disputes*, 1932, chap. v.

many instances to do more than enforce the law as written, that is, the judge who issued an injunction seemed often to be actually "making the law."

The features of injunction procedure perhaps most frequently attacked were three: (1) A judge might issue a temporary "restraining order" on an *ex parte* basis; that is, for a short period until a hearing could be held, he might forbid all sorts of strike activities solely on complaint of the employer, without giving the workers any opportunity to answer the charges made. (2) Temporary injunctions (often lasting many months) were usually issued on the basis of affidavits, without the appearance of witnesses in open court where they could be cross-examined by the opponent's lawyer.[143] (3) When strikers were tried for contempt (or violation) of the injunction the trial was usually conducted by the judge who issued the injunction, and there was no opportunity for a jury trial.

As for the content of injunctions, in theory a judge can only enjoin illegal acts. But in a strike the illegality of acts is by no means a simple matter to determine. As discussed above, it depends not only on the acts themselves, but on the purpose of the strike, the prior existence of contracts, and so forth. Hence the same acts may be permitted under some circumstances and enjoined under others. Moreover, the substantive law is by no means definite at all points, and judges who granted injunctions almost necessarily exercised considerable discretion. It follows from all this that injunctions varied widely in content, not only from state to state, but even in the same state. For example, as to picketing, sometimes large numbers of pickets were expressly permitted; sometimes one or two pickets at each entrance; sometimes no pickets at all, if the purpose of the strike was held to be illegal.[144] In that event many other activities might be forbidden—even the payment of strike benefits.[145] If workers were employed under yellow-dog contracts, even peaceful persuasion of these workers might be enjoined.[146] Blanket injunctions sometimes even forbade en-

[143] See criticism of this practice by Judge Amidon in Great Northern Ry. Co. *v.* Brosseau, 286 Fed. 414, 416 (1923).
[144] See illustrative cases cited above, pp. 397-400.
[145] See illustrative cases cited above, note 73, p. 397.
[146] See above, p. 406.

COLLECTIVE BARGAINING 415

couragement of a strike in any way. If really enforced, they would have completely crippled the strike. Labor felt that the provisions of most injunctions were grossly unfair.

The Norris-La Guardia Act, first introduced in Congress in 1930, was designed to remove the worst abuses in the use of injunctions: (1) by specifying in detail the procedure to be followed by the inferior federal courts in issuing injunctions in labor disputes; and (2) by setting up certain limitations and requirements as to the content of such injunctions, and certain conditions under which injunctions should not be issued. A model state statute along the same lines was passed in Pennsylvania and Wisconsin in 1931;[147] the federal act was passed in 1932.[148] Up to December 1, 1935, sixteen states had passed similar laws.[149] The constitutionality of this legislation has not been finally settled by the courts.

Under this new legislation temporary *ex parte* restraining orders are prohibited except under unusual circumstances, and then for no longer than five days. Otherwise notice and oppor-

[147] Pennsylvania Laws of 1931, No. 310-311; Wis. Stat. 1935, Secs. 103.51-103.63, Laws 1931, C. 376.
[148] 47 U. S. Stat. at Large 70 (1932), 29 U. S. C. A., Secs. 101-115.
[149] In addition to Pennsylvania and Wisconsin, see *Colorado*, Laws 1933, C. 59; *Idaho*, Laws 1933, C. 215; *Indiana*, Baldwin's Ind. Stat. 1934, 10155-10168, Acts 1933, C. 12; *Louisiana*, General Stat. 1935 Supp. Secs. 4379.5-4379.17, Acts 1934, No. 203, p. 600; *Maryland*, Code 1924, Art. 100, Secs. 65-77, Laws 1935, C. 574; *Maine*, Laws 1933, C. 261, p. 439; *Massachusetts*, Acts 1935, C. 407; *Minnesota*, Laws 1933, C. 416; *New York*, Laws 1935, C. 477, amending Civil Practice Act, Sec. 876-a, Laws 1935, C. 298, C. P. A., Sec. 882-a, Laws 1935, C. 299, Sec. 1, Penal Law, Sec. 600 (4), (5), Laws 1935, C. 299, Sec. 2, Jud. Laws Sec. 753-a; *North Dakota*, Laws 1935, C. 247; *Oregon*, Code 1935 Supp. 49-1901-49-1914, Laws 1933, C. 355; *Utah*, Laws 1933, C. 15; *Washington*, Remington's Revised Stat. Supp. 1935, Secs. 7612-1-7612-15, Laws 1933, Ex. Sess., p. 10; *Wyoming*, Laws 1933, C. 37.

The yellow-dog feature of the act was absent from the original act in Pennsylvania but was added in 1933. Pennsylvania, Laws 1933, C. 219. It is not a part of the Maine and Wyoming statutes. All of the statutes contain some form of the injunction and contempt features of the federal act.

For a comparison of state and federal legislation, see Riddlesbarger, "State Anti-Injunction Legislation" (1935), 14 *Ore. L. Rev.* 501. For an excellent general discussion of the acts, see Fraenkel, "Recent Statutes Affecting Labor Injunctions and Yellow-dog Contracts" (March, 1936), 30 *Ill. L. Rev.* 854, 864-881.

416 PRINCIPLES OF LABOR LEGISLATION

tunity for the other party to be heard are required. Temporary or permanent injunctions can be issued only after oral testimony in open court. Persons charged with contempt are entitled to a jury trial unless the contempt was committed in the presence of the judge. They are also entitled to demand a trial by a different judge from the one who granted the injunction. Other matters of procedure designed to protect the rights of the workers are also specified. The conditions under which injunctions can be issued are also set forth.[150] The employer must show real need for injunctive relief and the inadequacy of other remedies to afford him adequate protection.[151]

This new legislation has had a decided effect in restricting the use of injunctions in labor disputes. During 1933 and 1934 very few injunctions were granted by the federal courts, if we consider how many strikes occurred during those years. In quite a number of cases the courts either refused to issue injunctions or carefully restricted their scope.[152] Of course the new

[150] Sec. 8 of the Norris-La Guardia Act provides that: "No restraining order or injunctive relief shall be granted to any complainant who has failed to comply with any obligation imposed by law which is involved in the labor dispute in question, or who has failed to make every reasonable effort to settle such dispute either by negotiation or with the aid of any available governmental machinery of mediation or voluntary arbitration."

[151] The significance of the public policy declaration of the Norris-La Guardia Act is discussed below, p. 422. The yellow-dog provision is discussed above, p. 407.

[152] In inferior federal courts injunctions have been denied in the following cases: Levering & Garrigues Co. *v.* Morrin, 71 F. (2d) 284 (1934); Cinderella Theater Co., Inc., *et al., v.* Sign Writers' Local Union No. 591, 6 F. Supp. 164 (1934), 6 F. Supp. 830 (1934); Knapp-Monarch Co. *v.* Anderson, *et al.,* 7 F. Supp. 332 (1934); Miller Parlor Furniture Co., Inc., *v.* Furniture Workers' Industrial Union, 8 F. Supp. 209 (1934). The Levering and Cinderella Theater Co. cases upheld the power of Congress to limit federal equity jurisdiction. The Cinderella case stressed the fact that the plaintiff had not attempted to settle the dispute. That case and the Knapp-Monarch Co. case referred to the fact that there was no showing that local authorities were unable or unwilling to handle the situation. In all four cases the court found a "labor dispute" within the broad definition of the act.

In the following cases picketing was enjoined: Dean *v.* Mayo, 9 F. Supp. 459 (1934), reversing 8 F. Supp. 73 (1934); Laclede Steel Co. *v.* Newton, 6 F. Supp. 625 (1934), 80 F. (2d) 636 (1935); United Electric Coal Co. *v.* Rice, 80 Fed. (2d) 1 (1935), reversing

COLLECTIVE BARGAINING

legislation has not been passed on or interpreted by the United States Supreme Court. We do not know whether the present situation will continue.

4. **Toleration the Attitude of the Law.**—The law of collective bargaining as it stood before the advent of the New Deal may be characterized by the word *toleration*. The workers were free to bargain collectively; their right to organize and bargain collectively was recognized and repeatedly affirmed by legisla-

---

9 F. Supp. 635 (1934); *In re* Cleveland & Sandusky Brewing Co., 11 Fed. Supp. 198 (1935). In Dean *v.* Mayo the injunction was denied on the first hearing, no effort on the part of the complainant to settle the dispute being found. This was reversed on rehearing, a showing of a *bona fide* attempt to settle the dispute being made. There was mass picketing, violence, failure of local police to furnish protection, and interference with interstate commerce. In the other three cases cited, the court found that there was not a labor dispute within the meaning of the act. The plaintiff had the support of the majority of its employees in the Laclede case; the dispute was between two unions in the United Electric Coal Co. case; and the plaintiff was the receiver of a bankrupt corporation against whom a sympathetic strike was being carried on, in the last-mentioned case. In all of these cases there was violence.

State acts were involved in the following cases: Dehan *v.* Hotel & Restaurant Employees, etc., 159 So. 637 (La. 1935), injunction denied; Micamold Radio Corp. *v.* Beedie, 156 Misc. 390, 282 N. Y. Supp. 77 (1935), injunction granted, the court finding that the act was not retroactive and that the acts on which the injunction was based occurred before the statute was passed (federal courts and Louisiana contra); Kronowitz, *et al., v.* Schlansky, *et al.,* 282 N. Y. Supp. 564 (1935), injunction granted for same reason as in preceding case, but contempt feature of act held constitutional; La Rose *v.* Possehl, *et al.,* 282 N. Y. Supp. 332 (1935), injunction granted because no labor dispute was found where plaintiff sued a union for refusal to recognize him as a member in good standing; Penn Anthracite Mining Co. *v.* Anthracite Miners of Pa., *et al.,* 114 Pa. Super. 7, 174 Atl. 11 (Pa. 1934), contempt feature of act held constitutional; Safeway Stores, Inc., *v.* Retail Clerks' Union, Local No. 148, *et al.,* 51 P. (2d) 372 (Wash. 1935), and Jensen *v.* St. Paul M. P. Machine Operators' Local Union, 194 Minn. 58, 259 N. W. 811 (1935), injunctions granted because no labor dispute found within the meaning of the act.

In Massachusetts and New Hampshire, advisory opinions were secured of the state courts, and both said such an act would be unconstitutional. *In re* Opinion of the Justices, 271 Mass. 598, 171 N. E. 234 (1930); *In re* Opinion of the Justices, 86 N. H. 597, 166 Atl. 640 (1933). Massachusetts, however, enacted both the yellow-dog and general anti-injunction acts.

tures and by courts. Their right to strike was also recognized, though, as we have seen, it was by no means unqualified. But the rights of employers and non-union workers were also recognized and affirmed. Non-union workers had the right to get and hold jobs; employers had the right to use yellow-dog contracts, to hire and fire for any or no reason, and to organize company unions. They also had the right of access to the commodity and labor markets, the right to operate their plants, and the general right to do business.

Now these rights of workers and employers were bound to come into conflict. And the courts who were supposed to enforce the rights of both groups very frequently had to decide which rights to enforce. On the whole, their decisions in such cases tended to favor the employers, largely because their rights were better understood by lawyers and judges, and were more susceptible of protection through court procedures.

The right to bargain collectively certainly includes the right to join a union. Yet the protection of this right by forbidding discriminatory discharges and yellow-dog contracts was held to be an infringement of the employer's right to hire and fire. Similarly, the right to strike for a closed shop (believed by many labor organizations to be essential to effective collective bargaining) was sometimes held to infringe the rights of employers and non-union workers. While the courts enforced yellow-dog contracts which enabled employers to maintain *shops closed to union labor,* they often held illegal strikes to secure shops *closed to non-union labor.* Again, collective action by workers cannot be effective unless it extends beyond the confines of a local craft union. Yet the courts, ignoring economic realities, condemned many kinds of sympathetic action on the ground that these workers had no legitimate interest in the dispute.

Collective action by workers is more likely to interfere with the rights of the public than are the methods which employers use to combat it. Pickets must use the streets, agitation may lead to violence; but the firing of employees or the procuring of new ones is but an incident to the regular conduct of business. Hence the courts were more likely to interfere with the activities of workers.

Injunctions theoretically could be used to protect workers'

COLLECTIVE BARGAINING

rights as well as employers'. But the injunction can only be used to protect property rights from irreparable injury. For the most part, workers' rights were not recognized as property rights which could be protected in this way. Very few injunctions were ever granted to unions.

Finally the courts insisted on treating employers and workers with formal "equality," completely ignoring the gross economic inequality prevailing between them. A law which treats alike the giant corporation and the single laborer employed or seeking employment therein is bound to produce anomalous results.

Thus in actual practice before the New Deal the law operated to protect those employers who strove to prevent organization among their workers, who refused to bargain collectively, or who were trying to break a strike. The workers had the right to bargain collectively, but in seeking to achieve this end they were allowed to use only those methods which did not interfere with the rights of employers and of non-union workers.

IV. THE LAW OF COLLECTIVE BARGAINING UNDER THE NEW DEAL

New Deal legislation relating to collective bargaining exemplifies the attitude of *encouragement*. It treats collective dealing by labor as sound public policy. Further, it recognizes that the right to bargain collectively must include the right to organize and choose representatives for bargaining purposes, and that these rights must be protected against interference by employers. It accepts the fact that employers must be restricted in the exercise of certain rights long possessed by them, if labor's right to bargain collectively is to have any reality.[153]

1. Precursors of New Deal Legislation.—The New Deal attitude toward collective bargaining was embodied in statute form in Section 7a of the National Industrial Recovery Act

[153] At the present writing the constitutionality of New Deal legislation relating to collective bargaining has not been determined. Section 7a of the N. I. R. A. was invalidated as part of an unconstitutional statute in Schechter Poultry corp. *v.* U. S., 295 U. S. 495, 55 Sup. Ct. 837 (1935), but the court did not pass on the constitutionality of that particular section. The National Labor Relations Act has not reached the United States Supreme Court—the decisions of lower federal courts as to its constitutionality are conflicting.

passed in 1933.[154] But it was clearly foreshadowed in certain earlier legislation. In a sense it is to be found in the early anti-discrimination and anti-yellow-dog laws, since they obviously placed restrictions on the employer's right to hire and fire, in the interest of protecting the worker's right to join a union. But little attempt was ever made to enforce these laws and, as discussed above, both types were held unconstitutional. A more direct precursor of New Deal legislation is to be found, not in a statute, but in the statement of principles formulated by the War Labor Board, an agency set up to settle labor disputes during the World War. That statement contained the following: "The right of workers to organize in trade unions and to bargain collectively, through chosen representatives, is recognized and affirmed. This right shall not be denied, abridged, or interfered with by the employers in any manner whatever."

After according employers the right of organization, there followed the proposition: "Employers should not discharge men for membership in trade unions, nor for legitimate trade union activities."[155]

The Railway Labor Act of 1926 went further in this direction by stating explicitly that railway workers should be free to choose their own representatives for the purpose of collective bargaining. After making it the mutual duty of the carriers and their employees to exert every reasonable effort to make and maintain agreements concerning rates of pay, rules and working conditions, the act provided:

Representatives, for the purposes of this act, shall be designated by the respective parties in such manner as may be provided for in their corporate organization or unincorporated association or by any other means of collective action, without interference, influence, or coercion exercised by either party over the self-organization or designation of representatives by the other.[156]

The importance of this provision in encouraging *bona fide*

[154] 48 U. S. Stat. at Large 198 (1933), 15 U. S. C. A., Sec. 707 (a).
[155] This statement of principles is quoted by Lorwin and Wubnig, *Labor Relations Boards,* Brookings Institution, 1935, p. 10. Interestingly enough, the War Labor Board in a number of its decisions formulated the principle of "majority rule" later so important an issue in the interpretation of Section 7a. See *ibid.*
[156] 44 U. S. Stat. at Large 577, Sec. 2 (3), 45 U. S. C. A., Sec. 152 (3).

COLLECTIVE BARGAINING

labor organizations became apparent in 1930, when the United States Supreme Court not only held this provision constitutional, but on the basis of it upheld an order of a federal district court which directed the disbanding of a company union set up by the Texas and New Orleans Railroad among its shop employees.[157] The company was charged with having violated the Railway Labor Act, on the ground that, in setting up a company union for its clerks, it interfered with their free choice of representatives for collective bargaining purposes. The United States Supreme Court declared:

> It has long been recognized that employees are entitled to organize for the purpose of securing the redress of grievances and to promote agreements with employers relating to rates of pay and conditions of work. . . . Congress was not required to ignore this right of employees but could safeguard it. . . . Collective action would be a mockery if representation were made futile by interference with freedom of choice.[158]

After this decision it was clear that the Railway Labor Act of 1926 outlawed company unions, in the sense of company-dominated organizations set up and controlled by the railroad. Although no case arose on the subject, it seemed equally clear that the act outlawed yellow-dog contracts, since to require workers seeking employment to sign such contracts would clearly constitute "interference or coercion" exercised by the employer over the "self-organization" of his workers.

The Norris-La Guardia Act of 1932—previously discussed in connection with its restrictions on the issuance of injunctions—also contained provisions clearly tending to *encourage* collective bargaining. Its yellow-dog provision was of this character.[159] It declared such contracts "contrary to public policy" and hence made them unenforceable in the federal courts. This put a stop to the issuance by those courts of sweeping injunctions virtually prohibiting all kinds of union activity where workers were employed under yellow-dog contracts, based on

---

[157] Brotherhood of Railway and Steamship Clerks *v.* Texas & N. O. Ry. Co., 24 Fed. (2d) 426 (1928), 25 F. (2d) 873 (1928), 33 F. (2d) 13 (1929).

[158] Texas & N. O. Ry. Co. *v.* Brotherhood of Railway & Steamship Clerks, 281 U. S. 548, 570, 50 Sup. Ct. 427, 434 (1930).

[159] 47 U. S. Stat. at Large 70, Sec. 3, 29 U. S. C. A., Sec. 103.

the theory that such activity might induce such workers to break their anti-union contracts. In effect, Congress was directing the federal courts to refuse to enforce contracts, the enforcement of which would necessitate serious restriction on attempts to organize workers for collective bargaining purposes.[160]

As foreshadowing New Deal legislation the public policy declaration of the Norris-La Guardia Act was perhaps even more significant. It stated that:

Whereas, Under prevailing economic conditions, developed with the aid of governmental authority for owners of property to organize in the corporate and other forms of ownership association the individual unorganized worker is commonly helpless to exercise actual liberty of contract and to protect his freedom of labor, and thereby obtain acceptable terms and conditions of employment, wherefore, although he should be free to decline to associate with his fellows, it is necessary that he have full freedom of association, self-organization, and designation of representatives of his own choosing to negotiate the terms and conditions of his employment, and that he shall be free from the interference, restraint, or coercion of employers of labor, or their agents, in the designation of such representatives or in self-organization or in other concerted activities for the purpose of collective bargaining or other mutual aid or protection; . . .[161]

In this statement Congress took an affirmative position. It virtually declared collective bargaining to be *good public policy* —something to be *encouraged,* not merely tolerated. To be sure, this declaration of policy was not fully implemented. No machinery was set up to prevent the exercise of "interference, restraint or coercion" by employers. In fact, such interference was not specifically forbidden. The act merely prescribed the conditions under which the federal courts should grant injunctions in labor disputes. But to place restrictions on the issuance of injunctions did increase labor's chance of making effective its

[160] For a list of the states enacting anti-yellow-dog statutes of this type up to December 31, 1935, and citations to the statutes, see above, note 119, p. 407. Federal legislation making yellow-dog contracts unenforceable is a part not only of the Norris-La Guardia Act but of the railroad reorganization and of the corporate reorganization sections of the Federal Bankruptcy Act. 47 Stat. 1474, 1481, Sec. 77 (p.), (q), (1933); 11 U. S. C. A., Sec. 205 (n); 48 Stat. 912, 922, Sec. 77B (l), (m), (1934), 11 U. S. C. A., Sec. 207 (l) (m).

[161] 47 U. S. Stat. at Large 70 (1932), 29 U. S. C. A., Sec. 102.

COLLECTIVE BARGAINING

right to bargain collectively. Though Congress did not at this time order employers to stop trying to defeat collective bargaining, it did in effect order the federal courts to cease lending employers their aid.

2. **Section 7a.**—The famous Section 7a of the National Industrial Recovery Act[162] borrowed much of its language from the public policy declaration of the Norris-La Guardia Act. Its first two parts read as follows:

> Every code of fair competition, agreement, and license approved, prescribed, or issued under this title shall contain the following conditions: (1) that employees shall have the right to organize and bargain collectively through representatives of their own choosing, and shall be free from the interference, restraint, or coercion of employers of labor, or their agents, in the designation of such representatives or in self-organization or in other concerted activities for the purpose of collective bargaining or other mutual aid or protection; (2) that no employee and no one seeking employment shall be required as a condition of employment to join any company union or to refrain from joining, organizing, or assisting a labor organization of his own choosing.[163]

The wording of 7a was vague and general. Until it was interpreted and applied to specific situations no one could tell just what it would amount to. It might prove as disappointing as the high-sounding phrases of Sections 6 and 20 of the Clayton Act, which the American Federation of Labor had hailed as labor's Magna Charta nearly twenty years before. In the early days of the N. R. A. the interpretations of 7a were varied and confused. At one time the National Labor Board (set up by the executive order of the President in the summer of 1933) and the Administrator of the N. R. A. were far apart as to what it meant. No attempt can be made here even to indicate the

---

[162] 48 U. S. Stat. at Large 198 (1933), 15 U. S. C. A., Sec. 707 (a).

[163] How Congress came to enact such a provision cannot be adequately discussed here. It was, of course, part of a measure in which industry was accorded certain rights of collective action long forbidden under the anti-trust laws. It may be said that an extension of the right of collective action by labor was an offset designed both to win labor's support for the measure in Congress and to make the act work effectively in promoting recovery. For an interesting analysis of the genesis of 7a, see Lorwin and Wubnig, *Labor Relations Boards,* Brookings Institution, 1935, chap. ii.

nature of the controversies.[164] One thing, however, was soon apparent, namely, that if the attitude 7a expressed were to be made effective, it should be clarified and amplified by statute and some permanent administrative agency should be set up with power to apply it. Much clarification of its meaning and implications was achieved through the decisions of the National Labor Board set up in 1933 and its successor, the National Labor Relations Board created in July, 1934.[165] But these agencies had no power to enforce their decisions and no one knew whether their interpretation of the meaning of 7a would be accepted by the courts. In May, 1935, 7a as part of the National Industrial Recovery Act was invalidated by the United States Supreme Court in the Schechter Case.[166]

3. **The National Labor Relations Act.**—The National Labor Relations Act, passed in July, 1935, embodied in statute form Section 7a as it had been interpreted by the agencies set up to administer it.[167] The new act also provided for enforcement by a new board which was given power to issue orders to employers—these orders, like those of the Federal Trade Commission and the Interstate Commerce Commission, to be enforced when necessary by the federal courts. At the present writing the constitutionality of this act has not been determined, and interpretation of its specific provisions by the courts is still lacking.

A summary of the National Labor Relations Act will provide the best means of indicating the changes in the law of collective bargaining which it represents. To justify a federal act applying not merely to transportation but to industry generally, the act recites the interference to the flow of interstate commerce arising from strikes arising from the "denial by employers of the right of employees to organize and the refusal

---

[164] For a discussion of these differences of interpretation, see *ibid.*, especially chap. iii.

[165] See *Decisions of the National Labor Board,* Parts I and II, 1934, and *Decisions of the National Labor Relations Board,* Parts I and II, 1935.

For an interesting discussion of the "common law" of 7a built up by these boards, see Lorwin and Wubnig, *op. cit.,* especially pp. 450-452.

[166] Schechter Poultry Corp. *v.* U. S., 295 U. S. 495, 55 Sup. Ct. 837.

[167] 49 U. S. Stat. at Large 457, 29 U. S. C. A., Sec. 151-166.

by employers to accept the procedure of collective bargaining," and declares it:

> ... to be the policy of the United States to eliminate the causes of certain substantial obstructions to the free flow of commerce and to mitigate and eliminate these obstructions when they have occurred by encouraging the practice and procedure of collective bargaining and by protecting the exercise by workers of full freedom of association, self-organization, and designation of representatives of their own choosing, for the purpose of negotiating the terms and conditions of their employment or other mutual aid or protection.[168]

To protect the workers in the exercise of their right of self-organization for the purpose of collective bargaining, the act makes certain activities of employers, which would interfere with the exercise of that right, "unfair labor practices," and empowers the National Labor Relations Board after hearing and due procedure to order an employer to "cease and desist" from such practices. The board has also the power to order the reinstatement of employees discharged because of union membership or activities. The federal circuit courts are directed to enforce the orders of the board. Appeal from an order of the board to a federal circuit court is provided for, but "the findings of the board as to the facts, if supported by the evidence, shall be conclusive."[169] The board is composed of three persons, no representation of employers or employees being provided for.

Most important are the list of activities declared to be "unfair labor practices."[170] First, it is an unfair labor practice to interfere with, restrain, or coerce employees in the exercise of their rights of self-organization, etc. Second, it is an unfair labor practice "to dominate or interfere with the formation or administration of any labor organization or contribute financial or other support to it." This is definitely aimed at the organization of company unions by employers. Third, it is an unfair labor practice "by discrimination in regard to hire or tenure of employment to encourage or discourage membership in any labor organization." Yellow-dog contracts are obviously out-

[168] *Ibid.*, Sec. 1.
[169] *Ibid.*, Sec. 10 (e).
[170] *Ibid.*, Sec. 8.

lawed by this provision. But the sentence quoted above would also bar closed-shop agreements, which organized labor in many industries regards as indispensable to the maintenance of effective collective bargaining. So a proviso is added stating that this does not preclude an employer from making an agreement with a labor organization to require, as a condition of employment, membership in that organization, if the organization actually represents the employees (in accordance with requirements to be discussed below), and if the organization was not built upon any unfair labor practices. This rather complicated provision permits a closed-shop agreement with a union genuinely representing the workers, but not with a company-dominated union (which would have been built up through unfair labor practices). It is also an unfair labor practice for an employer to refuse to bargain collectively with the representatives of his employees.

How can the employer know who are the proper representatives of his employees? Experience in applying 7a had demonstrated the importance of definite rules on this subject. The new act provides that the representatives selected "by the majority of the employees in a unit appropriate for such purposes shall be the exclusive representatives of all the employees in such unit"; and the board is to decide in each case where dispute arises the appropriate unit to be used as the basis of representation—"the employer unit, craft unit, plant unit, or subdivision thereof." The board where necessary is to conduct an election to select representatives and certify the name or names of the representatives that have been designated or selected.[171]

Just what the employer's duty to bargain collectively amounts to cannot be found in the statute. On this point the new board will probably follow the decisions of the first National Labor Relations Board which held in a number of cases that the employer must meet with the chosen representatives of the workers and in good faith try to reach a collective agreement.[172] He

[171] *Ibid.*, Sec. 9.

[172] *Decisions of the National Labor Relations Board* for the period July 9, 1934-December, 1934: In the matter of Eagle Rubber Co. and United Rubber Workers' Federal Labor Union #18683 (decided November 8, 1934); In the Matter of Atlanta Hosiery Mills and American Federation of Hosiery Workers' Local #76 (decided November 5, 1934); In the Matter of Whiting Milk Co. and Milk Drivers' and Creamery Workers'

COLLECTIVE BARGAINING 427

must be willing to discuss the terms presented by the workers' representatives and, if not willing to accept them, must present counter proposals of his own.[173] Obviously the law cannot require him to have a certain state of mind and cannot prevent a secret determination on his part not to reach agreement. If an agreement is reached, the board may, in the interest of avoiding future controversy, require that it be embodied in a written document and that it provide for machinery to interpret its provisions in case of dispute. The old National Labor Relations Board recognized that collective bargaining was seriously incomplete if not carried to this point.[174] If no agreement can be reached, "individual bargaining" or a strike remains the only alternative. The act provides definitely that no limitation is placed on the right to strike.[175] There is no provision for arbitration of any kind.

This act embodies a genuine attempt to give affirmative protection to workers in the exercise of their right to organize and bargain collectively. In consequence it calls for special administrative agencies to carry it into action. The ordinary machinery of government—the police and the courts—could not possibly

---

Union Local #214 (decided October 27, 1934); In the Matter of Johnson Bronze Co. and International Brotherhood of Foundry Employees Local #92 (decided October 27, 1934); In the Matter of Ely & Walker Dry Goods Co. and Wholesale House Workers' Union Local #18316 (decided September 25, 1934).

[173] See *ibid.*: In the Matter of Eagle Rubber Co. and United Rubber Workers' Federal Labor Union #18683 (decided November 8, 1934). Also *Decisions of National Labor Board*, Part II, In the Matter of Conn. Coke Co. and United Coke and Gas Workers' Union #18829 (decided June 30, 1934).

[174] *Decisions of the National Labor Relations Board* for July 9, 1934-December, 1934: In the Matter of the Eagle Rubber Co. and United Rubber Workers' Federal Labor Union #18683 (decided November 8, 1934); In the Matter of Atlanta Hosiery Mills and American Federation of Hosiery Workers Local #76 (decided November 5, 1934); In the Matter of National Aniline and Chemical Co. and Allied Chemical Workers' Local #18705 (decided October 3, 1934); In the Matter of Ely and Walker Dry Goods and Wholesale House Workers' Union Local #18316 (decided September 25, 1934); In the Matter of Houde Engineering Corp. and United Automobile Workers' Federal Labor Union #18839 (decided August 30, 1934).

[175] 49 U. S. Stat. at Large 457, Sec. 13 (1935), 29 U. S. C. A., Sec. 163.

do the job. For the government has undertaken to determine in case of dispute what organization does represent the workers in any plant, large or small. This involves determining the proper bargaining unit, and in many cases the holding of an election to permit that unit a fair chance to choose its representatives. Further, if any employer is engaging in any of the unfair labor practices listed above, the workers may appeal to the government to put a stop to it. Thus among other things the government promises to protect every wage earner (in a plant covered by the act) from discriminatory treatment. Any worker who believes he was discharged because he joined a union or was active in it has a right to have the case investigated. If his claim is substantiated, the government undertakes to secure his reinstatement.

The National Labor Relations Board with its regional offices and agents has been set up to carry out this law. The courts are merely to enforce its orders or hear appeals therefrom. Whether even such a special administrative tribunal can cope with the task ahead of this body remains to be seen. Of course the board will act only on complaint, and the volume of complaints will depend on the strength of unionism throughout the country and the success of the board in handling such complaints as are made.

On its face, the National Labor Relations Act makes a number of important changes in the law of collective bargaining, as compared with the law as it stood in 1932. These changes are mostly restrictions on rights long exercised by employers. Chief among them are the following: (1) The employer is restricted in his right to hire and fire. He can no longer use that general right in such a way as to interfere with the organization of his workers. He must not use yellow-dog contracts, he must not refuse to hire men because they belong to a union nor fire them for that reason. (2) The employer is restricted in his right to organize a company union. His employees may form any kind of organization they want, but he must keep his hands entirely off. (3) The employer is restricted in his right to refuse to deal collectively with his employees. If they organize and choose representatives, he must meet with those representatives and endeavor to reach a collective agreement as to terms and conditions of employ-

COLLECTIVE BARGAINING 429

ment. (4) The new act sets up a special administrative agency. The enforcement of the law of collective bargaining is no longer left to the police and the courts.

It is too early to say how important these changes will prove in actual practice. We do not yet know what scope, if any, the courts will accord this new law, or how they will interpret its provisions. Nor do we know how important these statutory changes—even if allowed to stand as written—will prove in promoting the growth of labor unions. In any case, the National Labor Relations Act of 1935 constitutes a significant experiment in government *encouragement* of collective bargaining.

v. Intervention by Government

The development of large-scale production and the growing complexity and interdependence of the social order have vastly increased the number and disastrousness of strikes and lockouts.[176] Today society in general often suffers acutely from interruptions to production and the disorder which may accompany them. This is especially true where essential services such as transportation are involved. Hence there exists a public interest in preventing strikes, or shortening their duration; and demands arise for government *intervention* to accomplish these aims. Government intervention in the United States has not gone very far, except in the railroad industry, and for a short period more generally in one state, Kansas. Australasia furnishes the leading example of government intervention to settle labor disputes and as such warrants somewhat full description in this chapter. By way of introduction, however, methods and degrees of intervention should be listed and explained. Four methods are usually recognized: (1) mediation or conciliation; (2) voluntary arbitration; (3) compulsory investigation; (4) compulsory arbitration.

[176] For recent figures on the extent of strikes and lockouts and the number of workers involved, see International Labor Office, *The I. L. O. Year Book*, 1934-35, vol. ii, Labour Statistics, pp. 164-165. From 1927-1932 there were in Germany 3,587 disputes involving 2,048,949 workers, with 37,871,790 working days lost. From 1927-1934 there were in Great Britain 3,100 disputes involving 2,211,000 workers, with 30,750,000 working days lost. In the United States for the same period there were 7,923 disputes with 3,783,026 workers involved and 129,038,575 working days lost.

By *mediation* or *conciliation* is usually meant the bringing together of employers and employees for a peaceable settlement of their differences by discussion and negotiation. The mediator, either a private or an official individual or board, makes inquiries without compulsory powers, trying to induce the two parties by mutual concessions to effect a settlement. The successful mediator never takes sides and never commits himself as to the merits of a dispute. He acts purely as a go-between, seeking to ascertain, in confidence, the most that one party will give and the least that the other will take without entering on either a lockout or a strike. If he succeeds in this, he is really discovering the bargaining power of both sides, and bringing them to the point they would arrive at if they made an agreement without him.

Where the difficulty is due to the parties not having thoroughly discussed the situation together, the mediator is often able to bring them into joint conference. In practice, most of the settlements have been arranged through compromise. In other cases, the parties are unwilling to admit to each other the utmost concession they will make, fearing to weaken their position. In such cases a mediator whom both sides can trust can render invaluable service as an intermediary. Occasionally parties refuse to treat with each other, but each will consent to make a separate settlement with the mediator. Finally, mediators, through their familiarity with methods for dealing with analogous difficulties in different trades, are sometimes able to suggest a solution. In all cases the mediator is merely a confidential adviser. Even when he is a state authority, he does not exercise any of the compulsory powers of the state; and if he even endeavors, by public investigations and recommendations, to bring public opinion to bear upon the disputants, he disqualifies himself for further mediation.

Voluntary arbitration occurs when the two parties, unable to settle the controversy by themselves or with the assistance of a mediator, agree to submit the points at issue to an umpire or arbitrator, by whose decision they promise to abide. The complete procedure of arbitration consists of a number of steps: (1) the submission of the dispute to the decision of a third party; (2) submission to an investigation; (3) refraining from strike or lockout pending investigation; (4) drawing

COLLECTIVE BARGAINING 431

up an award; (5) enforcement of the award and refraining from strike or lockout during its life. Arbitration remains strictly voluntary even if at every step except the first the state uses its compulsory power. The essential thing is that *both* parties consent in advance to calling in the powers of government. Hence, it is not inconsistent with the idea of voluntary arbitration for the state to use its power of compelling testimony, or even of enforcing an award, provided both sides have previously agreed that this be done.

Under the system of *compulsory investigation*, a board created by the state summons witnesses and takes testimony on the initiative of one party to the dispute without the consent of the other, or upon its own initiative without the consent of either. The board is one of investigation and recommendation, without legal power to enforce its awards. Compulsory investigation is sometimes accompanied by prohibition of strikes or lockouts pending the completion of the investigation and the publication of the recommendations. This compulsory postponement is the characteristic feature of the Canadian Industrial Disputes Investigation Act of 1907,[177] copied by Colorado in 1915,[178] designed to prevent sudden strikes or lockouts. It is not essential to compulsory investigation. The alternative is compulsory investigation without the prohibition of strikes and lockouts, and this is provided for in the laws of several American states. These laws are generally thought to establish voluntary systems of mediation, but they go beyond that point when they take testimony without the consent of either side.

Compulsory arbitration consists in the government's directly or indirectly compelling employers and employees to submit their disputes to an outside agency for decision. In a complete system of compulsory arbitration, government coercion is exercised at all five of the steps previously mentioned. Differences *must* be submitted to arbitration; witnesses *must* testify and produce papers; the parties *must* refrain from strike or lockout during the investigation; the board *must* reach a decision and announce an award; the parties *must* observe the

[177] Canadian Industrial Disputes Investigation Act (1907), 6-7 Edw. VII, C. 20.
[178] Colorado Compiled Laws, 1921, Secs. 4341-4374.

award and refrain from strike or lockout during its life. The penalties for violation are fine and imprisonment; however, they are not imposed on a workman for ordinarily quitting work or on an employer for the ordinary discharge of a workman, but for quitting or discharging collectively, or with intent to obstruct any of the steps essential to the arbitration.

1. **State Mediation Laws.**—A majority of American states have agencies of some kind for the mediation and voluntary arbitration of labor disputes.[179] Many of the states have permanent boards, usually called boards of "conciliation and arbitration," made up of three or six members representing employers, workers, and the public. In other states, the labor commissioner acts as a mediator, or a chief mediator is appointed under an industrial commission. In some states these agencies function very infrequently; in a few they have played quite a part in preventing strikes or bringing them to a close. Obviously this kind of government intervention is limited in character. It functions only with the consent of the parties to the dispute. Government merely helps the parties to reach a collective bargain, or, if they are willing, may itself settle the terms of employment. In about a dozen states provision is made for the legal enforcement of an arbitration award when arbitration has been agreed to by representatives of both sides.[180]

[179] Alabama, Arizona, Arkansas, Colorado, Connecticut, Georgia, Illinois, Indiana, Iowa, Kansas, Louisiana, Maine, Maryland, Massachusetts, Michigan, Minnesota, Missouri, Montana, Nevada, New Hampshire, New Jersey, New York, Ohio, Oklahoma, Oregon, Pennsylvania, South Carolina, South Dakota, Texas, Utah, Vermont, Washington, West Virginia, Wisconsin, and Wyoming have some kind of agency for mediation or voluntary arbitration. Alaska, the Philippine Islands, and Puerto Rico also have agencies for mediation or voluntary arbitration. See *Bulletin 370*, Labor Laws of the United States Series, published by the U. S. Bureau of Labor Statistics in 1925, and also *Bulletins 403, 470, 528, and 590* of the same series.

[180] In Colorado, Kansas, Maryland, Nevada, Ohio, and Texas there are specific provisions for filing the award and the enforcement of it by the court. In Illinois, a court may order compliance with an award, in which case failure to obey is punished as contempt, but not by imprisonment. In Iowa, Michigan, Missouri, Montana, and New Hampshire, the award is binding for a certain length of time and may probably be enforced by injunction and contempt proceedings, although the statute does not specifically provide for it. In fourteen states the voluntary agreement to arbitrate must contain a promise to abstain from strike

COLLECTIVE BARGAINING

Somewhat more drastic government intervention is provided for in the twenty-two states with compulsory investigation laws.[181] But this power has in fact been very rarely invoked. Colorado's compulsory investigation law entails the most compulsion. It forbids strikes or lockouts pending investigation and recommendation.

2. **Railway Labor Laws.**—Government intervention in the United States has gone furthest and been most frequently employed in relation to labor disputes on the railroads.[182] The public interest in uninterrupted operation in this field is readily apparent. In consequence, through a long series of federal statutes the attempt has been made to use government agencies to prevent strikes of railroad workers. The first act, passed in 1888, provided for voluntary arbitration and compulsory investigation.[183] It was on the statute book for ten years, but its arbitration provisions were never used and its investigation provisions were used only once. A new act was passed in 1898,[184] another in 1913,[185] another (when the railroads were returned to private hands) in 1920.[186] The basic features of the present system for handling labor disputes on the railroads were enacted in 1926,[187] with important changes added in 1934.[188]

---

or lockout pending arbitration proceedings: Alabama, Connecticut, Illinois, Indiana, Iowa, Louisiana, Maine, Massachusetts, Montana, New Hampshire, Ohio, Texas, Utah, and Vermont. See United States Bureau of Labor Statistics, *Bulletins 370, 403, 470, 528,* and *590.*

[181] Alabama, Colorado, Connecticut, Georgia, Illinois, Indiana, Iowa, Louisiana, Maine, Maryland, Massachusetts, Minnesota, Missouri, Montana, New Hampshire, New York, Ohio, Oklahoma, Oregon, South Dakota, Utah, and Vermont have compulsory investigation laws. See United States Bureau of Labor Statistics, *Bulletins 370, 403, 470, 528,* and *590.*

[182] Except for the brief experiment in compulsory arbitration in Kansas. See below, pp. 437-439.

[183] 25 U. S. Stat. at Large 501 (1888).

[184] 30 U. S. Stat. at Large 424 (1898).

[185] 38 U. S. Stat. at Large 103 (1913), 45 U. S. C. A., Sec. 101 *et sequitur.*

[186] 41 U. S. Stat. at Large 469 (1920), 45 U. S. C. A., Sec. 131 *et sequitur.*

[187] 44 U. S. Stat. at Large 577 (1926), 45 U. S. C. A., Sec. 151.

[188] 48 U. S. Stat. at Large 1185 (1934), 45 U. S. C. A., Sec. 151 *et sequitur.*

434   PRINCIPLES OF LABOR LEGISLATION

The present set-up and its functioning is significant: (1) because it exemplifies the most comprehensive attempt made in the United States to *encourage* and promote collective bargaining; (2) because it provides a carefully worked-out system by which government *intervenes* to help the parties to reach and maintain agreements without resort to compulsory arbitration. It is too soon to tell whether these provisions facilitating collective bargaining and removing causes of dispute will actually prevent all strikes.

As indicated in the preceding section, the Railway Labor Act of 1926 was a forerunner of 7a and the National Labor Relations Act. It provided very definitely that for purposes of collective bargaining and the settlement of disputes "representatives shall be designated by the respective parties . . . without interference, influence or coercion by either party over the self-organization or designation of representatives by the other."[189] This provision was the basis of the very important decision of the United States Supreme Court in the Texas and New Orleans Railway case.[190] The act of 1934 elaborates the provisions in the act of 1926 designed to protect the workers in the exercise of this right. It provides that

> it shall be unlawful for any carrier to interfere in any way with the organization of its employees or to use funds of carriers in maintaining or assisting or contributing to any labor organization, labor representative or other agency of collective bargaining . . . or to influence or coerce employees in an effort to induce them to join or remain, or not to join or remain members of any labor organization, or to deduct from wages of employees any dues, fees, assessments, or other contributions payable to any labor organization, or to collect or assist in the collection of any such dues, fees, assessments, or other contributions.[191]

This is clearly aimed at methods used to promote company unions and has sounded their death knell in the railroad field.

The new act also provides definitely for "majority rule,"

---

[189] 44 U. S. Stat. at Large 578, 45 U. S. C. A., Sec. 152 third.
[190] 281 U. S. 548, 50 Sup. Ct. 427 (1930). For discussion of this decision and its significance, see above, p. 421.
[191] 48 U. S. Stat. at Large 1187 (1934), 45 U. S. C. A., Sec. 152 fourth.

COLLECTIVE BARGAINING 435

with an agency to certify as to the accredited representatives for dealing with the employer.[192]

In these respects the act may be said to be merely *encouraging* collective bargaining and to go little further than the National Labor Relations Act. But additional provisions clearly constitute government *intervention* to prevent interruptions to commerce and the operation of the railroads. The act recognizes that there are two kinds of disputes which may threaten interruption to railroad operation: (1) disputes as to the interpretation or application of agreements covering wages, hours and working conditions; (2) disputes arising over attempts to arrive at new agreements on these matters. It therefore provides for two independent agencies, the National Railroad Adjustment Board[193] and the National Mediation Board.[194]

The first is to function as far as possible on a bipartite basis without any participation by outsiders. Government intervention is here limited to requiring the setting up of such adjustment machinery and to enforcing the decisions arrived at by that machinery. The decisions of the National Adjustment Board are enforceable through the federal courts. If this bipartite adjustment board becomes deadlocked when trying to settle a grievance or interpret an agreement, a referee is to be added, chosen if possible by the two sides, if necessary by the non-partisan Mediation Board.

This Mediation Board of three members is the instrument of government intervention when there is danger that a new collective agreement may not be arrived at by direct negotiations.[195] As its name implies, it acts as mediator between the parties, with no powers of compulsion. In the first year of its existence it was successful in mediating seventy disputes.[196]

[192] 48 U. S. Stat. at Large 1187 (1934), 45 U. S. C. A., Sec. 152 fourth.
[193] 48 U. S. Stat. at Large 1189 (1934), 45 U. S. C. A., Sec. 153.
[194] 48 U. S. Stat. at Large 1193 (1934), 45 U. S. C. A., Sec. 154.
[195] The National Mediation Board also performs for the railroad industry one of the important functions performed by the National Labor Relations Board for industry generally. In case of dispute on the question, it decides the proper unit for choosing representatives, conducts the election where necessary, and certifies the accredited representatives. See 48 U. S. Stat. at Large 1188 (1934), 45 U. S. C. A., Sec. 152 ninth.
[196] See First Annual Report of the National Mediation Board for the year ending June 30, 1935, Table II, p. 10.

The act provides that where mediation fails, the parties be urged to accept arbitration. If they cannot agree on the arbitrators to represent the public, they will be selected by the Mediation Board. In the first year of operation mediation was unsuccessful in two instances, but voluntary arbitration was refused. However, strikes did not follow.[197]

The act further provides for compulsory investigation by a special board to be appointed by the President if the Board of Mediation finds that there is danger of a substantial interruption in transportation service.[198] This power has not been invoked under the new act.

The question may be asked whether the new Railway Labor Act restricts the right to strike. There is no such explicit provision in the act. Employers are forbidden under severe penalty to change wage rates or working conditions without recourse to the prescribed forms of negotiation, including action by the Mediation Board if requested by the employees or proferred by the board.[199] There is no corresponding restriction on employees not to strike until after recourse to negotiation and mediation. If compulsory investigation is resorted to, for sixty days "no change except by agreement shall be made by the parties to the controversy in the conditions out of which the dispute arose."[200] The act contains no explicit affirmation of the right to strike, such as is found in the National Labor Relations Act. There is merely a provision:

Nothing in this chapter shall be construed to require an individual employee to render labor or service without his consent, nor shall anything in this act be construed to make the quitting of his labor or service by an individual employee an illegal act; nor shall any court issue any process to compel the performance by an individual employee of such labor or service, without his consent.[201]

Whether a strike called before all the various methods of settling the dispute had been resorted to would be declared illegal by the courts remains to be seen. At all events, there

---

[197] *Ibid.,* p. 10.
[198] 44 U. S. Stat. at Large 586 (1926), 45 U. S. C. A., Sec. 160.
[199] 48 U. S. Stat. at Large 1188, 1189, 1197 (1934), 45 U. S. C. A., Sec. 152 seventh, tenth, Sec. 156.
[200] 44 U. S. Stat. at Large 586 (1926), 45 U. S. C. A., Sec. 160.
[201] 44 U. S. Stat. at Large 586 (1926), 45 U. S. C. A., Sec. 159 eighth,

COLLECTIVE BARGAINING

are no penalties against such strikes. It appears, then, that the new Railway Labor Act merely provides carefully worked-out forms of government action to prevent strikes, but, in the last analysis, no coercion.

3. **Compulsory Arbitration in Kansas.**—The only really coercive measure attempted in the United States was the short-lived compulsory arbitration statute of Kansas.[202] Organized labor and organized employers have both opposed compulsory arbitration in this country. The Kansas act was passed (largely by farmer votes) at a special session of the legislature, called after a nation-wide coal strike in 1919 had caused public suffering and created a public opinion favorable to coercive government action to prevent strikes. Organized labor bitterly opposed the measure. The employers of Kansas were divided.

The Kansas act created a "court of industrial relations," composed of three judges appointed by the governor for three-year terms. The manufacture of food products, the manufacture of "clothing and all manner of wearing apparel in common use by the people," the mining or production of fuel, "the transportation of all food products and articles or substances entering into wearing apparel or fuel," and all public utilities and common carriers, as defined under the general statutes of Kansas, were declared to be affected with a public interest and therefore subject to supervision by the state "for the purpose of preserving the public peace, protecting the public health, preventing industrial strife, disorder, and waste, and securing regular and orderly conduct of the business directly affecting the living conditions of the people." In case of a serious controversy in any of the industries covered, the Court of Industrial Relations was authorized on its own motion, or on complaint of any ten taxpaying citizens in the locality, to summon the parties before it and to investigate the conditions of the industry. The findings of the court were to state "specifically the terms and conditions upon which said industry . . . should be thereafter conducted." The court was to "order such changes, if any, as are necessary to be made in and about the conduct of said industry . . . in the matter

[202] Kansas Industrial Relations Court, Acts of 1920 Special Session, C. 29.

of working and living conditions, hours of labor, rules and practices, and a reasonable minimum wage or standard of wages."

Under the Kansas act the right of collective bargaining was expressly recognized, but strikes, picketing, boycotting, and similar acts to enforce labor's claims were forbidden. On the other hand, the discharge of employees for bringing controversies to the attention of the court, or for testifying before it, was prohibited, and the right of workmen to quit their employment individually was not restricted. In case of actual suspension or limitation of operation in any industry covered by the act, the court was to take it over and operate it during the emergency.

The Kansas Industrial Relations Act was the subject of extensive litigation. Both employers and workers were unfavorable to the act and both contested it in the courts. In 1923 the United States Supreme Court declared unconstitutional, at least for industries which are not public utilities, the provisions undertaking to give the industrial court power to fix wages.[203] Fixing of wages by compulsory arbitration in the packing industry was held inconsistent with the due process of law clause of the Fourteenth Amendment. In April, 1925, the law was again passed on by the Supreme Court.[204] The court unanimously held that the meat packing industry was not affected with a public interest, and the fixing of hours of work through a system of compulsory arbitration by a state agency was described as infringing the liberty of contract and rights of property guaranteed by the due process of law clause of the Fourteenth Amendment.

Even before the Kansas court was finally invalidated, it had ceased to function, having largely lost public support. It was a leading political issue in 1922. The Republican platform praised it highly and the Democratic platform repudiated the whole act. The verdict at the polls was somewhat inconclusive, since the voters elected a Democratic governor and an overwhelmingly Republican legislature. The governor sought to

[203] Wolff Packing Co. v. Court of Industrial Relations, 262 U. S. 522, 43 Sup. Ct. 630 (1923).

[204] Wolff Packing Co. v. Court of Industrial Relations, 267 U. S. 552, 45 Sup. Ct. 441 (1925).

COLLECTIVE BARGAINING 439

abolish the court; the legislature reduced its appropriation. In 1922 it heard but few cases; after 1923, none at all.

4. **Compulsory Arbitration in Australasia.**—Thoroughgoing coercive intervention by government to settle labor disputes and prevent strikes is to be found in Australasia, dating from the first compulsory arbitration act passed in New Zealand in 1894.[205] New South Wales passed a similar statute in 1901, Western Australia in 1902, the Commonwealth in 1904, South Australia and Queensland in 1912.[206]

This Australasian development in relation to collective bargaining diverged widely from that in the rest of the English-speaking world. No single reason explains the difference. The adoption of coercion in Australasia was the result of a development—economic, social and political—sharply in contrast to that in the United States.

The employer in Australasia was not as far separated from his men as the capitalist in America. The eight-hour day was the general rule even before the adoption of compulsory arbitration, and wages were much more nearly equal from one class of workers to the next. While our labor standards were depressed and wage differentials increased by the introduction

[205] The Industrial Conciliation and Arbitration Act, 1894, New Zealand Statutes, 58 Victoria, No. 14.

[206] Industrial Arbitration Act, 1901, 1901 Statutes of New South Wales, No. 59; Industrial Conciliation and Arbitration Act, 1902, Western Australia Acts of Parliament, 1st and 2nd Edwardi VII, No. 21; Commonwealth Conciliation and Arbitration Act 1904, Commonwealth Acts, Vol. III, No. 13; The Industrial Arbitration Act, 1912, Acts of the Parliament of South Australia, III Georgii V, No. 1110; The Industrial Peace Act of 1912, The Queensland Statutes, 3 George V, No. 19. In the same period the other two Australian states, Victoria and Tasmania, adopted a wage-board system for fixing minimum wage rates for men as well as women (The Wages Boards Act, 1910, Tasmania Acts of Parliament, 1 George V, No. 62; Factories and Shops Act, 1896, Victoria Acts of Parliament, 60 Victoria, No. 1445). These laws differed in basic principle from the compulsory arbitration statutes since they involved no restriction on the right to strike and were originally designed to protect sweated workers from excessively low wages, presumably in the absence of any collective bargaining. In subsequent developments, however, the wage-board system and the compulsory arbitration system tended to approach each other as the wage boards came to fix wages and hours for all occupations and as increasing reliance under compulsory arbitration statutes came to be placed on mediation and conciliation rather than compulsion.

of Negro and immigrant labor with lower standards of living and willing to work for lower wages, the immigration in Australia was comparatively light and mostly from England, where wages were the highest in Europe. Australasian labor escaped the difficulties presented by conflicting races and different languages. There was greater racial homogeneity and social equality. Land ownership, always an antidote for radical economic theories, was not diffused in Australia, and even farm laborers were organized in unions. There was no large body of disfranchised or unnaturalized laborers. The entire labor force, not merely the skilled workmen as in some of our eastern and southern states, could be mobilized at the polls. As a result, the ballot became in Australasia a class weapon.

The power of labor at the polls was first shown during the very years when labor proved impotent in collective bargaining. From 1890 to 1893 labor was defeated in four disastrous strikes. In Australia during these four years the number of parliamentary seats held by the Labor Party greatly increased. In New Zealand there was never a large Labor Party, but after the failure of the maritime strike of 1890, a progressive Liberal Party favorable to labor came into power to hold office for the next twenty years. Strikes had meant loss to the public and defeat to the employees. In a number of strikes voluntary arbitration had been refused by the employers. So organized labor in both countries turned to government for coercive assistance in determining wages and conditions of employment, and because of their political strength they secured the assistance they sought. Thus it was that New Zealand passed the first compulsory arbitration act in 1894,[207] a measure supported by labor and opposed by the employers.

In Australia the Labor Party grew rapidly from 1890-1893 and then suffered a temporary setback. After the creation of the Commonwealth in 1899, it continued its development and soon became one of the two dominant political parties. In fact, Australia has been for years divided politically between employers and employees. The first compulsory arbitration

[207] For an account of the background of the New Zealand Act, see Broadhead, Henry, *State Regulation of Labour and Labour Disputes in New Zealand,* Whitcombe and Tombs Ltd., Melbourne and London, 1908, pp. 3-10.

COLLECTIVE BARGAINING 441

law in Australia was passed in New South Wales in 1901;[208] the Commonwealth Act applicable to interstate disputes came in 1904.[209] The other states enacted similar legislation—except for Victoria and Tasmania which undertook to raise wages and improve working conditions through the less coercive wage-board system.

a. *Operation of the New Zealand Act.*—A brief sketch of the New Zealand law[210] and its operation may give some idea of the functioning of a compulsory arbitration system. The New Zealand act applied only to unions of employers or employees who registered under the act. Registration could be withdrawn on short notice. The act provided for district boards of conciliation made up of representatives of employers and employees nominated by the registered unions in the district, and a Court of Arbitration consisting of one Supreme Court judge assisted by a representative of employers and a representative of employees, also nominated by the registered unions. If a labor dispute arose it was referred to the appropriate district conciliation board. If it could not be settled by conciliation the dispute went to the Court of Arbitration which made a binding award. The typical award of the New Zealand arbitration court contained a detailed schedule of wage rates for the many different occupations in the industry, specified the hours to be worked, contained rules as to overtime and other labor conditions.[211] Strikes and lockouts by registered unions of employees or employers were prohibited under substantial penalties.

From 1895 to 1906 was a period of prosperity in New Zealand. Employees in various industries appealed to the arbitration court and secured a series of awards raising wages and otherwise improving conditions. The coercion of the system operated entirely on the employers, and labor was well

[208] Industrial Arbitration Act, 1901, 1901 Statutes of New South Wales, No. 59.
[209] Commonwealth Conciliation and Arbitration Act 1904, III Commonwealth Acts, No. 13.
[210] The Industrial Conciliation and Arbitration Act, 1894, New Zealand Statutes, 58 Victoria, No. 14.
[211] These details are to be found in practically all awards, as will be seen by examining any volume of the *Awards Made Under the Industrial Conciliation and Arbitration Act of New Zealand* (Wellington, New Zealand).

satisfied.[212] But in 1907 the period of prosperity came to an end and wage increases stopped. There followed a number of illegal strikes and a reorganization of the system in 1908.[213] The boards of conciliation organized on a district rather than an industry basis had been rather unsuccessful, because of a lack of expert knowledge for handling disputes in particular industries. The revised act provided for commissioners of conciliation who should appoint advisers to assist them in individual disputes, these advisers to be nominated by the parties to the dispute and to be men with practical experience in the trade concerned.[214] After 1908 the penalties against illegal strikes were increased by providing for attachment of the wages of individual workers and heavy fines on the unions. And certain restrictions on striking were laid on unions, whether registered or not, in public utilities and certain other industries.

Compulsory arbitration did not operate to prevent all strikes in New Zealand. Of course strikes by unregistered unions remained legal, and many of the strikes were of this character. But some illegal strikes occurred and penalties were applied.[215]

The effect of this system of compulsory arbitration on unionism may be noted. The whole system, of course, encouraged and promoted collective bargaining. Individual workers had no standing before the arbitration court.[216] And registered unions

[212] See Rankin, Mary Theresa, *Arbitration and Conciliation in Australasia*, G. Allen & Unwin, Ltd., London, 1916, pp. 160-168; and Research Report Number 23 of the National Industrial Conference Board, *Conciliation and Arbitration in New Zealand*, Boston, 1919, pp. 22-27. Both sources divide this into two periods of six years each, labor being well satisfied and heartily in favor of the act during the first six years, and neutral during the second six years of its operation.

[213] Mary Rankin, *op. cit.*, pp. 168-177. After 1908 a large section of labor was in open revolt against the act.

[214] The commissioners of conciliation sitting with the assessors (who represented the employers and employees) formed a Conciliation Council. It was the duty of this council to try to effect a settlement of the dispute for which they were brought together. Their decision was not binding, but disputes had to be referred to a council before they could be referred to the arbitration court.

[215] For a more detailed account of the operation of the New Zealand act, see Rankin, *op. cit.*, pp. 133-177.

[216] Initially this was also true of employers, but by a later amendment the individual employer was permitted to apply to the court for intervention in case of an industrial dispute.

COLLECTIVE BARGAINING 443

gained "union preference," which amounted to the closed shop, in most arbitration awards. Obviously the growth of unions was immensely stimulated by the operation of the compulsory arbitration statute. On the other hand, only registered unions were recognized by the court, and registration led inevitably to government supervision and control of the internal affairs of unions. Initiation fees, membership fees, fines, procedure, and relations to other unions came to be regulated by awards. Of course registration was voluntary and could be canceled at any time. But it appears that employers usually refused to recognize unregistered unions, thus forcing registration.

For many years all parties in the New Zealand Parliament, though they differed as to details, were committed to compulsory arbitration, the only opposition being from groups not represented in Parliament, like the socialists and syndicalists. After 1929 opposition to the system arose, chiefly because of its inflexibility. Apparently the court could not or did not act fast enough in reducing wages to meet depression conditions.[217] In 1932 the opposition won the day, and the first country to adopt compulsory arbitration practically abolished it.[218]

The only important respect in which compulsion is retained in New Zealand is that any organization of female workers may still secure from the court an award fixing the basic wage in its industry. Otherwise the act as amended requires recourse to the conciliation machinery by registered unions, but arbitration is purely voluntary. Under the old act, if conciliation proceedings broke down, the dispute was automatically referred to the Court of Arbitration which issued an award binding the parties. Today, if conciliation fails, unless there is unanimous (or in some cases majority) agreement among the members of the Council of Conciliation to refer the dispute to the Court

[217] See the *I. L. O. Year-Book*, 1931 (Geneva, 1932), p. 498. Riches, E. J., "The Depression and Industrial Arbitration in New Zealand," in the *International Labor Review*, November, 1933, vol. xxviii, pp. 617-634; pp. 623-628 give an account of the growing opposition of farmers and employers to the act during the depression. Awards were ordinarily made for three years, without any provision for changes in rates to meet falling prices, and no reduction could be effected during the currency of an award except by special legislative action.

[218] Industrial Conciliation and Arbitration Amendment Act, 1932, New Zealand Statutes, 22-23, Geo. V, No. 4.

of Arbitration, all awards and collective agreements binding the parties in dispute expire automatically (one month after conciliation has failed to secure agreement). Employers will then be free to reduce wages or workers to strike. Moreover, existing collective agreements and awards will be reviewed by conciliation councils promptly on request of employers—to make for more flexibility in wage rates. And obviously, if agreement as to changes cannot be reached and arbitration is not agreed to by both groups on the conciliation council, government intervention will terminate at that point. As a result of the act of 1932 it is apparent that the Court of Arbitration will funcion only rarely. Compulsory arbitration has been virtually abolished in New Zealand after nearly forty years of operation.

b. *Operation of Australian Laws.*—In Australia compulsory arbitration still prevails, though in that country, too, there has been some reaction against it, particularly since 1929.[219] The history of compulsory arbitration in Australia begins with the act passed in New South Wales in 1901.[220] New South Wales had suffered from many widespread and often violent strikes. In the attempt to mitigate them, it enacted a voluntary arbitration act in 1892.[221] But in the next few years when labor disputes arose, employers refused to accept arbitration; the voluntary act having thus proved completely ineffective, compulsion was resorted to in 1901. The original New South Wales act provided no conciliation machinery, but merely a single arbitration court. Strikes and lockouts were forbidden, but no prosecutions could be commenced for violation of this provision without the consent of the arbitration court. This feature, as well as the general plan of a single arbitration court without conciliation machinery, was copied in the Common-

[219] See Comonwealth Bureau of Census and Statistics, *Official Year Book of the Commonwealth of Australia* (Melbourne, 1908 et. seq.), No. 24, 1931, p. 388, and No. 25, 1932, pp. 787-788. See also the *New International Year Book* for 1931 (ed. by Herbert Treadwell Wade, New York, 1932), pp. 80-81; and "The Attack on Compulsory Arbitration," in *Labour Monthly*, June, 1929, vol. x, pp. 443-445.
[220] Industrial Arbitration Act, 1901, 1901 Statutes of New South Wales, No. 59.
[221] Labour Settlements Act, Statutes of New South Wales, 56 Victoria, No. 34.

COLLECTIVE BARGAINING

wealth Act of 1904.[222] The Commonwealth Court was given jurisdiction over "disputes extending beyond the limits of any one state." By 1912 all the Australian states had passed compulsory arbitration laws except Victoria and Tasmania which adopted instead a wage-board system involving no restriction on the right to strike.[223]

No attempt can be made here to trace the changes in structure and functioning under the various Australian acts.[224] Only a few contrasts to New Zealand can be indicated. In one respect the Australian laws are more stringent. Since all unions are subject to the acts regardless of "registration," it follows that (except in Victoria and Tasmania) no strikes or lockouts are legal in Australia. On the other hand, penalties against strikers have been invoked more rarely than in New Zealand. In fact, the Commonwealth Court of Arbitration has never given the necessary consent to the prosecution of unions or strikers. Its awards have thus operated as coercive on employers but not on labor.

Union preference has been an exceedingly controversial issue in most of the Australian states and in the Commonwealth. Ministries have been wrecked on both sides of the question.

In Australia the difficulties of compulsory arbitration have been enhanced by conflicts over jurisdiction as between the state and the commonwealth courts. In many cases both federal and state awards have operated in the same industry, sometimes applicable to the members of different unions working in the same factory. Attempts to avoid such overlapping by either expanding or curtailing the power of the Commonwealth Court have proved unavailing. In 1929 the anti-labor

---

[222] Commonwealth Conciliation and Arbitration Act 1904, III Commonwealth Acts, No. 13.

[223] For a statement of the essential differences between the wage-board and compulsory arbitration systems, see above, note 206, p. 439.

[224] For the best general discussion of the various Australian acts, see Anderson, George, *Fixation of Wages in Australia* (University of Melbourne Publications, No. 12), Macmillan & Co., Melbourne, 1929. See also, by the same author, "Regulation of Industrial Relations," *Annals of the American Academy,* November, 1931, vol. clviii, pp. 156-165; and Ko, Ting Tsz, *Governmental Methods of Adjusting Labor Disputes in North America and Australia* (Columbia University Studies in History, Economics, and Public Law, No. 271), New York, 1926, chap. vi.

ministry was overturned when it attempted to abolish federal compulsory arbitration in all except maritime industries.[225] But in 1931 when the labor ministry tried to extend the power of the Commonwealth and get full federal jurisdiction over industrial disputes, it too was defeated and the anti-labor party returned to power.[226] And so the system of dual regulation has continued.

One of the major problems faced under compulsory arbitration is what standards should be used in fixing wage rates and other conditions. Under mediation and voluntary arbitration, since the alternative trial of economic strength remains, the relative economic strength of the parties really determines the terms arrived at. One or the other party to the dispute will refuse to agree to a wage that seems far out of line with the probable outcome of a strike. Where strikes are completely outlawed, this measuring rod or standard disappears. In Australia (more than in New Zealand) the attempt has been made to substitute another standard, namely, the cost of living, in fixing a "basic" wage, with differentials above it based on differences in skill. Justice Higgins, for many years President of the Commonwealth Court of Arbitration, first set up this standard in the famous Harvester decision in 1907, and for years thereafter most Australian awards started from that base —taking into account changes in cost of living, differentials for skill, and so forth. The difficulties were great, but on the whole that basis has been continued up to the present time.[227]

Many changes have been made in the organization of the arbitration machinery in the Commonwealth and the various states. Until 1930 the changes seemed to be mostly in the direction of elaborating the conciliation features of the various acts and reducing so far as possible the resort to compulsory arbitration. Since 1930 the conciliation machinery has been simplified and in some respects the use of coercion has been in-

---

[225] *The New International Year Book* for 1929, ed. by Herbert Treadwell Wade, New York, 1930, p. 77.
[226] *Ibid.* for 1931 (1932), pp. 80-81.
[227] Harvester Judgment (*ex parte* H. V. McKay), 2 C. A. R. 1. The substance of this judgment and a complete discussion of this and other similar decisions are included in Anderson, George, *Fixation of Wages in Australia* (Melbourne, 1929), pp. 188 ff. See also the *Official Year Book of the Commonwealth of Australia*, No. 27, 1934, pp. 718-723.

COLLECTIVE BARGAINING

creased—largely in order to make possible more rapid changes to meet changing industrial conditions. In general, the tendency since the advent of the depression has been to adjust wages and hours in conformity with the needs of industry, with less regard to preserving or enhancing standards of living.[228]

It is well-nigh impossible to draw general conclusions as to the success of the Australasian experiment in government *intervention*. Assuredly it served to increase union organization and collective dealing between employers and workers. Probably it somewhat retarded the gains which labor, if untrammeled in the right to strike, might have won in the period of rising prices and general prosperity. On the other hand, it undoubtedly protected labor from losses which it would have suffered in the depression period. It did not serve to prevent strikes, though perhaps it reduced their number. To some extent, at least, it transferred the conflict between labor and capital from the economic to the political level. It offers no conclusive evidence of the social desirability of that transfer.

[228] See Foenander, O. de R., "The New Conciliation and Arbitration Act in Australia," in *International Labor Review*, February, 1929, vol. xix, pp. 151-174, pp. 162-163, and, by the same author, "The New Commonwealth of Australia Conciliation and Arbitration Act," in *International Labor Review*, December, 1931, vol. xxiv, pp. 699-712, pp. 709-710.

CHAPTER VIII

ADMINISTRATION

NOTWITHSTANDING ALL THAT HAS BEEN SAID REGARDING THE progress of legislation for the protection of the workers, it is scarcely worth consideration if the laws are not enforced. More important than the hasty enactment of additional laws is the adoption of methods of administration that will enforce them. It is easy for politicians, or reformers, or trade union officials to boast of the laws which they have secured for labor, and it is just as easy to overlook the details, or appropriations, or competent officials that are needed to make them enforceable. It is easy to say that little or nothing can be done by changing the "machinery of government" and that the real thing to do is to get "better officials" to enforce the laws, and better judges to interpret them; but it is only through the "machinery of government" that such officials are found and selected, and that judges can have the facts needed for interpretation. Administration is more than mechanism. It is a method of legislation. It is the means of investigating, drafting, and adopting enforceable laws. It is the means of getting and keeping competent officials. It is the method of determining what authority or powers the officials shall have, how they shall execute the laws, what procedure they shall follow in court, what facts they shall investigate for the use of the court in its duty of interpretation. Administration is legislation in action.

In a constitutional government, executive officers are not supposed to go out with a club and, on their own initiative, force people into obeying what they happen to think is the law. Before they act, they are supposed to investigate. The legislature, too, is assumed to be a body possessed of all the facts, and its acts are unconstitutional when they disregard essential facts that could be ascertained by investigation. The court, through many centuries of experience, has developed the law of evidence and the procedure of investigation for the trial of indi-

ADMINISTRATION

viduals who are charged with the violation of law. Finally, when the higher court passes upon the constitutionality of the law itself, it does so with reference to whether the facts are such as call for the law and whether the law deals with the facts in accordance with the higher law of the Constitution.

Thus, each department of government is an investigating body. Only by investigation can each be restrained from the arbitrary and capricious acts that make despotism abhorrent. This is the significance of "reasonableness," which runs through every requirement of the Constitution. Reasonableness is ascertained by investigating *all* the facts and giving to them "such weight as may be just and right in each case."[1] Thus, we have executive, judicial, and legislative investigations designed to guide each department of government in dealing with all the facts in its own field.

But modern industrial conditions have become so complex, and the laws deal with such a variety of facts, that a fourth department of government is emerging whose purpose is primarily investigation. This is administration. If administration is legislation in action, it is because administration is investigation. It unites in one department the investigating activities of all departments. Let us first consider the executive department and its field of investigation.

1. The Executive

The history of the so-called "factory acts" shows the beginnings of the special kind of investigation needed for the enforcement of labor law. The term "factory act" or "factory legislation" covers all legislation, whether applied to factories or to other establishments, respecting such matters as health and safety of workers, hours of labor, child labor, payment of wages, company stores, and so on. Factory acts are distinguishable from those laws which determine the fundamental rights and duties of master and servant, employer and employee, in the labor contract, such as mechanics' lien, wage exemption, employers' liability, and the law of conspiracy. The distinction is not always clear because the line between the two is drawn differently at different times and in different countries. In

[1] Smyth *v.* Ames, 169 U. S. 466, 18 Sup. Ct. 418 (1897); Freund, *Police Power*, 1904, p. 58.

general, we may say that by factory legislation is meant that side of labor legislation which requires officials for continuous inspection and enforcement, whereas other labor laws are enforced only when a private individual brings a case in court. The distinction tends to disappear in proportion as special administrative machinery is adopted for the enforcement of other laws. For this reason the term "labor legislation" is taking the place of "factory acts."

The early factory laws provided no special officers for their enforcement. It was assumed that complaints would be made by the injured employees, and it was merely provided that the ordinary officers attached to the court, such as sheriffs, policemen, prosecuting attorneys, should attend to the prosecutions on complaint. Such is even now the theory and practice in some states, especially in the South.

It required several years to discover the futility of this kind of administration. Employees would not make complaints for fear of being discharged. The officials had other duties more urgent. They were local officials, usually afraid of the voters.

The next step, beginning in the decade of the 'sixties, was the creation of a class of special state police, known as factory inspectors, whose duty it was to investigate the conditions in the factories, to get their own evidence of violations and then to conduct the prosecutions without calling upon employees to testify.

The first state to appoint this class of special police was Massachusetts, in 1867. Since that time the method has been adopted in most of the states, and the largest force of inspectors in any state is that in New York, where 161 were employed on January 1, 1936.

The creation of this special type of police was not a complete solution of the problem of effective administration. So long as these inspectors are considered as executive officials, they have a limited and special purpose. The chief object is to secure evidence for prosecutions against violators of the law. Having secured their evidence, they must take it to the prosecuting attorney or district attorney, who then reinvestigates the facts in order to determine if there is a case made out that will probably result in a conviction when tried in court. Finally,

ADMINISTRATION   451

when the case is brought to trial, the court again investigates all the facts, calling witnesses on both sides and providing for their cross-examination. It follows precise rules of evidence, rejecting what is immaterial to the point to be decided. This evidence may be heard and passed upon by a jury. The entire procedure of the executive, the prosecutor, and the court in reaching a decision and enforcing the law turns upon an investigating of the facts of violation.

For various reasons, the enforcement of labor law in American states through investigations by the old type of factory inspectors has come to be recognized as ineffective. The inspectors were not trained for their work; they were frequently changed; they were poorly paid, and they had but little opportunity for promotion and a professional career. Their number was usually inadequate for the amount of work required. Much of their time was often given to gathering and publishing large volumes of belated statistics that had but little value as an aid either to their own administration or to the legislature in improving the laws. Considerable attention has been given to these deficiencies and they are justly considered to be the most important problem of labor legislation. Useless statistics are giving way to timely bulletins on safety, health, and other specific conditions of labor. The New York State Factory Investigating Commission was created, after a deadly factory fire, to inquire why it was that the laws were not enforced.[2] The United States Bureau of Labor investigated the enforcement of woman and child labor laws.[3] The American Association for Labor Legislation devotes a large part of its attention to the improvement of administration.[4] Out of these investigations and a widespread distrust of the existing methods of factory inspection have come serious attempts to improve the character of administration. The more promising of these attempts are described in the following pages. They involve not only the

[2] See New York State Factory Investigating Commission, *Preliminary Report*, 1912, pp. 13, 14.
[3] *Report on Condition of Woman and Child Wage-earners in the United States* (Senate Doc. 645, Sixty-first Congress, Second Session), 1910-1913.
[4] See its official organ, the *American Labor Legislation Review*, published quarterly, beginning 1911.

executive branch of government, but also the legislative and judicial branches.

11. THE LEGISLATURE

In an executive investigation no question is raised as to the reasons for the enactment of the law itself. The question is merely whether the law was violated or not. Investigations take a much wider scope when the matter is being prepared for the legislature upon which it shall proceed to enact a law. The first investigations on a subject of legislation are usually made by private parties or by persons whose object it is to secure legislation. In the field of labor the American workingmen's organizations, as early as 1832, published reports upon the conditions of labor showing the need of new laws for their correction. These crude investigations have been followed and multiplied by a great variety of associations and organizations. In the decades of the 'forties and 'fifties industrial congresses were held in different cities and investigations of shop and factory conditions were made. The International Workingmen's Association, founded by Karl Marx and the British trade unionists in 1864, and spreading to the United States, included as one of its objects the collection of information and carrying on of investigations of labor conditions in different countries of the world. The National Labor Union in 1868, the industrial congresses of 1873 and 1874, the Knights of Labor and the American Federation of Labor have all in turn conducted investigations on all the aspects of labor problems that in their opinion needed legislation.

In the decade of the 'eighties private organizations like the Consumers' League began investigations, especially of child labor and sweating systems. The National Child Labor Committee, founded in 1904, has had a systematic plan and a wide field of investigation. In 1900 the first international association for the investigation of labor conditions in all countries was organized at the Paris Exposition, under the name of the International Association for Labor Legislation. Up to the time of merging with the International Association on Unemployment and the International Committee on Social Insurance in September, 1925, it had organized sections in fifteen coun-

ADMINISTRATION

tries.[5] In some cases affiliations were made with previously existing private organizations. The object for which the International Association was founded was to bring about uniform legislation through treaties entered upon by independent governments. The procedure adopted was to hold international biennial congresses in Switzerland, at which the conditions of labor and the laws of different countries were reported upon and plans for uniform laws were drafted. Through the courtesy of the government of Switzerland the diplomatic representatives of the different nations would then be invited to meet and formulate "conventions" carrying out, as far as possible, the plans recommended by the preceding congress of the association. When these "conventions" were agreed upon, the several countries were expected to enact the desired legislation and enforce it in their own jurisdiction. When any country adopted the recommendations of a convention, it became equivalent to a treaty between that and other countries which had acted in the same way. The first international "conventions" of this kind were those of 1906, forbidding the night work of women[6] and the use of poisonous phosphorus in the manufacture of matches.[7] The former was quickly adopted by fourteen nations, and the latter by eleven.

The characteristic activities of the International Association and its fifteen national sections have been scientific investigations conducted with the definite object of securing needed legislation. Like other private associations, its work has been largely propagandistic and did not carry official weight. However, the International Association, with permanent headquarters in a government building at Basle, Switzerland, was in receipt of subventions from twenty-two different national governments. In this respect it marked the beginning of an affiliation between private investigations and those conducted by government.[8] As frequently occurs with pioneer social organizations, certain of the activities of the International Association

[5] Austria, Belgium, Denmark, England, Finland, France, Germany, Holland, Hungary, Italy, Norway, Spain, Sweden, Switzerland, and the United States.
[6] See "Night Work," p. 142.
[7] See "Prohibition of Substances or Instruments," p. 194.
[8] See Bibliography under "VIII. Administration."

have now been taken over officially, in this case by the International Labor Office instituted under the League of Nations.

There were two other allied associations, the International Association on Unemployment and the International Committee on Social Insurance. In 1922 steps were taken to merge the three associations, and this was finally brought about in September, 1925, at a representative meeting at Berne. The name of the present organization is the International Association for Social Progress.

The American section of the International Association for Labor Legislation was organized in 1906 with the object of investigating conditions underlying labor laws and disseminating information leading to the enactment and efficient enforcement of protective legislation. It has conducted investigations, held national conferences, published reports, drafted bills, and secured the enactment into law of progressive standards. While known as the American Association for Labor Legislation, it has served as the American arm of all three international associations, social insurance and unemployment as well as labor legislation. It continues as the American section of the International Association for Social Progress.

Governmental study of labor conditions in America also dates back to the early part of last century. As early as 1838 the state legislature of Pennsylvania conducted an investigation of woman and child labor in the factories of that state.[9] Massachusetts followed in 1845. Many states and the national government have at different times carried on investigations of this kind for special purposes by temporary committees of the legislature or by commissions appointed for the purpose. During the years 1910 to 1915 there were nearly thirty state commissions and one federal commission for the study of industrial accidents and the drafting of laws on workmen's compensation. Another notable example is the Factory Investigating Commission of New York, whose careful studies led to the adoption in 1914 of a large number of labor laws by the legislature of that state. In the broader field of federal investigations, a committee of the Senate of the United States in 1885 held extended hearings on the subject of capital and labor. The Industrial Commission, composed of members of Congress

[9] Pennsylvania Senate, *Journal*, vol. ii, 1837-1838.

ADMINISTRATION 455

and appointees of the President, made a report of nineteen volumes on the same and other subjects in 1901. Other temporary federal commissions have been the one on Immigration in 1911, and the Commission on Industrial Relations of 1913.

The origin of these temporary legislative investigations was a demand on the part of private organizations either for definite legislation or for official inquiry which would have greater weight through the power of compelling witnesses to testify and the conclusiveness which could not be secured by private societies. Their intent was both to inform the public and to aid the legislature.

The first state in the world to establish a permanent bureau for the investigation of labor conditions was Massachusetts in 1869. Under the names of bureau of labor statistics, bureau of labor, and similar names, such permanent machinery of investigation has been established in almost all of the states, by the federal government with its Department of Labor, first established in 1884, and by all national governments where the problem of labor and capital has become prominent. These bureaus were at first established primarily on the petition of labor organizations.[10] Their scope has been broadened in some cases, but their largest activity has been the collection of statistics of wages, hours, and conditions of labor. At times they are called upon by the legislature to make investigations which otherwise would have been conducted by legislative committees or temporary commissions.

A certain ineffectiveness of these bureaus has sprung from their desire, as permanent bureaus, to maintain a non-committal attitude in presenting facts, and they generally refrain from making recommendations for legislative action. Most of these bureaus, moreover, also have charge of the enforcement of the various labor laws, or are a part of a labor department that is charged with the enforcement of labor laws. Because of inadequate appropriations and the necessity of giving first attention to the enforcement of the laws, the tendency has been to abandon special studies and the collection of statistics, except as a by-product of the work of enforcing the laws.

The fullest development to date of official bureaus created for the sole purpose of ascertaining facts as a basis for legis-

[10] Powderly, *Thirty Years of Labor,* 1889, p. 303.

lative enactment is found in the International Labor Organization set up by the treaty which concluded the World War. Part XIII of the treaty declares that permanent peace such as is sought by the League of Nations "can be established only if it is based on social justice," and that the failure of any nation to adopt humane labor standards "is an obstacle in the way of other nations which desire to improve the conditions in their own countries." To arrive at desirable international minimum protective standards, a permanent International Labor Office is created, with quarters at the seat of the League of Nations. The office is in charge of a governing body of thirty-two persons, sixteen representing the governments, eight the employers, and eight the workers of the affiliated countries, selected for three-year terms. Eight of the sixteen government members are to represent the eight nations of chief industrial importance.[11] The governing body appoints a director of the office, who chooses the staff, "a certain number" of whom must be women. The duties of the organization include collecting and distributing labor data, conducting investigations, publishing a periodical on employment problems, and preparing the order of business for the International Labor Conferences.

The International Labor Conferences which the office thus assists in conducting are held at least yearly at the seat of the League of Nations or at some other place previously selected. They are composed of four delegates from each country attached to the league, divided among the government, the workers, and the employers, in the same proportion as the members of the governing body, namely, two, one, and one, respectively. The labor and employer delegates are named by the governments "in agreement with the industrial organizations, if such organizations exist, which are most representative of employers and workpeople" in the respective countries. Delegates may be accompanied by advisers, and when questions affecting women are before the conference at least one of the advisers "should be" a woman. The first annual conference, held in Washington, D. C., in 1919, had representatives from some thirty countries. At the twentieth annual conference held in Geneva in 1936 fifty countries were represented. Recom-

[11] In June, 1936, Canada, France, Great Britain, India, Italy, Japan, the United States, and Russia were the eight nations represented.

mendations and draft conventions have been adopted on such matters as the eight-hour day and forty-eight-hour week, public employment offices, workmen's compensation, unemployment insurance, health insurance, old-age pensions, reduction of child labor, prohibition of women's work immediately before and after childbirth, prohibition of night work for women and young persons, protection against anthrax, lead poisoning, and white phosphorus poisoning, and establishment of government factory inspection and health services.

The International Labor Office has also established commissions to aid in its work and it has secured the assistance of experts and technical advisers who are members of various commissions or correspondence committees. In 1920 the Joint Maritime Committee was set up. This is presided over by the chairman of the governing body and consists of two members of that body, five representatives of shipowners, and five representatives of seamen. It advises the office on all maritime questions and considers measures to be adopted to give effect to the decisions of the second session of the conference in 1920 which dealt with maritime questions. The Agricultural Advisory Committee was created in 1922, the Correspondence Committee on Industrial Hygiene in 1922, a Correspondence Committee on Social Insurance in 1923, and a Permanent Emigration Committee in 1925.[12]

Although the first International Labor Conference was held in Washington in 1919, with the United States participating, rejection of the Treaty of Versailles and the League of Nations by the United States Senate involved also rejection of the International Labor Organization. In 1933, however, the United States sent a delegation of four "observers" who participated in the work of the conference; and on June 16, 1934, Congress authorized the President "to accept membership" for the United States Government in the organization. An invitation was promptly voted by the conference then in session at Geneva, and this was officially "accepted" by the President in August, 1934. The United States was for the first time officially

[12] For a history of the organization and operation of the International Labor Organization, see Shotwell, James T., *The Origins of the International Labor Organization*, vol. i, History; vol. ii, Documents, 1934; and Wilson, Francis G., *Labor in the League System*, 1934.

represented by a full delegation at the Nineteenth International Labor Conference in 1935.

III. THE JUDICIARY

In the United States the judicial branch of government may be called upon to make investigations of labor conditions in order to render decisions on the constitutionality of laws enacted by the legislature. These investigations are quite different in character from those, previously described, in a trial for the violation of statutes. In a trial the question to be decided is that of a particular violation of a law. In questions of constitutionality the question is the conformity of the law with the Constitution. Here the court must investigate the question as to whether there is really an evil condition that needs to be remedied; whether this condition is a menace to the public or whether the statute is merely a benefit to private individuals without a public purpose; whether under the actual conditions the legislature confiscates property, discriminates between individuals, and thus denies the equal protection of the laws.[13]

In making such an investigation the court might appoint a referee or master in chancery to take evidence and investigate the facts. This procedure is often followed in the regulation of public utilities. The referee, usually a lawyer appointed by the court, calls before him accountants, engineers, experts, as

---

[13] "The principle involved in these decisions is that where the legislative action is arbitrary and has no reasonable relation to a purpose which it is competent for government to effect, the legislature transcends the limits of its powers, in interfering with liberty of contract; but where there is reasonable relation to an object within the governmental authority the exercise of legislative discretion is not subject to judicial review." (Chicago, B. & Q. R. Co. v. McGuire, 219 U. S. 549, 31 Sup. Ct. 259 [1911]).

"In every case that comes before this court, therefore, where legislation of this character is concerned, and where the protection of the federal Constitution is sought, the question necessarily arises: Is this a fair, reasonable, and appropriate exercise of the police power of the state, or is it an unreasonable, unnecessary, and arbitrary interference with the right of the individual to his personal liberty, or to enter into those contracts in relation to labor which may seem to him appropriate or necessary for the support of himself and his family." (Lochner v. New York, 198 U. S. 45, 25 Sup. Ct. 539 [1905]). See also "Public Benefit," p. 523, and "Equal Protection of the Laws," p. 528.

ADMINISTRATION 459

needed, and makes a report to the court of the facts. Such a practice, however, has not been followed in cases where the constitutionality of labor laws is called in question. This is probably owing to the fact that legislation of this character covers a large variety of subjects, requires a variety of witnesses and extended technical investigations, and that the court is not itself equipped with the staff of investigators competent to secure and furnish the information. The result is that social and economic conditions are not investigated by the court and it is compelled to fall back upon the principles of constitutional law, without full knowledge of the conditions to which the statute applies. Examples of decisions without investigation of conditions are as follows:

The Colorado Supreme Court, in declaring unconstitutional a law which limited the hours of labor in smelters to eight a day, said:

> This act is an unwarrantable interference with, and infringes, the right of both the employer and employee in making contracts relating to a purely private business, in which no possible injury to the public can result.[14]

Likewise, Judge Gray explained in the following language why the New York court nullified a law prohibiting night work for women:

> I think that the legislature, in preventing the employment of an adult woman in a factory, and in prohibiting her to work therein before six o'clock in the morning, or after nine o'clock in the evening, has overstepped the limits set by the constitution of the state to the exercise of the power to interfere with the rights of citizens. . . . It is clear, as it seems to me, that this legislation cannot, and should not, be upheld as a proper exercise of the police power. It is, certainly, discriminative against female citizens, in denying to them equal rights with men in the same pursuits.[15]

In the following cases the court clearly states that sufficient facts have not been presented to prove that legislation of that character is necessary to conserve the public welfare.

In the first Ritchie case the Illinois Supreme Court said:

> There is no reasonable ground—at least none which has been made

[14] *In re* Morgan, 26 Colo. 415, 58 Pac. 1071 (1899).
[15] People *v.* Williams, 189 N. Y. 131, 81 N. E. 778 (1907).

460   PRINCIPLES OF LABOR LEGISLATION

manifest to us in the arguments of counsel—for fixing eight hours in one day as the limit which woman can work without injury to her physique, and beyond which, if she works, injury will necessarily follow. But the police power of the state can only be permitted to limit or abridge such a fundamental right as to make contracts, when the exercise of such power is necessary to promote the health, comfort, welfare, or safety of society or the public, and it is questionable whether it can be exercised to prevent injury to the individual engaged in a particular calling.[16]

In the Lochner case, where a ten-hour law for bakers was tested, the court had before it only a limited amount of general information on the subject, without any special investigation. The majority ruled that the facts were not conclusive to warrant such legislation for the following reasons:

We think the limit of the police power has been reached and passed in this case. There is, in our judgment, no reasonable foundation for holding this to be necessary or appropriate as a health law to safeguard the public health, or the health of the individuals who are following the trade of a baker. . . . We think that there can be fair doubt that the trade of a baker, in and of itself, is not an unhealthy one to that degree which would authorize the legislature to interfere with the right to labor, and with the right of free contract on the part of the individual, either as employer or employee. In looking through statistics regarding all trades and occupations it may be true that the trade of a baker does not appear to be as healthy as some other trades, and is also more healthy than still others. To the common understanding the trade of a baker has never been regarded as an unhealthy one. . . . There must be more than the mere fact of the possible existence of some small amount of unhealthiness to warrant legislative interference with liberty.[17]

The foregoing cases illustrate the attitude of the courts where investigations of the facts have not been brought to their attention, or where they have been compelled to depend upon such knowledge as they themselves might have regarding such facts. In such a case the court might take what it calls "judicial notice" of facts even though they are not presented in evidence, and might rely upon what it considers "common knowledge," or that kind of knowledge which a reasonable

[16] Ritchie v. People, 155 Ill. 98, at p. 113, 40 N. E. 454 (1895).
[17] Lochner v. New York, 198 U. S. 45, at p. 58, 25 Sup. Ct. 539 (1905).

ADMINISTRATION 461

person ordinarily well informed might be supposed to have upon the subject. Common knowledge may go still further and include investigations made by private societies or by individuals or attorneys which appear to the court as presenting the facts pertaining to the case. "Courts will take notice of whatever is generally known within the limits of their jurisdiction."[18] "A common belief, like common knowledge, does not require evidence to establish its existence, but may be acted upon without proof by the legislature and the courts. While the power to take judicial notice is to be exercised with caution and due care taken to see that the subject comes within the limits of common knowledge, still, when according to the memory and conscience of the judge, instructed by recourse to such sources of information as he deems trustworthy, the matter is clearly within those limits, the power may be exercised by treating the fact as proved without allegation or proof."[19]

The first notable example of a decision on the constitutionality of a law based upon investigations of this kind is that of the Holden v. Hardy case, in 1898. In that case the attorney in defense of the law made an investigation of the health of workmen in mines and smelters which was presented in his brief to the court. Upon this information the court took exactly the opposite view of the Colorado court above cited, and held that the law was constitutional upon the following grounds:

While the general experience of mankind may justify us in believing that men may engage in ordinary employments more than eight hours per day without injury to their health, it does not follow that labor for the same length of time is innocuous when carried on beneath the surface of the earth, when the operative is deprived of fresh air and sunlight, and is frequently subjected to foul atmosphere and a very high temperature, or to the influence of refining or smelting.[20]

It is to be noticed that while the Supreme Court held that

[18] Quoted from Brown v. Piper, 91 U. S. 37 (1875), in People v. Charles Schweinler Press, 214 N. Y. 395, 108 N. E. 639 (1915).
[19] Quoted from Viemeister v. White, 179 N. Y. 235, at p. 240, 72 N. E. 97 (1904), in People v. Charles Schweinler Press, 214 N. Y. 395, 108 N. E. 641 (1915). See also cases quoted in Mr. Brandeis' brief, published by the National Consumers' League, in Muller v. Oregon, 208 U. S. 412, 28 Sup. Ct. 324 (1908).
[20] Holden v. Hardy, 169 U. S. 366, at p. 395, 18 Sup. Ct. 383 (1898).

the questions of law—that is, the principles of public benefit and equal protection of the laws—were identical in the Lochner case and the Holden v. Hardy case, the former was declared unconstitutional, while the latter was upheld because of difference in fact. Similarly, Mr. Brandeis in his brief in Muller v. Oregon quotes the law as propounded in the Lochner case but argues that the facts "establish . . . conclusively, that there is reasonable ground for holding that to permit women in Oregon to work in a 'mechanical establishment, or factory, or laundry' more than ten hours in one day is dangerous to the public health, safety, morals, or welfare." The court, which sustained the law, concurred in counsel's contention, as indicated by the following quotation:

In patent cases counsel are apt to open the argument with a discussion of the state of the art. It may not be amiss, in the present case, before examining the constitutional question, to notice the course of legislation, as well as expression of opinions from other than judicial sources. In the brief filed by Mr. Louis D. Brandeis for the defendant in error is a very copious collection of all these matters, an epitome of which is found in the margin. . . . The legislation and opinions referred to in the margin may not be, technically speaking, authorities, and in them is little or no discussion of the constitutional question presented to us for determination, yet they are significant of a widespread belief that woman's physical structure, and the functions she performs in consequence thereof, justify special legislation restricting or qualifying the conditions under which she should be permitted to toil. . . . When a question of fact is debated and debatable, and the extent to which a special constitutional limitation goes is affected by the truth in respect to that fact, a widespread and long-continued belief concerning it is worthy of consideration. We take judicial cognizance of all matters of general knowledge.[21]

A supreme court may even squarely reverse itself when it finds that a former decision was made without full knowledge of the facts. We have quoted above the language of the New York court, in 1907, in the case of People v. Williams, in which the court, without the aid of official investigation, held that a law prohibiting night work for women was unconstitutional. Eight years later the same court overthrew its former decision, when the legislature had again enacted a similar law, this time,

[21] Muller v. Oregon, 208 U. S. 412, 28 Sup. Ct. 324 (1908).

ADMINISTRATION 463

however, following the recommendations of the state factory investigating commission. The court justified itself as follows:[22]

It is urged that whatever might be our original views concerning this statute, our decision in People v. Williams . . . is an adjudication which ought to bind us to the conclusion that it is unconstitutional. While it may be that this argument is not without an apparent and superficial foundation and ought to be fairly met, I think that a full consideration of the Williams case and of the present one will show that they may be really and substantially differentiated, and that we should not be and are not committed by what was said and decided in the former to the view that the legislature had no power to adopt the present statute. . . . While theoretically we may have been able to take judicial notice of some of the facts and of some of the legislation now called to our attention as sustaining the belief and opinion that night work in factories is widely and substantially injurious to the health of women, actually very few of these facts were called to our attention, and the argument to uphold the law on that ground was brief and inconsequential.

Especially and necessarily was there lacking evidence of the extent to which, during the intervening years, the opinion and belief have spread and strengthened that such night work is injurious to women; of the laws, as indicating such belief, since adopted by several of our own states and by large European countries, and the report made to the legislature by its own agency, the factory investigating commission, based on investigation of actual conditions and study of scientific and medical opinion that night work by women in factories is generally injurious and ought to be prohibited.[23]

Not only have the courts changed their opinion as to actual conditions because of investigations, but as the investigations educated the public and created sentiment in favor of such legislation, courts have even indirectly reversed themselves on principles of law. The two Ritchie cases in Illinois offer an instance. In the first case (1895), one of the determining ob-

[22] People v. Charles Schweinler Press, 214 N. Y. 395, 108 N. E. 639 (1915).
[23] See also McLean v. Arkansas, 211 U. S. 539, 29 Sup. Ct. 206 (1909), in which the court upholds a screen law on the basis of investigations made by a commission; and State ex rel. Yaple v. Creamer, 85 Ohio St. 349, 97 N. E. 602 (1912), where the court accepts the findings of a special investigating committee as conclusive "to sustain the exercise of the police power" in workmen's compensation legislation.

jections that the court raised was that "it is questionable whether it [the police power] can be exercised to prevent injury to the individual engaged in a particular calling."[24] In other words, the court ruled that legislation protecting the health of the public or society was a proper exercise of the police power, but that it was improper when aimed to protect individuals against themselves.[25] The court, in the second Ritchie case (1910), found it convenient to avoid reference to this principle and scrupulously omits that portion in quoting from the case. According to the second opinion, the difference turned, not on principle, but on fact. The court said:

> The second proposition upon which the cases differ is this: the act of 1893 provides for an eight-hour day in which women shall be permitted to work in mechanical establishments, or factories or laundries. Can it be said if the limitation upon the number of hours which women were permitted to work in the designated callings in the act of 1893 had been fixed at ten hours instead of eight hours the court would have held the act unconstitutional as an unreasonable exercise of the police power of the state or that the act would have been held obnoxious to the Constitution as special or class legislation? We do not think it can be so said, as there is throughout the opinion a veiled suggestion which indicates that it was the opinion of the court that the limitation of the right to work longer than eight hours was an unreasonable limitation upon the right of contract.[26]

The principle that the police power cannot be exercised to protect individuals against themselves would overthrow a ten-hour law as well as an eight-hour law; but the fact that a ten-hour law is less restrictive than an eight-hour law causes the Illinois court to abandon the principle and to inquire into the facts. By a similar reliance on facts the Supreme Court of the

---

[24] Ritchie v. People, 155 Ill. 98, 40 N. E. 454 (1895).

[25] For a critical discussion of this principle, see Freund, *Police Power*, p. 141; for an acceptable presentation, see *In re* Morgan, 26 Colo. 415 58 Pac. 1071 (1899); and *In re* Jacobs, 98 N. Y. 98 (1885). In Holden v. Hardy the United States Supreme Court repudiates this principle, holding that it is constitutional under the police power to enact legislation either to protect the public or to protect individuals against themselves or acts of others. See "Public Benefit," p. 523.

[26] Ritchie v. Wayman, 244 Ill. 509, 91 N. E. 695, at p. 700 (1910).

ADMINISTRATION

United States held that an eight-hour law was constitutional and reasonable.[27]

The foregoing illustrations have been cited, among many that might be given, on account of the peculiarly high position occupied by American courts through their power to veto legislation on the ground of unconstitutionality. There has been abundant criticism of the courts for exercising this power, and insistent demands for constitutional amendments abrogating the power have been repeatedly made for more than a hundred years. Without pretending to enter upon a full discussion of these criticisms and demands, except to note the reactionary opinions on later laws during recent years, one thing is apparent—the courts ascribe great importance to reliable and complete investigations of actual conditions. The foregoing illustrations, as well as others found in this book, indicate that criticism also should be directed against legislatures and administrative authorities who enact and administer laws without reliable knowledge of the conditions with which they are dealing. During the past twenty-five years there has been a steady improvement in the quality and methods of administration. Nevertheless, in a majority of states, there is a great need for more efficient administration of labor laws, which will provide for continuous investigation, as well as law enforcement. Thus we come to a consideration of the modern department of labor, the functions of which are not only of an executive nature, but are also quasi-judicial and quasi-legislative in character, all based upon continuous investigation.

IV. THE MODERN LABOR DEPARTMENT

In all of the investigations above mentioned, even those carried on by the best-qualified experts, there is lacking the important feature of *prima facie* evidence, or of evidence that is conclusive as to the facts in a trial in court. Those investigations were not conducted under the rules of evidence which the court relies upon, and it therefore treats them merely as common knowledge. Even the factory investigating commission of New York, although created by the legislature, did not make an investigation that, in the eyes of the law, had binding force

---

[27] Miller *v.* Wilson, 236 U. S. 373, 35 Sup. Ct. 342 (1915). See "Maximum Hours, Women," p. 115.

upon the court. It indicates, however, the kind of investigations which are the next step in the administration of labor laws. This involves the transformation of the bureaus of labor statistics into an integral part of the department of government charged with the enforcement of the labor laws, with the object, not only of furnishing information to the legislature and to the people, but also of furnishing conclusions or findings of fact which shall be *prima facie* evidence of the truth, or even conclusive and binding upon the court. This object is sought to be obtained through the powers granted to the modern department of labor.[28]

1. **Administrative Investigations.**—One reason for the breakdown of administration is the failure to provide for that executive discretion which is as inevitable and necessary as legislative discretion. The American theory of separation of branches of government assigns to the legislature the investigation of conditions upon which its policy or principle is adopted and enacted into statute law. With the growing complexity of conditions the legislature has been compelled to go into the investigation of minute details, legislation on which, if applied to every establishment, would be unenforceable. Consequently, the old-type factory inspectors or special police are compelled to decide upon their own executive investigations whether or not they will enforce these details.

The situation is similar to the history of railroad regulation. In the early "Granger laws" of sixty years ago it was attempted to enact a detailed actual schedule of each rate for every shipment on every road, and then it was left to the individual shipper to bring suit in the courts to enforce the schedule. The later legislatures of the past forty years have omitted these technical details and have contented themselves with laying down general rules such as that all rates and services shall be reasonable as between the roads and the shippers. They have then created railroad, or public utility commissions,

[28] To what extent this object can be accomplished constitutionally is not here discussed. The court is itself both an investigating body and independent of the legislature. It can evidently refuse to be bound by a creature of the legislature. At the same time the ingenuity of bill-drafters has worked out methods of procedure which go far toward accomplishing the object. These are considered below.

ADMINISTRATION

whose powers, in the light of the Constitution, are not legislative, executive, or judicial, but *investigational*.

The problem which the legislature sets to these commissions for investigation is that of reasonable rates and services in each particular case where the question arises. The *principles* which enter into reasonableness are being continually laid down by the courts in long lines of decisions. Consequently, the commission needs no power of discretion. It must follow the law—that is, the principles. It only investigates and ascertains the *facts* which those principles call for. The legislature meanwhile has enacted that, *when* these facts are ascertained and published, *then* the law shall go into effect. The *fact* is the rate or service which has been ascertained by the investigations of the commission to be reasonable. It is announced and published as a finding of fact, a "rule," or "regulation," or "order," not a statute, but having the force of a statute. This is the finding or conclusion of the commission's investigations. It is *prima facie* valid in court and cannot be overthrown except by overwhelming evidence to the contrary.

Labor legislation has now reached an even more voluminous and technical stage than that which applies to railroad regulation. The legislature cannot possibly consider all the facts and details. Yet the legislature alone should determine the policies and the standards, and should go only into such details as have general application. The modern department of labor corresponds to the public utility or railroad commission. The latter passes upon the opposing interests of corporations and consumers or shippers, epitomized in the price bargain. The former passes upon the interests of employer and employee, epitomized in the wage bargain. The modern department of labor investigates the facts and works out the details which the legislature cannot pass upon.

Some thirty states have given their labor departments such rule-making power in widely varying extent.[29] The problem is much more diversified than that of establishing reasonable rates and services. "Reasonableness" in railroad regulation has a comparatively definite meaning; but reasonableness in labor legislation is as complicated as human life and modern indus-

[29] See Andrews, John B., *Administrative Labor Legislation*, Harpers, 1936.

try. A reasonable standard in one field has no meaning in another. There are health, safety, and welfare, for example, which require a variety of standards. There are hours of labor, days and periods of rest, age and sex of workers, with varying standards. There are private employment offices, workmen's compensation for accidents, and many other matters.

An Ohio statute of 1913, following the example of Wisconsin, merely requires that: "Every employer shall furnish employment which shall be safe for the employees therein; and shall furnish a place of employment which shall be safe for the employees therein and for frequenters thereof; and shall furnish and use safety devices and safeguards, and shall adopt and use methods and processes, follow and obey orders and prescribe hours of labor reasonably adequate to render such employment and places of employment safe; and shall do every other thing reasonably necessary to protect the life, health, safety, and welfare of such employees and frequenters." The law then gives to a commission the authority to ascertain and "fix such reasonable standards and to prescribe, modify and enforce such reasonable orders for the adoption of safety devices, safeguards, and other means or methods of protection to be as nearly uniform as possible, as may be necessary to carry out all laws and lawful orders relative to the protection of the life, health, safety, and welfare of employees in employments and places of employment or frequenters of places of employment."[30] The orders of the commission go into effect thirty days after publication and are *prima facie* reasonable and lawful. By means of this procedure the laws may be adapted to every detail of modern industry. They can be changed at any time when a further investigation shows new dangers or new methods of prevention. The commission is continually in session, but a legislature meets only at stated times. The commission is continually investigating while it is enforcing the laws, but the legislature investigates only when lobbyists, petitioners, or members succeed in getting a hearing. Included among the states which have adopted a similar method are California, Colorado, Massachusetts, New York, Oregon, Pennsylvania, and Wisconsin.

The above illustration particularly pertains to safety regu-

[30] Ohio, General Code, 1921, Sec. 871-15, and Sec. 871-22 (4).

lations, but the same principle has been developed with reference to other phases of labor legislation.[31]

For compensation in case of accident the legislative standard may require "reasonable" medical and surgical care, 70 per cent of the average weekly earnings lost during disability, and so on, to be determined and awarded by the commission.

For private employment offices the legislative standard may prohibit misleading statesments, discriminatory fees, and the like, and then give the commission power to "fix and order such reasonable rules of conduct of the business of any employment agent as may be necessary adequately to carry out" the sections of the law.

For the wages of minors the legislature may require employers to pay a "living wage," or such compensation "whether by time, piecework, or otherwise," as shall be "sufficient to enable the employee receiving it to maintain himself or herself under conditions consistent with his or her welfare." The commission, then, must carry on extensive investigations, must make various classifications, and determine for each the amount of the wage that the legislature intended.

In the case of adult women the legislature may provide that no woman shall be paid less than "reasonable and adequate compensation for the services rendered," and require the commission to ascertain whether the remuneration in a given instance is reasonable and adequate.[32]

For the hours of labor for women the legislature may prohibit the employment of any female "for such a period or periods of time during any day, night, or week, as shall be dangerous or prejudicial to the life, health, safety, or welfare of such female," and then authorize the commission to "investigate, ascertain, determine, and fix such reasonable classification" and such periods of time as shall carry out the purposes of the law.

---

[31] The illustrations following are taken from the laws of Wisconsin, but are more or less typical of laws in other states.

[32] Prior to 1925 the minimum wage law applied to adult women as well as minors. The commission, however, was enjoined from enforcing the law because of the decision in the Adkins case, 261 U. S. 525. The legislature then repealed the sections making it applicable to adult women, and substituted the so-called "oppressive-wage" law, from which these quotations are taken. See C. 176 Wisconsin Session Laws, 1925.

For dangerous employments the legislature may provide that "no employer shall employ, require, permit, or suffer any minor or any female to work in any place of employment, or at any employment, dangerous or prejudicial to the life, health, safety, or welfare of such minor or female," and then authorize the commission to investigate, classify, and determine the specific occupations from which women and minors shall be excluded.

For the regulation of apprenticeship the legislature may require an indenture stipulating the hours for work, the hours for attendance at school, the compensation, etc., and authorize the commission to draft, approve, and enforce it.

For industrial and vocational education, the legislature may require employers to permit children to attend continuation schools a certain number of hours each week in the daytime, without deduction of pay, and then authorize the commission to issue and revoke permits to work based on investigations showing what is necessary to secure compliance with the law.

The foregoing illustrations show the distinction between a legislative policy which sets up a standard, and an administrative investigation which applies the standard to each case or each class of cases. The principles of standardization have two aspects, which may be designated as *diversity* and *generality*. There is a wide diversity of standards, simply because there is a wide diversity in the subject matter of legislation, all the way from safety and health to wages and education. Diversity requires specialization on the part of investigators; and consequently the staff of a labor department requires physicians and hygienists for some of the standards, accountants and actuaries for others, engineers and mechanics, economists and statisticians, business men and workingmen according to the peculiarities of each subject and the special or general knowledge required.

Much more difficult and debatable is the question of generality of the standards. The most general standard is "reasonableness." Reasonableness, in law, means simply that *all of the facts* must be investigated and *due weight* must be given to each. If the legislature merely required that wages or hours should be "reasonable," then the labor department would have almost as wide discretion as the legislature itself. If, at the

ADMINISTRATION

other extreme, the legislature prescribes minute details, then the investigations are reduced to those executive investigations already described as the means of securing evidence of violations for prosecution. Between these two extremes of generality and particularization there is room for wide differences of opinion and policy. In some subjects the legislative standards must necessarily be much more general than in others. A "living wage" can scarcely be ascertained as precisely as the age of a child. The number of hours of continuous work that are injurious to the health of women cannot be as accurately determined as the dangerous character of a set screw or a circular saw. Only this is to be noticed: if the legislature goes too far in specifying details of each standard, it forces widely different factories, shops, ages, conditions, into the same mold, and assumes to have an intricate knowledge of conditions and a foresight of changing conditions which its brief and crowded sessions do not permit. Consequently, the law is unenforceable. On the other hand, the labor department is continuously in session. It is not hurried. It can adopt a general rule or can go into the details as far as it has information. It has its staff of investigators and inspectors who are continually furnishing new information, and it can change its rules as needed. It has its representatives of employers and employees who testify to the actual conditions that need remedying and the actual workings of the rules already adopted. It can make classifications and issue different rules for different conditions, and can change its rules when the conditions change or when it discovers new and more effective remedies.

The principal value and importance of administrative investigations is their conclusiveness. No matter how indefinite or general is the legislative standard, it must be reduced to a definite rule upon which prosecutions and penalties can be based. A decision must be reached and enforced. We have seen that the investigations of private associations, of experts, of attorneys on either side of a case, or even of legislative committees and temporary commissions, are not conclusive. If the court accepts these investigations it does so as facts of "common knowledge" of which the judge takes "judicial notice" without proof; and, in so doing, every reasonable doubt is resolved against them and in favor of the alleged violator. To be conclusive, an investigation must be clinched by proof, and the procedure by which this is accomplished is prescribed by the courts in their decisions on due process of law. An administrative investigation must usually follow this procedure: First, the inspectors and investigators assemble their facts. Tentative conclusions are drafted and notice given of a public hearing for all persons whose interests will be affected by the rule. Opportunity to be heard is essential to due process of law. After the public hearing the rules are drafted in final form, and, when they are officially published, they go into effect on such date as the legislature has previously designated. Even with this procedure, the rules and orders are not legally conclusive and binding on the court. If an employer violates them and then attacks them in court, he does so on the ground that they are unreasonable in some respect, such as class legislation or discrimination, instead of reasonable classification. If they are unreasonable, then they are unconstitutional. The court may decide to reinvestigate the facts on its own account. It is an independent branch of government and cannot be deprived of its powers by the legislature; but the legislature may prescribe the court's procedure and may give to the rules of the labor department, when based on full investigation, a preferential position as proof. It makes them *prima facie* lawful, valid, and reasonable, so that the burden of proof is on the employer to prove affirmatively that they are unreasonable. It may require the court to send the case back to the labor department for reinvestigation if the employer attempts to bring to the court any evidence that he had withheld from the department. The department may then, if it so decides, change its orders to cover the omitted facts. In these and various other ways suggested by the ingenuity of bill-drafters, the investigations, findings, and orders of administrative bodies are given, not actually binding and conclusive weight on the courts, but such a high degree of conclusiveness that for ordinary, practical purposes they are final.[33]

[33] For different methods of securing different degrees of conclusiveness, consult the minimum wage laws of various states, the laws already referred to, and the laws creating state public utility commissions, the Interstate Commerce Commission and the Federal Trade Commission.

See also "Penalties and Prosecutions," p. 490.

ADMINISTRATION

In this respect, administrative investigations are a necessary aid to the court and serve to place in evidence the industrial facts which otherwise would not receive due weight. The court is intrusted with the final authority to apply the principles of justice and the Constitution to the acts of legislatures and administrative bodies. It decides whether or not the act accomplishes a public purpose and affords equal protection of the laws. These are questions of fact in each particular case. A question of fact resolves itself into a question of classification. Does the particular act apply to some people and not to others who are similar? Or does it enforce the same arbitrary rule on a variety of persons who are not really similar? If so, it is discriminatory and unequal in that it is based on a false classification. Does the act benefit a class of people who do not need the aid of the police power and whose private benefit is not a public benefit? Does the act impose burdens on some that are so far in excess of the benefits to others that they are unreasonable?[34] These are some of the questions of classification asked by the courts, and, evidently, they require accurate investigation and well-established facts in order to avoid the charge of false classification. Speaking of the need of administrative investigations that shall approach the standard of conclusiveness in establishing the facts for classification, Professor Ernst Freund in 1913 said:[35]

The equal protection clause of the Fourteenth Amendment will, of course, be thought of at once as a possible weapon of defense against unwarranted class legislation. However, a study of the operation of this clause in the past must produce considerable skepticism as to its availability in the future. There are some states in which it plays a considerable part in the judicial overthrow of statutes, and Illinois is conspicuous in this respect. In that state, however, the application of the rule of non-discrimination has been so capricious that the impossibility of foretelling what kind of

---

[34] In upholding the law prohibiting night work for women, the New York court said: "The only chance for debate would be whether the prohibition is so wide and so universal that it can be said it is so out of proportion to the benefits sought that it is burdensome and unreasonable to a degree which transcends the discretion of the legislature." People v. Charles Schweinler Press, 214 N. Y. 395, 108 N. E. 639 (1915).

[35] "Problems of the Police Power," *Case and Comment*, vol. xx, 1913, p. 303.

classification for purposes of welfare legislation will stand the test of judicial scrutiny has become a notorious grievance. The Supreme Court of the United States, on the other hand, having applied the rule in one case (that of the antitrust act of Illinois, Connolly v. Union Sewer Pipe Co., 184 U. S. 540, 46 L. ed. 679, 22 Sup. Ct. 431) with surprising strictness, has since practically taken the position that a legislative classification will be sustained if there is any reasonable possibility of its justification, and in the last ten years no measure has been declared invalid by reason of undue partiality or discrimination. No jurisdiction has developed any constructive theory of classification which might serve for guidance or protection.

The reason for this failure is tolerably clear. The legitimacy or illegitimacy of classification can be established only on the basis of social or economic data of great complexity. It presents a question of fact for the examination of which the courts are not equipped. It is always a condition as well as a theory which underlies public welfare legislation; and while the courts can deal adequately with the theory, the condition must elude them unless it is notorious, and at present the causes of social or economic grievances are rarely notorious.

Conceivably this defect of judicial action might be overcome by new powers or facilities for independent inquiry placed at the disposal of the courts; but it is not likely that these will be resorted to if experience shows that the same function can be better performed by other organs. And the remedy appears to be coming from another direction. In an increasing number of cases important legislation is being prepared by commissions of inquiry composed of experts and having adequate resources for investigation at their command. The conclusions of such a commission will carry weight which unfortunately has long ceased to attach to the mere fact of the enactment of a statute. The courts may of course still reject an act thus recommended; but the case of the workmen's compensation law of New York shows not merely with what unfeigned respect the work of such a commission will be commented on by a court, but also that public opinion will not be inclined to treat a decision adverse to its conclusions as final. A proper development of scientific methods of legislation will reduce the conflict between legislation and adjudication to a minimum.

A similar result may be expected from the growing legislative practice of delegating in appropriate cases powers of quasi-legislative or quasi-judicial determination to administrative commissions. It is now generally conceded that no other form of railroad control is adequate or satisfactory, and the superseding of the Massa-

ADMINISTRATION

chusetts advisory railroad commission—for many years the model of its type—by the mandatory commission act of the present year, marks the final victory of this phase of railroad legislation. Again, the establishment of an industrial board in New York, likewise in the present year, and in pursuance of the recommendations of a notable commission, marks the adhesion of the leading state of the Union to a similar method of labor legislation, first introduced in Wisconsin. And it is noteworthy that of the minimum wage laws enacted during the year only one does not pursue the commission plan.

In proper hands and under proper safeguards the system of leaving to an administrative commission the development of principles laid down by the legislature in broad terms carries with it guaranties of reasonableness and impartiality which a political body can never afford. The system is based upon the theory that when once an agreement has been reached regarding the principle of a measure, the development of that principle into detailed rules is a process determined by the logic of ascertained facts. It thus represents a separation of that which is matter of choice, or expediency, *viz.*, the adoption of a policy, from that which is matter of argument and judgment, namely, the application of the policy to particular circumstances. Viewed in this light, the delegation constitutes not a violation, but a more perfect development of the principle of the separation of powers, and this should be borne in mind when the system is attacked as an unconstitutional delegation of the legislative power.[36] In any event some such method of dealing with complex social and economic problems seems an almost indispensable corrective of the possible abuse of a police power extending to every interest that can be reached or affected by governmental action.

2. **Representation of Interests.**—From what precedes, it will be seen that the highest place in the American scheme of constitutional government is that occupied by investigation. But the investigations required are not merely those of experts, as seems often to be assumed when the term "scientific" legislation is used. The investigations of experts, such as physicians, engineers, economists, statisticians, and lawyers, are likely to

[36] The law which was invalidated by the decision cited in "One Day of Rest in Seven," p. 152, was not of this class. It made no provision for investigation and ascertaining of facts, but merely stated that certain action might be taken by the commissioner of labor "in his discretion." The law as later amended to overcome this weakness has not been passed upon by the courts.

end in conclusions that may be ideally perfect from a technical point of view, but not *reasonable* from the constitutional point of view. They do not include *all* of the facts. The latter can be ascertained only through adding the experience and testimony of employers and employees—those who are daily in contact with the facts, and whose common knowledge corrects the narrow knowledge of specialists. The public hearings required by due process of law are the legal and constituted devices contrived to make sure that all sides will be heard. These public hearings are formal, disputatious, indiscriminate, and indecisive. They do not offer the common man an equal opportunity with the lawyer or expert to get his common experience written into the conclusions. The commission is not bound in any direct way by what was offered at the public hearing. The latter becomes a formality and a mere technical compliance with the constitutional requirement of "due process." The officials withdraw and formulate their own rules as they please.

This is the essence of bureaucracy. It is often charged that the efficient methods of administration employed in leading European countries are not adapted to American democracy because they are "bureaucratic"; but American officials, as a rule, are as bureaucratic as those of Europe. It is not rotation in office that cures bureaucracy. The most democratic of Americans often become bureaucrats as soon as installed in office. Bureaucracy is just the ordinary human instinct for exclusive possession of power. Its essence consists in imposing its will upon others without really consulting them. Whether the officeholder is an expert, a democrat, or a politician, makes little difference. It seems easier to reach a decision in one's mind and then to force others to obey than to submit to the criticism or to profit by the advice of those who are not officials.

The situation is different in a legislature where each member is compelled to listen to his opponents as well as his partisans, and to modify his individual opinion in order to get a majority opinion. A similar arrangement is called for in the administration of labor law. Here the conflict of interest is often more intense than it is in a legislature, rising at times to the pitch of incipient civil war. It is not surprising, therefore, that, in many states and countries, the officials who administer labor law are required to submit their investigations and proposals, before

ADMINISTRATION

action, to the representatives of employers and employees. These representatives owe allegiance, not to the government officials, but to the interests which select them. Wherever these interests are organized into employers' associations and trade unions, there the representatives may be elected or designated and recalled in some way by the organizations. In American states the substitution of administrative rules for legislative details makes it possible to adopt representation of interests. If the legislature lays down the general rule that every place of employment shall be made "safe," it naturally follows that those who can best pass upon the safety devices and processes, as to whether they are *practical*, in addition to being *scientific*, are the employers and employees who must install and use them. In the states which have adopted the principle of administrative investigations these joint committees actually draw up the rules for safety and health, assisted by the staff of the commission and the various classes of experts who may be called in.

In New York, for example, there is a Division of Industrial Codes, to which is left the preparation of regulations for the conduct of industry, supplementing and amplifying the provisions of the law itself. When a new set of rules or amendments to existing ones is to be undertaken, the Industrial Commissioner appoints a committee of experienced persons who are acquainted with the particular industry or problem under consideration, including representatives from both employer and employees, who serve voluntarily and without compensation. One of the Industrial Code referees acts as chairman, and technical experts of the Engineering Division and Division of Industrial Hygiene act as advisors. The committee holds meetings as a whole. In addition, there are many subcommittee meetings and conferences with individual members and inspections of factories for the purpose of working out in a practical manner subjects on which the committee could not otherwise agree, and for the purpose of getting first-hand knowledge of conditions in and about a particular industry under consideration. After the proposed rules are drawn up there is a public hearing where suggestions and objections are heard. The committee then reconsiders the proposed rules, and makes such modifications as are considered necessary in the light of such suggestions and objections. A report is then submitted to the Industrial Commissioner, for action by the Industrial Board.[37]

Thus there are two kinds of publicity, the public hearing usually required by the formalities of due process of law, and the *representative publicity* participated in by the chosen agents of the interests. The latter is the more effective, because it is carried on with experiments and tests, over a period of time, by those whose personal interests and knowledge are keen. It is a process of cooperative investigation. When an investigation of this kind is completed it fulfills all the constitutional requirements of "reasonableness." It includes all of the facts, because it is conducted by those whose interests are opposite on some points and common in others. It gives "due weight" to the interests of employer and employee, and thus conforms to the "equal protection of the laws." Furthermore, a rule thus agreed upon has the backing of the representative employers of the state, and their approval carries such weight in court that other employers, who would ordinarily violate the laws enacted by a legislature, do not violate the administrative rules approved in joint conference.

What is true of safety is also true in a greater or less degree of all branches of labor legislation where administrative rules can be substituted for legislative statutes. As we have seen, this is possible in minimum wage laws, hours of labor, excluded employments, public and private employment offices, and workmen's compensation. In some of these branches the opposition of interests is less reconcilable than it is in others, and there the commission itself must exercise greater authority. For the representative committees are, after all, only advisory. They have no legal power, no veto, on the commission. The rules and orders that carry penalties are the commission's rules and orders, and not those of the representatives. But, while the committees are advisory, the legislature may make it mandatory upon the commission to consult them. The industrial commission law of New York, enacted in 1915, took this further step in the recognition of representatives. It required the commission to submit its proposals and investigations to an

[37] *Annual Report,* Industrial Commissioner, New York, 1925, pp. 132-136. See also Andrews, John B., *Administrative Labor Legislation,* 1936, chap. iv on "Procedure."

"industrial council" of representative employers and employees, for their advice.[38]

The economic principle underlying this representation of interests is the well-known fact that competition tends to drag down all employers to the level of the worst. Labor legislation is designed to bring the worst employers up to the level of the best; yet it cannot be expected that legislation will ever be able fully to accomplish this. Individuals here, as elsewhere, always will be ahead of what the state can do. With each rise in the level of standards required by the legislature, individual employers will be free to rise still higher. Here is exactly where the field of administration lies. A labor department, with representation of interests, can do what the legislature cannot do. If it is given leeway in drafting rules and regulations, it can call upon the more advanced employers and the representatives of labor to assist in setting higher standards, and it can then enforce these standards on the more backward ones. It can bring out the divisions that already exist among employers, and, instead of permitting the worst to set the standards for the best, it can assist the best in setting standards for the worst. The legislative method treats all employers alike as criminals, and forces all to combine and to support the same lobbyists, in order to resist what they consider destructive laws. The administrative methods permits the leading representatives of employers to consult with the representatives of labor and with the officials who represent the state, regarding all of the details necessary to carry the law into effect and to adjust it to all conditions. The method is practically that of the voluntary joint conference of collective bargaining in which a trade agreement between an employers' association and a union is drawn up. Neither the union, the employer, nor the politician dominates. The decisions are not hastily adopted by a majority vote, but are given sufficient consideration, accompanied by thorough investigation and complete publicity. The process is educational and cooperative, rather than argumentative and coercive. It is not the struggle of two lobbies to win over a committee or a legislature, but it is a substitute for the lobbies, sitting in continuous con-

[38] Although the industrial commission has been superseded by the industrial commissioner, with an Industrial Board, provision for such an advisory council still remains.

480   PRINCIPLES OF LABOR LEGISLATION

ference, under state supervision, working out the rules and regulations which give effect to the legislature's standards of industrial welfare.

This representation of organized interests in the administration of law is peculiarly fitted to bridge the gaps caused by our constitutional separation of the branches of government. In other parliamentary countries the heads of executive departments, such as cabinet officers and ministers of labor, are also members of the legislature. Any member of the legislature, or the opposition parties in the legislature, can call them to account on the floor of the house and before the audience of the people, for their methods of administration. A hostile vote can dismiss them from office. Thus their acts are scrutinized and their responsibility is enforced.

In the American system the "minister of labor" is the "commissioner of labor," the "state factory inspector," or the "Secretary of Labor." In theory he is responsible, but in practice the machinery is lacking to enforce responsibility.[39] Those who are most concerned in holding him responsible are not "the public" at large, but the employers and employees who must obey the laws which he enforces. At the same time they have no voice, no *representation*, that is theirs as a matter of right and law. They can only exert themselves through the devious ways of "politics" and lobbyists.

For this reason, in American states and the federal government, it has been necessary to create "commissions," where in foreign countries the same duties would be intrusted to political departments. The Interstate Commerce Commission, the Federal Trade Commission, the Federal Reserve Board, the public utility commissions of the states are fourth branches of government, separated from the other branches and performing duties which in other countries are under a cabinet officer, such as the chancellor of the exchequer, or the minister of commerce and industry, who has a seat in parliament. A leading object in all of these American cases is to take the question "out of politics"—that is, out of the partisan contests that go on in the

[39] An interesting adaptation of the European system is found in the Wisconsin statutes, which provide that the legislature may interpellate appointive officers, and remove them from office, after being examined. Sec. 13.23, 13.24 and 13.245, Wisconsin Statutes.

ADMINISTRATION

legislature. This would probably not be necessary if the chief executive officer having them in charge were a member of the legislature, as in parliamentary countries, liable to be dismissed if he and his colleagues fail to get a majority vote in the legislature.

The situation is even more serious in dealing with labor legislation. Here, the conflict of classes is more menacing to peace than it is in matters of railroads, trusts, and banks. The labor question, of course, cannot and should not be taken out of the legislature. It is always a question of politics—that is, of public policy—as to what shall be the standards and what laws shall be enacted. But the modern department of labor takes out of the legislature the intricate details of investigation, after the standards have been enacted into law, and, most important of all, it permits the creation of an inferior industrial legislature, composed of the real representatives and leaders of both interests, continually in session under state supervision, and working upon those details of administration which, after all, are the actual substance of such legislation as is enforced.

Of course, various problems arise in the constitution of these representative councils. One is the representation of unorganized workers. As yet, no device has been discovered by which they can be directly represented. It may be said, perhaps, that they are partly represented by employers who need them to offset the unions, partly by the unions, many of whose demands would benefit both organized and unorganized labor, and partly by the administrative body which represents the public.

In all cases it is found by experience that the representatives on either side should not be lawyers. The object is not to win a case in court, but to reach an agreement by conference. Neither should the employers' representatives come from the financial or commercial side of the business. They should be the men in charge of production, who have grown up in the industry and know the labor conditions. The amount of time required is not so great as to prevent attendance. The investigations are made by a staff continuously employed and are then laid before the representatives, and their familiarity with the business enables them immediately to pick out the weak spots. These are referred back for further investigation, so that the various brief meetings of the representative council are enough to accomplish the purpose. Such investigations are not hastily made, as they are in the cases of legislatures in session. The conferences are not required to act within a limited time, and if they cannot cover the whole ground they cover a part of it and wait for future investigations to make the necessary amendments. The representatives do not need to be officials with governmental powers to enter factories, but they must have a staff in which they have confidence. This is the problem of civil service to be discussed later.

3. **Types of Labor Departments.**—The earliest and most universal development of the new class of commissions has occurred in the field of workmen's compensation. More than thirty states have a workmen's compensation act administered by a commission, which determines, under the rules laid down by the legislature, just how much the loss of wages is due to an industrial accident for which the employer shall make compensation. Usually, these compensation commissions have been created in addition to the existing bureaus or officials enforcing labor laws. The existing departments continue to follow their old line of executive procedure, and consequently there is often an overlapping and uncorrelated administration of the various laws. On July 1, 1935, more than twenty-five states had two or more independent agencies dealing with labor laws. In some of these states an attempt has been made to bring about a coordination of functions, by making the executive official an *ex-officio* member of the new board. In California in 1921 the four bureaus were designated divisions of the newly created department of labor and industrial relations. A member of one of the bureaus was elected commissioner, and monthly meetings of division representatives are held. These representatives have the power to transfer functions and funds.

There is a well-defined tendency toward centralization, the idea of economy and fixation of responsibility making a strong appeal to legislatures. This centralization process has proceeded along two distinct lines. In some states, as in Michigan, Minnesota, Utah, and Wisconsin, a commission, usually consisting of three members, is created to take over all functions—the executive, as well as the quasi-legislative and quasi-judicial functions already described. Sometimes the individual members

ADMINISTRATION 483

of these commissions are appointed as directly representative of employers, workers, or the public, as the case may be. When the members are not representative, representation of interests is obtained through the appointment of advisory committees. Besides centralizing administrative responsibility in one body, the commission form of organization is designed to insure greater continuity of experience and policy in labor law administration. This is accomplished by providing that only one commissioner's term of office shall expire in any two-year period. Such "overlapping" terms also help to prevent political upheavals in departmental personnel after the election of a new governor. This form of organization is well illustrated by the Wisconsin Industrial Commission (see chart on page 484).

In other states, as in Illinois, New York and Pennsylvania, the centralization has occurred through the creation of a department of labor headed by one person, variously designated as director, secretary, or commissioner. The New York department of labor and industry, the organization of which is shown on page 485, is a good example of this form. It should be observed that within the department there is usually a board of three or five members to hear appeals in compensation cases and to adopt the rules under the general legislative standard. In Pennsylvania, there are two such boards, one to consider appeals in compensation cases only, and one for the approval of rules and consideration of appeals on the application of such rules and labor laws other than the compensation law. Usually, the commissioner of labor is *ex officio* a member of such a board, but in New York he is not. Apparently, it was the intention of the New York legislature to divorce entirely the executive and judicial functions, for the reason that when the functions are combined the accusation is sometimes made that the same official or board is prosecutor, judge, jury, and executioner.

The exact structure or form of organization of the labor department is not so important as observance of the principles which are discussed in this chapter. It is of course necessary to eliminate overlapping of functions and to correlate the work of the various officials and bureaus charged with the administration of the labor laws; but unless there is scientific investigation of

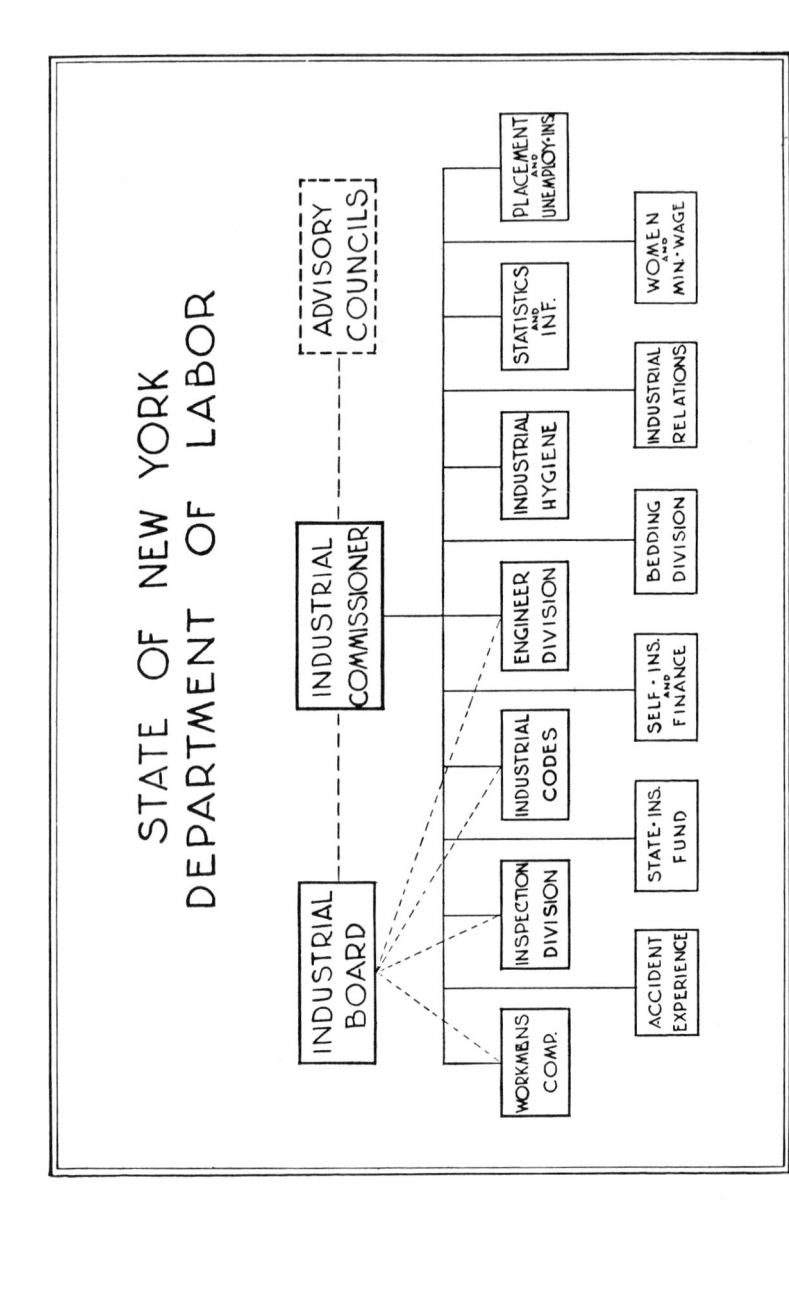

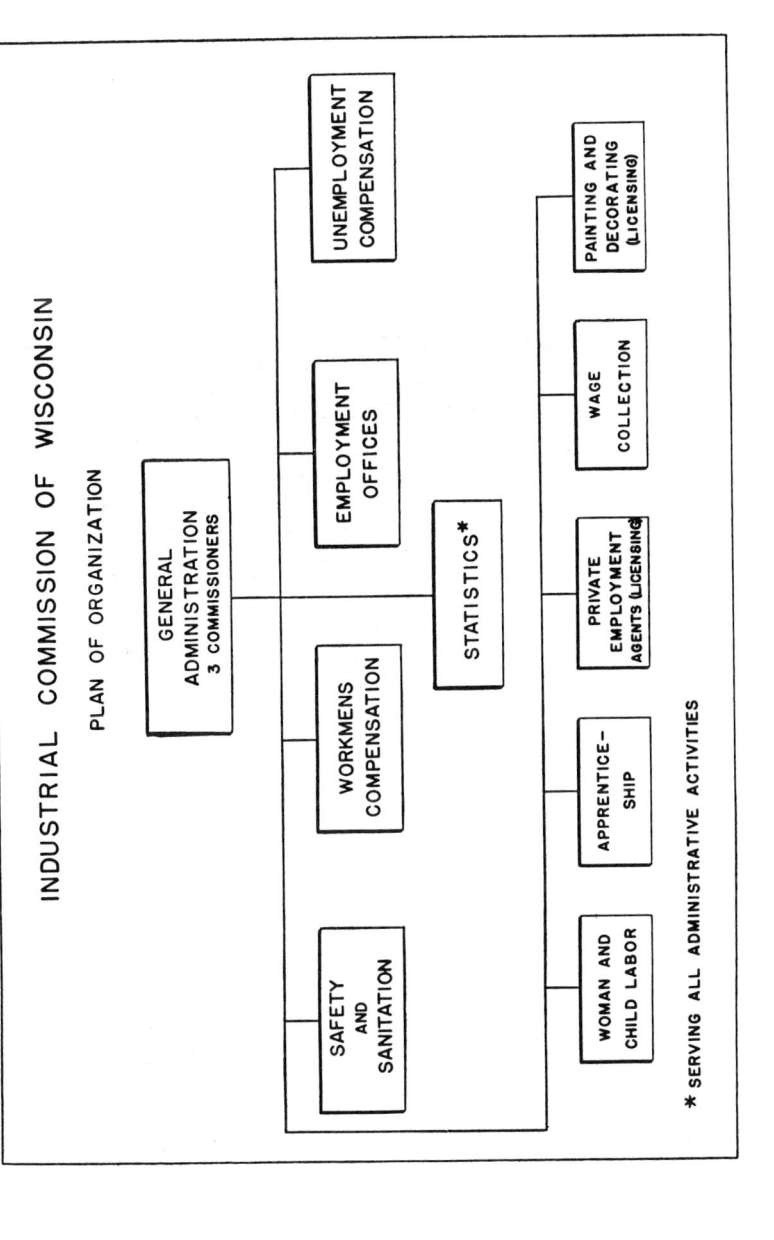

486 PRINCIPLES OF LABOR LEGISLATION

facts, representation of interests, and a trained personnel, there cannot be efficient administration.

4. **Civil Service.**—We have already seen how the administration of labor laws has required the building up of a special police. This was an advance over the enforcement of law by general officers, but it brought many difficulties. It created salaried positions, which political parties seized upon for political

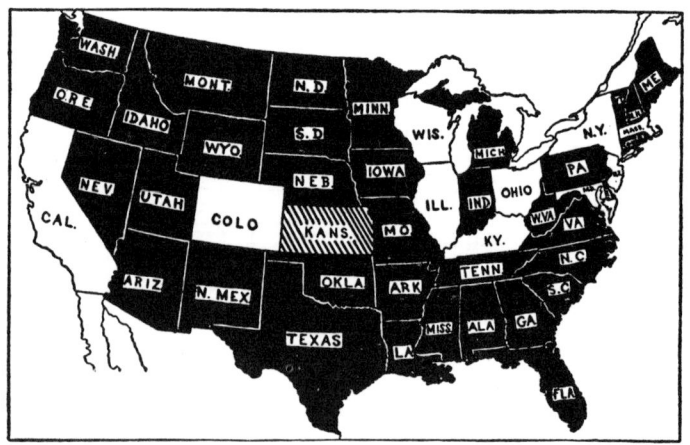

CIVIL SERVICE LAWS

By July 1, 1936, eleven states and the federal government had civil service laws requiring appointment of public employees on a merit basis. In Kansas, however, the legislature had not appropriated funds to put its law into effect.

purposes, and a mere ostensible enforcement of the law. Even more serious than party politics was the struggle of employers and employees to get control of these offices. The trade unions claimed the right of appointment, because largely through their efforts the positions had been created, and because they considered that the laws would not be enforced except by friendly inspectors. The result has been that, in many states, the unions themselves have been split by internal politics over the personal candidacies of their members for the positions. The unions also have been compelled to make alliances or compromises with the political parties, and thus has resulted the "labor politician"

—selected, not to enforce the law effectively, but to get the "labor vote." On the other hand, the employers also make their political alliances, and then the selection of factory inspectors is often designedly made to prevent the enforcement of the laws. Thus, both political and industrial partisanship have joined, either to defeat altogether the factory laws through hostile inspectors, or to make them ineffective through political trade union inspectors.

The next step is the effort, made in a few states and by the federal government, to adopt civil service examinations, tenure of office on good behavior, and promotion in the service, as a substitute for political appointments. These civil service laws, beginning in the decade of the 'eighties, were designed primarily to prevent the use of public offices as a part of the political "machine." Indirectly, they have secured greater efficiency, in so far as they have been able to prevent officials from being changed at each change in the elections, but it has required several years for the more experienced civil service commissions to reach the point where they could learn to conduct examinations directly for efficiency and for the peculiar fitness of the applicant for the particular position. Industrial antagonism must be recognized, just as political antagonism has been recognized and provided against. Factory inspectors, who do not have the confidence of both employers and employees, as to either their practical knowledge or their impartiality, are as inefficient for their positions as those who are avowed politicians. Just as civil service reform is designed to secure officials who are non-partisan as respects political antagonism, so it should secure factory inspectors who are impartial as respects industrial antagonism. It is in the legislatures and Congress that organized labor and organized capital should fight out their legal battles. There it is proper that each side should have its lobbies and its recognized leaders, and should carry its fight "to a finish." It is there that public policy is determined and that opinions, partisanship, and prejudice have full play in working out that legislative discretion which constitutes public policy. When the law is once enacted the battle should cease, and the officials selected to enforce the law should enforce it efficiently, exactly as it stands, in harmony with its policy and yet impartially as between the two interests. This is the present problem of "civil service reform" as respects labor legislation. Labor law cannot be enforced if either employers or trade unionists distrust the officials on account of their incompetency, their politics, or their partiality. Even in states having civil service commissions this distrust sometimes exists. This is partly due to the bureaucratic exclusiveness of the administrative bodies themselves. An essential thing in their method of administration is that they should admit the recognized leaders of employers and unions to a share in conducting the examinations. This is partly provided for in the department of labor law of New York, which makes the advisory council of employers and employees the assistants to the civil service commission for the examination of applicants. It has been provided for in the public employment offices of Wisconsin, where the employment officials are selected by the joint committees of employers and employees.

It has been implied above that the inspectors of the modern department of labor become investigators as well as police. They cooperate with the employers and workmen in drafting the rules. Their work consists more of instructing employers and workmen in the devices and processes of safety, sanitation, and welfare than in mere prosecutions; but they can occupy this enviable position only to the extent that they are skillful, efficient, and impartial. "Politics" is fatal. As soon as organized employers and employees, have become accustomed to cooperate in the administration, they tend to exclude the politician because he drives capital and labor apart instead of bringing them together.

5. **Bill Drafting.**—The history of labor legislation is the history of an art as highly technical and expert as that of engineering science or that of an inventor in electricity or chemistry. Like other arts, it is a history of trial, experiment, failure, until something workable is produced. In early days an inventor might be merely an ingenious mechanic; now he is frequently a scientist, with a staff of assistants, supported and financed by large expenditures of money. Great private corporations keep ahead of competition by means of their laboratories, scientists, investigators, inventors. When the government takes up in-

vention, as has been done in agriculture, it supports costly experiment stations and sets scientists and inventors to work.

Yet, in the equally technical field of legislation, the drafting of bills remains largely in the stage of the mechanic. There are two very distinct divisions in the process of legislation. One is the discussion of policy, the other the framing of bills that give effect to policy. The former is the division belonging to the legislature, drawn from the ranks of the people. The latter is the technical work of experts. In a private corporation the line of demarcation corresponds to that between the board of directors and the engineers, architects, or lawyers. In lawmaking it corresponds to that between the legislature and an administrative commission. The latter is conducting experiments in a great laboratory. The enforcement of law is, in fact, a series of experiments and tests upon the actual workings of the law. The commission's investigations reveal the gaps and defects. When the legislature meets, these tests and investigations furnish the technical information for amendments. The commission, indeed, when it drafts its own rules and orders, is doing the same kind of technical work as when it assists the legislature in drafting its bills.

But administrative commissions are like the courts in that they follow precedents, and are conservative in that they do not willingly take up new things. Their administrative problems are sufficiently great so that they will not of their own volition initiate and push new lines of public policy. Their work is the perfection and elaboration of policies already adopted.

The business of pioneering new lines of labor policy belongs to the legislature and to private associations, or to a legislative reference bureau; but when there is sufficient public opinion, and a legislative demand for these new lines of legislation, then administrative investigation is superior to any that has been devised for ascertaining the facts and preparing machinery for administration. It follows that private societies, such as labor unions, associations for labor legislation, child labor committees, and consumers' leagues are needed not only to watch the existing administrative machinery, but to pioneer on new lines of legislation. The functions of such private associations are now even greater than they have been before. They criticize where needed and assist where practicable.

6. **Penalties and Prosecutions.**—Behind all laws and administrative rules having the force of law lies the penalty for violation. No matter how efficient the administration or how actively employers and employees may assist, the administration would remain but a voluntary cooperative society if not supported by penalties imposed on those who refuse or neglect to assist.

Yet, too much reliance is generally placed on penalties and punishment. Officials sometimes point to their record of numerous prosecutions as evidence of their efficiency in office. Such a record may prove exactly the opposite. Penalties should be looked upon as only a *potential* power, whose strongest evidence of *actual* power is sometimes found in the least necessity of resorting to them. A record of a small number of prompt and impressive convictions may mean more for the enforcement of law than several pages of statistics of prosecutions. At the other extreme, many factory inspectors who in American states furnish little or no evidence of any prosecutions are probably not enforcing the laws. No subject of labor legislation is more uncertain and unsatisfactory than this of penalties and prosecutions.

The difficulty sometimes experienced in securing convictions is shown by a statement of the commissioner of labor in New York in 1908.[40] In thirty-two cases of illegal employment and overtime work of women and children tried before juries in a period of three months, not a single conviction was obtained, although it was shown in one instance that a woman worked seventeen hours in one day, and in another that a child was only seven years old. The inspector's report for 1907 showed that in one-half of the 294 cases where conviction was secured, the court remitted the fine, and in most of the other cases only the minimum fine was imposed, averaging about $26 a case.[41] Other states showed a similar leniency.

Today the situation is not much changed in New York so far as leniency of the courts is concerned; but improvement in the laws themselves, the development of administrative codes,

---

[40] *Report on Condition of Woman and Child Wage-earners in the United States* (Sixty-first Congress, Second Session, Senate Doc. No. 645), p. 44.

[41] *Ibid.*, p. 48.

ADMINISTRATION

and better methods of enforcement have brought more effective compliance with the laws without resort to prosecution. Therefore, the methods used in New York which have reduced prosecutions to a minimum are set forth in detail. After an inspection has been made, orders are issued by the industrial commissioner to remedy the violations of the law which have been observed. Reinspections are later made to determine whether there has been compliance. In the majority of cases, compliance is rather easily secured. When cooperation by the employer is not forthcoming, however, a "counsel letter" is sent to him, fixing a final date for compliance if he desires to avoid prosecution. Another method used is to issue a summons to the person failing to comply, requiring him to appear at a fixed time and place to show cause why prosecution should not be commenced. When he appears at the hearing, if the orders are not already complied with, a final date for compliance is fixed. If he fails to comply with the orders at the time fixed, prosecution ensues. During a single year 7,386 cases were thus set for hearing. The result of this procedure was that the cases in which prosecution was necessary numbered only 2,752. Of the 2,775 cases disposed of by the courts in 1934, including some instituted in the previous year, convictions were secured in 2,541 cases. The leniency of the courts, however, is evidenced by the fact that in 1,756 of the convictions, sentence was suspended; while the fines for the 785 other convictions amounted to only $17,802.30.[42]

An interesting method of enforcing compliance, which is found in some states, is to give the authorities power to stop work on a machine or in an establishment which violates the law. Thus in several states inspectors may place upon machinery a notice forbidding its use until specified safety measures have been taken. In some states mines may be absolutely closed, and several states have extended the same principle to certain factories and workshops. According to a Delaware statute, a cannery violating the law may upon a third conviction be closed by the court, and the person convicted may be prohibited from engaging in the cannery business until further court order. California, in 1915, authorized the closing

[42] See *Annual Report,* Industrial Commissioner, New York, 1934, pp. 6, 7. A similar procedure prior to prosecution is followed in Wisconsin.

by the courts of labor camps, upon their failure to comply within a reasonable time with the sanitary provisions laid down for them. The California statutes also give the industrial accident commission the power to prohibit the use of dangerous machinery and to apply for an injunction to close a dangerous place of employment.[43]

It may be desirable that the administrative body charged with the enforcement of the labor laws should have the power to order the discontinuance of a building or machinery that is manifestly dangerous. It is questionable, however, whether this summary power should be placed in the hands of the inspector. In order to eliminate personalities and arbitrariness, provision should be made for a hearing before the same body that has the power to adopt industrial code rules and grant variations from such rules. Perhaps the same results can be obtained by simply giving the administrative body the right to apply for an injunction.

In American labor legislation, little attention has been paid to the careful adjustment of penalties to offenses. The amount of penalty seems to be determined very largely at random, and there is a great variety of penalties in the same state and in different states. Too frequently the idea seems to be that the more severe the penalty the greater the likelihood of enforcing compliance. This frequently fails of its purpose, because courts and juries often permit an offender to escape entirely rather than subject him to a penalty out of proportion, as they see it, to the offense.

Yet a distinction must be made between penalties for a single offense and penalties for a continuing offense. Failure to return a child worker's employment permit may be treated as a single offense; but employment of the child beyond working hours may be treated as a continuing offense, repeated every day that the child is so employed. Here is a cumulative injury to the child which the law seeks to prevent, and, very properly, a cumulative penalty might be imposed, making each day for each child a separate and distinct offense. If the penalty, for example, is $10 to $100 for each offense, even

[43] Other states that have similar provisions are Michigan, Minnesota, New York, Ohio, and Pennsylvania.

ADMINISTRATION

the minimum penalty would accumulate effectively. Otherwise, if treated as a single offense for each child, no matter how long continued, the penalty might bear no adequate proportion to the profit derived from the child's labor.

This method of cumulative penalties has been more or less adopted, thereby making each day during which an employer fails to observe or comply with any order of the commission or any section of the statute a separate violation.[44] Cumulative penalty provisions, however, are construed very strictly by the courts, and the language of the statute must be made perfectly clear.

Another distinction of importance is that between a criminal action and a civil action. Formerly, when employers were mostly small employers with but little property, the criminal penalties of fine or imprisonment, which are the ordinary penalties for violation of police regulations, seemed to be appropriate. These criminal penalties are practically out of date when it comes to enforcing the law against corporations. In criminal prosecutions, moreover, the individual employer has many technical defenses based on the presumption of innocence. A readier and simpler method is the "action of debt," a civil action employed to recover taxes or penalties under the guise of a debt owing the state.[45] This form of action is now generally adopted in the case of railroad commissions and industrial commissions, along with the cumulative penalty. It is more effective against corporations, and it recognizes the cold fact that courts and juries are loath to impose criminal penalties on employers when their offense is the violation of laws enacted for the protection of labor.

Prosecutions generally are brought in justice courts or other inferior criminal courts. It is obvious that such courts are not equipped to decide technical questions, and the limitations imposed by rules of evidence on the admissibility of testimony make it practically impossible for the court to obtain the ex-

[44] California, General Laws 1920, Act 2781, Sec. 50; Colorado, Laws 1921, Sec. 4369; Ohio, Laws 1921, Sec. 871-44; Oregon, General Laws 1920, Sec. 6780; Wisconsin, Statutes 1925, Secs. 101.18 and 103.15.

[45] Stockwell v. U. S., 13 Wall. 531 (1871); Chaffee v. U. S., 18 Wall. 516 (1873); Florida Central R. Co. v. Reynolds, 183 U. S. 471, 22 Sup. Ct. 176 (1902).

pert information and opinion essential to intelligent decision of such cases.

There are two classes of questions, often equally technical. One is the question of fact, the other of constitutionality of a statute or of reasonableness and validity of an administrative rule. A technical question of fact is, for example, whether a certain room is sufficiently ventilated or sufficiently lighted. A question of constitutionality or reasonableness is whether a statute or administrative rule limiting a woman's work to a certain number of hours is valid. Both involve questions of fact, but the two questions can be separated. If a justice's court, or a jury, as in the instance above referred to, refuses to convict an employer who is shown to have allowed a woman to work seventeen hours in face of a law restricting her work to ten hours, it is really deciding not only the fact of violation, but also the reasonableness of the law. Hence it is that in states which have labor departments with power to issue rules the attempt is made to separate the two questions. The question of fact is determined in a lower court; but the question of reasonableness or validity can be raised only in a different suit in a higher court. The employer is permitted first, by the provisions of the law, to test the reasonableness or validity of the rule in a hearing before the administrative body. Next, he has a right to appeal to a higher court on questions of law. If no such hearing or appeal is taken within a specified time, then no question can be raised in the inferior court except the fact of compliance or non-compliance with the rule or order of the labor department.[46]

A similar facility is afforded to the inferior court, in passing upon questions of fact, by the provision that the labor department may draw up specific standards fitted to each occupation, or even to a single shop, where the legislative standard is liable not to take into account real differences. These standards, if previously passed upon by representative committees of employers and employees, can be made both definite and practica-

---

[46] California, General Laws 1920, Act 2107, Sec. 12, and Act 2781, Sec. 67; Massachusetts, Laws 1921, C. 149, Sec. 9; New York, McKinney's Consolidated Laws 1925, C. 31, Secs. 110-112; Ohio, General Code 1921, Sec. 871-29, 871-38, 871-40; Oregon, General Laws 1920, Sec. 6776; Wisconsin, Laws 1925, Sec. 101.11 and 101.13.

ble, and therefore not a matter of such controversy or opinion as to require expert testimony in the lower court.

This simplifies the work of the factory inspector in the field. He is the prosecuting witness. His opinion of whether the law is violated or not is set up against the opinion of the employer or his representative. All doubts are resolved in favor of the defendant. But with the more precise standards there is less dependence on weight of opinion. If a statute merely says that workshops shall be "sufficiently lighted," the factory inspector must set up his opinion against the employer's opinion as to whether the light in his shop is sufficient. The jury must then pass upon both the fact of violation and the opinion of the inspector. But if the administrative body upon investigation ascertains that one-quarter candle-power for every square foot of floor space is sufficient for that class of shops, then the inspector needs to prove only that the amount of light was less than this standard.

These provisions do not mean that less competent inspectors may be employed. They mean that much more time may be given to actual inspection and less to prosecutions. The inspector, in the ordinary prosecutions, wastes an incalculable amount of time in assembling and producing in court the evidence of the alleged violation. His current inspection work must be neglected in order that he may attend court, awaiting the trial of the case, or attempting to convince a court or jury of the accuracy and honesty of his observation of conditions out of which the alleged violation grew. Where he should be engaged in discovering violations and suggesting means of compliance, he is marshaling evidence and trying to convince third parties of deviations from ambiguous standards.

Various devices have been invented in the drafting of labor laws to determine whether the provisions of the law are being complied with. The possibility of detecting all violations by official inspection is obviously limited. An army of inspectors making constant visits would be required. The prosecution may be relieved of a portion of its burden of proof by a provison that certain facts shall constitute *prima facie* evidence. The burden is always on the prosecution to prove circumstances which constitute a violation of a statutory provision. Thus, where a statute forbids the employment of children under sixteen except under specified conditions, the prosecution for an alleged offense must prove the employment of the child, must prove that the child was under sixteen, and must prove that the circumstances authorizing the employment of a child of that age were not present. This ordinary rule respecting the burden of proof, however, may be altered by the legislature. The difficulty of enforcing the one-day-of-rest-in-seven law[47] has been considerably lessened in New York by a requirement that the employer shall post "a schedule containing a list of his employees who are required or allowed to work on Sunday and designating the day of rest for each," and shall file a copy of the schedule with the industrial commissioner. This provision reduces the necessity of inspection to the single question of whether any employee named on the schedule as entitled to rest on any day is at work on that day. That in itself constitutes a violation of the substantive provision that "no employee shall be required or allowed to work on the day of rest so designated for him." Similar provisions are employed in enforcing laws regulating hours of labor.[48] The California law regulating the employment of children under the age of sixteen requires the employer of such children to keep a record of the name, age, and residence of such children and to produce such record for inspection by the agents of the industrial relations department. The employer is also required to keep on file and to furnish on demand of the department the child's employment permit. The employer's failure to produce such permit is made *prima facie* evidence in a prosecution for the violation of a provision of the law that the child is under sixteen and unlawfully employed.[49]

Of the devices to assist the officials which have been made use of in this country, those which impose upon the employer the duty to keep some sort of current record of conditions or happenings in his plant are the most important aids to official inspection. Records of accidents, certified daily time reports, registers, and account books are often required by labor laws.

There is, however, a limitation on the extent to which the

---
[47] See "One Day of Rest in Seven," p. 149.
[48] See "Maximum Hours, Women," p. 109.
[49] California, Acts 1929, C. 23, Secs. 1.221, 1.280.

employer may be compelled to collect and record for official use the evidence of his own violation of the law. Our constitutions generally protect the individual against a requirement that he testify against himself. When the requirement of records becomes practically a system of compelling testimony against himself, the employer may refuse to comply and depend upon his constitutional guaranty.

Licensing a business practice or place of employment affords another means of increasing the possibilities of enforcement, especially if the licensee be required to give bond. This method is employed in the regulation of employment agencies and sweatshops. License requirements are ordinarily supplemented by a prohibition of action without the license. Failure to produce the license is thereby made proof of violation. The license is usually issued on condition that the standards imposed by the law be complied with.[50] Fear of loss of the license and of summary recovery on the bond affords strong inducement for compliance. The license, however, does not entirely obviate the necessity for inspection or other means of obtaining evidence as to compliance by the licensee with the requirements of the law or the conditions of the license.

In the effort to secure enforcement of laws prohibiting or regulating sweatshops, resort has been had to the device of tagging the products of sweatshops that do not comply with the law.[51] In some cases the value of the tag is not due so much to the fact that it aids enforcement of provisions regulating the sweatshop industries as to the discouragement of that industry by branding its products and discouraging their purchase by the public.

After the evidence of violation of the requirements of the law is secured, the marshaling and presentation of that evidence to the court in which a prosecution is conducted are of the greatest importance. Ordinarily, it is the business of the district attorney or the attorney-general to conduct prosecutions. The department, however, which administers the law violated is under obligation to secure the evidence of viola-

[50] See U. S. Department of Labor, Bureau of Labor Statistics, *Bulletin No. 581,* "Laws Relating to Employment Agencies in the United States."
[51] Missouri, Revised Statutes 1919, Sec. 6835; New York, McKinney's Consolidated Laws, C. 31, Sec. 357.

tion and present it to the prosecuting officer. In practice, other duties so absorb the time and attention of the attorney-general and the district attorney that they give little consideration to the preparation of prosecutions for violation of police regulations. The rules of evidence, especially in criminal prosecutions, are very technical. It is difficult even for a lawyer to determine what is relevant testimony. It frequently happens that a factory inspector, without legal training or sympathetic legal advice, bases a prosecution on testimony which, because of technical rules, will not be admitted by the courts, and therefore the prosecution fails. This need of sympathetic, constant legal assistance to administrative officials in securing and furnishing the evidence of violation has resulted, in many jurisdictions, in the assignment of a special assistant attorney-general, district attorney, or city counsel to attend to prosecutions for violations of laws enforced by a particular administrative department. In New York, instead of having a special deputy attorney-general assigned to the industrial commission, the legislature provided for a counsel and three assistants whose duty it was to assist in the preparation of prosecutions and in the conduct of such prosecutions in the courts.[52] By arrangements with district attorneys, counsel to the commission actually conducted the prosecutions in the criminal courts, but he did this subject to the control of the district attorney. When the New York labor law was recodified in 1921, the legal division in the labor department was abolished and the work turned over to an assistant counsel in the office of the attorney-general.

7. **Cooperation by Pressure.**—Penalties and prosecutions are coercive methods of administration. But the workmen's compensation laws adopted in several states indicate a new and important administrative principle. Prior to the adoption of these laws, the only inducements offered to the employer to prevent accidents to his employees were the liability laws and the factory acts. The employer was treated as a criminal, and naturally he revolted and obeyed only as little of the laws as he might be exposed to on account of his lack of political influence or the efficiency of inspectors. But the compensation laws, by requiring him to pay for *all* accidents, instead of merely those he cannot escape, tend to bring upon him a uni-

[52] New York, McKinney's Consolidated Laws 1916, C. 31, Sec. 48.

ADMINISTRATION

versal pecuniary pressure, like that of taxation, which induces him to prevent *all* accidents and to provide for early recovery of the victims. This is especially true if the law is so drafted as to lay the emphasis on prevention and medical and surgical treatment.

This class of legislation is *cooperative,* instead of *coercive.* The employer now takes as much interest as the employee in having the factory inspectors efficient and helpful. Furthermore, he establishes his own "safety department," which is always watchful and far more efficient than the small number of state inspectors that the taxpayers will allow. In this way "social insurance" in its many forms of accident, health, invalidity, old-age, and unemployment insurance may be expected, if the laws are properly drafted and then properly administered, to bring about the cooperation of employer, employee, and the state, where the older methods of coercion were ineffective and productive of antagonism.

The insurance principle also provides an inducement for employers and employees to give sufficient of their time to the administration of labor law. This is the peculiar need and weakness of American administration. Private citizens leave administration to professional politicians. Employers hire attorneys to represent them in legislation. A kind of constant pressure is needed that will induce them to take part themselves in public administration exactly as they do in the administration of their factories. Financial gain or loss is this universal pressure, not depending on exhortation or public spirit. Social insurance, properly organized and administered under the supervision of those who pay the bills, converts the prevention of accidents and the preservation of health from sentiment and humanitarianism into business and profits. It makes it worth while for employers to give time to public service.

Thus, social insurance, accomplishes what, in France, is called *solidarism,* as a correction of individualism.[53] The health and welfare of every wage earner are "affected by a public interest" when the industry or the community is required to make good the loss. Each laborer then becomes a "public utility." Individualism, while it highly rewards the fortunate individual,

[53] Bourgeois, Léon, "International Organization of Social Policies," *American Labor Legislation Review,* March, 1914, p. 186.

carries with it the sole responsibility and liability for his own misfortunes. The solidarism of social insurance enforces the joint responsibility of employer, employee, and the community.

But social insurance is an administrative rather than a judicial problem. It takes the question of individual liability out of the hands of the courts and places it in the hands of executives. It avoids litigation over past misfortunes and substitutes "social prevention" of future misfortunes. For this reason, the administrative officials of the state cannot successfully deal with social insurance except through the cooperation of employers and employees, and the latter will not effectually cooperate except through the inducement of financial gain. Hence it is that well-considered schemes of social insurance often distribute the burden of expense among employer, employee, and the state. This is plain in the form of health insurance, where the employee contributes a share of the insurance premiums. It may also be brought about in non-contributory schemes of accident compensation, where, in place of denying the employee any compensation at all in case of "willful misconduct," his compensation is reduced, say, 10 or 15 per cent. This minimizes contests in court over "willful misconduct," but at the same time forces the workman to contribute when he is plainly responsible.

This and other devices illustrate the differences between legislation with its court procedure, which penalizes the individual for past acts, and administration based on insurance, which induces him to avoid future acts. The matter resolves itself into a series of adjustments which balance the motive of pecuniary gain or loss against the carelessness, greed, or oppression that produces misfortune and suffering. These nice adjustments can be worked out only through the accumulated tests and trials of administrative investigations, where employers, employees, and officials join together, and not through partisan conflicts in legislatures or legal battles in court.

Thus "solidarism" is that goal of labor legislation where it can be truly said that "an injury to one is the concern of all." On the financial side it is such an arrangement that all will equitably bear the burdens that fall upon each individual. On the side of human motives it is a departure from litigation and the fear of occasional criminal penalties to the adoption of continuous inducements for the prevention of misfortune and oppression. On the side of administration it is the cooperative investigation of conditions by employers, employees, and the state through representatives and officials in whose ability and integrity all have confidence. On the side of a broader social philosophy it is the recognition both of class struggle and of common interest as permanent facts, and then the adjustment of laws and administration so as to equalize the struggle and utilize the common interest for a public benefit.

CHAPTER IX

THE BASIS OF LABOR LAW

MODERN INDUSTRY IS MAINLY A MATTER OF BUYING AND SELLing. Scarcely any person lives on the things which he alone produces with his own property. Formerly the protection of his person and his physical property was the principal part of the law. Now the protection of that intangible property, which arises through buying and selling and is defined in the law of contract, occupies the attention of lawmakers, courts, and the administrative authorities.

1. THE LABOR CONTRACT

The labor contract is one of several kinds of contracts, which until recently has differed from the others but little in the eyes of the law. Like the others, it originates in an agreement, implies a promise, creates rights and duties, and is enforced, if need be, by the power of the state.

But the labor contract, in course of time, has come to be recognized as something peculiar. When a bushel of wheat is bought and sold, when a factory or farm is transferred, when a banker receives deposits or lends his credit, when a corporation issues stocks or bonds, the rights and duties created thereby can be fulfilled by delivering something external and non-human. But when a laborer agrees to work he must deliver himself for a time into the control of another. He earns his living, not by working upon his own property, but by working upon the property of another, and by accepting all the conditions he finds there. And, if he has no property of his own sufficient to fall back upon, he is under an imperious necessity of immediately agreeing with somebody who has. This peculiar relation between a propertyless seller of himself, on the one hand, and a propertied buyer, on the other, coupled as it is with equal suffrage of both in the politics of the country, has gradually acquired recognition as something sufficiently

THE BASIS OF LABOR LAW

important for the government to take notice of. While the courts and law books have dealt with the labor contract as similar to other contracts, legislation goes behind the legal face of things and looks at the bargaining power which precedes the contract. It distinguishes the price bargain, the investment bargain, the real estate bargain, and others, from the wage bargain. The former are dealings between property-owners. The latter is a bargain which involves not only wages, but also hours of labor, speed and fatigue, safety and health, accident and disease, even life itself. Unemployment is failure to make such a bargain; immigration, child labor, education, prison labor, collective bargaining, and so on, are conditions which determine the bargaining power of the laborer. Every topic in labor legislation is a phase of the wage bargain, and it is because a large class of people have come to depend permanently, not on their property or resources, but on these bargains with property-owners, that labor legislation has significance.

This spectacle of the free laborer, without property but with the ballot, bargaining for his livelihood but electing his rulers, is something new and unaccustomed, measured by the life of nations. It has come about through what may be called industrial, legal, and political changes.

1. **Industry.**—Little more than a generation has passed since the natural resources of the country were sufficiently free to permit people without property to acquire ownership merely by labor. The homestead laws, culminating in 1862, may be looked upon as early labor legislation, for they were intended to provide "free land" by preventing the public domain from falling into the hands of capitalists and slave-owners and so to furnish an outlet to laborers from the East. Workmen who could not become farmers or miners could become tradesmen and independent mechanics in the new towns. But since the lands have been closed by occupation, and their values have increased, money or credit is required to purchase them. This means that laborers without capital must seek capitalists to employ them.

In 1869 the first Pacific railway was completed, and immediately Chinese coolies made their appearance in Massachusetts as strike breakers, and the manufactured products of Massachusetts contributed to unemployment in California. The railway and steamship have made labor almost as movable as capital, and any bargaining advantage which wage earners have in one section of the country is quickly leveled by migration.

Huge factories and corporations were almost unknown two generations ago, but now the United States Steel Corporation has some 200,000 employees, and single establishments have thousands and ten thousands. The special bargaining power of skilled mechanics is leveled down to that of the lesser skilled.

Thus the three industrial factors of closed land, labor mobility, and large-scale production have produced a class permanently dependent on wages.

2. **Labor Law.**—When land and natural resources were free, labor was not always free. Slave labor in the South, indentured labor and apprenticeship in the North and South, contract labor from abroad, were based on legal devices by which the laborer could be kept from running away. Not until the enactment of the Thirteenth Amendment, following the Civil War, did slavery and involuntary servitude, except as a punishment for crime, become everywhere illegal.[1] The labor contract henceforth has its peculiar significance. Although in theory it is like other contracts, yet it cannot in fact be enforced. The laborer cannot sell himself into slavery or into involuntary servitude. He retains the right to change his mind, to quit work, to run away. Certain other contracts can, in the absence of any other sufficient remedy, be enforced by the courts by compelling "specific performance."[2] But specific performance of the labor contract is involuntary servitude. Business contracts, if violated, are ground for damages which the court orders paid even to the extent of taking all of the business property of the debtor. The labor contract also, if violated, is ground for damages, but for the court to order

[1] Constitution of the United States, Amendments, Art. XIII:

"SEC. 1. Neither slavery nor involuntary servitude, except as a punishment for crime, whereof the party shall have been duly convicted, shall exist within the United States, or any place subject to their jurisdiction.

"SEC. 2. Congress shall have power to enforce this article by appropriate legislation."

The exception in the case of the seaman's contract has been noted on page 324.

[2] See Andrews, *American Law,* 1908, vol. i, pp. 582, 1586.

damages paid out of labor property would be to order the laborer to work out the debt. This is involuntary servitude. Hence the employer is left with the empty remedy of bringing suit against a propertyless man. He can protect himself by making contracts which he also can terminate at any time by discharging the workman without notice.

Thus the labor contract becomes, in effect, a new contract every day and every hour. It is a continuous process of wage bargaining. It carries no effective rights and duties for the future and is as insecure as it is free. After land has ceased to be free the laborer becomes free. Closed resources and freedom with insecurity produce in time a permanent class of wage earners.

3. **Politics.**—In the northern states, the suffrage was granted to all male wage earners during the years preceding 1845 by removing the property qualifications.[3] This was as much as forty to sixty years in advance of other nations, and was, in fact, the first experiment in the world's history of universal admission of the propertyless laborer to an equal share in government with the propertied capitalist or employer. A similar experiment was made in the South after the slaves were freed by war. Henceforth the laborer not only shares in electing the legislature that makes the law, but he shares in selecting the judges who interpret it, and the governors, factory inspectors, sheriffs, marshals, and constables who enforce it. The labor contract and the wage bargain become as much a question of the control of politics as they are of large-scale industry and the mobility of labor. Wherever property-owners or employers can deprive the laborer of his suffrage or can control his vote, there they can more effectively control his bargaining power. He may be disfranchised, as in the South, or intimidated, as in some towns controlled directly by corporations, or manipulated and bought, as in towns controlled indirectly through the political "machine." So the struggle for the suffrage, begun more than a century ago in the North, renewed in the struggle of forty years ago for the secret ballot, and kept up in the struggle against political corruption, is both a cause and a consequence of the appearance of wage earners as a class in modern industry.

[3] Rhode Island was the only northern state that retained the property qualification.

II. INDIVIDUAL RIGHTS

Federal and state constitutions contain the fundamental laws and create the authorities of government with the power to interpret, amend, and enforce them. The Declaration of Independence and most of the state constitutions declare that all men are created equal. Prior to the Civil War, certain of the southern states declared only that "all freemen" are equal. Those constitutions were afterward changed to read "all men" are equal. Some constitutions say that they are "equally free and independent." If they are equal, they have equal rights. Some of these rights are declared to be natural, essential, indefeasible, inalienable. Among the inalienable rights mentioned in different constitutions are life, liberty, the pursuit of happiness, acquiring, possessing and protecting property, reputation, and enjoyment of the gains or proceeds of a man's own labor.[4]

The Federal Constitution guarantees certain means for protecting these rights, and prohibits certain measures that violate or impair them. Among the protective measures are the writ of *habeas corpus*, trial by jury, a republican form of government, freedom of speech or of the press, the right peaceably to assembly and to petition the government for a redress of grievances, the right to keep and bear arms, security against unreasonable search and seizure of persons, of houses, papers or effects, indictment by a grand jury, speedy and public trial, compensation for property taken for public use, due process of law, equal protection of the laws. Among the prohibited measures are bills of attainder, *ex post facto* laws and laws impairing the obligation of contracts. Finally, the enunciation of certain rights cannot be construed to deny or disparage others retained by the people. These restrictions, however, with the exception of those insuring equal protection of the laws and the obligation of contracts, are binding on Congress and not on the states. The Fourteenth Amendment prohibits any state from denying due process of law and equal protection

---

[4] The Declaration of Independence is "read into" the constitutions, where it says: "We hold these truths to be self-evident, that all men are created equal, that they are endowed by their Creator with certain inalienable rights, that among these are life, liberty, and the pursuit of happiness."

of the laws, but under the decisions of the courts this protection does not extend to other rights guaranteed in the early amendments to the Constitution, which, as has just been said, are protected only against infringement by Congress.[5]

If certain rights, such as life, liberty, and property, are strictly and literally "inalienable," then they cannot either be given away by any person or taken away by any other person or by government, either by coercion or by persuasion, either by violence or by voluntary sale and compensation. If the owner sells them, they are worthless to the buyer because he gets no title. Of course, it follows that these rights were never considered strictly "inalienable." Only an impossible anarchist could believe this. The Fourteenth Amendment partly clears the atmosphere. "Privileges and immunities" are substituted for inalienable rights. Life, liberty, and property can be taken provided it be done according to "due process of law." "Equality" becomes "equal protection of the laws." In other words, rights become "relative," not "absolute," *alienable* but *protected*.

If rights are relative, then their meanings and definitions are liable to change when the relationships to which they refer happen to change. The rights of property are defined in several constitutions as the right of acquiring, possessing, and protecting property. These were the significant points in the definition when people were isolated, as they were in colonial and pioneer times. At that stage, their main concern was in getting and holding physical property, like lands, crops, or even human beings, if the definition of property included slaves. But in modern society, based, as it is, mainly on buying and selling, the right to withhold property from others becomes significant. It is this that protects the individual in his power of bargaining—his power, protected by law, to hold back and wait until an agreement can be reached upon the exchange value of the property before permitting others to take it or use it.

This right to withhold property is like the laborer's right to withhold his labor by refusing to work or by quitting work. In both cases this is also "liberty"—a "personal" right rather

[5] Willoughby, *Constitutional Law of the United States,* 1910, vol. i, pp. 175 ff.

than a "property" right. It is his right to withhold his services from the use of others until their value can be agreed upon. This is the legal basis of his wage bargain.

Hence property and liberty change places and merge their meanings when industry changes from the agricultural stage of production for self to the modern stage of bargaining with others. The wage-earner's "property" becomes his right to seek an employer and to acquire property in the form of wages; his property in the sense of liberty is his right to refuse work or to quit work if the conditions are not satisfactory. The employer's "property" is, in part, his right to seek laborers and acquire their services; his property, in the sense of "liberty," is his right to run his business in his own way, that is, in part, to withhold employment or to discharge the laborer if the bargain is unsatisfactory.

These definitions of property rights are evidently quite different from the older ideas of property in physical things, such as lands, buildings, machinery, or slaves. They signify rights of buying and selling, of access to a market. They are "intangible" property, and not "tangible." They are like the "good will" of a business. They are defined as "property" because they are necessary to give to things and services that value in exchange which in modern industry depends as much on selling them as it does on "producing" them.

Only within the past half-century have courts and legislatures distinguished and protected such intangible property as good will, trade-marks and trade names, based on the right of access to a commodity market; and still more recently has "access to a labor market" been treated in effect as a property right of both the laborer and the employer, in addition to a personal right.[6] Not merely the contract after it is made is property, but the right to be unhindered by others in order to make a labor contract is a property right. It is "intangible" property both of the laborer who seeks employers and of the employer who seeks laborers. It is intangible, because it is merely the act of offering and yet withholding services or commodities. It is property and becomes capital in the sense that

[6] See also *ibid.*, vol. ii, p. 872; Hall, *Constitutional Law*, 1914, pp. 134, 135. "Doctrine of Conspiracy," p. 106. Commons, John R., *Legal Foundations of Capitalism*, 1924, chaps ii and viii.

it is the power of getting value in exchange. Just as the employer's property is both his physical factory and his intangible business, so the laborer's property is both his physical body and his intangible labor. This "intangible" property has come to mean a part of what was formerly known as personal liberty. It is that kind of liberty that has money value. It gives value alike to the laborer's labor and the employer's business.

If meanings of property and liberty change with changes in industry, so does the meaning of equality. Equality for the colonist and the pioneer signified mainly equal right to acquire property *through labor*—now it signifies equal right to acquire it *through bargaining*. But where bargaining power on the one side is power to withhold access to physical property and the necessaries of life, and on the other side is only power to withhold labor by doing without those necessaries, then equality of rights may signify inequality of bargaining power. The gradual recognition of inequalities of waiting power has required changes to be made in the legal means of protecting equality, and these changes underlie the history of labor legislation. They occur within limits prescribed by "due process of law."

III. Due Process of Law

The constitutions, which declare private rights inalienable, yet provide methods and standards both to abridge them and to protect them. A right has two sides. It is a *right* of one and a *duty* of another, or of all others. One person signs a note agreeing to pay $20 to another person. The second person has a right to receive $20—the first is under a duty to pay it. One person owns a piece of land. He has a right to use it as he pleases—all other persons are under the duty to keep off and let him alone. To protect the rights of one is to enforce the duties of others. If a right of one is abridged or reduced, the corresponding duty of another or of all others is reduced. If a debt is reduced from $20 to $10, both the right to receive and the duty to pay are reduced. If a person's right to use his land as he pleases is restricted, then the corresponding duties of others are reduced. On the other hand, a person's duties are just so much subtracted from the total of his liberties, and so to reduce the amount of his duties is to enlarge the total amount of his liberties. To reduce the rights of one is to enlarge the liberties of others.

Here must be noted the distinction already made between the labor contract and the wage bargain. The two may be diametrically opposed. From the standpoint of the wage bargain, if an employer's right to require a woman to work unlimited hours is reduced, then the woman's duty is consequently reduced and her liberties enlarged. But, from the standpoint of the labor contract, she loses the liberty to contract for unlimited hours. This may be a mere fictitious liberty for her, existing only in the eyes of the law, whereas it is in reality the right of the employer to compel her to work. From the legal standpoint her liberties are abridged—from the economic standpoint they are enlarged. Likewise, from the legal standpoint the employer's duty is reduced when her hours of service are reduced. From the economic standpoint his duty may be increased if her bargaining power is increased. It is this contradiction between the labor contract and the wage bargain that labor legislation attempts to reconcile.[7]

The state exercises the great and sovereign power of enlarging and abridging rights and liberties without consent of the parties. This power is intended, under our constitutions, to be safeguarded most minutely and accurately. The safeguards are developed with reference to an all-inclusive term, "due process of law."

Due process of law, along with the provisions of the constitutions, determines both the substance and the procedure of government in three principal aspects: first, the *public powers*, or the powers of government under which authority is granted to protect, enlarge, or abridge rights and duties; second, the *public authorities*, or the powers of officials acting within that authority; and third, the *principles*, standards or "maxims" that determine the limits beyond which public powers and public authorities shall not go. Each of these aspects affects labor legislation.

1. **Public Powers:** a. *Power to Preserve Peace and Execute the Laws.*—Government exists, first of all, to enforce the duty

[7] See "Public Benefit," p. 523; "Equal Protection of the Laws," p. 528; "Maximum Hours, Women," pp. 112-116. John R. Commons, *Legal Foundations of Capitalism*, chap. iv.

THE BASIS OF LABOR LAW 511

to keep the peace. To do this it may use force. It is the custodian of physical coercion and the authority that may threaten violence. Only in actual self-defense or in extreme urgency has an individual the right to resort to violence. He must confine himself to persuasion in every other case. Groups of individuals may go on strike, may get together for free discussion, or for agitation and joint action, but they must assemble and act peaceably. Even though they suffer the greatest injustice, they must not go beyond the duty of obedience to law and order. The authorization, or "power," of the state to use or threaten violence in order to execute the laws, to protect person and property, to punish for crime, is its first and highest justification, without which no other power could exist, and all government would be impossible. This is its exclusive authority, and it cannot compromise the question or permit private violence, except at the peril of its own existence. Under the justification of preserving the peace and executing the laws, the state may deprive individuals of life, liberty, or property without consent or compensation.

b. *The Taxing Power.*—The taxing power is an authorization under which government takes private property for public purposes without compensation. By this authority the state provides for the most fundamental legislation for or against labor. It provides free schools, compulsory education for future workers, and pays the salaries and expenses of all officials who enforce the labor laws. A labor law is defeated as surely by voting against taxes to enforce it as by voting outright against the law itself. The taxing power is used, not only for revenue, but also for purposes which otherwise are justified under the police power. A tariff on the products of foreign pauper labor is designed to strengthen the bargaining power of American labor. A tax on poisonous phosphorus matches is placed so high that it brings in no revenue at all, and serves only to protect the health of employees. Under our form of government the police power belongs to the states and not to the federal government; but the federal government does, under the justification of the taxing power, what the states might do under the police power.

c. *Guardianship.*—The state is the universal trustee or guardian, and exercises the remnants of the authority which the monarch had as *parens patriæ*, the "father of his country." In mediæval times the property of a chief tenant, reverted at death to the king, and the children became the wards of the king, for the king's benefit. Now the state is trustee for the benefit of the children and the people. This power justifies child labor legislation. In the early law of *patria potestas*, or "power of the father," the natural father was the owner of his child, as he was owner of his wife, lands, slaves, and chattels. It was the child's duty to obey. Now, the child has many rights against its parent, and, since it is unable to enforce these rights itself when the parent violates them, the state intervenes as its guardian on behalf of the people of the future.[8] It takes the child away if necessary; it deprives the parent of his right to the child's earnings by prohibiting its employment or by reducing its hours of labor; it enforces the parent's duty of education by compulsory school attendance. *Patria potestas* yields to the authority of *parens patriæ*.

This authority of the state is nowadays treated as a branch of the police power.[9] As such, it is a justification for an extreme use of the police power not permitted in other cases. It deals with children unable to make bargains for themselves. The police power primarily interferes with the bargains of adults. Restrictions which the courts would not permit under other classifications within the police power are unquestionably approved when the justification of guardianship is merged with that of police.

d. *Eminent Domain.*—The state may be an owner of property and business, like a private person. It may acquire ownership by various methods, all of which rest ultimately on its sovereign power of coercion. Some of its properties are acquired by conquest. Others are purchased by voluntary bargain; others, by compulsory bargain, under the power of eminent domain. In either case the power of taxation may furnish the funds.

Eminent domain is a justification of the state in taking property from its own citizens without their consent. It differs from the other powers in that it applies to an individual rather than to a class, and therefore our constitutions require that

[8] See Andrews, *American Law*, pp. 652-654, and cases there cited.
[9] Freund, *Police Power*, 1904, pp. 246-253.

compensation be made when property is taken. The individual has no inalienable right to withhold his property from the state, if the state desires it for a public purpose. But the constitutions protect the individual against the state by requiring just compensation.

e. *Proprietorship.*—Whether it acquires physical property or not, the state, in its various divisions of town, city, county, state, and nation, becomes an employer of thousands of wage earners. It fixes their wages, hours, and conditions of labor according to its own ideas as determined by its legislatures, executives, or courts. It is not restricted, as it is when exercising the police power, because it is not taking away private property (except perhaps as it falls back on the taxing power to pay the wages). Consequently, the American state, under universal suffrage and the power of proprietorship, or public ownership and operation of public business, supported by the taxing power, has gone far ahead of private owners in raising wages, shortening hours, and improving the conditions of its employees. Even contractors, or private employers who work for the state, are required, under laws that provide for "fair wages," as in England, or for the "prevailing rate of wages," as in America, to pay higher wages or observe shorter hours than they might in their work for private capitalists.[10]

f. *The Police Power.*—The police power is an indefinite authorization for the American state to abridge liberty or property without consent or compensation, in addition to its other more definite powers. An individual is sick with diphtheria. The state draws the line of quarantine beyond which his family and friends are deprived of their liberty of movement. Valuable animals have the foot-and-mouth disease. The state may order them to be shot and buried without consent or compensation. A public utility corporation has the valuable bargaining power of fixing its prices for gas, electricity, water, or transportation, and withholding service if the price is not paid. The state reduces the price and compels the company to continue or increase the service. The employer has valuable rights in his defenses of assumption of risk, fellow servant, and contributory negligence in suits brought against him for

[10] See "Historical Development of the Minimum Wage, United States," p. 54; "Maximum Hours, Men," p. 117.

damages caused by accident. The state takes away his defenses and increases by so much the value of the rights belonging to his employees.[11] Other examples might be given. The bulk of labor legislation by the states looks for authorization to the police power.

The police power in the United States differs from other powers in the miscellaneous and indefinite range of subjects that it may cover. It is defined rather by what it does not cover than by what it does. It differs from the taxing power in that it reduces the owner's liberty to use, acquire, or own property, rather than the revenues derived from it. It differs from eminent domain in that it applies to a class rather than to an individual and does not require compensation to be made. While it includes guardianship, it differs from it in that it abridges or enlarges the rights of adults and full citizens instead of those of children. It differs from public ownership and operation, or proprietary power, in that it abridges or enlarges the powers of private persons over their own persons or property instead of the power of the state over its own property or business. It differs from the power to use violence in order to keep the peace and execute the laws, in that it is one of the justifications or reasons advanced according to which the state is authorized to enact the laws themselves, rather than the physical power to enforce them after enactment. It is the police *power*, not the police *man*.

The other powers of the state, previously mentioned, are in theory definitely limited. Either they accomplish only a specific object of government, such as conquest, peace, the execution of laws, the acquisition of revenues, or the purchase of property, or they extend only to a limited class of people, such as children or public employees. But, in addition to these objects and persons, there are those large and indefinite purposes of public safety, health, morals, welfare, and prosperity, and those many but indefinite classes of producers and consumers, buyers and sellers, employers and employees, who often are restrained by government under the police power. These purposes and classes, moreover, are continually changing as industry changes from agriculture to commerce, or as property changes from physical things to bargaining and contracts, or

[11] See "Industrial Accident Insurance," p. 227.

THE BASIS OF LABOR LAW 515

as population becomes more congested and people interfere with one another, or as public opinion regarding rights and duties, morals and welfare, advances from ignorance to intelligence, from servitude to liberty. It is the police power, for the most part, that affords, in the case of the state governments, that elastic justification by which the state abridges or enlarges liberty or property without compensation, in order to achieve a newly recognized public purpose through a newly recognized class of persons or things.

g. *Commerce Power and Federal Powers.*—The police power is not isolated from the other powers. All of them are but different ways of looking at the single power of sovereignty. But, under our system of government, sovereignty is divided between the federal government and the state governments. The federal government has specific delegated powers of taxation, of regulation of foreign and interstate commerce, while the states have the taxing power, and, in addition, the "police power." But the federal government uses its delegated powers to accomplish the same purposes that the states accomplish with their reserved police power. The taxing power is used by the federal government, not merely to secure revenue, but to protect industry and labor against foreign competition, or to suppress state bank notes, colored oleomargarine, or poisonous phosphorus matches. The "commerce" power is used to regulate railroad rates and services, to restrict hours of labor, and to require the adoption of safety devices by railroad or steamship companies. New lines of legislation protecting labor, such as child labor and workmen's compensation laws, if adopted by state governments, are justified by the police power —if adopted by the federal government, they are justified by the taxing power or the commerce power. Yet all powers are but the single power of sovereignty split up to fit the constitutional divisions of government.[12]

h. *Police Power and the Constitution.*—From the foregoing, it will be seen how impossible it is accurately to define the police power, the taxing power, or the commerce power. Com-

[12] For a detailed history of the conflict between the commerce and police powers, see Hastings, "The Development of Law as Illustrated by the Decisions Relating to the Police Power of the State," in *Proceedings of the American Philosophical Society,* 1900, vol. xxxix, p. 349.

paring the police power with the principles of the common law, Freund says:[13] "[the state] exercises its compulsory powers for the prevention and anticipation of wrong by narrowing common-law rights through conventional restraints and positive regulations which are not confined to the prohibition of wrongful acts. It is the latter kind of state control which constitutes the essence of the police power. The maxim of this power is that every individual must submit to such restraints in the exercise of his liberty or of his rights of property as may be required to remove or reduce the danger of the abuse of these rights on the part of those who are unskillful, careless, or unscrupulous."

Describing this power as developed under American institutions, Ely says:[14] "It is that power of the courts committed to them by American constitutions whereby they must shape property and contract to existing social conditions by settling the question of how far social regulations may, without compensation, impose burdens on property."

Comparing it with other powers of government, Hastings says:[15] "It is not necessary to adopt Treitschke's oft-repeated declaration, that the state is force, in order to conclude that the 'police power' is a fiction. Every judge whom we have seen attempt to analyze it finds in it Madison's 'indefinite supremacy' of the state. The doctrine of faculties and separate powers of the state may not be as essentially absurd as Treitschke thinks, but in our case the term is certainly a mere abstract and collective one for the state, where regarded as employed in certain functions." Hastings also says that the police power is "a branch of constitutional law peculiar to countries having legislatures with limited power. It is an outgrowth of the American conception of protecting the individual from the state."[16]

We may not say that the police power is a fiction, for it is a necessary part of the reasoning by which, under our federal Constitution, the distinction is made by the courts between

[13] *Police Power*, p. 8.
[14] *Property and Contract in Their Relations to the Distribution of Wealth*, 1914, vol. i, p. 220.
[15] Hastings, *op. cit.*, p. 349.
[16] *Ibid.*, p. 360.

THE BASIS OF LABOR LAW

those powers that belong to the states and those that belong to the federal government. Yet, from another point of view, it is a fallacious distinction if it pretends to assign to the states a different kind of power from that exercised by the federal government. We have just said that the federal government accomplishes, under the name of "taxing power" or "commerce power," what the states accomplish under the name of police power. While the refinements of legal logic may seem to make these powers different, they are identical from the standpoint of the kind of legislation and the public purpose which they justify. The police power has sometimes narrowly been held to be limited to matters of health and morals. But legislatures and Congress refuse to be limited in this way, and are held in restraint by the courts. They regulate the bargaining power of individuals and corporations where no justification can be found in the protection of health and morals. From this standpoint, the theory of the police power is used by the courts to determine how far the state legislature may be permitted to go. But they use similar standards or principles to determine how far Congress may go in using the taxing power and the commerce power.

For our purposes, therefore, in speaking of the police power, we often use the term in this broad sense, to imply all the powers of government, whether state or federal, whether of police, taxation, or interstate commerce, in so far as they are used to justify that indefinite extension of power to abridge liberty or property without compensation for some newly recognized public purpose. The practical problem with which we are concerned is not so much the technical legal distinctions between different powers, as the extent to which these powers are increasingly used to determine the bargaining relations between employers and employees. In this way, without formal amendment, the American constitutions are unconsciously amended by the police power through the change of public opinion regarding the rights and liberties of labor. This change works its way into the constitutions, partly through the discretion of public authorities, and partly through the application of old principles of justice to new conditions.

2. **Public Authorities.**—Here the issue is between the amount of discretion, or power to enforce one's own opinion,

allotted to the executive, legislative, and judicial branches of government. Shall the legislature or Congress use its sovereign power to the extreme limit of equalizing fortunes and giving labor a high preference over capital, or shall it be restricted to narrower limits? In other words, can the legislature, under whatever power of taxation, commerce, or police, put into force its own notions of "general welfare" and "social expediency," or must it be limited to the notions held by the courts?

In monarchical countries, or countries whose executives inherit monarchical powers, executive discretion still remains to the monarch, or president, or the executive council,[17] after legislative powers have been taken away by Parliament. This power of discretion is the executive's power to decide when and where a law applies, and to issue rules, regulations, ordinances, or orders which have the effect of law, which are needed to enforce the law, or even are thought by the executive necessary to fill any gaps which Parliament has left in the scheme of laws. Indeed, in enforcing a law, every executive officer must exercise some discretion, which he does as his own opinion directs. Discretion is the power to act without interference according to one's own opinions, or policy, or theory of things. It is not supposed to be capricious or changeable. It is power to adopt and follow a policy, not power to be arbitrary and unreasonable. Even a policeman must make up his mind whether a man is drunk or not, before applying the law against public intoxication. Policemen may differ in their opinions on this matter, even though the facts do not differ; and their differences are the little germs of what, in the case of a mayor, governor, president, or king, would be called executive policy, or executive discretion.

Under the theory of our Constitution, however, the executive officers have no discretion to follow a policy of their own. The legislature is the policy-making branch of government. It has discretion; it can put its opinions into effect; it can adopt a policy, because it is supposed to represent all interests in society and to know all the facts. The effort is therefore made in our country to limit the executive discretion as narrowly as possible, in order that it may be said that the executive merely enforces the law as he finds it. To do other-

[17] Switzerland.

THE BASIS OF LABOR LAW

wise would be to delegate legislative power to an authority that is not legislative under the Constitution.

But with us, not even the legislature is the supreme legislative power. The written constitutions are the fundamental laws, enacted directly by the people themselves. Being laws, they also express a policy, based on the opinion of the people who adopted them. And their policy must prevail against the legislative discretion. The policy of the constitutions is extremely individualistic. It asserts inalienable and natural rights of individuals against all others and against the state itself. When a policy of the legislature set forth in a statute comes into conflict with this individualistic policy of the constitutions, someone must be called upon to decide which shall prevail. The supreme courts, at first with hesitation, but afterward with assurance, have made these decisions. If a statute of the legislature fixing the hours of labor or the minimum wage of women, conflicts with the Constitution, the courts merely refuse to enforce it—they enforce the Constitution itself. They declare the law "unconstitutional."

There is a principle of our courts to the effect that a law is not unconstitutional if a way can be found to sustain it. Hence, if there is an apparent conflict between the Constitution and the attempt of the legislature to abridge private rights, and if the court cannot support the legislature under the other limited justifications of taxation, guardianship, proprietorship, eminent domain, or protection of person and property, it may see its way to support it under the elastic justification of the police power. Thus the police power in America may be looked upon as the courts' justification for gradually *amending the Constitution by interpretation* so that it may conform to the new objects and new restrictions on property which the legislature deems important. A similar justification and gradual amending of the Constitution takes place when the court permits Congress to extend the taxing power or the commerce power to the regulation of rates, services, wages, hours of labor, safety, health, and compensation for accidents.

This distinction between discretion on the part of the legislature and interpretation on the part of the courts is a distinction not so much between the several powers of government as between the functions peculiar to the several branches of government. It leads us to distinguish the public authorities who share in the exercise of the public powers.

Government can interpret and exercise its powers only through individuals. Each of these individuals takes an oath appropriate to his office, agreeing to support the Constitution, to execute the law, to maintain order. For the time being, his acts are the acts of the state, provided he keeps within the authority granted to him. To the legislature is granted the authority of deciding on public policy for the future, and, in doing so, it exercises discretion. To the courts belongs the power of deciding particular cases as they arise, and in doing so they interpret the laws. The executive enforces the law. But to a fourth and new branch of government, unrecognized in the original constitutions, which may be called the administration,[18] is coming to be assigned the function of investigation of those economic and social conditions upon which the several branches of government base their decisions. While these functions cannot be separated in practice, yet they stand out as characteristic of each branch of government. *Execution, discretion, interpretation,* and *investigation* are the four great divisions in the functions of officials, and the *executive*, the *legislature*, the *judiciary*, and the *administration* are the four branches that are specialized for these functions.

a. *The Executive.*—The executive authorities are entitled to use violence if necessary, and to deprive individuals of life, liberty, and property without their consent. Private individuals may not even resist an officer of the law. The army, navy, and militia may be called upon by the governor or President in time of strike or riot. Sheriffs, marshals, their deputies and policemen, may arrest and imprison individuals in order to prevent violence and to execute the orders of the court in the administration of civil and criminal justice. They belong to the military or "police" force of the state, which, under our theory, is subordinate to the civil authorities. The police force, as already stated, differs from the police power, in that the police

[18] *Die Verwaltung.* The term "administration" has been used by the Supreme Court in this sense: Interstate Commerce Commission *v.* U. S. *ex rel.* Humboldt Steamship Co., 224 U. S. 474 (1911) 32 Sup. Ct. 556; Pennsylvania R. R. Co. *v.* International Mining Co., 230 U. S. 196, 274 (1912).

THE BASIS OF LABOR LAW

power is the authorization, or justification, under which civil authorities are entitled to exercise discretion in enacting laws and issuing orders, while the police force is the agency which exercises coercion as directed by these laws and orders.

While in law the military and police forces have no discretion, but must follow orders, yet, in the urgency of immediate action, they must exercise discretion before their acts can be passed upon by the civil authorities. Only in case of war can executives legally set aside the superior authority of the courts, but war can be declared only by the legislature, a civil authority.[19] The arbitrary discretion of the executive is sought to be held in check by that greatest instrument of freedom, the writ of *habeas corpus*. By means of this writ the court, a civil authority, orders the executive, or military power, to bring out a prisoner for hearing and for release if wrongly imprisoned. If the executive refuses, then the civil authority *ipso facto* becomes subordinate to military force. In so far as the executives and the military and police authorities exercise discretion, their opinion of the rights and duties of employer and employee is sometimes the deciding factor one way or the other in determining the relative power of the two in the wage bargain as affected by strikes, lockouts, public assembly, public speaking, agitation, arrest of leaders, protection of strike breakers, picketing, the use of the streets, and otherwise.

b. *The Legislature.*—The legislature is the authority which, acting within limits, is entitled to exercise discretion in deciding upon public policy and enacting laws to carry the policy into effect. It is the one branch of government where the representatives of conflicting opinions are entitled to express their joint opinion in the form of law that shall be enforced on all persons with or without their consent. Other branches of government are considered to be impartial and limited to the execution of the law as the legislature prescribes. But the legislature may be partisan in politics and partial between employers and employees. It is considered that, if partisans

---

[19] This has apparently been denied by the Supreme Court of West Virginia, which sustained the acts of a "military commission" in sentencing strikers to prison: State *ex rel.* Mays *v.* Brown, 71 W. Va. 519, 77 S. E. 243 (1912); *ex parte* Jones, 71 W. Va. 567, 77 S. E. 1029 (1913).

meet and discuss in an orderly way their points of antagonism, the outcome will be a compromise in which the arbitrary power of no individual or class will dominate others. Yet, in fear that the legislature may not act justly, and may override minorities or those not represented, the people have enacted the higher law known as the Constitution, with its bill of rights and its limitations on the legislature. This leads to the judiciary.

c. *The Judiciary.*—Under our constitutional system the judicial branch holds a high and unique position. In order that it may be removed from the heat of partisanship and partiality, it is made independent of the executive and legislative branches. In order that the federal system of a central government and forty-eight state governments, each supreme in its own field, may operate in harmony, the federal court is made the final authority to determine how far the field of each extends. By the Fourteenth Amendment to the Constitution, all persons born or naturalized in this country enjoy a double citizenship—that of the United States and of the state wherein they reside. By this amendment the federal courts have authority to prevent any state from abridging the rights which the federal Constitution and laws grant to them as citizens of the United States, and to prevent any state from depriving any person of life, liberty, or property without due process of law. The federal courts interpret and apply treaties with foreign nations and protect the rights of aliens. Finally, since the acts of the federal Congress or executive may conflict with the Constitution, the federal court may declare them unconstitutional and hence refuse to apply them, in order to protect the Constitution.

In this many-sided jurisdiction over states, over Congress, over the executive, over inferior courts, and over private citizens, and in the interpretation of these many laws, the Supreme Court of the United States exercises authority not only judicial, but also, in fact, legislative and executive; so also with the supreme courts of the states within their proper jurisdictions. When deciding between a law of the legislature and the law of the constitution, they necessarily decide between the policy of the legislature and their own opinion, based on previous decisions, of the policy contained in the constitution. When nullifying an act of the executive they interpose their opinion of the law and the constitution against the executive's opinion. Yet they are but performing the judicial function of interpreting the laws and making their application to the facts of each particular case, as it arises. Their legislative and executive functions arise because they have authority to apply their interpretation to cases in which the acts of legislatures and executives are called in question, as well as cases where only private citizens are the litigants. In this way is established, as the court has said, "a government of laws and not of men."[20]

The courts, just like legislatures and executives, are composed of men. They, too, are guided by opinions, and their opinions change with change in experience and change in judges. The difference consists in the procedure, the standards, and the safeguards by which the judges arrive at their opinions, compared with those which restrain the more hasty opinions of lawmakers and executives. It is merely "opinions," after all, rather than written constitutions, that protect, enlarge, and abridge rights and liberties.

d. *The Administration.*—Opinions of individuals are so capricious, fluctuating, and uncertain, so liable to be bent by bias, passion, and interest, that our constitutional system of government imposes methods and principles designed to reduce them to an orderly system based on reason. These methods are *investigation* or the accurate discovery of facts and conditions, and in more recent times the administrative branch of government has been devised with investigation as its main purpose. Investigation is so involved in all the topics of labor legislation that the topic of administration has been treated in a separate chapter.

3. **Principles.**—The other essential to an orderly system of reason in place of capricious opinion is the principles, standards, or "maxims" that underlie due process of law. Under the theory of our courts, the principles of law and justice are immutable and unchanging. Facts and conditions change, and these are revealed by investigation; but the principles remain the same, though their application changes when the facts change. The leading principles that concern us are "public benefit" and "equal protection of the laws."

a. *Public Benefit.*—The effect and purpose of the police power

[20] Marbury *v.* Madison, 1 Cranch 137, at p. 163 (1803).

are to impose a duty on some individual which rebounds to the benefit of other individuals.[21] In despotic or oligarchic governments these benefited individuals are likely to be the favorites and courtiers of the monarch or the privileged and aristocratic classes. In a democratic or republican government they are likely to be political partisans, monied interests, employers' organizations, trade unions, or other classes who get control of the legislature and enact laws merely for the benefit of their private interest, at the expense of other private interests. But if a thing of this kind happens, then the legislature is doing the very thing which revolutions and written constitutions were designed to prevent when despots and aristocrats were the offenders. Hence it is that every act of the legislature must be tested by a standard which shall determine whether the persons or classes of persons to be benefited are so benefited merely because they have power in the legislature to impose burdens on others, or because the benefit to them is also a benefit to that body of the whole people which we call "the public." If the benefit goes only to private persons for their private benefit then the legislation is unconstitutional, because it employs the sovereign power of government for private purposes. If those persons who are benefited are either the entire population or such a significant part of the population that their benefit is also a public benefit, then the powers of government are put to their proper use of performing a public purpose.[22]

Thus we have a series of terms closely related or synonymous, all of them implying public benefit, such as public utility, public interest, public use, public value, public service, public welfare, public purpose. These indicate the most fundamental principle, standard, or maxim, which measures or limits the extent to which the legislature may go in exercising its police power.

Public benefit is not something fixed and unchangeable. The police power particularly is that justification by which the definition of public benefit may be changed or enlarged as

[21] See "The Police Power," p. 513.
[22] The term "public purpose" is usually limited to taxation and eminent domain, but in this book it is also applied to other powers, especially the police power.

time goes on. In the final analysis this enlargement of the definition of public benefit is merely an enlargement of the court's opinion as to what constitutes a public purpose. But, behind the change in the court's opinion is the change in *conditions* and the change in *public opinion*. Among the changes in conditions which lead to changes in opinion are those industrial changes already mentioned, such as the change from free land to closed land, the changes in transportation and mobility of labor, the development of large-scale industry, all of them throwing large masses of labor together into active competition. The increasing congestion of population, whether in towns or factories, has brought a change of opinion as to the need of extending the police power in matters of health, safety, and morals.

Accompanying these changes in outward conditions may be noted significant changes in public opinion and court opinion regarding labor. In the *colonial* or *agricultural* stage of industry, the man without property was looked upon as partly shiftless, partly vagabond, partly criminal; and the opinion of the time supported many kinds of coercive laws by which both adults and children might be captured or enslaved or otherwise compelled to work. In this way it was considered that propertyless laborers would be trained in the habits of industry and thrift by which they could rise to the position of proprietor and could share in the rights and civilization of their superiors.

A *citizenship* stage followed, beginning in the decade of 1820, when the propertyless man was granted the suffrage. This produced at once a revolutionary change in the attitude of labor toward itself, shown in the first series of strikes on a large scale for reduction of hours of labor, with the demand for more leisure for the duties of citizenship, as well as the demand for free schools, for the abolition of imprisonment for debt, of indentured service, and other remnants of the servile stage.

Immediately, following this period and the failure of aggressive methods, after the panic of 1837, came what may be called the *humanitarian* period. Labor, for the time being, lost its power of attack and became incapable of self-help. So the long period of unemployment, until the gold discoveries of 1849, produced a class of eminent men in sympathy with labor, and brought about the beginning of legislation abolishing imprisonment for debt, providing wage and homestead exemptions, free schools, protective tariffs against foreign pauper competition, and generally removing the opinions of servility, dissoluteness, and criminality theretofore held regarding propertyless labor. This remarkable period culminated in the Civil War, which freed the slaves. It was accompanied by similar movements in Europe, and altogether was nothing less than a revolution in public opinion regarding labor.[23]

With the decade of the 'sixties began again an aggressive movement of labor, headed in Europe by the International Workingmen's Association, which later split into socialism, anarchism, and trade unionism, and in the United States by the National Labor Union, which finally split into greenbackism, socialism, and trade unionism. This period, extending into the twentieth century, may properly be characterized as a period of *class struggle*, in which new and enormous fortunes derived from industry were pitted against unprecedented organizations of labor in many deadly struggles, and in which legislatures responded to the demands of labor for legislation, and the courts responded to the demands of capital by declaring such laws "class legislation" and therefore unconstitutional.

This period, to a considerable extent, continues to the present time; but the beginning of another, which may be called the *public benefit* period of labor legislation, dates from 1898, when the Supreme Court decided the case of Holden v. Hardy.[24] Hitherto the police power was recognized mainly as an authority to enforce protective restrictions against producers in behalf of consumers. This decision affirmed the power to enforce such restrictions on employers and consumers in behalf of producers. In other words, whereas formerly, for the most part, the health of consumers, but not the health of producers, was a public benefit, now the health of the laborer as a producer is considered to be as much a public benefit as the health

[23] See chaps. vi, "Individual Bargaining," and vii, "Collective Bargaining," of this book.

[24] 169 U. S. 366, 18 Sup. Ct. 383 (1898). The decisions affirmed the constitutionality of legislation reducing the hours of labor of *men* who work in smelters and underground.

THE BASIS OF LABOR LAW

of the consumer of his product. If this be so, then the liberty of both the employer and the employee to make a labor contract may be restricted and regulated, if it is found that the contract is injurious to the laborer. The protection of labor becomes a public purpose.[25]

In the Holden v. Hardy case, the court also stated the principles on which the powers of government are enlarged as conditions change and new facts are brought to the attention of the court through investigation: "This court has not failed to recognize the fact that the law is, to a certain extent, a progressive science; that in some of the states methods of procedure which, at the time the Constitution was adopted, were deemed essential to the protection and safety of the people, or to the liberty of the citizen, have been found to be no longer necessary; that restrictions which had formerly been laid upon the conduct of individuals, or of classes of individuals, have proved detrimental to their interests, while, upon the other hand, certain other classes of persons (particularly those engaged in dangerous or unhealthful employments) have been found to be in need of additional protection. . . . It is impossible to forecast the character or extent of these changes; but in view of the fact that, from the day Magna Charta was signed to the present moment, amendments to the structure of the law have been made with increasing frequency, it is impossible to suppose that they will not continue, and the law be forced to adapt itself to new conditions of society, and particularly to the new relations between employers and employees, as they arise."[26] Two state courts have said: "While the principles of justice are immutable, changing conditions of society and the evolution of employment make a change in the application of principles absolutely necessary to an intelligent administration of government."[27]

Finally a justice of the Supreme Court, in 1911, was able to

---

[25] This, of course, was not the first time that this doctrine was asserted. Indeed, it was implied whenever a court sustained a law protecting labor. It was the first broad statement by the highest court in such a way as to make it "the law of the land."

[26] Holden v. Hardy, 169 U. S. 366, at pp. 385-387, 18 Sup. Ct. 383 (1898).

[27] Ritchie v. Wayman, 244 Ill. 509, 91 N. E. 695 (1910); quoted with approval from State v. Buchanan, 29 Wash. 602, 70 Pac. 52 (1902).

identify a public benefit with public opinion regarding not only the health of a class of producers, but also regarding the welfare of any class of people, and to declare that the police power is shaped "by the prevailing morality or the strong and preponderant opinion" as to what is "greatly and immediately necessary to the public welfare."[28]

b. *Equal Protection of the Laws.*—Another respect in which the case of Holden v. Hardy is the headlight of a new period is found in its opinion regarding the inequality of bargaining power of employer and employee. The opinion declared that a law, such as the one then before the court, limiting the working hours of men, was not class legislation and therefore did not conflict with the Constitution, which guarantees to each individual the equal protection of the laws. The reason is, as declared by the court, that the employers and their laborers do not stand upon an equality; that "the proprietors lay down the rules and the operatives are practically constrained to obey them"; that "the latter are often induced by the fear of discharge to conform to regulations which their judgment, fairly exercised, would pronounce to be detrimental to their health and strength," and that, even though "both parties are of full age and competent to contract," yet the legislature may interfere "where the parties do not stand upon an equality, or where the public health demands that one party to the contract shall be protected against himself."[29]

[28] Noble State Bank v. Haskell 219 U. S. 104, 31 Sup. Ct. 186 (1911). Also contrary opinion in Ives v. South Buffalo R. R. Co., 201 N. Y. 271, 94 N. E. 431 (1911), at p. 448, where the highest court of New York said in part: "As to the cases of Noble State Bank v. Haskell, and Assaria State Bank v. Dolly, we have only to say that if they go so far as to hold that any law, whatever its effect, may be upheld because by the 'prevailing morality' or the 'strong and preponderant opinion' it is deemed 'to be greatly and immediately necessary to the public welfare,' we cannot recognize them as controlling of our construction of our own constitution."

[29] A similar opinion had been stated in 1892 by a state court (Peel Splint Coal Co. v. State, 36 W. Va. 802, 15 S. E. 1000 [1892], at p. 1009): "When a few persons are engaged in an extensive business and they have a multitude of customers or dependent employees and it appears that the business is of such a character that the parties do not deal upon an equal footing and that the many are at a disadvantage in their contractual relations with the few, the legislature may regulate these rela-

In this opinion the court recognized, what had been dimly seen or implied from the beginning of labor legislation, that inequality of bargaining power is a justification under which the state may come to the protection of the weaker party to the bargain. In earlier periods the courts had often held that capital and labor were equal, that laws favoring labor against capital were class legislation; and, even where certain courts held otherwise, the law books severely criticized them as yielding to the pressure of politics instead of bravely standing by the Constitution.[30] Inequality of bargaining power has long been a ground for legislative and judicial protection of the weaker party, even though the courts found other grounds on which to base their opinions. It was early conceded as a justification of usury laws, protecting the weak debtor against the strong creditor; latterly, of public utility laws, protecting the weak consumer, farmer, or shipper against the powerful corporation; and now it only needs a recognition of facts to justify labor legislation protecting the weak wage earner against the more powerful capitalist. Such legislation could be held to deny equal protection of the laws only where the facts showed that both parties were actually equal. But where the parties are unequal (and a public purpose is shown),[31] then the state which refuses to redress the inequality is actually denying to the weaker party the equal protection of the laws.

It is by recognizing this inequality of bargaining power, coupled with a public purpose, that the courts pass over, in any particular case, from the theory of *class legislation* to the theory of *reasonable classification*. The two are identical in one respect: all classification is class legislation, but the kind

---

tions, with a view to prevent fraud, oppression, or undue advantage." See also State *v.* Brown & Sharpe Manufacturing Co., 18 R. I. 16, 25 Atl. 246 (1892); Avent Beattyville Coal Co. *v.* Commonwealth, 96 Ky. 218, 28 S. W. 502 (1894).

[30] Eddy, *Law of Combinations,* 1901, vol. i, pp. 245-247, 277; vol. ii, p. 1023.

[31] In the case of Coppage *v.* Kansas, 236 U. S. 1, 35 Sup. Ct. 240 (1915), the Supreme Court denied the application of the doctrine of inequality of bargaining power, but this was a case where the purpose was to protect trade unions against disruption by employers. What the court in effect decided was that a trade union performed a private and not a public purpose.

of class legislation which the courts condemn is that which they consider to be "unreasonable" classification. Class legislation benefits or burdens one class against others where there is no real inequality or no public benefit. "Reasonable" classification benefits or burdens a class where there is real inequality to be overcome and a public benefit to be attained.[32] That which is class legislation at one time may become reasonable classification at a later time, if the court perceives that what it once thought was equality is really inequality, and what it once thought was merely private benefit is also public benefit.

Thus the history of the constitutionality of labor legislation in the United States has been a history of the *theory of classification*. The conflicting opinions of various courts on the extent of the police power over private property are usually conflicting opinions on the equality or inequality of bargaining classes and on the public or private purpose subserved by the legislation. In proportion as certain classes of laborers, such as women or mine workers, are recognized by the courts as suffering an injury, and in proportion as the injured persons are deemed to be of importance to the public as well as unable to protect themselves, then legislation requiring the employer to remove the injury and prohibiting the laborer from even voluntarily consenting to the injury ceases to be overruled as "class legislation" and begins to be sustained as "reasonable classification." Even though the individual liberty of both employer and employee to make so-called voluntary contracts is restricted by the law, yet each continues to have "equal protection of the laws" because each individual is treated equally with all other individuals *of his own class*. The bargaining power of the employee is increased while that of the employer is reduced, yet all employers in a given class are treated alike and all employees in their class are similarly treated alike.[33]

[32] See also Freund, *Police Power*, pp. 626-755.
[33] This principle may be seen in the workmen's compensation laws. Under the former law of employers' liability the laborer carried all the expense incurred by reason of the risk of accident. The employer had certain defenses by which he could throw the cost of accidents on the employee. (See "Rules of Employers' Liability," p. 228.) These defenses were held to be property rights, because they were valuable to the employer. But the legislature abolished these defenses and requires the employer to compensate *all* laborers for *all* disabling accidents. The

THE BASIS OF LABOR LAW

This gradual transition from the time when labor was treated as equal to capital to the modern time when labor is given privileges superior to those of capital may be described as a transition from the law of *master and servant* to the law of *employer and employee*. Prior to the decade of the eighteen-thirties the laborer could be imprisoned for debt. In other words, his creditor had rights over his body, which was looked upon as property justly belonging to the creditor as was the laborer's other property sufficient to pay the debt. This reduced the laborer to a servile state while pretending that he was equal and free. No distinction was made between the fraudulent debtor and the unfortunate debtor. Now the laborer is not treated as a criminal unless proved to be so, and his creditor consequently has no remedy which reduces the laborer to the servile state.

Next, in the decade of the 'forties, the law went further and the wage exemption laws prevented the creditor from taking even the minimum wages of the laborer in payment of a debt. Finally, the Thirteenth Amendment to the Constitution, by prohibiting involuntary servitude except for crime, confirmed the preceding privileges as well as the privilege of a laborer even to break his contract to labor without being forced to "specific performance." In these respects labor has been given a preference over capital, in that while both the employer and the employee can bring suits for damages on account of breaking a contract, the employer's suit is against the laborer whose small property is exempt from attachment, but the laborer's suit is against an employer whose business property as such has no exemption.[34]

Other laws were mentioned in the preceding chapters, showing the transition from the master-servant notion of law to the employer-employee notion. The master and servant law,

---

employers are thus compelled to pay the cost of insurance against all of these risks, where formerly the laborer carried the insurance as best he could. In this way the employer's increased cost of insurance may be said, so far as the law is concerned, to have increased the bargaining power of the employee and reduced the bargaining power of the employer or of the consumer to the same extent.

[34] Of course, the bankrupt employer has the same exemptions as the laborer.

while pretending to treat employer and employee alike, retained marks of that servile status in which the laborer's body was the physical property of employer or creditor. The law of employer and employee, as it develops, not only gradually removes those vestiges of past servitude when the master could compel the servant to work, but also gives the latter a preference over capital in bargaining and a privilege to break contracts without effective penalty which the employer does not possess. In other words, the natural inequality of employer and employee reduces the latter to a servile state, reinforced by the law of master and servant; but the legislature, by giving preference to the weaker party, overcomes in part the inequalities of nature and secures a more real equality protected by the law of employer and employee.[35]

Thus it may be affirmed that the equality of bargaining power toward which the law of employer and employee is directed is a principle so important for the public benefit that it becomes in itself a public purpose. Many decisions of the courts base the justification of the police power, not merely upon the protection of health, safety, and morals, but squarely upon strengthening the bargaining power of laborers. In sustaining a law requiring wages to be paid in cash, the Supreme Court of Tennessee said: "The legislature evidently deemed the laborer at some disadvantage under existing laws and customs, and by this act undertook to ameliorate his condition in some manner by enabling him, . . . at his election and at a proper time, to demand and receive his unpaid wages in money rather than in something less valuable. Its tendency, though slight it may be, is to place the employer and employee upon equal ground in the matter of wages."[36] The court again ap-

---

[35] This distinction between the law of master and servant and that of employer and employee is not technically correct. The law books include both under "master and servant." But the legislatures have broken away from these terms. In recent legislation of the more industrial states the terms used are employer and employee. This goes along with popular usage and serves to bring out, not so much the legal form of the labor contract, as the underlying purpose of equality in the wage bargain.

[36] Knoxville Iron Co. v. Harbison, 183 U. S. 13, 22 Sup. Ct. 1 (1901). For cases declaring similar laws unconstitutional, see Freund, *Police Power*, pp. 305, 306.

THE BASIS OF LABOR LAW 533

proved the passage in Holden v. Hardy bearing on bargaining equality.

An Arkansas law, forbidding coal operators "from using screens or other devices to reduce the amount of wages that would be due on the basis of weight of coal actually mined and accepted by the operator," was upheld as constitutional upon similar grounds. The court said: "We are unable to say, in the light of the conditions shown in the public inquiry referred to, and in the necessity for such laws, evinced in the enactments of the legislatures of various states, that this law had no reasonable relation to the protection of a large class of laborers in the receipt of their just dues and in the promotion of the harmonious relations of capital and labor engaged in a great industry in the state."[37]

The court argued in a like tenor in upholding an Iowa statute denying effect to any contract restricting liability or the acceptance of any insurance benefits as a defense to personal injury actions brought against railroads by their employees. In dealing with the relation of employer and employed, the court held that "the legislature has necessarily a wide field of discretion in order that there may be suitable protection of health and safety, and that peace and good order may be promoted through regulations designed to insure wholesome conditions of work and freedom from oppression. What differences as to the extent of this power may exist with respect to particular employments, and how far that which may be authorized as to one department of activity may appear to be arbitrary in another must be determined as cases are presented for decision. It is well established that, so far as its regulations are valid, not being arbitrary or unrelated to a proper purpose, the legislature undoubtedly may prevent them from being nullified by prohibiting contracts which, by modifications or waiver, would alter or impair the obligation imposed."[38] The court here also quotes with approval the passage from Holden v. Hardy relating to inequality and conflicting interest.

[37] McLean v. Arkansas, 211 U. S. 539, at p. 550, 29 Sup. Ct. 206 (1909), reprinted in Hall, *Cases on Constitutional Law*, 1913, p. 424.

[38] Chicago, Burlington & Quincy R. R. Co. v. McGuire, 219 U. S. 549, at p. 570, 31 Sup. Ct. 259 (1911), reprinted in Hall, *Cases on Constitutional Law*, p. 518.

As summarized by Ernst Freund:[39] "Our whole economic system is based upon a very wide liberty of dealing and contract, and it is deemed perfectly legitimate to use liberty for the purpose of securing special advantage over others. The resulting disparity of conditions is not, on the whole, regarded as inconsistent with the welfare of society. Yet a different view seems to be taken of this liberty of dealing, where economic superiority is used to dictate oppressive terms, or where a degree of economic power is aimed at that is liable to result in such oppression. The theory of legislative interference seems to be in some cases that oppression in itself, like fraud, is immoral and wrong either against the individual affected thereby or against the public at large; in other cases, that the excessive dependence of whole classes of the community threatens, though perhaps only remotely, the social fabric with grave disturbance or ultimate subversion and ruin."

[39] *Police Power,* p. 285. For more recent checks which the Supreme Court has placed on the extension of the police power, taxing power, and commerce power, see "Minimum Wage," p. 74, and "Child Labor," p. 172.

SELECT CRITICAL BIBLIOGRAPHY

In preparing the following select critical bibliography, arranged by chapters, an effort has been made to bring together only the most helpful and the most accessible works on labor legislation.

I. EMPLOYMENT AND UNEMPLOYMENT

American association for labor legislation. American labor legislation review. Quarterly, 1911-
  For articles relating to unemployment see Index to volumes I to XX and annual volume indexes thereafter.

Andrews, John B. A practical program for the prevention of unemployment in America. New York, American association for labor legislation, 1914. 24 p.
  Practical constructive suggestions for reducing unemployment through public employment offices, public works planning, regularization of industry, unemployment compensation, and other measures.

Astor, J. J., and others. Is unemployment inevitable? London, Macmillan, 1924. viii, 388 p.
  A general survey of basic economic factors with special reference to Great Britain, with separate memoranda on special problems by outstanding economists.

Barnett, George E. Machinery and labor. Cambridge, Harvard university press, 1926. viii, 161 p.
  A study of the displacement of men by machinery.

Beveridge, William H. Unemployment; a problem of industry. London, Longmans, Green, 1930. 514 p.
  Discusses the problem and its limits, sources of information, seasonal fluctuations, and the reserve of labor, the personal factor, remedies of the past, and principles of future policy. A critical analysis of British experience with unemployment insurance is included.

California. Unemployment commission. Report and recommendations. San Francisco, 1932. 809 p.
  Comprehensive survey of unemployment problem in one state, and proposed remedies.

Chase, Stuart. The tragedy of waste. New York, Macmillan, 1925.
  Chapters III and VIII describe graphically the industrial and human waste caused by unemployment.

Chegwidden, T. S., and Myrddin-Evans, G. The employment exchange service of Great Britain; an outline of the administration of placing and unemployment insurance. New York, Industrial relations counselors, 1934. xiv, 310 p.

    Authoritative history and description of the British public employment office system.

Davison, Ronald C. The unemployed; old policies and new. London, Longmans, Green, 1929. xxiii, 292 p.

    Critical discussion of British methods of dealing with unemployment.

Douglas, Paul H., and Director, Aaron. The problem of unemployment. New York, Macmillan, 1931. xix, 505 p.

    Surveys causes, effects, and programs for prevention and relief.

Federated American engineering societies. Committee on elimination of waste in industry. Waste in industry. New York, McGraw-Hill, 1921.

    Chapter XI describes the part played by unemployment in the sources and causes of economic waste.

Feldman, H. Regularization of employment. New York, Harper, 1925. 437 p.

    An excellent presentation of the evil effects of insecurity in employment and the methods used by some business men in regularizing employment in their own plants.

Fitch, John A. Causes of industrial unrest. New York, Harper, 1924. xiv, 424 p.

    Chapter V treats unemployment as a cause of industrial unrest.

Gayer, Arthur D. Public works in prosperity and depression. New York, National bureau of economic research, 1935. xx, 460 p.

    Outstanding American study of federal, state, and city public works, with emphasis on their utilization as an agency of economic stabilization.

Great Britain. Ministry of labor. Labour gazette. London, monthly, 1893- .

    Regularly contains sections on the labor market, unemployment insurance, employment in the principal industries, and public employment offices.

——— *Royal commission on poor laws and relief of distress.* Report of the Royal commission on the poor laws and relief of distress. Part VI, "Distress due to unemployment," pp. 303-445. London, 1909.

——— The Minority report of the Poor law commission. London. Printed for the National committee to promote the break-up of the Poor law, 1909. 2 v.

    Minority report by Sidney and Beatrice Webb; Part II, "Public organization of the labor market" contains: The able-bodied under the

SELECT CRITICAL BIBLIOGRAPHY 537

unemployed workmen act, the distress from unemployment, proposals for reform.

Harrison, Shelby M., and associates. Public employment offices. New York, Russell Sage foundation, 1924. xvii, 685 p.

A notable survey of the need, the development, and the methods of public employment offices.

Hill, A. C. C., and Lubin, Isador. The British attack on unemployment. Washington, Brookings institution, 1934. xiv, 325 p.

History of policies, and description of employment offices, relief works, transference, and unemployment insurance, with concluding critical comment.

Hurlin, Ralph G., and Berridge, William A. Employment statistics for the United States; a plan for their national collection and a handbook of methods recommended by the committee on governmental labor statistics of the American statistical association. New York, Russell Sage foundation, 1926. xvi, 215 p.

Includes statement of the value of employment data.

Industrial relations counselors, inc., and others. Administration of public employment offices and unemployment insurance: Canada, France, Sweden, Switzerland. New York, Industrial relations counselors, 1935. xi, 395 p.

Describes the public employment office systems of these countries, with special reference to their relation to unemployment insurance.

International labor office. Abolition of fee-charging employment offices. (First discussion report. International labor conference, 1932.) Geneva, 1932. iv, 141 p.

Survey of laws and regulations relating to fee-charging employment agencies throughout the world.

——— Employment exchanges; an international study of placing activities. (Studies and reports, series C, no. 18.) Geneva, 1933. iv, 231 p.

Analyzes public employment office organization, policies and procedure in many countries.

——— I. L. O. yearbook. Geneva, 1930- .

Includes description of current developments in efforts to deal with unemployment in the various countries.

——— Public works policy. (Studies and reports, series C, no. 19.) Geneva, 1935. iii, 166 p.

Describes trends, financial problems, methods of operation, and coordination of public works for the prevention of unemployment.

——— Unemployment and public works. (Studies and reports, series C, no. 15.) Geneva, 1931. 186 p.

International survey of public works programs for unemployment prevention, with special emphasis on the need for advance planning.

Jerome, Harry. Mechanization in industry. New York, National bureau of economic research, 1934. xxxi, 484 p.

    A notable study of the introduction of labor-saving devices in industry, with conclusions as to the effects upon labor.

Kellogg, Ruth M. The United States employment service. Chicago, University of Chicago press, 1933. xiv, 192 p.

    History and critical description of the federal employment service just prior to the Employment Service Act of 1933.

Lescohier, Don D. The labor market. New York, Macmillan, 1919. 338 p.

    Notable analysis of causes of fluctuations in American labor supply and demand, and discussion of methods of reducing them.

Lescohier, Don D., and Brandeis, Elizabeth. History of labor in the United States. New York, Macmillan, 1935. xxx, 778 p.

    Chapters VII and VIII, on "Unemployment"; Chapter X on "The Labor Market"; Chapters XI and XII, on "Unemployment Relief"; and Chapter XIII, on "Unemployment Insurance, Private Plans."

Lewisohn, Sam A., Draper, Ernest G., Commons, John R., and Leschohier, Don D. Can business prevent unemployment? New York, Knopf, 1925. 226 p.

    Two business men and two economists describe 114 outstanding experiments in employment stabilization by American companies.

Massachusetts. Special commission on stabilization of employment. Final report. Boston, 1932. 250 p.

    Discusses causes of unemployment and proposed method of stabilizing employment, with recommendations including unemployment compensation.

Mess, H. A. Casual labor at the docks. London, Bell, 1916. 147 p.

    The scramble for work, irregular earnings and their consequences; suggestions for decasualization.

Mitchell, Wesley C. Business cycles; the problem and its setting. New York, National bureau of economic research, 1927. xxii, 489 p.

    Outstanding analysis of the basic economic factors in booms and depressions.

Mitchell, Wesley C., and others; edited by Edie, Lionel D. Stabilization of business. New York, Macmillan, 1923. xii, 399 p.

    The problem of business policies as they relate to business cycles is here analyzed by a group of specially qualified writers, with emphasis on control through improved business policies.

New York. Department of labor. Bulletins. Albany.

    For those concerning unemployment, see index of publications.

Parker, C. H. Casual labor and other essays. New York, Harcourt, 1920. 199 p.

SELECT CRITICAL BIBLIOGRAPHY 539

Graphic description of some aspects of the problem of casual labor in America.

President's conference on unemployment. Report. Washington, Govt. print. off., 1921. 178 p.

────── Business cycles and unemployment. New York, McGraw-Hill, 1923. 405 p.

Report and recommendations by a committee of the conference including an investigation made under the auspices of the National bureau of economic research.

────── Planning and control of public works; report of the Committee on recent economic changes, including the report of Leo Wolman of the National bureau of economic research, inc. New York, National bureau of economic research, 1930. xxviii, 260 p.

A survey of public works in the United States, with recommendations looking toward a program of advance planning.

────── Recent economic changes; report of the committee on recent economic changes, including the reports of a special staff of the National bureau of economic research, inc. New York, McGraw-Hill, 1929. 2 v.

Chapter VI, "Labor," by Leo Wolman, includes an estimate of the extent of unemployment in the United States, 1920-1927.

────── Seasonal operation in the construction industries. New York, McGraw-Hill, 1924. 213 p.

Report and recommendations of a committee of the conference.

Royal institute of international affairs. Unemployment; an international problem. New York, Oxford university press, 1935. viii, 478 p.

A world view of unemployment and efforts to mitigate the problem, including public works, work relief, shorter hours, placement services, unemployment insurance, and relief.

Slichter, Sumner H. The turnover of factory labor. New York, Appleton-Century, 1919. xiv, 460 p.

Notable treatment of the amount, cost, causes, and means of reducing the shifting of working forces.

Smelser, D. P. Unemployment and American trade unions. Baltimore, Johns Hopkins press, 1919. 154 p.

Describes the trade union theory of unemployment and operation of union employment bureaus.

Smith, Edwin S. Reducing seasonal unemployment; the experience of American manufacturing concerns. New York, McGraw-Hill, 1931. xvii, 296 p.

Survey of methods by which some manufacturers have attempted to stabilize employment.

Stewart, Annabel M., and Stewart, Bryce M. Statistical procedure of public employment offices. New York, Russell Sage foundation, 1933. 327 p.

A study of employment office record systems as developed in Europe and America, with a plan for the United States.

United States. Bureau of labor statistics. Bulletins. Washington, Govt. print. off., 1912- .

See series on "Employment and Unemployment" in list on final pages of latest bulletin.

────── Laws relating to employment agencies in the United States as of January 1, 1933 (Bulletin no. 581). Washington, Govt. print. off., 1933. 164 p.

Gives text of state and federal laws relating to public offices and fee-charging agencies.

────── Monthly labor review. Washington, Govt. print. off., 1915- .

Each issue includes articles and statistics on various phases of employment and unemployment.

────── *Department of labor.* Employment service news. Washington, Govt. print. off., 1934- . Monthly.

Articles and statistics on the placement activities of the federal-state employment service.

────── *Federal reserve board.* Federal reserve bulletin. Washington, Govt. print. off., 1915- . Monthly.

Contains indices of production and employment and valuable summaries of current economic conditions.

Weigert, Oscar. Administration of placement and unemployment insurance in Germany. New York, Industrial relations counselors, 1934. xiv, 241 p.

Operation of public employment offices in Germany described by a German labor law administrator.

Williams, R. First year's working of the Liverpool docks scheme. London, King, 1914. 192 p.

Account of an outstanding attempt to abolish casual labor.

II. MINIMUM FAIR WAGE

American association for labor legislation. American labor legislation review. Quarterly, 1911- .

See "minimum wage" in Index to volumes I to XX, and annual volume indexes thereafter.

Anderson, George. Fixation of wages in Australia. Melbourne, Macmillan, 1929. 568 p.

Describes administrative organization and powers, principles of wage determination, and special problems arising under Australian legislation.

SELECT CRITICAL BIBLIOGRAPHY 541

Andrews, Irene Osgood. Minimum wage legislation. Albany, Lyon, 1914. 219 p. (Printed also as Appendix III of the Third report of the New York State factory investigating commission. Albany, 1914. pp 169-385.)

History, text, analysis, and operation of American and foreign laws; decision of Oregon supreme court upholding the state law.

——— The relation of irregular employment to the living wage for women. (American labor legislation review, June, 1915. v. 5:287-418. Printed also as Appendix X of the Fourth report of the New York State factory investigating commission. Albany, 1915. pp. 497-635.)

Need for considering income losses of women workers through unemployment and underemployment in making minimum wage awards.

Armstrong, Barbara Nachtrieb. Insuring the essentials; minimum wage plus social insurance—a living wage program. New York, Macmillan, 1932. xvii, 717 p.

Part II describes development of minimum wage legislation throughout the world and includes economic analysis.

Broda, Rudolph. Minimum wage legislation in various countries. (U. S. Bureau of labor statistics, bulletin no. 467.) Washington, Govt. print. off., 1928. 125 p.

Describes development of legislation and administration.

Burns, Eveline M. Wages and the state; a comparative study of the problems of state wage regulation. London, King, 1926. ix, 443 p.

Comprehensive survey of wage regulation by law, with sections on existing legislation, methods, and principles.

The *Case* for the minimum wage. (Survey, Feb. 6, 1915, v. 33:487-575, 521-524.)

Symposium, containing articles on the need, extent, and operation of minimum wage legislation in this country and abroad by experts, including Florence Kelley, Louis D. Brandeis, M. B. Hammond, John A. Hobson, Howard B. Woolston, N. I. Stone, and Esther Packard.

Clark, John Bates. The minimum wage. (Atlantic monthly, Sept., 1913, pp. 289-297.)

Theoretical discussion setting forth the probable operation of the legal minimum wage, with particular emphasis upon those who might be thrown out of work by such laws.

Douglas, Paul H. Real wages in the United States, 1890-1926. Boston, Houghton Mifflin, 1930. xxviii, 682 p.

A statistical study of changes in wage rates, earnings, hours, unemployment, and the cost of living.

Fisher, A. G. B. Some problems of wages and their regulation in Great Britain since 1918. London, King, 1926. xvii, 281 p.

Includes chapter on "Trade Boards and a Minimum Wage."

Frankfurter, Felix; Dewson, Mary W., and Commons, John R. State minimum wage laws in practice. New York, National consumers' league, 1924. 179 p.

Brief in support of the constitutionality of the California minimum wage law, and a description of the operation of such laws in Massachusetts and Wisconsin.

Frankfurter, Felix, and Goldmark, Josephine. Brief for defendants in error upon reargument in the case of Stettler v. O'Hara, et al., constituting the industrial welfare commission. Oregon, 1916. 783 p.

Revised and enlarged edition of original brief prepared by Louis D. Brandeis. Selected extracts favorable to the legal minimum wage; sets forth evils of low wages, benefits of adequate wages, benefits of legal minimum wage, and analogy with other labor legislation.

Great Britain. Ministry of labor. Report of the committee appointed to enquire into the working and effects of the Trade boards acts. London, 1922.

The so-called "Cave committee report" on the operation of minimum wage legislation in Great Britain from 1909 to 1922.

Hohman, H. F. Development of social insurance and minimum wage legislation in Great Britain. Boston, Houghton Mifflin, 1933. xi, 441 p.

Chapter VII traces development of minimum wages under the trade boards acts.

International labor office. I. L. O. yearbook. Geneva, 1930- .

Reports current developments in minimum wage legislation.

——— Minimum wage fixing machinery; an international study of legislation and practice. (Studies and reports, series D, no. 17.) Geneva, 1927. 155 p.

Title adequately indicates scope of the study.

Massachusetts. Commission on minimum wage boards. Report. Boston, 1912. 326 p.

The report which led to the passage of the first American minimum wage law.

Merchants and manufacturers of Massachusetts. Executive Committee. The minimum wage, a failing experiment; together with some sidelights on the Massachusetts experience. Boston, 1916. 58 p.

Effort to prove that to encourage the minimum wage law is to "sign a preliminary death warrant for many Massachusetts industries."

Morris, V. P. Oregon's experience with minimum wage legislation. New York, Columbia university press, 1930. 236 p.

A study of the history of the legislation, its administration, and effects on employees and employers in one state.

SELECT CRITICAL BIBLIOGRAPHY 543

National consumers' league. The Supreme Court and minimum wage legislation. New York, New republic, 1925. xxviii, 287 p.

A collection of important articles discussing the United States Supreme Court's decision in the District of Columbia minimum wage case, with an introduction by Roscoe Pound.

National industrial conference board, inc. Minimum wage legislation in Massachusetts. New York, National industrial conference board, 1927. xiii, 243 p.

A study of the administration and effects of minimum wage legislation under the Massachusetts non-mandatory law of 1912, made by an employers' research organization.

Richardson, J. H. A study on the minimum wage. New York, Adelphi, 1927. 198 p.

Presentation of basic problems in minimum wage legislation and its administration based on the experience of various countries. Includes chapter on family allowances.

Ryan, John A. A living wage. New York, Macmillan, 1920. 182 p.

Emphasizes especially the ethical and economic bases and the need for minimum wage legislation in the United States.

Seager, Henry R. The theory of the minimum wage. (American labor legislation review, Feb., 1913, v. 3:81-91.)

A statement of the underlying theory of minimum wage legislation together with its probable results upon the organization of industry and upon other problems of labor legislation; contains discussion by John R. Commons, Paul U. Kellogg, M. B. Hammond, George W. Anderson, and others.

Sells, Dorothy M. The British trade boards system. London, King, 1923. vi, 293 p.

Includes description of the effect of the trades boards system upon wages, hours, employment, production, and costs.

Snowden, Philip. The living wage. London, Hodder and Stoughton, 1913. 189 p.

Discussion of the benefits of the legal minimum wage, including experience under the British trade boards.

United States. Bureau of labor statistics. Bulletins. Washington, Govt. print. off., 1895- .

See series on "Labor Laws" and on "Women and Children in Industry" in list on final pages of latest bulletin.

——— Monthly labor review. Washington, Govt. print. off., 1915- .

Reports on cost of living, wage investigations, legislation, and minimum wage orders.

——— *Women's bureau.* Bulletins.

For list of bulletins on wages and minimum wage legislation, see final pages of recent bulletin.

United States. The development of minimum wage laws in the United States, 1912 to 1927. (Bulletin no. 61.) Washington, Govt. print. off., 1928. 635 p.

    Thoroughgoing review of legislation and its administration, including list of all wage orders issued in the various states.

——— Summary of state hour laws for women and minimum wage rates. (Bulletin no. 137.) Washington, Govt. print. off., 1936. 54 p.

    Describes status of minimum wage legislation and rates at the end of 1935.

Vibart, Hugh H. R. Family allowances in practice; an examination of the development of the family wage system and of the compensation fund, principally in Belgium, France, Germany and Holland. London, King, 1926. x, 237 p.

    Subtitle adequately describes contents.

Waggaman, Mary T. Family allowances in foreign countries. (U. S. bureau of labor statistics, bulletin no. 401.) Washington, Govt. print. off., 1926. vi, 192 p.

    Summary of experience in more than a score of countries.

Webb, Sidney. The economic theory of a legal minimum wage. (Journal of political economy, 1912. v. 20:973-998.)

    Summary of the theoretical and practical arguments in favor of the minimum wage.

III. HOURS OF LABOR

American association for labor legislation. American labor legislation review. Quarterly, 1911- .

    See Index to volumes I to XX and annual volume indexes thereafter.

Baker, Elizabeth F. Protective labor legislation. New York, Columbia university, 1925. 467 p.

    Written with special reference to women in the State of New York with application to a wider field. Discusses attitude of courts, enforcement and effects of hour legislation.

Beman, Lamar T. (compiler). Five-day week. New York, Wilson, 1928. 150 p.

    A debater's handbook on the subject.

Bogardus, E. S. The relation of fatigue to industrial accidents. (American journal of sociology, 1911-1912. v. 17:206-222, 351-374, 512-539.)

    Study of the effect of fatigue on the system and an attempt to correlate working hours and accident frequency.

Brandeis, Louis D., and Goldmark, Josephine. Brief in the case of Ritchie *v.* Wayman. Illinois, 1909. 610 p.

SELECT CRITICAL BIBLIOGRAPHY 545

The dangers of long hours, benefits of short hours, desirability of uniformity, reasonableness of the ten-hour law for women.

———— Brief in the case of People v. Charles Schweinler press. New York, 1915. 529 p.

Argues the constitutionality of prohibiting night work for women.

Cahill, Marion Cotter. Shorter hours; a study of the movement since the Civil war. New York, Columbia university press, 1932. 300 p.

The history of the hours movement, with appropriate attention to legislative regulation.

Callcott, Mary Stevenson. Child labor legislation in New York. New York, Macmillan, 1931. xv, 267 p.

Describes the growth of child labor laws with emphasis on the period since 1905.

Commons, John R., and Andrews, John B. Documentary history of American industrial society. Cleveland, Clark, 1910.

V. 8:81-210, contains documents illustrative of the movement to decrease hours of labor; v. 9:24-33, the growth of the philosophy of hour limitation.

Dahlberg, Edward. Jobs, machines, and capitalism. New York, Macmillan, 1932. xviii, 252 p.

An argument in support of the shorter work week as a means of eliminating depressions.

Dana, R. T., and Ackerman, A. P. The human machine in industry. New York, Codex, 1927. xiv, 312 p.

Includes chapters on fatigue, economic hours of work, rest periods, and occupational age limits.

Daugherty, Carrol R. Labor problems in American industry. Boston, Houghton Mifflin, 1933. xviii, 959 p.

Chapter IX deals with the problem of hours and work periods.

Federated American engineering societies. Committee on work periods in continuous industry. Twelve-hour shift in industry. New York, Dutton, 1922. 302 p.

Contains an authoritative account of hours of work in continuous industries of the United States and effects upon production where a change has been made from the twelve-hour to shorter shifts.

Fitch, John A. Causes of industrial unrest. Chap. II. New York, Harper, 1924.

———— Sunday and rest day labor laws in the United States. (New York department of labor bulletin no. 45:377-403. Albany, 1910.)

A review of court decisions on Sunday rest day laws showing that their justification by virtue of the police power applies even more clearly to the one-day-of-rest-in-seven laws.

Fitch, John A. Judicial basis for legislative restriction of hours of labor of adult males. (New York department of labor bulletin no. 46:90-121. Albany, 1911.)
  Critical review of court decisions.

——— The steel workers. The Pittsburgh survey. New York, Charities publication committee, 1911. 380 p.
  Treats of the results of a seven-day week and twelve-hour day.

Florence, P. Sargent. Individual variations in efficiency and the analysis of the work curve. Archin für Weltwirtschaft, Kiel university, Jan., 1924.

——— Economics of fatigue and unrest, and the efficiency of labor in industry. New York, Holt, 1924. 426 p.
  Analyzes large collection of data derived from experiments and practical experience and makes a scientific estimate of business losses caused by fatigue and unrest of workers. In regard to hours, a conclusion is that reduction of hours increases hourly output and decreases absence and accidents.

Frankfurter, Felix, and Goldmark, Josephine. Brief for defendant in error in the case of Bunting v. Oregon. Oregon, 1915. 2 v. 984 p.
  Successful argument, based on economic data, for constitutionality of Oregon ten-hour law for men.

Freund, Ernst. Constitutional aspects of hour legislation for men. (American labor legislation review, March, 1914. v. 4:129-132.)
  Suggestion of possible principles on which to base hour legislation.

——— Constitutional limitations and legislation. (Proceedings of third annual meeting of the American association for labor legislation, pp. 51-71. New York, 1910.)
  Critical discussion of development of theory of constitutionality of hour legislation.

——— The constitutional aspects of the protection of women in industry. (Publications Academy of political science, 1910. v. 1:162-184.)

Goldmark, Josephine. Fatigue and efficiency; a study in industry. New York, Charities publication committee, 1912. xvii, 591 p.
  Shows necessity for regulation of working hours to prevent overfatigue and exhaustion.

——— The inalienable right to rest. (Survey, May 24, 1913. v. 30:264-266.)
  Comment on favorable decision of Mississippi supreme court upholding state's ten-hour law for factory workers.

——— U. S. Supreme Court and the eight-hour day. (Survey, Mar. 20, 1915. v. 33:677-678.)
  Brief statement of court decisions.

Goldmark, Josephine, and Hopkins, Mary D. Comparison of an eight-hour plant and a ten-hour plant. Bulletin No. 106, Public health service. Washington, 1920.

Great Britain Industrial health research board. Reports. London, 1919-

    Among important reports concerning hours are: No. 5, "Fatigue and efficiency in the iron and steel industry," 1920; No. 24, "Comparison of different shift systems in the glass trade," 1924; No. 32, "Studies in repetitive work with special reference to rest periods," 1925; No. 42, "Rest pauses in industry," 1927.

——— Home office. Report of departmental committee on the night employment of male young persons in factories and workshops. Minutes of evidence and appendices. London, Wyman, 1913. 289 p.

——— Report on the acts for the regulation of the hours of employment in shops in Australia and New Zealand, by Ernest Aves. 1908. 218 p.

    The advantages and risks of limiting hours of labor compared; decision in favor of limitation based on increased efficiency of service.

——— Ministry of munitions. British health of munition workers' committee memoranda. London, 1915, 1916. (Also reprints by United States Bureau of labor statistics, Bulletins no. 221, 222, 223, 230, 249.)

    Strong recommendations, on basis of war experience, for shorter hours and better conditions as a means of securing larger output.

Hoopingarner, Dwight L. Labor relations in industry. Chap. XVII. New York, McGraw-Hill, 1925.

Interchurch world movement. Commission of inquiry. Report on steel strike of 1919. New York, Harcourt, 1920. 277 p.

——— Public opinion and the steel strike. New York, Harcourt, 1921. 346 p.

    Both these books contain considerable information concerning hours in the steel industry.

International association for labor legislation. Report of the special commission on hours of labor in continuous industries. London, Pioneer press, 1912. 26 p.

    Comparison of actual conditions in different countries and the results obtained by introducing the eight-hour, three-shift system.

International labor office. I. L. O. yearbook. Geneva, 1930-

    Gives annual summary of world progress in the shorter hours movement.

——— Studies and reports, series D (wages and hours) and special reports on hours. Geneva, 1919-

Kelley, Florence. The sex problems in industrial hygiene. (American journal of public hygiene, June, 1910. v. 20:252-257.)

Brief plea for legal regulation of the hours of labor of women to prevent excessive fatigue.

Lee, Frederic S. The human machine and industrial efficiency. New York, Longmans, Green, 1918. 119 p.

Scientific data reinforcing the case for short hours and good working conditions.

Lescohier, Don D., and Brandeis, Elizabeth. History of labor in the United States. New York, Macmillan, 1935. xxx, 778 p.

Under "Working Conditions" Chapter VI is on "The Hours They Work." Under "Labor Legislation," Chapter II is on "Child Labor Legislation," Chapter III is on "Women's Hour Legislation," and Chapter V is on "Hour Laws for Men."

Lever, William H. L. (Lord Leverhulme). The six-hour day and other industrial questions. London, Allen, 1918. 331 p.

Proposal by a prominent soap manufacturer for the introduction of six-hour shifts in his plant.

Leverhulme, Lord. The six-hour day. New York, Holt, 1919. 344 p.

Lippman, Otto. Hours of work and output (International labour review, April, 1924, v. 9:481-506.)

Survey of data on relation between hours of work and output.

Manly, Basil M. Work periods in continuous night and day occupations. (American labor legislation review, March, 1914. v. 4:109-116.)

Argues for eight-hour shifts in continuous industries.

Mayo, Elton. The human problem of an industrial civilization. New York, Macmillan, 1933. 194 p.

Includes results of investigations of fatigue, monotony, and morale of industrial workers.

Milhaud, Edgar. Results of the adoption of the eight-hour day: 1. The eight-hour day and technical progress. 2. The eight-hour day and the human factor in production. (International labour review, Dec., 1925, pp. 820-853, and Feb., 1926, pp. 175-210.)

Summarizes the report of an investigation authorized by the International labor office regarding the effects of the introduction of the eight-hour day in European countries following the war. The gist of the conclusion is that "the view is gaining ground that the value of this reform from the view of output consists in the fact that it stimulates energy on the part of the workers and initiative on that of the employers."

Mills, Charles M. Vacations for industrial workers. New York, Ronald press, 1927. viii, 328 p.

A comprehensive study of vacations for workers throughout the world.

National industrial conference board. The five-day week in manufacturing industries. New York, National industrial conference board, 1929. xi, 69 p.

A study of the movement for the five-day week as practiced in American industries, made by an employers' research organization.

——— Research reports. New York and Boston. 1918- .

For other reports concerning hours see list of publications.

New York. Department of labor. Bulletins. Albany.

For those concerning hours see index of publications.

——— *State factory investigating commission.* Second report. "Night work of women in factories," pp. 193-215. Albany, 1913.

Summarizes investigations and the legal status of night work.

Persons, Charles E.; Parton, Mabel, and Moses, Mabelle. Labor laws and their enforcement. "The early history of factory legislation in Massachusetts; from 1825 to the passage of the ten-hour law in 1874," pp. 1-129. "Hours of labor: Of women and children—Of public employees," pp. 314-315. New York, Longmans, Green, 1911.

Gives history of the agitation for shorter hours in Massachusetts and the situation in 1911.

Price, George M. Night work of women. (In Second report of the New York state factory investigating commission, Albany, 1913, pp. 439-459.)

Investigations in a cordage mill, and analysis of the personal histories of 100 women night workers.

Princeton university. Industrial relations section. The five-day week in industry, statement of fact and opinion. Princeton, n. d. 28 p.

A compilation of statements for and against the five-day work week.

——— Hours of work and recovery; summary of fact and opinion. Princeton, 1934. 52 p.

Brief survey of hours movement, with special stress on NRA codes; and arguments for and against shorter hours as a method of providing employment.

Spalding, Henry S. Social problems and agencies, Part I, chap. IX and bibliography. New York, Benziger, 1925.

Tillyard, Frank. The worker and the state. London, Routledge, 1936. x, 308 p.

A survey of labor legislation in Great Britain, with chapters on hours regulation.

United States. Report on condition of woman and child wage-earners in the United States. (Senate doc. no. 645, 61st Cong., 2d sess.) Washington, Govt. print. off., 1910-1912. 19 v.

Report of extensive official investigations into the cotton, clothing, glass, and silk industries, laundries, etc.

United States. Report on conditions of employment in the iron and steel industry in the United States. (Senate doc. no. 110, 62d Cong., 1st sess.) Washington, Govt. print. off., 1911-1912.

V. 1 deals with wages and hours of labor; v. 2 gives detailed tables in regard to the same; v. 3 treats of the various factors affecting the health and efficiency of the working force, such as the seven-day week and the twelve-hour day.

——— *Bureau of labor.* Bulletins. Washington, Govt. print. off., 1895-1912.

No. 52, "Child labor in the United States," H. R. Sewell; No. 96, "Working hours, earnings, and duration of employment of women workers in Maryland and California, 1911," Marie L. Obenauer.

——— *Bureau of labor statistics.* Bulletins. Washington, Govt. print off., 1912- .

See series, "Wages and hours of labor," in list on final pages of latest bulletin.

——— *Monthly labor review.* Washington, Govt. print. off., 1915- .

Gives digests of investigations into hours in various industries, and legislation on the subject.

——— *Children's bureau.* Bulletins and charts. Washington, Govt. print. off., 1912- .

See annual lists of publications issued by bureau.

——— *Coal commission.* Report submitted to legislative committees on mines and mining, Dec., 1923. Washington, Govt. print. off., 1925. 5 v.

Reports thorough investigation of conditions in anthracite and bituminous coal mines; see "Hours of labor" in index at end of v. 1.

——— *House committee on labor.* Hearings on thirty-hour week bills. (Seventy-third Congress, first and second sessions, April and May, 1933, and Feb., 1934.) Washington, Govt. print. off., 1933 and 1934.

Labor and employers argue for and against federal legislation to reduce hours of work for all wage earners.

——— *Industrial commission.* Final report. "Hours of labor," v. 19:763-793. Washington, Govt. print. off., 1902.

Effect of reduction of working time on output and development of legal theory.

——— *National war labor board.* Memorandum on the eight-hour working day. Washington, Govt. print. off., 1918.

Actual effects of shorter work day in increasing production; summary of existing eight-hour legislation for men.

——— *Treasury Department. Public health service.* Comparison of an eight-hour plant and a ten-hour plant. (Public health bulletin no. 106, Josephine Goldmark and Mary D. Hopkins.) Washington, Govt. print. off., 1920. 213 p.

Careful experimental study, showing superiority of eight-hour plant in maintenance of output, reduction of lost time, more incentive to individual output, and fewer accidents.

——— *Women's bureau.* Bulletins and charts. Washington, Govt. print. off., 1918- .

See list of publications issued by bureau.

Van Kleeck, Mary. Working hours of women in factories. (Charities, 1906-1907. v. 17:13-21.)

Describes actual conditions, non-enforcement of ten-hour law, and results in physical condition of working women.

Vernon, H. M. Industrial fatigue and efficiency. London, Routledge; New York, Dutton, 1921.

——— The shorter working week; with special reference to the two-shift system. London, Routledge, 1934, viii, 201 p.

A notable British study of working hours and the practical effect upon industry and workers of their reduction.

Watkins, Gordon S. Labor problems. New York, Crowell, 1929. xvi, 726 p.

Chapter XI is on hours of labor.

IV. SAFETY AND HEALTH

American academy of political and social science. Industrial safety annals. V. cxxiii, no. 212. Concord, 1926.

Forty-two papers on the industrial safety problem. Includes sections on: (1) The need for safety in industry. (2) The organized accident prevention movement. (3) Safety code development and enforcement. (4) Safety in specific industries. (5) Accident prevention for certain hazards. (6) Educating the workers in safety. (7) The relation of safety, compensation, and rehabilitation.

American association for labor legislation. American labor legislation review. Quarterly, 1911- .

See Index to volumes I to XX and annual volume indexes thereafter.

American engineering council. Safety and production; an engineering and statistical study of the relationship between industrial safety and production. New York, Harper, 1928. 414 p.

A statistical study of accident and production trends in various industries, with conclusions and recommendations by a committee of experts.

Anderson, Adelaide Mary. Women in the factory. New York, Dutton, 1922. 316 p.

Women's work, the legislation pertaining thereto, and the factory inspection problems involved, discussed by a former chief lady factory inspector of Great Britain.

Andrews, John B. Administrative labor legislation. New York, Harper, 1936. 231 p.

Describes method of administrative rule-making in safety legislation, and includes draft of enabling act.

Aub, Joseph C.; Minot, A. S.; Farrhill, Lawrence T., and Reznikoff, Paul. Lead poisoning. Baltimore, Williams & Wilkins, 1926. 265 p.

Technical study made at the Harvard medical school.

Baker, Elizabeth Faulkner. Protective labor legislation, with special reference to women in the state of New York. New York, Columbia university press, 1925. 467 p.

Study of the history, administration, and results of certain labor laws. Concludes that the modern trend is toward protective legislation for both sexes alike.

Bowers, Edison L. Is it safe to work? A study of industrial accidents. Boston, Houghton Mifflin, 1930. xiii, 229 p.

Discusses the problem of accidents and their prevention and compensation.

Cathcart, E. P. Human factor in industry. London, Oxford university press, 1928. 105 p.

Discusses the problem of work fatigue and its alleviation.

Dana, R. T., and Ackerman, A. P. The human machine in industry. New York, Codex, 1927. xiv, 312 p.

Includes chapters on fatigue, hours, age limits, occupational diseases, and sickness.

DeBlois, Lewis A. Industrial safety organization for executive and engineer. New York, McGraw-Hill, 1926. xiii, 328 p.

Discussion of the accident problem in industry and methods of promoting safety.

Dublin, Louis I. Health and wealth; a survey of the economics of world health. New York, Harper, 1928. xiv, 361 p.

Includes chapters on the health of workers.

Eastman, Crystal. Work accidents and the law. New York, Charities publication committee, 1910. xvi, 345 p.

Chapters on the "Personal factor in industrial accidents," "Distribution of the burden of income loss," and "The effect of industrial fatalities upon the home."

Fuller, Raymond G. Child labor and the constitution. New York, Crowell, 1923. 323 p.

Discussion of the extent of child labor and its social and legal aspects. Contains extended bibliography.

Goldberg, Rosamond W. Occupational diseases; in relation to compensation and health insurance. New York, Columbia university press, 1931. 280 p.

SELECT CRITICAL BIBLIOGRAPHY 555

New South Wales. Board of trade. Report on white lead as used in the painting industry. Sydney, Gullick, 1921. 778 p.

Embodies the results of a special inquiry undertaken in order to determine the government's position on the proposed international white-lead convention.

New York. Department of labor. Special bulletins. Albany, 1914- .

Special bulletins dealing with many industrial safety and sanitation problems and with child labor, women's work, etc. (For full list of titles see covers of recent bulletins.)

——— *State factory investigating commission.* Reports. Albany, 1912-1915.

Results of investigations into fire hazard, tenement labor, occupational diseases, sanitary conditions, and accident prevention in mercantile and manufacturing establishments.

Oliver, Thomas. Dangerous trades: the historical, social, and legal aspects of industrial occupations as affecting health, by a number of experts; edited by Thomas Oliver. London, Murray, 1902. 891 p.

Authoritative discussions by specialists of international reputation.

——— Diseases of occupation from the legislative, social, and medical points of view. London, Methuen, 1908. xix, 427 p.

Comprehensive clinical and industrial descriptions.

——— Health of the workers. London, Faber & Gwyer, 1925. 226 p.

Condensed treatment of occupational-disease problems by a well-known author of more extended works in this field.

Persons, Charles E.; Parton, Mabel, and Moses, Mabelle. Labor laws and their enforcement. "Unregulated conditions in women's work," pp. 131-155. New York, Longmans, 1911.

Conditions of work in rubber, cordage, and twine factories, and instances of violation of health laws.

Price, George M. The modern factory. New York, Wiley, 1914. xx, 574 p.

Safety, sanitation, and welfare in the work places as affected by private effort and by legislation.

Resnick, Louis, and Carris, Lewis H. Eye hazards in industrial occupations. New York, National committee for the prevention of blindness, 1924. 247 p.

A handbook for safety experts and industrial operators.

Schwedtman, Ferdinand C., and Emery, James A. Accident prevention and relief. New York, National association of manufacturers, 1911. xxxvi, 481 p.

An investigation of the subject in Europe, with special attention to

England and Germany, and with recommendations for action in the United States.

Thompson, W. Gilman. The occupational diseases, their causation, symptoms, treatment, and prevention. New York, Appleton-Century, 1914. 724 p.

    Detailed study of causes and symptoms, with methods of treatment and prevention.

Tillyard, Frank. The worker and the state. London, Routledge, 1936. x, 308 p.

    A survey of labor legislation in Great Britain, with chapters on health and safety.

Tolman, William H., and Kendall, Leonard B. Safety; methods for preventing occupational and other accidents and disease. New York, Harper, 1913. 422 p.

    The philosophy of safety, and suggestive descriptions of the need for and success of preventive devices.

United States. Report on condition of woman and child wage-earners in the United States. (Senate doc. no. 645, 61st Cong., 2d sess.) Washington, Govt. print. off., 1910-1912. 19 v.

    Discusses the working hours and hazards in the cotton textile industry, clothing, glass, silk industry, and laundries.

——— Report on conditions of employment in the iron and steel industry in the United States. (Senate doc. no. 110, 62d Cong., 1st sess.) Washington, Govt. print. off., 1911-1913. 4 v.

    V. 3 treats of various factors affecting the health and efficiency of the working force, such as heat, speed, and severity of work. V. 4 treats of accident rates, relation of night work and long turns to accidents, and organization for safety.

——— *Bureau of labor statistics.* (Bureau of labor, 1895-1912.) Bulletins. Washington, Govt. print. off., 1912- .

    Series on women in industry, industrial accidents and hygiene, labor laws of the United States, labor as affected by the war, and safety codes, contain material on safety and health problems. (See last pages of recent bulletins for full list.)

——— Monthly labor review. Washington, Govt. print. off., 1915- .

    Contains valuable articles on safety and health problems.

——— *Bureau of Mines.* Bulletins and technical papers. Washington, Govt. print. off., 1910- .

    Studies on extent, causes, and prevention of mine accidents and diseases of the mining trades.

——— *Children's bureau.* Bulletins and charts. Washington, Govt. print. off., 1912- .

    Series on child labor and industrial problems of child welfare con-

SELECT CRITICAL BIBLIOGRAPHY 557

tains material on safety and health. (See list of publications published by the bureau for titles.)

——— *Coal commission.* Report. (Senate doc. no. 1955, 86th Cong., 2d sess.) Washington, Govt. print. off., 1925. 5 v.

Contains, among other things, reports on safety in anthracite and bituminous coal mining.

——— *House judiciary committee.* 68th Congress, 1st sesssion. Hearings before the house judiciary committee on the proposed child labor amendment to the Constitution of the United States, Feb. and Mar., 1924. (Serial no. 16.) Washington, Govt. print. off., 1924. 307 p.

Contains valuable data on child labor conditions as well as on the nature of the forces supporting and opposing the amendment.

——— Report on child labor amendment to the Constitution of the United States. (Report no. 395.) Mar., 1924. 21 p.

Favorable report. A brief for federal action.

——— *Women's bureau.* Bulletins. Washington, Govt. print. off., 1918- .

Studies of working women and their problems.

——— State reporting of occupational diseases; including a survey of legislation applying to women. (Bulletin no. 114.) Washington, Govt. print. off., 1934. vi, 99 p.

Summary and analysis of state legislation and of occupational disease statistics.

Watkins, Gordon S. Labor problems. New York, Crowell, 1929. xvi, 726 p.

Includes chapters on child labor, women in industry, and human waste in industry.

White House conference on child health and protection. Child labor; report of the subcommittee on child labor. New York, Century, 1932. xix, 592 p.

Includes discussion of laws and regulations affecting health and safety of working children, and makes recommendations.

Williams, Sidney J. The manual of industrial safety. New York, McGraw-Hill, 1927. viii, 207 p.

A study of safety engineering methods based on best practices in industry.

Woodbury, Robert Morse. Workers' health and safety: a statistical program. New York, Macmillan, 1927. xii, 207 p.

Constructive criticism of available sources of accident and health statistics, with recommendations for improvement.

V. SOCIAL INSURANCE

American association for labor legislation. American labor legislation review. Quarterly, 1911- .

   Contains articles and reports on current developments in social insurance. See Index to volumes I to XX and annual indexes thereafter.

——— An American plan for unemployment reserve funds; tentative draft of an act. (American labor legislation review, Dec., 1930, v. 20:349-356.)

   A proposed measure for state legislation.

——— Standards for workmen's compensation laws. Revised ed. Jan., 1935.

   Essential features of satisfactory law, with annotations showing states already possessing such provisions.

American federation of labor. Report of the executive council to the fifty-second annual convention. Washington, 1932. 100 p.

   Includes the statement of "principles" adopted by the federation's convention in 1932 on the subject of unemployment insurance.

American medical association. Social insurance. Report of the Special committee of the American medical association for 1919. Chicago, Council on health and public instruction of the American medical association, 1919. 59 p.

   Treats sickness as a social problem and discusses universal workmen's health insurance as a means of distributing the cost and providing improved medical care. Urges physicians to take constructive part in shaping pending legislation.

Andrews, John B. Limitations of occupational disease compensation. (American labor legislation review, Dec., 1918. v. 8:311-315. Also reprint.)

   Shows that inclusion of occupational diseases under workmen's compensation laws would meet only slight fraction of the sickness among wage earners.

——— The protection of family life through accident prevention and compensation. (Reprint from Annals of American academy of political and social science, Sept., 1925. 9 p.)

   The social effects of workmen's compensation legislation described with comments on the shortcomings of existing American laws and standards yet to be obtained.

Armstrong, Barbara Nachtrieb. Insuring the essentials. New York, Macmillan, 1932. xvii, 717 p.

   Includes comprehensive treatments of minimum wage, workmen's compensation, unemployment insurance, old age pensions, and health insurance.

Astor, J. J., Bowley, A. L., and others. The third winter of unemployment. London, King, 1923. 350 p.

SELECT CRITICAL BIBLIOGRAPHY 559

Detailed impartial report of a study of unemployment conditions in Great Britain during the fall of 1922, with an evaluation of existing relief methods including unemployment insurance.

——— Unemployment insurance in Great Britain, a critical examination. London, Macmillan, 1925. 68 p.

Careful study of operation of the British act, especially during the post-war period.

Bakke, E. Wight. Insurance or dole? New Haven, Yale university press, 1935. xii, 280 p.

An American sociologist's survey of British experience with unemployment insurance.

Blanchard, Ralph H. Liability and compensation insurance. New York, Appleton-Century, 1917. xii, 394 p.

Excellent analysis of existing workmen's compensation legislation and administrative practice. Strong argument for more liberal standards and wider application of the laws.

——— Workmen's compensation in the United States. (International labour office, Studies and reports, series M, no. 5.) Geneva, 1926. 103 p.

Survey of compensation legislation and its administration.

British medical association. Insurance acts committee. Interim report on the future of the insurance acts. London, 1917. 12 p.

Based on replies to questionnaire sent to each branch of the association. Shows wide agreement among physicians on beneficial results of health insurance act and suggestions for its expansion.

Cahn, Reuben D. Civilian vocational rehabilitation. (Reprint from Journal of political economy, Dec., 1924. 24 p.)

History, description, and criticism of the federal act and its administration. Contains valuable data on past experience as well as suggestions for improvement.

California. Social insurance commission. Report of the Social insurance commission of the State of California. Sacramento, 1917. 339 p.

First official American report on the subject. On data secured through two years' study the commission finds for compulsory, contributory, non-commercial system.

——— *Unemployment commission.* Report and recommendations. San Francisco, 1932. 809 p.

Comprehensive survey of unemployment problem in one state, and proposed remedies. Recommends unemployment compensation.

Canada. Alberta. Final report of legislative commission appointed to make recommendations for adequate medical and health services. Edmonton, 1934. 39 p.

Subsequent to this report, Alberta adopted a plan for health insurance permissive to localities in the province.

Canada. British Columbia. Provincial secretary. A plan for health insurance for British Columbia. Victoria, 1935. 54 p.

Draft of a bill with supporting arguments submitted to the legislature which in 1936 adopted the first compulsory health insurance law on the American continent.

Carroll, Mollie Ray. Unemployment insurance in Austria. Washington. Brookings institution, 1932. ix, 52 p.

——— Unemployment insurance in Germany. Washington, Brookings institution, 1930. xii, 140 p.

Describes the development of unemployment insurance in Germany as enacted in 1927 and amended in 1929.

Carstens, C. C. Public pensions to widows with children; a study of their administration in several American cities. New York, Russell Sage foundation, 1913. 36 p.

An adverse analysis of the workings of widows' pensions in several states and cities, with suggestions for other methods of meeting the problem. An advance report by Mr. Carstens appeared in the Survey, Jan. 4, 1913. v. 29:459-466.

Cohen, Joseph L. Insurance against unemployment. London, King, 1921. 536 p.

History of the subject, with critical consideration of the British act and American proposals.

——— Insurance by industry examined. London, King, 1923. 120 p.

Criticism of existing British scheme of unemployment insurance and analysis of "insurance by industry" as a substitute. Concludes that the present scheme with certain suggested amendments is preferable.

——— Social insurance unified. London, King, 1924. 157 p.

Criticism of present British social insurance schemes and pleas for their unification.

——— Workmen's compensation in Great Britain. London, Post magazine, 1923. 232 p.

Critical description of the workings of the British act.

Committee on the costs of medical care. Medical care for the American people; the final report of the committee on the costs of medical care. Chicago, Chicago university press, 1932. xvi, 213 p.

A representative committee presents compromise program for improving medical services, but divides on subject of health insurance.

Conant, Luther. A critical analysis of industrial pension systems. New York, Macmillan, 1922. 262 p.

Description and critical comparison of various types of establishment funds for pensioning aged employees.

Davison, Ronald C. The unemployed; old policies and new. London, Longmans, 1929. xxiii, 292 p.

SELECT CRITICAL BIBLIOGRAPHY 561

Contains an excellent critical statement of British experience with unemployment insurance.

Dawson, William H. Social insurance in Germany, 1883-1911. New York, Scribner, 1912. xi, 283 p.

An historical and critical treatise on social insurance legislation in Germany, with special emphasis on prevention.

Devine, Edward T. Report of an investigation of matters relating to the care, treatment, and relief of dependent widows with dependent children in the city of New York. New York, The committee, 1914. 58 p.

Recommends social insurance to prevent commitment of children.

Dodd, Walter F. Administration of workmen's compensation. New York, Commonwealth fund, 1936. xviii, 845 p.

A notable survey of administrative problems and practice under American compensation laws. Includes an excellent brief historical background.

Duke University. School of law. The old-age security and the welfare titles of the social security act. (Law and contemporary problems, April, 1936, v. III, no. 2.) Durham, 1936.

Helpful discussions by various authorities on old age benefits and assistance, mothers' pensions, maternal and child welfare, and other provisions of the federal social security act.

——— Unemployment compensation. (Law and contemporary problems. Jan., 1936, v. III, no. 1.) Durham, 1936.

A symposium on leading questions relating to unemployment compensation.

Eastman, Crystal. Work-accidents and the law. New York, Charities publication committee, 1910. xvi, 345 p.

A study of the causes of industrial accidents, and the remuneration therefor, in Allegheny county, Pa., in 1906-1907, with argument for a more just law.

Epstein, Abraham. Facing old age. New York, Knopf, 1922. x, 352 p.

A study of old-age dependency and foreign pension laws, with a plea for old-age pension legislation in the United States.

——— Insecurity—a challenge to America. New York, Smith and Haas, 1936. xv, 821 p.

A survey of the entire field of social insurance.

Falk, I. S. Security against sickness; a study of health insurance, America's next problem in social security. Garden City, Doubleday, Doran, 1936. xii, 423 p.

An excellent survey of European experience and discussion of its lessons for America. Favors health insurance with medical care and cash benefits separated.

Falk, I. S., Rorem, C. Rufus, and Ring, Martha D. The costs of medical care; a summary of investigations on the economic aspects of the prevention and care of illness. Chicago, University of Chicago press, 1933. 648 p.

One of the studies published under the auspices of the Committee on the costs of medical care.

First national conference on vocational rehabilitation of persons disabled in industry or otherwise. Report of proceedings. Washington, Govt. print. off., 1922. 138 p.

Papers delivered and general discussion on various phases of the rehabilitation problem.

Frankel, Lee K., and Dawson, Miles M. Workingmen's insurance in Europe. New York, Charities publication committee, 1910. xviii, 447 p.

A study of insurance systems in force in Great Britain, Holland, Belgium, France, Switzerland, the Scandinavian countries, Italy, Germany, Austria, with numerous tables. Convenient for reference and international comparison.

Gilson, Mary B. Unemployment insurance in Great Britain. New York, Industrial relations counselors, inc., 1931. xiii, 560 p.

The most exhaustive American study of British unemployment insurance.

Gordon, Alban. Social insurance, what it is and what it might be. Westminster, Fabian society, 1924. 150 p.

A plea for unification and extension of the British social insurance schemes.

Great Britain. Committee appointed to consider position of outworkers in relation to unemployment insurance. Report. London, His Majesty's stationery office, 1923. 14 p.

Official report on one of the most difficult problems of unemployment insurance.

——— *Departmental committee on sickness benefit claims under the national insurance act.* Report. London, Unwin, 1914. 87 p.

Excellent report upon the alleged excessive claims on the sickness benefit funds, with an analysis of causes and suggestions for readjustment.

——— *Ministry of labor.* Memorandum on proposal to use unemployment benefit in aid of (*a*) wages on relief work, or (*b*) wages in industry. London, His Majesty's stationery office, 1923. 8 p.

Official study of the merits and demerits of these proposals; deciding against both.

——— Report on national unemployment insurance to July, 1923. London, His Majesty's stationery office, 1923.

SELECT CRITICAL BIBLIOGRAPHY 563

Official data on experience under the British act during the height of the post-war unemployment crisis.

——— *National health insurance joint committee.* Reports on the administration of the national insurance act, Part I, health insurance. London, Darling, 1912-1913, 1913-1914- .

Detailed descriptive and statistical reports on numbers insured, methods of operation, finances, and administrative problems.

——— *Royal commission on unemployment insurance.* Final report. London, His Majesty's stationery office, 1932. 529 p.

An important survey of the operation of British unemployment insurance with recommendations for changes. Includes a minority report.

——— *Unemployment grants committee.* Second (interim) report of proceedings, Mar. 3, 1922, to June 28, 1923. (Includes also text of first report, Dec., 1920, to Mar., 1922.) London, His Majesty's stationery office, 1923. 21 p.

Report of the committee appointed to administer funds for assisting local authorities in carrying on useful work schemes for unemployment relief.

Hansen, Alvin; Murray, Merrill; Stevenson, Russell, and Stewart, Bryce. A program for unemployment insurance and relief in the United States. Minneapolis, University of Minnesota press, 1934. viii, 201 p.

Discusses pros and cons of various proposals for unemployment insurance and develops a program.

Hohman, Helen Fisher. The development of social insurance and minimum wage legislation in Great Britain. Boston, Houghton Mifflin, 1933. xxi, 441 p.

Historical and critical treatment of British experience.

Illinois. Health insurance commission. Report of the health insurance commission. Springfield, 1919. viii, 647 p.

Valuable first-hand investigation into sickness, including its economic results and the experience under existing insurance plans.

Industrial relations counselors, inc. An historical basis for unemployment insurance. Minneapolis, University of Minnesota press, 1934. vi, 306 p.

Concise treatment of unemployment insurance systems and proposals in Great Britain, Germany, Belgium and Switzerland, and the United States.

International labor office. Compulsory pension insurance; comparative analysis of national laws, and statistics. (Studies and reports, series M, no. 10.) Geneva, 1933. xii, 782 p.

The most comprehensive comparative analysis of the old age pension laws of all countries.

——— Compulsory sickness insurance; comparative analysis of

national laws and statistics. (Studies and reports, series M, no. 6.) Geneva, 1927. xvi, 794 p.

    Comparison of benefits, financial resources, insurance institutions, and settlement of disputes under health insurance laws.

——— Documents of international labor conference. Geneva, 1919- .

    Stenographic record of proceedings, conventions and recommendations adopted, questionnaires issued and answers thereto, etc.

——— Industrial and labour information. Geneva, weekly, 1922- .

    Contains brief notes on labor news throughout the world, including legislative developments.

——— International labour review. Geneva, monthly, 1921- .

    Contains valuable articles, reports, and legislative notes relating to labor problems.

——— Legislative series. Geneva, yearly, 1920- .

    Contains translated texts of important laws and regulations pertaining to labor adopted in various countries.

——— Official bulletin. Geneva, 1920- .

    Quarterly publication (formerly more frequent) containing texts of official documents and information on official action pertaining to the office, the conventions, etc.

——— Studies and reports, series M, social insurance, and series C, unemployment. Geneva, 1921- .

    Special studies on social insurance problems. Unemployment insurance is grouped under the unemployment series.

——— I. L. O. yearbook. Geneva, 1930- .

    Contains summary of important developments in social insurance in all countries.

Kessler, Henry H. The crippled and the disabled; rehabilitation of the physically handicapped in the United States. New York, Columbia university press, 1935. xiii, 337 p.

    A study of the problem and existing legislation on vocational training for cripples.

Kiehel, Constance. Unemployment insurance in Belgium. New York, Industrial relations counselors, inc., 1932. xiv, 509 p.

    Belgian experience under the Ghent system of subsidized voluntary unemployment insurance.

Latimer, Murray W. Industrial pension systems in the United States and Canada. New York, Industrial relations counselors, inc. 1932. 2 v.

    Exhaustive study of old age pension systems in industry as developed by voluntary employer action.

SELECT CRITICAL BIBLIOGRAPHY 565

Latimer, Murray W. Trade union pension systems. New York, industrial relations counselors, inc., 1932. xvi, 205 p.

Most complete survey of trade union provision for old age pensions.

McCleary, George F. National Health insurance. London, Lewis, 1932. 185 p.

The former chief medical officer describes the British system.

Massachusetts. Special commission on stabilization of employment. Final report. Boston, 1932. 250 p.

Advocates unemployment reserve funds with employer contributions only.

Michelbacher, G. F., and Neal, Thomas M. Workmen's compensation insurance. New York, McGraw-Hill, 1925. 503 p.

A brief description of the history and present status of workmen's compensation laws in the United States, with more extended discussion of some technical workmen's compensation insurance problems.

Morley, Felix. Unemployment relief in Great Britain. Boston, Houghton Mifflin, 1924. 203 p.

Criticism of British act, and plea for insurance by industry. Contains valuable data, but draws somewhat too sweeping conclusions therefrom.

National industrial conference board. Industrial pensions in the United States. New York, 1925. 157 p.

History and analysis of existing establishment funds for pensioning aged employees, with examination of their advantages and disadvantages.

National joint council representing the general council of the trade union congress and the executive committee of the labor party. Unemployment insurance by industry. Westminster, 1923. 32 p.

Argument for and against unemployment insurance by industry with summary of position of various British trade unions on this question.

New York. State commission on relief for widowed mothers. Report. Albany, Lyon, 1914. 584 p.

A careful study of the provisions for the support of dependent widows and children in New York State and in European countries. Recommendations for county boards of child welfare with power to grant allowances to deserving widows with children.

New York State federation of labor. Reports on health insurance. 1918-1920.

These pamphlets present the attitude of a state federation of labor which has given long and careful study to the subject. No. 1, "Official endorsement of the New York state federation of labor." No. 2, "Discussion of the bill." No. 3, "Advantages to industry." No. 4, "A demand for the passage of a health insurance law." No. 5, "Progress toward health insurance legislation." No. 6, "Opposition attempts to mislead workers." No. 7, "Digest of the speech of Hon. Frederick M. Davenport on April 10, 1919, immediately preceding the passage of labor's bill." No. 8, "What's Your Health Worth?" No. 9, "Sickness in Industry as a Cause of Poverty—and a remedy Therefor," by James M. Lynch.

Newsholme, Arthur. Medicine and the state; the relation between the private and official practice of medicine; with special reference to public health. Baltimore, Williams & Wilkins, 1932. 300 p.

A prominent British physician discusses health insurance and other aspects of medical care.

Ohio. Commission on unemployment insurance. Report. Part I, Conclusions and recommended bill. Part II, Studies and reports. Columbus, 1932 and 1933. 99 and 304 p.

Favors single pool fund insurance with worker contributions.

——— *Health and old-age insurance commission.* Health, health insurance, old age pensions; report, recommendations, dissenting opinions. Columbus, 1919. xiii, 448 p.

Approves compulsory contributory health insurance, carried exclusively through mutual funds and associations, as a means of distributing the cost of sickness.

President's unemployment conference. Special committee. Report on business cycles and unemployment. (Chap. xvii, Trade union out-of-work benefits, 9 p. Chap. xviii, Unemployment insurance, 40 p.) New York, McGraw-Hill, 1923.

Carefully considered articles forming part of a very valuable study.

Ramsey, William T., and Tead, Ordway. Report of investigation into the operation of the British health insurance act. Pennsylvania health insurance commission of 1921.

A critical study made for the Pennsylvania health insurance commission of 1920.

Rhodes, J. E., 2d. Workmen's compensation. New York, Macmillan, 1917. 300 p.

Traces development of workmen's compensation legislation in the United States, with special reference to insurance, administration, and constitutionality.

Rubinow, I. M. The quest for security. New York, Holt, 1934. vii, 638 p.

Surveys critically the movement for social insurance in the United States.

——— Social insurance, with special reference to American conditions. New York, Holt, 1913. vii, 525 p.

Study of the social results of industrial accident, sickness, old age, invalidity, death, and unemployment, with the principles and development of social insurance against these contingencies.

——— Standards of health insurance. New York, Holt, 1916. 322 p.

Brisk and progressive discussion of such points as the justice of

SELECT CRITICAL BIBLIOGRAPHY 567

compulsion, coverage, amount of medical and cash benefit, and exclusion of commercial insurance companies.

Schwedtman, Ferdinand C., and Emery, James A. Accident prevention and relief. New York, National association of manufacturers, 1911. xxxvi, 481 p.

    An investigation of the growth of workmen's compensation systems in Europe, especially in England and Germany; with illustrations and charts.

Seager, Henry Rogers. Social insurance. New York, Macmillan, 1910. 175 p.

    A sympathetic discussion of the need and the principles of social insurance and the extent to which it can and should be introduced in the United States.

Simons, A. M., and Sinai, Nathan. The way of health insurance. Chicago, University of Chicago press, 1932. ix, 215 p.

    A survey of health insurance experience in other countries with discussion of its application to American conditions.

Spates, T. G., and Rabinovitch, G. S. Unemployment insurance in Switzerland. New York, Industrial relations counselors, inc., 1931. xii, 276 p.

    A complete history and careful analysis of Swiss unemployment insurance.

Stewart, Bryce. Unemployment benefits in the United States: the plans and their setting. New York, Industrial relations counselors, inc., 1930. xviii, 727 p.

    The most thoroughgoing study of American experiments with unemployment insurance, covering employer, trade union, and joint voluntary plans up to 1930.

Tillyard, Frank. The worker and the state. London, Routledge, 1936. x, 308 p.

    A survey of labor legislation in Great Britain, with a chapter on workmen's compensation and unemployment insurance.

Trade-union congress and the labor party. The administration of the unemployment insurance acts. Westminster, 1923. 24 p.

    Labor's criticisms of the provisions and administration of the British unemployment insurance act with recommendations for its improvement.

Turner, G. V. M. Unemployment insurance. Sydney, Gullick, 1921. 71 p.

    A study of unemployment insurance laws of various countries prepared for the New South Wales board of trade.

United States. Bureau of the census. Paupers in almshouses, 1923. Washington, Govt. print. off., 1924. 8 p.

    Statistics of United States almshouse population.

United States. Bureau of labor statistics. (Bureau of labor 1895-1912.) Bulletins. Washington, Govt. print. off., 1912- .

Series on workmen's insurance and compensation contains material on social insurance.

———— *Monthly labor review.* Washington, Govt. print. off., 1915- .

Contains valuable articles and news notes on social insurance problems.

———— *Children's bureau.* Bulletins and charts. Washington, Govt. print. off., 1912- .

Series on mothers' pensions presents valuable studies in this field.

———— *Mothers' aid,* 1931. (Bureau publication no. 220.) Washington, Govt. print. off., 1933. v, 39 p.

A survey of legislation and administration of state mothers' pensions.

———— *Federal board for vocational education.* Bulletins. Industrial rehabilitation series and civilian vocational rehabilitation series; also annual reports.

Official data on various phases of rehabilitation problems.

———— *House committee on the District of Columbia.* Subcommittee hearings and report on workmen's compensation for the District of Columbia. 67th and 68th Congresses. Washington, Govt. print. off., 1926. 550 p.

Exhaustive discussion of model workmen's compensation bill with special reference to exclusive state fund insurance.

———— Report on workmen's accident compensation for the District of Columbia. 69th Congress, 1st session (Report no. 859). Washington, Govt. print. off., 1926. 7 p.

Brief for exclusive state fund bill.

———— *House Committee on ways and means.* Hearings on economic security act. (74th Cong., 1st session.) Washington, Govt. print. off., 1935. 1141 p.

Views of proponents and opponents of federal security act during its passage through Congress.

———— *President's committee on economic security.* Report to the President. Washington, Govt. print. off., 1935. 74 p.

Recommendations which led to the enactment of the federal social security act.

———— *Senate Committee on finance.* Hearings on economic security act. (74th Cong., 1st session.) Washington, Govt. print. off., 1935. 1354 p.

Valuable source for points of view of proponents and opponents of the federal social security act.

———— *Treasury department. Public health service.* Health insurance; its relation to the public health. (Public health bulletin no. 76, B. S. Warren and Edgar Sydenstricker.) Washington, Govt. print. off., 1916. 76 p.

Searching statistical study of economic conditions conducing to sickness, adequacy of existing provisions for care and relief, benefits of universal health insurance.

Van Doren, Durand Halsey. Workingman's compensation and insurance. New York, Moffat, Yard, 1918. viii, 332 p.

Well-written stimulating discussion of the history and practice of workmen's compensation, together with current problems. Special attention to insurance leads to conclusion in favor of state funds.

Wisconsin. Insurance investigation committee. Report. Majority report of the senate committee on the practicability of government and state insurance. iv, 52 p. Minority report of the senate committee on the practicability of government and state insurance. ii, 18 p. (Printed separately but bound in back of joint committee report.) Madison, 1907.

Majority report gives arguments for and against state life insurance, and recommends postponement. Minority report makes a vigorous argument for immediate steps toward establishing state life insurance.

Wolman, Leo. A proposal for an unemployment fund in the men's clothing industry. Amalgamated clothing workers of America, education department, 1922. 27 p.

Memorandum presented to the Chicago board of arbitration explaining the union demand for an unemployment fund.

Woodbury, Robert M. Social insurance; an economic analysis. New York, Holt, 1917. 171 p.

Finds that the possible disadvantages of economic burden, decrease in thrift, and increase in accidents, are relatively unimportant and are outweighed by the gains through compulsory insurance.

VI. INDIVIDUAL BARGAINING

Anson, William R. Principles of the law of contract. (Edited with American notes by Arthur L. Corbin.) New York, Oxford university press, 1924. ix, 592 p.

Standard English work on the subject, edited for American use.

Ballagh, James C. White servitude in the colony of Virginia; a study of the system of indentured labor in the American colonies. (Johns Hopkins university studies in historical and political science, v. 13:259-357.) Baltimore, Johns Hopkins press, June-July, 1895.

Representative picture of the conditions of indentured service in the south; includes a chapter on "The freedman."

Byer, Herman B. Prison labor in the United States. (United States Bureau of labor statistics, bulletin no. 595.) Washington, Govt. print. off., 1933. 216 p.

Report of a survey of extent and character of prison labor in 1932.

Champion, F. C. Gurney. Justice and the poor in England; an account of the position of the poor in legal matters in England and Wales and a study of the inequality in the administration of justice where they are concerned, and of the remedies which have been attempted and suggested. London, Routledge, 1926. x, 245 p.

Subtitle describes scope of the book.

Commons, John R. Races and immigrants in America. New York, Macmillan, 1913. xiii, 242 p.

An estimate of the contribution made by each race to the nation as a whole.

Coolidge, Mary R. Chinese immigration. New York, Holt, 1909. x, 531 p.

Sketches the history of the anti-Chinese movement, with conclusions in favor of non-restriction.

Davie, Maurice R. World immigration; with special reference to the United States. New York, Macmillan, 1936. x, 588 p.

An historical and descriptive account of immigration, its effect on American society, and its regulation through legislation.

Eaves, Lucile. A history of California labor legislation, with an introductory sketch of the San Francisco labor movement. (University of California, publications in economics.) Berkeley, the university press, 1910. xiv, 461 p.

Several chapters on the Chinese, with special reference to California.

Garis, Roy L. Immigration restriction; a study of the opposition to and regulation of immigration into the United States. New York, Macmillan, 1927. xv, 376 p.

Traces the history of restrictive regulation from colonial times, with chapters on the Chinese and Japanese problems.

Geiser, Karl F. Redemptioners and indentured servants in the colony and commonwealth of Pennsylvania. New Haven, Conn., Tuttle, Morehouse and Taylor co., n. d. (Supplement to the Yale review, v. 10, no. 2, Aug., 1901.) 128 p.

Account of the countries whence the early immigrants came, the conditions of their voyage, and their mode of living in this country; doing for the north what Ballagh's book (*q. v.*) does for the south.

Goldman, Mayer C. The public defender; a necessary factor in the administration of justice. New York, Putnam's, 1919. xiii, 98 p.

Describes the need, functions and progress of the public defender movement.

Gulick, Sidney L. American democracy and Asiatic citizenship. New York, Scribner, 1918. 257 p.

Plea for a reasonable immigration policy, based on capacity for assimilation, and applied to all races alike.

Hourwich, Isaac A. Immigration and labor; the economic aspects

SELECT CRITICAL BIBLIOGRAPHY 571

of European immigration to the United States. New York, Putnam, 1912. xvii, 544 p.
>Presents the argument against restriction.

Hurd, John C. The law of freedom and bondage in the United States. Boston, Little, Brown, 1858. 2 v.
>Deals exclusively with the legal aspect of the question.

Ingram, John K. A history of slavery and serfdom. London, Black, 1895. xiv, 285 p.
>Deals with slavery in ancient Greece and Rome, the serfdom of the middle ages, the African slave trade and slavery in Russia and the east.

Jenks, Jeremiah W., and Lauck, William J. The immigration problem. (Revised and enlarged by R. D. Smith.) New York, Funk and Wagnall, 1926. xxvii, 717 p.
>Survey of immigration problem in the United States. Advocates restriction.

Legal aid society of New York. Annual reports. Also Legal aid review, quarterly.

Lescohier, Don D., and Brandeis, Elizabeth. History of labor in the United States. New York, Macmillan, 1935. xxx, 778 p.
>Chapter XIV on Apprenticeship, Employee Training, and Vocational Education.

Maguire, John MacArthur. The lance of justice; a semi-centennial history of the Legal aid society, 1876-1926. Cambridge, Harvard university press, 1928. 305 p.
>Traces the development of legal aid in the United States.

Motley, James M. Apprenticeship in American trade unions. (Johns Hopkins university studies in historical and political science, v. 25:482-604.) Baltimore, Johns Hopkins press, 1907.
>Chapter on the governmental regulation of apprenticeship.

Parry, Edward A. The law and the poor. New York, Dutton, 1914, xxi, 316 p.
>A London county court judge's criticism of the law's treatment of the working class; with a chapter on imprisonment for debt.

Ross, Edward Alsworth. The old world in the new; the significance of past and present immigration to the American people. New York, Appleton-Century, 1914. 327 p.
>Analyzes in turn the racial characteristics of each immigrant group.

Scrimshaw, Stewart. Apprenticeship; principles, relationships, procedures. New York, McGraw-Hill, 1932. xv, 273 p.
>Thoroughgoing discussion of apprenticeship, with chapters on public regulation.

Sharkey, Charles F., and Patterson, George D., Jr. Laws relating to prison labor in the United States as of July 1, 1933. (United

States Bureau of labor statistics, bulletin no. 596.) Washington, Govt. print. off., 1933. 146 p.

Text of laws with brief introductory survey of court decisions.

Smith, Reginald Heber. Justice and the poor. New York, Carnegie foundation for the advancement of teaching, 1919. xiv, 271 p.

Severe arraignment of modern civil and criminal procedure, with discussion of remedial agencies and legal aid societies.

─────── and Bradway, John S. Growth of legal aid work in the United States; a study of our administration of justice primarily as it affects the wage earner and of the agencies designed to improve his position before the law. (U. S. Bureau of labor statistics, bulletin no. 607.) Washington, Govt. print. off., 1936. vii, 223 p.

Includes discussion of legal aid, the public defender, and the small claims court.

Taylor, H. C. Outlines of agricultural economics. New York, Macmillan, 1931. xii, 614 p.

Chapters XX to XXV discuss the problem of farm tenancy; Chapter XIV is on farm labor, and Chapter XV is on farm credit.

Underhill, H. Clay. A treatise on the law of landlord and tenant, including leases, their execution, surrender, and renewal; the parties thereto, and their reciprocal rights and obligations; the various kinds of tenancy, the use and possession of the premises, the character of rent and the remedies for its recovery, the tenant's right to fixtures, etc., etc.; with full references to the latest American and English cases and to relevant American and English statutes, both ancient and modern. Chicago, T. H. Flood, 1909. 2 v.

Seeks to give a treatment of the subject in the light of modern conditions and especially to bring out more clearly the contractual character of the landlord-tenant relationship.

United States. Report on condition of woman and child wage-earners in the United States. (Senate doc. no. 645, 61st Cong., 2d sess.) V. 6, "The beginnings of child labor legislation in certain states: a comparative study," Elizabeth Lewis Otey. Washington, Govt. print. off., 1910.

Chapter on apprenticeship.

─────── Bureau of labor statistics. Bulletins. Washington, Govt. print. off., 1895- .

See list of titles on final pages of most recent bulletin.

─────── Monthly labor review. Washington, Govt. print. off., 1915- .

Contains frequent articles and summaries of reports on immigration, convict labor, wage payment legislation, and related topics.

SELECT CRITICAL BIBLIOGRAPHY 573

United States. Department of justice. Annual report of the attorney-general. Exhibit 17, p. 207-215. Washington, Govt. print. off., 1907.

    Short report on peonage conditions resulting from an investigation by the assistant attorney-general.

——— *Immigration commission.* Reports. (Senate doc. no. 747, 61st Cong., 3d sess.) Washington, Govt. print. off., 1911. 41 v.

    Contain reports on contract labor, the padrone system, peonage, and immigrant banks.

Whitney, Edison L. Cooperative credit societies (credit unions) in America and foreign countries. (United States Bureau of labor statistics, bulletin no. 314.) Washington, Govt. print. off., 1922. 60 p.

    Describes Raiffeisen and Schulze-Delitzsch plans, and extent of credit cooperation in foreign countries and its growth in the United States.

Wilson, Henry. History of the rise and fall of the slave power in America. Boston, Houghton Mifflin, n. d. 3 v.

    A history of slavery in America from colonial times to the passage of the fifteenth amendment, the most detailed part being concerned with the Civil War.

Wilson, Walter. Forced labor in the United States. New York, International, 1933. 192 p.

    Includes chapter on convict labor and peonage.

Wolff, Henry W. Cooperation in agriculture. London, King, 1912. x, 378 p.

    Describes in detail the methods of cooperation used in different countries. The author is a leading authority on cooperation.

VII. COLLECTIVE BARGAINING

Allen, Henry J., and Gompers, Samuel. The Allen-Gompers debate. New York, Dutton, 1920.

    A debate upon the Kansas industrial relations court act, with Governor Allen of Kansas and Samuel Gompers, president of the American federation of labor, on opposite sides.

Anderson, George. Regulation of industrial relations. (Annals of American academy of political and social science, Nov., 1931, v. 158:156-165.)

    A brief summary of the history of compulsory arbitration in Australia.

Askwith, Lord. Industrial problems and disputes. London, Murray, 1920. 494 p.

    Experiences of the man who for twenty years was the foremost industrial arbitrator in England.

Barnett, George E., and McCabe, David A. Mediation, investigation, and arbitration in industrial disputes. New York, Appleton-Century, 1916. 209 p.

A study for the United States commission on industrial relations upon the mediation and arbitration machinery developed in this country.

Berman, Edward. Labor and the Sherman act. New York, Harper, 1930. xviii, 332 p.

A thorough study of the Sherman anti-trust act as applied to labor union activities by court interpretation.

——— Labor disputes and the President of the United States. New York, Longmans, Green, 1924. 284 p.

Historical account of intervention by the President in labor disputes, with particular attention to the war period.

Canada. Department of labor. Labour gazette, Ottawa, 19-

Monthly bulletin which always includes an account of all proceedings under the Canadian industrial disputes investigation act.

Commons, John R., and Gilmore, Eugene A. (ed.). A documentary history of American industrial society. v. 3, 4, and supplement. Cleveland, Arthur H. Clark, 1910. 10 v.

Reprints in full the records of the labor cases in the United States prior to Commonwealth *v.* Hunt (1842).

Feis, Herbert. The Kansas court of industrial relations, its spokesman, its record. (Quarterly journal of economics, Aug., 1923. v. 37:705-733.)

An important account, written before the United States Supreme Court virtually destroyed the court.

Fisher, Clyde V. Use of federal power in the settlement of railway labor disputes. (Bulletin no. 303, United States Bureau of labor statistics.) Washington, Govt. print. off., 1922. 121 p.

An historical account of conciliation and arbitration in railroad labor disputes in the United States, with text of acts and bibliography.

Fitch, John A. The causes of industrial unrest. (Chaps. xv, xvi, xvii.) New York, Harper, 1924. 424 p.

The existing law of labor combinations as a cause of industrial unrest.

Foenander, O. de R. The new commonwealth of Australia conciliation and arbitration act. (International labour review, Dec., 1931, v. 24:699-712.)

Frankfurter, Felix, and Greene, Nathan. The labor injunction. New York, Macmillan, 1930. 343 p.

A study of the origin, development, use and abuses of the injunction in labor disputes, including discussion of legislation on this subject.

Frey, John P. The labor injunction: an exposition of government by judicial conscience and its menace. Cincinnati, Equity pub. co., 1922. 197 p.

A criticism of the use of injunctions in labor disputes from the point

SELECT CRITICAL BIBLIOGRAPHY 575

of view of organized labor. Valuable as an expression of labor's feeling toward injunctions.

Gompers, Samuel. And yet they would "wish" it on us. (American federationist, 1915. v. 22:333-337.)
   Criticizes the industrial arbitration court of New South Wales for its action in reducing wages owing to the war.

———— Australasian labor regulating schemes. (American federationist, 1915. v. 22:253-263.)
   Expresses the view that the arbitration courts and wages boards constitute a "judicial despotism."

Hale, William G. Injunction against interference with freedom of trade or employment; combinations, strikes, boycotts, etc. (In Pomeroy's Treatise on equitable remedies, 2nd ed., 1919. v. 5, chap. xviii, pp. 4564-4646.)
   An account from a legal point of view of the law of labor combinations in the United States.

Hammond, Matthew B. British labor conditions and legislation during the war. New York, Carnegie endowment for international peace, 1919. 335 p.
   Includes study of war-time anti-strike legislation and its results.

———— The Australian system of compulsory arbitration. (Proceedings American academy of political science, New York, 1917. v. 7:19-30.)
   Favorable account of Australian law.

Hedges, R. Y., and Winterbottom, A. The legal history of trade unionism. New York, Longmans, Green, 1930. xix, 170 p.
   The history of the legal status of trade unions and trade union activities in Great Britain.

Higgins, Henry Bourne. A new province for law and order. London, Constable, 1922. 181 p.
   An account of the compulsory arbitration in Australia by the man who was chief justice of the commonwealth arbitration court from 1907 to 1921.

Huggins, William L. Labor and democracy. New York, Macmillan, 1922. 213 p.
   An argument for the Kansas industrial relations court by its first presiding judge and author of law creating this court.

International labor office. Studies and reports, series A, Industrial relations. 1927- .
   Reports issued include "Freedom of Association," 5 vol. (1927-30); "Conciliation and Arbitration in Industrial Disputes" (1933); "Labor Relations in Great Britain" (1933).

International labor office. I. L. O. yearbook. Geneva, 1930-   .
   Includes annual summary of world developments in legislation relating to collective bargaining.

Ko, Ting Tsz. Government methods of adjusting labor disputes in North America and Australasia. New York, Longmans, 1926. 221 p.
   Historical and descriptive account of arbitration, conciliation, and mediation in labor disputes in the United States, Canada, New Zealand, and Australia, with general conclusions.

Lorwin, Lewis L., and Wubnig, Arthur. Labor relations boards. Washington, Brookings institution, 1935. xiv, 477 p.
   A thorough analysis of the work of the labor relations boards set up under the National industrial recovery act of 1933.

Martin, W. A. A treatise on the law of labor unions. Washington, Byrne, 1910. xxv, 649 p.
   Trade union law as applied by conservative courts. Gives sample forms of bills of complaint and injunctions.

Mason, Alpheus T. Organized labor and the law with especial reference to the Sherman and Clayton Acts. Durham, N. C., Duke university press, 1925. 265 p.
   Historical account, which stresses the interpretations given by the courts to the Clayton act.

Merritt, Walter G. The struggle for industrial liberty. New York, League of industrial rights, 1922. 98 p.
   Advocates a governmental policy toward labor unions and labor disputes, which is almost directly opposite to that presented in this book.

Murphy, H. M. Wages and prices in Australia. Our labor laws and their effects. Melbourne, Robertson, 1917. 144 p.
   A criticism of Australian compulsory arbitration and wage regulation by the chief inspector of factories in Melbourne.

National industrial conference board. Arbitration and wage fixing in Australia. (Research rept. no. 10.) Boston, 1918. 52 p.

——— Conciliation and arbitration in New Zealand. (Research rept. no. 23.) Boston, 1919. 46 p.

——— The Canadian industrial disputes investigation act. (Research rept. no. 5.) Boston, 1918. 28 p.

——— The Kansas court of industrial relations. (Research rept. no. 67.) New York, 1924. 103 p.
   Studies by the leading employers' research organization of the country. Concise and fair.

National mediation board. Annual report, including the report of the National railroad adjustment board. 1935-   .

Describes settlement of disputes by machinery created under the federal railway labor act.

Nicod, Jean. Freedom of association and trade unionism. An introductory survey. (International labour review, Apr., 1924. v. 9:467-480. Also, in Law and labor, Feb., 1925. v. 7:38-43.)

A review of the law regarding the right to form labor organizations in all countries.

Oakes, Edwin Stacy. The law of organized labor and industrial conflicts. Rochester, N. Y., Lawyers cooperative publishing co., 1927. xxxii, 1333 p.

A compendium of the law on labor unions, employers' associations, union labor contracts, union labels, and similar subjects.

Perlman, Selig. The principle of collective bargaining. (Annals of the American academy of political and social science. v. 184, March, 1936, pp. 154-160.)

Rankin, Mary Theresa. Arbitration and conciliation in Australasia. London, Allen and Unwin, 1916. 192 p.

History and analysis of arbitration in Victoria and New Zealand.

———— Arbitration principles and the industrial court; an analysis of decisions, 1919-1929. London, King, 1931.

Describes British experience with the arbitration of industrial disputes.

Riches, E. J. The depression and industrial arbitration in New Zealand. (International labour review, Nov., 1933, v. 28:623-628.)

Sayre, Francis B. A selection of cases and other authorities on labor law. Cambridge, Harvard university press, 1922. 1016 p.

A case book which includes all leading cases in the American and British law of labor combinations as well as many of the leading critical comments.

Seidman, Joel I. The yellow-dog contract. Baltimore, Johns Hopkins press, 1932. 96 p.

Describes the development, use, and attempts at legislative control of anti-union labor contracts.

Selekman, Ben M. Law and labor relations; a study of the industrial disputes investigation act of Canada. Cambridge, Harvard university graduate school of business administration, 1936. 65 p.

Brief account of experience under the Canadian act up to 1935.

———— Postponing strikes; a study of the Industrial disputes investigation act of Canada. New York, Russell Sage foundation, 1927. 405 p.

A study of the operation of the Canadian Industrial disputes investigation act during its first eighteen years.

Sells, Dorothy M. The development of state wage regulation in Australia and New Zealand. (International labour review, 1924. v. 10:607-629, 789-799, 962-1004.)

Deals with both the compulsory arbitration and trades boards act.

Slesser, Henry, and Baker, Charles. Trade union law. London, Nisbet, 1927. xxvii, 424 p.

History and analysis of British law relative to trade unions and their activities.

Tillyard, Frank. The worker and the state. London, Routledge, 1936. x, 308 p.

A survey of labor legislation in Great Britain, with a chapter on trade disputes.

Twentieth century fund, inc. Labor and the government; an investigation of the rôle of the government in labor relations. New York, McGraw-Hill, 1935. xii, 413 p.

Includes critical survey of methods of government intervention in labor disputes, and outlines a program prepared by a selected committee.

United States. Board of mediation and conciliation. Railroad strikes and lockouts. A study of the laws of the principal countries of the world providing machinery for the peaceable adjustment of disputes between railroads and their employees, and the laws of certain countries for the prevention of strikes. Washington, Govt. print. off., 1916. 367 p.

Subtitle accurately describes scope.

——— *Bureau of labor statistics.* Decisions of courts affecting labor. Washington, Govt. print. off., 1913- .

Annual or biennial bulletins reproducing all decisions of the United States and state supreme courts relating to labor law.

Webb, Sidney, and Webb, Beatrice. Industrial democracy. London, Longmans, Green, 1920. xxxix, 899 p.

Analyzes trade union structure, function and theory. The classic work on collective bargaining.

——— The history of trade unionism. London, Longmans, Green, 1920. xviii, 784 p.

A narrative of the facts of trade union history in England, forming the complement to "Industrial democracy."

Witte, Edwin E. The government in labor disputes. New York, McGraw-Hill, 1932. xi, 352 p.

Outstanding treatment of the injunction and other phases of government intervention in industrial disputes.

Wolf, H. D. The railroad labor board. Chicago, University of Chicago press, 1927. x, 473 p.

An account of the operations of the board created in 1920 and abolished in 1926, with discussion of their significance to the problem of governmental intervention in railway labor disputes.

VIII. ADMINISTRATION

Altmeyer, A. J. The industrial commission of Wisconsin. Madison, University of Wisconsin, 1932. xiii, 324 p.

Historical description of labor law administration under the outstanding state industrial commission.

American association for labor legislation. American labor legislation review. Quarterly, 1911- .

See Index to volumes I to XX and annual volume indexes thereafter.

American bar association. Special committee on legislative drafting. Report. (Senate doc. no. 262, 63d Cong., 2d sess.) Washington, Govt. print. off., 1913.

Andrews, John B. Administrative labor legislation. New York, Harper, 1936. 231 p.

Describes and evaluates actual experience with administrative rule-making by labor departments over a period of twenty-five years, with chapters on statutory authorization, administrative organization, procedure, records, accomplishment, and constitutionality.

────── *and Andrews, Irene Osgood.* Scientific standards in labor legislation. (American labor legislation review, June, 1911. v. I, no. 2:123-134.)

Defects of early legislation and advantages of advisory board method.

Blackly, Frederick F., and Oatman, Miriam E. Administrative legislation and adjudication. Washington, Brookings institution, 1934. xv, 296 p.

A discussion of the quasi-legislative and quasi-judicial functions of administrative officials.

Bourgeois, Leon. The international organization of social policies. (American labor legislation review, March, 1914. v. 4:186-202.)

Necessity for international cooperation in labor legislation.

Brown, Edward F. The efficiency of present factory inspection machinery in the United States. (American labor legislation review, Feb., 1913. v. 3:24-28.)

Inadequacy of then existing administrative agencies.

Calder, John. Scientific accident prevention. (American labor legislation review, Dec., 1911. v. I, no. 4:14-24.)

Emphasizes need for cooperation between employer, employee, and engineering expert.

Commons, John R. Labor and administration. New York, Macmillan, 1913. vii, 431 p.

Essays on various labor questions, the last in the book taking up the subject of administration in connection with the Wisconsin workmen's compensation act.

────── The industrial commission of Wisconsin. (American labor legislation review, Dec., 1911. v. 1, no. 4:61-69.)

Principles of commission plan.

────── How the Wisconsin industrial commission works. (American labor legislation review, Feb., 1913. v. 3:9-14.)

Operation of commission plan.

Dodd, Walter F. Administration of workmen's compensation. New York, Commonwealth fund, 1936. xviii, 845 p.

A notable survey of administrative problems and practice under American compensation laws, including description of commission administration.

Gettemy, Charles F. The Massachusetts bureau of statistics, 1869-1915; a sketch of its history, organization, and functions, together with a list of its publications and illustrative charts. Boston, 1915. 115 p.

Written by the director in connection with the exhibit of the bureau of statistics at the Panama-Pacific exposition.

Kaiser, John Boynton. Law, legislative, and municipal reference libraries. Boston, Boston book co., 1914.

Comprehensive exposition of the legislative drafting research movement.

Kingsbury, Susan M. (ed.). Labor laws and their enforcement, with special reference to Massachusetts. New York, Longmans, Green, 1911. xxii, 419 p.

Historical and critical studies on the administration of labor laws in Massachusetts, special chapters being devoted to woman and child labor and employment offices.

McNeill, Joseph H. The Massachusetts board of boiler rules. (American labor legislation review, Dec., 1911. v. 1, no. 4:70-80.)

Description of the joint board plan and its operation.

Mess, Henry A. Factory legislation and its administration, 1891-1924. London, King, 1926. xii, 228 p.

An account of British experience with the enforcement of labor laws.

Shotwell, James T. (ed.). The origins of the International labor organization. Vol. I, history. Vol. II, documents. New York, Columbia university press, 1934.

Authoritative treatment of the beginning of the I. L. O. See list of bulletins on final pages of recent bulletin.

SELECT CRITICAL BIBLIOGRAPHY 581

Stewart, Frank Mann. The national civil service reform league; history, activities, problems. Austin, University of Texas, 1929. viii, 304 p.

The history of an organization which has labored since 1881 to establish and extend the merit system in American government.

United States. Report on condition of woman and child wage-earners in the United States. (Senate doc. no. 645, 61st Cong., 2d sess.) V. 19, "Labor laws and factory conditions." Washington, Govt. print. off., 1912. 1125 p.

Summary of laws on child labor, safety, health, and comfort, and study of their enforcement.

――――― Senate hearings on a legislative drafting bureau and legislative reference division of the library of Congress. (Senate rept. no. 1271, 62d Cong., 3d sess.) Washingtin, Govt. print. off., 1911.

Testimony of experts from all parts of the country.

――――― *Bureau of labor statistics.* Bulletins. Washington, Govt. print. off., 1895.

Especially concerned with administration of labor legislation are: No. 142, "Administration of labor laws and factory inspection in certain European countries," George M. Price; No. 211, "Labor laws and their administration in the Pacific States," Hugh S. Hanna; No. 254, "International labor legislation and the society of nations," Stephen Bauer.

――――― Monthly labor review. Washington, Govt. print. off., 1915- .

Reviews reports of federal, state, and foreign bureaus administering labor laws.

――――― *Children's bureau.* Publications. Washington, Govt. print. off., 1913- .

Issues give investigations of administration of child labor laws in Connecticut, New York, Maryland, and other states.

――――― *Commission on industrial relations.* Final report. "Report of commissioners John R. Commons and Florence J. Harriman," pp. 307-403. Washington, 1915. 448 p.

Breakdown of existing labor laws and proposals for securing more thorough enforcement.

Willoughby, W. F. Principles of public administration. Washington, Brookings institution, 1927. xxii, 720 p.

A comprehensive treatise on the basic problems, administrative organization and operation in government.

Wilson, Francis G. Labor in the league system; a study of the International labor organization in relation to international administration. Stanford university press, 1934. xii, 384 p.

An excellent critical survey of the I. L. O. from an American point of view.

IX. THE BASIS OF LABOR LAW

American association for labor legislation. American labor legislation review. Quarterly, 1911- .

One issue each year summarizes new labor legislation enacted by Congress and by the several states.

Andrews, J. deWitt. American law, a commentary on the jurisprudence, constitution, and laws of the United States. Chicago, Callaghan, 1908. 2 v.

"Constructed in accordance with the institutional or analytical method, with the object of producing an elementary treatise possessing as much of the practical as is possible within the space devoted to the work." Intended to provide a classification that will fit American conditions.

Andrews, John B. Labor problems and labor legislation. New York, American association for labor legislation, 1932. 135 p.

Brief popular treatment, heavily illustrated.

Beard, Charles A. The supreme court and the constitution. New York, Macmillan, 1912. vii, 127 p.

Judicial supremacy discussed in the light of the views of the founding fathers.

Bowden, Witt. The industrial history of the United States. New York, Adelphi, 1930. x, 511 p.

Clark, Lindley D. The law of the employment of labor. New York, Macmillan, 1911. xiv, 373 p.

Deals with the principles underlying the common law and legislation as far as these affect the relation between employer and employee. Written from a legal standpoint. Appendix, giving a code of the common law affecting employment.

Commons, John R. Industrial good will. New York, McGraw-Hill, 1919. 213 p.

Treats of labor legislation as supplementing good will by raising the general level of competition.

——— Legal foundations of capitalism. New York, Macmillan, 1924. x, 394 p.

——— *Saposs, David J.; Sumner, Helen L.; Mittelman, E. B.; Hoagland, H. E.; Andrews, John B.; Perlman, Selig.* History of labor in the United States. New York, Macmillan, 1918. 2 v.; xxv, 623; xx, 620 p.

Recounts by successive periods the efforts of American wage earners to improve their conditions by trade union activity and through labor legislation.

Corwin, Edward S. The constitution and what it means today. Princeton, Princeton university press, 1930. xxviii, 160 p.

The constitution is discussed section by section as interpreted by court decisions.

Ely, Richard T. Property and contract in their relations to the distribution of wealth. New York, Macmillan, 1914. 2 v.

Gives a wide survey of the theories of property and contract held at different times; interprets cases on police power according to a progressive theory. Many references.

——— Economic theory and labor legislation. (Proceedings American association for labor legislation, 1st annual meeting, pp. 10-39.) Madison, Wis., 1908.

Examines the attitude of the classical economists toward social reform. First presidential address of the American association for labor legislation.

Farnam, Henry W. Some fundamental distinctions in labor legislation. (Proceedings American association for labor legislation, 2d annual meeting, pp. 29-42.) Madison, Wis., 1909.

Discusses the different types of labor laws and the purposes for which they are enacted. Second presidential address of the American association for labor legislation.

Freund, Ernst. The police power, public policy, and constitutional rights. Chicago, Callaghan, 1904. xiii, 819 p.

A thorough and learned study of the police power in its various aspects.

Goodnow, Frank J. Social reform and the constitution. New York, Macmillan, 1911. xxi, 365 p.

An attempt to determine how far the constitution is a bar to social progress; with a chapter on the attitude of the courts.

Groat, George G. The attitude of American courts in labor cases. (Columbia university studies in history, economics, and public law, v. 42, no. 108.) New York, Longmans, Green, 1911. 400 p.

Analysis and criticism of court decisions on trade union activities and protective labor legislation.

Hastings, William G. The development of law as illustrated by the decisions relating to the police power of the state. (Proceedings of the American philosophical society, 1900, v. 39:359-554.)

Original and suggestive treatment.

Hutchins, B. L., and Harrison, Amy. A history of factory legislation. London, King, 1911. xviii, 301 p.

History of factory legislation in England from the Elizabethan poor law to 1910. Preface by Sidney Webb.

Jevons, William Stanley. The state in relation to labor. London, Macmillan, 1882. 174 p.

An effort to define the extent to which protective labor legislation and laws establishing the rights of trade unions may be carried in a *laissez-faire* society.

Lescohier, Don D.; Brandeis, Elizabeth; Perlman, Selig, and Taft, Philip. History of labor in the United States. Vols. III and IV. New York, Macmillan, 1935.

Brings down to 1932 the history begun in two earlier volumes by Commons and Associates. Volume III deals with working conditions and labor legislation. Volume IV deals with the labor movement.

McBain, Howard Lee. The living constitution; a consideration of the realities and legends of our fundamental law. New York, Workers education bureau press, 1927. vii, 284 p.

A discussion of the basic principles of the United States Constitution in the light of history.

Mess, Henry A. Factory legislation and its administration, 1891-1924. London, King, 1926. xii, 228 p.

A critical account of English factory legislation, with stress on safety laws and their enforcement.

Pic, Paul. Traité élémentaire de législation industrielle; les lois ouvrières. Paris, Rousseau, 1922. xxv, 1043 p.

A scholarly collection and arrangement of laws on labor, with a theoretical and historical introduction. Deals primarily but not exclusively with France.

Rice, William G., Jr. The constitutionality of labor legislation in the United States of America. (International labour review, 1925. v. 14:619-639, 779-782.)

Seligman, E. R. A., and Johnson, Alvin (ed.). Encyclopedia of the social sciences. 15 vols. New York, Macmillan, 1929-35.

Contains authoritative articles on many phases of labor and labor legislation.

United States. Bureau of labor statistics. Monthly labor review. Washington, Govt. print. off., 1915- .

Contains summaries of labor laws under discussion and enacted in the United States and abroad.

——— *Children's bureau.* Publications. Washington, Govt. print. off., 1913- .

Give summaries and tabular analyses of legislation on child labor.

——— *Women's bureau.* Publications. Washington, Govt. print. off., 1918- .

Give summaries and tabular analysis of legislation affecting women in industry.

Webb, Beatrice. The case for the factory acts. London, Richards, 1902. 233 p.

Economic and social justification for social regulation of labor conditions.

Willoughby, W. W. The constitutional law of the United States. New York, Baker, Voorhis, 1929. 3 v.

Deals with the general principles underlying constitutional law.

TABLE OF CASES CITED

In the following table of cases, wherever possible, the reference to the official (state, circuit court, or United States) report is given first; for the convenience of those to whom the official reports are inaccessible, references to the unofficial (sectional, federal, supreme court, etc.) reports are added.

Aberthaw Construction Co. v. Cameron, 194 Mass. 208, 80 N. E. 478 (1907) 391
Adair v. U. S., 208 U. S. 161, 28 Sup. Ct. 277 (1908) 377, 387, 406
Adams v. Tanner, 244 U. S. 590, 37 Sup. Ct. 662 (1917) 9
Adkins v. Children's Hospital, 261 U. S. 525, 43 Sup. Ct. 394 (1923) 55, 78-81, 469
Aeolian Co. v. Fischer, 27 F. (2d) 560 (1928) 394
Allis Chalmers Co. v. Iron Molders, 166 Fed. 45 (1908) 399
Almand v. Scott, 80 Ga. 95, 4 S. E. 892 (1888) 341, 342
American Steel Foundries Co. v. Tri-City Central Trades Council, 257 U. S. 184, 42 Sup. Ct. 72 (1921) 387, 400
American Steel & Wire Co. v. Davis, 261 Fed. 800 (1919) 404
Androff v. Building Trades Employers Assoc., 7 *Law & Labor* 178 (Ind. App. 1925) 404
Arkansas Stave Co. v. State, 94 Ark. 27, 125 S. W. 1001 (1910) 330
Arthur v. Oakes, 11 C. C. A. 209, 63 Fed. 310 (1894) 325, 396
Atchison, Topeka & Santa Fe Ry. Co. v. Gee, 139 Fed. 582 (1905) 398
Atkin v. Kansas, 191 U. S. 207, 24 Sup. Ct. 124 (1903) 75, 132
Atkins v. Fletcher, 65 N. J. Eq. 658, 55 Atl. 1074 (1903) 404
Auburn Draying Co. v. Wardell, 227 N. Y. 1, 124 N. E. 97 (1919) 402
Avent Beattyville Coal Co. v. Commonwealth, 96 Ky. 218, 28 S. W. 502 (1894) 529

Bailey v. Alabama, 219 U. S. 219, 31 Sup. Ct. 145 (1910) 323, 324
Bailey v. Drexel Furniture Company, 259 U. S. 20, 42 Sup. Ct. 449 (1922) 173
Baldwin Lumber Co. v. Local 560, 91 N. J. Eq. 240, 109 Atl. 147 (1920) 393
Baltimore and Ohio Railroad Co. v. Interstate Commerce Commission, 221 U. S. 612, 31 Sup. Ct. 621 (1911) 133
Barnes v. Typographical Union No. 16, 232 Ill. 424, 83 N. E. 940 (1908) 397
Bausback v. Reiff, 244 Pa. 559, 91 Atl. 224 (1914) 393
Bausch Machine Co. v. Hill, 231 Mass. 30, 120 N. E. 188 (1918) .. 391

586   PRINCIPLES OF LABOR LEGISLATION

Beattie v. Callanan, 67 App. Div. 14, 73 N. Y. Supp. 518 (1901);
  82 App. Div. 7, 81 N. Y. Supp. 413 (1903) 393
Bedford Cut Stone Co. v. Journeymen Stone Cutters Association,
  274 U. S. 37, 47 Sup. Ct. 522 (1927) 394, 395
Beekman v. Marsters, 195 Mass. 205, 80 N. E. 817 (1907) 399
Belfi v. U. S. 259 Fed. 822 (1919) 386
Bemis v. State, 12 Okla. Crim. 114, 152 Pac. 456 (1915) 407
Berry v. Donovan, 188 Mass. 353, 74 N. E. 603 (1905) 391
Best Service, etc., Co. v. Dickson, 121 Misc. 416, 20 N. Y. Supp.
  173 (1923) 396
Bittner v. West Virginia-Pittsburgh Coal Co., 15 F. (2d) 652 (1926) 406
Bixby v. Dunlap, 56 N. H. 456 (1876) 399
Blum & Co. v. Landau, 23 Ohio App. 426, 155 N. E. 154 (1926) 390
Bomes v. Providence Local No. 223, 51 R. I. 499, 155 Atl. 581 (1931) 398
Booth v. Burgess, 72 N. J. Eq. 181, 65 Atl. 226 (1906) 394
Bossert v. Dhuy, 221 N. Y. 342, 117 N. E. 582 (1917) 394
Boston Store v. Retail Clerks, 216 Ill. App. 428 (1920) 398
Bowman v. Bradley, 151 Pa. St. 351, 24 Atl. 1062 (1892) 342
Boyer v. Western Union, 124 Fed. 246 (1903) 408
Boyle v. U. S., 259 Fed. 803 (1919) 386
Bricklayers', Masons', and Plasterers' International Union v. Seymour Ruff & Sons, Inc., 160 Md. 483, 154 Atl. 52 (1931) 393
Brotherhood of Railway and Steamship Clerks v. Texas & N. O. Ry.
  Co., 24 Fed. (2d) 426 (1928); 25 F. (2d) 873 (1928); 33 F.
  (2d) 13 (1929) 421
Brown v. Piper, 91 U. S. 37 (1875) 461
Bunting v. Oregon, 243 U. S. 426, 37 Sup. Ct. 435 (1917) 137
Burgess v. Ga., etc., Ry. Co., 148 Ga. 415, 96 S. E. 864 (1918) 396
Burgess v. Stewart, 112 Misc. 347, 184 N. Y. Supp. 199 (1920), 114
  Misc. 673, 187 N. Y. Supp. 873 (1921) 393
Burke v. Fay, 128 Mo. App. 690, 107 S. W. 408 (1908) 396
Burnham v. Dowd, 217 Mass. 351, 104 N. E. 841 (1914) 394
Butterfield v. Forester, 11 East 60 (England 1809) 231
Butterick Publishing Co. v. Typographical Union, 50 Misc. 1, 100
  N. Y. Supp. 292 (1906) 399, 402

Carew v. Rutherford, 106 Mass. 1 (1870) 396
Carter v. Carter Coal Company, 56 Sup. Ct. 855 (1936) 128
Chaffee v. U. S., 18 Wall. 516 (1873) 493
Chamberlain v. Andrews, et al., 241 N. Y. 1 (1936) 314
Chase v. McDonnell, 24 Ill. 237 (1860) 342
Chicago, Burlington & Quincy R. R. Co. v. McGuire, 219 U. S. 549,
  31 Sup. Ct. 259 (1911) 458, 533
Chicago, Rock Island and Pacific R. Co. v. Arkansas, 219 U. S. 453,
  31 Sup. Ct. 275 (1911) 218
Children's Hospital v. Adkins, 284 Fed. 613 (1922) 78
Church Shoe Co. v. Turner, 218 Mo. App. 516, 279 S. W. 232 (1926) 412
Cinderella Theater Co. Inc., et al. v. Sign Writers' Local Union No.
  591, 6 F. Supp. 164 (1934), 6 F. Supp. 830 (1934) 416

TABLE OF CASES CITED

City of Chicago v. Sturges, 222 U. S. 313, 32 Sup. Ct. 92 (1911) .. 404
City Trust, etc., Co. v. Waldhauer, 47 Misc. 7, 95 N. Y. Supp. 222
    (1905) 403, 404
In re Cleveland & Sandusky Brewing Co., 11 Fed. Supp. 198 (1935) 417
Clyatt v. U. S., 197 U. S. 207, 25 Sup. Ct. 429 (1904) 317, 318
Coffeyville, etc., Co. v. Perry, 69 Kan. 297, 76 Pac. 848 (1904) 405
Cohen v. Garment Workers, 35 Misc. 748, 72 N. Y. Supp. 341 (1901) 402
Commonwealth v. Beatty, 15 Super. Ct. (Pa.) 5 (1900) 114
Commonwealth v. Boston Transcript Company, 249 Mass. 477, 144
    N. E. 400 (1924) 68
Commonwealth v. Clark, 14 Pa. Super. 435 (1900) 405
Commonwealth v. Hamilton Mfg. Co., 120 Mass. 383 (1876) 113
Commonwealth v. Hunt, 4 Metcalf 111, 45 Mass. 111 (1842) 383
Commonwealth v. Lancaster Mills, 212 Mass. 315, 98 N. E. 864
    (1912) 337
Connally v. General Construction Co., 269 U. S. 385, 46 Sup. Ct. 126
    (1926) 76
Cook v. Wilson, 108 Misc. 438, 178 N. Y. Supp. 463 (1919) 396
Coppage v. Kansas, 236 U. S. 1, 35 Sup. Ct. 240 (1915) 377, 388, 407, 529
Coronado Coal Co. v. United Mine Workers, 268 U. S. 295, 45 Sup.
    Ct. 551 (1925) 386
Cote v. Murphy, 159 Pa. 420, 28 Atl. 190 (1894) 403, 404
Crisler v. Crum, et al., 115 Neb. 375, 213 N. W. 366 (1927) 389
Cunningham v. Northwestern Improvement Co., 44 Mont. 180, 119
    Pac. 554 (1911) 236
Curran v. Galen, 152 N. Y. 33, 46 N. E. 297 (1897) 392
Curran Printing Co. v. Printing Council, 5 Law & Labor 91 (1923) 386
Cusumano v. Schlessinger, 152 N. Y. Supp. 1081 (1915) 392
Cutting v. Cox, 19 Vt. 517 (1847) 342

Danbury hatters' case. See Loewe v. Lawlor.
Davis v. Mercer Lumber Co., 164 Ind. 413, 73 N. E. 899 (1905) .. 197
Dean v. Mayo, 8 F. Sup. 73 (1934) ; 9 F. Supp. 459 (1934) 416
In re Debs, 158 U. S. 564, 15 Sup. Ct. 900 (1895) 384
Dehan v. Hotel & Restaurant Employees, etc., 159 So. 637 (La.
    1935) 417
De Minico v. Craig, 207 Mass. 593, 94 N. E. 317 (1911) 390
Donham v. West Nelson Mfg. Co., 273 U. S. 657, 47 Sup. Ct. 343
    (1927) 56, 78
Dorchy v. Kansas, 272 U. S. 306, 47 Sup. Ct. 86 (1926) 396
Duplex Printing Press Co. v. Deering, 254 U. S. 443, 41 Sup. Ct. 172
    (1921) 384, 387, 394
Dyer Bros., etc., v. Central Iron Works, 182 Cal. 588, 189 Pac. 445
    (1920) 403

Eagle Glass & Mfg. Co. v. Rowe, 245 U. S. 275, 38 Sup. Ct. 80
    (1917) 406
Ellis v. United States, 206 U. S. 246, 27 Sup. Ct. 600 (1907) 119

588   PRINCIPLES OF LABOR LEGISLATION

Empire Theatre Co. *v.* Clarke, 53 Mont. 183, 163 Pac. 107 (1917) 399, 402
Employing Printers' Club *v.* Doctor Blosser Co., 122 Ga. 509, 50 S. E. 353 (1905) 399
Englemeyer *v.* Simon, *et al.,* 148 Misc. 621, 265 N. Y. Supp. 636 (1933) 402
Epperson *v.* Howell, 28 Idaho 338, 154 Pac. 621 (1916) 33
Erdman *v.* Mitchell, 207 Pa. 79, 56 Atl. 327 (1903) 393
Erie R. R. Co. *v.* New York, 233 U. S. 671, 34 Sup. Ct. 756 (1914) 124, 135, 142
Evansville Hoop & Stave Co. *v.* Bailey, 43 Ind. App. 153, 84 N. E. 549 (1908) 198
Everett-Waddey Co. *v.* Typographical Union, 105 Va. 188, 53 S. E. 273 (1906) 398
Exchange Bakery & Restaurant, Inc., *v.* Rifkin, 245 N. Y. 260, 157 N. E. 130 (1927) 392

Farwell *v.* Boston & W. R. Co., 4 Metcalf (Mass.) 49, 57 (1842) 229, 230
Fenske Bros., Inc., *v.* Upholsterers' Union, 358 Ill. 239, 193 N. E. 112 (1934) 399
Flaccus *v.* Smith, 199 Pa. 128, 48 Atl. 894 (1901) 399
Floersheimer *v.* Schlesinger, 115 Misc. 9, 187 N. Y. S. 891 (1921) 406
Florida Central R. Co. *v.* Reynolds, 183 U. S. 471, 22 Sup. Ct. 176 (1902) 493
Folding Furniture Works *v.* Industrial Commission of Wisconsin, 300 Fed. 991 (1924) 56
Folsom Engraving Co. *v.* McNeil, 235 Mass. 269, 126 N. E. 479 (1920) 392
Folsom *v.* Lewis, 208 Mass. 366, 94 N. E. 316 (1911) 391
Foster *v.* Retail Clerks, 39 Misc. 48, 78 N. Y. Supp. 860 (1902) .. 402
Frank *v.* Herold, 63 N. J. Eq. 443, 52 Atl. 152 (1901) 398
Franklin *v.* United Railways and Electric Co. of Baltimore, Baltimore Common Pleas Ct., April 27, 1904 236
Franklin Union *v.* People, 220 Ill. 355, 77 N. E. 176 (1906) 398

Gevas *v.* Greek Restaurant Workers' Club, *et al.,* 99 N. J. Eq. 770, 134 Atl. 309 (1926) 393, 398, 411
Gillchrist Co. *v.* Metal Polishers, 113 Atl. 320 (N. J. Ch. 1919) .. 396
Gillespie *v.* People, 188 Ill. 176, 58 N. E. 1007 (1900) 405
Gitlow *v.* People of New York, 268 U. S. 652, 45 Sup. Ct. 625 (1925) 388
Glass Co. *v.* Glass Blowers, 77 N. J. Eq. 219, 79 Atl. 262 (1911) .. 399
Godcharles *v.* Wigeman, 113 Pa. St. 431, 6 Atl. 354 (1886) 113
Goldfield Consolidated Mines Co. *v.* Miners' Union, 159 Fed. 500 (Nev. 1908) 398, 407
Goyette *v.* Watson Co., 245 Mass. 577, 140 N. E. 285 (1923) 390
Grant Bros. Construction Co. *v.* U. S., 232 U. S. 647, 34 Sup. Ct. 452 (1914) 350

TABLE OF CASES CITED 589

Grant Construction Co. v. St. Paul Building Trades Council, 136 Minn. 167, 161 N. W. 520 (1917) 393
Gray v. Building Trades Council, 91 Minn. 171, 97 N. W. 663 (1903) 393
Great Northern Ry. Co. v. Brosseau, 286 Fed. 414 (1923) 401, 414
Greenfield v. Central Labor Council, 104 Ore. 236, 192 Pac. 783 (1920) 399
Greenlee v. Southern R. Co., 122 N. C. 977, 30 S. E. 115 (1898) .. 215
Greenwood v. Building Trades Council, 71 Cal. App. 159, 233 Pac. 823 (1925) 393
Gregg v. Starks, 188 Ky. 834, 224 S. W. 459 (1920) 390
Grisson v. Pickett, 98 N. C. 54, 3 S. E. 921 (1887) 343
Gulla v. Barton, 164 App. Div. 293, 149 N. Y. Supp. 952 (1914) .. 390

Haley v. Chicago & Northwestern R. Co., 21 Iowa 15 (1866) 231
Hall v. Johnson, 87 Ore. 21, 169 Pac. 515 (1917) 399
Halsell v. First National Bank, 109 Okla. 220, 235 Pac. 532 (1925).. 342
Hammer v. Dagenhart, 247 U. S. 251, 38 Sup. Ct. 529 (1918) 173
Hammock v. Creekmore, 48 Ark. 264, 3 S. W. 180 (1886) 341
Harrison v. Ricks, 71 N. C. 7 (1874) 341
Haskins v. Royster, 70 N. C. 601 (1874) 399
Hawkins v. Bleakley, 243 U. S. 210, 37 Sup. Ct. 255 (1917) 238
Hennington v. Georgia, 163 U. S. 299, 16 Sup. Ct. 1086 (1896) 153
Hennington v. State, 90 Ga. 396, 17 S. E. 1009 (1892) 153
Henry v. Century Shoe Co. 12 *Law & Labor* 7 (Mass. Super. Ct., 1929) 392
Hilton v. Sheridan Coal Co., 132 Kan. 525, 297 Pac. 413 (1931) .. 409
Hitchman Coal & Coke Co. v. Mitchell, 202 Fed. 512 (1912); 245 U. S. 229, 38 Sup. Ct. 65 (1917) 389, 406
Hoban v. Dempsey, 217 Mass. 166, 104 N. E. 717 (1914) 392
Holcombe v. Creamer, 231 Mass. 99, 120 N. E. 354 (1918) 77
Holden v. Hardy, 169 U. S. 366, 18 Sup. Ct. 383 (1898) 114, 136, 238, 461, 462, 464, 526, 527, 528
Hopper v. Haines, 71 Md. 64, 18 Atl. 29, 20 Atl. 159 (1889) 343
Hudson v. Cincinnati, etc., Ry. Co., 152 Ky. 711, 154 S. W. 47 (1913) 389
Hughes v. Motion Picture Operators, 282 Mo. 304, 221 S. W. 95 (1920) 399, 402

Illinois Central R. R. Co. v. International Association of Machinists, 190 Fed. 910 (1911) 412
Interborough Rapid Transit Co. v. Green, 131 Misc. 682, 227 N. Y. Supp. 258 (1928) 407
Interborough Rapid Transit Co. v. Lanvin, 247 N. Y. 65, 159 N. E. 863 (1928) 407
International Organization, U. M. W. A. v. Leevale Coal Co., 285 Fed. 32 (1922) 406
International Organization U. M. W. A. v. Red Jacket C. C. & C. Co., 18 F. (2d) 839 (1927) 397, 406
Interstate Commerce Commission v. U. S. *ex rel.* Humboldt Steamship Co., 224 U. S. 474 (1911) 32 Sup. Ct. 556 520

Ives v. South Buffalo R. Co., 201 N. Y. 271, 94 N. E. 431 (1911)
237, 240, 528

Jackson v. Berger, 92 Ohio St. 130, 110 N. E. 732 (1915) 405
Jackson v. Brown, 3 *Law & Labor* 53 (1921) 392
In re Jacobs, 98 N. Y. 98 (1885) 206, 464
Jacobs v. Cohen, 183 N. Y. 207, 76 N. E. 5 (1905) 392
Jeans Clothing Co. v. Watson, 168 Mo. 133, 67 S. W. 391 (1902) .. 402
Jensen v. St. Paul M. P. Machine Operators' Local Union, 194 Minn.
    58, 259 N. W. 811 (1935) 417
Jersey Printing Co. v. Cassidy, 63 N. J. Eq. 759, 53 Atl. 230 (1902) 398
Jetton-Dekle v. Mather, 53 Fla. 969, 43 So. 590 (1907) 394
Johnson v. Aetna Life Ins. Co., 158 Wis. 56, 147 N. W. 32 (1914) 409
Johnson v. Goodyear Mining Co., 127 Cal. 4, 59 Pac. 304 (1899) 331
Ex parte Jones, 71 W. Va. 567, 77 S. E. 1029 (1913) 521

Kelly v. Rummerfield, 117 Wis. 620, 94 N. W. 649 (1903) 342
Kemp v. Division 241, 255 Ill. 213, 99 N. E. 389 (1912) 393
Keoleg v. Phelps, 80 Mich. 466, 45 N. W. 350 (1890) 343
Keuffel & Esser v. Machinists, 93 N. J. Eq. 429, 116 Atl. 9 (1922) 399
Kimpton v. Bronson, 45 Barb. 625 (1866) 315
Kirmse, et al., v. Adler, et al., 311 Pa. 78, 166 Atl. 566 (1933) 399
Kisson v. Printing Co., 199 N. Y. 76, 92 N. E. 214 (1910) 392
Knapp-Monarch Co. v. Anderson, et al., 7 F. Supp. 332 (1934) 416
Knickerbocker Ice Co. v. Stewart, 253 U. S. 149, 40 Sup. Ct. 438
    (1920) 242
Knoxville Iron Co. v. Harbison, 183 U. S. 13, 22 Sup. Ct. 1 (1901) 532
Kolley v. Robinson, 109 C. C. A. 247, 187 Fed. 415 (1911) 399
Kronowitz, et al., v. Schlausky, et al., 282 N. Y. Supp. 564 (1935) . 417

Laclede Steel Co. v. Newton, 6 F. Supp. 625 (1934), 80 F. (2d)
    636 (1935) 416
LaFrance Electrical & Supply Co. v. Electrical Workers, 108 Ohio
    St. 61, 140 N. E. 899 (1923) 399
In re Langell, 178 Mich. 305, 144 N. W. 841 (1914) 398
LaRose v. Possehl, et al., 282 N. Y. Supp. 332 (1935) 417
Larsen v. Rice, 100 Wash. 642, 171 Pac. 1037 (1918) 77
Lawler v. Loewe, 187 Fed. 522 (1911) 412
Lehigh Structural Steel Co. v. Atlantic, etc., Works, 92 N. J. Eq.
    131, 111 Atl. 376 (1920) 393
Lenahan v. Pittston Coal Mining Co., 218 Pa. 311, 67 Atl. 642 (1907) 175
Levering & Garrigues Co. v. Morrin, 71 F. (2d) 284 (1934) 416
Levy v. Rosenstein, 66 N. Y. Supp. 101 (1900) 398
Lindsey & Co. v. Montana Federation of Labor, 37 Mont. 264, 96
    Pac. 127 (1908) 402
Lisse v. Local Union No. 31, 2 Cal. (2d) 312, 41 Pac. (2d) 314
    (1935) 399, 402
Local Union v. Stathakis, 135 Ark. 86, 205 S. W. 450 (1918) 399
Lochner v. New York, 198 U. S. 45, 25 Sup. Ct. 539 (1905)
138, 458, 460, 462

TABLE OF CASES CITED 591

Loewe v. Lawlor, 208 U. S. 274, 28 Sup. Ct. 301 (1908) 385, 401, 402, 412
Lohse Patent Door Co. v. Fuelle, 215 Mo. 421, 114 S. W. 997 (1908) 402
Louisville, Henderson & St. Louis R. Co. v. Lyons, 155 Ky. 396, 159 S. W. 971 (1913) 175
Low v. Reese Printing Co., 41 Neb. 127, 59 N. W. 362 (1894) 139

McCord v. Thompson-Starrett Co., 198 N. Y. 587, 92 N. E. 1090 (1910) 392
McGrath v. Norman, 221 App. Div. 804, 223 N. Y. Supp. 288 (1927) 404
ex parte H. V. McKay, 2 C. A. R. 1 (Australia) 446
McLean v. Arkansas, 211 U. S. 539, 29 Sup. Ct. 206 (1909)
332, 463, 533
McMichael v. Atlanta Envelope Co., 151 Ga. 776, 108 S. E. 226 (1921) 398
Magee v. Chicago & Northwestern R. Co., 82 Iowa 249, 48 N. W. 92 (1891) 228
Malette v. City of Spokane, 77 Wash. 205, 137 Pac. 496 (1913) 75
Marbury v. Madison, 1 Cranch 137 (1803) 523
Matthews v. People, 202 Ill. 389, 67 N. E. 28 (1903) 14
Matthews v. Shankland, 25 Misc. 604, 56 N. Y. Supp. 123 (1898) 402
Maxwell v. Reed, 7 Wis. 582 (1859) 75
Mayer, *et al.*, v. Journeymen Stone Cutters' Assn., *et al.*, 47 N. J. Eq. 519, 20 Atl. 492 (1890) 389
Metropolitan Water District v. Whitsett, 10 Pac. (2nd) 751 (California, 1932) 76
Metzler v. Kaminer, 131 Misc. 813, 227 N. Y. Supp. 459 (1927) 390, 396
Micamold Radio Corp. v. Beedie, 156 Misc. 390, 282 N. Y. Supp. 77 (1935) 417
Michaels v. Hillman, 112 Misc. 395, 183 N. Y. Supp. 195 (1920) .. 412
Michaelson v. U. S., 266 U. S. 42, 45 Sup. Ct. 18 (1924) 387
Middleton v. Stark, 2 *Law & Labor* 121 (Super. Ct. Wash. 1920) 403
Miller v. Wilson, 236 U. S. 373, 35 Sup. Ct. 342 (1915) 115, 465
Miller Parlor Furniture Co., Inc., v. Furniture Workers' Industrial Union, 8 F. Supp. 209 (1934) 416
Miller Telephone Co. v. Minimum Wage Commission, 145 Minn. 262, 177 N. W. 341 (1920) 77
Millet v. People, 117 Ill. 294, 7 N. E. 631 (1886) 113
Mills v. U. S. Printing Co., 99 App. Div. 605, 91 N. Y. Supp. 185 (1904) 402
Minasian v. Osborne, 210 Mass. 250, 96 N. E. 1036 (1911) 392
Minneapolis, St. Paul and Sault Ste. Marie R. Co. v. Railroad Commission of Wisconsin, 136 Wis. 146, 116 N. W. 905 (1908) 219
Minnesota Rate Cases, 230 U. S. 352, 33 Sup. Ct. 729 (1913) 135
A. J. Monday Co. v. Automobile Workers, 171 Wis. 532, 177 N. W. 867 (1920) 399
Montgomery, *et al.*, v. Pac. Elec. Ry. Co., 293 Fed. 680 (Cal. 1923)
406, 407
Moody v. Model Window Glass Co., 145 Ark. 197, 224 S. W. 436 (1920), 150 Ark. 142, 233 S. W. 1092 (1921) 390

592   PRINCIPLES OF LABOR LEGISLATION

Morehead v. People, ex rel. Tipaldo, 56 Sup. Ct. 918 (1936) 57, 80
In re Morgan, 26 Colo. 415, 58 Pac. 1071 (1899) 136, 459, 464
Mountain Timber Co. v. Washington, 243 U. S. 219, 37 Sup. Ct. 260 (1917) 238, 239, 240
Muller v. Oregon, 208 U. S. 412, 28 Sup. Ct. 324 (1908) . 114, 461, 462
Mullins Body Corp. v. International Assoc., 3 *Law & Labor* 149 (1921) 404
Murphy v. Sardell, 269 U. S. 530, 46 Sup. Ct. 22 (1925) 56, 78
Murray v. South Carolina R. Co., 1 McMullan 385 (1841) 230

Nann v. Raimist, 255 N. Y. 307, 174 N. E. 690 (1931) 398
National Employment Exchange v. Geraghty, U. S. Circuit Court of Appeals, Second Circuit, July 29, 1932 10
National Protective Assoc. v. Cumming, 170 N. Y. 315, 63 N. E. 369 (1902) 392
Neal v. Brandon, 70 Ark. 79, 66 S. W. 200 (1902) 342
New England, etc., Co. v. McGivern, 218 Mass. 198, 105 N. E. 885 (1914) 393
New York Central R. Co. v. White, 243 U. S. 188, 37 Sup. Ct. 247 (1917) 238
Newton Co. v. Erickson, 126 N. Y. Supp. 949 (1911); 129 N. Y. Supp. 1111 (1911), 221 N. Y. 632, 117 N. E. 1059 (1917) 394
Noble State Bank v. Haskell, 219 U. S. 104, 31 Sup. Ct. 186 (1911) 528
Noe v. Layton, 69 Ark. 551, 64 S. W. 880 (1910) 343
Northern Pacific Ry. v. Washington, 222 U. S. 370, 32 Sup. Ct, 160 (1912) 135

O'Brien v. People, 216 Ill. 354, 75 N. E. 108 (1905) 393
O'Brien v. U. S., 290 Fed. 185 (1923) 386
O'Neil v. Behanna, 182 Pa. 236, 37 Atl. 843 (1897) 399
In re Opinion of the Justices, 86 N. H. 597, 166 Atl. 640 (1933) . 417
In re Opinion of the Justices, 271 Mass. 598, 171 N. E. 234 (1930) 417
Otis Steel Co. v. Molders, 110 Fed. 698 (1901) 399

Panama Refining Co. v. Ryan, 293 U. S. 388, 55 Sup. Ct. 241 (1935) 91
Parker Paint & Wall Paper Co. v. Local Union, 87 W. Va. 631, 105 S. E. 911 (1921) 404
Parkinson Co. v. Building Trade Council, 154 Cal. 581, 98 Pac. 1027 (1908) 390, 394, 402
Parrish v. West Coast Hotel Company, 55 Pac. (2d) 1083 (1936) .. 81
Patterson v. Building Trades Council, 11 Pa. Dist. 500 (1902) 394
Peel Splint Coal Co. v. State, 36 W. Va. 802, 15 S. E. 1000 (1892) 528
Penn Anthracite Mining Co. v. Anthracite Miners of Pa., et al., 114 Pa. Super. 7, 174 Atl. 11 (Pa. 1934) 417
Pennsylvania R. Co. v. Ewing, et al., 241 Pa. 581, 88 Atl. 775 (1913) 218
Pennsylvania R. R. Co. v. International Mining Co., 230 U. S. 196, 274 (1912) 520
People v. Balofsky, 167 N. Y. App. Div. 913 (1915) 207
People v. Barondess, 133 N. Y. 649, 31 N. E. 240 (1892) 396

TABLE OF CASES CITED 593

People v. Chicago, Milwaukee and St. Paul Railway Company, 306 Ill. 486, 138 N. E. 155 (1923) 370
People v. Elerding, 254 Ill. 579, 98 N. E. 982 (1912) 115
People v. Erie R. R. Co., 198 N. Y. 369, 91 N. E. 849 (1910) 134
People v. Ewer, 141 N. Y. 129, 36 N. E. 4 (1894) 99
People v. Fisher, 14 Wendell 9, N. Y. (1835) 382
People v. Klinck Packing Co., 214 N. Y. 121, 108 N. E. 278 (1915) 152, 154
People v. Kostka, 4 N. Y. Crim. 429 (1886) 401
People v. Marcus, 185 N. Y. 257, 77 N. E. 1073 (1906) 407
People v. N. Y. C. & H. R. R. Co., 163 App. Div. (N. Y.) 79 (1914) 142
People v. Radt, 15 N. Y. Cr. 174, 71 N. Y. Supp. 846 (1900) 402
People v. Ruggles, 8 Johnson (N. Y.) 289, 5 Am. Dec. 335 (1811) 153
People v. Charles Schweinler Press, 214 N. Y. 395, 108 N. E. 639 (1915) 142, 146, 461, 463, 473
People v. Steelik, 187 Cal. 361, 203 Pac. 78 (1921) 389
People v. Walczak, 315 Ill. 49, 145 N. E. 660 (1924) 396
People v. Western Union Tel. Co., 70 Colo. 90, 198 Pac. 146 (1921) 407
People v. Williams, 189 N. Y. 131, 81 N. E. 778 (1907) 145, 459, 462, 463
People v. Wilzig, 4 N. Y. Crim. 403 (1886) 401
People ex rel. Armstrong v. Warden of the City Prison of N. Y., 183, N. Y. 223, 76 N. E. 11 (1905) 9
People ex rel. Cossey v. Grout, 179 N. Y. 417, 72 N. E. 464 (1904) 132
People ex rel. Tipaldo v. Morehead, 270 N. Y. 233 (1936) 56, 80
People ex rel. Williams Eng. and Cont. Co. v. Metz, 193 N. Y. 148, 85 N. E. 1070 (1908) 133
Pickett v. Walsh, 192 Mass. 572, 78 N. E. 753 (1906) 392, 393
Pierce v. Stablemen, 156 Cal. 70, 103 Pac. 324 (1909) 398, 402
Plant v. Woods, 176 Mass. 492, 57 N. E. 1011 (1900) 391
Thomas G. Plant Co. v. Gould, 2 *Law & Labor* 276 (1920) 392
Price v. People, 193 Ill. 114, 61 N. E. 844 (1901) 9
Priestly v. Fowler, 3 Meeson and Welsby 1 (England, 1837) .. 228, 229
Purvis v. Carpenters, 214 Pa. 348, 63 Atl. 585 (1906) 394

Radice v. New York, 264 U. S. 292, 44 Sup. Ct. 325 (1924) 146
Railroad Retirement Board v. Alton Railroad Co., 295 U. S. 330, 55 Sup. Ct. 758 (1935) 284
Randall v. Ditch, 123 Ia. 582, 99 N. W. 190 (1904) 343
Reed Co. v. Whiteman, 238 N. Y. 545, 144 N. E. 885 (1924) 401
Reynolds v. Davis, 198 Mass. 294, 84 N. E. 457 (1908) 391, 396
Ribner v. Rasco Co., 135 Misc. 616, 238 N. Y. Supp. 132 (1929) 390
Ribnick v. McBride, 277 U. S. 350, 48 Sup. Ct. 545 (1928) 10
Rice, Barton & Fales Machine, etc., Co. v. Willard, 242 Mass. 566, 136 N. E. 629 (1922) 406
Riley v. Commonwealth, 232 U. S. 671, 34 Sup. Ct. 469 (1914) 109
Ex parte Riley, 94 Ala. 82, 10 So. 528 (1891) 323
Ritchie v. People, 155 Ill. 98, 40 N. E. 454 (1895) .. 113, 460, 463, 464

Ritchie v. Wayman, 244 Ill. 509, 91 N. E. 695 (1910) 115, 463, 464, 527
Robertson v. Baldwin, 165 U. S. 287, 17 Sup. Ct. 326 (1897) 324
Root v. Anderson, 207 S. W. 255 (Mo. App. 1918) 402
Ryan v. Hayes, 243 Mass. 168, 137 N. E. 344 (1922) 392

Safeway Stores, Inc., v. Retail Clerks' Union, Local No. 148, et al., 51 P. (2d) 372 (Wash. 1935) 417
St. Germain v. Bakery Workers, 97 Wash. 282, 166 Pac. 665 (1917) 399
Schechter Poultry Corp v. United States, 295 U. S. 495, 55 Sup. Ct. 837 (1935) 57, 419, 424
Schlesinger v. Quinto, 201 App. Div. 487, 194 N. Y. Supp. 401 (1922) 390
Segenfeld v. Friedman, 117 Misc. 731, 193 N. Y. Supp. 128 (1922) 398
Shaughnessy v. Jordan, 184 Ind. 499, 111 N. E. 622 (1916) 399
Shinsky v. O'Neil, 232 Mass. 99, 121 N. E. 790 (1919) 392
Shoemaker v. Crawford, 82 Mo. App. 487 (1900) 342
Simpson v. O'Hara, 70 Ore. 261, 141 Pac. 158 (1914) 77
Sinsheimer v. Garment Workers, 77 Hun. 215, 28 N. Y. Supp. 321 (1894) 402, 404
Smith v. Alabama, 124 U. S. 465, 8 Sup. Ct. 564 (1888) 134
Smith v. Atchison, Topeka and Santa Fe Railway Co., 39 Tex. Civ. App. 468, 87 S. W. 1052 (1905) 123
Smith v. Bowen, 232 Mass. 106, 121 N. E. 814 (1919) 392
Smythe v. Ames, 169 U. S. 466, 18 Sup. Ct. 418 (1897) 449
Snow Iron Works v. Chadwick, 227 Mass. 382, 116 N. E. 801 (1917) 391
Southern California Iron & Steel Co. v. Iron & Steel Workers, 186 Cal. 604, 200 Pac. 1 (1921) 398
Southern Pacific Co. v. Jensen, 244 U. S. 205, 37 Sup. Ct. 525 (1917) 242
Spokane Hotel Co. v. Younger, 113 Wash. 359, 194 Pac. 595 (1920) 77
State v. Ankham, et al., 31 Pac. (2nd) 888 (Arizona, 1934) 76
State v. Barba, 132 La. 768, 61 So. 784 (1913) 139
State v. Brown & Sharpe Mfg Co., 18 R. I. 16, 25 Atl. 246 (1892) 331, 529
State v. Buchanan, 29 Wash. 602, 70 Pac. 52 (1902) 114, 527
State v. Crowe, 130 Ark. 272, 197 S. W. 4 (1917) 77
State v. Daniels, 118 Minn. 155, 136 N. W. 584 (1912) 407
State v. Employers of Labor, 102 Neb. 768, 169 N. W. 717, 170 N. W. 185 (1918) 403
State v. Hennessy, 114 Wash. 351, 195 Pac. 211 (1921) 389
State v. Julow, 129 Mo. 163, 31 S. W. 781 (1895) 405
State v. Kassay, 126 Ohio St. 177, 184 N. E. 521 (1932) 389
State v. Kreutzberg, 114 Wis. 530, 90 N. W. 1098 (1903) 405
State v. Lange Canning Co., 164 Wis. 228, 160 N. W. 57 (1916) 157
State v. Martin, 193 Ind. 120, 139 N. E. 282 (1923) 331
State v. Napier, 63 S. C. 60, 41 S. E. 13 (1902) 9
State v. J. J. Newman Lumber Co., 102 Miss. 802, 59 So. 923; 103 Miss. 263, 60 So. 215 (1912) 139
State v. Nicholls, 77 Ore. 415, 151 Pac. 473 153
State v. Pocock, 161 Minn. 376, 201 N. W. 610 (1925) 155

TABLE OF CASES CITED 595

State v. Roberson, 136 N. C. 587, 48 S. E. 595 (1904) 9
State v. Van Pelt, 136 N. C. 633, 49 S. E. 177 (1904) 394
State Board of Control v. Buchstegge, 18 Ariz. 277, 158 Pac. 837 (1916) 277
State of Washington v. Dawson & Co., 264 U. S. 219, 44 Sup. Ct. 302 (1924) 242
State ex rel. Buell v. Frear, 146 Wis. 305, 131 N. W. 832 (1911) 157
State ex rel. Mays v. Brown, 71 W. Va. 519, 77 S. E. 243 (1912) 521
State ex rel. Yaple v. Creamer, 85 Ohio St. 349, 97 N. E. 602 (1912) 463
A. T. Stearns Lumber Co. v. Howlett, 260 Mass. 45, 157 N. E. 82 (1927), 163 N. E. 193 (1928) 392, 394
Steel v. Frick, 56 Pa. St. 172 (1867) 341
Steffes v. Motion Picture Operators, 136 Minn. 200, 161 N. W. 524 (1917) 399
Stettler v. O'Hara, 69 Ore. 519, 139 Pac. 743 (1914); 243 U. S. 629, 37 Sup. Ct. 475 (1917) 76, 116
Stivers v. Blethen, 124 Wash. 473, 215 Pac. 7 (1923) 389
Stockwell v. U. S., 13 Wall, 531 (1871) 493
Sun Printing & Publishing Assoc. v. Delaney, 48 Ap. Div. 623, 62 N. Y. Supp. 750 (1900) 402
Sutton v. Unity Button Works, Inc., 144 Misc. 784, 258 N. Y. Supp. 863 (1932) 390
In re Sweitzer, 13 Okla. Crim. 154, 162 Pac. 1134 (1917) 399
Swift v. Hague, 2 *Law & Labor*, 9 (1919) 404

Taylor v. Bradley, 39 N. Y. 129 (1868) 342
Texas & N. O. Ry. Co. v. Brotherhood of Railway and Steamship Clerks, 281 U. S. 548, 50 Sup. Ct. 427 (1930) 411, 421
Thomas v. Cincinnati, etc., R. R. Co., 62 Fed. 803 (1894) 393
Topeka Laundry Co. v. Court of Industrial Relations, 119 Kans. 12 (1925) 56
Tracy v. Osborne, 226 Mass. 25, 114 N. E. 959 (1917) 390
Trade Press Publishing Co. v. Milwaukee Typographical Union, 180 Wis. 449, 193 N. W. 507 (1923) 403
Truax v. Bisbee Local No. 380, 19 Ariz. 379, 171 Pac. 121 (1918) 399, 401, 402
Truax v. Corrigan, 20 Ariz. 7, 176 Pac. 570 (1918) 402
Truax v. Corrigan, 257 U. S. 312, 42 Sup. Ct. 124 (1921) 377, 384, 387, 400
Truax v. Raich, 239 U. S. 33, 36 Sup. Ct. 7 (1915) 351
Tunstall v. Stearns Coal Co., 192 Fed. 808 (1911) 398

United Chain Theaters v. Philadelphia M. P. M. O. Union, 50 F. (2d) 189 (1931) 401
United Electric Coal Co. v. Rice, 9 F. Supp. 635 (1934); 80 Fed. (2d) 1 (1935) 416, 417
United Hat Manufacturers v. Baird-Unteidt Co., 88 Conn. 332, 91 Atl. 373 (1914) 403
United Mine Workers v. Coronado Coal Co., 259 U. S. 344, 42 Sup. Ct. 570 (1922) 412

596 PRINCIPLES OF LABOR LEGISLATION

United States v. Atchison, Topeka and Santa Fe Railway Co., 220 U. S. 37, 31 Sup. Ct. 362 (1911) 134
U. S. v. Bricklayers' Union, 4 *Law & Labor* 95 (1922) 386
United States v. Chicago, Milwaukee and Puget Sound R. R. Co., 197 Fed. 624 (1912) 133
United States v. Edgar, 1 C. C. A. 49, 48 Fed. 91 (1891) 350
United States v. Gay, 37 C. C. A. 46, 95 Fed. 226 (1899) 350
United States v. Kansas City Southern R. R. Co., 202 Fed. 828, 121 C. C. A. 136 (1913) 133
U. S. v. Norris, 255 Fed. 423 (1918) 386
U. S. v. Northern Commercial Co. and George A. Coleman (1918) 140
U. S. v. Railway Employees' Dept. A. F. of L. 283 Fed. 479 (1922); 286 Fed. 228 (1923); 290 Fed. 978 (1923) 386, 397
United States v. Southern Pacific Co., 136 C. C. A. 351, 220 Fed. 745 (1915) 134

Vandalia R. Co. v. Public Service Commission of Indiana, 242 U. S. 255, 37 Sup. Ct. 93 (1916) 219
Vandalia R. Co. v. Railroad Commission of Indiana, 182 Ind. 382, 101 N. E. 85 (1913) 219
Vandell v. U. S., 6 Fed. (2d) 188 (1925) 386
Vegelahn v. Guntner, 167 Mass. 92, 44 N. E. 1077 (1896) 397, 398
Viemeister v. White, 179 N. Y. 235, 72 N. E. 97 (1904) 461
Vonnegut Machinery Co. v. Toledo Machine & Tool Co., 263 Fed. 192 (1920) 399

Walters v. City of Indianapolis, 191 Ind. 671, 134 N. E. 482 (1922) 399
Weber v. Nasser, 286 Pac. 1074 (Cal. App. 1930) 390
Wenham v. State, 65 Neb. 394, 91 N. W. 421 (1902) 114
Western Union v. International Brotherhood, 2 F. (2d) 993 (1924) 396
White Mountain Freezer Co. v. Murphy, 78 N. H. 398, 101 Atl. 357 (1917) 397, 399
Whitey v. Bloem, 163 Mich. 419, 128 N. W. 913 (1910) 115
Whitfield v. State of Ohio, 56 Sup. Ct. 532 (1936) 361
Whitney v. California, 274 U. S. 357, 47 Sup. Ct. 641 (1927) 388
Williams v. Evans, 139 Minn. 32, 165 N. W. 495 (1917) 77
Williams v. Fears, 110 Ga. 584, 35 S. E. 699 (1900); 179 U. S. 270, 21 Sup. Ct. 128 (1900) 9
Ex parte Williams, 158 Cal. 550, 11 Pac. 1035 (1910) 398
Wilson v. New, 243 U. S. 332, 37 Sup. Ct. 289 (1917) 136
Wilson v. Stewart, 69 Ala. 302 (1881) 343
Wiseman v. Tanner, 221 Fed. 694 (1914) 9
Wolff Packing Co. v. Court of Industrial Relations, 262 U. S. 522, 43 Sup. Ct. 630 (1923); 267 U. S. 552, 45 Sup. Ct. 441 (1925) 377, 438

Yalenezian v. City of Boston, 238 Mass. 538, 131 N. E. 220 (1921) 404
Yazoo & M. V. R. Co. v. Sideboard, 161 Miss. 4, 133 So. 669 (1931) 390

INDEX

Accident prevention, exclusion of persons, 169-194; prohibition of substances or instruments, 194-196; regulation, 196-219; in relation to workmen's compensation, 255, 256, 498

Accident reporting, 161-164, 257

Accidents, statistics, 163-165

Action of debt used in enforcing labor laws, 493

Adamson law, 124, 125, 135

Administration, employment offices, 13-17; minimum wage laws, 64-68; hours laws, 96, 109-112; child labor laws, 96, 181-185; workmen's compensation laws, 233, 234, 251-253; health insurance laws, 258-264; old age insurance laws, 280-282; unemployment insurance laws, 296, 297, 312-313; importance of, 448; the executive, 449-452; the legislature, 452-458; the judiciary, 458, 465; the labor department, 465-483; and civil service, 486-488; and bill drafting, 488-489; and prosecutions, 490-548; cooperation by pressure, 498-501; and public authorities, 523

See also Enforcement of labor laws.

Administrative regulation, of hours, 106-109, 115, 116, 129, 144, 152, 157; constitutionality, 115, 116, 152, 157; exclusion of children from dangerous employments, 175; boiler rules, 199; lighting codes, 201; railroad safety, 215, 216, 219; growth of, 219-223; and collective bargaining, 378; in labor legislation, 467-483; and representation of interests, 475-482

Advisory committees, for employment offices, 13, 14, 15, 17, 22, 25; in minimum wage fixing, 66, 67; in labor law administration, 475-482

Agricultural workers, employment offices for, 16, 22, 24, 26; accidents, 164; classes described, 339-343; labor legislation for, 343-345

Alien contract labor. *See* Induced immigration.

American Association for Labor Legislation, unemployment survey, 29; one-day-of-rest-in-seven study, 152; drafts accident reporting law, 162; drafts occupational disease reporting law, 166; study of court administration in New Jersey, 252; health insurance standards, 269; and labor law administration, 451; organization of, 454

Apprenticeship, and minimum wages, 63, 72; in colonial times, 169; unfree status of, 316, 504; characteristics, 321, 332; Wisconsin regulations for, 470

Arbitration, voluntary, 430, 431; compulsory, 431, 437-447; in Kansas, 437-439; in Australasia, 439-447; in New Zealand, 441-444; in Australia, 444-447

Assignment of wages, 329

Assumption of risk, 231, 240, 513; and child labor, 175; and safety, 197

Aviation, safety regulations, 212

Bargaining power, and minimum wage laws, 43; and collective bargaining, 372-373; and equality, 509; and equal protection of the laws, 528-534

Bill drafting, 466, 472, 488, 489

Blacklist, legal status of, 408, 409

Blue laws for Sunday observance, 149

Boiler explosions, measures against, 199

Boycott, legal status, 401-403; damage suit against, 411, 412

Bureaucracy in the administration of labor laws, 476

Casual laborers, decasualization, 40, 41

Child labor, employment offices for juveniles, 15, 19; and minimum wages, 57, 63, 64, 78, 469; hours legislation, 95-99, 146, 152; federal regulation, 98, 172-174; night work, 146; age requirements, 169-178; extra compensation for illegally employed minors, 175, 176; physical requirements, 178-180; educational requirements, 180, 181; enforcement problems, 181-185; and tenement-house manufacture, 206-208; in indentured service, 321; competition of, 345, 503; safety regulations, 470

Child labor legislation, federal, 98, 172-174, 185; problems of enforcement, 181-186; cumulative penalties, 492; justified by guardianship power of state, 512; in relation to commerce and police powers, 515

Childbirth, protection of women before and after, 188

Chinese exclusion laws, 354-355

Citizenship, voting rights protected, 370, 371; stage in labor legislation, 525

Civil service, for employment offices, 26; in labor law administration, 486-488

Civilian Conservation Corps, 31

Class legislation, 473; and equal protection of the laws, 528-534

Class struggle in labor legislation, 481, 500, 526

Closed shop, strikes for, 391-393

Collective bargaining, defined, 372-374; legal attitudes toward, described, 374-376, 417-419; government agencies affecting, 376-379; evolution of law on, 379-388; the law before the New Deal, 388-419; the rights of labor, 388-403; rights of employer, 403-411; enforcement of rights in, 411-417; precursors of the New Deal, 419-423; under Section 7a, 423, 424; under the National Labor Relations Act, 424-429; government intervention in, 429-447; and representation of interests, 479

Colonial stage of labor legislation, 525

Commerce power, 515

Commission plan, applied to safety regulations, 199, 221; under workmen's compensation, 252; of labor law administration, 466-486

Company houses, regulated, 333

Company stores, in relation to peonage, 319; regulated, 333, 334

Company unions, employer's right to organize, 409-411; restrictions in National Labor Relations Act, 425

Competition, of women and children, 48, 345; in relation to labor legislation, 345-361, 503; of immigrants, 346-357; of Orientals, 353-355; of convict labor, 357-361

Compressed air work, hours regulated, 129, 142; workers barred from, 189; safety regulations, 191, 211, 212

INDEX 599

Conciliation in labor disputes, 430
Congress, organized labor and capital in, 487; and the police power, 520; in relation to Constitution, 522
Conspiracy, doctrine of, 381-383
Constitutionality of laws, employment agency laws, 8-10; of minimum wage laws, 55-57, 74-81; federal hours law for children, 98, 99; hours laws for women, 112-116; of administrative regulations, 115, 116; hours laws for men, 124, 132-140; night work restrictions, 145, 146; rest-day laws, 153-155; federal laws fixing minimum age limit for child labor, 172, 173, 175; labor contract, 232, 233; workmen's compensation, 238-242; wage payment laws, 331, 332; of compulsory arbitration, 439; how determined, 449, 458-465, 494, 519, 524, 526; and judicial investigations, 458-465; of labor laws, 530, 531
Continuation schools, 181
Contract, yellow-dog, 387, 389, 406-408
Contract labor, servile characteristics, 316, 321-325
Contributory negligence, and child labor legislation, 175; under employers' liability, 230, 231, 240
Convict labor, extent, 357-358; competition of, 359; regulation by state laws, 359, 360; federal legislation, 360, 361
Corporations and collective bargaining, 381
Court administration of workmen's compensation, 251, 252
Courts, small claims, 369; and collective bargaining, 377, 378
Croppers, 340-343

Damage suits in labor disputes, 385, 411-413
Debt, imprisonment for, and contract labor, 322, 323; abolished, 326, 327
Deductions from wages regulated, 334-337
Discharge, penalty for, without notice or cause, 42; employer's right, 405, 406
Dockers, decasualization of, 40
Dressing-rooms, legislation providing, 203, 212
Due process of law, 506, 509; and minimum wage laws, 74, 76; and investigations, 470, 476, 478

Education, requirements in child labor laws, 180, 181-185
Efficiency, and minimum wages, 73, 74; and hours of work, 85, 87, 88
Eight-hour day, in the United States, 83-85, 89; in foreign countries, 92, 94; international convention on, 94; for children, 97; in public work, 118, 121, 132; constitutionality, 132-140, 459
Election day holiday laws, 370, 371
Emergency work as unemployment relief, 27-32
Eminent domain, 512, 513
Employer and employee, law of, 316, 531
Employers' advances, 319, 323
Employers' associations, employment bureaus of, 6; right to form, 403; and representation of interests, 477
Employers' liability, rules of, 228-231; results, 231-232; and wage deductions, 336
Employment, statistics, 2; methods of finding, 5-6; regularization, 37-42; effect of minimum wages on, 71-72
Employment agencies, numbers, 6, 7; abuses, 7; restrictive legislation, 7-11; prohibition of, 8, 9, 11; constitutionality of legislation on, 8-11; international convention on, 11, 12; oppose public offices, 23

INDEX

Employment certificates for working children, 171, 179, 181-185
Employment offices, state and municipal, 12-17, 24; federal, 12, 13; number, 12, 13; standards, 13-17, 25, 26; advisory committees, 13, 14, 19, 25; policy in strikes, 14, 15; for juveniles, 15; transportation advances, 15, 17, 19; clearing, 16; for farm labor, 16, 22, 24, 26; foreign systems, 17-21; national subsidies for, 21, 25; international convention on, 21; federal-state system, 21-27; for longshoremen, 22; for veterans, 23, 24, 26; national reemployment service, 27; and public works, 27-37; and decasualization of labor, 40, 41; and seasonal employment, 42; and unemployment compensation, 297, 312
Enforcement of labor laws, hours, 96, 101, 102, 109-112, 145; child labor, 170, 178, 179, 181-185; effect of workmen's compensation on, 243; on collective bargaining, 411-417; importance of, 448; and the executive, 449-452; and the legislature, 452-458; and the judiciary, 458-465; and the labor department, 465-501; penalties and prosecutions, 490-498
Equality, and labor contract, 509; before the law, 528-534
Evidence in labor law enforcement, 495-498
Executive, and collective bargaining, 376, 377; and enforcement of labor laws, 449-452; and public authorities, 517-521
Exemption, wage, 327; homestead, 328

Factory inspection, 450, 451
Factory legislation, 449, 450
Fair wage. *See* Minimum wage.
Family allowance system, 54, 58
Fellow servant rule under employers' liability, 229, 240
Feudalism, 317

Fines, wage deductions, 334, 336, 337
Fire regulations, 199, 200
Firemen, hours regulated, 121

Garnishment, 327, 328, 362
Ghent system, unemployment insurance, 293, 294
Gilds, and collective bargaining, 379, 380; early health insurance, 454
Government, may use force, 511, 520, 521; as employer, 513; branches of, 517-523; intervention in bargaining, 528
Guardianship of state, 511, 512, 514

Habeas corpus, writ of, 506, 521
Head tax on immigrants, 347
Health, justification for minimum wage, 76; and hours of labor, 86, 87; and women's work, 103, 105, 112-116, 186-189; a social question, 158-160; types of legislation, 160; legal protection against infectious diseases, 204-208; and immigration legislation, 346
Health insurance, subsidized systems, 258; compulsory systems, 258-264; benefit funds, 259, 263, 264; coverage, 259-260; contributions, 260, 261, 264; benefits, 261-263; maternity insurance, 264-267; movement for, in the United States, 267-273
Heating regulations, 201, 202
Holidays, 147-149
Homestead laws, 328, 503, 526
Homework, regulated, 206-208
Hours of labor, shorter hours movement, 83-85, 88-95; federal legislation, 83, 85, 90, 92, 98; in relation to efficiency, 85, 87, 88; in relation to health and welfare, 86-88; laws for women, 86, 87, 99-116, 141, 152; foreign legislation, 92-94, 103, 128, 130, 150; laws for children, 95-99, 146, 152; regulation by administrative or-

der, 106-109; constitutionality, 112-116, 123, 132-140, 145, 146, 153-155, 459-464; laws for men, 116-138, 141; on public works, 117-121; in transportation industry, 122-127, 134, 135, 141; in mines and tunnels, 127-129; 136, 137; in factories and workshops, 130-132, 137-140; rest period requirements, 140-156; vacations, 155, 156

Humanitarian stage of labor legislation, 525, 526

Humidity in factories, 202

Immigration, immigrant employment offices, 21-22; Bureau of Immigration, 22; and low wages, 47, 48; purposes of regulation, 346-348; induced, 348, 349; the quota system, 350-352; exclusion of Orientals, 353-355; literacy test, 355-357

Imprisonment for debt, 322, 323, 326, 327, 526, 531

Indentured service, 316, 320, 321, 348, 504, 525

Individual bargaining and collective bargaining, 372-374

Induced immigration, laws against, 348-350

Industrial commission. *See* Commission plan.

Industrial courts in Europe, 367-368

Industrial education, and competition, 345; regulation of, 470

Industrial insurance, 290

Industrial pensions, 274, 275

Injunctions in labor disputes, early use of, 384; statutory restriction of, 385-387, 415-417; nature of, 413-415

Inspection, under child labor laws, 182-185; mines, 210, 211; new methods, 222, 493-498; partisanship in appointments, 486-488

Insurance, principle of, 224; in connection with workmen's compensation, 253-257; under health insurance, 259, 263, 264; voluntary life, 289, 290; under unemployment compensation, 307-309; in administration of labor legislation, 499-501

See also Social insurance.

International Association for Labor Legislation, convention on night work of women, 142, 143; convention on poisonous phosphorus, 194; history of, 452, 453

International Association for Social Progress, 454

International Association on Unemployment, 454

International Committee on Social Insurance, 454

International Labor Conference, on employment agencies, 11, 12; on employment offices, 14, 21; on public works, 37; on hours of labor, 94, 129, 130; on night work of women, 143; on night work of children, 146; on night work in bakeries, 147; on weekly rest days, 150, 151; on vacations with pay, 156; on child labor, 174, 175; on women's work in mines, 188; on childbirth protection, 188; on poisonous phosphorus, 194; on white lead in paint, 195, 196; on anthrax, 205; on maternity insurance, 267; on immigration, 350

International Labor Office, and employment offices, 21; on hours, 86; history of, 456, 457

International Labor Organization, and public works, 37; history of, 456, 457

Interstate Commerce, in relation to child labor, 172; hour regulations, 172; and convict labor, 359

Interstate compact on minimum wages, 57, 58

Invalidity insurance, 280-289

Investigation, compulsory in labor disputes, 431; state laws on, 433; by the executive, 450-452; by the legislature, 452-458; by private organizations, 452-454; by commissions, 454, 455; by labor bureaus, 455; by international labor organizations, 456, 457; by the judiciary, 458-465; administrative, 466-475

Judiciary, defines "cropper," 341; and contract labor laws, 349, 350; inadequacy to secure laborers' rights, 361, 362; in relation to investigation, 458-465, 527; and the police power, 516; and the legislative, 517-520; interprets laws and constitutions, 519, 520; authority, 522, 523; guided by opinions, 522-525, 528; changing opinions on labor, 525-528; considers labor legislation class legislation, 529; uses theory of reasonable classification, 529-532

Kansas industrial relations act, 437-439
King, as *parens patriae*, 512

Labor camps regulated, 333, 334
Labor contract, characteristics, 502-505; in relation to politics, 505; in relation to liberty and property, 507-509; in relation to equality, 509; restrictions on, 527; specific performance, 531
Labor Department, and employment offices, 16, 22, 25; types of, 482-486; and bill drafting, 489
Labor legislation, aims at equality, 316; relation to agriculture, 339, 343-345; relation to competition, 345-361; enforcement, 448-452, 490-498; solidarism in, 499-501; in relation to labor contract, 503, 510; relation to taxing power, 511, 515; relation to police power, 513-517; stages, 525-528; considered as class legislation, 528-530
Labor market, disorganized, 5; right of access to, 507, 508; influences on, 525

Land, laborer's lien on, 337; in relation to labor market, 503, 504, 525
Landlord and tenant, law of, 340-345
Lead trades, women barred from, 187; examination of workers, 190, 191; prohibition of white lead, 195; wash-rooms and dressing rooms for workers, 204
Legal aid, private organizations for, 363-364; public defenders, 364, 365; by labor departments, 365, 366; League of Nations' study of, 166, 167
Legislation, when constitutional, 449, 458-465, 494, 519, 524, 526
  See also Labor legislation.
Legislature, and collective bargaining, 377; and labor legislation, 452-457; function, 467; and administrative rule-making, 471; in relation to judiciary, 517-520; and public authorities, 521, 522
Liberty, of contract, 113-116, 132, 140, 331; in relation to property, 507-509; in relation to labor contract, 508-510; in relation to police power, 514
Licenses, for qualified workers, 192-194; in labor law enforcement, 497
Liens. *See* Mechanics' lien laws.
Life insurance, voluntary, 289, 290
Lighting regulations, 200, 201
Literacy test, for child workers, 180; for immigrants, 347, 355-357
"Living-in" system, 332
Lockout, employer's rights to, 404
Longshoremen, employment office for, 22; decasualization of work, 40, 41; workmen's compensation for, 242

Machine guards required, 197-199
Map, unemployment offices, 26; child labor amendment ratification, 99; workmen's compensation laws, 237; rehabilitation laws, 251; old-age pension laws, 278; mothers' pension laws, 292; un-

INDEX

employment compensation laws, 300; civil service laws, 486
Master and servant as stage in labor history, 316, 320-329·
Matches, poisonous phosphorus in manufacture of. *See* Phosphorus.
Maternity insurance, connection with childbirth protection, 188; provision for, 264-267
Mealtime, laws requiring rest period, 141-142
Mechanics' lien laws, 329, 337, 338
Mediation, in labor disputes, 430; state laws on, 432
Medical benefit, under workmen's compensation, 244-246; under health insurance, 262, 263; under invalidity insurance, 281
Merit-rating, under workmen's compensation, 255; under unemployment compensation, 305-307
Minimum wage, compared with other · labor laws, 43; economic basis, 44-48; in Australasia, 48-51, 58, 59; in Great Britain, 51-54; in Canada, 54; in South America, 54; in South Africa, 54; in the United States, 54-58, 60; in government contracts, 57; interstate compact on, 57, 58; standards, 58-64; rates established, 60-62, 64, 65; administration, 64-68; flat-rate laws, 64, 65; wage-board laws, 65-68; results achieved, 68-74; constitutionality, 74-81
Mining, hours of labor regulated, 127-129, 136, 461; accident statistics, 164, 165, 208, 209; occupational diseases, 166; women's work forbidden, 186, 188; miners licensed, 193; safety regulations, 208-211; wage payment, 332
Minors. *See* Child labor.
Mothers' pensions, 291, 292
Motor vehicles, hours of labor regulated, 126

National Guard duty, 371
National Industrial Recovery Act, and minimum wages, 57; hours of labor, 83, 85, 90, 92, 122, 128; child labor regulations, 174, 177; and collective bargaining, 423, 424
National Labor Relations Act, 424-429
Night work, of women restricted, 106, 142-146, 459, 462; of children restricted, 146; of men restricted, 147
Norris-La Guardia Act, 415, 421, 422

Occupational diseases, phosphorus poisoning, 159, 194, 195; reporting, 164-168; classification of causes, 165, 166; statistics, 167, 168; examinations required, 189-192; compensation for, 235, 236, 243, 244
Old-age insurance, private schemes, 273-275; assisted state plans, 275, 276; straight pensions, 276-280; compulsory systems, 280-289
One day rest in seven, 149-155
Orientals, exclusion of, 353-355
Orphans, social insurance for, 289-292

Padrone system, 325, 326
Patria potestas, 512
Pawnbrokers, abuses by, 362
Payment of wages, time of, 330, 331; place of, 331; basis of, 332; medium of, 332-334; deductions prohibited, 334-337; mechanics' liens provided, 337, 338; wage preference, 338, 339
Penalties for violating labor laws, 490-498; cumulative, 492, 493; civil and criminal actions, 493.
Pensions. *See* Old-age insurance.
Peonage, in other countries, 317; in the United States, 318-320; and contract labor, 322
Phosphorus, prohibition of poisonous, 159, 194, 195
Physical examination, required in child labor laws, 178-180; required as condition of employment, 189-192

Picketing, legal status of, 397-401; prosecution for, 411
Poisons, list of industrial, 165, 166 *See also* Lead trades, Occupational diseases, Phosphorus.
Police power, and minimum wage legislation, 74-77; and hours regulation, 116, 132, 153, 154; in child labor legislation, 175; and wage payment laws, 332; in relation to investigation, 464; and labor legislation, 473, 513, 514; belongs to states, 511, 513; and guardianship, 512, 514; and eminent domain, 512; defined, 513; and taxing power, 513; and liberty and property, 515; indefinite character, 515, 516; and other government powers, 516; and public benefit, 524; and health, 526; and inequality of bargaining power, 532
Politics and labor contract, 505
Postal employees, hours regulated, 119, 120
Prison labor. *See* Convict labor.
Property, varying conceptions, 502, 507-509, 525, 526; and the labor contract, 507-510; and eminent domain, 512, 513; and proprietorship, 513; and the police power, 513-515
Prosecutions, 450, 490-498; against strikers, 411
Public benefit, 473, 523-528
Public employment, and unemployment, 27-37; minimum wages for, 55, 75, 76; hours regulation, 117-121; annual vacations, 156; and workmen's compensation, 236, 237, 241; pensions, 282
Public opinion on labor, 525-528
Public works, employment offices and, 26-27; emergency relief work, 27-32, 36; federal aid to states, 30; "civil works administration," 30; "works progress administration," 30; advance planning, 32-37; and unemployment insurance, 36; minimum wage for, 55, 75, 76; hours regulation, 117-121

Raiffeisen banks, 344
Railroad commission laws, 218, 219, 512, 513
Railroad Retirement Act, 284, 285
Railroads, hours of labor regulated, 122-125; safety regulations, 214-219; old-age pensions, 284, 285; workers' right to quit regulated, 325; and collective bargaining, 420-421, 433-437
Railway Labor Act, and collective bargaining, 420-421; constitutionality upheld, 421; background and operation of, 433-437
Reasonableness, in administrative regulation, 467-471, 475; and classification, 529, 530
Regularization of industry, 37-42; recommendations of President's conference on unemployment, 38; by credit control, 38; in construction industry, 38, 39; decasualization of longshoring, 40, 41; government encouragement, 41, 42; seasonality, 42; and unemployment insurance, 42
Rehabilitation of industrial cripples, 250, 251
Representation of interests, in employment offices, 13, 14, 17, 26; in minimum wage, 66, 67, 478; in labor law administration, 475-482
Rest periods, 140-156
Rights, of individuals, 506-509; of property, 507-509; and duties, 509, 510
Rock dusting of coal mines, 210
Rural credits law, 344

Safety, types of legislation, 160; prohibitive method, 169-196; regulative methods, 196-219; defects of statute laws, 219-221; administrative regulation method, 221-223; effect of workmen's compensation, 256

INDEX 605

Saturday half-holiday, 147-149
Schultze-Delitsch banks, 344
Scientific management. *See* Time study.
Seamen, employment agencies for, 11; hours regulated, 126, **127**; safety provisions, 213, 214; seaman's contract regulated, 324, 325
Seats required, 203
Self-insurance under workmen's compensation, 253
Separation of powers, 520-523
Serfdom, 316, 317
Servitude, transition from, 531
Seven-day week, 88-90, 149
Shuttles, laws regulating, 196
Slavery, 315, 316, 318; and the labor contract, 504
Social insurance, defined, 224, 225; principle of, 225, 226; against industrial accidents, 227-257; health insurance, 257-273; maternity insurance, 264-267; old age and invalidity, 273-289; widows and orphans, 289-292; unemployment compensation, 293-314; cooperative character of, 499-500
Social Security Act, old-age pension provisions, 279; old-age benefit provisions, 286-289; mothers' aid provisions, 292; unemployment compensation provisions, 299, 300, 307, 313
Solidarism in labor legislation, 500, 501
Specific performance of contracts, 504, 505, 531
State fund insurance under workmen's compensation, 253-255
"State use" system of convict labor, 360
Street railways, hours of labor regulated, 125, 126
Street trades of children, 176
Strikes, the right to strike, 390, 391; closed shop, 391-393; sympathetic, 393-396; court action against, 396, 397; methods of conducting, 397; picketing in, 397-401; prosecutions in, 411
Suffrage, 503, 505, 525

Sunday rest laws, 149, 150, 153
Supreme Court, and judicial investigation, 458-465; powers, 522, 523
  See also Constitutionality.
Survivors' insurance. *See* Widows' and orphans' insurance.
Sweating system, in Victoria, 48-50; in Great Britain, 51; in the United States, 54, 205-208; licenses, 497; tagging products, 497

Tariff in relation to labor, 511, 515, 526
Taxation, and child labor regulation, 173; for health purposes, 195; as basis of labor legislation, 511, 515; and government property, 512; place in constitutional system, 514
Tenants, agricultural, 340, 343-345
Tenement house manufacture, regulated, 206-208
Thrift and social insurance, 225
Time study of federal employees forbidden, 120
Toilets required, 204
Tools, exemption from seizure, 328; charges for, 335
Trade disputes. *See* Strikes.
Trade unions, and unemployment statistics, 2; and employment offices, 6; and minimum wage laws, 57, 73; and hours laws for men, 116; and safety, 159; and health insurance, 257; and unemployment insurance, 293; opposed contract labor, 348; and representation of interests, 475-482; and civil service, 486-488; as controlling legislation, 524; development, 526; judicial opinion of, 529
  See also Collective bargaining.
Transportation, hours of labor regulated, 122-127
  See also Motor vehicles, Railroad, Seamen, Street railways.
Truck system, 333, 334

Tunnel workers, hours regulated, 129
Twelve-hour day, 88-90

Unconstitutionality of legislation. *See* Constitutionality.
Unemployment, extent, 1; statistics, 2; causes, 2; costs, 3-4; defined, 4; remedies, 5; and public works, 27-37; President's conference, 29, 38, 39; international conference on, 36; and regularization of industry, 37-42; and minimum wage, 62, 63, 71, 72; insurance against, 298-314.
See also Employment, Employment agencies, Employment offices.
Unemployment insurance, and public works, 36; Ghent system, 293, 294; growth of compulsory systems, 294-296; British system, 295-297; in the United States, 298-314; Social Security Act on, 299, 300; state laws, 300-314; coverage, 302; contributions, 303, 304; merit rating, 305-307; reserve funds, 308, 309; benefits, 309-311; administration, 312, 313; constitutionality, 314
Unionism. *See* Trade unions.

Vacations, 155-156
Vagrancy laws and peonage, 319, 320
Ventilation regulations, 202
Veterans, employment offices for, 23, 24, 26
Vocational guidance and employment offices, 15, 19
Voluntary defenders, 365
Voting, legislation on, 370, 371

Wage, prevailing, 55; exemption, 327; garnishment, 327; assignment, 329; time of payment regulated, 330, 331; place of payment regulated, 331; basis of payment regulated, 332; medium of payment regulated, 332-334; deductions prohibited, 334-337; preference, 338, 339; collection of unpaid, 365, 366
See also Minimum wage.
Wage boards, 65-68
See also Minimum wage.
Wage collection by state labor departments, 365, 366
War Labor Board, policy on collective bargaining, 420
Washrooms required, 204
Widows' and orphans' insurance, 289-292
Women, wages and living costs of, 44-47; minimum wage for, 54-58, 60-63, 65-68, 76-82; budgets, 62; hours legislation, 99-116, 141, 152, 459, 462-464, 469; organizations, 100-102; freedom of contract, 112-114; basis of legislation for, 186, 203, 530; employments forbidden, 186-188; childbirth protection, 188; maternity insurance, 264-267; as competitor, 345
Work accidents. *See* Accidents, Employers' liability, Workmen's compensation.
Workmen's compensation, for illegally employed minors, 175, 176; for occupational diseases, 192, 209, 226, 235, 236, 243, 244; basic theory, 227; development of, 232-236; American legislation, 236-238; constitutionality, 238-241; employments included, 241-243; injuries included, 243; scale of benefits, 244-250; rehabilitation, 250, 251; second injury fund, 250; administration, 251-253; security of payment, 253-257; and accident prevention, 256, 257, 498-501; and the police and commerce powers, 515; and equalization of bargaining power, 530

Yellow-dog contracts, laws on, 387, 389, 406-408